D0349793

NO MORE WACOS

NATIONAL UNIVERSITY
LIBRARY   SAN DIEGO

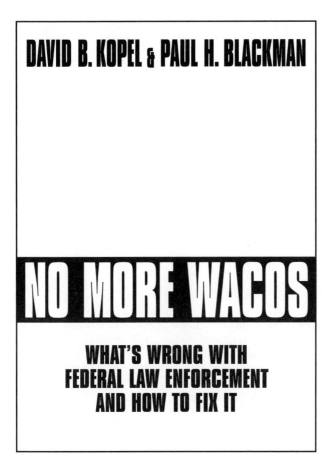

DAVID B. KOPEL & PAUL H. BLACKMAN

NO MORE WACOS

WHAT'S WRONG WITH FEDERAL LAW ENFORCEMENT AND HOW TO FIX IT

Prometheus Books
59 John Glenn Drive
Amherst, New York 14228-2197

Published 1997 by Prometheus Books

No More Wacos: What's Wrong with Federal Law Enforcement and How to Fix It. Copyright ©
1997 by David B. Kopel and Paul H. Blackman. All rights reserved. No part of this publication
may be reproduced, stored in a retrieval system, or transmitted in any form or by any means,
electronic, mechanical, photocopying, recording, or otherwise, without prior written permission
of the publisher, except in the case of brief quotations embodied in critical articles and reviews.
Inquiries should be addressed to Prometheus Books, 59 John Glenn Drive, Amherst, New York
14228–2197, 716–691–0133. FAX: 716–691–0137.

01 00 99 98 97   5 4 3 2 1

Library of Congress Cataloging-in-Publication Data

Kopel, David B.
    No more Wacos: what's wrong with Federal law enforcement, and how to fix it / David B.
Kopel and Paul H. Blackman
        p.   cm.
    Includes bibliographical references and index.
    ISBN 1–57392–125–4 (cloth : alk. paper)
    1. Law enforcement—United States. 2. Waco Branch Davidian Disaster, Tex., 1993.
I. Blackman, Paul H. II. Title.
HV8141.K67   1997
363.2′0973—dc21   96–37639
                                                                            CIP

Printed in the United States of America on acid-free paper

To my late brother, Stephen. "All he lost he shall regain." (Robert Hunter)

D.B.K.

To my sister, Beth, for her encouragement when we discovered the only national issue on which we agreed.

P.H.B.

Contents

Appendices

Acknowledgments

We would like to acknowledge our many friends in the law enforcement community who have spontaneously come forward to express their dismay about the events in Waco. Out of concern for their careers, we will not acknowledge them by name, but they, like the vast majority of American law enforcement officers, have earned our respect and gratitude. Like them, we strongly support law enforcement, and recognize that the foundation of law and order is compliance with the Constitution.

We would like to thank Steve Aeschbacher, Mark Benenson, David Bordua, Roger Charles, Deron Dilger, Richard E. Gardiner, Stephen P. Halbrook, David A. Heiner, Jr., Deirdre Kopel, Gerald H. Kopel, Shawn Mitchell, Steven L. Mitchell, Mary A. Read, Dick Reavis, Mark Ruggiero, Lisa C. Halbrook-Stephenson, and Richard Wahl for their help.

Thanks to Jasmin Lee Cori for permission to reprint an excerpt from her poem "Flame of God," which appears in chapter 6. The poem appears in *Freefall to the Beloved: Mystical Poetry for God's Lovers* (Boulder, Colo.: Golden Reed, 1996), available from P.O. Box 20815, Boulder, CO 80308.

A Note on Sources

This book may be long, but we do not believe that it is the final word on Waco. The full truth about Waco will only be discovered when documents, videotapes, and other evidence that have been withheld from the public are released, and when witnesses who have lied under oath, confident that perjury charges will not be brought, finally tell the truth. For reasons detailed in chapter 5, we believe that the appointment of a special prosecutor is the most likely strategy for revealing all the truth about Waco.

This book is intended as a starting point. It is based on documents in the public record, particularly government documents. (In one case, however, the government report has not yet been published. A secret Department of Justice internal review of the Ruby Ridge killings was leaked to the Internet.) Whenever possible, we provide not only the ordinary citation, but also a citation to where a document may be found on the Internet.

Recognizing that something went tragically wrong at Waco does not require buying into silly conspiracy theories about flamethrowing tanks and the like. The facts already in the public record speak for themselves.

We hope that this book is not understood as an insistence that law enforcement personnel never make mistakes. This book does, however, insist that they should obey the law.

Introduction

Suddenly, in the midst of the brilliant civilization of the twentieth century, all the worst attributes of humanity have come to the front; all the most evil passions have been unleashed; all the evil spirits some thought were exorcized centuries ago have returned sevenfold, more loathsome and diabolical than of old.

Seventh-day Adventist writer Arthur Maxwell, *History's Crowded Climax*[1]

. . . a raging riot of blood and murder, theft and deceit, corruption, faithlessness, tumult, perjury, confusion over what is good, forgetfulness of favors, defiling of souls, sexual perversion, disorders in marriage, adultery, and debauchery.

Wisdom of Solomon 14:25–26

On February 28, 1993, the Bureau of Alcohol, Tobacco and Firearms (BATF[2]) sent seventy-six BATF agents to storm the Mount Carmel Center, near Waco, Texas.[3] The Center housed the Branch Davidian[4] followers of David Koresh. Although it is unclear whether Koresh and his followers or the BATF agents fired first, four BATF agents were killed and many others wounded (some probably struck by "friendly fire"), as were six Branch Davidians. BATF field commanders knew before the raid began that the element of surprise had been lost.

The raid was followed by a fifty-one-day standoff led by the Federal Bureau of Investigation (FBI), including negotiations, the surrender of some of the adult and child residents of the Mount Carmel Center, and psychological warfare by the FBI, such as bombarding the Branch Davidians with loud music, the sounds of rabbits being slaughtered, and other unpleasant noises. Then, on April 19, 1993, FBI tanks began ramming holes into the structure in order to pump in CS chemical warfare agent, purportedly because of threats to the twenty-seven children remaining in the residence. A conflagration broke out, killing most persons at Mount Carmel, although Koresh and some of his followers were killed by gunshots rather than fire.[5] Some Branch Davidians may have died from inhalation of hydrogen cyanide, which is produced when CS burns under

15

certain conditions, and others may have been asphyxiated or incapacitated by the CS itself. The government reports that the fire was started by Koresh and his followers. The siege ended with the deaths of all the children and almost all the adults remaining inside.

The number of deaths resulting from the events at Waco is over 50 percent of the total American casualties in the Gulf War. But unlike the Gulf War, the Waco disaster resulted from people being killed by Americans, rather than by foreign troops. And unlike the many deaths or injuries inflicted on innocent children every day by abusive parents, incompetent doctors, or criminals, the deaths of the children at Waco would not have occurred but for the acts of the federal government of the United States, which most Americans expect to be under the control of the laws of the United States.

The Waco raid was not merely the largest in the history of the Bureau of Alcohol, Tobacco and Firearms. It was the largest federal armed entry ever against an American home, resulting in the largest number of law enforcement officer deaths in a single operation, as well as the largest number of civilian deaths ever resulting from a law enforcement operation. Not since the Wounded Knee massacre in 1890 had so many Americans been killed as a result of a conflict with the federal government.[6] Rep. Charles Schumer explained that "mistakes in outcome are not always the results of mistakes in judgment. . . . We are not dealing with a corrupt or dishonest Government agency, we are not dealing with acts of . . . coverup. . . ."[7] Representative Schumer was mistaken.

As this book will detail, the adult Branch Davidians, particularly David Koresh, played a large role in the disaster. But while most Americans are not surprised to find poor judgment displayed by self-proclaimed prophets and their followers, the federal government is generally held to a higher standard. The government gave David Koresh unnecessary help in his misguided quest for martyrdom.

After a prologue that sets forth the background of some of the major characters in the Mount Carmel tragedy, chapter 1 of this book analyzes the procurement of the warrant to search the Branch Davidian compound, a warrant which was based on a combination of falsehoods, legal error, and apparent bad faith. The BATF assault on the Branch Davidian compound is detailed in chapter 2, with a particular focus on the lack of justification for an armed, military assault to serve a search warrant. Chapter 3 examines the siege, the FBI's psychological warfare tactics, and the FBI's decision to ignore a surrender offer by David Koresh. While the siege was in progress, the FBI deceived Attorney General Janet Reno in order to obtain her approval for an assault to end the siege militarily. Chapter 4 studies the FBI tank and chemical warfare attack which brought the fifty-one-day standoff to its horrifying finale. In chapter 5, the investigations which the Departments of Treasury (overseeing BATF) and Justice (overseeing the FBI) performed on their bureaus are analyzed, and found to be lacking in candor. We also look at the criminal prosecution of the Branch Davidians, the congressional hearings into Waco, and the role of the "fourth branch"—the news media. Throughout the book, when we identify problems in federal law enforcement, we propose specific solutions. Chapter 6, the conclusion, proposes additional, broader reforms to prevent the recurrence of mass deaths such as those which took place at Waco. An appendix offers a proposed "Comprehensive Public Safety and Federal Law Enforcement Reform Act" with specific statutory language to implement the reforms discussed in the book.

Throughout the book, we place Waco in the broader context of the breakdown in the lawfulness of federal law enforcement. While Waco was a sensational, highly publicized case, there are many other cases of federal law enforcement lawlessness which do not receive national attention. We will discuss some of them, and also discuss the Randy Weaver incident, at Ruby Ridge, Idaho, which revealed law enforcement problems similar to those at Waco.

As the book jacket notes, one of us (Blackman) works for the National Rifle Association. We want to emphasize that the reforms advocated or the arguments advanced in this book are *not* official policy of the NRA. The opinions expressed in this book do not necessarily reflect the viewpoints of the authors' employers or, from time to time, each other.

Prologue

I had made up my mind to do what God said, even though I could see only destruction and ruin.

Vernon Wayne Howell

THE BOOK OF REVELATION

You could blame it all on Domitian, the despotic ruler of the Roman Empire from 81 to 96 C.E. Styling himself as "Master and God" of the Roman Empire, the Emperor Domitian built a large network of informers and prosecutors, whose repression inspired further resistance, which in turn inspired further repression, until Domitian was assassinated in 96 C.E. by a group of conspirators that included his wife.[8] Although the historical evidence is not definitive, it is generally believed that Domitian was the first emperor to practice empire-wide persecution of Christians for refusing to participate in the cult of the emperor and recognize him as a god.[9]

The last book of the New Testament, the Book of Revelation, is thought to have been written as a response to the mobilization of the vast resources of the Roman Empire against the struggling Christian communities of the late first century. Revelation is an apocalyptic book, describing the climactic battles between the forces of good and evil that will usher in the final triumph of Christianity, and the destruction of the forces of evil, at the end of time. Replete with fantastic imagery of angels, beasts, battles in the sky, massively destructive wars on the earth, fires, bottomless pits, and immense cataclysms, Revelation is the most difficult book of the Bible to interpret. Martin Luther, who wrote a commentary on every other book of the Bible, omitted Revelation from his own Bible, and warned that study of Revelation would drive the student mad.

Mainline religions have rarely focused their teaching on Revelation, perhaps because of its complexity and incomprehensibility, and perhaps because of the subver-

19

sive tone of the book. The beasts in Revelation who rule the world (before being destroyed in the end) were certainly intended on one level to represent the persecuting Roman Empire; and Revelation was written to give first-century Christians hope of an eventual victory over the evil empire that was murdering them for refusing to accept the supremacy of the state. But Revelation has over the centuries been seen as foretelling the triumph and ultimate doom of various empires, including the Holy Roman Empire, the Third Reich, the United States, and the one-world government that is feared to be the objective of the "New World Order." For the last nineteen hundred years, the groups which have clung most fervently to Revelation have usually been groups marginalized from the existing power structure, groups who are radically dissatisfied with the existing order of society, who look to Revelation for the hope of the imminent destruction of an evil world and its replacement with a holy one. This perspective was shared by members of the Branch Davidian Seventh-day Adventist faith.

THE BRANCH DAVIDIANS

The Seventh-day Adventist church grew out of the teachings of William Miller, an American religious leader who predicted the Second Advent and end of the world to take place on or before October 22, 1844.[10] Although Miller's prediction did not come true, many of his followers continued to observe his teachings. There are approximately eighty-four groups of churches which have historical ties to the Miller movement, with over ten million members worldwide. Miller is the founder of the largest homegrown religious movement in American history, larger even than the movement founded by Joseph Smith.[11] By far the largest Millerite group is the Seventh-day Adventists, whose doctrines were molded in the late nineteenth century by Ellen G. White. Mrs. White is recognized as a prophet by the Seventh-day Adventist church.

In 1935, Bulgarian immigrant Victor Houteff, who had declared himself the new Adventist prophet and had founded the Shepherd's Rod Church, established a Mount Carmel Center near Waco, Texas. Houteff saw himself in a line of prophets who had successively restored crucial biblical doctrines: Luther (faith), Knox (holy spirit), Wesley (grace), Campbell (baptism), Miller (second coming), and White (sabbath).[12] Houteff's followers expected the establishment of the "Davidic Kingdom," a special society of pure righteousness. Although the world did not end by 1936, as Houteff had expected, the sixty people living at Mount Carmel made their community a success, and won new followers from all over the United States. After the enactment of the military draft in 1942, the group incorporated as Davidian Seventh-day Adventists in order to certify their status as conscientious objectors. The Adventist church denied that the Davidians were authentic Adventists; Houteff had been disfellowshipped from a California Adventist congregation in 1930.[13]

Victor Houteff died in 1955. His followers, who believed that he was the new Elijah, were shocked to see him pass away before his mission was completed.[14] After some struggle, he was succeeded by his wife, Florence, who established a new Mount Carmel Center further outside Waco. As religious historian Bill Pitts observes, the Branch Davidian movement never deviated from the essential shape which Houteff had given it. From 1935 until 1993 (and thereafter), the Branch Davidian religion has been "millenarian, sabbatarian, authoritarian, and communal."[15] To these four key traits might be added one other: a belief that the Bible is a complex document which can only be truly understood by a select group of persons who know how to decode it. This is why the sect was so heavily oriented toward prophetic leadership; it rejected the idea that individuals could read the Bible by themselves and fully understand it. The Bible was written by inspiration, and must be understood through inspired teaching.[16]

David Koresh would later radicalize the Branch Davidians by pushing all of the religion's key traits to an extreme, but Koresh could do so only because he was moving the Branch Davidians along a path that had been established for nearly half a century before he discovered the group.

Under Mrs. Houteff's leadership, the Branch Davidian religion of the late 1950s attracted approximately ten thousand followers throughout the world. But many "branches" left the religion when the predicted Second Coming of Jesus Christ (and massacre of mainstream Seventh-day Adventists pursuant to Ezekiel 9) failed to materialize on April 22, 1959. The event became known in Davidian circles as "The Great Disappointment."[17]

The group split, with the largest contingent following self-proclaimed prophet Ben Roden. Roden considered himself the messianic "Branch" foretold in Zechariah.[18] He introduced the Branch Davidian practice of observing the Old Testament feast days from the Book of Leviticus.[19] The Roden group retained control of Mount Carmel, while other groups fanned out to various parts of the United States, where they continue to this day to follow their visions.[20]

Roden was succeeded upon his death in 1978 by his wife, Lois. The Branch Davidian religion stagnated, as a smaller and smaller contingent of the faithful watched Lois Roden draw the same seven-year prophecy chart on the chalkboard every day. A major change was, however, predicted by Mrs. Roden for 1984, growing out of something that would begin in 1981.

Lois Roden was known in Texas Adventist circles for her doctrine that the Holy Spirit was female.[21] Attracted by this doctrine, and in search of a living prophet, Vernon Wayne Howell joined the Branch Davidian community at Mount Carmel during the Holy Days of June 1981.[22]

VERNON WAYNE HOWELL

My time coming, any day, don't worry about me no.
It's gonna be just like they say, them voices tell me so . . .
You will follow me and we will ride to glory, way up, the middle of the air!
And I'll call down thunder and speak the same.
My word fills the sky with flame.
Might and glory gonna be my name . . .

"Estimated Prophet," The Grateful Dead

Vernon Wayne Howell was born on August 17, 1959, the illegitimate son of a fifteen-year-old mother.[23] Young Vernon was remembered by his mother as "a smart young boy. Very intelligent for his age. . . We nicknamed him Sputnik, after the Russian satellite. . . . He couldn't be still; he was so energetic, hyper."

When Vernon was two, his mother married a man who quickly became abusive. He beat little Vernon until he was black and blue, and held his bare feet on a hot furnace grating. The mother obtained a divorce after a year of marriage. The mother moved to Dallas, and left Vernon with his grandmother. Two years later, the mother remarried, and reclaimed Vernon, who had come to consider his grandmother as his mother. "Don't take me from my mama," he pleaded to no avail. "I don't want you to be my mother."

According to what Vernon later privately told some fellow Branch Davidians, from the age of five until age nine, he was frequently raped by one of his mother's male relatives.

When Vernon was nine, he and his mother began attending Seventh-day Adventist services in Dallas. Vernon loved Adventism, and embraced Adventism's theory of a small remnant of godly people in a faithless world, emphasis on prophecy, and recognition of modern-day prophets. He eventually memorized large passages from difficult prophetic books such as Isaiah, Jeremiah, and Ezekiel, all in the King James Version of the Bible, with its seventeenth-century English.

The last recognized Adventist prophet, Ellen G. White, had died in 1915, and Vernon was frustrated by the idea that there were no current prophets. He began to wonder if there was an unbroken prophetic chain that continued to the present.[24] Vernon had two great interests: the Bible and the electric guitar, and he devoted himself to both passionately. As a teenager, he often got into scriptural arguments with local Adventist ministers, and he believed that the modern Adventist church had become too mainstream and worldly, and fallen away from its prophetic mission. According to his mother, he would spend hours in prayer, crying and begging God to send the people a living prophet.[25]

In 1979, at the age of twenty, Howell began attending a Seventh-day Adventist (SDA) church in Tyler, Texas. Howell attended a church-sponsored revival meeting featuring traveling evangelist Jim Gilley's "Revelation Seminars." Gilley's multimedia events warned that the fantastic, frightening Apocalypse foretold in the Book of Revelation could take place soon. Howell was fascinated.[26]

A friend in the Tyler congregation told Howell about the Mount Carmel community.[27]

When Vernon first arrived at Mount Carmel in 1981, he tried to help out as a handyman.[28] But he was also a stuttering, insecure, pesky young man, given to tearful confessions of what he saw as his horrible sins, including his problem with compulsive masturbation. Day after day, he would lie on his bed, not just crying, but sobbing and flailing.[29]

For a while, Howell participated in both the Branch Davidian community in Waco and the mainstream Seventh-day Adventist community in Tyler. But Howell was disfellowshipped from the SDA church in 1983, "after a succession of conflicts that precipitated when he announced that God intended him to marry the pastor's daughter, incessantly witnessed to other church members, and on one occasion took over the pulpit to propound his own theological views."[30]

In retrospect, it seems apparent that one of Vernon Howell's most serious problems was the conflict between his natural sexual urges and his belief in the wickedness of sexuality—a belief that has been an element of some parts of the Judeo-Christian tradition for many centuries. As a victim of repeated childhood sexual abuse, Howell's internal conflicts would likely have been all the more severe.

The result appears to have been Howell's consistent pattern of entering or attempting to enter into sexual relationships that were "blessed" by what seemed to Howell to be some kind of command from God. His first sexual encounter, as a teenager, not only violated his religious beliefs, causing a temporary break in the relationship, but resulted in a pregnancy the responsibility for which Howell first denied, claiming he was sterile. He eventually decided that the relationship meant that he and the girl were married in God's eyes and went back to living with her. For that, he had the permission of her father, who would not allow a marriage, and who had approved the abortion but apparently not realized Howell's involvement until he again impregnated her. When this led to Howell's mentioning his role in the first pregnancy, the girl's father ended the relationship. After some turmoil, Howell convinced himself that God had told him that God would give her to him again later. God did not.

Based on the available evidence, it would be overly simplistic to claim that all that was going on was Howell cynically using religion as a pretext for his repulsive sexual behavior. To the contrary, a special dispensation from God appeared to be the only way in which Howell could deal with sex.

Howell's announcement that God wanted him to marry the SDA preacher's daughter had been rebuffed. There would only be one more time when anyone who knew Howell well would reject his sexual message.

Now living full-time at Mount Carmel, Howell was a rising force in the community. He developed a sexual relationship with Lois Roden, who was then in her sixties.[31] While the relationship was not publicly acknowledged, even to other Branch Davidians, Roden apparently believed that Howell and she would miraculously conceive a child.[32]

Leadership was slipping from Lois Roden, who had presided over years of torpor and decline, into the dynamic hands of Vernon Howell. When the main administration building burned down in 1983 (according to some allegations, after Howell started a fire), Howell announced that the fire was God's punishment for the Branch Davidians' spiritual laziness. He began announcing new dietary rules, sticking his nose into everyone else's business and condemning their sins, and injecting excitement into what had been a dying movement.[33] The other residents of Mount Carmel, observing Howell's growth into a mature, well-liked member of the community, attributed Howell's beneficial changes to God's work.[34] Howell said, and Lois Roden and almost everyone else agreed, that Howell was the "Seventh Angel" (prophet) of the Book of Revelation. Under this theory, the first six angels had been William Miller (preaching the messages of the First and Second Angels), Ellen G. White (Third Angel), Victor Houteff (Fourth Angel), Ben Roden (Fifth Angel), and Lois Roden (who had long proclaimed herself the Sixth Angel).

One night Howell snuck out of Lois Roden's bed, and went to the nearby home of Perry Jones, a long-time Branch Davidian, and one of the most respected members of the community. (Jones eventually served as vice president of the Branch Davidians; he was killed on February 28, 1993, the day of the Bureau of Alcohol, Tobacco and Firearms raid.[35]) Howell told Perry Jones that God had told Howell to marry Jones's fourteen-year-old daughter Rachel. Rachel, a dutiful daughter, did as her father asked and married Vernon Howell the next day.

When Lois Roden found out, she went berserk. She revealed to the entire group the sexual relationship between herself and Howell. Rachel Jones Howell said she never would have married Vernon if she had known about his relationship with Lois Roden.

George Roden, Lois's son, drove Howell and the Jones family away from Mount Carmel at the point of an Uzi. The Mount Carmel community eventually split between followers of George Roden and followers of Howell. Lois Roden died in 1985.

In control of Mount Carmel, George Roden set up a methamphetamine lab, and amassed a large collection of guns.

The Howell group set up a separate community, under Spartan conditions, near Palestine, Texas. They also acquired group homes in Pomona and La Verne, California, which Howell used as bases for his attempts to become a rock star. At one point, an effort was made to contact Madonna, with the hope that she would become one of his wives.

While visiting Israel in 1985 and studying the Bible with several rabbis, Howell experienced what he described as "a miraculous meeting with God," in which he was instructed to study and then fulfill the prophecies contained in the Seven Seals of the Book of Revelation.[36] Howell believed that he heard God talking directly to him, as God had spoken to Moses from the Burning Bush.[37] Koresh's stutter disappeared forever, and the quality, energy, and intensity of his preaching improved tremendously. The voice stayed with Howell and instructed him while he read the Bible. At other times, he would see pictures in his head. He believed that a heavenly "vehicle" transported him past the constellation Orion.[38] In a 1987 teaching session, Howell described one of his experiences with the voice:

> What—what if you turned on the water in the shower and all of a sudden it said, "Drop down ye waters from above, let the faucets pour out righteousness. I the Lord have created it." Huh? You know. Sh- and, and the songs of blessing, showers of blessing, starts being heard in your room or in the bathroom, right? I mean let's face it. Let's be realistic now. This guy is freaked out now, isn't he? OK? He's—this—Cyrus has an experience which none—very few and far in between have had.[39]

Around Passover in 1986, Vernon heard a voice say "Give seed to Karen." After some inner struggle, reported Howell, "I had made up my mind to do what God said, even though I could see only destruction and ruin." And so Vernon took thirteen-year-old Karen Doyle, with her consent and her family's blessing, as his second wife.[40] This was the beginning of the "House of David," as Howell, who later called himself "David Koresh," eventually dubbed his growing collection of wives.

Howell was a far more charismatic preacher than George Roden, and his group thrived while Roden's withered. Roden refused to pay property taxes for Mount

Carmel, while Howell's group strengthened their claim to ownership by paying $68,000 in back taxes. (The property is legally owned by the General Association of Davidian Seventh-day Adventists;[41] the legal issue was who was the proper representative of this group.)

George Roden produced two wills by his mother, Lois, which left Mount Carmel to him, but neither will was properly authenticated. The younger Roden, who had run for president in 1984 on the platform of starting a nuclear war with the Soviet Union, filed court motions filled with obscenities and threatened judges with herpes and various other plagues. Ignoring repeated orders to improve his behavior, Roden was sentenced to six months in jail. Howell's group moved into Mount Carmel the next day, March 23, 1988.[42]

Howell's group was conditionally granted possession of the Mount Carmel property, but they were required to occupy the property for a five-year period in order to perfect title. This five-year possession period ran through March 22, 1993, a date which happened to fall three-and-half weeks after the BATF raided Mount Carmel on February 28, 1993. The property issue would make the Branch Davidians extremely reluctant to comply with FBI orders for a complete surrender in early March. They feared that their sacred home would be left unoccupied, and likely seized by the federal government or other hostiles.[43]

Taking over Mount Carmel from George Roden, Howell's group cleared away the neglected, crumbling buildings, dismantled the methamphetamine lab, turned the drug equipment and manuals over to the sheriff,[44] and began building a large new building which would house everyone in the community.

Over the years, Vernon and the Branch Davidians grew increasingly confident of his prophetic role, and of the special role that they would play in history.

Vernon decided that his true name was David Koresh. The name "David" was an easily recognizable reference to King David, the greatest King of Israel, and the antitype for the Messiah expected by the Jews.

"Koresh" has a more obscure origin, at least for people who (unlike the Branch Davidians) are not immersed in the Bible.

Around 600 B.C.E. in Persia, a child named "Kurush" was born. The name is rendered as "Cyrus" in Latin (and in English Bibles), and as "Koresh" in Hebrew. In the Old Testament, Kurush/Cyrus/Koresh seized control of the Persian Empire, and then conquered the Middle East all the way to the Aegean Sea.[45] In the process, King Cyrus destroyed the Babylonian Empire, which had previously conquered Jerusalem and taken the Jews into captivity. Cyrus allowed some Jews to return to Jerusalem and begin rebuilding the Temple which had been the center of Jewish worship. Although not a Jew, Cyrus was highly regarded by the Jews; the Book of Isaiah calls Cyrus God's "anointed," a term applied to persons, including the Messiah, chosen by God for a special purpose.[46]

Later, Howell decided that "Koresh" had an additional meaning: death. God's first name was "life" (*Yahweh* in Hebrew), and his last name was "death" (*Koresh* by Howell's interpretation). And thus David Koresh saw himself as rider on the pale horse in Revelation 6:8: "his name that sat on him was Death."

Vernon Wayne Howell saw himself as the messianic fulfillment of both Cyrus and the

Hebrew King David. King David played a "stringed instrument," and David Koresh played the guitar. King David (while leading the rebellion against King Saul) hid out in the wilderness with his band of followers, while Koresh had his own remote headquarters.[47]

David Koresh also saw in himself the fulfillment of the prophecies in the Song of Solomon. In a passage favored by Koresh, King Solomon (David's son and successor), like other Old Testament kings, was surrounded by fierce warriors: "Behold his bed, which is Solomon's; threescore valiant men are about it, of the valiant of Israel. They all hold swords, being expert in war; every man hath his sword upon his thigh because of fear in the night."[48]

King Solomon set Koresh's standard for how many wives Koresh should have: "threescore queens, and fourscore concubines, and virgins without number."[49] As in Old Testament times, girls as young as twelve were considered old enough to be married.[50]

Koresh's sexual practices were loathsome, but, unfortunately, not unique in the history of religious leaders. King Solomon, for example, is revered as one of the wisest men who ever lived, and one of Israel's greatest kings, second only to King David. He is the purported author of the Book of Proverbs, and the Book of Ecclesiastes. But, as the Bible teaches, he was apparently sexually insatiable, needing sixty "wives," eighty concubines, and "virgins without number." The sixteenth-century Anabaptist movement (ancestor of today's Mennonite and Hutterite sects) was for a time led by a tailor named Jan Bockelson, who enjoyed free sexual access to his female devotees.[51] We will not catalogue the numerous sexual misadventures of some of the medieval popes, but we will suggest that wrongful sexual behavior by the head of a religion does not mean that the followers of that religion—be they Jews, Anabaptists, Catholics, or Branch Davidians—are fools or "cultists," or that they deserve to be persecuted.

Nor was Koresh unique among religious leaders in believing that he received bizarre instructions from God. Minister Louis Farrakhan, who considers himself to be the Messiah,[52] has spoken of his 1985 trip on a UFO.[53] Ellen G. White believed in space travel. As Branch Davidian Livingstone Fagan notes,[54] according to the Bible, God instructed the prophet Isaiah to walk barefoot and naked for three years,[55] the prophet Hosea to marry a prostitute,[56] and the prophet Ezekiel to make a mixture of cow dung and grain and to eat it before the public (Ezekiel had talked God out of God's original order to use human dung, rather than cow dung).[57] Further, God killed Ezekiel's wife and ordered Ezekiel not to mourn,[58] and instructed Abraham to kill his only son, Isaac, by slitting his throat with a knife, as a human sacrifice to God.[59]

Messianically, Koresh saw himself third in line, following Melchizedek, a "high priest" from the book of Genesis who blessed Abraham, and who was "Without father, without mother, without descent, having neither beginning of days, nor end of life; but made like unto the Son of God . . ."[60]—and following Jesus, who had no earthly paternal lineage. In contrast to Melchizedek and Jesus, Koresh "had both a very worldly father and mother."[61] Thus, Koresh described himself as "the sinful messiah" because he, unlike Jesus, was riddled with sin, and therefore could fulfill the biblical prophecies which Koresh thought called for a Messiah with the full scope of human frailty. He identified himself as the character in Psalm 40 who "preached righteousness in the great congregation" but who also knew that "mine iniquities have taken hold upon me . . . they are more than the hairs of mine head."

Branch Davidian theology was premised on the idea that the Bible is the infallible word of God. Like previous "Angels," Koresh examined the prophetic books of the Bible, and found numerous prophecies, including prophecies about a Messiah, which had never been fulfilled. (For example, Psalm 45 predicts a Messiah who will have children, and Jesus never did.) Like many other Christians throughout history, the Branch Davidians believed that they were living in the end-times. The climax of history was foretold in the Book of Revelation, the book in which all the other books of the Bible, especially the prophetic books of the Old Testament, came together.

While the Branch Davidians were unique in seeing Koresh as the Messiah, they were not unique in much of their general orientation. For example, the Jehovah's Witnesses (another Millerite group) also believe in an impending but frequently postponed Armageddon, believe that only members of their sect are living according to God's truth, and believe that only the top leaders of their sect can interpret Scripture, which everyone else in the sect must obey unquestioningly.[62]

Koresh knew the Bible inside out, and his preaching held an obvious attraction to potential converts who already believed that all truth is contained in the Bible. Koresh's proselytization was especially geared toward mainstream Seventh-day Adventists, who already believed that God could send prophets as in the days of old. And, like mainstream Christianity for most of its history, Koresh's preaching relied heavily on hellfire. Potential converts were offered a last chance to save themselves from eternal torture, and warned of the consequences of not heeding God's word. Fear of hellfire also played an enormous role in keeping Branch Davidians with doubts from renouncing the faith.[63]

Although street-corner preaching never attracted any Branch Davidian converts, missions did. Converts came from places as diverse as England, Australia, Hawaii, and California. The Mount Carmel Center became a multiracial, multicultural community, with large numbers of blacks, Hispanics, Asians, and whites. Over half the population were people of color; adult women, adult men, and children each comprised about a third of the 130 people present.[64] In contrast to the stagnant group which had clustered around Lois Roden, Koresh brought in a far more dynamic, expanding group of followers. Although Koresh himself was dyslexic and poorly educated, with weak grammatical and spelling skills, many of the converts held degrees; these included a well-respected attorney who had graduated from Harvard Law School,[65] an electrical engineer,[66] and others with degrees or advanced degrees from Seventh-day Adventist theological academies.[67]

As with sex, Koresh had intensely puritanical, neurotic attitudes toward food. In his early days at Mount Carmel, he had fasted so severely that there was little more to him than skin and bones. The Branch Davidians had already been following Old Testament and Seventh-day Adventist dietary laws, but Koresh modified these, liberalizing them to allow meat, while adding other restrictions. Koresh thought that red meat and foods containing chemical additives were unclean, as were foods with high sugar content. Vitamins and other artificial dietary supplements were forbidden. Like the Mormons, the Davidians eschewed food containing caffeine.[68] Certain brands of beer were allowed, with consumption limited to two beers, one hour apart. Meals generally consisted of fresh fruits, vegetables, poultry, and breads. Turkey hotdogs and popcorn were especially popular. (Some days, popcorn would be the only food.)

The most complex dietary rules involved food combinations. Under Ellen G. White's teachings, certain permissible foods (such as oranges and raisins) could not be eaten together. Vegetables and fruit could only be consumed together if the vegetables were fresh cooked corn, and the fruit were lemons, pineapples, or avocados. Apples could be eaten with any vegetable if the apples were stewed first. From time to time, Koresh would change the rules about food combinations, forbidding new combinations, while authorizing other previously forbidden ones.

Perhaps the most important rule, in terms of its effects on the siege, was that drinks were forbidden with meals.[69] Having gotten used to restricting liquid intake, or to eating nothing but popcorn all day, and to rejecting many "worldly" pleasures of food, the ascetic Branch Davidians were extremely well prepared to withstand a long siege.

As with sex, Koresh managed to convince himself that all the worldly temptations which he protected the Branch Davidians from were meant to be experienced by him. He was supposed to suffer the "experience of all sin and degradation on earth" so that he would be ready to stand in judgment of the sinners on Judgment Day. While the Branch Davidians watched, Koresh would sometimes enjoy a large bowl of ice cream; he would tell how grateful they should be that he was taking on the sins of the world while they remained pure;[70] other times, he would order in ice cream for everyone, as a celebration.

Although Mount Carmel was intended to be distinct from the "Babylonian" outside world, life was not as entirely abnormal as anticult propagandists would suggest. While some Branch Davidians were alienated from their families, others kept in touch with frequent phone calls, letters, or visits.[71] People were free to leave, and over the years, many people did leave. Bible studies were, of course, the raison d'être for being at Mount Carmel; but there were also go-karts, music, and the ordinary chores of preparing meals, home-schooling the children, and construction work to expand the Mount Carmel Center.[72] McLennan County Sheriff Jack Harwell later recounted that he had met many Branch Davidians, and, although they believed in an odd religion, they all seemed to be likeable, normal people.

MARC BREAULT

What became of Vernon Wayne Howell after he began to be treated as an inerrant prophet confirms Lord Acton's adage that absolute power corrupts absolutely. Vernon Wayne Howell was an abused child who grew into an abuser named David Koresh. Two incidents, while not typical of Koresh's daily behavior, do illustrate the cycle of abuse.

One incident took place at Mount Carmel, when Vernon's mother, Bonnie, was living there. (At the time of the BATF raid, she was not living at Mount Carmel.) There was a well-liked, three-legged dog named Buddy tied to a rope outside the compound. Vernon's mother's dog spent hours sneaking up on Buddy, and then biting his leg. When Buddy at last bit back, "Vernon's mother witnessed this and flew into a rage. She picked up a shovel and repeatedly beat the wretched Buddy, eventually slicing open his remaining hind leg. Nobody dared intervene." Vernon came on the scene, declared that he would not tolerate troublemakers, executed Buddy with a rifle, and told the crying children not to be sissies. Later that night, Vernon preached a thirteen-hour sermon on love, forgiveness, and eternal life.[73]

As noted above, Vernon, at the age of five, had been taken away from his grandmother, whom he thought to be his mother, and forced to live with his real mother, despite his tearful protests. When Cyrus, the firstborn son of David Koresh, was three years old, Koresh decided that Cyrus's mother (Koresh's first wife, seventeen-year-old Rachel) was not raising him right, and sent him to live with another Koresh wife in California. Koresh demanded that little Cyrus acknowledge the new woman as his mother, which Cyrus refused to do, even after being severely beaten for a half hour by Koresh. Koresh then locked Cyrus in a dark garage for the night, warning him that giant rats that lived in the garage would attack him.

On a more mundane level, Koresh often had trouble taking personal responsibility. During jam sessions for his rock group, Messiah, if Koresh made a mistake with his guitar lead, he would blame it on the drummer or the bass player.[74]

But Koresh was not always malevolent. For example, one of his followers reports:

He once stood in the pouring rain for six hours while fixing a follower's pickup truck. He spent thousands of dollars buying new electric guitars for people and he even bought a couple of cars to give away. He gave Davidian Peter Hipsman, who died during the Feb. 28, 1993 ATF raid a newly restored 1968 Camaro![75]

Koresh's leadership position was significantly strengthened by his willingness to confess his sins to the rest of the group.[76]

In any case, the Branch Davidians were not unaware of Koresh's numerous personal flaws. They simply did not believe that it was their place to reject God's decision to choose a sinful Messiah. As Koresh's number-one follower Steve Schneider once asked, "Of all the people in the world, why did God have to choose a bum from Texas who can hardly speak English and who is always so rude to you?"[77]

In public discussion, "child abuse at Waco" means abuse perpetrated by David Koresh after he took control of the Branch Davidians. We will discuss the abuse in more detail in subsequent chapters. It is important to realize, however, what an essential role child abuse played in the Mount Carmel story long before David Koresh was running things.

The summer before Vernon Howell married fourteen-year-old Rachel Jones, he would give her guitar lessons, and her friend Debbie Bunds would come along as a chaperone. During these lessons, he would ask them intimate sexual questions, such as "Have you ever thought about what sex would be like?" or "When you get married, would you want to share your husband?" He even asked the girls if they had thought about marrying him, and whether they would mind sharing him.

The girls knew that Howell's comments were inappropriate, but they felt that there was no adult they could go to. Debbie Bunds (who left the Branch Davidians years later) explained that adults "just didn't listen to us ... we were nonhumans to them. ... They didn't look at us as human beings, as people with feelings and rights and minds. They just looked at us as their little clay. Lumps of clay I guess to mold and do with as they wished."

Rachel Jones had already been repeatedly sexually assaulted by her brothers, while their father, Perry Jones, remained oblivious. Debbie Bunds's older sister had been raped by their father, and he "was trying to get at me." Debbie Bunds's mother knew about it, but did nothing, while Perry Jones accused young Debbie of seducing her father.[78]

Put in a broader perspective, one of the reasons that some of the Branch Davidians put up with Koresh's behavior was that they had low expectations for how they deserved to be treated, and sometimes these low expectations were the result of some form of abuse they experienced as children.

To maintain one's own integrity—no matter how severe the external demands of authority—takes great courage for both children and adults. The courage, and the love, of a young man and a young woman were what set in motion the destruction of David Koresh's world.

Among the followers of David Koresh, two were preeminent, both as evangelists and as teachers of doctrine second only to Koresh: Steve Schneider and Marc Breault. After meeting Koresh in a chance encounter in a supermarket in 1986, Breault had recruited his best friend, Steve Schneider, who had been teaching comparative religion at the University of Hawaii.[79] Legally blind, but still possessing slight visual abilities, Breault was considered to have the gift of prophetic vision, and his dreams and visions were considered very important by his fellow Branch Davidians.

Breault and an Australian Branch Davidian, Elizabeth Baranyai, fell in love when she visited Palestine, Texas, in April 1986. Koresh, however, wanted her for one of his own wives, but she had no interest in marrying him.

Conflict began to develop between Breault and Koresh because Koresh refused to consent to Breault's marriage to Elizabeth. Finally, after Breault threatened to leave the group, Koresh acceded. Marc and Elizabeth Breault were married on April 28, 1989, and enjoyed a wedding meal that evening at a local Sizzlers' steakhouse. Elizabeth returned to Australia shortly thereafter when her tourist visa expired.[80]

On August 5 of that year, David Koresh began expounding a far more radical doctrine of polygamy: all of the Branch Davidians' marriages were invalid because they had been entered into for worldly, lustful reasons. Under the "New Light" revelation, all of the Davidian women should become the wives of David Koresh. (Later, he announced that their holy offspring would one day rule the world.[81])

Steve Schneider and his wife, Judy, were shocked. At first, Schneider refused to believe that Koresh really meant for married women to become Koresh's wives. He contemplated killing Koresh, but worried what would happen to Judy if he failed. But Steve and Judy talked together and with Koresh, and prayed and eventually concluded that they had no choice but to follow God's will. They knew that David Koresh was not very impressive as a person, but they believed that God could work through imperfect instruments, and, rather than lose their salvation, they accepted what seemed to be God's will. The sacrifice was seen as a "piercing test" of devotion to God.[82]

After Judy Schneider accepted Koresh's "New Light," all of the married Davidians at Mount Carmel, except for one, fell in line with the new doctrine. Including the offspring of Koresh's first wife, Rachel, Koresh eventually sired at least thirteen children, eleven of whom died on April 19, 1993.[83] These children were seen by all the Branch Davidians as the most important part of Mount Carmel's purpose.[84] After ten years of marriage, Steve and Judy Schneider had been unable to conceive, but Judy Schneider Koresh and David Koresh conceived rapidly.[85] To the Schneiders, and the rest of the Branch Davidians, it must have been seen as further proof of God's will.

"All right, then, I'll go to Hell," said Huck Finn, when he finally decided to help his slave friend, Jim, escape, even though Huck, in accordance with the Christian doctrine he had been taught, was certain that he would burn forever for helping a runaway slave.[86] At the end of the all-night study session in which Koresh had announced the New Light, Marc Breault—while still in the study session—had a dream of himself standing on a small patch of ground as the fires of hell converged on him.[87] Marc and Elizabeth Breault were afraid of hell, but they still knew that something was terribly wrong with the New Light. Breault left the United States, moved to Australia to join Elizabeth, and began what he described as a "vendetta" against David Koresh. Breault argued that the followers of David Koresh (whom he dubbed "the Vernonites") were not true Branch Davidians, but were following a false prophet. His counterpreaching eventually deprived Koresh of most of his followers in Australia and New Zealand. Koresh's followers claimed that Breault left because he lost a power struggle with Koresh over who would run the group.

Self-described as a "cult buster," Breault devoted his life to destroying the Koresh religion. He had all the emotional intensity of someone who has been through an angry divorce, and his view of his former "spouse," the Branch Davidian church, was just as one-sided and selectively focused as in a terrible divorce. The Branch Davidians had looked on the outside world as satanic, but now Breault reversed that vision, and saw Koresh as evil incarnate.

Along with about a dozen other disaffected Branch Davidians, Breault hired a private detective who tried to interest various local police departments, the Immigration and Naturalization Service, the Texas Department of Public Safety, the McLennan County (Waco) Sheriff, and the Internal Revenue Service into taking action against the Davidians.[88]

Breault's generally hysterical letters failed to prompt action by the government. But a sensational tabloid television program in Australia got interested and did a one-hour exposé on Koresh. The tabloid show in turn helped convince the Waco *Tribune-Herald* to begin a month-long investigation which, after numerous delays, finally began to run on February 27, 1993. The series, titled "The Sinful Messiah," was a lurid, one-sided summary of all of the charges made by Breault and other former followers of Koresh.[89]

The Waco *Tribune-Herald* series was the foundation for most of what the American public would know about the Branch Davidians during the fifty-one days of the siege, since the FBI blocked almost all Branch Davidian attempts to communicate with the public. Thus, the American people only knew the Branch Davidians as an apparently insane group of child-abusing, gun nut, sex nut, zombie "cultists" for whom there could be no empathy.

Today, most Americans maintain their one-dimensional view of the Branch Davidians. But as Marc Breault explained in 1995:

> I want to dispel the myth that Branch Davidians are stupid. I disagree with many of their interpretations of the Bible, but as a rule, they are far more advanced than your average Christian. Religious people should never mistake their complacency for superior intel-

lect or discernment. Branch Davidians, in their own way, actually gave up all to follow what they believed to be God's truth. In other words, they actually did what Christ commanded. How many others manage that? While Branch Davidians are by no means the only spiritual people around, many so-called religious people never take any risks.

My lament is that the Branch Davidians took risks for the wrong cause, and are now paying the price. I guess that's the chance you take. When you blitz the quarterback, you might give up a long bomb. But at least they tried. If more of us tried while maintaining open minds toward other viewpoints, this world would be a better place. Like everything else, the Branch Davidian movement has good and bad points. Perhaps people can learn from their spirit, dedication, and tenacity, while Branch Davidians can learn to exercise better judgment. In the end, their calamity befell them partly because the US government made a shambles of a law enforcement operation, and partly because of their pride, convinced that they alone had the truth and that no one else understood God as well as they did. I guess we can all learn from that mistake.[90]

Dress Rehearsal for Waco: The Randy Weaver Case

Randy Weaver was a white racist[91] who lived with his family[92] in a remote construction-grade plywood cabin—later described as "fortified" by the FBI director—in northern Idaho. In contrast to the Branch Davidians, over half of whom were people of color, Weaver was a follower of Christian Identity, a sect which believes that whites are the true Jews of the Old Testament, and that ordinary Jews and people of color are malign.

A frequent companion of Weaver, building a nearby cabin, was a young man named Kevin Harris. Weaver had no criminal record or predisposition to crime; he did have peculiar and repulsive views, but for the most part he simply wanted to be left alone. While he attended a few meetings of Aryan Nations, he was not a joiner.

He came to BATF's attention when he attended the Aryan Nations meeting in July 1986, where he met a BATF informant who befriended Weaver. The informant was a private investigator who was paid by BATF on a contingency basis, earning a $3,500 bonus when he got a conviction. After three years, in late 1989, the informant finally entrapped (a jury later found) Weaver into shortening two shotgun barrels and stocks to well below the legal limit. Weaver had shown no inclination to saw off shotguns but was eventually persuaded to do so by the informant and by Weaver's need for cash. According to the Weavers, the informant told Weaver precisely where to cut the stocks and barrels.

The practice of paying informants on a contingency basis was and is pervasive throughout federal law enforcement. As in the Weaver case (and other cases we will discuss below), contingency payments inflate the already enormous incentives for informants to lie and to manufacture crimes, thereby bringing down the full wrath of federal law enforcement on innocent persons.

At 1995 Senate hearings about Ruby Ridge, BATF Director John Magaw promised to end immediately BATF's practice of paying informants on a contingency basis.[93] This reform should be made permanent and applied throughout federal law enforcement. Specific statutory language carrying out this reform is included in Appendix A, along with statutory language to carry out the other reforms we will propose at various points.

Several months after the informant finally convinced Weaver to illegally shorten the shotgun barrels, BATF threatened to indict Weaver for six offenses involved in making, possessing, and transferring two sawed-off shotguns. BATF further threatened that conviction would result in his losing his property (this was false), his wife's being unable to support the family, and their losing custody of their children. BATF did not want to indict him so much as it wanted him to agree to serve as an informer on the Aryan Nations. Weaver refused.

When Weaver declined to cooperate, and his wife warned the Aryan Nations what BATF was up to, BATF revised its description of Weaver. Weaver was now claimed to be a violent conspirator against the government even though he was so reclusive that he could not—and so paranoid that he would not—-conspire with anyone except members of his household and his friend Kevin Harris. BATF also began to claim that Weaver was a bank-robbery suspect and was suspected of harboring another white-supremacist bank robber. Living about as far as possible from the federal government as is possible in the continental United States, Weaver was described as determined to seek a confrontation with the federal government. If BATF could not get Weaver to help them arrest violent racists, then BATF would claim that Weaver was one. And thus he was indicted in December 1990 for gun law violations.

Early in 1991, Randy and Vicky Weaver were driving down the snowy road from their mountain home when they saw a couple stranded with engine trouble, with their car blocking the road. The Weavers got out to help the couple—who turned out to be decoys—and were promptly surrounded and forcefully subdued by a team of BATF agents, which included a winter-camouflaged sniper. Although Weaver had never been arrested before and had never threatened violence in his previous conversations with BATF agents, and although the Weavers did not resist the BATF agents in any way, BATF planned for and executed a forceful arrest, which included shoving Mrs. Weaver into a snowbank.

After being held overnight, Randy Weaver was brought before Magistrate Stephen Ayers. BATF argued that Weaver should not be allowed to post bond, and instead should be held in jail until his trial. BATF's argument that Weaver was so dangerous that he must be denied the right to bail was ludicrous, considering that the only crime which Weaver had ever committed was a nonviolent regulatory offense which a BATF informant had spent three years convincing him to commit.

The magistrate allowed Weaver to post a personal bond, secured by the Weavers' only significant asset, their homestead. The magistrate correctly told Weaver that if he failed to attend the trial, the bond would be forfeit, meaning that the government could seize the Weavers' home. The magistrate also informed Weaver that an attorney would be appointed to defend him, and (incorrectly) warned Weaver that if he were convicted Weaver might lose his property to pay the government for the cost of the defense attorney.

Having been wrongly warned by both BATF and the magistrate that conviction would result in the loss of his home, and the consequent impoverishment of his children, and the government taking the children away from their mother, Weaver made no secret of his plans not to leave his home, not even to attend the trial, which he had been told was scheduled for March 20, 1991.

The proximate reason for his failure to attend his trial, however, was that it was actually scheduled for February 20, 1991, and the Assistant U.S. Attorney (AUSA), Ron Howen, knew that Weaver's absence could be explained by the error. Nonetheless, Howen obtained an additional indictment for Weaver's failure to appear and a bench warrant for his arrest. As a result, the law enforcement agency primarily concerned with Weaver changed from BATF to the U.S. Marshals Service (USMS), which is in charge of arresting fugitives from the U.S. courts.

The USMS spent the next sixteen months surveilling Weaver's home on Ruby Ridge, but made no attempt at a traditional arrest. To the violent background BATF had invented for Weaver, the USMS added suspicions of drug trafficking, thus explaining an imaginary $10,000 the impoverished Weaver supposedly received about the time his desperate desire to feed his children led him to sell a couple of sawed-off shotguns to BATF for a few hundred dollars.

The phony drug connection justified getting the military involved (as would also occur at Waco, on the basis of dishonest allegations about drugs), since there is a "drug exception" to the federal law against use of the military in domestic law enforcement. (The exception will be discussed in greater detail in chapter 2.) So a military aircraft was sent to overfly Weaver's property—a cabin and a few shacks on unfenced acreage, erroneously described as a "compound"—to see if there was evidence of drugs, and to assist in developing plans for arresting Weaver, who had made it clear he planned to remain secluded on his property and not to report for trial.

The USMS did engage in serious negotiations for ending Weaver's refusal to turn himself in, but negotiations were thwarted by the AUSA, who mandated that all negotiations had to go through Weaver's court-assigned lawyer, with whom Weaver was not in contact, and must be part of a plea-bargain arrangement. In other words, the AUSA would not allow any settlement by which Weaver would come down and go to trial. The only settlement terms permissible would have to include Weaver pleading guilty to a crime of which (a jury later found) he was innocent.

At Waco also, the U.S. Attorney's office may have played a role in setting up a needless violent confrontation. According to the BATF, the U.S. Attorney at Waco insisted that the BATF's arrest warrant at Waco could only be served through a "dynamic-entry" (violent break-in) arrest at the Mount Carmel Center.

Unable to negotiate a settlement because of the AUSA's intransigence, the USMS began to work on various apprehension plans, including kidnaping or arresting Weaver's teenage daughter Sara when she slept outside the cabin in the "birthing shed" used by women during menstruation and the final stage of pregnancy,[94] and holding her until he turned himself in. USMS remote surveillance teams took careful notes of Sara's menstrual cycle.

Finally, six deputy marshals—four of whom were new to the assignment—snuck onto the property in August 1992. While three were elsewhere on the property, one of the other group of three threw rocks toward the cabin, which eventually caused the Weavers' yellow Labrador to scurry barking in the direction of the unidentified, camouflaged marshals. Weaver, his neighbor Kevin Harris, and Weaver's fourteen-year-old son, Sammy, grabbed their guns to run and investigate what they thought was a deer (food). Sammy Weaver and Kevin Harris followed the dog while Randy Weaver ran to where he hoped his son and neighbor would drive the deer into range. Two of the marshals were armed with M16 automatic rifles and one with a silenced 9mm machine pistol.

There are two versions of what happened next. The one the jury believed is that one of the marshals shot the dog in the back, causing an outraged Sammy to curse the trespasser and fire a few shots wildly before responding to his father's shout that he run home. Randy Weaver—portrayed by the USMS and BATF as a man who had been seeking a violent confrontation with the federal government for nearly a decade—saw a marshal, turned and ran, firing shots into the air to get his son's and Harris's attention, to tell them to run home.

In response to Sammy's shooting, Marshal William F. Degan shot at Sammy, hitting and shattering his gun, and doing the same to his arm, which was nearly severed. Sammy dropped his gun, as his arm was no longer capable of holding anything. As Sammy ran, one barely attached arm flapping precariously, a second marshal, Larry Cooper, fired a 9mm burst, with one round to the back killing Sammy.

Harris's story is that he responded to the violence, firing a shot in the direction of a nearly invisible camouflaged man, killing Degan. The marshals' assertion is that they called out "U.S. Marshals, stop," and that Harris killed Deputy Marshal Degan in cold blood; the marshals also initially insisted Degan had fired no shots, although he had actually fired seven rounds.

Both sides disengaged. Three of the marshals stayed in the general area, and reported that they were pinned down, unwilling to leave their fallen comrade. Actually, no shots were fired at them for the rest of the day. The only shots were fired in the air by the distraught parents of the deceased Sammy. No shots were fired after early afternoon, although the description of the deputy marshals as "pinned down" was repeated throughout the afternoon, and into the night, until they were rescued by the FBI in the middle of the night.

During the day, Harris and a loudly mourning and cursing Randy Weaver and his wife, Vicki, took Sammy's body to the shed, somehow retrieving the body without being noticed by marshals who were supposedly pinned down nearby.

The USMS immediately called in the FBI, in addition to state and local law enforcement, for a massive siege. The marshals' briefing of the FBI was too brief and misleading. The FBI "Hostage Rescue Team" (HRT), headed by Richard (Dick) M. Rogers, who would later serve as HRT commander at Waco, was deceived about the nature of the shootout. Told of Weaver's military background, the FBI assumed Weaver had done everything the military had trained him to be capable of doing: booby-trapping the area (an area in which dogs, children, and a baby wandered), digging tunnels, fortifying the home, possessing grenades and automatic weapons—all of which the marshals knew to be untrue. The threat that the FBI perceived upon its arrival was thus drastically overblown.

When the FBI showed up, it proceeded to alienate many longtime residents of the area. For example, the FBI ejected Scott and Kim Dodge from their home, to turn it into an FBI facility. They were promised reimbursement, but they had to write letters for a year to get their motel costs paid. According to Mr. Dodge, the FBI agents assumed "everyone here was guilty until proven innocent." He said that FBI behavior "changed the whole community's feelings about the federal government."[95]

The FBI had been told that most residents of Ruby Ridge were armed (in full compliance with Idaho law) when they left the cabin. Despite that knowledge, but with at least partial approval from Larry Potts (the FBI supervisor in Washington, D.C., who had ultimate authority over the operation), Rogers changed the normal, constitutional rules of engagement, which allow use of deadly force only when necessary to protect an innocent person from imminent peril. The new rules called on FBI snipers to shoot any armed adult male outside the cabin.[96]

When the Ruby Ridge shootings were investigated by Congress in 1995, there was great attention paid to whether Potts (who had been promoted to the second-ranking position in the FBI) had approved illegal shoot-to-kill orders. Factually, the only dispute is whether Potts approved changing the language to "can and should" shoot or only to "can" shoot any armed male. "Can and should" would amount to orders to kill, but "can" would be a license to kill. It is not disputed that the license-to-kill language was approved by Potts before the HRT arrived at Ruby Ridge. The "can and should" order to kill was part of an operational plan sent to the FBI headquarters for approval, and was immediately rejected for want of any provision for negotiating an end to the siege. Since the "can and should" language was in a document which FBI headquarters rejected on other grounds, the order to kill language was never formally approved by Potts.

It is uncontradicted that Rogers proposed a plan that had no possibility of a peaceful, negotiated end to the conflict, and this plan is at least suggestive of problems that later occurred in Waco under Rogers's command. It is also uncontradicted that Larry Potts approved license-to-kill language, which was illegal.

At Weaver's trial in 1993, HRT Director Rogers was unable to cite any authority for allowing the FBI, in violation of state law, to shoot people who were posing no threat to anyone. (A provision in the 1994 federal crime bill, removed during the bill's final movement through Congress, would have immunized federal agents from state criminal prosecution for crimes committed while on the job.)

When the new license-to-kill rule went into effect, neither Harris nor Weaver, the adult males at Ruby Ridge, knew of such a rule, nor, indeed, that the FBI was surrounding the cabin.

Once the pro forma addition of a negotiation plan was sent to Washington, Rogers deployed his snipers. Soon after the six two-man sniper teams were in place, but before the rest of the perimeter had been secured for the siege, Harris, Weaver, and Weaver's sixteen-year-old daughter, Sara, left the cabin. Sara and Harris went to a high point to see what was happening. Randy Weaver went toward the birthing shed to prepare Sammy for burial, armed with a rifle, but with his back to FBI sniper Lon T. Horiuchi, who has said that he could hit a quarter at two hundred yards, about the distance from which he now fired. Horiuchi later testified that he shot at Weaver to keep him from shooting at a helicopter overhead. But other testimony revealed that the helicopter was not overhead; it was well behind Horiuchi, which meant it was also behind Weaver, who was shot in the back of his shoulder. In addition, the helicopter was engaged in defilade maneuvering, meaning it would dart up and then quickly down behind the wooded hills, so it was not exposed for long enough to make a decent target, even if Weaver wanted to shoot. Horiuchi knew the helicopter was thus in no danger, since he had ridden in the copter earlier in the day. At the trial later, charges that Weaver and

Harris threatened federal officials in the helicopter were so unsubstantiated that the judge directed a verdict of acquittal.

In response to the sniper, from a besieging force which had yet to announce that they were law enforcement officers demanding surrender—and certainly before announcing the new and unconstitutional rules of engagement already in effect—the three persons fled for the safety of the cabin. Sara ran in front of her father, hoping that whoever was shooting would be reluctant to shoot a child. Weaver's wife, Vicki, holding their ten-month-old daughter, Elisheba, opened the door, which stood between her and Horiuchi, and shouted at them to come back to the relative safety of the cabin.

Sniper Horiuchi fired again, at the man he says he incorrectly thought was Weaver, even though Weaver and Harris have noticeable height and age disparities. Horiuchi later testified that he could not identify his target clearly because he could not see through the curtains of the door. After Horiuchi testified, however, the government (illegally late) turned over Horiuchi's official report of the shooting, including a drawing, where two heads appear in the windows of the open door. The drawing suggests that Horiuchi believed, incorrectly, that Randy Weaver and his daughter were crouched behind the door. The cross hairs he drew on the window of the door, the location his shot was to hit, was thus less than a foot above where he thought Sara's head was located. Since even the aggressive license-to-kill rules of engagement allowed only shots which could be taken "without endangering the children,"[97] Horiuchi may have violated the altered FBI rules in addition to permanent FBI rules, state and federal law, and the Constitution.

Another theory is offered by investigative journalist James Bovard: "To shoot at a running target by aiming at the window of a door facing into a cabin would be an idiotic way to try to shoot Kevin Harris. However, the shot that hit Vicki Weaver—severing her carotid artery—was a perfect kill shot."[98]

The FBI sniper's .308 bullet crashed into Vicki Weaver's head with such force that skull bone fragments and bullet fragments went into Harris, seriously injuring him. Vicki fell to the ground, bleeding profusely, instantly dead.[99]

During the next week, "the FBI used the microphones to taunt the family. 'Good morning, Mrs. Weaver. We had pancakes for breakfast. What did you have?' asked the agents in at least one exchange. Weaver's daughter, Sara, 16, said the baby, Elisheba, often was crying for her mother's milk when the FBI's messages were heard."[100]

In defense of the negotiator, forced on Dick Rogers and the HRT by the FBI, he had no idea that Vicki Weaver was dead. He had apparently not been told that Horiuchi believed he had at least wounded one member of the household. The negotiator's good faith, however, could not have been perceived by the remaining Weavers.

Bo Gritz, a much-decorated Vietnam war hero who is now a talk-show host and a right-wing political figure, offered to try to negotiate with Weaver. Shortly before Gritz arrived at the FBI camp, the "Camp Vicki" sign was taken down.[101]

After Gritz's first negotiation session with Randy Weaver, he returned to the FBI camp and told Rogers that Vicki Weaver was dead. According to Gritz, Rogers expressed no surprise at this news. He mentioned an FBI psychological profile, prepared before the attack, which called Vicki Weaver the "dominant member" of the family, thus implying that if she were "neutralized" everyone else might surrender; further, there was a fear that Vicki Weaver would kill her own children rather than surrender.[102] Gritz testified to the Senate that there was never any indication that shooting Vicki Weaver was an accident. He suggests that the first shot at Randy Weaver was intended to bring him down in order to draw Vicki Weaver into the open.

During the eleven-day siege, the FBI repeatedly sent a robot with a telephone in one arm to the front door of Weaver's cabin. The FBI negotiators ordered Weaver to pick up the phone and talk to them, and the FBI press spokesmen criticized Weaver for refusing to pick up the phone and negotiate. But the FBI spokespersons neglected to inform the press of one crucial fact: the robot's other arm held a shotgun, pointed straight at Weaver's door.[103]

Eight days after Vicki Weaver was shot, Gritz succeeded in convincing Weaver to surrender based on a promise that Weaver could meet with famed criminal defense attorney Gerry Spence. Had Weaver not surrendered, the FBI had plans, the very next day, to launch a CS chemical warfare and armored vehicle assault on Weaver's home, similar to the assault which would take place April 19, 1993, on the Branch Davidians' home.[104]

Spence agreed to take Weaver's case pro bono, and in April 1993, Kevin Harris went on trial for murder, with Randy Weaver charged with conspiracy to commit murder.[105]

As with Koresh, the government attempted to portray Weaver as a political and religious zealot who prophesied and then sought to create a holy war with federal agents, even though Weaver's clear goal had been to avoid government agents.[106] Weaver and Harris claimed self-defense, and that the government had unjustifiably fired first. With no defense evidence even introduced, the jury acquitted the accused of all charges of criminal violence. The court fined the federal government for withholding evidence and for lying, and complained that the government had acted with "a callous disregard for the rights of the defendants and the interests of justice."[107] Weaver was convicted only of his failure to appear for the court hearing growing out of the BATF sting.[108] The jury was reportedly of the view that the wrong set of people was being prosecuted.

Sniper Horiuchi was decorated for his actions at Ruby Ridge; he later appeared at Waco with the Hostage Rescue Team. "I am very, very proud . . . particularly [of] the HRT snipers," said FBI Director Louis Freeh in January 1995.[109] Contrary to the findings of the 524-page Department of Justice report on Ruby Ridge, Freeh insisted that the FBI snipers were following standard rules, and not the shoot-to-kill rules of engagement.[110]

Months after the government settled the Weavers' civil suit for $3.1 million, the six deputy marshals who began the violence and the siege were honored as "heroes" for "their exceptional courage, their sound judgement in the face of attack [even though they had been under orders to avoid confrontation], and their high degree of professional competence during the incident" by the U.S. Marshals Service in March 1996. Awards included: a posthumous award for Degan, who fired at Sammy Weaver as he was running away and severed his arm; an award to Larry Cooper, who shot Sammy Weaver in the back with a silenced submachine gun, and later testified under oath that Weaver may have shot his own son; and an award to Arthur Roderick, who testified similarly, and who shot Weaver's dog.[111] The United States Senate subcommittee which investigated Ruby Ridge, and which issued its report months before the marshals received their awards, concluded that Cooper and Roderick had lied during their Senate testimony, and stated that there was no evidence to support Cooper and Roderick's testimony that Sammy Weaver had been shot in the back by his own father.[112]

Half a year after the killings at Ruby Ridge, Hostage Rescue Team Director Dick Rogers found himself in a command role of the FBI siege of Mount Carmel. Larry Potts, supervisor of the Ruby Ridge siege, also played a major role at Waco, and in formulating the plans for the FBI's tank and chemical warfare assault that brought the Waco siege to an end. In 1995, FBI Director Louis Freeh appointed Potts second-in-command of the FBI, but Potts was forced to step down not long afterward as a result of public criticism.[113]

At the end of each chapter, we will suggest particular reforms which would have prevented or mitigated the problems described in that chapter. Since many of the problems in the Randy Weaver case (inappropriate use of deadly force, covering up evidence) also occurred at Waco, we will postpone most Weaver-related reforms until later. We will, at this point, offer one reform which would have prevented the entire Weaver fiasco: government undercover agents should be entirely forbidden to attempt to entrap persons into committing crimes. Of course if an undercover agent observed a crime being perpetrated or planned, he could take action; he simply could not instigate crimes.

As Justice Felix Frankfurter put it: "The power of government is abused and directed to an end for which it was not constituted when employed to promote rather than detect crime and bring about the downfall of those who, left to themselves, might have obeyed the law. . . . Human nature is weak enough and sufficiently beset by temptations without government adding to them and generating crime."[114] And as the Weaver case illustrates, once the government begins generating the first crime, all sorts of crimes may spring from the poisonous root.

NOTES

1. Arthur S. Maxwell, *History's Crowded Climax: Prophecy Speaks to Our Time* (Mountain View, Calif.: Pacific Press, 1940), p. 13, quoted in Paul Boyer, *When Time Shall Be No More: Prophecy Belief in Modern American Culture* (Cambridge, Mass.: Harvard University Press, 1992), p. 110.

2. The Violence Policy Center, a research organization which supports stringent gun controls, including handgun prohibition, explains the Bureau's recent use of "ATF" instead of "BATF," as if the FBI dropped the "B" for "Bureau" and started calling itself the "FI":

> ATF has recently attained newfound respect by focusing on its law enforcement activities. With TV footage of agents in black jackets with large ATF letters on the back kicking in crack-house doors or interdicting gun runners on Interstate 95 now common, ATF hopes to be seen as a cadre of specialized lawmen—not as drab regulators leafing through gun store account books. (Originally known as BATF, the agency dropped the B so that its acronym would more resemble the better-known FBI and DEA.)

(Violence Policy Center, *More Gun Dealers than Gas Stations: A Study of Federally Licensed Firearms Dealers in America* [Washington, D.C.: Violence Policy Center, 1992], p. 42.)

The agency has not been uniformly successful in getting "ATF" accepted. See, for example, the

Treasury Department's Office of the Inspector General's report, *Review of the Bureau of Alcohol, Tobacco and Firearms's (BATF) Involvement in the Incidents at Ruby Ridge, Idaho* (June 30, 1994). The Justice Department's unpublished "Internal Review Regarding the Ruby Ridge Hostage Situation and Shootings of Law Enforcement Personnel" also used "BATF" to identify the bureau.

While three-initial abbreviations are common in the federal government, the usage is by no means universal (the United States Marshals Service is USMS, for example). Most federal abbreviations follow the rule that the abbreviation should specify the type of governmental entity. For example, it is important that the "Federal Bureau of Investigation" include a "B" in the abbreviation ("FBI"), to identify the entity as a bureau (rather than an agency, a department, a commission, or some other type organization). By the same principle that the Federal Bureau of Investigation is abbreviated "FBI" (rather than "FI"), the Internal Revenue Service is "IRS" (rather than "IR"), the United States Marshals Service is "USMS" (rather than "USM"), it is appropriate that the abbreviation for the Bureau of Alcohol, Tobacco and Firearms includes the "B" for Bureau. We shall use "BATF" throughout, unless quoting from a source which does not. In addition to "BATF," other commonly used abbreviations we shall be using are "FBI" for the Federal Bureau of Investigation, "DEA" for the Drug Enforcement Administration, "USMS," and "AUSA" for Assistant United States Attorney.

The Bureau of Alcohol, Tobacco and Firearms in its current form was created to enforce the federal Gun Control Act of 1968. The BATF is a descendant of the Bureau of Prohibition (which enforced alcohol prohibition in the 1920s and 1930s), and traces its lineage back to the federal "revenuers" who have waged a low-grade war with rural alcohol distillers since the founding of the United States.

3. Stephen Labaton, "Report to Fault Firearms Bureau for Raid on Cult," *New York Times*, August 30, 1993; U.S. Dept. of the Treasury, *Report on the Bureau of Alcohol, Tobacco and Firearms, Investigation of Vernon Wayne Howell also known as David Koresh* (Washington, D.C.: Government Printing Office, September 1993), cited as "Treasury Report." Although 76 agents participated directly in the raid, over 130 were involved in the overall operation in and around Waco. Ibid., p. 173.

4. By 1993, many members did not call themselves Branch Davidians, but instead "students of the seven seals." James D. Tabor and Eugene V. Gallagher, *Why Waco? Cults and the Battle for Religious Freedom in America* (Berkeley: University of California Press, 1995), p. 213.

When Kathy Schroeder left the besieged Mount Carmel Center and later telephoned in, Steve Schneider criticized her for identifying herself as a "Koreshian" or "Davidian," suggesting she could have said "Bible student" if the computer lacked space for the full name of the group, Branch Davidian Seventh-day Adventists. Transcripts of BATF Tapes of the Negotiations between Federal Law Enforcement and the Branch Davidians, February 28–April 19, 1993 (cited as "Negot. Tapes"), no. 126, March 13, 1993. We shall refer to the group as "Davidians" or "Branch Davidians," since that is how they are best known to the general public.

5. U.S. Department of Justice, *Report on the Events at Waco, Texas, February 28 to April 19, 1993* (Redacted version, Washington, D.C.: October 8, 1993), p. 7 (hereinafter "Justice Report").

6. See generally David Humphreys Miller, *Ghost Dance* (Lincoln: University of Nebraska Press, 1959).

7. *Events Surrounding the Branch Davidian Cult Standoff in Waco, Texas.* Hearing before the Committee on the Judiciary, U.S. House of Representatives, 103rd Cong., 1st sess., April 28, 1993, (hereinafter "Hearing"), p. 5.

8. Diana Bowder, ed., *Who Was Who in the Roman World* (New York: Washington Square Press, 1980), pp. 171–73.

9. Nero, one of Domitian's predecessors, had persecuted only the Christians in Rome.

10. See generally George R. Knight, *Millennial Fever and the End of the Word: A Study of Millerite Adventism* (Boise, Idaho: Pacific Press, 1993).

11. Tabor and Gallagher, *Why Waco?* pp. 44, 224 n. 47.

12. Ibid., p. 35.

13. Bill Pitts, "The Davidian Tradition," in *From the Ashes: Making Sense of Waco,* ed. James Lewis (Lanham, Md.: Rowman and Littlefield, 1993), pp. 34–35.

14. William L. Pitts, Jr., "Davidians and Branch Davidians 1929–1987," in *Armageddon in Waco: Critical Perspectives on the Branch Davidian Conflict,* ed. Stuart A. Wright (Chicago: University of Chicago Press, 1995), p. 30.

15. Pitts, "The Davidian Tradition," in Lewis, p. 36.

16. Pitts, "Davidians and Branch Davidians 1929–1987," in Wright, p. 34.

17. Clifford L. Linedecker, *The Massacre at Waco, Texas* (New York: St. Martin's, 1993), p. 57.

18. Pitts, "Davidians and Branch Davidians 1929–1987," in Wright, p. 32; Marc Breault and Martin King, *Inside the Cult* (New York: Signet, 1993), pp. 359–60. Zechariah 3:8, 6:12; Isaiah 11:1. Compare John 15:1–3 ("I am the vine, you are the branches").

All biblical quotations are from the King James Version, the text used by the Branch Davidians.

19. Breault and King, *Inside the Cult,* p. 361; J. Philip Arnold, "The Davidian Dilemma: To Obey God or Man?" in Lewis, *From the Ashes,* p. 30 (Leviticus as guide for holy days).

20. E.g., Daniel Cattau, "Davidians in Missouri Disavow Waco-area Cult," *Dallas Morning News,* March 14, 1993 (noting existence of groups in Mountaindale, New York; Spokane, Wash.; and Yucaipa, California).

21. Her prayers called on "Our Mother, who art in Heaven." Linedecker, *The Massacre at Waco,* p. 61. See generally Catherine Wessinger, ed., *Women's Leadership in Marginal Religions: Explorations Outside the Mainstream* (Urbana: University of Illinois Press, 1993).

Gnostic writings and some other early Christian documents also contain the belief that the Holy Spirit is female. Sally Cunneen, *In Search of Mary: The Woman and the Symbol* (New York: Ballantine, 1996), p. 79. The Gnostics addressed God as both "our Father" and "our Mother." Elaine Pagels, "God the Father, God the Mother," in *The Gnostic Gospels* (New York: Random House, 1979).

22. Kenneth Samples, Erwin de Castro, Richard Abanes, and Robert Lyle, *Prophets of the Apocalypse: David Koresh & Other American Messiahs* (Grand Rapids, Mich.: Baker, 1994); George W. Reid, "Sorting the Messiahs," *Liberty* (July/August 1993): 19; Carol Moore, *The Davidian Massacre* (Franklin, Tenn.: Legacy Communications and Gunowners Foundation, 1995), p. 16.

23. Breault and King, *Inside the Cult,* p. 27.

24. Samples et al., *Prophets of the Apocalypse,* pp. 17–27.

25. Tabor and Gallagher, *Why Waco?* pp. 40–41.

26. Thomas Robbins and Dick Anthony, "Sects and Violence: Factors Enhancing the Volatility of Marginal Religious Movements," in Wright, *Armageddon in Waco,* p. 239.

27. David G. Bromley and Edward D. Silver, "The Davidian Tradition: From Patronal Clan to Prophetic Movement," in Wright, *Armageddon in Waco,* p. 53.

28. Pitts, "Davidians and Branch Davidians 1929–1987," p. 37.

29. Samples et al., *Prophets of the Apocalypse,* pp. 32–34.

30. Bromley and Silver, "The Davidian Tradition," p. 53.

31. Dick J. Reavis, *The Ashes of Waco: An Investigation* (New York: Simon and Schuster, 1995), pp. 27–30.

32. Tabor and Gallagher, *Why Waco?* p. 41. Samples et al., *Prophets of the Apocalypse,* pp. 38–41. During the 1993 negotiations with the FBI, Koresh denied any sexual relationship with Lois Roden. Negot. Tape no. 7, March 1, 1993.

33. Samples et al., *Prophets of the Apocalypse,* pp. 33–39.

34. For example, Robyn Bunds observed that Vernon had become warmer, more considerate, and more capable. Linedecker, *The Massacre at Waco, Texas,* p. 68.

35. Jones was standing next to Koresh when the shooting began, according to the Davidians, and was seriously wounded in his abdomen. During the firefight, one of the Branch Davidians complied with Jones's request to put him out of his misery.

36. Treasury Report, p. 43.

37. Exodus 3.

38. Tabor and Gallagher, *Why Waco?* pp. 61, 230 n. 15.

39. David Koresh, "The Shower Head Tape," August 24, 1987 (Wisconsin teaching session; transcript available from The Research Center at http://www.ime.net/~mswett), p. 27. (We have changed some of the punctuation in the transcript, which the transcriber describes as a first draft.)

40. Samples et al., *Prophets of the Apocalypse,* pp. 47–48.

41. Pete Slover and Diane Jennings, "Source of Money for Davidian Sect Remains a Mystery," *Dallas Morning News,* March 8, 1993.

42. Pitts, "Davidians and Branch Davidians 1929–1987," in Wright, pp. 37–38. In 1988, an ex-

Branch Davidian who had been an alcoholic returned to the fold. He went to Koresh and Marc Breault (at the time Koresh's chief disciple), who conducted a Bible study designed to prove that Koresh was the Messiah. According to Breault, the man "got a glazed look in his eye. He stared up toward Heaven and said: 'My God, my God. After all these years I understand. I'm the Messiah, I'm the David. Now I know why I've suffered all these years.'" The man promptly headed off to see George Roden, who was then living in Odessa, Texas. Roden, who later claimed that the man was an assassin sent by Howell, split the man's head open with an axe. Breault and King, *Inside the Cult*, pp. 107–108. Acquitted of homicide on grounds of insanity, Roden is now incarcerated in a mental institution.

43. Moore, *The Davidian Massacre*, p. 221, citing *Day 51* video interview with Sheila Martin. One of the tasks of the attorney hired for Koresh during the siege, interpreted by the attorney as evidence Howell/Koresh was planning for a future on earth, was to perfect legal title to the property. United States House of Representatives, Subcommittee on Crime of the Committee on the Judiciary and the Subcommittee on National Security, International Affairs, and Criminal Justice of the Committee on Government Reform and Oversight, *Joint Hearings on Activities of Federal Law Enforcement Agencies Toward the Branch Davidians*, 104th Cong., 1st sess., July 19–August 1, 1995 (Washington, D.C.: Government Printing Office, 1996) (cited as "Joint Hearings"), testimony of Dick DeGuerin, part 2, p. 50.

44. Joyce Sparks, Joint Hearings, part 1, p. 611.

45. Isaac Asimov, *Asimov's Guide to the Bible: Old Testament* (1968), p. 435.

46. Isaiah 45:1.

47. 1 Samuel 22:1–2; The Chosen Vessel, *Seven Seals,* Book One (1996), p. 189 (explaining the next part of Rev. 6:8—"and Hell followed with him"—as meaning that Koresh had to be killed for the sins of people living under the New Testament period).

48. Song of Solomon 3:7–8; Karl Hennig, "'Apocalyptic Rock': My Days with David Koresh," *Liberty* (July/August 1993): 14.

49. Song of Solomon 6:8.

50. Ron Cole, "Davidian Tells the Truth about Waco," *Boulder Weekly*, July 27, 1995, p. 8; Tabor and Gallagher, *Why Waco?* p. 42 (Koresh's third wife was Michelle Jones, the twelve-year-old sister of his first wife).

51. Thomas Robbins and Dick Anthony, "Sects and Violence: Factors Enhancing the Volatility of Marginal Religious Movements," in Wright, *Armageddon in Waco*, p. 241.

52. Farrakhan:

> If the scholars agree that the Jesus of 2,000 years ago prefigured or gave us a picture of the real Jesus, then the historical Jesus is not the real Jesus, but the real Jesus is the one that the historical Jesus prefigures or gives us a type of.
>
> The historical Jesus was not the Messiah; the prophetic Jesus is the Messiah. The historical Jesus prefigured the Messiah, and that's why the Jews never accepted the historical Jesus. They continue to look for the Messiah. They are not wrong.
>
> He wasn't born in Bethlehem or Judea. He was born in Sandersville, Georgia. . . .
>
> When you close the Old Testament, you open the New Testament with the genealogy of Jesus. But the Old Testament closes saying Elijah's coming. God, my God, is coming. Then you open up with the genealogy of Jesus, so who is Jesus? Who is Elijah? Jesus and Elijah are one and the same.
>
> I am that Elijah that was to come and now is.

("The 700 Club," March 6, 1996 [Christian Broadcasting Network], transcript [Burelle's Information Services], pp. 9, 10.)

53. The UFO trip provided Farrakhan's inspiration for the Million Man March. Ken Ringle, "A Look at . . . Messages from the March," *Washington Post*, October 22, 1995, quoting *Million Man March Home Study Guide Manual* (Honorable Elijah Muhammad Educational Foundation: 1995)(reprinting Farrakhan's October 24, 1989 speech at the J.W. Marriott Hotel in Washington, describing his 1985 abduction, trip in a UFO with an invisible pilot, visit to a manufactured planet known as "The Mother Wheel," and meeting there with the voice of the late Elijah Muhammad, warning him that President Reagan and Joint Chiefs of Staff Chairman Colin Powell were planning a war against black Americans).

54. Livingstone Fagan, *Christ* (no date), p. 7, available from The Research Center, http://www.ime.net/~mswett/christ.html. All of Fagan's writings have been composed in federal prison, where he is currently serving a forty-year sentence. At his sentencing allocution, Fagan proudly stated that he had never attempted to distance himself from David Koresh. Fagan, the last Davidian to leave Mount Carmel before April 19, 1993, is the only incarcerated Branch Davidian who refused to appeal his sentence.

55. Isaiah 20:1–3.

56. Hosea 1:2.

57. Ezekiel 4:9–17.

58. Ezekiel 24:15–18.

59. Genesis 22. Just after Abraham "took the knife to slay his son," an angel from God called the whole thing off. The story is generally cited as an example of Abraham's magnificent obedience to the will of God, and modern readers insist that God never intended for the order to be carried out.

From our viewpoint, there is never an acceptable circumstance for human sacrifice; any god who would order the gratuitous killing of an innocent child is a god who does not deserve to be listened to.

60. Hebrews 7:3. See also Genesis 14:18–20 ("the high priest of the most high God"); Psalms 110:4 ("Thou art a priest for ever after the order of Melchizedek"); Hebrews 5–7.

61. Reavis, *The Ashes of Waco: An Investigation*, p. 108.

62. Jerry Bergman, "Paradise Postponed . . . and Postponed," *Christian Research Journal* (Summer 1996): 36–41.

63. Victoria Loe, "Ideas Vary on Cults' Appeal to Women," *Dallas Morning News*, March 21, 1993; David Koresh, "The Shower Head Tape," p. 12 (". . . I'm showing you the prophecies and telling you, you better learn them or you're going to hell").

64. Tabor and Gallagher, *Why Waco?* p. 23.

65. Harvard Law School graduate Wayne Martin had been the law librarian at the University of North Carolina Central Law School before joining the Branch Davidians: "Branch Davidians Living and Dead," *Dallas Morning News*, May 16, 1993. "Wayne Martin was recognized here as a good attorney": McLennan County Sheriff Jack Harwell, "Frontline" interview, August 3, 1995, available at http://www.wgbh.org.

66. "Branch Davidians Living and Dead," *Dallas Morning News*, May 16, 1993 (Graeme Craddock).

67. For example, Livingstone Fagan had a Master of Theology degree from NewBold College, an Adventist institution in England. Tabor and Gallagher, *Why Waco?* p. 24.

While everyone at Mount Carmel accepted the Branch Davidian religious doctrines, not everyone had started off with a primary interest in religion. David Thibodeau and Norman Allison had first been drawn by their interest in music and politics. Reavis, *The Ashes of Waco,* pp. 44–46, 193; David Thibodeau, Joint Hearings, part 1, p. 123; Negot. Tape no. 87, March 7.

68. Doctrines and Covenants 89:9 (Mormon scripture; "Hot drinks are not good for the body or belly").

69. All the food rules are from Alice Scott, *The Incredible Power of Cults* (Colorado Springs: Blue River Publications, 1994), p. 56.

70. Ibid., p. 56.

71. Diane Jennings, "Public Tragedy, Private Grief," *Dallas Morning News*, May 6, 1993 (Ruth Mosher, mother of Kiri Jewell; Isabelle Andrade, mother of Kathy and Jennifer Andrade). This undermines an assumption common to most defenders of the federal government's role, as stated by Rep. Barney Frank: "one of the things they [cults] do seem to have in common is that they don't get to family reunions much . . . one of the factors of cults is an isolation from the families." Hearing, p. 51.

72. "Frontline" interview with Clive Doyle, July 9, 1995. Available at http://www.wbgh.org.

73. Breault and King, *Inside the Cult*, pp. 174–75.

74. Darcey Steinke, "God Rocks," *Spin* (1993): 90.

75. Ron Cole, "Davidian Tells Truth About Waco," *Boulder Weekly*, July 27, 1995, p. 8.

76. Samples, et al., *Prophets of the Apocalypse*, p. 201.

77. Breault and King, *Inside the Cult*, p. 156. Koresh could, of course, speak English fluently, but his grammar and spelling skills were weak.

78. Samples, et al., *Prophets of the Apocalypse,* p. 36.

79. Tabor and Gallagher, *Why Waco?* p. 26.

80. Breault and King, *Inside the Cult,* pp. 166–70.

81. See Revelation 4:4, 5:9–10 ("And round about the throne were four and twenty seats: and upon the seats I saw four and twenty elders sitting, clothed in white raiment; and they had on their heads crowns of gold . . . And they sung a new song, saying, Thou are worthy to take the book, and to open the seals thereof: for thou wast slain, and hast redeemed us to God by thy blood out of every kindred, and tongue, and people, and nation.")

Koresh saw his "House of David" as the fulfillment of Psalms 8:2 and 45:16. J. Philip Arnold, "The Davidian Dilemma: To Obey God or Man?" in Lewis, *From the Ashes,* p. 30.

82. Livingstone Fagan, *Mt. Carmel: The Unseen Reality Part 2,* p. 31. Available from The Research Center, http://www.ime.net/~mswett. As partial compensation for the men, the beer rule was relaxed so that there was no limit on consumption. Breault and King, *Inside the Cult,* p. 187.

83. According to a lawsuit filed by, among other people, Koresh's mother, Bonnie Haldeman, the deceased children were named: Cyrus Ben Joseph, Star Hadassah Howell, Serenity Sea Jones Koresh, Chica Jones Koresh, Little One Jones Koresh, Startle Summers, Chanel Andrade, and Mayana Schneider. Surviving children are Jared Michael Okimoto and Sky Born Okimoto. Plaintiffs' complaint in *Brown* v. *United States,* (S.D. Texas, Houston Division), February 25, 1995, paras. 9, 15. The plaintiffs are represented by former United States Attorney General Ramsey Clark. For more on the suit, see chapter 5.

84. Tabor and Gallagher, *Why Waco?* p. 73.

85. Breault and King, *Inside the Cult,* p. 185. "Koresh" was the adopted last name of all of the Branch Davidians. To avoid unnecessary verbiage, we refer to them by their pre-Koresh names: e.g., "David Jones" rather than "David Jones Koresh."

86. Mark Twain, *The Adventures of Huckleberry Finn,* ch. 31 (1884).

87. Breault and King, p. 163.

88. Ibid., pp. 217–82. For examples, see Geoffrey N. Hossack, Director, ARM (All Risk Management) International, letter of January 3, 1992 to U.S. Consular Office, Melbourne; Hossack, fax of August 16, 1990 to Richard Ludwig, FBI liaison officer, United States Embassy, Australia; Hossack, letter of August 16, 1990, to Terry Lee, Texas Department of Public Safety, p. 3 (warning that "it is highly probable" that Vernon would murder/sacrifice one of his children and that "in all probability it will be performed during Yom Kipur [*sic*]").

Schneider said Breault was "constantly harassing them [the sheriff's office] in regards to getting some kind of charges on us . . . the guy was relentless." Negot. Tape no. 65, March 6.

89. Koresh's lieutenant, Steve Schneider, immediately thought of Breault when he saw the newspaper story, and thought, "Here we go again." Negot. Tape no. 56, March 5.

90. Marc Breault, *The Return of David Koresh* (1995), available on the World-Wide Web at: http://www.mainelink.net/~mswett/return.html.

91. When the BATF offered not to prosecute Weaver on firearms charges if he would become an undercover informant for the government, Vicki Weaver sent out a letter stating, "We cannot make deals with the enemy . . . ," which she addressed to "Aryan Nations & all our brethren of the Anglo Saxon race." George Lardner, Jr., and Richard Leiby, "Botched 'Anti-Terrorist' Operation Began with Series of Overreactions," *Washington Post,* September 3, 1995. At the U.S. Senate hearings, Mr. Weaver was asked by Sen. Dianne Feinstein if he owned any swastikas, and he replied "maybe."

92. Information on the Weaver incident at Ruby Ridge is based on research for a forthcoming book by James O.E. Norell, as well as from the marshals' logs, the trial transcript, and the 1995 hearings of the U.S. Senate Judiciary Subcommittee on Terrorism, Technology and Government Information. One other important source is the Department of Justice's internal investigation into Ruby Ridge; although the Department repeatedly refused to release the report, American Lawyer Media obtained a copy, and posted it on the World-Wide Web. United States Department of Justice, *Department of Justice Report Regarding Internal Investigation of Shootings at Ruby Ridge, Idaho, during Arrest of Randy Weaver* (hereafter, "DOJ Internal Investigation of Ruby Ridge"), available at http://www.courttv.com/library/government/ruby.html.

93. "Informer: Weaver Promised Guns," *Washington Post,* September 8, 1995 (Associated Press).

94. According to Old Testament law, which the Weavers apparently obeyed, menstruating women were considered unclean, and required to be separate from the rest of the population. Leviticus 15.

95. Mark Potok, "Ruby Ridge: Symbol of Government Intrusion," *USA Today*, September 14, 1995, p. A4.

96. According to the unpublished Department of Justice "Crisis Center Log: Degan Incident" for August 22, 1992, 4:50 P.M. EST: U.S. Marshall Michael Johnson "reported that . . . an operational plan has been agreed on and is being telephoned to the Department of Justice. The operational plan is as follows: . . . 3. If Weaver or his older son [Harris, the USMS thought] exit the residence armed, snipers will neutralize them."

97. Perhaps Horiuchi believed his expertise meant he was not endangering Sara by aiming about ten inches from where he suspected her invisible head to be. He had, however, just finished attempting to kill Weaver, whom he believed to be Harris, and failed. And then he fired again at a person whom he believed to be Harris and, again, did not believe he had killed him. When Dick Rogers testified at the Weaver/Harris trial, he noted he had been concerned that his sniper shot twice and apparently missed once and only wounded once.

98. James Bovard, "Hear No Evil," *American Spectator* (January 1996): 42.

99. Later, when the FBI was planning its final assault at Waco, and explaining what would happen if the adult Davidians attempted to use the children as shields, Attorney General Reno was assured that "our snipers are good enough to pick off the people who are holding the children." Hearing, p. 59. Sara Weaver could certainly bear witness to the accuracy of that statement. For those same hearings, BATF Director Stephen Higgins supplied a list of other sieges in which BATF had played some role, including "a support role in the Weaver standoff in Idaho. One U.S. marshal and two suspects were killed; two were wounded." Hearing, p. 122. It is unclear what Sammy and Vicki Weaver were suspected of.

100. Jerry Seper, "FBI Agents Waged War on Minds," *Washington Times*, September 22, 1993, p. A7.

101. Richard Leiby and George Lardner, Jr., "Siege Guided by Hastily Revised Rules of Engagement," *Washington Post*, September 4, 1995.

102. Alan W. Bock, "Ambush at Ruby Ridge," *Reason* (October 1993): 27; Richard Leiby and George Lardner, Jr., "Siege Guided by Hastily Revised Rules of Engagement," *Washington Post*, September 4, 1995.

103. James Bovard, "Hear No Evil," p. 79.

104. Jerry Seper, "Waco Plan Almost Used in Idaho," *Washington Times*, August 24, 1995, p. A1. During the 1995 House of Representatives hearings on Waco, Rep. Bob Barr questioned former FBI Assistant Director Larry Potts about an FBI document which read:

> On August 23, 1992, the above actions will be repeated. If no response from the compound is received, the APC's, armored personnel carriers, will be prepared to begin destruction of portions of the structure inside the compound. The destruction will not include the major living areas of the main residence. If no response is received at this time, ARC's [*sic*] will be prepared to deliver chemical agents into the residence in anticipation of conducting an entry into same.

(Joint Hearings, part 2, p. 574.) Mr. Potts refused to confirm or deny whether the above-quoted material was part of the official "ops" plan.

105. Jerry Seper, "The Shootout on Ruby Ridge," *Washington Times*, September 22, 1993, pp. A6–A7.

106. Louis Sahagan and Doug Conner, "Pair Acquitted of Murder in Idaho Mountain Shootout," *Washington Post*, July 9, 1993.

107. Sahagan and Conner, "Pair Acquitted of Murder"; Michele Ingrassia, "Is Deadly Force Justifiable?" *Newsweek* (June 21, 1993): 31; Timothy Egan, "U.S. Hits Snags in Idaho Siege Trial," *New York Times*, June 23, 1993; Jerry Seper, "FBI Official Called Unfit," *Washington Times*, April 14, 1995, p. A6.

108. Gerry Spence, *From Freedom to Slavery: The Rebirth of Tyranny in America* (New York:

St. Martin's, 1993); James L. Pate, "Standoff in Idaho: The Randy Weaver Incident," *Soldier of Fortune* (March 1993).

109. Press conference, January 6, 1995, quoted in Richard Leiby and George Lardner, Jr., "Siege Guided by Hastily Revised Rules of Engagement."

110. Jess Walter, "Ruby Ridge's Key Question," *USA Today*, September 6, 1995.

111. Sammy was killed by a 9mm round, with an upward trajectory. Weaver was uphill from his son when Sammy was killed, and carrying a shotgun, although he also had a 9mm pistol with him.

112. Jerry Seper, "Shootout Awards Anger Senator, Marshals Honored for Ruby Ridge," *Washington Times*, March 4, 1996, p. A3.

113. Potts was given a letter of censure for his role at Ruby Ridge, the same punishment meted out to Director Louis Freeh for losing his car phone. "While letters of censure can temporarily put a crimp in a bureau career, they are forgotten after a year or two." Ronald Kessler, *The FBI* (New York: Pocket Books, 1993), p. 112. See generally, Paul Marcus, *The Entrapment Defense*, 2d ed. (The Michie Co., 1995).

114. *Sherman* v. *United States*, 356 U.S. 369, 384 (1958) (Frankfurter, J., concurring).

1

The Unwarranted Warrant

In mid-November 1992, personnel from the "60 Minutes" television program began contacting BATF officials regarding a story that "60 Minutes" was producing about sexual harassment within BATF.[1] At the same time, BATF knew that a new president was coming to power—a president who had pledged to fight sexual harassment on every front, to "reinvent government," and to cut the federal budget deficit.

BATF had already been on the defensive about discrimination. In 1990, black agents had filed suit in federal court claiming that BATF racially discriminated in pay, hiring, and promotion. (The suit was settled in 1996, with BATF agreeing to pay 5.9 million dollars in damages to 241 current and former agents, and also agreeing to overhaul its personnel policies.) A fresh round of discrimination complaints by black BATF agents had come in October 1992, the month before "60 Minutes" began setting up interviews for the sex discrimination story.[2] The "60 Minutes" report, which would air on January 10, 1993, put BATF in a vulnerable position for the congressional budget hearing that would take place in early March.

The "60 Minutes" report was devastating. BATF agent Michelle Roberts told the television program that after she and some male agents finished a surveillance in a parking lot, "I was held against the hood of my car and had my clothes ripped at by two other agents." Agent Roberts claimed she was in fear for her life. The agent who corroborated Ms. Roberts's accusations recounted that he was pressured to resign from BATF. Another agent, Sandra Hernandez, said her complaints about sexual harassment were at first ignored by BATF, and she was then demoted to file clerk and transferred to a lower-ranking office. BATF agent Bob Hoffman said "the people I put in jail have more honor than the top administration in this organization." Agent Lou Tomasello said, "I took an oath. And the thing I find totally abhorrent and disgusting is these higher-level people took that same oath and they violate the basic principles and tenets of the Constitution and the laws and simple ethics and morality."[3]

BATF had investigated David Koresh in the summer of 1992. Like the Waco *Tribune-Herald* investigation, the BATF investigation began about a month after the Australian tabloid television program on Koresh.[4] Having lain moribund since the summer, the BATF investigation perked up in mid-November.[5] By early December, BATF was planning the raid on Mount Carmel.[6]

A BATF memo written two days before the February 28, 1993, raid explained, "this operation will generate considerable media attention, both locally (Texas) and nationally."[7] BATF public relations director Sharon Wheeler called reporters to ask them for their weekend phone numbers. The reporters contend, and Wheeler denies, that she asked them if they would be interested in covering a weapons raid on a "cult." Ms. Wheeler states that she merely told them "We have something big going down." After the raid, BATF at first denied there had been any media contacts.[8] Journalist Ronald Kessler reports that BATF told eleven media outlets that the raid was coming.[9]

The Department of the Treasury has refused to release the preraid memos which deal with publicity, asserting that they are exempt from the Freedom of Information Act.[10]

In any case, BATF's public relations officer was stationed in Waco on the day of the raid, ready to issue a press release announcing the raid's success.[11] A much-publicized raid, resulting in the seizure of hundreds of guns and dozens of "cultists" might reasonably be expected to improve the fortunes of BATF Director Stephen Higgins, who was scheduled to testify before the U.S. Senate Appropriations Subcommittee on Treasury, Postal Service, and General Government on March 10, 1993.[12] Writes investigative reporter Carol Vinzant:

> In the jargon of at least one BATF office, the Waco raid was what is known as a ZBO ("Zee Big One"), a press-drawing stunt that when shown to Congress at budget time justifies more funding. One of the largest deployments in bureau history, the attack on the Branch Davidians' compound was, in the eyes of some of the agents, the ultimate ZBO. . . .[13]

"Sixty Minutes" rebroadcast the BATF segment a few months later. Host Mike Wallace opined, "Almost all the agents we talked to said that they believe the initial attack on that cult in Waco was a publicity stunt—the main goal of which was to improve ATF's tarnished image."[14] The codeword for the beginning of the BATF raid was "showtime."[15]

While it is no crime for a federal agency to reap beneficial publicity from the execution of its lawful duties, it is, at the least, unethical for a federal agency to mislead a federal magistrate in procuring a warrant.

INITIAL INVESTIGATION

Nineteen ninety-two started badly for the Branch Davidians. The hostile Australian television crew had shown up in January. A court custody battle over Kiri Jewell (a girl living at Mount Carmel) took place in January and February, with custody terms being modified in favor of the non-Davidian father in Michigan. At the end of February, the

State of Texas Child Protective Services showed up and began a child abuse investigation. Then in March 1992, a local police SWAT (Special Weapons and Tactics) team conducted several days of noisy training near the Mount Carmel Center. Although there is no indication that the trainees had any thought of Koresh, Koresh apparently interpreted the training as a sign of an impending confrontation between the righteous (his followers) and the great Babylon (everyone else, especially the federal government)—perhaps as part of a raid to take all the Branch Davidians' children away. The Branch Davidians began a major weapons acquisition program, and adopted a siege mentality.[16]

June 1992 is when the BATF says that it began an investigation of possible violations of federal firearms laws by David Koresh and a few of his close associates. The official justification for the initial investigation was that a United Parcel Service (UPS) driver reported to the McLennan County sheriff's office several deliveries of firearms components and explosives which the driver considered suspicious.[17]

The driver found it suspicious that some deliveries to a place known as the Mag Bag (a garage rented by the Davidians) near Waco resulted in the driver being instructed to deliver the packages to Koresh's residence at the Mount Carmel Center.[18]

The UPS driver's suspicions were heightened when boxes broke open (by accident, according to the driver) and he could tell their contents were inert hand grenade hulls and a quantity of blackpowder.[19] (Both items are legal, although the UPS driver apparently did not know this; using blackpowder to build grenades is not legal, unless one has a license.) The Waco sheriff's office was informed of the "suspicious" deliveries, and the sheriff's office in turn notified BATF.

Koresh had a number of schemes for raising funds for the Branch Davidians; mounting inert grenade hulls on plaques and selling them at gun shows was one of their biggest moneymakers.[20] Custom-sewn magazine vests in tall and big sizes were another speciality, under the "David Koresh Brand" label.[21] Koresh also used gun shows as a way to make a profit on surplus meals-ready-to-eat (MREs). In addition, the Davidians assembled gun parts into complete guns, which they sold to the public through a licensed dealer. The Davidians also bought many semiautomatic rifles as an investment, assuming that an antigun president would act in such a way as to increase their value dramatically, just as President George Bush's ban on the imports of such rifles had increased the guns' value in 1989.[22] On the day of the BATF attack, many of the Davidian guns were on display miles away at a gun show.

While most guns owned by the Davidians were for investment purposes, the Davidians did own guns for protection. Koresh was concerned about a possible attack from George Roden, the person with whom Koresh and his followers had a shootout in 1987,[23] and from other persons who regularly sent hate mail to Koresh. Roden (who escaped from an institution for the criminally insane, and was later recaptured) had reportedly threatened to return, saying, "I'm not going to come back with BB guns."[24]

Ownership of machine guns in the United States is legal, but the owner must pay a federal tax and file a registration form with the Bureau of Alcohol, Tobacco and Firearms.[25] The BATF's legal reason for being involved in the Branch Davidian investigation was to see if Koresh were manufacturing machine guns illegally. If, on the other hand, Koresh had simply bought machine guns, rather than allegedly manufacturing them, and if Koresh had paid the appropriate tax ($200 per gun) and filed the appropriate paperwork, he would have been in full compliance with the law. In other words, the legal cause for the BATF investigation was not ownership of machine guns per se, but ownership of machine guns without registration and taxation. The seventy-six-person BATF raid Mount Carmel raid was, ultimately, a tax collection case.

The federal law requiring machine guns to be taxed and registered is the National Firearms Act of 1934 (NFA), which was enacted with little controversy after the National Rifle Association stated that it had no objection to the law.[26] If not for the National Firearms Act, there would probably not have been a BATF investigation and raid on Mount Carmel, and none of the needless deaths would have occurred.

The National Firearms Act of 1934 should be repealed.[27] States are perfectly capable of enacting their own laws regarding machine gun possession. Simple possession of an object within the boundaries of a single state is not usually an issue of legitimate federal concern. Repeal of the NFA would not mean that machine guns would be unregulated; state laws would remain in force, and states could enact additional regulations, or even prohibitions. State and local police would enforce state and local laws regarding machine guns. But the repeal of the NFA would mean that the federal BATF would not be in the business of enforcing a federal machine gun law. BATF would have to assign its personnel to more important matters, such as interstate gunrunning, and the risk of people being assaulted by BATF for violating a tax and paperwork statute would be reduced.

As part of the Branch Davidian investigation, BATF checked its records to determine whether "Vernon Howell" (but not "David Koresh") or Paul Fatta (who ran the Branch Davidian table at gun shows) had a federal machine gun license. BATF also checked its records to determine whether Mag Bag, Vernon Howell, David Koresh, David Jones (one of Koresh's in-laws), or Paul Fatta were federally licensed firearms dealers.[28] The records said they were not.[29]

On the other hand, BATF knew that its records of registered machine gun owners were grossly incomplete.[30] The federal database of machine gun owners, the National Firearms Registration and Transfer Record (NFR&TR), is maintained by BATF. In October 1995, in a BATF agent training videotape, Thomas Busey, who was then head of the National Firearms Act Branch at BATF, in charge of the machine gun records, made a startling admission.

When a person is charged with possessing an unregistered machine gun, the federal prosecutors call as a witness a BATF employee who testifies that the NFR&TR database was checked, and the defendant was not listed as a registered machine gun owner. As recorded for a videotaped BATF training session on October 18, 1995, Mr. Busey explained, "when we testify in court, we testify that the database is 100 percent accurate. That's what we testify to, and we will always testify to that. As you probably well know, that may not be 100 percent true." He elaborated: "when I first came in a year ago, our error rate was between 49 and 50 percent, so you can imagine what the accuracy of the NFRTR could be, if your error rate's 49 to 50 percent. The error rate is now down below 8 percent. . . ."

In other words, for many years BATF employees have testified hundreds of times per year in NFA prosecutions that the NFR&TR database is 100 percent accurate. That testimony has been consistently false.

Ever since the United States Supreme Court's 1963 decision in *Brady* v. *Maryland*,[31] prosecutors have been obliged to turn over to defendants any exculpatory material which is known to the prosecution. The United States Department of Justice, whose United States Attorneys prosecute all NFA cases, has commendably lived up to this obligation; in late 1996, the Department of Justice made a mass mailing to attorneys of convicted NFA defendants, admitting that false evidence may well have been used to convict those defendants. The Department of Justice eventually found out that BATF had known about the serious problems with the NFR&TR database since the 1970s, but BATF had failed to correct the problem.

The first case dismissed as a result of the disclosure of BATF's decades of false testimony came in May 1996. A Virginia machine gun manufacturer, John D. LeaSure, had received proper BATF authorization to manufacture and transfer five machine guns to a particular customer. After making the guns, LeaSure decided he wanted to keep them for himself, as a machine gun manufacturer is legally allowed to do. He voided out the transfer forms ("Form 3") to his customer, and faxed the voided forms to the BATF office. Thus, he ensured that the machine guns would be properly registered as belonging to him.

Long afterward, BATF raided LeaSure's home, and charged him with possessing the five machine guns without proper registration. BATF stated that the Form 3s showed that the machine guns were registered to someone else. LeaSure replied that the Form 3s had been voided, and the voided forms had been faxed to BATF. Telephone company records showed a twenty-one minute toll call from LeaSure's fax line to the fax line for BATF's NFA Branch on the day the LeaSure said he had faxed the voided Form 3s.

At trial, a BATF records custodian testified for the prosecution that BATF's official records did not show any voided transfers. But at a rehearing, the witness admitted that two BATF employees in the NFA Branch had received punitive transfers because they had thrown away faxed NFA registration documents in order to reduce their personal workload. After LeaSure's attorney produced a transcript of Busey's training session, the trial judge dismissed the charges against LeaSure.[32]

It is entirely possible to support registration and taxation of machine gun ownership while also believing that the federal government is not the proper entity to keep the registration records and collect the taxes. There is little public safety benefit from having a very troubled federal bureau perform a regulatory function which could easily be performed by state governments.

The BATF investigation of Koresh quickly led to Henry McMahon, doing business as Hewitt Handguns, Koresh's favorite gun dealer. The lead BATF agent on the Koresh case, Davy Aguilera, listed in his affidavit for the search and arrest warrants all of the relatively recent purchases by Koresh, including flare launchers, over one hundred rifles, an M-76 grenade launcher, various kits, cardboard tubes, blackpowder, and practice grenades.[33] All of those items may be lawfully owned without the government's permission.[34] Accordingly, the purchases, while listed in the affidavit, did not establish probable cause that Koresh or his followers had violated or were planning to violate any federal law.

To people who hate firearms, the idea of many dozens of firearms being in the same place is repulsive. Such people have every right to lobby for changes in current firearms law, so as to make it illegal to possess large numbers of firearms without special government permission.[35] But in the absence of such legislation, there is nothing criminal about owning a large number of guns.

Moreover, while the Branch Davidians did possess a huge cache of ammunition, the main reason that they seemed to have a large number of guns was because they had lived together. If the Branch Davidians had, as in their pre-Koresh days, all lived in separate houses on the same ranch, their gun ownership rate would have been unremarkable by Texas standards. Of Texans who own guns, 45 percent own two to five guns, while 18 percent own more than five.[36] There are many gun collectors in the United States who personally own more firearms than did the Branch Davidians collectively. A large gun collection is entirely lawful, and is no evidence of criminal activity.

Of course there is nothing illegal about believing in a false messiah such as David Koresh. Exercising one's First and Second Amendment rights to the fullest degree, and at the same time, is not against the law. For a government agent to insinuate in a search warrant application that the exercise of constitutional rights somehow allows the inference of criminal activity is a gross deviation from the agent's oath to uphold the Constitution. For an agency to tolerate such behavior on the part of an agent is a significant sign of the agency's own disregard for the Constitution.

The question for the magistrate was not whether the Branch Davidians were normal and righteous, or weird and sinful. The question was whether the warrant application presented probable cause to believe that evidence of a crime would be found at the Mount Carmel Center. Under our Constitution, an observation that people are heavily exercising their constitutional rights must not be an element in creating probable cause.

In evaluating the warrant application and magistrate's issuance of the warrant, the only facts that are relevant are those presented in the application. If a warrant application presents enough facts to create probable cause, but the resulting search turns up no evidence of a crime, the magistrate should not be criticized. The fact that nothing was found does not retroactively prove that there was not probable cause to search. Conversely, a bad warrant cannot be retroactively validated by the lucky discovery of evidence. Otherwise, there would be no point to the Fourth Amendment's requirement that searches must have a valid warrant based on probable cause. In chapter 5, we will discuss the evidence offered at the criminal trial that the Branch Davidians illegally possessed machine guns. But for purposes of evaluating the warrant, what matters is the evidence that was presented to the magistrate.

The BATF affidavit in the warrant application is filled with assertions which are dishonest, inadequate, or misleading. These flaws should not have been present in an affidavit prepared with the aid of two Assistant U.S. Attorneys.[37] The affidavit's acceptance by a federal magistrate—as the basis for one warrant to arrest Koresh and another warrant to search the entire seventy-seven acre property and the entire house, including the living quarters of over one hundred persons not mentioned in the affidavit— may be partly due to the fact that the warrant application was presented to a relatively inexperienced magistrate, Dennis G. Green, much of whose legal career was as a prosecutor.[38] The Supreme Court requires that the magistrate must "perform his 'neutral and detached' function and not serve merely as a rubber stamp for the police."[39]

A valid warrant may not be based on stale information; "the magistrate [must] conclude that what they are searching for is there now, not that it was there at some time in the past."[40] Thus, a key requirement of warrant applications is that they give some indication that the evidence is fresh.[41] Most of the Aguilera affidavit involves an investigation conducted in June and July 1992. Most of the investigation conducted in December 1992 and January 1993 involved reports of activities said to have occurred between 1988 and June 1992. Even such key issues as whether Koresh or his followers were registered owners of machine guns or "destructive devices" such as grenades (only unregistered possession constitutes a crime) was determined only in June 1992— and only regarding a few of the persons residing at the Mount Carmel Center. Indeed, there was apparently never a check to determine whether David Koresh had destructive devices registered to him under his chosen name; the check involved only Koresh's birth name, Vernon Howell.[42] It would have been perfectly lawful for Koresh to acquire items in the first half of 1992, which might be made into destructive devices, if the actual manufacture did not occur until after an appropriate federal license had been acquired or registration occurred. The BATF affidavit did not claim any effort to determine if any machine guns or destructive devices had been registered between June 1992 and February 1993.[43]

Unfortunately, while the Supreme Court has announced a clear rule that warrants may not use stale information, many lower federal courts have been lax in enforcing this rule, and have allowed search warrants based on information that was many months, or even two years, old.[44] To give courts appropriate guidance, federal law should specify a cutoff period (such as six months) beyond which information should automatically be considered stale.

More importantly, in a warrant affidavit filled with information irrelevant to the question of whether Koresh and his followers had violated any federal firearms laws,[45] most of the information was misleading regarding the law, guns, gun parts, gun publications, what Koresh and his followers had bought or not bought, and what would or would not constitute a violation of federal laws.

IGNORANCE OF THE LAW AND OF FIREARMS

The arrest and search warrant applications both misapplied the law. The search warrant alleged violation of two federal statutes, but the arrest warrant alleged that only one statute was violated: 26 U.S.C. § 5845(f). That statute, however, does not establish anything as a crime against the United States; it merely defines "destructive device." (A "destructive device" is defined as a bomb, grenade, mine, poison gas, or similar device. Regarding Waco, the destructive devices at issue were grenades.) The statute does not say that it is lawful or unlawful to manufacture, possess, use, or do anything else in relation to destructive devices. A different provision (§ 5861) establishes unlawful activities related to destructive devices.

Naming the wrong statute would not invalidate a warrant.[46] But the error does indicate either Agent Aguilera's ignorance of the law or his carelessness, and it set the stage for more misleading statements to the magistrate. The error also suggests that Magistrate Green did not so much as open the U.S. Code to determine whether BATF had asserted facts which fit within the definition of a federal offense. Nor did the Assistant United States Attorneys who helped Aguilera prepare the affidavit even bother to cite-check it.

The items to be searched for[47] included "machinegun conversion parts, which, when assembled, would be classified as machineguns." In fact, machine gun conversion parts are classified as machine guns even when not assembled. Under federal law, a "machine gun" is a functioning machine gun, or all the parts needed to make a machine gun, or the parts used to convert a regular gun to a machine gun.[48] In other words, if a person possesses a machine gun conversion kit, but does not possess any type of actual firearm, the person is considered by federal law to possess a machine gun. Similarly, if a person owns all in one place all the parts necessary to assemble a machine gun, then the person is a machine gun owner under federal law.

Further misstating the law, Aguilera, immediately after asserting that he was familiar with federal laws, asserted that a "machinegun conversion kit" is a combination of parts "either designed or intended" to convert a firearm into a machine gun. Actually, federal law defines a conversion kit as a combination of parts designed *and* intended to convert an ordinary gun into a machine gun.[49]

Also on the search list were items "which, when assembled, would be classified as destructive devices." Again, Aguilera and his two Assistant United States Attorneys were demonstrating that they did not even open the statute books. Potential assembly, while part of the definition of machine gun, is not part of the definition of "destructive device." Possession of all the parts necessary to make a grenade is not considered possession of a grenade.[50]

The legal distinction is eminently sensible. If one possesses all the parts necessary to make a machine gun, then one possesses an auto sear (the internal component that makes the machine gun fire repeatedly). There is no purpose to possessing an auto sear except for use in a machine gun. In contrast, millions, perhaps the majority, of American homes have all the components that are necessary to assemble a destructive device, since simple bombs can be assembled from common household goods and chemicals.

The above definitions are technicalities, but the fact that two Assistant United States Attorneys and one BATF agent made these sloppy errors in a case which they all knew would be very high profile may be indicative of the poor quality of work that is apparently tolerated by some BATF and U.S. Attorney offices in criminal cases. If the government's lawyers will not even look up a statute, it is unlikely that they are exercising appropriate diligence and care in regard to other matters on a warrant application.

The warrant application listed no actual machine guns or destructive devices among the items to be searched for, except for "sten guns"[51] and "pipe bombs." But the affidavit did not offer any evidence about pipe bombs.

The only allegation about a Sten gun (a type of machine gun) was a report of a conversation alleging that there was a drawing of a Sten gun on "an Auto Cad Computer located at the residence building at the compound. The computer has the capability of displaying a three dimensional rendering of objects on a computer monitor screen."[52] Rendering a gun on a computer monitor screen is no more a crime than playing with grenades on video games. There are many books which consist entirely of schematics of machine guns and unusual weapons which are restricted by federal law. Owning such drawings in a book (or an equivalent computer drawing) is not evidence that the owner has illegal machine guns or other weapons. No evidence asserted that the Sten gun went beyond the computer stage. Yet BATF would later describe its discovery of the computer drawing as "One of the last pieces of evidence that supported probable cause."[53]

The legal errors in the affidavit were compounded by much more serious factual errors. Besides asserting knowledge of federal weapons laws, Special Agent Aguilera asserted a knowledge of firearms. He then went on to claim that Koresh had ordered M16 "EZ kits."[54] Aguilera did not note that

- the kit is called an "E2" kit, not "EZ" (as in "easy" convertibility);
- the E2 kit is a spare parts kit, not a kit to convert a semiautomatic to full automatic;
- the E2 kit contains the same spare parts that fit in a semiautomatic Colt AR-15 Sporter or an automatic Colt M16 assault rifle (since the two guns use many common parts).

If the parts from the E2 kit are combined with the receiver from an AR-15 Sporter semiautomatic rifle, the result is a complete AR-15 E2 model semiautomatic rifle.[55] The reason that the E2 kit is not regulated by federal law is that it is not a gun, nor is it a kit designed to convert an ordinary gun to full automatic.[56] Yet the BATF affidavit gave the false impression that the "EZ" kit was made for turning semiautomatic guns into machine guns. Again, none of the spare parts actually alleged to have been delivered to Koresh were conversion kits.[57]

Aguilera explained in the affidavit that the AR-15 is a .223 caliber firearm[58] and that Koresh had ordered barrels for it in "various calibers."[59]

There are two distinct ways of turning an ordinary gun into a machine gun, and Aguilera confused the two. The easy way is to install a conversion kit. (As noted above, possession of a conversion kit is subject to the same legal requirements as possession of an actual machine gun.) Installation of a conversion kit is doable by anybody who has the patience and dexterity to disassemble a gun down to its very smallest parts (the trigger assembly) and then reassemble the gun with new parts, according to directions.

The hard way to create a machine gun—the way that must be used by persons without a conversion kit—is to perform extremely high-precision milling and lathing, in order to manufacture the necessary internal components for a machine gun.[60] Aguilera stated accurately that, in unrelated cases, persons have turned semiautomatic AR-15 rifles into machine guns, often using milling machines and lathes.[61] He also stated accurately that the Branch Davidians had "machinery and implements used or suitable for use in converting semi-automatic weapons to fully automatic and for constructing various destructive devices."[62] What Aguilera did not tell the magistrate is that hundreds of thousands, perhaps millions, of Americans own or have access to such basic machine tools in their home workshops or workplaces.

The Aguilera affidavit bounced back and forth between the two entirely different methods of creating a machine gun (conversion using a kit, and fabrication via milling and machining). Perhaps Aguilera was confused about the distinction between the two different processes; a magistrate unfamiliar with firearms manufacture would almost certainly be confused.

Months after the Branch Davidian residence was burned to the ground, the Treasury Department conducted a review of the conduct of its subdivision, the BATF, at Waco. The opinion of a firearms expert reprinted in the Treasury Department report noted that: "None of the many pieces of information available to me is sufficient, by itself, to answer the question as to whether Koresh and his followers inside the compound were engaged in assembling automatic weapons in violation of the National Firearms Act." The expert noted that the various parts Koresh ordered "do not convert the rifle to automatic fire, except in combination with an *automatic sear.* There is no automatic sear listed in the accounting. . . .[63] The material made available does not indicate that the Branch Davidians received shipments containing automatic sears. . . ."[64]

To suggest that Koresh was intending to convert AR-15 Sporters and semiautomatic imitations of the AK-47 into machine guns, Aguilera's affidavit asserted that Koresh made purchases from a South Carolina company which had in its inventory all the necessary parts to "convert AR-15 rifles and semi-automatic AK-47 rifles into machine-guns if their customers had the upper and lower receivers of those firearms. . . . I know that Howell possesses the upper and lower receivers for the firearms which he is apparently trying to convert to fully automatic."[65] It was highly unlikely, however, that Koresh really did possess "upper and lower receivers" for "semi-automatic AK-47 rifles." Such rifles have a solid block receiver, not separate upper and lower receivers.[66] In any case, Aguilera here was merely hinting that Koresh may have purchased the parts since there is no allegation that those necessary parts were purchased from the South Carolina firm.

In short, the only evidence that BATF offered the magistrate that the Davidians were converting semiautomatic guns into machine guns was

(a) the Davidians had bought the E2 spare parts kit, which BATF falsely claimed was an "EZ" conversion kit;

(b) the Davidians had made unspecified purchases from a company that sells conversion kits, and which also sells thousands of items which are not conversion kits; and

(c) the Davidians owned home workshop equipment such as lathes which can, in addition to many legal uses, be used for illegal fabrication of machine gun components.

Following the raid, Aguilera filed a new affidavit with more details about purchases from South Carolina.[67] Aguilera explained that Koresh had bought various spare parts for automatic M16 rifles. Aguilera incorrectly asserted that these spare parts are "used to convert an AR-15 semi-automatic rifle into a M-16 machinegun rifle."[68] To the contrary, all the parts were simply replacement parts, and have nothing to do with conversion. If Aguilera did not know exactly what the parts were for, he should have asked BATF technical staff.

Although not indicating evidence of illegal conversions, the purchase of the M16 spare parts did suggest that the Davidians owned automatic M16 rifles. On the other hand, most M16 spare parts are interchangeable with the AR-15 Sporter. A few M16 spare parts (such as those for the automatic sear on the M16) are unique to the M16. The affidavit did not disclose whether the spare parts were the parts that were interchangeable with semiautomatic rifles, or the parts that are unique to the M16.

And again, it should be noted that BATF only checked the names of a few of the many persons living at the Mount Carmel Center to see if they were registered owners of M16s; and the name check did not even involve running "David Koresh" through the computer file of registered machine gun owners.

The only time the investigation reached the point where it might have found probable cause that Koresh had purchased parts really capable of converting a semiautomatic into a machine gun, the investigation, amazingly, was not followed through. "Because of the sensitivity of this investigation, these vendors have not been contacted by me for copies of invoices indicating the exact items shipped to the Mag Bag," said the Aguilera affidavit.[69] Curiously, the decision not to investigate was praised by the Treasury Department, which noted that Agent Aguilera "sharply circumscribed his inquiries about Koresh to third parties, including arms dealers . . . for fear of alerting the Branch Davidians that they were under scrutiny."[70] It is hard legally to establish probable cause when the only source which might supply it is not pursued. If items purchased might have been lawful or might have been unlawful, some reason has to be given for presuming the items to have been unlawful.

In sum, the affidavit insinuated that there was something illegal about the practice of buying a large number of guns and spare parts for those guns; and that there was something illegal about possessing a computer drawing of a machine gun.[71] The evidence of conversion of the legal guns into illegal (unregistered) machine guns was Aguilera's false claims that various spare parts were actually conversion kits.[72]

Besides attempting to convince the magistrate that there was something illegal about Koresh's purchases of legal firearms parts, the affidavit also intimated that Koresh had sinister purposes in his acquisition of blackpowder. The affidavit quoted a BATF expert to the effect that blackpowder is routinely used when making grenades and pipe bombs.[73] The statement is not totally false, since BATF's Explosives Incidents System's analysis of 1991 pipe bombings notes blackpowder as the filler material in 41 percent of the investigations reported. On the other hand, 48 percent involved smokeless powder (the gunpowder used in most modern ammunition). Most persons would recognize the acquisition of modern smokeless powder as evidence only of intent to manufacture modern ammunition. (Home manufacture is legal, and not regulated by federal law.) Likewise, blackpowder is routinely used as gunpowder for antique and replica firearms which do not use commercially manufactured ammunition.

While a tiny percentage of modern smokeless powder and old-fashioned blackpowder is criminally misused, there is nothing suspicious about the acquisition of blackpowder, which is (like modern smokeless powder) largely unregulated by the federal government. Aguilera misled the magistrate into thinking such ownership unusual except in association with criminal manufacture of destructive devices.

The evidence regarding grenades was, however, much stronger than the evidence regarding machine guns. For machine guns, Aguilera never showed that Koresh possessed an automatic sear or a conversion kit—without which it is impossible to have a machine gun. In contrast, the affidavit did show that Koresh had all the ingredients necessary to manufacture destructive devices, such as grenades. Besides owning black-powder and grenade hulls, Koresh had also purchased various explosives ingredients, such as magnesium metal powder and potassium nitrate.

But Aguilera never offered evidence that Koresh had assembled these items to create a destructive device, or that he had even expressed an interest in doing so. Significantly, the affidavit left out an obvious, and innocent, reason for the possession of explosives. (Explosives may be legally purchased, but may not be assembled into destructive devices such as grenades.) The Branch Davidians were building a swimming pool. Perhaps the magistrate would have concluded that, despite the possible innocent explanation, there was probable cause regarding destructive devices. But the magistrate was never informed of all the facts.

WIDELY AVAILABLE "CLANDESTINE" PUBLICATIONS

Given the weak state of the evidence against Koresh, the authors of the affidavit seem to have decided to bolster it with a wide variety of accusations which were either patently false or presented in a misleading way.

The affidavit reported that a witness who had been at Mount Carmel in March–June 1992 (and was interviewed by BATF in January 1993) had "observed at the compound published magazines such as, the 'Shotgun News' and other related clandestine magazines."[74] There is nothing remotely clandestine about *Shotgun News*. *Shotgun News* is listed in the *Gale Directory of Publications and Broadcast Media* as being a trimonthly publication, with a reported circulation of about 165,000. Published by Snell Publishing Company of Hastings, Nebraska, subscriptions are available by mail or telephone (1-800-345-6923); VISA and MasterCard are accepted. Since the nearly two hundred pages of each issue consist largely of classified and display advertisements of firearms and accessories, as well as many types of other weaponry and collectibles, BATF, at headquarters and its various field offices, had sixty-five subscriptions to the "clandestine" publication, which in 1993 was forty-seven years old. One of those subscriptions was by the Austin, Texas, office, out of which agent Aguilera worked,[75] and for which Earl Dunagan (author of postraid affidavits) served as Acting Resident Agent-in-Charge. None of the other alleged "clandestine" publications is identified.[76]

Lying on a sworn warrant affidavit is a federal felony.[77] A warrant based on deliberately falsified information is generally invalid.[78]

In addition, the same witness reportedly heard talk of, but apparently saw no evidence of, the entirely legal *The Anarchist Cookbook*—available from Paladin Press in Boulder, Colorado, at 1-800-392-2400 or 1-800-872-4993 (they, too, take VISA or MasterCard).[79] There was no evidence that Koresh or anyone else in the Mount Carmel Center actually owned a copy of *The Anarchist Cookbook*.[80] The witness "heard extensive talk of the existence of the 'Anarchist Cook Book.'"[81]

While there is no law against owning *Shotgun News* or *The Anarchist Cookbook*,

BATF Agent Aguilera did think *The Anarchist Cookbook* was illegal.[82] His ignorance of the law says a lot about the poor quality of training given to some BATF agents, and their gigantic ignorance of constitutional law.

UNRELIABLE AND IGNORANT WITNESSES

Search and arrest warrants are supposed to be based upon reliable evidence; thus, government agents should assert that the witness interviewed is believed to be reliable. The Supreme Court has noted that "an informant's 'veracity,' 'reliability,' and 'basis of knowledge' are all highly relevant in determining the value of his report."[83] Aguilera (or whoever drafted the affidavit for him) did not assert that the sources were reliable. In fact, they were not.

Marc Breault, Koresh's angry former lieutenant, provided much of the information about Koresh. The fact that Breault is blind[84]—a fact which could clearly undercut Breault's reliability about his alleged observations—was never mentioned to the magistrate.[85]

Moreover, the warrant application never mentioned that Breault was a self-described "cult-buster" with a "vendetta" against Koresh, a fact which would certainly have affected a responsible magistrate's judgment of Breault's veracity.[86]

As a reform, affiants should be required to disclose evidence affecting the reliability or credibility of witnesses.

The affidavit repeated statements from several people who said they had heard or seen machine guns at Mount Carmel. With one exception, discussed below, there was no reason to believe that any of these witnesses knew what they were talking about.

The allegations that Koresh owned machine guns were made by persons who were clearly ignorant of firearms and could not reliably testify to whether the guns, or the pictures of guns, they saw were legal semiautomatic firearms or illegal machine guns. Aguilera attempted to establish that he believed one witness, Jeannine Bunds (who had once been one of Koresh's wives), was able to identify an AK-47, based on her descriptions, but he went on to assert: "She knew it was a machinegun because it functioned with a very rapid fire and would tear up the ground when Howell shot it."[87] In fact, almost any gun will tear up the ground when bullets are fired into the ground. And most guns which are *not* machine guns can be fired at the rate of over one shot per second, if the shooter doesn't bother aiming. Such a rate of fire would likely sound like a machine gun to a person who knows little about guns; but a BATF agent ought to know better. Slightly more credible was Deborah Sue Bunds's recollection of hearing guns firing more rapidly than the guns she was used to from the regular firearms training sessions.[88]

Other witnesses in the affidavit provided even weaker evidence. Robyn Bunds (an adult daughter of Deborah Bunds) stated that her brother, whom she reported "has some knowledge of firearms," had once seen something that he thought was a conversion kit. But Aguilera did not interview the brother.[89]

Hearsay is "proving" a fact by reporting what one person heard someone else say.[90] For example, Jones says "I heard Smith say that he bought a new sofa." If an attorney wants to prove in court whether Smith really has a new sofa, the attorney cannot call Jones to testify about what he heard Smith say; Jones's testimony would be inadmissible hearsay. The law frowns on hearsay because second- or thirdhand reports about what someone else saw or said tend to be unreliable. Instead of using hearsay, attorneys must use more direct, reliable evidence, such as a receipt from a sofa store, testimony from a neighbor who actually saw Smith's sofa, and so on. In the Waco case, Aguilera should have interviewed Miss Bunds's brother directly, to find out exactly what the brother saw.

In 1932, the United States Supreme Court, concerned about the invasions of private homes that had resulted from federal alcohol prohibition laws, unanimously ruled that search warrants must be based upon evidence that would be admissible in court.[91] (Hearsay evidence is generally not admissible.[92]) Unfortunately, the Court changed its mind seventeen years later.[93] Given the frequency of violent home invasions that result from thirdhand "information" supplied to law enforcement by dishonest informants (see chapter 6 for some examples), it would be appropriate for the Supreme Court to reinstate its rule against use of hearsay and other legally inadmissible evidence to obtain search warrants. Alternatively, Congress could by statute forbid the use of such evidence in federal courts for any purpose, including for search warrants. The prohibition on hearsay evidence in warrant application should include the same exceptions as does the courtroom rule against hearsay. For example, hearsay can be used if the actual witness (the Bunds brother) is unavailable by reason of death or incapacity.[94]

When a witness's knowledge of a particular subject (i.e., the difference between a real machine gun, and a gun which just looks like a machine gun) is necessary to establish probable cause, the warrant application should disclose the basis of the witness's knowledge. This requirement would have required Aguilera to disclose that most of the persons who claimed that they had seen machine guns at Mount Carmel would freely admit they knew almost nothing about guns.

Although Agent Aguilera presented reports from plainly ignorant witnesses to the magistrate as if they knew just what they were talking about, Aguilera did not hesitate to impeach an informant's knowledge—when impeachment suited Aguilera's purposes. "Mr. Block," Aguilera wrote, "told me that he observed a .50 caliber rifle mounted on a bi-pod along with .50 caliber ammunition. However, what Mr. Block described to ATF Agents, was a British Boys, .52 caliber anti-tank rifle (a destructive device)."[95] A firearm with a caliber larger than .50 is a "destructive device" under federal law, and can be possessed only if registered; hence the significance of whether the gun was a .50 or .52 caliber.[96]

The affidavit goes on to assert that Block heard talk of additional .50 caliber rifles and the possibility of converting the .50 caliber and other rifles to machine guns.[97] This conversation did provide some evidence towards probable cause. (And since warrants are not to be judged retrospectively, the value of the evidence in support of the warrant is not undercut by the fact, discovered much later, that the .50 caliber rifles had not been converted.)

The subsequent Treasury investigation of BATF's activities accidentally makes it clear that BATF and agent Aguilera should have known that some of Aguilera's witnesses were unreliable, which would have undermined the validity of the witnesses' evidence as a basis for a search or arrest warrant. Two of the six key witnesses who had at some point lived at Mount Carmel mentioned twenty-four-hour armed guards.[98] Yet the raid planners "concluded that neither armed guards nor sentries were posted at the Compound at any time."[99] The planners' conclusion means BATF doubted the reliability of the witnesses—but never shared those doubts with the magistrate.[100]

The one witness whom Aguilera quoted in the affidavit who actually did know something about guns was a farmer with property near the Mount Carmel ranch, who said he knew machine gun fire when he heard it, and he had heard the Branch Davidians shooting machine guns.[101] (He also offered law enforcement authorities his residence to be used as a surveillance post.[102]) What the BATF affidavit did not report to the magistrate was that farmer had already complained to the sheriff's office, which had investigated and found that the supposed machine-gun fire actually involved something similar to the "Hellfire device," an unregulated trigger attachment that makes guns sound (but not fire) like machine guns. BATF's affidavit also failed to note that the farmer may have been hostile toward Koresh, allegedly having been involved in a dispute regarding property lines.[103] Affiants should be required to divulge exculpatory evidence, such as the sheriff's investigation of alleged machine gun fire at the Mount Carmel Center.

Liberty magazine summed up the evidence in the warrant application:

> Let us suppose that you and your spouse had a horrible fight, characterized by fervent anger, ugly words and nasty accusations, resulting in your spouse moving out of the home. Let us suppose your spouse goes to the Bureau of Alcohol, Tobacco and Firearms and tells them that you are distilling alcohol without a proper license. The ATF checks with your supermarket and learns that you have over the past few years on numerous occasions purchased sugar and on a few occasions purchased yeast, and verifies with your local utility that you have purchased water. You have acquired all the ingredients needed to manufacture alcohol. The ATF also checks the Treasury's records and verifies that you have never acquired a license to make alcohol.
>
> In every detail, this situation is identical to the Davidians': there is testimony from an angry former close associate anxious to cause you trouble, there is evidence that you acquired the means to manufacture a product whose manufacture requires a license and there is evidence that you had not obtained the license. Is this evidence—"probable cause"—sufficient for you to lose your right to privacy in your home as guaranteed by the Fourth Amendment?[104]

Actually, the analogy is not quite identical to the Branch Davidian situation. There was no evidence that the Branch Davidians possessed auto sears or conversion kits, which are essential for converting a semiautomatic into an automatic.

IRRELEVANT, STALE, AND ABSURD ALLEGATIONS AGAINST KORESH

Among the more prominent irrelevant issues in the warrant application are reports involving child—particularly child sexual[105]—abuse by Koresh. Whether the allegations were valid or not, they do not involve the federal government. However, in the affidavit of BATF's Aguilera, the state of Texas's child abuse investigation is featured prominently; but the Aguilera affidavit does not mention that the child abuse investigation had been closed for lack of evidence on April 30, 1992,[106] nearly ten months before the assault on the Mount Carmel Center.

Another irrelevant and possibly misleading assertion in the affidavit was that a deputy sheriff heard a loud explosion, and observed "a large cloud of grey smoke dissipating from ground level."[107] Aguilera was presumably attempting to strengthen the notion that "explosive devices" were possessed by Koresh. Quite possibly, the explosion was related to the construction of the tornado shelter that the Branch Davidians were building. Aguilera's statement fails to note whether the deputy sheriff who told Aguilera of the explosion also told him if he had investigated the matter and what he had found, or why he had not bothered to investigate.

Other allegations were even weaker, such as a claim by Marc Breault (Koresh's disaffected former lieutenant who had left the residence in 1989) that Koresh had falsely imprisoned a woman in June 1991. The warrant application does not disclose that the FBI had investigated the case in April 1992, and closed the case in June 1992.[108]

After the BATF attack on Mount Carmel, Aguilera returned to court to ask for an expanded search warrant. In the second warrant application, Aguilera reported an incident of child sexual abuse which had been alleged by a Texas social worker. No time frame for the alleged abuse was given.[109] Even after a massive shootout, Aguilera was apparently still determined to prejudice the courts by bringing up possible violations of Texas state law which, nearly a year before, the state of Texas had found no cause to pursue further.[110]

The September 1993 Treasury Department review offers a justification for why BATF—which is not a child welfare agency—kept bringing up stale charges from the child abuse investigation: "While reports that Koresh was permitted to sexually and physically abuse children were not evidence that firearms or explosives violations were occurring, they showed Koresh to have set up a world of his own, where legal prohibitions were disregarded freely."[111] The Treasury Department theory would allow law enforcement agencies to use any allegations of any serious criminal activity to establish probable cause that any other crime was also being committed.

The Texas investigation of child abuse did, however, lead to the only bit of information in the warrant application which suggested that Koresh represented a danger to anyone except other Branch Davidians. According to the Texas social worker who had investigated child abuse allegations at Mount Carmel, Koresh "told her that he was the 'Messenger' from God, that the world was coming to an end, and that when he 'reveals' himself the riots in Los Angeles would pale in comparison to what was going to happen in Waco, Texas. Koresh stated that it would be a 'military type operation' and that all the 'non-believers' would have to suffer."[112] The social worker claims that this statement was made on April 6, 1992. Thus, the statement was allegedly made some three-and-a-half weeks *prior* to the start of the Los Angeles riots.[113]

THE LACK OF PROBABLE CAUSE

Despite the concerted BATF investigation, as of December 1992 the Bureau believed that it had failed to amass enough evidence to create probable cause for a search warrant.[114] In testimony before the House Judiciary Committee on April 28, 1993, BATF Director Stephen Higgins stated that the warrant was not served in 1992 because analysis of the investigation in December 1992 indicated that, at that time, there was no probable cause. According to Higgins's testimony: "We had a review in here at headquarters office in December with respect to whether we had probable cause. We decided at that point that we did not, and we continued to gather information. We brought people in from Australia; we got the undercover agent in; we interviewed any number of people." When asked by Rep. William Hughes: "When did you determine that you had probable cause?" the response was "I think it was mid-February." According to a confidential source, a memorandum from the FBI's San Antonio office dated five days prior to the BATF raid noted that "ATF intends to execute a warrant on 3/1[115] . . . to date no information has been developed to verify the allegations."[116]

The Fall 1993 Treasury Department review of the BATF investigation sees things differently, and asserts that probable cause existed much earlier. Assistant U.S. Attorney Bill Johnston determined that the threshold of probable cause had been met by late November.[117]

Yet even the chronology of events in the Treasury Department report contradicts the post hoc assertion that probable cause existed by December 1992. The Treasury Department chronology notes that in January 1993, the decision was made to use an undercover operation to seek additional evidence "to establish probable cause."[118] The chronology further notes that a reporter was told by one of Aguilera's superiors in February 1993 that "he had not yet obtained warrants and was not sure he would be able to get any."[119]

Regardless of Treasury's retrospective assertion of probable cause, BATF's belief that probable cause did not exist until February 1993 helps to explain the approach taken by the BATF affidavit for a search warrant. Much of agent Aguilera's affidavit appears intended to convey a dislike and suspicion of Koresh and his followers without formally asserting that anything unlawful had been done. Some irony in the effort to condemn Koresh regardless of what he did appears in the final paragraph of the affidavit, where it is asserted both that persons engaged in violating the gun laws "employ surreptitious methods and means," and that they also "maintain records of receipt and ownership."[120]

Lacking probable cause, BATF began an undercover operation at Mount Carmel in early 1993.

On January 10, BATF agents set up surveillance cameras at a house three hundred yards away from the Davidian residence. After less than two weeks, the agents decided that "we weren't getting what we wanted" and decided to send an undercover agent into Mount Carmel.[121] The remote and undercover surveillance revealed no evidence of anything illegal.[122]

Unsuccessful efforts were also taking place away from Mount Carmel. In the December 1992 and January 1993 interviews, the only informants whom BATF could find were disenchanted ex-Davidians with very stale information. Three members of the Bunds family, who had left Mount Carmel before 1992, were interviewed, and described events occurring around 1989–91. The three women were not knowledgeable about firearms and identified firearms by looking at pictures and remembering how rapidly the guns fired. All of the information from the Bunds, and from a woman from New Zealand, was old.[123] The information added staleness to unreliability.

One witness, Marc Breault, did indicate that Koresh thought "gun control laws were ludicrous, because an individual could easily acquire a firearm and the necessary parts to convert it to a machinegun, but if a person had the gun and the parts together they would be in violation of the law."[124] Koresh was not quoted as having confessed to any such conjunction of events. Koresh was wrong about the law; acquiring the crucial parts to assemble a machine gun is exactly as difficult under federal law as acquiring a full machine gun.[125] Still, Koresh's incorrect belief that the machine gun law was easy to evade might be considered as some evidence of an interest in evading the law.

EXERCISING FIRST AMENDMENT RIGHTS AS "PROBABLE CAUSE"

BATF sent an undercover agent, Robert Rodriguez, inside Mount Carmel. His was, apparently, the only information obtained during the month of February, all of the other interviews in the revived investigation having been completed by January 25th.[126] Rodriguez was never really a covert agent; as detailed in chapter two, Koresh was on to him from the start.

Koresh played the guitar for Rodriguez, read from the Bible, and invited him to take training preparatory to joining the group. Koresh warned Rodriguez that "if he joined the Branch Davidians, he would be disliked because the Government did not consider the group religious and that he (Koresh) did not pay taxes or local taxes because he felt he did not have to."[127] Aguilera went on to explain what seems to have been the basis for BATF's belief that probable cause existed:

> David Koresh told Special Agent Rodriguez that he believed in the right to bear arms but that the U.S. Government was going to take away that right. David Koresh asked Special Agent Rodriguez if he knew that if he (Rodriguez) purchased a drop-in-Sear for an AR-15 rifle it would not be illegal, but if he (Rodriguez) had an AR-15 rifle with the Sear that it would be against the law. David Koresh stated that the Sear could be purchased legally.[128] David Koresh stated that the Bible gave him the right to bear arms. David Koresh then advised Special Agent Rodriguez that he had something he wanted Special Agent Rodriguez to see. At that point he showed Special Agent Rodriguez a video tape on ATF which was made by the Gun Owners Association (G.O.A.).[129] This film portrayed the ATF as an agency who violated the rights of Gun Owners by threats and lies.[130]

Based on the rambling fifteen-page affidavit climaxed by the report of agent Rodriguez, Aguilera announced, "I believe that Vernon Howell, also known as David Koresh and/or his followers . . . are unlawfully manufacturing and possessing machineguns and explosive devices."[131] Magistrate Green apparently agreed and, on February 25, 1993, issued a search warrant for machine guns and destructive devices (among other things) and an arrest warrant for Vernon Howell a.k.a. David Koresh for possession of destructive devices.

The key evidence in BATF Director Higgins's mind—based on his testimony before the House Judiciary Committee [132]—appears to have been Koresh's religious views, pro–gun rights views, criticism of federal gun laws, and hostility toward the BATF, all of which are protected by the First Amendment. Higgins testified that the necessary probable cause was not obtained until mid-February; the only evidence after January involved religious and political views expressed by Koresh.

A conspiracy of two or more persons to "injure, oppress, threaten, or intimidate" any person because of the person's exercise of constitutional rights is a criminal offense. If death results from the conspiracy, a sentence of life imprisonment may be imposed.[133]

The day after the search and arrest warrants were issued, Assistant U.S. Attorney William W. Johnston, chief of the Waco Division, who had assisted Aguilera in preparing the affidavit, obtained an order to seal the affidavit and search and arrest warrants against Koresh "to ensure the integrity of an ongoing criminal investigation. . . . It is believed that evidence may be altered or destroyed should the direction of the investigation become evident."

Nine days after the BATF assault, Magistrate Green issued another sealed warrant dramatically expanding the items to be searched for at Mount Carmel Center. Some of the expansion was to items relevant to investigation of the possible charges related to the Branch Davidian resistance to the BATF's serving of the first warrant (spent cartridges, bullets, bullet holes, blood, and the like), but the new warrant was also for video- and audiotapes which would indicate criticism "of firearms law enforcement and particularly the Bureau of Alcohol, Tobacco and Firearms (ATF)," as "evidence [of] Howell or other cult members' motive for wanting to shoot and kill ATF agents."

The second search warrant also authorized a search for photographs, because, the BATF agent explained, "I know that often times persons who violate firearms laws take or cause to be taken photographs of themselves displaying their weapons. . . ."[134]

What the BATF agent who procured the second warrant neglected to note to Magistrate Green was that photographs of inert grenade hulls look identical to those of live grenades, and that photographs of semiautomatic firearms generally look identical to photographs of semiautomatic firearms unlawfully converted to full-auto. And, while persons who violate gun laws have photographs taken of themselves with their firearms—certainly true of criminals such as Billy the Kid and Lee Harvey Oswald—so do children posing with their cap guns in hand or holster, successful hunters and target shooters, and politicians seeking the votes of sportsmen.[135]

THE EXCLUSIONARY RULE

Magistrate Green was apparently quite sloppy, but his decision to issue the warrant was not necessarily incorrect. Because Green relied on Aguilera's false statements that Koresh's spare parts purchases were actually purchases of conversion kits, it was not unreasonable for Green to conclude that Koresh might be converting semiautomatics into machine guns. On the other hand, if Magistrate Green had been careful, he might have immediately noticed small problems with the warrant application (such as getting statutory definitions wrong), which might have led him to interview Aguilera thoroughly enough to find the big problems with the warrant, such as Aguilera's often misleading presentation of the facts.

The Fourth Amendment envisioned an independent judiciary exercising oversight of the executive branch, making sure there existed probable cause before privacy rights could be infringed by government. In conformity to the Fourth Amendment, the Supreme Court has long insisted that a warrant may only issue upon the determination of a neutral and detached magistrate that probable cause exists to believe that the search will yield evidence of criminality. The magistrate is to serve as something more than a rubber stamp.[136]

Magistrate Green did not so much as open the United States Code to determine that the statute Koresh was alleged to have violated was merely a definition of "destructive device." He apparently did not notice that virtually no one who claimed to have seen or heard Koresh's machine guns was alleged to have knowledge of firearms, or that most of the allegations did not assert possible violations of federal law, or that almost all the evidence was over six months old.

Defenders of BATF's raid took heart in the testimony of Gerald Goldstein, president of the National Association of Criminal Defense Lawyers, that the warrant application was probably valid under existing federal law: "It . . . is not terribly atypical . . . it is chock full of irrelevant, highly inflammatory material. That's not unusual. . . . It definitely has matters that fall well beyond . . . either the expertise or jurisdiction of the particular agency. . . . The fact that the warrant may lack probable cause . . . quite frankly to the lawyers that were out there in the trenches trying this case, it didn't make a hill of beans."[137] Goldstein also noted that deliberately inflammatory statements would not matter, nor would the fact that outright lies and perjured statements were used: "the judge would simply excise that out, and you'd redact it." He went on to complain that virtually none of the flaws in the warrant, including staleness and overbreadth, were uncommon or would be used to exclude evidence in most real-world situations.

The most important reform, he suggested, was to eliminate the "good faith" exception to the exclusionary rule. The exclusionary rule, first announced in 1914, prohibits the use of evidence seized as a result of government conduct in violation of the Constitution.[138] The exclusionary rule has four purposes: first, it deters illegal conduct by the police, since they know that evidence that is illegally seized cannot be used.[139] Second, the rule protects "the imperative of judicial integrity," by ensuring that courts do not become "accomplices in the willful disobedience of a Constitution they are sworn to uphold."[140] Third, the exclusionary rule reinforces "popular trust in government" by "assuring the people—all potential victims of government conduct that the government would not profit from its lawless behavior."[141] This third purpose is distinct from the first purpose (to affect government behavior); the third purpose aims to reassure the people about how the government will behave, so as to increase popular confidence in government.

Fourth, besides promoting popular support for the government, the exclusionary rule promotes popular adherence to the rule of law. As Justice Louis Brandeis wrote:

> If the government becomes a lawbreaker, it breeds contempt for law; it invites every man to become a law unto himself; it invites anarchy. To declare that in the administration of criminal law, the end justifies the means . . . would bring terrible retribution.[142]

All of these purposes were undermined by the 1984 Supreme Court decision in *United States* v. *Leon*. That decision allows the introduction of evidence seized by police relying in "good faith" on a search warrant, even when the warrant is later found to lack the constitutionally required probable cause.[143] Since the BATF agents conducting the Waco raid were acting in "good faith" on a warrant issued by a neglectful magistrate, no evidence they found could be excluded—even if there were no probable cause.

When creating the "good faith" exception, the Supreme Court majority reasoned that "the exclusionary rule is designed to deter police misconduct rather than to punish the errors of judges." Since "there exists no evidence suggesting that judges and magistrates are inclined to ignore or subvert the Fourth Amendment," there would be only "marginal or non-existent benefits" to excluding evidence found as a result of good-faith reliance on a warrant.

Whatever appeal the Supreme Court majority's reasoning may have had in the abstract in 1984, the *Leon* rationale has been disproven by the sad experience of law enforcement since then, including at Waco.

First of all, *Leon* argued that judges and magistrates do not seek to subvert the Fourth Amendment. Yet while judges or magistrates may not be hostile to the Fourth Amendment, many are indifferent to it. Like Magistrate Green, they make little effort to review a warrant application for accuracy. Observed Koresh's attorney, Dick DeGuerin:

> As practicing lawyers, we know that usually judges rubber stamp the applications for search warrants. . . . [T]he way we made progress in the jurisprudence of this country, was requiring search warrant applications to be accurate and to have enough probable cause in them to justify a supposedly neutral and detached magistrate into authorizing a search. But *Leon* wipes that out. If you have got some judge that doesn't carefully read such warrants—and, cynically I say, that happens all the time—then he just rubber stamps it and that's the end of the inquiry.[144]

Leon removes the incentive for a magistrate to be sure that he only issues search warrants when there is probable cause, since his issuance of the warrant cannot be meaningfully challenged later.

Second, *Leon* promotes police misconduct. The "good faith" means that there is little incentive for officers seeking search warrants to tell the whole truth, and not to rely on informants' tips which they suspect to be lies. When other officers conduct a search resulting from the warrant, all the evidence will be admitted, since they were acting in "good faith" on the warrant. The "good faith" exception does not apply if the police knowingly or recklessly misled the magistrate, but proving that a police officer actually knew an informant was lying is nearly impossible. Whether the magistrate issues the warrant because he is too lazy to examine it carefully, or because he does examine the warrant application carefully, and is deceived by an informant's lies in support of the application, the evidence will still be admissible. In chapter 6, we examine other instances of sloppy or dishonest work by police and magistrates, low-quality work which has been encouraged by *Leon*'s exception to the exclusionary rule.

The third purpose of the exclusionary rule—promoting popular confidence in government—has also been undermined. As we detail in chapter 6, Waco is merely the tip of the iceberg of persons subjected to violent "searches" and "dynamic entries" into their homes as a result of warrants that are based on lies and which lack probable cause. Such constitutional misconduct has played a major role in creating the current climate of mistrust of government.

Finally, it is sadly true that many criminals purport to excuse (to themselves) their own criminality by telling themselves that the government also commits crimes.

DeGuerin was correct to tell Congress: "If you can undo *Leon,* that will be a giant step in the right direction."[145] While the Supreme Court sets the minimum standards for what kind of evidence can be admitted in court, Congress can set higher standards for federal courts. Thus, Congress should enact a statute which prohibits all use in federal courts of evidence seized in violation of the Constitution. If a search was illegal, the product of the search should not be allowed in court. Period.

Unfortunately, some persons in Congress, wrapping themselves in the mantle of "law and order," are pushing legislation which would go even further than *Leon* in promoting bad-faith, lawless police conduct. For example, a 1995 bill sponsored by Senator Robert Dole would wipe out the exclusionary rule entirely in federal courts. Instead, persons victimized by illegal searches would be allowed to sue the government, although the suit could recover no more than $30,000 in actual damages, no matter how great the damage that was caused by the illegal search.[146] In other words, evidence would be admitted, even when it was clear that the police acted in bad faith, in knowing violation of the Constitution.

Another bill, H.R. 666, which passed the House but never came up in the Senate, went further than *Leon,* but not as far as the Dole bill. This bill would allow use of evidence when the police officer reasonably believed that seizing the evidence was lawful, even when the police officer did not first obtain a search warrant. Amendments to the bill specified that the expansion of immunity from the exclusionary rule would not apply to the BATF and the IRS.

Supporters of legislation such as Senator Dole's S.3 claim that they are only objecting to the exclusionary rule, which they deride as a "technicality." But really, their objection is to the Fourth Amendment itself. The exclusionary rule merely establishes a practical mechanism to enforce the Fourth Amendment's warrant and probable cause requirements. The Fourth Amendment is not a "technicality." Government conduct in violation of the Constitution is a far more serious breach of law and order than is the conduct of a lone individual who violates a mere statute or regulation.

The proponents of exclusionary rule destruction assert that allowing the victims of illegal searches to sue the government will actually be a better deterrent to police misconduct than is the current exclusionary rule. It is difficult to believe that they take this argument seriously, when they propose tort remedies which do not even allow the victims of illegal conduct to recover their actual damages. An effective tort remedy would be a good supplement to the exclusionary rule, especially if it forced rogue agencies to pay the full cost of their misdeeds. But because most victims of illegal searches would rather put the incident behind them—rather than spend years in court, and thousands of dollars in attorneys' fees—suing the most powerful litigant in the world (the United States government), it is implausible to suggest that a tort remedy could fully replace the benefits of the exclusionary rule.

A streamlined administrative action should be established to allow victims of illegal searches to recover their damages, without having to go through the years-long process of a lawsuit in federal court. This administrative remedy should supplement, not replace, the exclusionary rule.

Persons hostile to the Fourth Amendment exclusionary rule are wrong when they tell the public that keeping illegal evidence out of court harms law enforcement. A 1979 study (conducted before the weakening of the exclusionary rule that took place in the 1980s and 1990s) found that in only 1.3 percent of federal prosecutions was even a single piece of evidence excluded as a result of the exclusionary rule.[147] The impact is even lower in violent crimes, for search and seizure violations disproportionately cluster in the investigation of victimless crimes, including possession of firearms without proper paperwork.

In chapter 6, we will return to the topic of search warrant policy. After examining additional case histories of search warrants based on flimsy or nonexistent evidence, we will propose additional Fourth Amendment enforcement tools.

The search warrant changes we have proposed would not alter the substance of the law. They would simply enforce the Fourth Amendment's promise that Americans should not be subjected to searches without genuine probable cause.

NOTES

1. Daniel Wattenberg, "Gunning for Koresh," *American Spectator* (August 1993): 39. An internal Treasury Department investigation, which was later obtained by the Associated Press pursuant to the Freedom of Information Act, confirms that BATF failed to prevent sexual harassment, and disciplined employees who complained about it. For example, one criminal investigator who had filed a sexual harassment complaint was threatened with a thirty-day suspension for "engaging in repeated criminal conduct." The "repeated criminal conduct" was three separate guilty pleas to failure to control his barking dog. "Treasury Report Confirms BATF Harassment," *Gun Week*, June 24, 1993, p. 3.

2. Stephen Labaton, "Saved from Extinction, Agency Faces New Peril," *New York Times*, March 4, 1993.

3. "60 Minutes" (CBS television broadcast, January 10, 1993). See also Bob Lesmeister, "Bad Influence: Corruption within the Ranks of BATF," *American Firearms Industry*, June 1995, pp. 53, 55.

4. Stuart A. Wright, "Construction and Escalation of a Cult Threat," in *Armageddon in Waco: Critical Perspectives on the Branch Davidian Conflict*, ed. Stuart A. Wright (Chicago: University of Chicago Press, 1995), p. 88; John R. Hall, "Public Narratives and the Apocalyptic Sect: From Jonestown to Mt. Carmel," in Wright, *Armageddon in Waco*, p. 219 (*Tribune-Herald* investigation sparked by Australian media).

5. Davy Aguilera, Application and Affidavit for Search and Arrest Warrants for Vernon Wayne Howell and the Residence of Vernon Wayne Howell, and others. Waco, Texas, February 25, 1993 (hereinafter "Aguilera").

6. U.S. Department of the Treasury, Report on the Bureau of Alcohol, Tobacco and Firearms, Investigation of Vernon Wayne Howell also known as David Koresh (Washington, D.C.: Government Printing Office, September 1993) (hereinafter "Treasury Report"), pp. 32, 37.

7. Christopher Culyer, memorandum of February 26, 1993 to Michael D. Langan, Office of the Assistant Secretary for Enforcement, reprinted in Treasury Report, at E-3. A BATF employee told Congress that the purpose of the memo was to keep the front office from being surprised "should ATF's execution of search and arrest warrants near Waco, Texas receive public attention that would reach the Office of the Assistant Secretary for Enforcement." Ronald K. Noble, Testimony of Assistant Secretary for Enforcement, Department of the Treasury, before the Subcommittee on Treasury, Postal

Service, and General Government, Committee on Appropriations, U.S. House of Representatives, June 9, 1993, p. 2.

8. Testimony of Sharon Wheeler, U.S. House Appropriations subcommittee, June 9, 1993, pp. 144–45; United States House of Representatives, Subcommittee on Crime of the Committee on the Judiciary and the Subcommittee on National Security, International Affairs, and Criminal Justice of the Committee on Government Reform and Oversight, *Joint Hearings on Activities of Federal Law Enforcement Agencies Toward the Branch Davidians*, 104th Cong., 1st sess., July 19–August 1, 1995 (Washington, D.C.: Government Printing Office, 1996) (hereinafter "Joint Hearings"), part 1, pp. 762–63; Walter Williams, "Waco Wildfire Update," *Washington Times*, February 11, 1994, p. A–21; Lewis, "Showdown at the Waco Corral: ATF Cowboys Shoot Themselves in the Foot," in *From the Ashes: Making Sense of Waco*, ed. James R. Lewis (Lanham, Md.: Rowman and Littlefield, 1993), p. 92; Clifford L. Linedecker, *The Massacre at Waco, Texas* (New York: St. Martin's, 1993), p. 168 (Wheeler contacted NBC and ABC affiliates in Dallas the day before the raid and told them that something major would take place).

9. Ronald Kessler, *The FBI* (New York: Pocket Books, 1993), p. 420.

10. Joe Rosenbloom, III, "Waco: More than Simple Blunders?" *Wall Street Journal*, October 17, 1995.

11. BATF agent Barbara Maxwell, testimony at January 1994 Branch Davidian trial, reported in "At Cultists' Trial, Fights and Tears," *New York Times*, January 24, 1993, p. A9.

12. Wattenberg, "Gunning for Koresh," p. 39.

A BATF manual orders agents to help create photos and movies of raids that will assist BATF's public relations efforts:

> Due to an ever continuing need for photographs for use with newspaper and magazine articles, district offices should furnish still photographs and movies which relate to significant activities (raids, arrests, searches, etc.) to regional headquarters. These are to be taken with an eye to publication rather than law enforcement. It is recommended that these photographs be "action" oriented as opposed to the evidence-type photographs needs for case report work.

(Bureau of Alcohol, Tobacco and Firearms, *Public Affairs Guidelines, ATF Order 1200.2.*)

13. Carol Vinzant, "ATF-Troop," *Spy* (March 1994): 47.

14. "60 Minutes" (CBS television broadcast, May 23, 1993).

15. BATF's public information officer, Sharon Wheeler, emphasized in testimony that "showtime" was not the name of the operation, but the word "to be used to alert everyone that the agents had stepped off the trucks." Joint Hearings, part 1, p. 795.

16. John R. Hall, "Public Narratives and the Apocalyptic Sect," in Wright, *Armageddon in Waco*, p. 220.

17. Many innocent people would still be alive today if the sheriff's office had handled the investigation itself, rather than turning it over to a federal agency.

18. There is a fairly simple, nonsuspicious explanation: The deliveries not accepted at the Mag Bag were Cash on Delivery (C.O.D.). Aguilera, pp. 1–2. Firearms components, ordered in quantity, cost money. The safer place to keep the large sum of money for which to pay for a delivery which might come at any time was at the Mount Carmel Center, rather than at the Mag Bag, which was just a rented garage. And large sums were kept there. As soon as the siege began, Koresh sent out $1,000 to take care of the children, and promised more money if and as needed. Transcripts of BATF Tapes of the Negotiations between Federal Law Enforcement and the Branch Davidians, February 28–April 19, 1993 (hereinafter "Negot. Tapes"), no. 141, March 20.

19. Treasury Report, pp. 17, 74.

20. Jim McGee and William Clairborne, "The Transformation of the Waco 'Messiah,' " *Washington Post*, May 9, 1993, p. A19. Committee on Government Reform and Oversight, in conjunction with the Committee on the Judiciary, *Report on the Investigation into the Activities of Federal Law Enforcement Agents Toward the Branch Davidians*, U.S House of Representatives, 104th Cong., 2d sess., August 2, 1996, p. 13 (hereinafter "Committee Report"); Negot. Tapes no. 108, March 10; no. 243, April 18.

21. Testimony of Karen Kilpatrick, in Ken Fawcett, *Blind Justice: A Chronology of the Historic*

Trial of Eleven Branch Davidians in January 1994, 2d ed. (Royse City, Tex.: Electropress, 1994), p. 26; *United States* v. *Brad Branch,* Crim. No. W-93-CR-046 (W.D.Tex., 1994) (hereinafter "Trial Transcript"), pp. 4881–84.

22. Henry Stanley McMahon, Jr., and Karen J. Kilpatrick, *In re: Interviews of Henry Stanley McMahon, Jr., and Karen J. Kilpatrick,* May 25, 1993, pp. 3, 26, 108–109 (on file with coauthor Paul Blackman); James L. Pate, "Waco: Behind the Cover-Up," *Soldier of Fortune* (November 1993): 38. The expectation of skyrocketing prices was also given as the reason for investing in a huge quantity of ammunition. Negot. Tape no. 243, April 18, 1993.

23. McMahon and Kilpatrick, *In re: Interviews,* pp. 105–106.

24. Ibid. Roden's first escape was in 1993, and he was quickly recaptured. Moore, *The Davidian Massacre,* p. 18; Pete Slover and Diane Jennings, "Source of Money for Davidian Sect Remains a Mystery," *Dallas Morning News,* March 8, 1993. Roden escaped again in September 1995, speedily picked up some cash (perhaps from his ex-wife, who currently gives tours of the Mount Carmel Center), and headed for New York. He was apprehended at the Israeli consulate, attempting to obtain a visa to Israel. Carol Moore, "Update on Waco," October 8, 1995, e-mail broadcast.

25. Some states, but not Texas, prohibit machine gun ownership entirely. About 15,500 machine guns are lawfully owned by Texans. Alan Korwin and Georgene Lockwood, *The Texas Gunowner's Guide* (Phoenix: Bloomfied Press, 1996), p. 84. A 1986 federal law bans possession of machine guns manufactured after May 19, 1986.

26. The original bill had proposed regulating handguns the same as machine guns, and the NRA had objected. When this provision was removed, the bill was speedily enacted.

27. This proposal is one of several in the book which are directly contrary to the policy of the National Rifle Association. This is one of several issues on which Blackman favors greater federal involvement than Kopel.

28. Aguilera, p. 5.

29. A Federal Firearms License is legally required in order to sell guns as a business; no license is required to sell merchandise at guns shows, as long as the merchandise is something other than guns.

BATF did not check whether Mike Schroeder (one of the regular recipients of UPS packages) was a licensed machine gun owner or a licensed gun dealer. (He was not.) In the official Treasury Department Report of the BATF investigation, the Treasury Department misleadingly suggested that Aguilera checked lots of names—"neither Koresh nor any of his known followers owned such a registered weapon"—whereas Aguilera's affidavit suggested only a few names known and few checked. Treasury Report, p. 24. BATF Director Higgins later reported, inconsistent with Aguilera's affidavit, in a letter to Rep. Jack Brooks on June 17, 1993, that on January 25, 1993, BATF checked the names of all adults known to be at Mount Carmel to determine whether they were licensed to deal in firearms or registered National Firearms Act weapons owners, with negative results. Hearing, p. 193. It is possible that Aguilera's initial check of a small number of names was supplemented later with an incomplete but longer list, perhaps based on intelligence gleaned by the undercover agent. The accuracy of Higgins's statement, however, seems dubious, because of inconsistency with the affidavit, because disclosure of a thorough name check would have strengthened the affidavit. Further, the poor surveillance work (Committee Report, pp. 11–12) and the FBI negotiators' unfamiliarity with the names and spelling of names of residents of Mount Carmel are evidence against the possibility of a thorough pre-raid check. In addition, the BATF records custodian testifying at the eventual trial of the surviving Branch Davidians noted only 14 names having been checked. Trial Transcript, pp. 4955–58. Finally, BATF underestimated the number of persons at the ranch by about one-third, and thus could not run checks on a large number of persons at the ranch.

30. The discussion of the NFR&TR is based on Tom Busey, "Roll Call Training," October 1995 (Washington, D.C.: BATF transcript); James H. Jeffries, III, "FOIA Produces Evidence of BATF Institutional Perjury," *Gun Week,* September 10, 1996, p. 4; and James L. Pate, "Shadows of Many Doubts," *Soldier of Fortune* (September 1996): 48–49, 70.

31. 373 U.S. 83 (1963).

32. *United States* v. *LeaSure,* criminal no. 4:95CR54 (E.D.Vir., Newport News Div., May 21, 1996).

33. Aguilera, p. 6.

34. Hearing, p. 145: BATF Director Higgins noted that the only unlawful item would be the grenade launcher if it were an M-79.

Koresh would later repeatedly insist to FBI negotiators that there were "yellow sheets"— BATF Form 4473, used for in-state retail transfers of ordinary firearms (machine gun transfer forms are white) on all of his guns. Negot. Tapes no. 52, March 5; no. 72, March 6. Dick Reavis interprets a vague reference on March 7 by Koresh that he has some things he should not have—"hey, if the Vatican can have its own little country, can't I . . . ?"—as a confession to possession of illegal weapons, and suspects the confession was not introduced into evidence because the prosecution wished to implicate the surviving defendants. Dick Reavis, *The Ashes of Waco: An Investigation* (New York: Simon and Schuster, 1995), p. 294. Koresh, however, never specified what he had that he should not have, or what sort of law he may have broken. He insisted throughout the siege that he purchased his guns legally. Negot. Tape no. 232, April 15.

Koresh further insisted he had done extensive research before he bought the guns, suggesting an effort to stay within the law. Negot. Tape no. 100, March 9. He noted that, once he realized BATF was investigating him, he had plenty of opportunity to flee, with any illegal weapons, had he been doing anything illegal. Negot. Tape no. 120, March 12. To show that there was nothing to hide, once the Davidians became aware that one of Koresh's houses in Southern California, the "white house," had been searched, Schneider provided the address of another house, the "rock house," where there were items stored. Negot. Tapes nos. 105 and 108, March 10. While maintaining all the firearms were purchased legally, Koresh declined to deny altering the guns, since Koresh said the negotiator would not have believed such a denial anyway. Negot. Tape no. 72, March 6.

35. Chapter 6 details the "arsenal" legislation being promoted by Handgun Control, Inc.

36. Chris Bird, "63% of Natives Found to Have Guns in Homes," San Antonio *Express News*, February 20, 1994.

37. Treasury Report, p. 73.

38. Ann L. Brownson, ed., *1992 Judicial Staff Directory* (Mount Vernon, Va.: Staff Directories, Ltd., 1991), pp. 701–702.

39. *Aguilar* v. *Texas*, 378 U.S. 108, 111 (1964).

40. See *Sgro* v. *United States*, 287 U.S. 206 (1932); *United States* v. *Ruff*, 984 F.2d 635 (5th Cir. 1993).

41. *United States* v. *Ruff*, 984 F.2d 635 (5th Cir. 1993).

42. Aguilera, p. 5.

43. Whether Koresh did or did not acquire such licenses is irrelevant to whether the February warrant could validly presume that he did not have such licenses, based on a June 1992 records check that did not look at his legal name.

44. At the 1995 Congressional hearings, defenders of the Waco warrant pointed to the following cases: *United States* v. *McCall*, 740 F.2d 1331 (4th Cir. 1984) (seven months, possession of a handgun); *United States* v. *Brinklow*, 560 F.2d 1003 (10th Cir. 1977) (eleven months, firearm); *United States* v. *Rahn*, 511 F.2d 290 (10th Cir. 1975)(two years); *United States* v. *Mariott*, 638 F. Supp. 333 (N.D. Illinois 1986) (thirteen months). Testimony of AUSA William Johnston, Joint Hearings, part 1, p. 267. See also University of Chicago Law Professor Albert W. Altschuler, letter to Rep. John Conyers, Jr., reprinted in Joint Hearings, part 1, p. 812 (arguing that whether evidence is "old" is distinct from whether it is "stale"; in contrast to drugs, which are consumed, guns observed in a building are relatively likely to still be in the same building months later).

While it is true that guns are much more durable than drugs, evidence that is more than half a year old is stale enough so that it simply should not be allowed. If there is some real threat to public safety, the federal government ought to be able to finish an investigation in half a year.

45. Most of the federal machine gun laws are nominally tax laws, because they date from 1934. At the time, Congress did not imagine that the interstate commerce clause gave Congress a general police power to regulate simple firearms possession. Accordingly, the machine gun registration laws were enacted as supposedly necessary to carry out Congressional power to tax machine gun transfers.

46. Gerald Goldstein, of the National Association of Criminal Defense Lawyers would later testify: "No question, it's sloppy. I would suggest that day in and day out courts affirm arrests of individuals even though the citation to the Code is wrong. . . . Convictions are even upheld when an indictment contains the wrong citations." Joint Hearings, part 1, p. 165.

47. Aguilera, Attachment D.

48. 26 U.S.C. § 5845(b).

49. Aguilera, p. 1; 26 U.S.C. § 5845. The "designed *or* intended" language is applicable only to "destructive devices" (such as bombs), which are an entirely separate legal category.

50. 26 U.S.C. § 5845(f).

51. A "Sten gun" is a type of British submachine gun used during World War II. Ian V. Hogg, *The Illustrated Encyclopedia of Firearms* (Secaucus, N.J.: Chartwell, 1978), pp. 288–89.

52. Aguilera, pp. 13–14.

53. Hearing, p. 163.

54. Aguilera, p. 5.

55. Properly speaking, an "AR-15" refers only to a machine gun. There are a large number of semiautomatics which use designs derivative of the AR-15, but the guns are never formally designated as simply an "AR-15." Rather, the designation usually includes "AR-15" as part of a longer name (e.g., "Colt AR-15 Sporter"). It is common, although inexact, for the semiautomatic guns to be called AR-15s. Such imprecision in gun magazines, where semiautomatics are often called automatics, is more acceptable than in legal documents where different words suggest different legal restrictions.

56. Moorman Oliver, Jr., "Killed by Semantics: Or Was It a Keystone Kop Kaleidoscope Kaper?" in Lewis, ed., *From the Ashes*, pp. 83–84.

57. The Treasury Report got the kits' name right, but still insisted that they were "conversion kits": "The parts in the kit can be used with an AR-15 rifle or lower receiver to assemble a machinegun. . . . The parts in the E-2 kit also can be used to convert an AR-15 into a machinegun." Treasury Report, pp. 23–24. The statements are plainly false. Treasury is required by law to regulate actual conversion kits as if the kits were machine guns. 26 U.S.C. § 5845(b). Treasury so regulates actual conversion kits, but does not apply the regulation to E2 kits.

58. Aguilera, p. 3.

59. Ibid., p. 4.

60. A machine gun expert explains the complexity of converting a semiautomatic rifle to automatic:

If time and effort are of no consequence, any firearm, even a lever-action rifle, can be converted to fully automatic fire. Converting a semiautomatic-only AK to automatic fire requires a great deal of skill and knowledge and no small amount of effort and equipment. Without being too specific, the procedure is more or less as follows:

1) A portion of the receiver must be modified. A hole through each side of the receiver (larger on one side than the other) must be precisely located (to within 0.0015″) and drilled to accept the axis pin for the auto safety sear and its coil spring. This special coil spring also retains the hammer and trigger pins. If not installed correctly, the hammer and trigger axis pins will not be retained, and these components will fall out of the receiver. A slot must also be carefully milled into the rightside bolt-carrier rail to accept the auto safety sear. The three new components required are not easily procured or fabricated.

2) The hammer must be built up by welding and then with great skill re-shaped to provide a notch not present on the semiautomatic-only version.

3) An extension must be added at the rear of the sear by welding and then re-shaped to contact the selector lever.

4) A portion of the selector-lever stop on the rightside exterior of the receiver must be removed and another detent milled into the receiver for the new semiauto position.

5) The bolt carrier must be built up by welding and then re-shaped to actuate the auto safety sear.

If welded components are not subsequently and properly heat-treated, wear will be accelerated and these parts will fail in a short period of time, often with dangerous consequences. Furthermore, if this conversion is performed on an AKM type with a sheet-metal receiver, failure to install a completely unavailable five-component, anti-bounce mechanical drag device on the hammer (especially if the firing pin is not spring-retracted) will probably result in a disastrous ignition out of battery.

(Peter G. Kokalis, "Full Auto," *Soldier of Fortune* [December 1989]: 16.)

61. Aguilera, p. 3. As discussed above, Aguilera's use of the phrase "AR-15" to identify semi-automatic firearms was a technical error.

62. Aguilera, attachment D.

63. The expert goes on to point out that automatic sears (which are the key component for turning a semiautomatic into an automatic) could have been manufactured by the Branch Davidians; alternatively, the lower receivers of a semiautomatic could be unlawfully modified to allow automatic operation. Treasury Report, Appendix B-164–65. The BATF affidavit, it should be remembered, provides no evidence of the Davidians building their own automatic sears, or illegally modifying the lower receivers of any firearm.

The sear is a pivoting bar that forms the link between the trigger and the hammer. In an automatic, the hammer falls repeatedly, even though the trigger is not pressed repeatedly; accordingly, automatic firearms require a special sear.

64. Treasury Report, Appendix B-182.

65. Aguilera, p. 13.

66. Oliver, p. 84. The receiver is the part of a rifle or shotgun that holds the bolt, firing pin, mainspring, trigger group, and ammunition feed system. R. A. Steindler, *The Complete Firearms Dictionary* (1970), p. 189.

67. These details obviously could not retroactively validate the warrant for the initial raid.

68. Earl Dunagan and Davy Aguilera, Application and Affidavit for Search of Residence of Vernon Wayne Howell, and others. Waco, Texas, April 4, 1993, p. 17.

69. Aguilera, p. 7.

70. Treasury Report, p. 123.

71. Aguilera, *passim.*

72. Ibid.

73. Ibid., pp. 11–12.

74. Ibid., p. 14.

75. Ibid., p. 1.

76. Statements made by Koresh's gun dealer, Henry McMahon, suggest that *Gun List*, a publication similar to *Shotgun News*, was also used by Koresh and might be the, or one of the, other "clandestine" publications seen in Koresh's house. McMahon and Kilpatrick, *In re: Interviews,* p. 122.

77. 18 U.S. Code § 1621 *et seq.*

78. *Franks* v. *Delaware*, 438 U.S. 154 (1978).

79. *Paladin Press, Publishers of the Action Library* (catalogue), vol. 23, no. 4 (1993), p. 19.

80. *The Anarchist Cookbook* includes recipes for growing, harvesting, and cooking with marijuana, information on various drugs, and the admonition: "When going to make a deal for dope, do not take a weapon with you. This is provoking violence and legal hassles. If you don't trust the guy, then don't deal with him." William Powell, *The Anarchist Cookbook* (Secaucus, N.J.: Barricade Books, 1971), pp. 39, 40. The book also provides information on firearms. There is no information on converting semiautomatic firearms to fire full auto. There is extensive information on making explosives, but (a) with many admonitions against doing so for safety reasons unless one knows more than is in the pages of the book, and (b) generally not with the materials Aguilera established that Koresh owned. Powell, *The Anarchist Cookbook*, ch. 4.

81. Aguilera, p. 14. The witness not only did not see a copy, but the assertion does not expressly state that the talk involved the book's presence at the compound, only its existence.

82. Marc Breault and Martin King, *Inside the Cult* (New York: Signet, 1993), p. 305.

83. *Illinois* v. *Gates*, 462 U.S. 213, 230 (1983).

84. Wattenberg, "Gunning for Koresh," p. 34; Testimony of Davidian David Thibodeau, Joint Hearings, part 1, p. 178.

85. Testimony of Davidian David Thibodeau, Joint Hearings, part 1, p. 179. Thibodeau also testified that, in general, Breault had a reputation as a person who liked to "tell some whoppers." It is not clear whether Aguilera knew or had reason to believe Breault had such a reputation. Breault, who fancied his conflict with Koresh to be a cloak and dagger suspense similar to a Robert Ludlum novel, reports his meetings with Davy Aguilera as rendezvous with BATF agent "Derek Anderson (not his real name)." Breault and King, *Inside the Cult,* p. 294.

The warrant application gave the impression that Breault had been one of Koresh's combat troops. Breault "participated in physical training and firearm shooting exercises conducted by Howell. He stood guard armed with a loaded weapon." Being blind, Breault would probably have been more a threat to fellow Davidians than to intruders.

86. Committee Report, p. 13.

87. Aguilera, p. 9.

88. Ibid., p. 10.

89. Ibid., p. 9. Bunds reported having found some gun parts in her parents' Los Angeles, California, home. Aguilera, p. 9. Three members of Koresh's group eventually came to pick them up. No reason is given for Aguilera's not having interviewed the brother, David Bunds.

90. Federal Rules of Evidence 801(c): "'Hearsay' is a statement, other than one made by the declarant, while testifying at a trial or hearing, offered in evidence to prove the truth of the matter asserted."

91. *Grau v. United States*, 287 U.S. 124 (1932). For the Court's increasing concern about the civil liberties price exacted by prohibition, see Kenneth M. Murchison, *Federal Criminal Law Doctrines: The Forgotten Influence of National Prohibition* (Durham, N.C.: Duke University Press, 1994).

92. Fed. Rules. Evid. 802.

93. *Brinegar v. United States*, 338 U.S. 160 (1949).

94. Fed. Rules Evid. 803, 804 (listing numerous exceptions to Rule against Hearsay).

95. The Treasury Department review said the gun was "either a .50 caliber rifle mounted on a bi-pod or a 'British Boys' .52-caliber antitank rifle." Treasury Report, p. 33. Block had been in the Mount Carmel Center during the spring of 1992, and had attended gun shows with Koresh, McMahon (Koresh's gun dealer), and other Branch Davidians. Block was unfamiliar with and uncomfortable around guns, and it was the gun activities which caused him to leave in June 1992. McMahon and Kilpatrick, *In re: Interviews*, pp. 50–52.

96. There are some exceptions to the .50 caliber rule, not relevant here, for "elephant rifles" and other "sporting" weapons. The Boys rifle was initially produced in .55 caliber, not .52; it is unlikely there is such a version as the .52. Hogg, *The Illustrated Encyclopedia of Firearms*, p. 94.

When the Gun Control Act of 1968 was enacted, defining rifles of caliber above .50 as "destructive devices," most guns like the Boys were rebarreled in .50 caliber to remove them from the highly regulated "destructive device" category. Thus, if Koresh owned a Boys, there would be no reason, absent other evidence, to believe it to be an illegal version rather than the much more readily available .50 caliber version—especially since Aguilera's witness described it as a .50 caliber gun.

At the 1994 trial of the Davidians, the prosecution introduced evidence showing that the Davidians owned two .50 caliber rifles. No evidence was introduced regarding .52 caliber firearms. "Rangers Tell of Weapons Stockpile," *Washington Times*, January 14, 1994, p. A–5.

97. Aguilera, p. 14. Koresh's .50 caliber rifles were Barretts. According to Barrett Firearms Manufacturing, "It's designed as a rifle and not as an automatic weapon. Converting it would require major design changes." Lee Hancock, "Gun Dealer, Koresh called Partners," *Dallas Morning News*, March 10, 1993.

98. Aguilera, pp. 9, 12.

99. Treasury Report, p. 53. Treasury goes on to note that the raid planners determined that Koresh never left the residence, but the source for that information was Joyce Sparks, who investigated the allegations of child abuse, and Treasury "was unable to identify a reliable source for this common assumption." Ibid., pp. 53, 136. In other words, Treasury concluded that Sparks, who was Aguilera's key witness on the violence Koresh intended for the Waco area, was not reliable.

100. It was only after the raid that a supplemental affidavit at last recognized the desirability of claiming a witness was reliable. Some of the information in the postraid affidavit relates to items which are lawful to own, like m10 and m11 semiautomatic pistols, as well as the unlawful manufacture of silencers and live grenades, and the possession of machine guns. Dunagan and Aguilera, p. 16.

101. Aguilera, p. 4.

102. Ibid.

103. McMahon and Kilpatrick, *In re: Interviews*, pp. 46-50. The devices were ACTs, according to McMahon, but Koresh referred to them as Hellfire devices in talking to the FBI negotiators. And he

said he had told BATF's undercover agent Robert Rodriguez about them, and that the issue had been cleared up with the sheriff. Negot. Tape no. 59, March 5.

104. R.W. Bradford, "There's No Kill Like Overkill," *Liberty* (August 1993): 31. There are actually some differences, since a license is not needed to produce small quantities of alcohol for personal use. Professor Albert W. Altschuler's defense of the warrant used almost the same example as justifying a warrant for bootlegging. The example was changed to subtract the hostile wife, and to add a suspect who denounced alcohol taxation and the BATF, and who expressed a love of moonshine. Altschuler, Joint Hearings, part 1, p. 811.

105. The affidavit stated the ex-Davidian Jeannine Bunds said that Koresh had sex with girls as young as eleven years old, and fathered children with girls as young as twelve. Aguilera, pp. 9–10. Long after the fact, Treasury Undersecretary for Enforcement Ron Noble told Fox Morning News (July 20, 1995) that the child sexual abuse allegation was placed in the affidavit to prove that Koresh controlled what went on at Mount Carmel, "to show the magistrate judge that if there were machine-guns and hand grenades in that compound, they were there because David Koresh wanted them there."

106. Wattenberg, "Gunning for Koresh," p. 37. The department's summary stated:

> None of the allegations could be verified. The children denied being abused in any way by adults in the compound. They denied knowledge of other children being abused. The adults consistently denied participation in or knowledge of any abuse of children. Examinations of the children produced no indication of current or previous injuries.

(Gustav Nieguhr and Pierre Thomas, "Abuse Allegations Unproven: Koresh was Investigated in Texas, California," *Washington Post*, April 25, 1993, p. A20.) An affidavit stating that Koresh severely beat an eight-month-old baby is contained in U.S. Department of Justice, *Report on the Events at Waco, Texas, February 28 to April 19, 1993* (Redacted Version, Washington, D.C.: October 8, 1993) (hereinafter "Justice Report"), pp. 224–26.

107. Aguilera, p. 7.

108. Ibid., pp. 10–11; Carol Moore, *The Davidian Massacre*, p. 61. The woman, who claimed to hear a disembodied voice telling her that she was the only person worthy of bearing Koresh's children, was either (1) seriously mentally ill, or (2) possessed by a demon, depending on one's interpretive framework. Kenneth Samples, Erwin de Castro, Richard Abanes, and Robert Lyle, *Prophets of the Apocalypse: David Koresh & Other American Messiahs* (Grand Rapids, Mich.: Baker, 1994), pp. 72–75, 191–92.

109. Kiri Jewell's testimony to the Joint Committee gives the year of the alleged incident as 1991. Joint Hearing, part 1, p. 149. From the Justice Department review, it appears that the social worker's interview occurred on February 22, 1993. Social worker Joyce Sparks, from the Texas Department of Child Protective Services, reported that on February 22, 1993, a girl (later identified as Kiri Jewell) told Sparks that when the girl was ten years old, Koresh had taken off her clothes and his clothes, and gotten on top of her. The girl reported feeling "scared but privileged," and was unwilling to testify against Koresh. Justice Report, pp. 215, 219; Treasury Report, p. 64. (For more, see chapters 4 and 5.) The social worker's interview was related to an effort to lure Koresh off his property by having local charges of child abuse brought; that effort was given up on February 22, when the girl told a state prosecutor she would not testify against Koresh. Treasury Report, Appendix D–12.

110. Dunagan and Aguilera, Application and Affidavit, pp. 18–19. Assistant U.S. Attorney Johnston stated that he refrained from making the original affidavit even more deliberately irrelevant: "Had I wanted to prejudice the affidavit and the warrant, . . . I knew Kiri Jewell's story before the affidavit and I would have put in all the details, the gory details about . . . what he did to her. I didn't want to prejudice the magistrate, but I did want to put the context of Ms. Sparks' visit." Joint Hearing, part 1, p. 212.

111. Treasury Report, p. 27.

112. Aguilera, p. 9. The comment is consistent with Koresh's overall theology. If he made the comment, he was two-thirds right. Deaths at Waco were greater than in the Los Angeles riots, and it was a "military type operation."

113. The witness stands by her statement that Koresh made the threat, if that is what it was. She disapproved of her agency's decision to close the case and continued to have telephone contacts with

Koresh. Wattenberg, "Gunning for Koresh," p. 37. The Treasury Department explanation is that the statement was not made in early April, but on April 30, the day after the riots began and the day the investigation was closed despite the social worker's objection. Treasury Report, p. 126.

114. According to Marc Breault, on December 15, 1992, Aguilera stated that there was "circumstantial" evidence about Koresh, but Aguilera "could not do anything because he lacked direct evidence." Breault and King, *Inside the Cult,* pp. 299–300.

115. The date of the assault was moved from a weekday to a Sunday, February 28, because the Waco newspaper began an exposé of Koresh, "The Sinful Messiah," earlier than BATF had expected or wanted. The result was that more men, and at least one additional child, were at the Mount Carmel Center.

116. James L. Pate, "Gun Gestapo's Day of Infamy," *Soldier of Fortune* (June 1993): 63.

117. Treasury Report, p. 37.

118. Ibid., p. 44.

119. Ibid., p. 71.

120. Aguilera, p. 15.

121. Sue Anne Pressley, "Federal Agent Describes Undercover Role before Deadly Texas Raid," *Washington Post,* January 28, 1994, p. A–3, Trial Transcript, p. 3451.

122. Committee Report, pp. 11–12; James L. Pate, "We Have Truth on Our Side: Jailhouse Interviews with Branch Davidians," *Soldier of Fortune* (July 1994): 48.

123. Aguilera, pp. 9–11.

124. Ibid., p. 12.

125. 26 U.S.C. § 5845(b)("machine gun" is defined to include "any part designed solely and exclusively, or combination of parts designed and intended, for use in converting a weapon into a machine gun").

126. Aguilera; Treasury Report, Appendix D.

127. Aguilera, pp. 14–15. Koresh thought the entire seventy-seven acres should, as religious property, be exempt from taxation, while the government considered only the two acres of the building to be tax-exempt.

128. Koresh, who owned AR-15 Sporters, did not acknowledge to Agent Rodriguez that he owned a sear. Checks with the various companies BATF identified as having done business with Koresh indicate no purchase by Koresh of a sear. None of the gun-part company representatives who testified at the Branch Davidians' trial indicated sale of such a sear, or of enough other parts to convert a semiautomatic to full-auto capability, aside from the significant exception of one "grandfathered" pre-1981 auto-sear. Testimony of Cynthia Eileen Aleo (Nesard Gun Parts), Peter Waltzman (Sarco, Inc.), Tammy Smith (Shooter Equipment Co.), Ron Jones (Global Sales). Trial Transcript, pp. 4296–4302, 4766–4821, 4920–25.

The federal government's treating automatic sears the same as machine guns (for which the auto sear is the essential component) dates to 1981. Automatic sears manufactured before 1981 are "grandfathered," and are not subject to the same restrictions as machine guns; the policy was not to suddenly turn the owners of old auto sears into felons. Koresh's possession of the single grandfathered auto sear—while legal—demonstrates his capability of converting one semiautomatic rifle to full automatic. Because BATF had decided not to ask Koresh's firearms parts suppliers exactly what firearms parts Koresh had bought, the evidence about the grandfathered auto sear was not presented to the magistrate in the warrant application. This evidence would have been the strongest evidence in the application.

129. Actually, "G.O.A." stands for Gun Owners of America, and was a group of which Koresh was much fonder than of the NRA. According to testimony of BATF undercover agent Rodriguez: "He [Koresh] denounced the Government many times, denounced the NRA, called it as corrupt as our Government." Joint Hearings, part 1, p. 802.

130. Aguilera, p. 15. The film includes interviews of police officers and other citizens who believe that they were unfairly prosecuted by BATF for alleged gun law violations. Gun Owners of America, *Breaking the Law . . . in the Name of the Law: The BATF Story* (Springfield, Va.: Gun Owners of America, 1989).

131. Aguilera, p. 15. He meant "destructive devices."

132. "The last factual pieces of information that were to be included in the affidavit for Koresh's arrest warrant were not obtained until February 22, 1993, during our undercover contacts with Koresh.

This led us to seek the U.S. Attorney's concurrence for the issuance of the arrest warrant that was issued on February 25, 1993." Letter to Representative Brooks, in Hearing, p. 193.

133. 18 U.S.C. § 241.

134. Earl Dunagan, Application and Affidavit for Search Warrant for the Residence of Vernon Wayne Howell, and others, Waco, Texas, March 9, 1993, p. 4.

135. In a popular biography of the young Theodore Roosevelt, one-third of the photographs of Roosevelt show him wearing or carrying a firearm. David McCullough, *Mornings on Horseback* (New York: Simon and Schuster, 1981). About one-sixth of the photos in a collage inside the front cover of the *Theodore Roosevelt Cyclopedia* also show him armed. Albert Bushnell Hart and Herbert Ronald Ferleger, *Theodore Roosevelt Cyclopedia* (New York: Roosevelt Memorial Association, 1941).

136. *Aguilar* v. *Texas*, 378 U.S. 108 (1964); *United States* v. *Leon*, 468 U.S. 897 (1984).

137. Testimony of Gerald Goldstein, Joint Hearings, part 1, p. 128. Goldstein was concerned that the situation was likely to get worse as a result of antiexclusionary rule legislation being considered by Congress. Some Democratic representatives noted the irony of Republicans attacking the affidavit and warrant used against David Koresh and Mount Carmel Center while those same Republicans were generally opposed to the exclusionary rule, and had actively worked for H.R. 666 to weaken it still further. As Rep. John Conyers put it:

> [J]ust recently in the GOP Contract With America, and specifically H.R. 666, we voted out a bill with nearly unanimous Republican support. . . . We [Democrats] pointed out that this was eroding the whole Constitution. And now I am so pleased to find that the same people that voted to further erode the exclusionary rule, of which Mr. Goldstein has very adequately complained of, are now very worried that there aren't any teeth in it. . . .

(Joint Hearings, part 1, p. 197.)

Inconsistencies were not a problem for the groups which most seriously questioned the Waco search warrant. The American Civil Liberties Union (ACLU) unsuccessfully lobbied against H.R. 666. The NRA remained neutral at the time since its board of directors had not specifically created a policy on such Fourth Amendment issues. Since then, a policy has been articulated which would require the NRA to lobby against such legislation.

138. *Weeks* v. *United States*, 232 U.S. 383 (1914).

139. *Mapp* v. *Ohio*, 367 U.S. 643 (1961).

140. *Elkins* v. *United States*, 364 U.S. 206 (1960).

141. *United States* v. *Calandra*, 414 U.S. 338, 357 (1974) (Brennan, J., dissenting).

142. *Olmstead* v. *United States*, 277 U.S. 438 (1928) (Brandeis, J., dissenting).

143. *United States* v. *Leon*, 468 U.S. 897 (1984). *See also Illinois* v. *Krull*, 480 U.S. 340 (1987); *Arizona* v. *Evans*, 115 S.Ct. 1185 (1995)(reliance on defective computer records).

144. Joint Hearings, part 2, p. 40.

145. Ibid.

146. S. 3, 104th Cong., § 507. The bill also allows no more than $10,000 in punitive damages, no matter how flagrant and malicious the police misconduct.

147. Comptroller General of the United States, *Impact of the Exclusionary Rule on Federal Criminal Prosecutions* (April 19, 1979).

2

A Search Warrant or a Death Warrant?

Truth shall go farther away, and falsehood shall come near. For the eagle that you saw in the vision is already hurrying to come.

2 Esdras 14:18

On February 28, 1993, BATF sent seventy-six agents to storm the Branch Davidians' home. In the ensuing shootout, four BATF agents were killed, and another twenty-eight received injuries ranging from minor to serious.[1] Some Branch Davidians were also killed. More were wounded, including Koresh himself. Even if it is hypothesized that the search and arrest warrants were valid, BATF's execution of the warrants was gratuitously violent, especially considering that an arrest warrant for one person was executed by invading and assaulting a home of 127 persons. According to the official BATF orders on Searches and Examinations: "The special agent is liable if he/she exceeds his/her authority while executing a search warrant and must be sure that a search warrant is sufficient on its face, even when issued by the magistrate."[2]

COULD KORESH HAVE BEEN ARRESTED OUTSIDE THE MOUNT CARMEL CENTER?

Some critics of BATF suggested the bureau should have attempted to arrest Koresh when he was alone, or almost alone, outside of the Branch Davidian home.[3] BATF responded that it was difficult to find Koresh off the grounds of the Mount Carmel Center: "In January 1993, BATF initiated a surveillance of the compound. Koresh was never seen leaving the property by BATF. Additionally, an undercover operation by ATF indicated that Koresh had no intention of leaving the compound."[4] The two sources for the allegation that Koresh rarely left Mount Carmel were the social worker, Joyce Sparks, and a former Branch Davidian who said Koresh feared arrest by the sheriff's department.[5]

If BATF really never saw Koresh leave the property, BATF was extremely unobservant. The Waco *Tribune-Herald*, which was preparing an exposé of Koresh, noted that Koresh had been in town as recently as February 22, when he went to an auto repair shop.[6] Koresh was reportedly served at the Chelsea Bar & Grill about once a week during February 1993.[7] He had also been seen at another nightspot in January; and a businessman who wished to remain anonymous showed the newspaper a sales slip indicating Koresh had been in his shop on January 5, 1993.[8] He visited a junkyard three days before the February 28 raid.[9] Koresh also went shopping, to music stores, among other places.[10]

Branch Davidian Paul Fatta stated that on several occasions in the weeks leading up to the raid, Fatta, Koresh, and others had gone jogging down the road.[11] This was confirmed by David Thibodeau: "I recall that approximately two weeks before the raid he was going through a period of time when he wanted to get back into health and back into shape. And so he would go out running, and some of the guys would go jogging with him. . . . And he would jog directly in front of the two houses that are across the street—one, of course, was the surveillance house—all the way down to the stop sign, maybe about a mile or so."[12]

During the siege, Koresh and others pointed to numerous occasions when he might have been arrested away from Mount Carmel; Koresh and the others also suggested that the undercover agent inside Mount Carmel could simply have served a warrant on February 28 while he was there, or BATF could have telephoned or knocked or sent the sheriff.[13]

BATF itself knew that Koresh was not a recluse. The BATF warrant application referred to Koresh's attending gun shows, and Koresh reportedly attended a gun show in Waco in February.[14] The agents in BATF's surveillance house next door to Mount Carmel made a log entry stating that Koresh left Mount Carmel Center on January 28.[15] BATF's insistence that he could not have been arrested outside the "compound" was untrue.

Eventually, BATF admitted it had not kept close tabs on Koresh and did not know whether or how often he left Mount Carmel.[16] One reason BATF did not "see" Koresh leave was that they did not know what they were seeing; "during the period of constant surveillance the agents within the house did not know what Koresh looked like." The surveillance operation included taking—but not developing—nine hundred photographs from the surveillance house, and failing to review videotapes of the movements of the Davidians. Moreover, the surveillance operation lasted little more than one week in January, although most BATF agents involved in planning the assault mistakenly believed that the surveillance was continuing.[17]

BATF's only effort to arrest Koresh off the compound involved trying to talk Texas authorities into issuing an arrest warrant for child abuse.[18] Notably, BATF's efforts to convince the state of Texas to issue an arrest warrant for Koresh presumed that Koresh would cooperate with such a warrant.

Clearly, BATF did not care much whether Koresh could be arrested away from the Mount Carmel Center. Later on, BATF agents would explain that there was no real point to trying a peaceful off-site arrest. Phillip Chojnacki, the BATF agent in charge of the raid, said: "We felt at that time that if we arrested him outside the compound, we still had to bear the brunt of attempting to execute the search warrant inside that location, because that's where the evidence was."[19]

Koresh's attorney testified, "They abandoned the idea of arresting him outside, I think, because they wanted to arrest him with a big show."[20] The congressional joint subcommittees which looked into the matter years later concluded that BATF was predisposed toward a confrontational arrest.[21]

Aside from the efforts to have Texas order Koresh to turn himself in, the only two options seriously considered for arresting Koresh were a siege of the compound and a "dynamic entry" (a paramilitary assault).[22] Assistant U.S. Attorney Johnston was reportedly strongly opposed to a siege approach for fear the days involved would allow Koresh to destroy evidence of weapons law violations.[23]

The fall 1993 Treasury investigation into BATF conduct at Waco offers no indication that BATF raid planners were concerned about—or even discussed—how different arrest strategies might minimize the risk of possible injury or death to innocent civilians, including the children. Instead, materials obtained from the U.S. Special Operations Command under the Freedom of Information Act provide the smoking gun for BATF's culpability in the deaths of February 28. To carry out the raid, BATF had obtained the assistance from the U.S. Army (more on this below), which is allowed to participate in domestic law enforcement when asked to do so by a "Drug Law Enforcement Agency" (DLEA). In this case, the civilian DLEA was BATF. According to the Army memo: "DLEA recognizes that casualties are probable. . . . Casualties will be DLEA, bad guys and civilians."[24]

Thus, BATF and the military expected "probable" casualties to BATF agents and to "civilians," and yet proceeded anyway. Executing search and arrest warrants in which casualties to innocent persons, including children, is "probable" can be justified in extreme emergencies. It is not justifiable when the underlying crimes are federal tax offenses, there is no urgency to arrest a fleeing suspect, and there is no violent crime in progress. It is a federal misdemeanor to exercise authority under a search warrant "with unnecessary severity."[25]

Rather than try to isolate Koresh, BATF managed, with almost complete success, to consolidate the Branch Davidians. BATF did so by selecting Sunday rather than a weekday for the raid. If BATF were really observing the activities at Mount Carmel, it should have known that many of the men left during the day for work. BATF's surveillance had made it clear that a school bus stopped there regularly to pick up at least one of the children during the week.[26]

THE ARRESTING DIFFERENCE BETWEEN ORDINARY CRIMINALS AND MARTYRS

Most ordinary criminals are inclined to stay alive as long as possible. But for virtually all religions, there are times where death may be preferable to a prolonged life, certainly with a good death preferable to a bad life. Thus, deeply religious persons, particularly if they see government agents as serving the devil, may die willingly, if they believe that death is what God wants for them. Eternal bliss, after all, is just around the corner. BATF's maximum force "dynamic entry" arrest procedures are well geared to arresting ordinary criminals. But BATF failed to adjust its strategy to take into account the completely different nature of the Branch Davidians. People expecting the apocalypse will not necessarily just raise their hands in surrender when a large contingent of federal agents invades their property. If law enforcement does not take into account the importance of religion for many people, more Wacos are on the horizon.

One religious scholar observed:

> As we edge inexorably toward the end of the 20th century, we bring closure to the second millennium since the birth of Christ. We are on the verge of a new millennium, a new age. I don't need to tell you that there is a rich religious symbolism attributed to this historical event. There are an estimated 30 million Protestants—evangelicals, fundamentalists, and charismatic Christians—most of whom hold fast to the doctrine of biblical literalism . . . and await the return of the historical Jesus of Nazareth in a cataclysmic episode referred to as the Second Coming.
>
> Many believe this event could take place in the near future, perhaps before the year 2000. These themes are preached in pulpits all over the country on any given Sunday. . . .
>
> Within this sector of the population, there are hundreds of religious groups not unlike the Branch Davidians: Independent, proud, defiant, religiously devout believers who think the larger, secular world is morally bankrupt.
>
> Historians and sociologists know that dissident millenarian and apocalyptic ideas will become more widespread in the next few years, and this raises an alarming question: Could there be another Waco on the horizon?[27]

To BATF, David Koresh was simply a religious fraud. Long after the botched raid, Ron Noble, Undersecretary of Treasury for Law Enforcement, who oversaw BATF during the Waco episode and who oversaw the Treasury review of BATF, stated: "This was not a religious group. This was a group of criminals engaged in serious violations of Federal criminal laws . . . though they might call it religion, there is no protection for any group that attempts or in fact does manufacture machineguns and grenades in this country."[28] Whether or not Koresh was a fraud, his followers were not frauds; they deeply believed in his teachings. And that belief should have been taken into account in determining how to proceed against the Branch Davidians. But instead, the Branch Davidians were "repeatedly referred to and vilified . . . as a cult."[29] Since BATF did not bother to try to understand the belief system of the "cult," it was hardly surprising that BATF so badly miscalculated how the Branch Davidians would react.[30]

BATF's simplistic "cult" view of Koresh's followers justified, to the agency, arresting him at the Mount Carmel Center. Otherwise, they reasoned, if the Branch Davidians found out he was in custody, "what would their reaction be? They would know we were coming with a warrant. They would have plenty of time to set up a defensive position, if that was their intention. We did not know what their mindset was going to be. Would they be collapsed because we had their messiah, or would they come to his defense? Would they possibly come into the community to get him out of the county jail? We did not know what they would do."[31]

Joyce Sparks, the social worker, understood that Koresh's followers were religiously sincere, and tried to convince BATF, and later the FBI. At first, she tried to avoid biblical references and interpretations in her investigation—as the BATF and FBI managed to do also. But:

He repeatedly told me that you can't understand me unless you understand what I believe, and I came to understand that, so I started watching how his beliefs manifested in his actions. It was real clear . . . he said that the enemy will surround the camp, and the saints will die. . . . And he believed that, and the people that followed him believed it as well. So once you set in motion the enemy surrounding the camp, he and his followers would have believed that that was the end of time. . . . He was adamant that suicide was not in their plan. You have to understand the way that he was. Christ came and he was the gentle messiah. He tried to tell us the truth, and we didn't listen. So he [Koresh] thought that he was here as a military intervention. So that was his position. He thought that he was here to militarily intervene, and that colored a lot of the things that he did.[32]

As Sparks understood Koresh's prophecies, arresting Koresh away from the "compound" would have meant the search following would not have been resisted.[33] "My point is that if they had separated him from his followers . . . , the prophecy could not have been fulfilled because the prophecy was that he had to die with the saints. So they wouldn't have acted on this. He had been arrested before. . . . No [there was not a junior or second prophet[34]], David was the only lamb and they would not have acted because they had to die with him. That was the prophecy."[35] In other words, the Branch Davidians were ready, willing, and able to die with David Koresh. But if he could not die with them (i.e., if he were in federal custody, following a peaceful arrest), they would have no theological motive for martyrdom.

Sparks's efforts to convince authorities to take seriously his religious teachings in figuring out how to arrest him failed: "all through all the agencies, State and Federal, there were people who didn't think they needed to listen. They thought they had all the answers. They had a task to do and they were going to do it. You couldn't get them to even stop and listen to information that could have been very vital. They just thought they were above it."[36]

But rather than defuse the situation by arresting Koresh, BATF fulfilled Koresh's prophecies when BATF launched its raid while Koresh and his followers were together, so that they could die together. No one is suggesting the religious zealots should be above law. Instead, law enforcement is "to avoid a catastrophe which takes the lives of law enforcement agents or innocent people. . . . The way to do that is to bring in religious translators . . . and ATF did not do that. Neither . . . did the FBI earnestly contact and consult religious experts."[37]

As one religious scholar who would later attempt to help the FBI to negotiate with the Branch Davidians, Dr. Philip Arnold, put it:

Without a correct understanding of the Branch Davidians religious faith, law enforcement was acting in a vacuum. . . . They were not able to understand the actions that the Branch Davidians took. They were not able to know which precise course of action would be of more value than another course of action. And they were unable to know which particular steps could precipitate disaster. Had they had knowledge of the religious faith of the Branch Davidians, this story could have ended in a much better and happier way . . . it is crucial to understand the world view, the ideological world view of a religious group if we are going to deal with them in the act of law enforcement.

Not that they are in any way exempt from existing laws. . . . But if we are going to deal
with someone from a different culture or someone who has a different religious language or even a different language linguistically speaking, you want a good translator
present to help you understand the culture of those people you are dealing with.[38]

As Dr. Arnold's colleague, Dr. James Tabor, put it: "They [the FBI] are trained in
hostage barricade rescue not the Book of Revelation."[39]

Failure to adjust standard law enforcement thinking to the religious views of the
Davidians adversely affected all aspects of the planning and acting for February 28
onward. It meant BATF did not adequately appreciate the importance of arresting
Koresh away from the Mount Carmel Center.

It also meant BATF's commanders in the field—chosen by seniority rather than
experience—were not concerned with the loss of the element of surprise. When arresting ordinary criminals, surprise is not usually necessary: "In theory, the criminals are
overwhelmed so quickly by police, who are using superior firepower, that they are psychologically overcome. According to this strategy, they then surrender with little or no
resistance."[40] Writes journalist Dick Reavis:

ATF raiding teams had routinely succeeded because ordinarily, when suspects look out
their windows and see an overwhelming show of force, they throw up their hands.
Survival is their paramount concern. Ordinarily, when raiders go into action, they don't
know whether their quarry has been forewarned or not: that's the kind of detail that
they usually learn only after a raid is over, from the confessions of defendants, for
example. That forewarning does not doom a raid is a point sometimes championed in
ATF literature with references to an action in which one hundred and fifty members of
a California motorcycle gang surrendered uneventfully, despite knowing that a raid
was imminent. The element of surprise isn't necessary to the kind of success that the
somewhat unheralded ATF has known, largely because the dope dealers who are its
quarry are pragmatic and streetwise souls.[41]

As the agent in charge of the Waco operation explained: "[I]n almost every situation, where we use a rapid entry and an overwhelming force, and what we think is overwhelming firepower . . . the people surrender rather than fight law enforcement."[42]
BATF had seventy-six armed personnel, invading property they believed to contain
seventy to eighty men, women, and children,[43] which would have meant BATF out-
numbered adult males at least three to one. But the Branch Davidians were not motorcycle gang members who wanted to stay alive as long as possible. They were ready to
be martyrs with David Koresh, as he had long taught they would.[44] When the BATF
showed up acting as if it wanted to kill them all, they did not fall on their knees to beg
BATF for mercy. To save their lives in this way would have been to lose their souls.

Failure of law enforcement to account for sincere, passionate, spiritual worldviews
unnecessarily endangers lawmen, endangers true-believer adults who are not the subjects of warrants for worldly crimes (i.e., as of the morning of the raid, all adults other
than Koresh), and endangers children, who may not have firm religious views of any
kind. All these dangers were ignored when BATF failed seriously to consider arresting
the lone suspect away from his flock.

MILITARIZING AMERICAN DRUG LAW ENFORCEMENT

The Posse Comitatus Act of 1878 was passed to outlaw the use of federal troops for civilian law enforcement.[45] The law made it a felony to use "any part of the Army or the Air Force . . . to execute the laws" except where expressly authorized by the Constitution or by act of Congress. The act of 1878, as amended, provides:

> Whoever, except in cases and under circumstances expressly authorized by the Constitution or Act of Congress, willfully uses any part of the Army or the Air Force as a posse comitatus or otherwise to execute the laws shall be fined no more than $10,000 or imprisoned not more than two years, or both.[46]

The idea was that law enforcement and the military are completely different, with the army largely geared toward destroying enemies of a different nationality, while law enforcement is serving persons largely friendly, who are guaranteed presumptions of innocence and rights not appropriate when dealing with the enemy. Anything which made law enforcement seem militarized was un-American; our citizens are not supposed to perceive themselves as subjects of an occupying force.[47]

As one modern court stated, the Posse Comitatus Act "is not an anachronistic relic of an historical period the experience of which is irrelevant to the present. It is not improper to regard it, as it is said to have been regarded in 1878 by the Democrats who sponsored it, as expressing 'the inherited antipathy of the American to the use of troops for civil purposes.' "[48] Indeed, during the debate over ratification of the Constitution, the Federalist Papers assured Americans that the military would never be used against the American people.[49]

In *Laird* v. *Tatum*, Chief Justice Warren Burger referred to "a traditional and strong resistance of Americans to any military intrusion into civilian affairs. That tradition has deep roots in our history and found early expression, for example, in the Third Amendment's explicit prohibition against quartering soldiers in private homes without consent and in the constitutional provisions for civilian control of the military."[50]

As another court put it:

> Civilian rule is basic to our system of government. The use of military forces to seize civilians can expose civilian government to the threat of military rule and the suspension of constitutional liberties. On a lesser scale, military enforcement of the civil law leaves the protection of vital Fourth and Fifth Amendment rights in the hands of persons who are not trained to uphold these rights. It may also chill the exercise of fundamental rights, such as the rights to speak freely and to vote, and create the atmosphere of fear and hostility which exists in territories occupied by enemy forces.[51]

Use of the military in domestic law enforcement has repeatedly led to disaster. In 1899, the army was used to break up a miners' strike at Couer d'Alene, Idaho, arrest all adult males in the area, imprison men for weeks or months without charges, and keep the area under martial law for two years.[52] During and after World War I, the army was used to break peaceful labor strikes, to spy on union organizers and peaceful critics of the war, and to respond to race riots by rounding up black "Bolshevik agitators."[53] Historian Jerry M. Cooper observes that the army's efforts "substantially slowed unionization for a decade."[54] One of the most egregious abuses of power in American history—President Truman's illegal seizure of the steel mills—was carried out with the military, which obeyed a plainly unconstitutional order.[55] During the Vietnam War, military intelligence was again deployed against domestic dissidents. "Military investigation of civil protest activity was precisely the kind of abuse of standing armies that eighteenth-century antimilitarists had feared," Cooper observes.[56] The 1970 killings of student protesters at Kent State University were, of course, carried out by a National Guard unit.

While the framers of the American Constitution would have found David Koresh repulsive, they would have been far more disturbed at, among other things, the use of the military against American citizens.

One of the reasons for the "law enforcement" disasters of February 28 and April 19, 1993, was that they were both run as military exercises, planned and executed with the advice of the U.S. Department of Defense. As Rep. John Conyers mentioned in his initial impressions of the final assault, "The root cause of this problem was that it was considered a military operation, and it wasn't."[57] Attorney General Janet Reno, on the other hand, discussed the incident, and the president's involvement, as similar to her acting as a general during World War II, where the president was not expected to exercise constant oversight.[58] And she acknowledged that, while "Plan A" for the final assault was the work of the FBI, the implementation of "Plan B" (which was put into effect a few minutes after the April 19 tank assault began) meant that "in effect [the U.S. Army] Delta Force's recommendation was carried out."[59]

Judicial interpretation and acts of Congress have sharply reduced the Posse Comitatus Act's limitations and have allowed much in the way of militarizing of law enforcement to occur. For one thing, the prohibition on the use of military personnel and equipment does not mean personnel cannot be used to assist law enforcement, only that they cannot be used directly[60] for enforcing the law itself. Thus, throughout the Waco standoff, military personnel, with express legal authority,[61] trained FBI and other law enforcement officials to use military vehicles.[62] In addition, the proscription on use of the military is limited to personnel; military equipment can be used,[63] although the usual procedure is to remove or cover military markings. The civilian agency must pay the military for use of the equipment.[64]

But these exceptions are minor compared to largest loophole in the Posse Comitatus Act: the "drug law" exception. Normally, the obligation to reimburse the military for the loan of equipment is a powerful incentive *not* to use military equipment in domestic law enforcement. A police chief will be hesitant to borrow military helicopters if his department will have to pay for them. But when drug laws are involved, the military assistance is free. In addition, greater use of military personnel is allowed.[65] As if to make the "drug war" a literal war, the U.S. military has created special Joint Task Forces (JTF) whose primary mission is to assist civilian drug law enforcement agencies.[66] Some JTF leaders foresee that not-far-distant day when restrictions against use of the military in domestic law enforcement will be abolished completely.

As part of the planning for the Waco raid, BATF went to the Joint Task Force which covers Texas, JTF-6, and asked for training, medical, communications, and other support. The JTF staff explained that JTF could only be involved if the case were a drug case.[67] If the case were not a drug case, BATF could obtain assistance from other parts of the military, but would have to pay for it.

Immediately, BATF claimed that the Waco case was a drug investigation. Koresh was supposedly running a methamphetamine laboratory. The military should have known that the drug allegation was merely a guise; BATF came up with the allegation only after being told of the benefits of such an assertion. In addition, the military prepared a memorandum for BATF on methamphetamine labs, and the precautions essential for dealing with such a lab. But when the paper was presented to BATF agents, they openly ignored the information in front of the soldiers who prepared it. Further, agents from the civilian Drug Enforcement Administration (DEA) who were assisting BATF also expressed no concerns about how BATF was addressing the risks of a meth lab in its operational planning, which similarly should have indicated to the military that the allegation was not valid.[68]

JTF-6, though, signed onto the mission of "training a National Level Response Team [BATF strike-force] for Counter Drug operations," in "Support of BATF Takedown of Meth Lab."[69] According to documents received from the U.S. Special Operations Command under Freedom of Information Act requests, the Joint Training operation (JT002-93) was approved due to a request from BATF dated February 2, 1993, requesting U.S. and Texas National Guard assistance, in serving a federal search warrant "to a dangerous extremist organization believed to be producing methamphetamine."[70] The army assistance at Waco would supposedly be "in direct support of interdiction activities along the southwest border."[71] (Waco is approximately 300 miles from the southwest border. Besides, the claim was that Koresh was manufacturing methamphetamine, not that he was importing it from Mexico.)

Had BATF actually been planning to take down a methamphetamine lab, its plans would have been far different and the involvement of experts greater. Testimony at the 1995 congressional hearings indicated the potential dangers of an explosion if a meth lab is not taken down properly. For instance, because a stray bullet could cause a major explosion, a dynamic entry would be an extremely risky, disfavored approach.[72] In addition, the chemicals in methamphetamine production are toxic, capable of injuring lungs, skin, liver, kidneys, central nervous system, and potentially causing genetic damage.

DEA protocol for seizure of meth labs require that agents wear special clothing and bring other specialized equipment. BATF not only made no such plans, but made express advance plans to use flashbang grenades—grenades which could set off a massive explosion in a real meth lab. When requesting flashbangs for use in the raid, BATF omitted mention of any possible presence of a meth lab.[73] Had BATF really thought there were a drug lab at Mount Carmel, BATF should have taken advantage of the DEA offer of assistance by a DEA Clandestine Certified Laboratory Team. But the offer was rejected.[74]

When JTF-6 was not looking, BATF did not even bother to pretend that drugs were involved. Notably, the initial warrant application included nothing regarding drug law violations—even though the presence of a drug lab would have given BATF clear legal authority to search for the presence of any type of firearm (not just machine guns), and even though the warrant affidavit threw in all sorts of other unsubstantiated allegations about Koresh.[75] In March, the BATF sought and obtained a warrant expanding the authorized scope of the search of Mount Carmel. Even the second warrant application did not include allegations of illegal drug activity.

After the botched raid, BATF still tried to use the drug claim to receive free military assistance. Richard L. Garner, Chief, BATF Special Operations Division, wrote to the Pentagon on February 28, 1993, asking for additional assistance related to "an on-going investigation in Waco, Texas involving apparent drug and firearms violations."[76] Although BATF maintained that pretense into late March,[77] the army had come to believe that its assistance to BATF and the FBI would be reimbursed[78]—as is required when there is no drug nexus. By May 15, 1993, the military suspected the "possibility that drug-connection was overstated to secure cost-free SOF training and assistance. No mention of drugs in public media."[79]

The drug enforcement exception to the Posse Comitatus Act has been very effective at undermining the honesty of law enforcement, who are encouraged to allege a drug nexus in many investigations for the purpose of getting, gratis, federal military assistance.[80] The U.S. Marshals Service claimed a possible drug problem involved with the Weavers at Ruby Ridge in order to get military reconnaissance flights over the cabin, which revealed no evidence of drugs.

According to an anonymous JTF-6 employee, JTF is often aware that civilian agencies are fabricating a pretext for military involvement, but, "the JTF doesn't even care, because there is little or no oversight involved. There's no independent authority looking over anyone's shoulder."[81]

What was the basis for the claim that Koresh was running a drug lab? First, one person associated with the Branch Davidians had been convicted of using drugs, and was paroled to McLennan County (Waco), Texas.[82] Second, ten Branch Davidians had been arrested or at least investigated for some "drug activity" at some time in their lives—apparently with no convictions.

In the mid-1980s, after the schism between George Roden and David Koresh, Roden had taken over the Mount Carmel Center, driving Koresh's followers away at gunpoint. Roden, currently confined in an institution for the criminally insane, did in fact set up a meth lab. But in March 1988, when Roden was sent to jail and Koresh's group took back the Mount Carmel Center, they found the meth lab, and promptly reported it to the sheriff.[83]

The fall 1993 Treasury Report insisted that the investigation of alleged drug use was valid.[84] Treasury reasoned that the sheriff's office had planned to collect the lab equipment but found no record it had done so, "raising the possibility that the illegal equipment might still have been at the Compound."[85] The Treasury Report ignores the fact that Marc Breault, the source for BATF's information that there had once been a meth lab at Mount Carmel, simultaneously told Davy Aguilera that the building in which it was housed had burned down in Spring 1990.[86] Koresh was thoroughly anti-drug, and it is implausible that he would have started operating a methamphetamine lab *after* telling the sheriff about its presence.

The limit of the Treasury criticism was that there should be clearer standards about what constitutes a drug nexus, and that BATF probably should have told the Texas National Guard more than a day in advance that their pilots might be shot at.[87] Treasury noted, accurately, that BATF could have had just as much military assistance without any alleged drug nexus had it been willing to reimburse the Defense Department. (Although the assistance could not have come from JTF-6.) That fact should raise some concerns about the viability of the Posse Comitatus Act as modified and interpreted. There are few real limits on the further militarization of American law enforcement. We will return to this topic in chapter 6.

What kind of military support did BATF get? Throughout February 1993, BATF agents learned at Fort Hood how to carry on a surprise military raid against the Mount Carmel Center.[88] The training was conducted by Army Special Forces (Green Berets) from Fort Bragg, North Carolina. According to unnamed "military sources," the training included not only use of flashbang grenades, but also "after hours" training in subjects which are not supposed to be taught to civilian law enforcement, including "Close Quarter Combat," "room-clearing, fire-and-maneuver, and building takedown." These are techniques for house-to-house urban combat (as at Stalingrad), not for service of a search warrants under the Constitution. The Green Berets also allegedly wrote a specific assault plan for BATF to use at Mount Carmel, and four Green Berets were allegedly present at Mount Carmel as observers on the day of the raid.[89]

To carry out the raid, BATF had procured helicopters from the Texas National Guard.[90] Unlike the federal government, which allows some reimbursed use of the military even when drugs are not involved, Texas law only allows the use of its National Guard helicopters for law enforcement when there is a drug nexus.

BATF also made use of the Alabama National Guard for aerial photography. The use was authorized by a "memorandum of agreement" between the Adjutants General of the Texas and Alabama National Guards. Even if the drug nexus had been real, there are a number of problems with employing the Alabama National Guard in Texas. Texas law expressly requires the governor's approval for the entry of a military force which, like the Alabama National Guard, is not part of the U.S. armed forces.[91] But Texas Governor Ann Richards never knew about the use of the Alabama or Texas National Guards until after the raid. Alabama law limits the operation of the Alabama National Guard to the state boundaries of Alabama. Thus, the deployment of the Alabama National Guard in Texas was a flagrant breach of the laws of Alabama and Texas. In addition, the "memorandum of agreement" providing for use of the Alabama National Guard in Texas violated the United States Constitution. Agreements between two or more states require congressional consent, and Congress has not consented the Alabama/Texas "agreement."[92] In other words, the Adjutants General of the National Guards of Alabama and Texas executed a "memorandum of agreement" which purported to authorize cross-border use of the Alabama National Guard, even though the "agreement" as implemented was in defiance of the law of Alabama, the law of Texas, and the Constitution of the United States. It is precisely such military usurpation of civil authority—the destruction of the rule of civil law—which is the ultimate, and real danger posed by use of the military in law enforcement.

Shortly after the raid, Governor Richards blasted the BATF for having lied to obtain the Texas helicopters. BATF then claimed that a British surveillance airplane, recently brought onto the Waco scene, had found new thermal evidence of the methamphetamine lab. Later, a law enforcement expert from the federal government's Sandia

National Laboratories would describe evidence of a methamphetamine lab as based on "an overflight using some very unsophisticated, forward-looking infrared devices" and detecting "the so-called hot spot on the compound. That hot spot could have come from any number of heat sources," but the government chose it to be indicative of a meth lab.[93] (At Ruby Ridge, the thermal "hot spot" which was asserted to be the site of Weaver's drug lab was actually a dog house.) An anonymous BATF source told a reporter that the new drug allegation "was made up . . . out of whole cloth . . . a complete fabrication" to avoid further criticism from Governor Richards.[94]

In commenting on the multitude of errors and distortions in the affidavit for the search and arrest warrants, attorney Gerald Goldstein noted that if BATF "had spent as much time worrying about the warrant as they had in amassing military-type equipment to execute the warrant, they probably wouldn't have made those kinds of mistakes."[95] They managed, unfortunately, to make other kinds of mistakes in executing the warrants.

WHY AN ELEMENT OF SURPRISE?

BATF was supposed to be serving a warrant to arrest Koresh and search the seventy-seven-acre property and all structures there and to seize automatic rifles, conversion parts, metal lathes and milling machines, grenade launchers, various chemicals, pipe bombs, grenades, and computer hardware and software.[96] Unless there is fear that the evidence might be destroyed while police identify themselves and give notice of why they are at a particular place, warrants are not usually supposed to be served with surprise. Under federal law, some force may be used by an officer to "execute a search warrant, if, after notice of his authority and purpose, he is refused admittance or when necessary to liberate himself or a person aiding him in the execution of the warrant."[97] In other words, "no-knock" is the exception, not the rule.[98]

In this case, the crimes alleged were all nonviolent offenses—felonies with the cumulative potential of decades of prison time, but generally crimes in and of themselves victimless. The core of the case was unregistered machine guns. (The alleged destructive devices were peripheral to the gun investigation.) The issue was not the number of machine guns per se. Individual gun collectors in Texas can and do own legally registered collections of dozens of machine guns. All of Koresh's alleged machine guns could have been legally possessed if Koresh had registered the guns, filled out the appropriate paperwork, and paid the $200 per gun federal tax. Thus, the crux of the Waco raid involved tax evasion—a serious federal felony, but not serious enough to merit an armed assault to serve a search warrant.

Koresh's Prior Cooperation with Law Enforcement

Significantly, BATF disregarded clear evidence that if BATF had simply asked to search the premises (even without a warrant), Koresh would have let them. Back in the summer of 1992, when BATF had been inspecting the records of and questioning Henry McMahon (Koresh's gun dealer), the following transpired:

While [agents] Skinner and Aguilera pored through McMahon's records, the dealer excused himself and telephoned Koresh. "I told him there were ATF agents at my house asking a lot of questions about him," McMahon said. "He said, 'If there's a problem, tell them to come out here. If they want to see my guns, they're more than welcome.'"

"So I walked back in the room, holding the cordless phone and said, 'I've got [Koresh] on the phone. If you'd like to go out there and see those guns, you're more than welcome to.' They looked at each other and Aguilera got real paranoid, shaking his head and whispering, 'No, no!'—so I went back to the phone and told David they wouldn't be coming out."[99]

Koresh's invitation to BATF to come out and inspect his guns suggests (a) no search warrant was needed, nor was an assault by seventy-six BATF agents needed in order to carry out a search warrant; and (b) Koresh either was in compliance with federal gun laws, believed he was in compliance, or believed he could hide any violations from invited guests. It has been suggested that accepting such invitations violates normal investigative techniques. There are, however, a few arguments against that explanation.

First, although BATF was investigating Koresh, not McMahon, BATF was pretending it was only conducting an ordinary compliance inspection of McMahon, the licensed gun dealer.[100] Such inspections involve checking to see if inventory is accounted for or properly logged out. There were sixty-five lower receivers in Koresh's custody but not yet recorded out of McMahon's dealer inventory, presumably because Koresh was going to make them into complete guns before having McMahon sell them (and share the profits with the Davidians). Under the circumstances, accepting the offer to see what was being done with the guns would not have been out of line.[101]

Notably, while the September 1993 Treasury Report offered justifications for other BATF actions which had been criticized,[102] the Treasury Report did not offer an explanation for why BATF declined Koresh's offer to visit. Instead, Koresh's invitation is simply omitted from the Treasury Report's discussion of the BATF's visit to gun dealer McMahon.[103]

Two years later, different explanations were offered. Phillip Chojnacki, the BATF agent in charge of the raid on Mount Carmel, said there was no point in going to see the firearms, because "at that particular point in time, the weapons in question were completely legal firearms . . . they were title I firearms that were being transferred from a licensed firearms dealer to an individual."[104] It is unclear what, exactly, BATF was investigating if it believed Koresh's firearms were lawful. At any rate, at those same congressional hearings, two law enforcement experts indicated that they would have accepted the offer, if only for the purpose of gathering intelligence.[105] Later, BATF's Charles Sarabyn did not assert that visiting Mount Carmel would violate normal investigative techniques; instead, if BATF paid a visit, Koresh "would put the armed guards out and it would be harder for us to be able to execute any type of warrant."[106] An additional fear was expressed that anyone sent in might have been taken hostage by Koresh.[107]

Was Koresh's invitation valid? Would he have cooperated with federal agents without a warrant? Or, later, could a warrant have been served without violence? One indication that there was no need for violence was that in 1987 Koresh had submitted without incident to arrest and to seizure of his guns.

The incident grew out of a schism between Koresh and George Roden (the son of Lois Roden, Koresh's predecessor as leader of the Davidians) about which of the two was the true prophet. Most Davidians opted to go live with Koresh in Palestine, Texas, rather than with Roden at the Mount Carmel Center. Roden challenged Koresh to a contest to see who could raise a corpse from the dead.[108] Preparatory to the contest, Roden dug up the body of a Branch Davidian who had died twenty years before. Koresh informed the police of Roden's unlawful abuse of a corpse; the police decided not to act until more evidence was available. Koresh and his followers snuck onto Mount Carmel to photograph the corpse, were caught by Roden, and a gun battle broke out. Koresh claimed that he shot Roden only in self-defense, with most rounds fired into the ground. (Wounded slightly, Roden survived.) When the sheriff's deputies arrived, Koresh and his aides offered no resistance, welcoming the law enforcement intervention they had sought earlier.[109] The trial jury in the attempted murder case hung, and Koresh was not retried. All of Koresh's followers were acquitted.[110]

The former McLennan County District Attorney who had prosecuted Koresh called the BATF raid unnecessary: "If they'd called and talked to them, the Davidians would've given them what they wanted."[111]

But BATF insisted to Congress that if they attempted to serve the warrant by knocking on the door, "he would meet that with violent resistance."[112] The Treasury Report rejects the local prosecutor's observation, and essentially denies that Koresh cooperated peacefully with his 1987 arrest, which took place immediately at the scene of the shooting. Accordingly, the Treasury Report asserts: "There was, in fact, no evidence that Koresh was prepared to submit to law enforcement authorities or that he had done so in the past."[113] The Treasury Report ignores the fact that the shootout was never determined to be unlawful; and the shootout did not involve law enforcement officers, but, indeed, occurred in part because law enforcement refused to intervene in response to Koresh's expressed concerns about possible violations of the law until Koresh could provide more evidence.[114] Most importantly, the shootout resulted not only in Koresh's immediate arrest, but also the later seizure of firearms pursuant to a warrant, which was served without resistance.[115] Thus, there was a precedent for the Branch Davidians allowing a search of their premises and the seizure of their guns after Koresh had been arrested off-site.

In addition to the 1987 incident, Koresh had more recently submitted peacefully to law enforcement, as the chronology provided in the Treasury Report indicates.

In 1992, Koresh was requested to visit and did visit a government social services agency regarding allegations of child abuse.[116] Koresh had also submitted to a warrantless search by Joyce Sparks, of the Texas Department of Child Protective Services, who went to Mount Carmel on at least two occasions to investigate possible child sexual abuse charges against Koresh. On the second visit, on April 6, 1992, he escorted her through the residence and showed her some of his guns, and showed her where he did some target shooting.[117] BATF decided that her visit was limited, that she did not have access to all rooms at the Mount Carmel Center, and any visit by BATF would similarly be limited, that they would not really have gotten access. Even with limited access, a BATF visit would have obtained additional information about the layout of the house.[118]

Also in 1992, in compliance with a Michigan court order in a child custody dispute, Koresh had allowed a child to be removed from Mount Carmel.[119]

In addition, after a neighboring farmer complained to the sheriff's office that he had heard machine gun fire in January and February 1992,[120] the sheriff's office investigated the incidents. Koresh "escorted local sheriff's deputies . . . through the compound after they had called beforehand to say they were coming. Koresh even invited one of the deputy sheriffs to come back and fish in their lake, according to McLennan County Sheriff Jack Harwell."[121] Koresh showed the sheriff that he was using a trigger attachment similar to the Hellfire device, which makes a semiautomatic rifle sound like a machine gun, but does not make it fire like a machine gun. (The trigger attachment amounts to selling the sizzle without the steak.) Koresh and the Branch Davidians checked with the sheriff to make sure that the devices were legal and did not require registration or federal tax payment.[122] As the *Christian Science Monitor* noted: "In the past, upon learning that local authorities were concerned about the types of weapons the Branch Davidians might possess, sect members elected to take samples in for examination to prove the weapons were legal."[123] After the BATF raid, during the early negotiations, Koresh insisted there was no need for the raid: "It would have been better if you just called me up or talked to me. . . . Then you could have come in and done your work."

Misguided as the Branch Davidians were, they nevertheless lived peaceful lives, bothering no one except each other.[124] Local law enforcement saw them as private and territorial but no threat to the surrounding community.[125]

On the other hand, Sheriff Jack Harwell later recounted: "Vernon Howell sent word to me—I didn't talk to him personally, but I received word, oh, two years prior to the raid—that he said he would never be taken into custody again." The sheriff explained that from then on, whenever he went to the Mount Carmel Center, there were always additional officers in cars waiting nearby, in case of trouble. Of course there never was any trouble during any of these visits.[126]

From Koresh's standpoint, violence may have appeared inevitable based upon how BATF proceeded. Koresh knew that he had always cooperated with the authorities before, and knew he had made it clear to BATF (when they visited McMahon's gun shop) that they could investigate without objection. He may have known of instances where government raids began with violence regardless of the likely reactions of the persons being investigated, such as the attacks on Randy Weaver by the FBI and U.S. Marshals in 1992. And (as detailed in the next section) about an hour before the February 28 raid, Koresh told a BATF agent he knew that BATF was coming, and that Koresh would submit peacefully to a peaceful arrest.[127] It would not necessarily be unreasonable to conclude that if seventy-six armed people, some in helicopters, storm your home—after you have told them you will cooperate—their intentions are not peaceable and self-defense may be a rational reaction (as a jury eventually found it to be in the case of Randy Weaver).

Violence could also have appeared inevitable to Koresh because he knew the government was expecting violence. The tip-off about the raid (discussed in the next section) had told him that a "shootout" was in the offing.

Violence from the government was something Koresh had preached and his followers expected. When an FBI negotiator later asked Sherri Jewell why the Davidians had so many guns, she responded: "If we didn't, we would have been slaughtered." "Before Sunday, we were preparing for this event. We knew it was going to happen," said Koresh. During the siege negotiations, Koresh aide Steve Schneider asserted repeatedly his and the Davidians' view that BATF came intent on murder.[128]

Evidence of Koresh's Possible Dangerousness

Neither the affidavit nor the arrest or search warrants make any reference to dangers Koresh might pose to arresting officers.[129] Even postraid affidavits indicating a "predisposition toward violence" apparently referred to his fondness for violent movies.[130]

In the Treasury Report, while there are frequent assertions of Koresh's hatred of law enforcement and a tendency toward violence, reasons to expect violence in response to a search or arrest warrant are weak.[131] BATF apparently expected Koresh to respond violently to the exposé which began in the Waco newspaper the day before the raid. BATF seemed surprised that "the article had not caused the cult to arm itself." But the Davidians' passive response did not make BATF wonder if BATF's perception of the Davidians' inclination for offensive violence might have been exaggerated.[132]

While one former Branch Davidian said Koresh would tell his flock that they might have to resist local or federal authorities, there was no indication the Branch Davidians would seek out a confrontation. Moreover, "as far as the former cult members knew, Koresh had not specifically trained his followers to repulse law enforcement officers or other visitors perceived to be hostile."[133]

There has been only one real allegation of any intention by Koresh to seek violent confrontation (as opposed to responding defensively to someone else's violence). It was what prosecutors of the surviving Branch Davidians called

> the McDonald's plan. And in that, he encouraged them to go out in the community in order to force a confrontation with law enforcement, to go out in the community, take over a public facility, a McDonald's, or, if you recall, there was an incident in Killeen involving a Luby's Cafeteria. Take over a facility. Take the people inside hostage. Hold them at gunpoint, and force them to admit that David Koresh was the lamb of God. . . . [H]e encouraged and directed his followers to . . . kill them if they refused. He later backed off on that . . . and said . . . it was just a test.[134]

The McDonald's plan story came from Marc Breault and the Bunds, and was vigorously denied by the Branch Davidians. If true, the plan provides further evidence that the Davidians were willing to kill for Koresh. Such willingness was never really in doubt. The issue for the BATF planners was whether Koresh would resist peaceful service of a search warrant.

Just as BATF and the U.S. Marshals Service perceived the hermit Randy Weaver's isolation in his cabin to be part of a years-long plan to achieve a violent confrontation with the federal government, the federal government somehow came to believe the same thing of David Koresh: "He went out of his way to attract the attention of law enforcement so that there would have to be some sort of a response in the future."

Among the ways Koresh supposedly carried out his master plan to invite a violent confrontation was having "his followers get credit cards and run up the limits so he knew somebody was going to be investigating that."[135] But most people expect that accumulating high credit card debt while making the minimum monthly payment will not lead to any adverse response, and certainly not a seventy-six-person armed assault.

Similarly, the acts of child abuse were said be part of Koresh's effort to be investigated. But when he was investigated, he tried to convince Joyce Sparks and her superiors—successfully, with regard to her supervisors—to call off the investigation.

Finally, Koresh "collected so much arms and ammunition beyond what is necessary for your own self-defense that he knew sooner or later either ATF, the sheriff's department or somebody was going to have to investigate that particular matter."[136] In general, gun owners and collectors, especially those working openly through a federally licensed dealer, do not believe that purchasing large quantities of firearms and ammunition will make an investigation inevitable. And, of course, when Koresh learned of the BATF investigation, he peacefully invited the investigators to come to the Mount Carmel Center.

Had religious analysis been solicited, it would also have undermined the fear BATF had of Davidian violence. "They . . . definitely had religious reasons [for having guns] . . . to protect themselves when the prophecy would one day be fulfilled that they would be attacked. It was not an attempt to go on the offensive and go to war against people, but all the prophecies that they quoted, and I have listened to 51 days of negotiation tapes, almost all of them by now, and they were not intending to have those weapons in order to go to war, but to defend themselves when they were attacked. They did believe it would happen."[137]

If BATF feared violence, there might have been a reason to attempt to achieve the element of surprise, but such fears are inconsistent with the minimal efforts to keep the news media away, both because the news media are not secretive in their actions and because government agencies are not in the business of endangering the lives of reporters.[138] If BATF was not expecting violence, a massive raid would produce good television and other media coverage, but be a poor justification for a massive show of force.[139]

Aside from fearing violence, a second reason for an element of surprise would be the possibility that evidence might be destroyed. Neither firearms nor conversion equipment are easy to destroy. There was nothing in the application for the warrants which indicated a concern that the guns would, or could, somehow be destroyed.[140]

BATF is left with the explanation offered by bureau spokesman Jack Killorin: "The warrant is for an imminent threat to the life and safety of everybody in that compound. The warrant is for the illicit manufacture of explosives and explosive devices which right away is an immediate threat to the life and safety of every person in there."[141] Whatever threat that the possible illegal manufacture of weapons posed to the children was probably outweighed by the threat created by the actual use of weapons in an assault against the children's home.

A third and perhaps more plausible explanation for the raid was eventually revealed. Assistant United States Attorney Bill Johnston, in a December 1992 meeting with BATF, had allegedly told them that he would not support a search warrant unless it were executed with a raid, a "dynamic entry."[142] As noted above, BATF also had important financial reasons for wanting to execute a high-profile, massive raid on "heavily armed cultists" just before the March 1993 congressional budget hearings.

WHAT ELEMENT OF SURPRISE?

The BATF assault was code-named "Operation Trojan Horse" because the agents would be hidden in cattle trailers.[143] Despite the name, the raid never had an element of surprise, as BATF was well aware before the raid began.

The assault by BATF was in the planning stages for over two months. Under the supervision of Green Berets at Fort Hood, BATF agents staged practice raids on a mock Mount Carmel. The pattern was always the same: a military attack from several directions, continuous firing of weapons, breaking into the home with ladders and crowbars, and use of concussion grenades. According to the military personnel who helped to train BATF, the BATF agents clearly expected to be met with gunfire when they served the warrant.[144]

Yet drilling had been done so that some of the timing was down to the second—so long as the Branch Davidians did not interfere with the BATF scripting. As quoted in the *Houston Chronicle*, "We had practiced to where it took seven seconds for us to get out of the tarp-covered cattle trailers we rolled up in, and 12 seconds to reach the front door."[145] Full control was to be achieved within 60 seconds.[146] There was no contingency plan for loss of surprise.[147] Peaceful entry was not rehearsed, nor was announcement of who the raiding party was, or the existence of a search warrant.

At the Davidians' trial, several BATF agents admitted they knew the element of surprise had been lost.[148] An hour before the attack began, Robert Rodriguez, the undercover agent who had been in the Mount Carmel Center, told his superior, Chuck Sarabyn, that Koresh was aware of the impending attack: "Chuck, they know, they know." Sarabyn responded by simply asking what Koresh was wearing and if he was armed. The Treasury Report later acknowledged that Sarabyn and raid director Phillip Chojnacki had falsely claimed that Rodriguez had not told them the element of surprise had been lost.[149]

Sarabyn commenced the raid by running out to the staging area and shouting: "Let's go! Come on, hurry up! They know we're coming!" and "Koresh knows the ATF and National Guard are coming."[150] At the 1995 congressional hearings, Chojnacki testified that he thought that Rodriguez meant that Koresh expected a fierce battle with BATF "in the metaphysical" rather than the "physical" sense, something he spoke of all the time.[151] Even the most credulous person would have trouble believing that Sarabyn ran around yelling "hurry up! They know we're coming" in order to warn the BATF strike force that the Branch Davidians knew about the impending attack in the metaphysical sense.

Rodriguez rushed to the command center after completing his telephone report. When he discovered the raid had already begun despite his call, he went outside, sat down, and cried.[152]

Law enforcement experts found it beyond belief that persons could plan a dynamic entry without knowing that surprise was critical.[153] There are two explanations for why Sarabyn and Chojnacki could have considered Koresh's knowledge that they were coming not so important as to require canceling or postponing the raid. First, as noted by law enforcement expert Wade Ishimoto, part of the purpose of a dynamic entry is to intimidate so much—by numbers and by appearance (helmets, tactical vests, etc.)—that resistance becomes pointless.[154]

Second, the two leaders may have believed that the tarp-covered cattle trailers would serve as a sufficient disguise so that surprise could still be achieved. BATF agent Bill Buford believed the trailers were successfully "used . . . to surprise in order to get up there without them knowing we were in them," and that one of the Davidians had come out to "run these farmers off that had pulled into his driveway." The cattle trailers which the Davidians supposedly believed contained only cattle were part of an eighty-vehicle convoy which stretched over a mile—an unusual configuration for cattle transport.[155]

Former BATF Deputy Director for Enforcement Dan Hartnett agreed with Sarabyn and Chojnacki that the "element of surprise," which served as the basis for most Treasury Department criticism of the BATF, was not really as clear an issue in planning the raid. Hartnett insisted there was no discussion of the "element of surprise" until after the raid had failed, and it was discussed in the news media. He insisted, contrary to assertions by Treasury Undersecretary Ron Noble, that aborting the raid if the element of surprise were lost was never a part of the plan. He confirmed that secrecy and safety were parts of the plan, but not surprise.[156]

Another possibility is that BATF was not sure, when starting out, whether Koresh had responded to information about the raid with defensive action. For example, Sarabyn's questioning of Rodriguez told him that Koresh was unarmed, shaking, and reading the Bible when Rodriguez left, rather than organizing resistance; thus Sarabyn thought action before Koresh calmed down and got organized would be effective.[157] But according to BATF's James Cavanaugh, it was expected that the Branch Davidians would be armed and waiting: "[O]ur mistake was that we thought that the compound would bristle with guns. That he would be defiant. That he would get his mighty men and be defiant and not let law enforcement come on that property. And he was so diabolical that he laid an ambush."[158]

Branch Davidian suspicions had been aroused long before the raid began.

On January 27, 1993, a BATF agent posing as a trainee accompanied a UPS driver during a package delivery. When the "trainee" and the driver arrived at the Mag Bag, the trainee/agent demanded (in violation of UPS rules) that he be allowed into the building so that he could use the phone and the bathroom. The UPS truck then headed to the main building, insisting that the package could not be dropped off at the Mag Bag. The "trainee" was again going to insist that he use the bathroom, even though he had just used the Mag Bag bathroom a few minutes ago. Koresh and David Jones met the UPS truck, with Jones carrying a roll of toilet paper.[159] Assuming that Koresh and his followers had been stupid enough to fall for the BATF agent's ruse, the agent would not have learned much. The main building did not have indoor plumbing. Koresh told the UPS driver and his "trainee," "I know we're being watched." Koresh even complained to the sheriff's department about the "undercover" effort, which he apparently thought the sheriff's office was involved in.[160]

Months before BATF agents moved into the "undercover house," friendly neighbors had warned the Branch Davidians that government agents had asked for permission to install surveillance equipment on the neighbors' property.[161]

Then, eight "college students" moved into the undercover house. The supposed student leader, Rodriguez, was over forty, but he and the others were chosen for their youthful appearances.[162] The "students" were supposed to have come from west Texas to attend Texas State Technical College. But they drove new cars. The Branch Davidians checked the registration of the three vehicles and found, surprisingly for students, "no ownership liens. All were registered to the same address in Houston—a long way from West Texas."[163] According to the surveillance notes, Davidian David Jones came to visit, said he had gone to TSTC, and started discussing various teachers. The surveillance notes fail to indicate if the undercover agents thought they answered correctly. Wayne Martin, a Davidian with a Harvard Law degree and a Waco law practice, checked the "students'" names with the registrar at Texas State, and found there were no such students.[164]

One evening, a few Davidians decided to welcome the new neighbors, and brought over a six-pack of beer. The house was dark, but there were cars in the driveway, so the Davidians knocked. "Who is it?" came a hoarse, conspiratorial voice from inside the house.

The Davidians said that they were from across the street, and had brought over some beer as a welcoming gift. Could the Davidians come in? "No! You can't!" said the same hoarse voice. "I got my girl in here." The door then opened a crack; a hand sprang out and grabbed the beer, and the door slammed shut.[165]

Several days later, Koresh told the family that lived next door to the undercover agents that he thought the "students" were FBI agents. Koresh thought the men were too old and articulate to be real students; their cars were too new; they carried briefcases; and the owner of the home, having previously refused to rent to anyone, would be unlikely to suddenly decide to rent to eight male college students.[166]

One of the undercover agents pretended to be a foreman in charge of cows; the man's obvious ignorance of the animals led Koresh's gun dealer to warn Koresh that Koresh needed to watch out.[167]

The day after the UPS trainee with his urgent needs had tried to get inside, "college student" and undercover agent Robert Rodriguez, using the fictitious name "Garcia,"[168] showed up at Mount Carmel. He was promptly invited to participate in group activities. Over the next month, Rodriguez listened to music, attended Koresh's Bible studies lectures, and spoke with Koresh frequently one-on-one. Koresh and the other Branch Davidians knew that Rodriguez was an undercover agent.[169] Koresh also showed Rodriguez the Gun Owners of America tape about BATF: *Breaking the Law in the Name of the Law*. (The tape's role in establishing probable cause for the raid is discussed in the previous chapter.)

Koresh was apparently quite persuasive since Rodriguez almost converted to the Branch Davidian faith: "'He was close,' he [Rodriguez] finally said, his voice cracking at the memory. 'The thing that probably saved me is I didn't have to stay there. I could come and go as I pleased.'"[170]

The Davidians knew something was up, but not until the morning of February 28 did they know an attack was planned. On the morning of February 28, KWTX television cameraman James Peeler asked a postman for directions to the Branch Davidian compound. The cameraman allegedly told the postman something like: "Well you better get out of here because there's a National Guard helicopter over at [Texas State Technical College] and they're going to have a big shootout with the religious nuts." Unbeknownst to the cameraman, the postman was David Jones (a Branch Davidian, and Koresh's brother-in-law), who immediately rushed to Koresh with a warning.[171]

BATF did not inform the public about the tip-off until August.[172] So not only did the Davidians know that the raid was coming, they also knew that the raiders had already planned for "a shoot-out."

Koresh had been giving undercover agent Robert Rodriguez a Bible study when a Branch Davidian called Koresh out of the room. Koresh returned, "breathing real hard," with his hands shaking so intensely that he could barely read from the Bible. He shoved his hands into his pockets, and looked out the window. Koresh turned to Rodriguez and said, "They're coming, Robert. The time has come." Rodriguez made a weak excuse about needing to meet someone for breakfast.[173] He was terrified that Koresh would hold him hostage or kill him. Indeed, few criminals—knowing that a violent raid was coming—would not hold on to a very valuable hostage such as a known undercover agent. But Koresh shook Rodriguez's hand, wished him "Good luck," and said to Rodriguez the same words that Jesus had said to Judas in parting: "What thou doest, do quickly."[174]

Koresh later explained that he was suggesting that he knew Rodriguez had to arrest Koresh—and he would not hold it against Rodriguez, nor would he resist. Koresh thought Rodriguez, knowing that Koresh would not resist, would see a duty to call off the raid as unnecessary.[175] Rodriguez did, of course, attempt to call off the raid, but for very different reasons. If Koresh meant to use the biblical quote to tell Rodriguez that there would be no resistance if the arrest warrant were served peacefully, the message was conveyed far too elliptically.

But if Koresh hoped for a peaceful resolution, the Branch Davidians still prepared for combat. While some, such as Winston Blake, ate breakfast, apparently unaware of what was coming, others, such as Jamie Castillo, dressed in black, and donned tactical vests designed to hold ammunition. "I looked like the ATF," Castillo later told a Texas Ranger.

Several minutes before the BATF "Trojan Horse" cattle trailers full of agents arrived at Mount Carmel, one of the three National Guard helicopters which BATF was using as command centers could be heard at the compound. The helicopter noise may have given the Davidians more evidence that a raid was imminent.[176] At the trial, the reporter and cameraman testified that they saw helicopters circling the building beginning at 9:30, long before the 9:48 beginning of the raid.[177]

There were many other indications that something was going to happen, although it is not known whether these signs were known to the Davidians. Radio talk shows shortly after the raid included callers who recalled Saturday night, February 27, with BATF agents drinking in local bars and, in Koresh's words, "talking about coming out here to Mount Carmel and . . . busting us up real good in the morning . . . and they were laughing about it."[178] Many Waco residents saw large numbers of BATF agents dressed in assault uniforms moving about hotel lobbies throughout Waco on the morning of the assault.[179] As was later observed, "even the hotel reservations that occurred on February 27 would have alerted someone as to the operational security risks involved . . . it's a theoretical premise, that you can both arrest someone and execute search warrants without the world finding out when the world is as modestly populated in that area."[180]

BATF did not use secure radio communications, so news media personnel and Waco residents using scanner radios and cellular phones heard extensive communications among BATF agents before and during the raid. According to the BATF conversations overheard during the raid, BATF had been searching mail and UPS packages coming in to the compound for months.[181]

It is possible that the BATF personnel who believed that incoming mail and packages had been searched for months beforehand were wrong. BATF might simply have been keeping records of the size and return address of incoming mail without opening it; such surveillance does not require a warrant. Alternatively, the BATF agents might have been repeating a distorted version of the story about the UPS driver who "accidentally" dropped a package and exposed its contents.

On the other hand, the BATF radio traffic might have been accurate. Perhaps BATF was in fact opening mail and packages sent to Mount Carmel. If so, there is no evidence BATF ever had a warrant to do so. Without a warrant, BATF's opening of the mail constituted not only a violation of the Fourth Amendment to the United States Constitution, but also criminal interference with the United States mail.[182]

SHOWTIME

Despite the many rehearsals, raid planning was very poor. The layout of the house, which was subject to constant expansion, was not known to BATF except by its undercover agent and by a former Branch Davidian who had left in 1989.[183] Both of those persons were males, and men were generally restricted to the first level of the house, with only women and children allowed upstairs.[184] The raid was scheduled for 10:00 A.M., on the assumption that most of the men would be outside working in the pit (a tornado shelter in progress), and separated from the firearms, which were stored on the second floor or in the living quarters of the men who had been issued arms.[185] But the surveillance indicated that men were working outside only about a third of the days during the surveillance, and no more than thirteen men worked even on those occasions.[186]

BATF scheduled its raid—on a seventy-seven-acre property with an observation tower[187] and "several manned observation posts [where it was] believed that the observers were armed"[188] —for daylight,[189] when everyone inside would be expected to be awake, on open plains, with numerous vehicles, noisy National Guard helicopters, and seventy-six agents.[190] The news media were known to be present, if they were not actually invited.

BATF agents were outfitted with soft (kevlar) body armor, rather than hard body armor made of steel or ceramic plates. Soft armor is more comfortable and easier to maneuver in, and stands up well against most handgun ammunition; but soft body armor is known to be incapable of stopping intermediate power rifles, which BATF knew were the Branch Davidians' main weapons.[191]

No time was allocated for the statutory obligation of BATF to identify its authority and purpose and to be refused admittance. At trial, BATF admitted that no agent was designated to announce the purpose of the raid and who the raiding party was.[192] BATF also admitted no peaceful entry was ever rehearsed.[193] BATF Special Agent Kenneth King, a member of the roof team, was asked, "Even if . . . the people at the front door had been welcomed in by David Koresh, none of that would have made any difference, as far as what you were doing was concerned?" "No, sir." ". . . [T]he flash-bang would have been thrown and you would have entered the window . . . ?"

"This is correct," King replied.[194] King further testified that his operational orders never included disclosing his identity or purpose for the entry before the entry, and the orders allowed him no discretion to retreat or otherwise change tactics, regardless of events. Lacking direct radio communication, King would have had no way of knowing if Koresh invited the raiding party to enter.[195] This lack of communications also delayed for several minutes achieving a ceasefire once Agent Jim Cavanaugh had negotiated it. With no direct link to the agents, he had to give the word separately to the various team leaders, who, in turn, had to communicate to their agents.[196]

Federal law states that an officer serving a search warrant "may break open any outer or inner door or window of a house, or any part of a house, or anything therein, *if, after notice of his authority and purpose, he is refused admittance*"(emphasis added).[197] Likewise, BATF's manual specifies that "Officers are required to wait a reasonable period of time to permit the occupants to respond before forcing entry."[198]

An FBI spokesman explained why BATF would not have identified itself at the outset: "You don't want to give these guys a chance to get to their guns. In Waco, there was no announcement of who was there and the fact they're there for the lawful purpose of executing a warrant."[199]

The common law has long been hostile to the use of force by a sheriff or other official to enter a home, or to an entry in which the sheriff fails to identify himself and to state his purpose. Such a standard dates back at least to 1603, and beyond that to the Magna Charta.[200] But today, even when knock and announce is enforced, officers are now allowed to break in within seconds after announcing themselves.[201] Violent entry into the homes of suspects has now become routine for much of federal law enforcement, including BATF.

Congress should specify by statute that all search or arrest warrants in a home must be preceded by a knock (or doorbell ring) and an announcement. A specified period of time (such as two minutes) should be required to elapse before entry can be forced. Unannounced break-ins should only be allowed when a magistrate or judge has specifically authorized them, based on unusual circumstances in the particular case, or when there is an unforeseeable emergency. Simply pointing out that the home to be searched contains firearms should not be taken as proof that the people in the home will kill law enforcement officers.

Further, applications for violent search warrants should be required to contain (in addition to the general requirements for warrants proposed in chapters 1 and 6) all known evidence regarding the defendant's cooperation or lack of cooperation with government investigations in the past. The application should also detail any potential threat to nonsuspect civilians that would be created by a violent "dynamic entry."

Proposals have been offered in state legislatures and in Congress to require federal law enforcement officials to notify or receive permission from local law enforcement before carrying out arrests or raids. One such measure was passed in Montana, but vetoed by Governor Marc Racicot. Had such a measure been in effect in Texas and Idaho, the many lives lost in the Waco and Weaver incidents might have been spared. The local notification/permission law should include an exception allowing a federal district court to issue a warrant which would not require local cooperation in cases where local law enforcement is corrupt.

WHO STARTED THE SHOOTING?

Supporting the BATF claim that Koresh started the shooting is BATF's report of his remarks on learning of the impending raid. According to BATF's version of a report by undercover agent Rodriguez (who was in the residence shortly before the attack), Koresh said, "Neither ATF or the National Guard will ever get me. They got me once, and they will never get me again. They are coming; the time has come."[202]

Later, during the siege, the attorneys for Koresh and for Steve Schneider were shown statements made by Rodriguez. When the attorneys met with Koresh and Schneider, and discussed Rodriguez's statements, the only thing which Rodriguez had said that Koresh claimed was wrong was the assertion that Koresh had said, in essence, "you're never gonna get me, copper." At the meeting, Steve and Judy Schneider, as well as other persons who were allegedly in the room at the time, agreed that they had heard no such language.[203]

According to Branch Davidian Clive Doyle, Koresh told his followers to "be cool" and to go to their rooms, and that Koresh would handle whoever was coming. Doyle said that he heard Koresh at the front door telling BATF to wait, because there were women and children inside, and the next sound he heard was incoming fire.[204] This version of Koresh's behavior at the door was repeated to FBI negotiators by Koresh, Steve Schneider, and other Davidians during the siege.[205]

Most participants on both sides probably did not know for certain who fired first, and most of those inside the house are now in no position to express their opinions; survivors' recollections might be self-serving, or they might not really have witnessed the first shots. BATF's legal obligation was to knock, identify itself, and give Koresh the opportunity to cooperate. Koresh and his supporters insisted that BATF started shooting before Koresh could either cooperate or defy, indeed, that the helicopters began firing before any knocking had been done. BATF insists the shooting began from the inside. One BATF account states that the first shots were fired at the helicopters, before the raid really began.[206] If so, it is hard to understand how the agents on the ground could be ambushed; the fact that helicopters were being shot at might be considered reason to believe that the Davidians were not going to be surprised.

Psychiatrist Robert Cancro, one of the independent experts reviewing both BATF's and the FBI's actions for the Justice Department, pointed out that it did not matter who fired first: "Certainly an armed assault by 100 agents had to be seen as an attack *independent* of who fired the first shot. If an armed individual enters your home by force and you have reason to believe that person represents a mortal threat, you are allowed to fire a weapon in self-defense in most states. The law does not usually allow the potential attacker to fire first before a response can be called self-defense."[207] Just as Cancro's analysis could justify a first shot by the Davidians, similar analysis could justify a first shot by BATF. As Chuck Sarabyn put it: "[A]n agent going forward there, if he's in fear of his life . . . could take the first shot."[208]

Five scenarios have been proposed.

The first is that the shooting began with shots fired from the helicopters, as some surviving Branch Davidians claim. (In a variant of this scenario, some BATF agents insist the gunfire began with Branch Davidians firing at the helicopters.)[209]

The second scenario, which was the government's theory at the trial of the Branch Davidians, is that as BATF approached, Koresh opened the door, grinned, closed the door, and the Branch Davidians began firing through the steel door before BATF had the opportunity to identify themselves and their purpose.[210]

The third scenario is that when Koresh opened the door and yelled that there were women and children inside, he was shot and wounded by a BATF agent assigned to him, whose MP-5 submachine gun was equipped with a silencer, after which the Branch Davidians responded with their unsilenced firearms.[211]

A fourth scenario is that accidental gunfire from BATF led to both sides shooting.[212] In one version, one of the BATF agents accidentally shot himself as he unholstered his gun, shouting "I'm hit! I'm hit!"[213]

At the 1995 congressional hearings, Rep. John Shadegg believed that BATF agents are too well trained to have accidental discharges, and "it is just as plausible a theory . . . that it was an accidental discharge by a nervous Davidian who was not as well trained to use that firearm." Steve Schneider's attorney responded that his reason for thinking it an accidental discharge from a BATF agent's gun was "information that was given to us by someone in the press who had a confidential source within the ATF who indicated that someone said that as he was coming out of the back of that, he tripped, his weapon wasn't on safe, and it discharged . . . supposedly if you looked at trajectory, the round went into the front of the pickup truck's engine compartment."[214] According to George R. Thacker, whose Pennsylvania Gunsmith School does work for the Energy Department's Central Training Academy in Albuquerque, shortly after the initial Waco raid, fifteen BATF agents who had participated took a SWAT (Special Weapons and Tactics) course at the school, and almost half failed.[215]

The final scenario is that the Branch Davidians' dogs, which were supposed to be controlled with fire extinguishers, but with firearms as backup, were shot at, leading each side to assume the other had begun firing. Hearing the noise, each side initiated what it assumed was defensive fire.[216]

According to the story Koresh told his attorney, Dick DeGuerin, the BATF agents arrived in their cattle trailers, screaming like Marines storming a beach, not identifying themselves or asserting a search or arrest.[217] Koresh opened the door, and told them "Get back! There's women and children here. Get back. I want to talk." Then, according to Koresh, after BATF started shooting, Koresh's people got their guns and responded.[218]

Koresh either believed the story or was good enough at bluffing to repeat it during the negotiations with BATF Agent Jim Cavanaugh, expressing the hope that the raid was videotaped (as it was supposed to have been): "My only hope would be . . . that those cameras actually were zooming in enough on that front door . . . to show . . . I waved out, and that's probably all in the film, too. And it says, you know, 'Get out of here, there's women and children. Let's talk, let's go. Get out.' "[219]

At the Davidians' trial, the defense introduced pictures taken by the Waco *Herald-Tribune*. Although BATF had testified that the first shots were fired through the front door, by the Davidians, immediately after Koresh slammed the door, the pictures showed no bullet holes in the door at the same time that agents were shooting toward the house. BATF had also testified that Davidians began shooting at them from every window.[220] The photographs showed BATF agents shooting before any Davidians were visible in the windows, and before any holes were visible in the front door.[221]

BATF agent Roland Ballesteros, the first agent to reach the Mount Carmel front door on February 28, testified at the Davidian trial that he raced toward the door yelling, "Police! Lay down!" Ballesteros could see Koresh standing, unarmed, in the doorway. Then Koresh "kind of smiled, then backed off and closed the door." On cross-examination, Ballesteros admitted that his statements to the Waco police on February 28, to the Texas Rangers on March 10, and at a September 30 pretrial hearing had not mentioned any sighting of Koresh. Agent Ballesteros had told the Waco police and the Texas Rangers that he assumed the first shots which Ballesteros heard were the dogs being shot. At the Davidians' trial, Ballesteros testified that the first shots came from within the "compound." Ballesteros explained that painkillers from a wound Ballesteros suffered during the raid had dulled his memory; his memory had been "jogged" when four U.S. Customs agents interviewed him during the Treasury Department investigation of the raid.[222]

Also supporting Koresh's claims are tapes from the telephone calls Koresh and his aide Wayne Martin made to 911 a minute after the shooting started, in the heat of battle, with the gunfight still in progress with the result unclear.[223] Martin called on the sheriff's office to get them to stop shooting, frantically screaming, "There's 75 men around our building and they're shooting at us! Tell 'em there's women and children in here and to call it off." While Sheriff's Lieutenant Lynch was trying to contact BATF, Martin yelled, "They keep on firing out there! They keep attacking!" Steve Schneider is heard in the background, as helicopters buzz the house, yelling, "Here they come!"[224]

Koresh's telephone call, also to Sheriff's Lieutenant Larry Lynch, included the words: "We told you we wanted to talk. No. How come you guys try to be ATF agents? How come you try to be so big all the time."[225] The second call to 911 included Wayne Martin's assertions "I have a right to defend myself" and "They started firing first."[226] Branch Davidian Wayne Martin had been the first to talk with the sheriff's office on the phone, and he also stated that the raiders had fired first.[227]

If the Davidians had really been planning to ambush the raiders, the Branch Davidian gunners "would have deployed in such a way as to be able to direct fire on the vehicles, annihilating the attacking force before it could exit the trailers."[228] As an attorney for one Branch Davidian later put it: "If the Branch Davidians intended to ambush those people with 48 machineguns and .50 caliber machineguns and they came up in unprotected cattle cars with nothing but tarps on them, they would have blown them away."[229] The FBI's Waco commander, Jeffrey Jamar, told a reviewer from the Department of Justice that the Branch Davidians "could have easily killed all of those agents before they even got out of the cattle cars with the kind of weapons they had."[230]

During the 1995 House of Representatives hearings on Waco, many government witnesses refused to confront the fact that the Branch Davidians chose not to kill the BATF raiders when it would have been easy to shoot them all. The fact must not be considered, the witnesses said, because to consider the possibility that the Davidians could have inflicted much more damage would be to suggest (supposedly) that the Davidians' killing four agents was not evil.

The one person who did seriously confront the concept that the Davidians had chosen not to open fire when they could have killed almost every agent at once was Agent Buford; he theorized that the Davidians were fooled into thinking the cattle trailers had erroneously strayed onto private property,[231] and, before the Davidians realized that the trailers contained the government agents they were expecting, all BATF personnel had a chance to leave the trailers and assume offensive positions. Agent Buford's theory depends on the Branch Davidians—who had been alerted that a raid was coming within minutes and who had already heard the helicopters—stupidly thinking that large cattle trailers which pulled onto the property just happened to be simple farm transport vehicles which had made a wrong turn.

There are two key pieces of evidence which might resolve the question of who opened fire first. One is the front door to the house. BATF claimed that the Davidian "ambush" included an opening fusillade through the front door. If the front door were examined, and holes showing numerous bullet entries originating inside the house were found, the BATF version would be supported. Although the left half of the metal door was found, the right half was not, a fact which the federal prosecutors later acknowledged was inexplicable.[232]

Jack Zimmermann, attorney for Koresh's aide Steve Schneider, visited Mount Carmel during the siege; he later testified that he saw the right side of the door, and the bullet holes were obviously from outside, since "the metal flared outward on the inside."[233] Koresh's attorney agreed: "and what I saw, and what I was told, it was very compelling that the ATF fired first. Understanding that those on the inside have a big stake in this and I might have been lied to, but what I saw confirmed that . . . ATF fired first. . . . Some people said that it was the dogs that were being killed, and there were dogs killed. . . . I saw the bullet holes in the front door. . . . Almost every bullet hole was an incoming round, and what I mean by that, it is a metal door, you could easily tell that the bullets were incoming rounds, they were punched in."[234]

The door was steel, not aluminum, and hence would not have melted during the April 19 fire. A photograph introduced at the trial of the bulldozer operating after the fire shows what appears to be the complete front door being pulled by the blade.[235] At the trial, evidence was introduced which proved that the other door from the pair of front double doors had survived the fire intact.[236]

At the 1995 congressional hearings, Rep. Charles Schumer scornfully said that the missing front door was irrelevant; the door would of course have only incoming bullet holes, since the Branch Davidians would not shoot through their own front door. Jack Zimmermann reminded Schumer that the Branch Davidians shooting through their own door was precisely the (incredible) theory proposed in both the Treasury Report, and in the criminal prosecution of the Branch Davidians. The Treasury Report claims that firing began when "Gunfire from inside the Compound burst through the door. The force of the gunfire was so great that the door bowed outward." The prosecutor argued that there was no way of telling when the photographs involving the door were taken. But if BATF had opened fire at *any* time before a bullet hole appeared in the front door, then BATF's story of an opening fusillade through the front door could not be correct.[237]

Even if it is assumed that the Branch Davidians fired first, the door was very important. Any bullet holes from outside through a closed door would have been inappropriate. BATF's standing orders "are to fire only at clearly identifiable targets."[238]

The second crucial item of evidence may be in the custody of BATF. In the spring of 1993, BATF announced it had a videotape which conclusively proved that the Branch Davidians started firing first; BATF later claimed that the video was inexplicably blank.[239] Jury forewoman Sarah Bain said that the jurors found the missing video particularly suspicious.[240]

Regardless of who fired first, a firefight broke out. Two-way radio communication between BATF commanders and agents broke down almost immediately.[241] At least some of the BATF agents began firing wildly. In all, BATF fired about 1,500 rounds.[242] Others followed official BATF procedures, and fired only at clearly visible targets who were armed. Inside, people were crying, "Go away, just leave us alone, just leave."[243]

Of the four BATF agents killed, at least one was likely the victim of "friendly fire."[244]

A ceasefire was finally negotiated after BATF had fired all but forty rounds of ammunition.[245] Within minutes after the shooting began, Wayne Martin and David Koresh had called 911, and were on the phone with the sheriff's office, trying to get BATF to stop shooting. But the firefight continued for forty-five minutes. One important reason was that phone communications with the sheriff's office (the sheriff had not been informed about the impending raid by BATF) were confused at first. Communications between the BATF commanders and the rest of the BATF agents were even worse, and it was very difficult to get orders to the various BATF teams which were spread out all over the property.

Reconstructing the details of a shooting is never easy, particularly when there are so many participants, none of whom saw everything, and almost all of whom have some incentive to remember events in a way that justifies their own group. Perhaps the most important evidence is what immediately preceded the shooting. If Koresh had wanted to massacre the BATF agents, he could have held Robert Rodriguez hostage, and perhaps prevented BATF from learning that the raid had been compromised. When the cattle trailers arrived on the property, he could have ordered that firing commence, and almost all the BATF raiders would have been instantly slaughtered.

Instead, Koresh shook Rodriguez's hand, and let him go. Rather than firing at the cattle trucks, Koresh let the BATF raiders pour out and run for their assault positions, and at that point he opened the door, exposing himself to the risk of sniper fire. (He was almost instantly shot.) His conduct is highly inconsistent with the conduct of someone who wanted to start a gunfight.

HELICOPTERS, MACHINE PISTOLS, AND OTHER WEAPONS

Although the National Guard helicopters were claimed to be used only as a distraction, one proposed plan called for the use of helicopters for an air assault on the Branch Davidians' house. While the helicopters were not armed, at least some of the BATF agents on board the helicopters were armed with MP-5 machine pistols, contrary to assertions by some government officials.[246] Significant evidence suggests that the BATF agents in the helicopters strafed the roof of the building.

Dr. Bruce Perry examined the Branch Davidian children who left the compound in the weeks following the BATF raid. One child drew a picture of a house beneath a rainbow. Perry asked, "Is there anything else?" and the child then drew bullet holes in the roof.[247] *Newsweek* magazine reprinted the Davidian girl's picture of her home with a dotted roof. "Bullets" the girl explained.[248]

Catherine Matteson, a seventy-two-year-old Branch Davidian woman not accused of any crimes, was interviewed by the *Las Vegas Review-Journal.* She clearly recalled seeing helicopters firing through the roof and walls of the residence. She recalled, "I saw the yellow flashes." When machine guns fire, there is a yellow flash of muzzle blast, visible even in daylight.[249] During the negotiations, Koresh and Schneider insisted that there were at least five witnesses who saw three helicopters come over and start shooting into Koresh's room, destroying his television set.[250]

Attorney Jack Zimmermann, who went into the house during the siege, later testified that he saw many bullet holes in the ceilings with a downward trajectory, indicating that the helicopters had been firing into the compound from above.[251] There is no nearby high ground from which BATF agents not in helicopters could have shot bullets into the building with a steep downward trajectory.

The BATF stated the helicopters were simply used as a "diversionary device" during the raid, and no shots came from the helicopters.[252] BATF agent Davy Aguilera, however, testified to Congress that the agents in the helicopters were armed, and had been told that they were allowed to fire in self-defense. But Aguilera maintained that no shots were fired from the helicopters.

At least during wartime, there are sound tactical reasons for beginning an assault on a building by strafing the second-story roof. The bullets coming through the ceiling will force people on the second floor to retreat to the first floor. It will therefore be easier for assault personnel to enter the second story. In addition, riflemen defending the building against ground attack will be deprived of the advantage of an elevated firing platform. Also, strafing the second-floor gun storage room would prevent the Davidians retrieving their guns prior to the imminent arrival of BATF land forces.

But strafing a building is not a particularly effective way to rescue children who are thought to be in danger. The second story of the Mount Carmel Center was known to be the living quarters for the women and children, and for Koresh; other men were not allowed up there.[253]

Strafing the roof, if it happened, might well be considered grotesquely excessive use of force for serving a search warrant. The persons who did the strafing might be considered guilty of reckless endangerment or homicide. If the Davidians fired first at the helicopters, then return fire at particular targets would be lawful, but not random firing through a roof. Branch Davidian rifle shots did hit at least one of the helicopters, forcing it to make an emergency landing.[254]

Whether lawful or not, the federal government's machine-gunning a roof that covered dozens of women and children would probably have been ill-received by the press and public. If there were hundreds of bullet holes in the roof, there would have been a motive for the federal government to destroy the evidence by having the building burned down, as Steve Schneider noted in the course of the negotiations.[255]

If BATF forces on the ground were using the armor-piercing 9mm Cyclone ammunition (and some anonymous source report that the Cyclone was used[256]), the action was in willful disregard for the safety of noncombatants. BATF knew, or should have known, that the armor-piercing ammunition it was using could easily penetrate the thin walls of the compound at the Mount Carmel Center, endangering the children whom the BATF claimed to be protecting from abuse.[257]

BATF's perception was very different, that they were expressly armed mostly with 9mm machine pistols "for a purpose. We knew there was a lot of children in there. And we knew there were a lot of women and innocents in there. . . . And with all these innocents in there, our teams . . . took mostly 9-mm firearms that they knew would not penetrate those walls, they knew would not go through and hit innocent children. And, so, in essence the beating we took was because we were trying not to have firearms that would go through the walls."[258] Actually, 9mm rounds can penetrate thin walls like those at the Mount Carmel residence.

More fundamentally, BATF's claim that it went into the Mount Carmel Center underarmed is ludicrous. Ten agents were carrying AR-15 semiautomatic rifles. This rifle, whose rounds can certainly penetrate walls, has been described by the BATF itself as an extremely powerful "assault weapon" primarily useful for mass murder.[259]

The majority of agents, though, were armed with Heckler & Koch MP-5 machine pistols.[260] These guns are sold almost exclusively to the military and police. The advertising to civilian law enforcement conveys the message that by owning the gun, the civilian officer will be the equivalent of a member in an elite military strike force, such as the Navy Seals. The ad copy links civilian law enforcement to military combat, with lines like "From the Gulf War to the Drug War." As one criminologist notes, "The MP5 series is the pride and staple of police tactical operations units, and it holds a central place in the paramilitary police subculture. Its imposing, futuristic style overshadows its utility as a superior 'urban warfare' weapon."[261]

Functionally, the MP-5 is a perfectly fine gun. But when law enforcement agencies are procuring weapons, they need to consider not only the mechanical characteristics of the gun, but also how officers in the field will react to having the gun. When a gun's advertising and styling deliberately blur the line between warfare and law enforcement, it is not unreasonable to expect that some officers—especially when under stress—will start behaving as if they were in the military. That is precisely what happened when the BATF agents began firing indiscriminately into the building. No one will ever be certain whether more agents might have obeyed BATF training and the law—to fire only at visible targets who pose a threat—if the agents had been armed with other guns. But it is hardly likely that Heckler & Koch's militaristic marketing of the MP-5 helped promote responsible law enforcement behavior at Waco.

AFTERMATH

A few hours after the raid, a BATF spokesperson insisted, "We had an excellent plan and we practiced it for months. Everything would have been fine, except their guns were bigger than our guns."[262] Whether the plan to serve a search warrant by firing automatic weapons, throwing concussion grenades and breaking into people's home without even announcing that a search warrant was being served is an "excellent plan," and whether it was a good idea to go ahead with an "excellent plan" after the element of surprise has clearly been lost, even when the "excellent plan" has no contingency for the loss of surprise, is not certain. One journalist labeled the BATF's blend of aggression and incompetence as "Keystone Kommando tactics."[263]

About a month later, BATF agents were quoted in the *New York Times* that BATF supervisors knew the element of surprise had been lost, and decided to go ahead anyway.[264] Yet BATF Director Stephen Higgins still insisted: "This was a plan that depended on the element of surprise. We would not have executed the plan if our supervisors felt like we had lost that element."[265]

During the assault, BATF had killed five of the Davidians' malamute dogs. Their dead bodies were lined up near the Davidian compound, apparently so the Davidians could see their former pets.[266]

Mike Schroeder (the drummer for Koresh's rock group) and two other Branch Davidians had been working at the Mag Bag on the morning of the BATF assault. (The Mag Bag, a garage rented by the Davidians, was located away from the Mount Carmel property.) After the firefight, Schroeder and the two others attempted to sneak past the BATF to get into the residence. The three ran into a BATF team; one Davidian was captured; another broke past and escaped for some days. Schroeder was fatally shot six times by a BATF agent with an MP-5 submachine gun.

BATF at first claimed that Schroeder had charged *out* of the residence with a gun, although the claim was eventually abandoned. It took several days before the body was removed and identified to the Branch Davidians in the residence.[267]

Texas Rangers were allowed to begin a limited crime-scene analysis of the shooting of Mike Schroeder. When they asked to make casts of footprints and gather other evidence, FBI commander Jamar refused; they were not allowed back on the crime scene for ten days, by which time rain had washed away much of the footprints.[268]

A helicopter photo of Schroeder's corpse, taken three days after his death, showed him wearing a blue stocking cap. Yet Schroeder's cap was never recovered, and no government witness at the trial acknowledged having seen it. Schroeder had died with two closely spaced bullet wounds to the head, and other disabling wounds. If Schroeder had been shot at close range (i.e., executed while he lay on the ground wounded), the cap would have absorbed most of the gunpowder traces.[269] It is illegal for a law enforcement officer to execute a wounded person, even a criminal, who is no longer a threat.

After the raid, the government procured a warrant to search the Mag Bag, the offsite garage rented by the Davidians. When the owner of the Mag Bag (Gary Welch, who was not a Branch Davidian) was informed, he offered them a key. But the Mag Bag was "searched" by a Bradley Fighting Vehicle smashing a hole in one wall, driving inside, and crushing two cars and a workbench. All the windows in the building were shattered. A destructive search tore apart what remained of the building's contents. One box of shotgun shells was discovered.[270]

The Davidians were not allowed to have doctors visit their sick and wounded.[271] Requests were repeatedly denied on the grounds of risk to the doctors, despite Davidian assurances they would no more shoot the doctors than would the FBI.[272] Had the Davidians been foreign troops invading the United States (rather than being American citizens or citizens of friendly nations such as England and Australia), they would have been entitled to medical care by international law.

NOTES

1. The initial reports indicated fifteen or sixteen injured. Janet Reno, testimony at U.S. House of Representatives, Events Surrounding the Branch Davidian Cult Standoff in Waco, Texas. Hearing before the Comm. on the Judiciary, U.S. House of Representatives, 103rd Cong., 1st sess., April 28, 1993 (hereinafter, "Hearing"), p. 13. The Treasury Report lists twenty gunshot or shrapnel wounds, six of which did not require hospital care, two "serious" non-gunshot-related injuries, one of which required some hospital care, and six minor non-gunshot-related injuries, including chipped teeth and heel irritation from "ATF boots." U.S. Department of the Treasury, *Report on the Bureau of Alcohol, Tobacco and Firearms, Investigation of Vernon Wayne Howell also known as David Koresh* (Washington, D.C.: Government Printing Office, September 1993) (hereinafter "Treasury Report"), pp. 102–103.

Speaking of boots, Democratic Representative John Dingell has referred to BATF agents as "jackbooted American fascists," and NRA Executive Vice President Wayne LaPierre used a similar phrase in a controversial 1995 fundraising letter. The *Washington Post* promptly came to BATF's defense, noting that the BATF "uniform does *not* include jackboots—above-the-knee footwear worn by 17th- and 18th-century cavalry officers, as well as fisherman and fascists." William F. Powers, "Dressed to Kill?" *Washington Post*, May 4, 1995, p. D8 (emphasis in original). See also BATF Agent Bill Buford, Joint Hearings, part 1, p. 456. But technically speaking, Dingell and LaPierre may have been correct. According to *Webster's New Collegiate Dictionary*, the first definition of "jackboot" is the over-the-knee cavalry boot. But the second, permissible, meaning is "a laceless military boot reaching to the calf." *Webster's New Collegiate Dictionary* (Springfield, Mass.: G. and C. Merriam Co., 1980), p. 612. Moreover, even if the BATF agents were barefoot, rogue agents could still be described as "jackbooted." The first definition of "jackbooted" is "wearing jackboots," but the second definition is "ruthlessly and violently oppressive." Ibid.

2. ATF Order 3240.1A (1981), p. 4.

3. If Koresh had been arrested away from Mount Carmel Center, the government would have been able to hold him for at least three days, just by asserting to a court that he might be a danger to the community. 18 U.S.C. §3142(f); Tim Evans, an attorney for the Branch Davidians, responding to questions from Rep. Bob Barr on the Bail Reform Act, United States House of Representatives, Subcommittee on Crime of the Committee on the Judiciary and the Subcommittee on National Security, International Affairs, and Criminal Justice of the Committee on Government Reform and Oversight, *Joint Hearings on Activities of Federal Law Enforcement Agencies Toward the Branch Davidians*, 104th Cong., 1st sess., July 19–August 1, 1995 (Washington, D.C.: Government Printing Office, 1996) (hereinafter "Joint Hearings"), part 1, p. 587.

4. Daniel Hartnett, BATF, letter to Rep. Jon Kyl, May 1993. According to Higgins' testimony, Koresh told undercover agent Rodriguez that he rarely left the Mount Carmel Center because he was keeping a low profile, since he was disliked, and that he had been keeping a low profile for two years. Hearing, p. 160. BATF Director Stephen Higgins's June 17, 1993, letter to Rep. Jack Brooks indicated that there was twenty-four-hour surveillance from January 11 until mid-February and that Koresh was never seen to leave the compound. Hearing, pp. 193–94. Higgins's statement is plainly false; Higgins was either lying, or passing on a lie that someone had told him. Surveillance actually lasted just over one week. United States House of Representatives, Committee on Government Reform and Oversight in conjunction with the Committee on the Judiciary, *Investigation into the Activities of Federal Law Enforcement Agencies Toward the Branch Davidians*, Report 104–179, 104th Cong., 1st sess. (Washington, D.C.: Government Printing Office, August 2, 1996) (hereinafter "Committee Report"), pp. 11–12.

The lying continued for some time. Treasury Undersecretary Ron Noble told "60 Minutes" in May 1995 that "Koresh was away from the compound . . . what you've heard over and over again is false. It's absolutely false." Joint Hearings, part 2, p. 12.

5. U.S. Department of the Treasury, Report on the Bureau of Alcohol, Tobacco, and Firearms, Investigation of Vernon Wayne Howell also known as David Koresh (Washington, D.C.: Government Printing Office, September 1993) (hereinafter "Treasury Report"), pp. 43, 51.

6. Trial Transcript, *United States* v. *Brad Branch*, Crim. No. W-93-CR-046 (W.D.Tex., 1994) (hereinafter "Trial Transcript"), p. 6718 (testimony of auto shop employee). James L. Pate, "Gun Gestapo's Day of Infamy," *Soldier of Fortune* (June 1993): 63.

7. Committee Report, p. 15.

8. Pate, "Day of Infamy," p. 63.

9. Dick Reavis, *The Ashes of Waco: An Investigation* (New York: Simon and Schuster, 1995), p. 180.

10. Daniel Wattenberg, "Gunning for Koresh," *American Spectator* (August 1993): 38; Treasury Report, Appendix D-10.

11. Robert W. Lee, "Truth and Cover-up: Sorting out the Waco Tragedy," *The New American*, June 14, 1993, p. 24 (hereinafter, "Lee, *Truth*"). Koresh's lawyer, Dick DeGuerin, states that Koresh also could have been arrested at a Waco automobile store, a Toys Я Us store, a Dairy Queen, a Western Steer restaurant, and a Dallas rock club, the last of which he appeared at two weeks before the raid. Maas, "None of This Had to Happen," p. 6. According to Director Higgins's letter to Representative Brooks, the jogger identified by some as Koresh was probably one of BATF's undercover agents. Hearing, p. 193.

12. David Thibodeau, Joint Hearings, part 1, p. 123.

13. Koresh and his associates added that he could have been arrested when he went to Dallas, or as part of the child abuse investigation, while jogging, or at Wal-Mart: "It's plainly known by . . . all the people around here that I'm always available on the premises or off the premises. . . ." Transcripts of BATF Tapes of the Negotiations between Federal Law Enforcement and the Branch Davidians, February 28–April 19, 1993 (hereinafter "Negot. Tapes"), no. 60, March 5; no. 51, March 5; no. 59, March 5; no. 65, March 6; no. 89, March 7; no. 96, March 9. Koresh even noted that agent Rodriguez knew that he jogged regularly and could have been arrested then. Negot. Tape no. 26, March 3. The negotiators' answers were that there was not yet a warrant, that Rodriguez's job was to leave the compound rather than to arrest Koresh, that the residence had to be searched anyway. The negotiators also made one brief claim, which Steve Schneider found unbelievable (and which was in fact false), that there was no arrest warrant, just a search warrant for the property.

14. Henry Stanley McMahon, Jr., and Karen J. Kilpatrick, *In re: Interviews of Henry Stanley McMahon, Jr. and Karen J. Kilpatrick*, deposition taken May 25, 1993, p. 171.

15. Reavis, *The Ashes of Waco*, p. 180.

16. Stephen Labaton and Sam Howe Verhovek, "U.S. Agents Say Fatal Flaws Doomed Raid on Waco Cult," *New York Times*, March 28, 1993, p. 20.

17. The tactical commander, Chuck Sarabyn, had decided to redirect activities toward infiltration of the residence. Committee Report, pp. 11–12.

18. Treasury Report, Appendix D-11–12.

19. Joint Hearings, part 1, p. 800. The leaders of the raid were unaware of any recommendations from social worker Joyce Sparks on the importance of arresting Koresh away from his flock; both Chojnacki and Sarabyn denied ever talking with Ms. Sparks, and said that most of her conversations were with Davy Aguilera. Questioning by Representative McCollum, Joint Hearings, part 1, pp. 800–801.

When the issue came up during the siege, Steve Schneider was told, "You can't arrest him outside and then expect to execute the search warrant there [at the residence]." Schneider's response: "That doesn't make sense. Of course you could." Negot. Tape no. 65, March 6.

20. Koresh's attorney, Dick DeGuerin, Joint Hearings, part 2, p. 35. The FBI would reportedly not have been so quick to limit the means of arresting Koresh to siege or dynamic entry. The FBI leader at Waco said, "the most disturbing thing to me, [arresting] someone with 100 automatic weapons, . . . you would do everything in your power to avoid a confrontation." He went on to say he did not know the best way, and was not necessarily saying Koresh should have been arrested away from the Mount Carmel Center, but that all options should be considered. He declined to criticize BATF, responding to a question from Rep. Bill Zeliff as to whether he would have continued once cover was blown, "It's hard to discuss that, but I wouldn't even think about being near a place with 100 automatic weapons." Jeffrey Jamar, Joint Hearings, part 3, p. 300.

21. Committee Report, pp. 13, 15, 17. The decision by BATF to limit considerations to the alternatives of dynamic entry and siege was not unanimous. BATF Agent James Cavanaugh—who would eventually become the first serious negotiator reaching some rapport with Koresh, until the FBI completely took over negotiations—had recommended using a ruse to arrest Koresh and his lieutenants away from the compound. He was later surprised to learn that the plan developed included no provision for a negotiator. Joint Hearings, part 2, p. 338. This is similar to the initial FBI plan for arresting Randy Weaver and Kevin Harris, which included no plan for a negotiated surrender.

22. The Treasury review merely found it unclear whether BATF's decision to assault rather than lay siege was well founded. Treasury Report, p. 134.

23. Treasury Report, p. 38. Mr. Johnston has denied under oath that he insisted on a dynamic entry.

24. The memorandum was written by Army Lt. Col. Philip Lindley. In the 1995 congressional hearings, the military made it clear that the casualties were expected to come from gunshot wounds, and the victims might include small children. Testimony of Col. Lindley, Maj. Mark Petree, and Sgt. Steve Fitts, Joint Hearings, part 1, pp. 390–91; Committee Report, p. 40.

25. 18 U.S. Code § 2234.

26. The school bus was the basis for one of the plans for arresting Koresh away from the rest of the Branch Davidians: "Staging a car wreck with a school bus, stating that some of the children were injured, hoping that he might come out. Not staging it, but at least stating that that had happened." William Buford, Joint Hearings, part 1, p. 484.

27. Stuart Wright, Joint Hearings, part 1, p. 81.

28. Joint Hearings, part 1, p. 900. Although not part of his formal list of improvements for BATF, Noble did indicate that, in the future, he would consult with "cult" experts where "cults" were involved as suspects. Part 1, pp. 858–60, 922.

29. Stuart Wright, Joint Hearings, part 1, pp. 82, 84.

30. To the extent BATF took religion into account, if their statements after the fact are credible, their misunderstanding was curious. One reason BATF agent William Buford opposed using a siege approach against the Branch Davidians was because of his experience with a siege against the Covenant, the Sword, and the Arm of the Lord (CSA) in Arkansas in 1985. That group, too, relied extensively on the Book of Revelation; a siege was used; it took three days, and ended successfully without a shot being fired. At Waco, he was convinced a siege operation would end in mass suicide, and that dynamic entry was the proper procedure. William Buford, Joint Hearings, part 1, pp. 424–25, 452–53. AUSA William Johnston reportedly opposed a siege-type operation, based upon the CSA experience, because the delay gave the suspects time to destroy evidence and make prosecution more difficult. Treasury Report, p. 38.

31. Phillip Chojnacki, Joint Hearings, part 1, p. 448. A federal arrest—unlike a local child abuse charge—could have resulted in Koresh's prompt removal to a federal detention facility anywhere in the United States, if necessary.

32. The quotation above partially follows the transcript of the hearings, rather than the published report of the hearings, because the published report erroneously alters Sparks's statement about the relationship between Koresh and Jesus. Koresh thought that Jesus was the gentle messiah, and Koresh the punitive, "military" one. The published report conflates the two, making Koresh, illogically, into both the gentle and the military messiah. Joint Hearings, part 1, pp. 576–78.

Representative Hyde: "This [BATF raid] was a fulfillment of the scriptures, but they had to fight back, and nobody understood that did they?" Sparks: ". . . they were looking forward to that." Hyde: "you are talking about the Davidians?" Sparks: "Yes." Part 1, p. 592

Representative Schumer found the whole issue offensive. He objected to the suggestion that "we have to understand these religious cults and these religious types of attitude to better deal with it. . . . [Representative Hyde] wasn't saying it justified their actions, but it was getting close. And I . . . remember my frustration when those on the left would do the same with people who were wanton murderers, saying, let's understand the horrible childhood they had." Joint Hearings, part 3, p. 471. In fact, of course, there was no suggestion by anyone that David Koresh's or the Branch Davidians' religious beliefs exempted them from enforcement of the laws, or justified breaking any laws, even "victimless crimes." The only criticism was of failing to take into account how religious beliefs would affect different sorts of efforts to arrest suspects.

33. Rep. Ed Bryant asked if the people left after the possible arrest of Koresh "were less likely to resist?" The response of Sparks was: "That is right, because they had to all be together for the prophecy to be fulfilled." Joint Hearings, part 1, pp. 595–96.

34. Steve Schneider's attorney would later testify that based on his getting to know the person called Koresh's "first lieutenant": "I can tell you without any reservation that Steve Schneider would not have organized any kind of violent resistance to a search warrant." Joint Hearings, part 2, p. 48. Schneider told the FBI negotiators that, although he was a strong supporter of the Second Amendment, he personally hated guns, had no gun in the initial shootout, heading straight for the telephone instead. The negotiators assured him that at his trial, he could probably count on sheriff's deputy Larry Lynch and chief day-to-day negotiator Byron Sage to testify as to Schneider's nonviolent activities on February 28. Negot. Tapes no. 108, March 10; no. 122, March 13.

35. Joint Hearings, part 1, pp. 596, 612. As Representative McCollum summarized her views, "if you captured Koresh outside the compound, it would have cut the head off, so to speak . . . under their religious tenets . . . they would never have killed themselves because they all had to die together." Joint Hearings, part 1, p. 800. Undercover BATF Agent Rodriguez disagreed, insisting that they would have had to arrest not just Koresh but his lieutenant Steve Schneider as well as Davidian aide and attorney Wayne Martin. Otherwise, they would have insisted in "negotiations that they wanted to talk to Koresh and wanted a sign from Koresh as to what to do. Therefore, in my own opinion, taking Koresh down would not have solved the problem." Joint Hearings, part 1, pp. 761–62, 775–76. Sparks would appear to have made a more thorough study of Koresh, with the conclusion that Davidian deaths had to occur with Koresh, not on his orders from a jail cell, where he was in custody and liable for anything his followers did—something attorney Martin would have advised him of.

Rodriguez would also insist that Koresh could not have changed his teachings in the middle of the siege and that, therefore, the deaths of all were largely inevitable. On the other hand, Rodriguez's expertise on religion and the Branch Davidians had limits. Despite the fact that several Davidians had jobs away from Mount Carmel, attended gun shows with Koresh, and went into town to shop and to see doctors, he testified "They didn't mingle with the public . . . they didn't go anywhere. These people were waiting for the time" when they would all die to fulfill Koresh's prophecies. Joint Hearings, part 1, p. 776. Interestingly, the subcommittee's minority viewpoint was that Koresh's views were quite malleable. Dissenting Views, Committee Report, p. 106.

36. Response to question by Rep. Steve Chabot, Joint Hearings, part 1, p. 611.

37. Philip Arnold, Joint Hearings, part 2, p. 152.

38. Ibid., pp. 144–45.

39. Joint Hearings, part 2, p. 145.

40. Vance McLaughlin, "Operation Trojan Horse: The Effects of Access to Information," paper delivered at the annual meeting of the Academy of Criminal Justice Sciences, Boston, March 1995, p. 5. Wade Ishimoto, Sandia National Laboratories, Joint Hearings, part 1, p. 314: "[W]earing certain kinds of helmets and tactical vests, in black uniforms, . . . intimidates a lot of people and causes them to use less lethal force in opposition to those making the raid."

41. Reavis, *The Ashes of Waco,* p. 183.

42. Phillip Chojnacki, Joint Hearings, part 1, p. 448.

43. Davy Aguilera, Application and Affidavit for Search and Arrest Warrants for Vernon Wayne Howell and the Residence of Vernon Wayne Howell, and others. Waco, Texas, February 25, 1993 (hereinafter "Aguilera"), p. 3.

44. Asserting that God calls America Babylon, Koresh said later to FBI negotiators that "Babylon the great is fallen . . . and has become the habitation of devils." Negot. Tape no. 71, March 6. He occasionally noted that he had been preparing for BATF's attack longer than BATF had, it being a regular part of his preaching for years. Negot. Tape no. 26, March 3.

45. See generally, 18 U.S.C. § 1385; S. Wisotsky, "Crackdown: The Emerging "Drug Exception" to the Bill of Rights," 38 *Hastings Law Journal* 889 (1987); Note, "Locked and Loaded: Taking Aim at the Growing Use of the American Military in Civilian Law Enforcement Operations," 26 *Loyola of Los Angeles Law Review* 1291 (1993).

46. 18 U.S.C. § 1385, as amended.

47. "[O]ur Founding Fathers intended this separation of the civilians and the military. They did

not want the military dominant, as it was in Europe and so the separation, the civilian control of the military became one of our tenets in the United States. And the Posse Comitatus Act is really a logical follow on to that." Brig. Gen. Michael Huffman, Joint Hearings, part 1, p. 366.

48. *Wrynn v. United States*, 200 F. Supp. 457, 465 (E.D.N.Y. 1961).

49. *The Federalist*, No. 29 (Alexander Hamilton).

50. 408 U.S. 1, 15-16 (1972). The case grew out of the U.S. Army's program of spying on anti-Vietnam political activists in the United States. A five-to-four majority of the Court refused to allow lower federal courts to hear the plaintiffs' complaints that the surveillance program violated their First Amendment rights. The Court majority held that use of the military within the United States against American citizens was "nonjusticiable" and within the sole discretion of the Executive branch. As the four dissenters explained, the majority holding is an abdication of judicial responsibility to enforce the Constitution; the decision should be reversed.

51. 776 F.2d 1384, 1385 (8th Cir. 1985), *adhered to on rehearing*, 788 F.2d 494 (1987), *aff'd Haig v. Bissonette*, 485 U.S. 264 (1988).

52. Jerry M. Cooper, "Federal Military Intervention in Domestic Disorders," in Richard H. Kohn, ed., *The United States Military under the Constitution of the United States, 1789–1989* (New York: New York University Press, 1991), p. 135.

53. Ibid., pp. 136–37.

54. Ibid., p. 137.

55. *Youngstown Sheet & Tube Co. v. Sawyer*, 343 U.S. 579 (1952).

56. Cooper, "Federal Military Intervention," p. 141.

57. Hearing, p. 25.

58. Ibid., p. 40.

59. Ibid., p. 65.

60. 10 U.S.C. § 375.

61. 10 U.S.C. § 373.

62. In the course of the siege, an FBI negotiator denied to Davidian Steve Schneider that the military was involved, but acknowledged that the military had trained FBI agents to drive tanks. Schneider indicated that he thought that was an erosion of the Constitution. Negot. Tape no. 103, March 10.

63. 10 U.S.C. § 372.

64. 10 U.S.C. § 377.

65. 10 U.S.C. § 374.

66. It is not entirely clear that BATF has the authority to request military assistance under the drug-law exception to the Posse Comitatus Act. The exception requires a "request from the head of a Federal law enforcement agency," defined as "an agency with jurisdiction to enforce" a variety of federal laws, none of which falls within the generally recognized jurisdiction of BATF. 10 U.S.C. § 374(b)(1) and (b)(4)(A). The House joint committees investigating Waco, though, believed that BATF is authorized as a DLEA ("drug law enforcement agency") by virtue of its investigations of "narcotics traffickers who use firearms and explosives as tools of their trade, especially violent gangs." Committee Report, p. 35 n. 177.

67. Maj. Gen. John M. Pickler, Joint Hearings, part 1, p. 400. "If it were not for some kind of drug connection, we would not have been participants. . . ." Rep. Bill McCollum: "But this particular unit was not, under the rules of the Army or DOD [Department of Defense], permitted to give training to anybody that didn't have a drug support connection like this, is that right? . . . If it had not been for the drug support, your particular unit would not have been permitted to train them?" Gen. Pickler: "That is correct, sir." All witnesses representing the Defense Department emphasized in testimony that no active-duty military personnel were present or participants in the BATF raid on February 28, 1993. Asst. Defense Secretary H. Allen Holmes, Generals John M. Pickler and Walter B. Huffman, Lt. Col. Philip Lindley, Maj. Mark Petree, Sgt. Steve Fitts, Sgt. Robert W. Moreland, and Chris Grain, U.S. Army Special Operations Command (Fort Bragg, N.C.), Joint Hearings, part 1, pp. 345–410.

68. Committee Report, pp. 41–42.

69. FRAGO "E" OpOrder, dated February 14, 1993; and largely blacked-out undated Memorandum for Record by Lt. Col. Douglas C. Andrews, Deputy Staff Judge Advocate. At the raid itself,

in addition to BATF personnel, there were representatives from the Immigration and Naturalization Service, and one agent from the Drug Enforcement Administration. Hearing, p. 164.

70. Maj. Gen. John M. Pickler testified that the request for military assistance came from both the Houston office and the Washington headquarters of BATF. Joint Hearings, part 1, p. 360.

71. The briefing of the Texas National Guard was to William R. Enney, Interagency Coordinator, Counterdrug Support. Hearing, p.164.

72. Army Staff Sgt. Steve Fitts, Joint Hearings, part 1, pp. 372, 395–96. Rep. John Shadegg (R-Ariz.): "Did the ATF ever, to your knowledge, express any concern about the dangers that were presented by a methamphetamine lab?"

Sgt. Fitts: "Not to my knowledge, no, sir."

Representative Shadegg: ". . . and the dangers that were exposed as a result of the lab being there?"

Sgt. Fitts: "No, sir. Nothing in the contact would indicate that."

Rep. Ed Bryant (R-Tenn.): "I understand you were assigned to draft a plan under the contingency that . . . there was a methamphetamine lab in there and what should occur in case there was an accident."

Sgt. Fitts: "My planning for the ATF did not include a methamphetamine lab."

Representative Bryant: ". . . there is a higher risk of danger, is there not, to . . . using a dynamic entry into a facility that has a methamphetamine laboratory in it?"

Sgt. Fritts: "Yes, sir."

Representative Bryant: "And that the risks . . . if there were a bullet shot into it . . . cause of it to explode, it could be a danger especially to children, to older people, to people around it?"

Sgt. Fitts: "I think there would be a danger to all people, regardless of age."

Similar testimony was provided by John Coonce of the Drug Enforcement Administration. Joint Hearings, part 1, pp. 311–12. BATF's response was that "we had a DEA lab team supervisor on board in the command post. His lab team was standing by for a call in case we did find . . . a lab, so that they could take over that very sensitive area of making that area safe, while we began our search of the premises." Phillip Chojnacki, the supervisor of the assault on Mount Carmel Center, Joint Hearings, part 1, p. 447. Such an invitation to the DEA would have followed the arrest expected to involve a shootout.

73. Committee Report, pp. 43–45, 48.

74. Ibid., p. 47.

75. Even if the drug allegations had been sincere, they would have provided no justification for conducting a "no–knock" raid to prevent the destruction of evidence. It is rather difficult to flush a methamphetamine lab down the toilet, and the Branch Davidians did not have flush toilets. David G. Bromley and Edward D. Silver, "The Davidian Tradition: From Patronal Clan to Prophetic Movement," in Wright, *Armageddon in Waco,* p. 55.

76. Richard L. Garner, Chief, Special Operations Division, BATF, letter to Headquarters, Department of the Army, February 28, 1993.

77. James L. Pate, "Waco's Defective Warrants: No Probable Cause For Raid on Ranch Apocalypse," *Soldier of Fortune* (August 1993): 48.

78. March 1, 1993, approval of Request for Helicopter Support to the FBI and Bradley Support to the Bureau of Alcohol, Tobacco, and Firearms (BATF), by Lt. Col Paul G. Marksteiner; Memorandum for the Record, March 25, 1993, from Major Alexander S. Wells, for the Acting Assistant Secretary of the Army Michael W. Owen.

79. From the mass of documents the Treasury Department eventually provided to the subcommittees investigating Waco, Rep. John Shadegg read into the record from an unsourced document with a stamp marked "00010228": "The use of the National Guard was a scam. . . . This was a scam initiated by Bureau [BATF] headquarters . . . in my opinion, to obtain the additional resources of the National Guard, air support assistance, etc." Joint Hearings, part 1, p. 379.

80. Most of the military assistance—including training, equipment, and expert advice—can be provided as long as there is reimbursement. But "the military is not to be involved in arrest, search or seizure or similar activities such as stop and frisk." Gen. Walter Huffman, Joint Hearings, part 1, p. 352. And there are certain units in the military, including JTF-6, which are geared toward drug-law enforcement and which would not get involved in assisting general law enforcement even with reimbursement. Gen. Pickler, Joint Hearings, part 1, p. 400.

81. James L. Pate, "No Peace without Justice," *Soldier of Fortune* (May 1995): 81.

82. Aguilera, p. 7. The affidavit does not indicate how serious the drug possession charges were, but the second conviction resulted in parole after three months.

83. Reavis, *The Ashes of Waco,* pp. 125–28. Branch Davidian David Thibodeau stated: "There was absolutely no drugs at Mount Carmel, period, other than alcohol." Joint Hearings, part 1, p. 125.

84. Treasury Report, pp. 16, 212.

85. Treasury Report, p. 212. Social worker Joyce Sparks, no avid fan of Koresh's, was in a position to reassure investigators regarding drugs: "David Koresh explained to me that the previous prophet had been involved in drugs, had a lab there, and [Koresh] said he had given that material, the needles and the drugs book explaining how to make drugs, he'd given that all to the sheriff's department in McLennan County." Joint Hearings, part 1, p. 611, responding to a question by Rep. Steve Chabot. Committee Report, p. 46.

86. Committee Report, p. 46.

87. Treasury Report, pp. 211–14.

88. Lee Hancock, "ATF Official Defends Raid Planning," *Dallas Morning News*, March 27, 1993.

89. James L. Pate, "Special Forces Involved in Waco Raid!" *Soldier of Fortune* (May 1994): 35–36; James L. Pate, "No Peace Without Justice," *Soldier of Fortune* (May 1995): 58–61. For the government's version of the training, see Treasury Report, pp. 73, 78, and Appendix B–56.

90. The Texas Army National Guard helicopters were two OH-58 Kiowas and a UH-60A Blackhawk. James L. Pate, "ATF's Bloody Sunday," *Soldier of Fortune* (June 1993): 52.

91. The National Guard is a complex entity which most of the time is under state control, and in that capacity would be known as the "Alabama National Guard." The president has the option of calling the National Guard into federal service, at which point the entity becomes known as the "National Guard of the United States." Most National Guard troops are dually enlisted in the state and federal guards, and take separate oaths of loyalty to each. (A few high-ranking officers may serve only in a state guard, and are not subject to induction into federal service.) The Alabama National Guard, not in federal service, was covered by the Texas law requiring the Texas governor's permission to enter Texas.

92. "No States shall, without the Consent of Congress . . . enter into any Agreement or Compact with Another State . . ." U.S. Constitution, art. I, § 10, cl. 3; Committee Report, pp. 34-35. The general rule of interpretation for this clause of the Constitution, as stated in *Virginia* v. *Tennessee*, 148 U.S. 503 (1893), and *United States Steel Corp.* v. *Multistate Tax Commission*, 434 U.S. 452 (1978), is that congressional consent is required for agreements which increase the political power of the states to the possible detriment of federal powers. Since the Alabama governor has no legal authority to command the Alabama National Guard beyond the boundaries of Alabama (Ala. Code § 31-2-7), and since the governor of Texas was not even aware of the Alabama Guard's presence in her state, the Alabama Guard was under the practical command of neither governor, and was thus, in essence, a rogue military force, answerable only to itself. The existence of such a force poses an obvious danger to federal supremacy, and hence would likely be unconstitutional under the principles of *Virginia* and *United States Steel.*

93. Wade Ishimoto, Joint Hearings, part 1, pp. 308–309.

94. Pate, "Day of Infamy," p. 50.

95. Gerald Goldstein, Joint Hearings, part 1, p. 165.

96. Aguilera, Attachment D.

97. 18 U.S.C. § 3109.

98. Ibid.

99. McMahon and Kilpatrick, *In Re,* pp. 75–76; Henry McMahon, Joint Hearings, part 1, p. 163; James L. Pate, "Waco: Behind the Cover-Up," *Soldier of Fortune* (November 1993): 37; Lee, "Truth," p. 24. At the Davidians' trial in February 1994, the court accepted into evidence a stipulation from the prosecution that if McMahon had been allowed to testify, he would have testified that the government refused an opportunity to speak with Koresh on the telephone on July 30, 1992. "Defense Rests Without Calling Cultists," *New York Times*, February 18, 1994.

100. Treasury Report, pp. 26, 180. As with much of the BATF operation, the McMahon inspection was poorly done. Compliance inspections are ordinarily preceded by telephone calls; this one was not. Aguilera was sloppily dressed, had no identification, and, although introduced as an inspector

trainee, not a special agent, made the decision not to visit Koresh's house. McMahon and his partner did not believe it to be a normal compliance inspection.

101. The September 1993 Treasury Report asserts that the igniter cord Koresh had was an "explosive" regulated by federal law, and legally requiring proper storage. Treasury Report, p. 124. If so, the BATF would have had every reason to visit Koresh's house, to see if the storage was in compliance with federal requirements.

The Treasury Report claimed that the gunpowder and igniter cord "were themselves explosives requiring proper registration and storage—neither of which Koresh provided." How Koresh could provide the registration or demonstrate the proper storage without being asked is unclear. In any case, the small amount of gun powder is expressly exempt from the law, and no registration is required for igniter cord. 18 U.S.C. § 841 et seq.; 26 U.S.C. § 5845(f). Apparently Treasury's comprehension of the laws it enforces is incomplete.

102. Treasury Report, pp. 26, 186.

103. The closest that report comes to anything of the sort is praise of Aguilera for attempting "to keep his investigation a secret from Koresh and his followers in order to ensure strategic and tactical flexibility in case search or arrest warrants needed to be served." Treasury Report, p. 123. Since Koresh had offered the invitation, the existence of BATF interest in his guns was likely no longer a secret to him.

104. Joint Hearings, part 1, p. 469. A Title I firearm is one regulated under Title I of the Gun Control Act of 1968, as opposed to Title II weapons, which are those regulated by the National Firearms Act, and include machineguns, short-barreled rifles and shotguns, and destructive devices.

105. Robert Sanders, former BATF Deputy Director for Enforcement, and Wade Ishimoto of Sandia National Laboratories testified that they would have accepted such an invitation as Koresh offered to Aguilera. Ishimoto was one of the law enforcement experts who reviewed the Treasury Report. He indicated he did not know when reviewing the report that BATF had been invited by Koresh to visit, and that such knowledge might have made a difference in his review of the report. Joint Hearings, part 1, p. 332. Two Texas Rangers also testified that they would have accepted the invitation, if only to gather intelligence. Captains Maurice Cook and David Byrnes, Joint Hearings, part 2, p. 182. By visiting Mount Carmel, Aguilera could have learned what Koresh looked like, so he could later point him out to the surveillance team, which reportedly lacked that piece of information. Committee Report, p. 11.

106. Charles Sarabyn, Joint Hearings, part 1, p. 417.

107. William Buford, BATF Resident-Agent-in-Charge, Little Rock, Joint Hearings, part 1, p. 424.

108. Roden's challenge evoked another miracle contest between competing religions that had taken place at Mount Carmel centuries before. See chapter 6.

109. Negot. Tape nos. 36 and 37, March 4.

110. Breault and King, *Inside the Cult* (New York: Signet, 1993), pp. 95–100. The jury voted nine to acquit Koresh, and three to convict. Breault and King, p. 103. All other defendants were acquitted. Aguilera's investigation of Koresh's criminal background concluded that he was "found not guilty by a jury trial." Joint Hearings, part 1, p. 990. The Davidians were offended that the news media would use the Roden shootout as evidence of how dangerous they were, since everyone but Koresh was acquitted on all charges, and Koresh was not reprosecuted. Negot. Tape no. 9, March 1.

111. Roy Bragg, "Ex-Prosecutor Laments Agents' 'Storm Trooper' Tactics," *Houston Chronicle*, March 2, 1993.

112. Hearing, p. 143.

113. Treasury Report, p. 135. In the March 1993 request for an additional search warrant, BATF cited Koresh's 1987 arrest as evidence BATF agents "were keenly aware of the dangerous nature of the search warrant to be executed. Several years ago, Howell and others, many of whom are still with the group, were involved in a fierce gun battle at the area of the compound with a former or rival cult member." Earl Dunagan, Application and Affidavit for Search Warrant for the Residence of Vernon Wayne Howell, and others, Waco, Texas, March 9, 1993, p. 2. According to Koresh, most of the fierce gun battle involved shooting into the ground, so that one minor wound was the extent of the injuries. Negot. Tapes no. 36 and 37, March 4.

114. Adam Nossiter, "Warning of Violence Was Unheeded After Cult Leader's Gun Battle in '87," *New York Times*, March 10, 1993.

115. Lee, "Truth," p. 23.

116. Treasury Report, Appendices D-3 and D-4.

117. Aguilera, pp. 7–9.

118. Discussion between Chuck Sarabyn and Rep. Steve Schiff, Joint Hearings, part 1, p. 417. Initially, of course, the BATF investigation dealt with particular firearms listed as being in McMahon's inventory but said to be in Koresh's possession. Those guns, at any rate, would presumably have had to be shown to the authorities for Koresh to able to pretend he was cooperating. And, while Sparks was not shown all of the residence, she was shown the children whose condition she was investigating.

119. Wattenberg, "Gunning for Koresh," p. 32. BATF would reinterpret that episode, suggesting a tie between the child refusing to touch a gun and her being "allowed to leave" the ranch. Dunagan, Howell Affidavit, p. 3.

120. Aguilera, p. 4.

121. Wattenberg, "Gunning for Koresh," p. 32.

122. McMahon and Kilpatrick, In Re, pp. 58–59; James L. Pate, "Waco's Defective Warrants: No Probable Cause For Raid on Ranch Apocalypse," Soldier of Fortune (August 1993): 47. Koresh said he had told undercover agent Rodriguez about the Hellfire-like device and about clearing it with the sheriff. Negot. Tape no. 59, March 5. Koresh was probably thinking of that gadget when he recounted going to the sheriff if he even heard through the grapevine that there was a question of the legality of something they were doing at Mount Carmel. Negot. Tape no. 51, March 5.

123. Scott Pendleton, "Waco Siege Prompts Scrutiny of Agency," Christian Science Monitor, March 8, 1993, p. 8; Michael deCourcy Hinds, "A Believer, Stranded in Battle, Says Sect Has Peaceful Goals," New York Times, March 6, 1993, p. 8.

124. Andrew Blum, "Waco Tragedy Spawns Litigation," National Law Journal, May 17, 1993, p. 31.

125. Wattenberg, "Gunning for Koresh," p. 32.

126. McLennan County Sheriff Jack Harwell, "Frontline" interview, August 3, 1995, available at http://www.wgbh.org.

127. Negot. Tapes no. 47, March 4; no. 76, March 7.

128. E.g., Negot. Tapes no. 64, March 6; no. 242, April 18.

129. One piece of evidence that Koresh might resist a search warrant was not cited in the warrant application. Marc Breault, Koresh's disaffected former chief aide, who had devoted himself to destroying the Koresh sect, recalled a conversation that Breault had with BATF on January 8, 1993. According to Breault, ATF asked, "If Vernon received a summons to answer questions regarding firearms, would he show up?" Breault replied "No way." BATF then asked "If the good guys came in with a search warrant, would Vernon allow it?" Breault answered: "If Vernon were not expecting it, no. If Vernon had prior warning, yes. He'd have time to shift all the firearms." Breault and King, Inside the Cult, pp. 306–307. Perhaps one reason that Breault's forecast was not contained in the warrant affidavit was that Koresh knew he was under surveillance, and BATF knew that Koresh knew, so Koresh already had plenty of time to conceal any illegal guns and consent to a search. In addition, Breault had an unreliable track record as a predictor of Davidian violence. In February 1992, Breault had told the U.S. Embassy in Australia that "there would be a shootout with authorities if they attempt to enter the cult's Waco property to take away any of the children living there, or investigate living conditions." Gustav Nieguhr and Pierre Thomas, "Abuse Allegations Unproven: Koresh was Investigated in Texas, California," Washington Post, April 25, 1993, p. A20. Contrary to Breault's forecast, a few weeks later Koresh complied fully and peacefully with a social worker's entry into the compound to investigate living conditions and with a court order to remove one of the children.

130. Earl Dunagan and Davy Aguilera. Application and Affidavit for Search of Residence of Vernon Wayne Howell, and others. Waco, Texas, April 4, 1993, p. 17. Ex-Davidian Robyn Bunds complained that Koresh made the group watch Vietnam war movies such as Hamburger Hill, Platoon, and Full Metal Jacket, referring to these movies as "training films." Wattenberg, "Gunning for Koresh," p. 36.

Fondness for violent movies was not unique to Koresh. "Today, large framed posters from the 1987 movie The Untouchables hang in many ATF offices." Erik Larson, "ATF Under Siege," Time (July 24, 1995): 23. The Untouchables glorifies lawless conduct by Elliot Ness and other Prohibition agents, who enforced the laws by engaging in machine gun battles with Al Capone's bootleggers.

131. It is unclear who invented the notion of a hatred of law enforcement. Koresh may have preached a fiery end when forces of the government attacked, but he expressed no hatred throughout the negotiations with the FBI. He indicated that, if he were not a preacher, he might have been a law enforcement officer. He expressed no hostility toward law enforcement in general. He praised the Texas Rangers and particularly local law enforcement. Regarding Sheriff Jack Harwell, he said, "Tell them I appreciate talking to Mr. Harwell because . . . that's like talking to a relative," and Harwell and one of his officers are "just real good down-to-earth people." Negot. Tape no. 97, March 9; Committee Report, p. 59.

Basically, Koresh refused to consider law enforcement officials as anything other than individuals. This meant that Koresh spent a lot of time trying to save the souls of every single negotiator. Early on, when a negotiator insisted that BATF negotiator Jim Cavanaugh was "just a voice for . . . the authorities here," Koresh demurred, "No, Jim is a person." And he expressed regret over the deaths of BATF agents who, in other circumstances, could have been friends. Negot. Tape no. 5, March 1.

The Branch Davidians' complaints about the sheriff's office expressed disappointment rather than anger. They believed they had been roughed up unnecessarily following the 1987 shootout with George Roden. They also believed the sheriff should have been willing to arrest Roden prior to the actions which led to the shootout, and they believed the sheriff should have used the evidence of a methamphetamine lab against those who had built it in Mount Carmel. Negot. Tapes nos. 51–52, March 5; Committee Report, p. 46. Koresh was hoping and expecting Rodriguez, known to be an agent, to call off the raid. Negot. Tape no. 47, March 4.

132. Treasury Report, pp. 10–11. At the trial, the undercover agent testified that the Davidians were all laughing at the article. Trial Transcript, p. 3404. Throughout the Joint Hearings, Rep. Gene Taylor (D-Miss.) wondered why the reporters who had exposed Koresh were not called to report his dangerousness and propensity for violence. Representative Taylor repeatedly noted that the reporters had left town to avoid Koresh's wrath, and that the newspaper had taken exceptional security precautions, including changing locks. He did not note that, whatever the concerns of the newspaper and its reporters, Koresh had apparently not reacted to the exposé with any threat of violence, and those concerns may have been unwarranted.

Still later, BATF Director Magaw was still insisting on Koresh's propensity toward violence in noting how "frightening" it was that undercover agent Rodriguez had to go to the Mount Carmel Center on both Saturday and Sunday, before the raid, "at risk of serious bodily injury or death." However real Rodriguez's concerns, or his bravery on facing Koresh despite those fears, the fact remains that nothing happened to Rodriguez although Koresh knew a raid was imminent and Rodriguez an undercover agent. John Magaw, Joint Hearings, part 1, pp. 907–908.

133. Treasury Report, p. 45. BATF's undercover agent testified that Koresh had never indicated he would, or had trained his followers to kill BATF agents. Trial Transcript, pp. 3397–98.

134. Assistant U.S. Attorney Ray Jahn, Joint Hearings, part 1, pp. 95, 101; Treasury Report, p. 127. A somewhat similar test of devotion was imposed on Abraham, with orders to sacrifice his son, Isaac; that test though, involved Abraham's being willing to kill his own beloved son, rather than to hold strangers hostage and then execute them. Genesis 22. The Treasury Report indicated that the alleged incident would be developed more fully in the trials of the Branch Davidians, but no evidence was introduced at trial regarding the incident. Lead prosecutor Ray Jahn noted that testimony regarding this plan was excluded from the trial as prejudicial because Koresh was not on trial. The sources for the story are not identified. In the course of the negotiations, Davidian Steve Schneider, without going into details, said that Marc Breault and other disaffected Davidians invented stories about Branch Davidian threats to attack the city of Waco. Negot. Tape no. 123, March 13. At Ruby Ridge, the allegations of potential violence were even more wildly exaggerated, with suggestions of a booby-trapped area—despite the free movement of animals and small children—and absurd exaggerations of the dangers posed by a man who never fired a shot at any law enforcement officer. Yet months after Randy Weaver's acquittal on all but minor charges, FBI Director Louis Freeh still spoke of "the known willingness of the Weavers to violently resist the lawful authority of the Federal government, [making] the crisis . . . one of the most dangerous and potentially violent situations to which FBI agents have ever been assigned." And he noted that the FBI approached the Weavers' cabin knowing or believing that Weaver had tried to wrestle a weapon from an officer at the time of his initial arrest, and

that he was prepared to place explosives on his property to defend against law enforcement officers. FBI Press Release, January 6, 1995. Director Freeh did not mention that all the things he said were false, and had been invented by other law enforcement officials in order to exaggerate the threat of violence from the Weavers.

135. Pete Smerick, Joint Hearings, part 2, p. 341. One explanation for the excess credit was that some followers believed, with the end imminent, they would not live to have to complete payments on the principal, although they were making appropriate minimum monthly payments. Carol Moore, *The Davidian Massacre* (Franklin, Tenn.: Legacy Communications and Gunowners Foundation, 1995), p. 27.

136. Ibid. This was from the FBI's behavioral scientist, who had opposed the anti-negotiation bias of the HRT and then felt pressured to advocate a more tactical approach to ending the siege. To him, Koresh was a "psychopathic criminal, a killer who used religion in order to exploit people for his own benefit." Jeffrey Jamar would note, "One of the descriptions of him as a psychopathic personality is that he is not really interested in dying for any cause, including his own . . . even to fulfill a prophecy." Joint Hearings, part 2, pp. 341, 359.

137. Philip Arnold, Joint Hearings, part 2, p. 154. James Tabor, too, concluded that "self defense" was a somewhat theological reason, supplementing investment, as a reason for Davidian gun ownership. Joint Hearings, part 2, pp. 153–54.

138. Stephen Labaton and Sam Howe Verhovek, "U.S. Agents Say Fatal Flaws Doomed Raid on Waco Cult," *New York Times*, March 28, 1993, p. 20; Paul Danish, "The Real Reason the Feds Stormed the Cult," *Soldier of Fortune* (August 1993): 3, 72; R.W Bradford, "There's No Kill Like Overkill," *Liberty* (August 1993): 30.

139. Danish, "The Real Reason," p. 72.

140. A follow-up affidavit by Agent Dunagan asserted as evidence of danger the shootout in 1987, but that, of course, was followed by arrest and search-and-seize warrants served peacefully. BATF Director Stephen Higgins told "Face the Nation" that a "no-knock" raid was necessary to prevent a mass suicide. *Lexington Herald-Leader* (Kentucky), March 6, 1993, p. A3. Of course the government's actions did a rather effective job of precipitating, rather than preventing suicide.

141. Wattenberg, "Gunning for Koresh," p. 38. Considering that BATF's Killorin insisted that the possession of explosives threatened the lives of everyone, that Mount Carmel was known to house numerous firearms, and that the agents were going in armed with guns drawn, the planners oddly failed to include a doctor or dispensary to treat wounded agents, a common practice for the FBI. There was one ambulance available, but it was kept away because BATF could not guarantee the driver's safety.

142. Treasury Report, p. 38 n. 16; James L. Pate, "Jury Acquits 11 Branch Davidians of Key Charges," *Gun Week*, March 11, 1994, p. 2. Assistant U.S. Attorney Johnston denied that he insisted upon a dynamic entry, and, indeed, denied knowing what a dynamic entry was. Joint Hearings, part 1, p. 206. One possible explanation would be that Johnston objected to a siege, without specifying an alternative, and BATF interpreted the objection as meaning that Johnston wanted a dynamic entry rather than a nonassaultive arrest. Johnston was clearly involved in all phases of the final months of the investigation. Charles Sarabyn indicated that the initial plans for the raid, made in December 1992, called for a siege rather than a dynamic entry. Joint Hearings, part 1, p. 222.

143. Treasury Report, Appendix B-40.

144. Maj. Mark Petree, in response to inquiry from Representative Schumer, Joint Hearings, part 1, p. 355.

145. Lee, "Truth," p. 23.

146. Wattenberg, "Gunning for Koresh," p. 32.

147. Treasury Report, pp. 148, 151. Agent Barbara Maxwell, to the contrary, testified that there was a contingency plan, to retreat in case shooting started, so as not to endanger the women and children. Ken Fawcett, *Blind Justice: A Chronology of the Historic Trial of Eleven Branch Davidians in January 1994,* 2d ed. (Royse City, Tex.: Electropress, 1994), p. 14; Trial Transcript, p. 2289. If retreat qualifies as a contingency plan, the plan was not followed.

148. Sue Anne Pressley, "Texas Raid Trial Focuses on Deadly 45 Minutes," *Washington Post,* January 23, 1994; Trial Transcript, pp. 2281–83 (Barbara Maxwell), 1805, 1814–18, 1871 (Dan Curtis), 1340 (Ballesteros).

149. Sue Anne Pressley, "Agent Testifies He Urged ATF to Cancel Waco Raid," *Washington Post,* January 29, 1994, p. A3. Trial Transcript, pp. 3519–24, 3556–64. Agent Ballesteros similarly noted that the agents in charge were lying, but he did not tell anyone. Trial Transcript, pp. 1414–16. Agent Rodriguez was emotional, and had been administratively disciplined by BATF in 1991 and in October 1992, so it is possible that his problems might have made him less credible to the raid commanders. Teresa Talerica, "Agent Disciplined Before Assignment," Waco *Tribune-Herald,* January 14, 1995, p. 1A.

150. Over sixty agents recalled Sarabyn's warnings that surprise had been lost. Treasury Report, pp. 91, 195. Adding to the confusion about what is meant by "element of surprise" and its significance for such a massive BATF raid, is testimony from Rodriguez, who indicated that, after telephoning Sarabyn, he headed for the command post. "I left for the sole purpose of contacting and talking to Mr. Sarabyn at the command post . . . because we didn't have a really long enough conversation on the telephone. . . . I wanted to stop the raid. . . . Unfortunately, I got there too late. When I got there, they had already proceeded with the raid." Joint Hearings, part 1, p. 761. The testimony suggests Rodriguez believed that merely telling Sarabyn that Koresh knew BATF was coming would not automatically cause Chojnacki and Sarabyn to cancel the raid.

151. Joint Hearings, part 1, p. 764. He probably meant to say "metaphorically."

152. Robert Rodriguez, Joint Hearings, part 1, p. 770.

153. McLaughlin, "Operation Trojan Horse," p. 7.

154. Joint Hearings, part 1, p. 314. Chojnacki indicated he shared this view, that "virtually everybody—not everybody, but virtually everybody" would respond passively to overwhelming force and law enforcement could take control before the situation became dangerous for either side. Testimony, Joint Hearings, part 1, pp. 773–74. Unfortunately, religious zealots may fall into the "not everybody" limitation.

155. Bill Buford, Joint Hearings, part 1, p. 786; Treasury Report, p. 81.

156. Notes from a BATF planning session, in BATF Director Stephen Higgins's handwriting, gave only one potential reason for aborting the raid: possible embarrassment to the Treasury Secretary if the raid should go wrong. The notes said nothing about loss of the element of surprise being a reason to abort, or about surprise even being part of the plan. Joint Hearings, part 1, p. 755.

157. Committee Report, pp. 18–21. This interpretation requires reading Koresh's supposed threatening language that BATF and the National Guard were coming as a repetition of the Koreshian prophetic mantras: The world is coming to an end; BATF is coming to get me; the Great Satan will attack; etc.

158. BATF Agent James Cavanaugh, Joint Hearings, part 2, p. 296.

159. Erik Larson, "How a Cascade of Errors Led ATF to Disaster at Waco," *Time* (July 24, 1995): 29.

160. Treasury Report, pp. 187–88. Although posing as a UPS trainee, the undercover agent declined to cut his hair to standard UPS length, insisted on parking at an unusual place at the Mag Bag, and attempted to enter both buildings to use the restrooms, untraditional UPS driver behavior. Stung by the criticisms of his actions in the Treasury Report, and unable to get corrected what he perceived as an injustice to him by that Report, the agent committed suicide. James Pate, "ATF Agent Commits Suicide; Despair over Waco Blame Cited," *Washington Times,* July 26, 1996, p. A6.

161. Clifford L. Linedecker, *The Massacre at Waco, Texas* (New York: St. Martin's, 1993), p. 16.

162. Treasury Report, p. 51. Rodriguez had previously been an undercover drug investigator for the Texas Department of Public Safety. Lee Hancock, "ATF Agent Says He Saw Disaster Loom," *Dallas Morning News,* May 13, 1993.

163. Reavis, *The Ashes of Waco,* p. 67.

164. Pate, "Jailhouse Interviews," p. 48; Thibodeau, Joint Hearings, part 1, pp. 174–75.

165. Pate, "Jailhouse Interviews," p. 48 (interview with Clive Doyle).

166. Treasury Report, p. 187, Appendix D 8–9; Negot. Tape no. 52, March 5.

167. Labaton and Verhovek, "U.S. Agents," p. 20; McMahon and Kilpatrick, *In Re,* p. 258; Pate, "Behind the Cover-Up," p. 39.

168. Reavis, *The Ashes of Waco,* pp. 67 *passim,* reported that Rodriguez's undercover name was Gonzalez, but Rodriguez pointedly corrected the record by noting that his undercover name was Garcia. Joint Hearings, part 1, p. 788. The misunderstanding occurred because Steve Schneider and David Koresh, who were never very good with names, referred to Rodriguez as Gonzalez in their

negotiations with the FBI. E.g., Negot. Tapes no. 59, March 5; no. 68, March 6. Indeed, at one point, Koresh corrects himself to get it wrong: ". . . Robert Garcia—Gonzalez, excuse me." Negot. Tape no. 97, March 9.

169. James D. Tabor, "The Waco Tragedy: An Autobiographical Account of One Attempt to Avert Disaster," in Lewis, *From the Ashes,* p. 17; video deposition of Branch Davidian Marjorie Thomas in Jack DeVault, *The Waco Whitewash: The Mt. Carmel Episode Told by an Eyewitness to the Trial* (San Antonio: Rescue Press, 1994), p. 129; Reavis, *The Ashes of Waco,* pp. 67–68; Trial Transcript, pp. 6190–92. An older Branch Davidian, Victoria Hollingsworth, testified that Koresh thought Rodriguez was "an agent," although she was not sure exactly what kind of agent. Trial Transcript, pp. 4068, 4146. Rodriguez did not believe that the Davidians knew he was an undercover agent. Joint Hearings, part 1, p. 770.

170. Lee Hancock, "ATF Agent Says He Saw Disaster Loom," *Dallas Morning News,* May 13, 1993, p. 8A. At the trial, Rodriguez described Hancock's reporting of his feelings as accurate. Trial Transcript, p. 3542. The night before the raid, Rodriguez told Chuck Sarabyn that Koresh was getting to him, and Rodriguez therefore did not want to go back in. Teresa Talerica, "Agent Disciplined Before Assignment," Waco *Tribune-Herald,* January 14, 1995, p. 1A.

Rodriguez's statements fit in more with Koresh's impression that Rodriguez was "deeply conflicted over what I was showing him" than with the FBI negotiator's assurances that the Rodriguez's near-conversion was just how undercover cops act. Negot. Tapes no. 55, March 5; no. 61, March 5. (Although the negotiation tape transcribes the word as "convicted," other discussions, noting Rodriguez's feelings "conflicting with his job," suggest that Koresh probably said or meant to say "conflicted." Negot. Tape no. 76, March 7.)

Rodriguez also testified that Koresh never indicated he had trained his followers to kill or ambush BATF members or that he would kill BATF agents, and that Rodriguez never saw automatic weapons. Trial Transcript, pp. 3397–98, 3446–49.

171. David McLemore and Lee Hancock, "Mailman Tied to Tip on Cult Is First Victim Identified," *Dallas Morning News,* April 26, 1993; Lee Hancock, "TV Cameraman Admits His Words Tipped Off Cult," *Dallas Morning News,* August 28, 1993.

KWTX had apparently learned about the raid from an employee of the ambulance company which BATF had hired for raid support. The Waco *Tribune-Herald* had also been tipped off, and sent reporters and photographers. Lee Hancock, "Key Review May Spur ATF Fallout," *Dallas Morning News,* September 26, 1993.

In May 1993, the Department of Justice (which controls the FBI, but not the BATF) issued guidelines forbidding advance notification of media about law enforcement actions, and forbidding invitations to media to attend such actions. Tracy Everbach, "Siege Prompts New Media Policy," *Dallas Morning News,* May 7, 1993. Such guidelines should be applied to all federal law enforcement.

172. Hancock, "Television Photographer Says He Tipped Waco Cult."

173. Joint Hearings, part 1, p. 761.

174. John 13:27; Tabor, "The Waco Tragedy," p. 17; Sue Anne Pressley, "Federal Agent Describes Undercover Role Before Deadly Texas Cult Raid," *Washington Post,* January 28, 1994, p. A-3.

175. "I'm pretty sure that he's going to realize, you know, to hold this thing off. . . . I thought for sure that he understood that . . . what I was asking from him was for him to go out and say, look, guys, let's hold off on this. Let's deal with it a different way." Negot. Tape no. 47, March 4. Koresh insisted he was trying to make it clear he could be arrested without incident when he told Rodriguez that he had to do what he had to do and Koresh had to do what Koresh had to do. Negot. Tape no. 60, March 5. "I says, Robert, they're coming now." His response? "He was confused. Same as Pilate. Pilate was confused. He wanted to let Christ go." Negot. Tape no. 76, March 7. Steve Schneider, Koresh's lieutenant, agreed that there was nothing aggressive or threatening in Koresh's warnings to Rodriguez. Negot. Tape no. 63, March 6. On the other hand, part of Koresh's hope that Rodriguez would recommend that BATF speak to Koresh and arrest him peacefully, and "see if he'll come out to us, . . . 'cause . . . aggression is going to cause aggression . . . these people believe in God and they do not believe in being pushed over." Negot. Tape no. 61, March 5.

176. Pate, "Day of Infamy," p. 50.

177. Moore, *The Davidian Massacre,* pp. 151–52.

178. Negot. Tape no. 48, March 4.

179. Moorman Oliver, Jr., "Killed by Semantics: Or Was It a Keystone Kop Kaleidoscope Kaper?" in Lewis, *From the Ashes*, p. 75.

180. Ron Noble, Joint Hearings, part 1, p. 924.

181. Oliver, "Killed by Semantics," p. 75; Linedecker, *Massacre at Waco*, p. 23 (scanner radios picked up walkie-talkie traffic).

182. 18 U.S. Code §§ 1701, 1702.

183. Pate, "Day of Infamy," p. 62; Aguilera, p. 12.

184. McMahon and Kilpatrick, *In Re*, pp. 174–75; Treasury Report, p. 46.

185. William Buford, Joint Hearings, part 1, p. 485.

186. Reavis, *The Ashes of Waco*, pp. 181–82; Erik Larson, "How a Cascade of Errors Led ATF to Disaster at Waco," *Time* (July 24, 1995); Treasury Report, pp. 146–47.

187. Aguilera, Attachment D.

188. Aguilera, p. 2. Professor Tony Cooper, a University of Texas scholar of terrorism and conflict, stated that Mount Carmel was "a location where surprise simply could not work." Pate, "Day of Infamy," p. 48.

189. Unless the magistrate had expressly authorized a nighttime raid, the warrant had to be served in daytime. Federal Rules of Criminal Procedure, Rule 41(c). A motion to supplement the warrant, filed on the night of February 28th, essentially repeated Aguilera's earlier affidavit verbatim adding a paragraph, with the request for a nighttime warrant, claiming that although BATF had "attempted to execute the warrant both on the main compound location and at the 'Mag Bag', we have been unable to search the premises and retrieve evidence because of heavy armed resistance." The destructive search of the Mag Bag was eventually conducted at 7:30 A.M. on March 3. Justice Report, pp. 25, 37.

190. There have been reports that BATF agents were known to be in local hotels, and that the activity was the talk of local radio scanners. Motel maids said that they knew a major raid would take place when they saw large numbers of agents leaving their rooms on the morning of February 28, wearing dark tactical clothing, and carrying weapons. Lee Hancock, "Inquiry of Lead to Cult Shifts to News Media," *Dallas Morning News*, March 18, 1993. There were sixteen BATF personnel in Waco the night before the raid. Treasury Report, pp. 185, Appendices B-71 and C-32-33. In addition, there were forty BATF support personnel staying in two Waco hotels, under instructions not to wear BATF clothing. BATF Director Stephen Higgins, letter to Rep. Jack Brooks, June 17, 1993, in Hearing, p. 186. BATF had reserved 150 rooms for the next night in Waco's three leading hotels. Reavis, *The Ashes of Waco*, p. 31.

191. Pate, *Day of Infamy*, p. 53. The Branch Davidians' ammunition was not particularly powerful. The Branch Davidians used 7.62 × 39 ammunition in many of their rifles. A 7.62 x 39 bullet (used in Kalashnikov rifles) weighs 110 to 125 grains, while the bullet for the popular .30-06 hunting rifle ranges from 55 to 250 grains (with 21 of the 22 bullet types being 100 grains or above); the bullet for the ubiquitous Colt .45 pistol weighs 185 to 230 grains; and bullets for the .458 Winchester magnum weigh between 300 and 510 grains. Frank C. Barnes, *Cartridges of the World*, 7th ed. (1993), pp. 59, 92, 110, 231, 249. One of the reasons that the ammunition for the military-style rifle is smaller, and hence less powerful, is that it was created for soldiers who would have to carry large quantities of ammunition over long distances; in contrast, standard hunting ammunition can be heavier, since a hunter will carry only a few rounds on a trip that is usually completed in a single day, or at most a few days. In addition, a hunter's goal is to kill game quickly and painlessly. A soldier's goal is to produce casualties, with fatalities not necessarily as desirable, for a wounded man may temporarily incapacitate more people, as soldiers are diverted from fighting to caring for the wounded.

Besides bullet weight, a second major factor in the force of a bullet's impact is its velocity. Other things being equal, a bullet traveling at high velocity will be more destructive than a bullet traveling at lower velocity. The muzzle velocities for the ammunition types listed above are: for the 7.62 x 39 from 2,100 to 2,500 fps (feet per second); for the .30-06 from 2,100 to 4,080 fps; for the Colt pistol 770 to 1140 fps; and for the .458 Winchester magnum from 2,100 to 2,500 fps.

A bullet's power to damage its target depends mainly on the kinetic energy delivered by the bullet. Kinetic energy is produced by the combination of bullet weight and velocity. A typical 7.62 x 39 bullet for the AKS rifle (a Kalashnikov variant) achieves 1,445 foot-pounds of kinetic energy. In contrast, the .30-06 hunting rifle bullet carries 2,820 foot-pounds of energy. "Firearms Market Thrives Despite an Import Ban," *New York Times,* April 3, 1989.

192. "Basically, we all announced," BATF agent Roland Ballesteros claimed. "Witness Says Cult Ambushed Agents but Acknowledges Blunders," *New York Times,* January 19, 1993; Trial Transcript, p. 1335.

193. Ibid. Other BATF agents who testified confirmed that no peaceful entry was ever rehearsed. Presley, "Texas Raid Trial"; Reavis, *The Ashes of Waco,* p. 139.

194. Special Agent Kenneth King, in Trial Transcript, pp. 2576–77.

195. Reavis, *The Ashes of Waco,* p. 154. BATF's Buford, who headed a four-man team on a different part of the roof from King's three-man team, testified that he and King each had radios, and that King had radio contact with other team leaders and could have known, in case of cooperation by Koresh below, that the use of flashbang grenades was not necessary, although the teams still would have made entry from the roof into the second-story rooms. Testimony, Joint Hearings, part 1, p. 461. Buford's testimony contradicts that of King, who testified he had no radio contact.

A reviewer of the Justice Department report noted the tactical flaw in continuing the second-floor assault once the shooting started: "The whole purpose of this raid was to get to the armory, which was supposedly locked on the second floor. Those poor officers are up on the roof, going into an armory that is supposedly locked. Well, as soon as they got shot at, they know that the armory is unlocked . . . the sheer stupidity of this is unbelievable." Alan Stone, Joint Hearings, part 1, p. 461. At least five agents entering the second floor were wounded, two fatally. Reavis, *The Ashes of Waco,* ch. 17.

196. Committee Report, p. 58 n. 401.

197. 18 U.S.C. § 3109.

198. Again, there was some question as to whether BATF's actions in Waco were unusual. Gerald Goldstein of the National Association of Criminal Defense Lawyers testified that "before . . . Justice Thomas' unanimous opinion in *Wilson* v. *Arkansas,* you probably couldn't have found a defense lawyer out there that would have thought that the knock and announce provisions of the fourth amendment had any teeth in them." Joint Hearings, part 1, p. 167.

199. Scott Pendleton, "Waco Siege Prompts Scrutiny of Agency," *Christian Science Monitor,* March 8, 1993, p. 8. The BATF agent who was to serve the warrant testified that he yelled: "Police search warrant, lay down," and, in response to Koresh's asking, "What's going on?" repeated, "Search warrant, lay down." It was further reported that he testified that BATF had "a plan to ram the door down, but there 'was not a plan to knock on the door and serve the warrant, in other words, the plan was to use force.'" Agent Robert Champion had not described any warrant announcement when the Texas Rangers had interviewed him March; at the Davidians' trial, Champion explained the omission by stating that the Rangers had not specifically asked him about it. Kathy Fair, "Witnesses Testify Koresh Cultists Fired First," *Houston Chronicle,* January 21, 1994, p. 23A; Trial Transcript, pp. 2096–2102 (Robert Champion), 1333–35 (Roland Ballesteros).

200. *Wilson* v. *Arkansas,* 115 S.Ct. 1914, 1917, n. 2 (1995), quoting *Semayne's Case*:

> But before he [the sheriff] breaks it, he ought to signify the cause of his coming, and to make request to open doors . . . , for the law without a default in the owner abhors the destruction or breaking of any house (which is for the habitation and safety of man) by which great damage and inconvenience might ensue to the party, when no default is in him; for perhaps he did not know of the process, of which, if he had notice, it is to be presumed that he would obey it. . . .

(77 English Reports 194, 195–96 [K. B. 1603].)

201. Response brief in *Wilson* v. *Arkansas,* 115 S.Ct. 1914 (1995), p. 127.

202. Dunagan, Howell Affidavit, p. 8; Rodriguez, Joint Hearings, part 1, pp. 749, 768.

203. Dick DeGuerin, Joint Hearings, part 2, p. 73.

204. Clive Doyle, part 3, p. 104. David Thibodeau had testified similarly, that Koresh had said, "'Don't do anything stupid. We want to talk to these people. We want to work it out. That's what we're all about here at Mount Carmel.' And I'll never forget those words, because I was really scared . . . it was like, OK, David's going to try to talk to them, maybe this can still be avoided. He went to the front door." Joint Hearings, part 1, pp. 175–76.

205. E.g., Negot. Tapes no. 55, March 5; no. 60, March 5; no. 80, March 7; no. 82, March 7.

206. Labaton and Verhovek, "U.S. Agents," p. 20; James L. Pate, "Waco Standoff Ends in Disaster," *Soldier of Fortune* (July 1993): 41.

207. Cancro, p. 3, in U.S. Department of Justice, *Recommendations of Experts for Improvements in Federal Law Enforcement After Waco* (Washington 1993).

208. Joint Hearings, part 1, p. 761. He was not asked whether that was part either of agent training in general or in the briefings for the raid for which he was operations coordinator.

209. Pate, "Day of Infamy," pp. 49–50; Pate, "Waco Standoff," p. 41.

210. Pate, "Day of Infamy," p. 51.

Other than BATF agents, the only person who testified that the Davidians fired first was a Waco *Tribune-Herald* reporter who was about 200–225 yards away. On cross-examination, however, the reporter stated that he had never said that the Branch Davidians fired first. Scott W. Wright, "Agents at Branch Davidian Trial Describe Blitz of Bullets at Raid," *Austin American-Statesman*, January 21, 1994, p. B3; Trial Transcript, pp. 1916–20, 1927–30.

211. Pate, "Day of Infamy," p. 51.

212. That is the opinion of Koresh's attorney. Dick DeGuerin, Joint Hearings, part 2, p. 26. And it was repeated frequently by Koresh and Schneider during the course of the negotiations, saying a BATF agent had admitted as much on the radio. E.g., Negot. Tapes no. 60, March 5; no. 121, March 12–13.

213. James L. Pate, "BATF's Magic Bullets," *Soldier of Fortune* (September 1993): 28.

214. Jack Zimmermann, Joint Hearings, part 2, p. 88; Tim Evans, Joint Hearings, part 1, p. 632; Reavis, *The Ashes of Waco,* pp. 137–38.

In the course of the negotiations, various Davidians recalled having heard radio reports of BATF agents admitting that their accidental gunshots began the shootout. Negot. Tapes no. 38, March 4; no. 41, March 4; no. 60, March 5; no. 104, March 10; and no. 140, March 19. On the last tape, Koresh opines that the accidental shooting might have been caused by an agent's hand being on the trigger too tightly, and suggesting that the fact should have been recorded by the guys in the surveillance house.

215. Personal communication, August 19, 1995.

216. The Davidian children were reportedly upset that "they shot these dogs right off." Negot. Tape no. 64, March 6. Attorney Jack Zimmermann asked: "Why did the ATF shoot five malamute dogs and let them whine and cry within sight and hearing of the children until their pets eventually died?" Joint Hearings, part 2, p. 130. That the planning for the raid included an initial effort to disable the dogs lends some credence to the supposition in the Ruby Ridge case, that the reason the three marshals threw rocks at the Weaver cabin was to lure the dog away and shoot him, preventing his either alerting the family or attacking marshals on future expeditions onto the property. Sammy Weaver was also upset that the arrest began by killing the dog, but he reacted more spontaneously and violently than the Davidian children.

217. When Koresh denied that the men identified themselves or announced a search or arrest warrant, he presumably really meant he could not hear any such thing. As he recalled, "they were all screaming at one time . . . you've been to a football game and you hear a roar but you don't know what anybody's saying. . . ." Negot. Tape no. 97, March 9.

218. Wattenberg, "Gunning for Koresh," p. 40; David Koresh, interview on KRLD radio, February 28, 1993, quoted in Moore, *The Davidian Massacre,* p. 124.

During the siege, there were reports indicating that BATF came to Mount Carmel Center believing that the women and children were all in one place rather than, as was the case, scattered all over. Negot. Tapes no. 38, March 4; no. 41, March 4. If BATF thought the women and children were all together, then the gunfire from the helicopters would be even more outrageous, since the second floor was the women's and children's quarters.

219. Negot. Tapes no. 60, March 5; no. 80, March 7; ABC News Nightline, "The Waco Tapes," July 5, 1995. Koresh's statements of what happened was supported by Judy Schneider. Negot. Tape no. 99, March 9. Ted Koppel went on, after playing that portion of the negotiation tapes, to report that the videotape "had, in fact, been shot, although at a considerable distance, from a government surveillance post more than 100 yards away. What that tape would have shown, we will never know. The government says the tape was blank." Koresh did lie, even when he knew that the lie was contradicted by tape. Early in the negotiations he had claimed a child was killed in the initial BATF raid; but on

Day 45, the negotiations tapes Koppel played indicate Koresh not only denied any such killing, but denied ever having asserted it, and he claimed the FBI would never find such a statement on any tape.

220. Likewise, the BATF follow-up affidavit for an expanded search warrant had stated that firing initiated by Koresh's followers came from "every window of the compound building." Dunagan, Howell Affidavit, p. 2.

221. The prosecutor argued that the pictures of the windows were too indistinct to tell if anyone were in the windows.

222. Kathy Fair, "ATF Testifies about Cult Ambush," *Houston Post*, January 19, 1994; "First Eyewitness Testifies at Branch Davidian Trial," *Washington Post*, January 19, 1994; Chip Brown, "Davidians Fired First, Agent Says," *Washington Times*, January 19, 1994; Trial Transcript, pp. 1338–39, 1378–79, 1394–1412. Ballesteros did not have the actual warrant. According to BATF's Chuck Sarabyn, he had brought the warrant with him. When the shooting started, he was about 75-100 feet from the door to Koresh's house, and the warrants were in the truck he had come in. He was prepared to bring the warrant once the situation was under control, but assumed the warrants were shot up when the truck was shot up. Joint Hearings, part 1, pp. 478–79.

223. Treasury Report, Appendix D-17.

224. Martin, an African-American graduate of the Harvard Law School, was known for a cool, reserved manner. But during the call to Sheriff Lynch, Martin's voice was high-pitched and frantic. (The call is discussed in Negot. Tape no. 122, March 13.) The judge at the Davidian trial suggested that Martin's performance on the tape was "self-serving." Sue Anne Pressley, "Branch Davidian Defense Cites Lawyer's Frantic Call During Raid," *Washington Post*, February 17, 1994; Trial Transcript, p. 6504. A sound excerpt from the tape is available at http://rampages.onramp.net/~djreavis/sndclips.html. Less easy to explain away is Steve Schneider's voice in the background yelling about choppers firing. "He didn't know Wayne Martin was on the telephone talking to 911 and being recorded." Jack Zimmermann, Joint Hearings, part 2, p. 138.

225. Wattenberg, "Gunning for Koresh," p. 40.

226. Ibid.

227. Transcript of 911 call in DeVault, pp. 208–35. The transcript can also be found at The Research Center, http://www.ime.net/~mswett. Some criticism has been voiced about the need for the sheriff's 911 line as intermediary. Other law enforcement experts expressed surprise that the raiding party lacked a mobile telephone and Koresh's number, in order to communicate if something unforeseen occurred. Reavis, *The Ashes of Waco*, p. 173. Referring to Reavis's book, Rep. Bill McCollum noted the lack of some equipment caused difficulty with the 911 communication, "At the same time they [BATF] had fax machines, telephones and computers and were ready for whatever PR [public relations] they had. That was a mighty strange operation, to say the least, and certainly a fatal flaw, not to pun a word." Joint Hearings, part 1, p. 622.

228. McLaughlin, "Operation Trojan Horse," p. 7.

229. Jack Zimmermann, Joint Hearings, part 2, p. 26.

230. Joint Hearings, part 2, pp. 402, 417–18.

231. Joint Hearings, part 1, p. 786.

232. "Much Evidence and Conflict in Branch Davidians' Trial," *New York Times*, January 17, 1994; Sue Anne Pressley, "Branch Davidian Defense Cites Lawyer's Frantic Call During Raid," *Washington Post*, February 17, 1994. One of the lawyers for the Branch Davidians found the missing door "troublesome," partly because of the "weakness of the excuse about why they couldn't come up with it. We were told it must have burned up in the fire. The trouble with that is it is a big metal door and there were other metal doors inside in hotter places that didn't burn up and there were cans of food in there that didn't burn up. A door like that isn't going to totally vaporize. Some remnant of it would be around." Tim Evans, Joint Hearings, part 1, p. 603.

233. Pressley, ibid. In addition, Zimmermann testified that there were bullet holes in the upper-level ceiling, which would lend support to the contention that the helicopter fired on the Davidian compound. DeVault, *The Waco Whitewash*, pp. 141–42; Trial Transcript, pp. 6609–11, 6646–48.

234. Dick DeGuerin, Joint Hearings, part 2, pp. 24–25.

235. James L. Pate, personal communication with Kopel, April 14, 1994.

236. On cross-examination, Texas Ranger Fred Cummings was shown a picture of the intact

door. DeVault, *The Waco Whitewash,* p. 66; Trial Transcript, pp. 1072–75. The missing door was an important issue to the jurors at the criminal trial of the Branch Davidians. They thought while the door might not have indicated who fired first, it would have indicated the size of the barrage in each direction. Moore, *The Davidian Massacre,* p. 129, citing Teresa Talerico, "Trial was Grueling, Juror Says," Waco *Tribune-Herald,* March 3, 1994.

237. Joint Hearings, part 2, pp. 32, 44; Treasury Report, p. 96.

238. Reavis, *The Ashes of Waco,* p. 142. In his overeager defense of coverup charges regarding the missing door, Representative Schumer conceded that of course there would have been gunshot holes from outside, since BATF was returning massive fire from within. "[T]he Davidians shoot from the windows. They are not going to shoot through the doors. . . . Then in response the ATF agents shoot back. Of course the majority of bullet holes would be . . . going in that direction, because the Davidians are not going to keep the door closed and shoot through it." Joint Hearing, part 2, p. 32. Representative Taylor similarly defended wild shooting toward the windows of the house: "if bullets are flying all over me, and there's one of me, . . . you don't really have the time to pick your shots, . . . basically . . . yes, you are going to empty your clip and hope you hit something and you don't get hit in the meantime. . . . So that could very well explain the very bad pattern of shots around those windows, couldn't it?" Ibid., p. 27. What Representatives Schumer and Taylor failed to recognize is that federal agents are not allowed indiscriminate fire in the general direction of bad guys intermingled with noncombatants, a point emphasized in trial testimony of Agent Roland Ballesteros, reproduced in the Joint Hearings, part 3, p. 88. He noted that no fire could be returned except at identified targets, not at windows or shadows which were sources of gunfire, not even at nonthreatening persons in mere possession of firearms.

239. Sam Howe Verhovek, "Eleven in Texas Sect are Acquitted of Key Charges," *New York Times,* February 27, 1994, p. A-1.

240. Moore, *The Davidian Massacre,* p. 134. She told attorney Zimmermann the jury could not decide who fired first. Joint Hearings, part 2, p. 29.

241. Treasury Report, pp. 143–56.

242. Hearing, p. 130. At the trial, a Texas Ranger testified that he found about forty used shell casings (in the same calibers as the BATF weapons) more than 300 yards from the house. "Much Evidence and Conflict," *New York Times,* January 17, 1994. Testimony of Ronny Griffith, Trial Transcript, pp. 1148–57. Agent Timothy Gabourie testified that he fired twenty-five to thirty shots in the direction of the house, without aiming or seeing exactly where he was shooting. "Lift for Defense in Cultists' Trial," *New York Times,* January 30, 1994; Trial Transcript, pp. 2469–70, 2482, 2499. Danny Curtis similarly suggested shooting about 20 rounds toward a window without seeing his target. Trial Transcript, pp. 1794, 1884.

243. Trial testimony of BATF Agent Ballesteros, on reexamination, in Fawcett, *Blind Justice,* p. 11; Trial Transcript, pp. 1505–1506.

244. BATF's Daniel Troy, like other BATF leaders, vehemently denied the friendly fire claims. Linedecker, *Massacre at Waco,* pp. 176–77. The only friendly fire that has been officially acknowledged was a single wounding. BATF agent Keith Constantino testified that he might have shot agent Glen Jordan, since the bullet found in Jordan's right biceps was the same 9mm HydraShok type that some BATF agents, including Constantino, were using. "ATF Agent Says He May Have Shot Comrade," *Washington Times,* January 26, 1994.

An anonymous, highly placed federal source was reported to have stated that "about half of ATF casualties in the raid apparently resulted from friendly fire." Pate, "Stand-off Ends," p. 53. BATF's reporting of the four fatalities to the FBI's Uniform Crime Reports section is vague, with all deaths attributed to rifle shots, but with no certainty as to any caliber, each death identified only "possibly" by caliber. FBI Uniform Crime Reports, *Law Enforcement Officers Killed and Assaulted, 1993* (Washington, D.C.: U.S. Department of Justice, 1994), p. 55. While most BATF agents attacking Mount Carmel were armed with 9mm handguns, ten were armed with either a .308 or .223 caliber rifle (Hearing, p. 189), calibers "possibly" involved in three of the four deaths.

The FBI and the Texas Rangers were even less forthcoming in sorting through the denouement: None of the deaths which occurred on April 19 is counted as a criminal homicide, with only three homicides recorded for suburban McLennan County for 1993, none from the Mount Carmel Center incident. *FBI Uniform Crime Reports, Crime in the United States, 1993* (Washington, D.C.: U.S.

Government Printing Office, 1994) p. 105; personal communication between Blackman and Uniform Crime Reports personnel, December 1994.

245. Oliver, "Killed by Semantics," p. 77.

246. Statement of Rep. Steve Chabot, Joint Hearings, part 1, p. 383. A heated discussion between BATF Agent Jim Cavanaugh and Koresh regarding guns on the helicopters ended with their calmly agreeing that there were no guns mounted on the helicopters but that agents on the 'copters had guns. Negot. Tape no. 42, March 4.

The government sometimes defines things differently for government and private use. At the trial of the Davidians, agents frequently testified that the MP-5 was a semiautomatic firearm even though it can fire a two-round burst, which would make it a machine gun under federal law. Testimony of agents Kevin Scott Richardson, Kenneth King, Bill Buford, and Kenneth Chisholm, Trial Transcript, pp. 2025, 2030–33, 2589, 2815–16, 3152–53.

247. Sue Anne Pressley, "Waco Cult's Children Describe Beatings, Lectures, War Games," *Washington Post*, May 5, 1993, p. A17.

248. "Someone Dropped the Ball," *Newsweek*, May 7, 1993, p. 51. See also Lynne Lamberg, "Children and Families Need Help After Disasters," *Journal of the American Medical Association* 275 (June 12, 1996): 1714–15.

249. Vin Suprynowicz (assistant editorial page editor, *Las Vegas Review-Journal*), "Speaking the Unpalatable Truth," available at http://www.nguworld.com/vindex/.

250. Negot. Tapes no. 50, March 4-5; no. 109, March 10–11. Some of the guns were at a gun show with Davidian financier and gun-show regular, Paul Fatta. He missed the shootout, made no effort to break in, and was arrested long after the battle, peacefully, and tried and convicted on gun-law violations. Reavis, *The Ashes of Waco*, pp. 37–38, 152–53, 291–92; Michael deCourcy Hinds, "A Believer, Stranded in Battle, Says Sect Has Peaceful Goals," *New York Times*, March 6, 1993, pp. 1, 8.

251. DeGuerin, Koresh's attorney, reported seeing "bullet holes in the ceiling of the highest room in the compound. . . . The only way those bullets could have been made was from someone standing on the roof shooting down, or someone shooting from the helicopters." Joint Hearings, part 2, pp. 25, 37. DeGuerin and Zimmermann said they saw bullet holes in Koresh's bedroom, in addition to bullet holes in the gun room. The bullet holes in the gun room, unlike those in the bedroom, could have come from agents who climbed onto the roof and who participated in the firefight at the gun room. Joint Hearings, part 2, pp. 105, 138.

The Texas Rangers testified that they found no evidence of shooting from helicopters, although the Rangers were unable to offer an alternative explanation for how the bullet holes described by DeGuerin could have been created. Joint Hearings, part 2, pp. 197–98.

252. "Defense Rests without Calling Cultists."

253. In the course of the negotiations, when the FBI suggested sending in a videotape showing the children who had left the residence, Koresh and his followers remarked that helicopter fire through the ceiling had damaged his television, and they would have to check to see if they had working TVs to use with their VCRs.

254. Pate, "Day of Infamy."

255. Negot. Tape no. 122, March 13.

256. Pate, "Day of Infamy," p. 62. The Treasury Report does not address the issue of Cyclone ammunition.

257. Stuart Wright, Joint Hearings, part 1, p. 91. The Treasury Report states that the Davidians killed by BATF agents were struck with 9mm HydraShok rounds, not the Cyclone. Treasury Report, p. 104. The Cyclone, as armor–piercing handgun ammunition, is banned from sale to civilians. Perhaps it is worth considering whether sale of such deadly ammunition to the government should also be prohibited.

258. BATF Agent James Cavanaugh, Joint Hearings, part 2, p. 329. BATF Deputy Director for Enforcement, Dan Hartnett, confirmed that he curtailed AR-15 use because of the rifle bullets' ability to penetrate, but some AR-15s were used since they were requested, and the assault was to occur in a nonurban setting. Joint Hearings, part 1, p. 266. In addition to 9mm rounds, which can penetrate thin walls, at least ten rifles were used in the assault. Hearing, p. 189.

259. We do not agree with this characterization of the AR-15, or of any other so-called assault weapon. The point is that BATF, while claiming to be only lightly armed, was using ten guns described by BATF officials as extremely powerful mass murder weapons.

260. A machine pistol is a machine gun that is also a pistol (as opposed to a rifle). Such guns are also called *submachine guns*.

261. Peter B. Kraska, "Enjoying Militarism: Political/Personal Dilemmas in Studying U.S. Police Paramilitary Units," *Justice Quarterly* 13, no. 3 (September 1996): 412.

262. Quoted in James T. Richardson, "Lessons from Waco: Will We Ever Learn?" in Lewis, *From the Ashes,* p. 181. Regarding BATF's weaponry, it was noted, "I can tell you at Ft. Hood, TX, we observed pistols, we observed submachine guns, we observed AR-15's, and we observed a long gun . . . I am trying hard not to use the word 'sniper' . . .—a long-range type of weapon like that with optics." Lt. Col. Philip Lindley, Joint Hearings, part 1, p. 379.

263. Pate, "Day of Infamy," p. 64.

264. Stephen Labaton and Sam Howe Verhovek, "U.S. Agents Say Fatal Flaws Doomed Raid on Cult," *New York Times*, March 28, 1993, p. 1

265. *NBC Today*, March 29, 1993, Burrelle's Information Services transcript, p. 15.

266. Ron Cole, *Sinister Twilight* (Longmont, Colo., self-published, 1994), p. 17.

267. Negot. Tapes no. 52, March 5; no. 62, March 6.

268. Justice Report, p. 229; Tim Evans, Joint Hearings, part 1, p. 635.

269. Testimony of Tarrant County Medical Examiner Nizan Peerwani, in DeVault, *The Waco Whitewash,* pp. 124–26; Treasury Report, p. 104; Reavis, *The Ashes of Waco,* pp. 196–98; Tim Evans, Joint Hearings, part 1, p. 635; Trial Transcript, pp. 6011–20, 6045. Some gunpowder might have been expected in such a wound, even through a cap.

270. William Daniel Wright, BATF, Trial Transcript, pp. 3911–14; Lee Hancock, "Koresh Trying to Provoke 'War,' Federal Officials Say," *Dallas Morning News*, March 9, 1993; Cole, *Sinister Twilight,* pp. 57–58.

271. Linedecker, *Massacre at Waco,* p. 204.

272. Negot. Tape no. 100, March 9. The FBI eventually suggested that the injured Judy Schneider could come out for medical care and return to the residence, in exchange for release of all of the remaining children. When this was rejected because most of the children were Koresh's, the FBI proposed sending out three, then two, adults who would remain while Judy returned. When this was rejected, the FBI offended the Davidians by reporting that the Davidians did not want medical treatment for Judy Schneider. The FBI's theory was that rejecting an item because of the price demanded meant that one did not want a particular item. Negot. Tape no. 124, March 13.

3

The Siege

THE RULES OF ENGAGEMENT AND THE HOSTAGE RESCUE TEAM

The FBI—with its Hostage Rescue Team (HRT)—was called into Waco to add some professionalism to a law-enforcement disaster. The initial FBI strategy was talking the Davidians out, no matter how long it took.[1]

As in Idaho, the Hostage Rescue Team had no hostages to rescue. They defined themselves as being in a "Complex Hostage Rescue Barricade Situation." But to the extent there were hostages at Mount Carmel, the Branch Davidians were hostage in their own home because they were afraid of what the Hostage Rescue Team and the federal government would do to them and their children. These fears were no doubt intensified by the fact that most adults who voluntarily left Mount Carmel were arrested and manacled, and children who left were taken away from their parents, and put in government custody under the supervision of an "anti-cult" specialist.[2]

As Koresh's attorney complained: "When adults came out, every one of them went to jail. . . . For instance, the first two ladies that came out, one of them was 77 years old and practically blind. She was charged with a false affidavit, with having participated in the shooting that occurred on February 28. An agent actually testified that she held a gun and pointed it. She . . . just couldn't have done it. When those on the inside, who were seeing the news reports, saw the treatment that people were getting when they went outside, well, it discouraged them from going outside."[3]

The Hostage Rescue Team's arrogance is a well-known problem in law enforcement. As Treasury Undersecretary for Law Enforcement Ron Noble observed, "when they come into an operation, they take over, and I've been with other law enforcement officers when that happens, and it is not something that makes law enforcement officers, who believe they're able, happy. That's just the way it is."[4] In Idaho, the HRT did not bother to debrief the marshals who had actually been involved in the shootout at Ruby Ridge, letting them depart to a hotel prior to any questioning. At Waco, the HRT rapidly established bad relations with the Texas Rangers.

Also as in Idaho, the HRT began with an anti-negotiation bias. In Idaho, the initial plans of attack included no mention of negotiations. Negotiation plans were only inserted when the FBI in Washington insisted.[5] Jeffrey Jamar, the special agent in charge of the San Antonio FBI office, was in charge of the entire operation at Waco, and of sorting out the conflicting views of the HRT and the FBI negotiation team. Jamar's immediate superior was Larry Potts, the assistant director of the Criminal Investigation Section.[6] Jamar personally had no training in negotiations; he "left that to the experts."[7] The advice of negotiators generally was ignored in favor the HRT's position to steadily increase pressure on the Branch Davidians. This proved to be a fatal error.[8]

One of the negotiators later noted that while sometimes negotiators and "tactical component" (the HRT or SWAT teams) agree about how to achieve success, in Waco "there was a fundamental strategy disagreement and what was the best way to proceed? . . . the negotiation team wanted to have a lower-keyed approach and the tactical team's approach was to apply pressure. Part of that . . . was driven by the fact that the team, as Mr. Jamar indicated, was exposed to open fire. We were dealing with the most complex situation we have ever had in the United States, where there had already been a demonstrated willingness to use force. . . . So the need to provide them with adequate cover to contain the situation had an impact on conveying perhaps the message that Mr. Koresh did not want to hear."[9]

The Hostage Rescue Team was originally created to rescue Americans abroad who were being held hostage by terrorists. The HRT is trained by Delta Force, the U.S. Army's counterterrorism team. But the HRT has frequently been deployed not to rescue hostages in other countries, or even in the United States, but instead as some kind of élite force to deal with particularly troublesome domestic criminals. This deployment—at Ruby Ridge, Waco, and elsewhere—has led to predictably disastrous consequences. A team trained to rescue hostages being held by foreign terrorists is an élite strike force of killers. They must attack rapidly, neutralize the terrorists (with not the slightest hesitation about killing them), and extricate the hostages. Rather than shooting only when clearly necessary to prevent harm to an innocent, a hostage rescue team must destroy the terrorists at the first opportunity, before the terrorists have an opportunity to pose an imminent threat.

Persons trained for this specific, important mission are mistrained for domestic law enforcement, in which the objective is to capture suspected criminals (not kill them), to minimize the use of force, and to act with a scrupulous regard for the United States Constitution.

Philip Heymann, who served as deputy attorney general in the first year of the Clinton administration, has suggested that the Hostage Rescue Team only be used for rescuing hostages. The problems caused by infrequent use of the HRT are far outweighed by use of the Hostage Rescue Team in nonhostage situations.[10] Professor Heymann's suggestion should be put into the United States Code.[11]

According to Attorney General Janet Reno:

From the start, the negotiation tactics focused on restricting the activities of those inside the compound, and depriving them of a comfortable environment so as to bring the matter to a conclusion without further violence.

Those inside the compound were advised of the FBI's rules of engagement. Under those rules, the agents conveyed the information that they would not use deadly force against any person except when necessary in self-defense or defense of another, or when they had reason to believe that they or another were in danger of death or grievous bodily harm.[12]

Attorney General Reno's statement about the FBI's use of force was consistent with the formal FBI rules of engagement, which allow a shooting only when a life is in danger or there is a risk of grievous bodily injury.[13] But these rules are not always obeyed, as illustrated by the case of Randy Weaver.

Two-and-a-half years after Waco, Attorney General Reno issued deadly force rules applicable to all federal law enforcement.[14] The rules are sensible, and not greatly different from the FBI rules which had nominally been in effect at Waco. It is good to have a rule stating that federal agents should kill people only when absolutely necessary. Enforcing that rule is another matter.

So thoroughly has militarization permeated federal law enforcement that the use of the term "rules of engagement" passes unnoticed. "Rules of engagement" is a military term, specifying how and under what conditions soldiers will strike at the enemy. The term—and its implicit sanction of imminent lethal destruction of foreign soldiers—should have no place in domestic law enforcement.

Regardless of Attorney General Reno's pronouncements about the official FBI rules of engagement, the Davidians were presented with a different set of rules. The Davidians were warned that if FBI agents perceived any threat to themselves or others, they would shoot; an additional rule was, "No one will be allowed to exit the building with a weapon."[15] This was amended after about ten days by prohibiting anyone's leaving the house without advance permission from the FBI.[16] The FBI used firecracker-like flashbang grenades, fired at violators, to enforce the rule against leaving Koresh's house without permission.[17]

Both BATF and the FBI used flashbangs at Waco. They are described by BATF as "diversionary devices that produce a flash and a bang but no fragments, and therefore do not cause injury."[18] To the FBI a flashbang, also called a "flash bang" or a "flash-bang grenade," "is a stunning device emitting bright light, sound and smoke to divert the activity and attention of the subject."[19] To the military, "Essentially, a flashbang is exactly what the name implies. It creates a very brilliant flash, it creates a very large noise. This noise and the flashbolt will disorient the eardrum."[20] In fact, a flashbang can cause serious injury, or even death.[21] According to federal law, it is a "destructive device," the unregistered possession of which is a serious felony. Under the 1994 changes to the criminal code in the Clinton crime bill, a flashbang was upgraded to the status of a "weapon of mass destruction" and any person "who uses, or attempts or conspires to use, a weapon of mass destruction . . . against any person within the United States" is subject to imprisonment for a term up to life.[22]

The use of flashbang grenades against the residents at the Mount Carmel Center was lawful and effective. No one violated the rule about leaving the house with a weapon.

NEGOTIATIONS AND PRESSURE

After the firefight had ended, the Branch Davidians claim that BATF threatened to call in artillery if the Davidians did not surrender that day. In case of a renewed assault, the group made plans to charge out of their home carrying guns and grenades, in a final effort to take as many BATF agents as possible with them to the grave.[23]

Koresh promised to surrender "immediately" if he could deliver a sermon on the radio and on the Christian Broadcasting Network.[24] But this surrender offer was not what it seemed. The plan was for the Branch Davidians to exit the building, and, when federal agents came close, blow up themselves and the agents with grenades. The suicide/murder plan may have been influenced by Koresh's thought that he was going to die from his gunshots wounds from February 28.[25] Although the radio sermon was broadcast, Koresh reneged on the surrender offer, thereby saving numerous lives, including his own. The FBI, not knowing of the hidden agenda in the March 2 surrender, was quite angry that Koresh had called it off. He said he had changed his mind because God had told him to wait.[26]

During the first week of the siege, the tone of the negotiations was generally positive, as FBI negotiators, and one from BATF, established what seemed to be a good rapport.[27] During this first, cordial, week, twenty-three persons left the Mount Carmel Center. Koresh ordered almost all children who were not his biological offspring to leave, overruling objections from their parents who wanted their children to stay with them, since Koresh felt he could not take responsibility for the children.[28]

Middle Period of Negotiations

In the next two weeks, negotiations grew more tense. There were a number of problems, in addition to some inconsistency in the quality of the various negotiators. Most of the discussions with David Koresh, personally, resulted in his expounding his views of the Bible and trying to save the negotiators' souls. Koresh's long monologues were described as "Bible babble" by the FBI. The FBI publicly denounced Koresh's "Bible babble," thus irritating Koresh and undermining negotiators' claims to take his religious views seriously. The other major negotiator for the Branch Davidians was Koresh's top aide, Steve Schneider, with whom the FBI team established a much better relationship, since Schneider engaged in conversation, rather than giving speeches.

The FBI told the public that negotiations involve "tit for tat," and complained that the Davidians were unwilling to negotiate in that way.[29] But to the Davidians, it appeared that the FBI was faithless to its bargains. For example, the initial negotiated cease-fire included the agreement that the dead and wounded would be taken away. But, when Branch Davidian Peter Gent's body was discovered, the negotiators refused to have the FBI take it away unless an adult accompanied it out of the compound, in which case "we'll be happy to take the body as a humanitarian gesture."[30]

For virtually any proposal, by whoever initiated, the FBI sought something from the Davidians, generally the surrender of a child or adult. Thus, the FBI suggested that the Branch Davidians make a videotape, because the FBI wanted to observe the health status of the people under siege. Seeing if the children's hair was clean would provide information about the water supply. But when the Branch Davidians agreed to make the video, the FBI stated that the Davidians should send out a child with the tape, as if the FBI accepting the tape were a favor to the Branch Davidians.[31]

Similarly, the FBI sent in videos of the already released children in order to satisfy concerns of their parents and thereby to encourage the exit of additional children or parents who wanted to join their children on the outside. Nonetheless, the FBI sought a quid pro quo for the videotapes it wanted to send in to the Davidians.[32] The net result was that the Davidians occasionally gave up children expecting no return, and other times expected something from the FBI without having to give up anything, while the FBI sought something from the Davidians even though at times both the "tit" and the "tat" were to benefit the FBI.[33]

Perhaps the most serious breach of an agreement, from the Davidian viewpoint, involved milk. As a result of the February 28 raid and the ensuing stressful siege, several mothers had stopped lactating. Late in the day on February 28, when Koresh sent out most of the children who were not his own, the Davidians also sent out $1,000. The FBI said that the money could be used to pay for care of the children who had left, and to pay for utilities. (The telephone which the FBI sent in could be used only for calls to and from the FBI negotiating room, but the electricity was still on for the building.[34]) The Branch Davidians wanted some of the $1,000 to be used for milk to be sent into the Mount Carmel Center.

In exchange for the milk, the Davidians sent out Mark and Kevin Jones, and then Heather Jones on March 5.[35] But rather than send in the milk, the FBI insisted that more children be sent out. There were two options, said the FBI: "You can send the children out . . . or two, you can send me out the kids and I will send the milk in."[36] The FBI demand for all the children was later reduced to four more children, and then to two children. When Steve Schneider said he could not send out children for milk without Koresh's approval, the negotiator sneered, "You can't do this yourself? I mean this is just milk."[37]

The games regarding the milk, as Steve Schneider and David Koresh repeatedly punned, "soured" after several days. The Davidians suggested the FBI should get ready for a long winter, meaning the following winter, or "just come and kill us like you would like to do."[38] Koresh also suggested, jokingly, that the FBI send in six gallons of ice cream instead, and return two children.[39] The Davidians finally rescinded their request for the milk. Eventually, the FBI sent the milk in anyway. The negotiators told the Davidians that the milk was delivered at the request of Sheriff Jack Harwell (whom the negotiators were using as an intermediary). The FBI press spokesman told the public that the FBI was delivering the milk as a humanitarian gesture to help the children, and said that the Davidians had previously refused to accept the milk.[40]

The FBI negotiators cannot be faulted for trying to use every possible transaction with the Davidians as a tool for getting more people, especially children, to come out. But at the same time, the FBI negotiation strategy made it much more difficult to build a trusting, honest relationship, which would be the foundation for getting all the Branch Davidians to come out together.

A variety of other FBI actions also made negotiations more difficult. The Branch

Davidians were frustrated that the FBI cut off all their contact with the outside world, even jamming their ham radio station. The frustration about the inability to communicate was exacerbated by the FBI and BATF daily press conference, in which the press spokespersons often misrepresented what was going on in the negotiations, or made false statements about the Branch Davidians.[41] For example, the Branch Davidians complained to the negotiators about the FBI press people claiming that Davidians were not free to leave Mount Carmel,[42] or that the Davidians on a tower were making obscene gestures at the Hostage Rescue Team.[43] Among the other falsehoods put out by the FBI during the siege were claims that the Branch Davidians had a tunnel and booby trap system in the back of the property, that the Branch Davidians were using illegal drugs, that most of the Branch Davidians were white (half were people of color), and that the siege was costing two million dollars a day (actually, $130,000).[44]

The Davidians were also upset by the actions of the Bradley tanks.[45] It was their understanding that the original cease-fire agreement included Davidians not threatening law enforcement with firearms in exchange for law enforcement staying off Davidian property. Instead, the tanks not only ran around the Davidian property, but damaged outbuildings and desecrated a cemetery.

The tanks also frightened the children remaining at the Mount Carmel Center.[46] The FBI negotiators insisted there was nothing to worry about since "nobody's going to run tanks through buildings that contain people."[47] In response to the expressed concerns of Cyrus Koresh (David Koresh's oldest child) about a tank assault on the building, the FBI negotiator promised "the last thing that's going to happen is for the government to take any type of offensive action here. It's just not going to happen. You know, we don't hurt babies. You know, we don't hurt women. We don't do those types of things."[48]

HRT commander Dick Rogers later testified that the sole purposes for the Bradley Fighting Vehicles (BFVs) was agent safety; some BATF agents had been wounded by grenades, and the Branch Davidians had a pair of .50 caliber rifles.[49] The nine Bradley Fighting Vehicles that were originally brought on-site were supplemented with two M-1A1 Abrams tanks and five M278 Combat Engineering Vehicles when Koresh told negotiators that he could destroy the BFVs.[50]

Once in place, however, the tanks were used for purposes which did not seem defensive. At various times, tanks would charge at the building. One person inside the building reported that men in the vehicles were shooting the finger at the children, and in at least one case "mooned" the Davidians.[51]

One of the most serious problems for the Davidians was that they did not like the treatment of the children who were sent out in the opening days of the standoff. They considered the mistreatment to violate the negotiated terms of the cease-fire. If the children could not be raised in the Branch Davidian "village," the parents wanted them sent to their nearest kin outside. Instead, the children were kept together in a Methodist church home, under the care of social workers and an "anticult" specialist. The FBI asserted that the children's living conditions were practically identical to the negotiated terms because the children were not sent to foster homes.[52] But to the Davidians, the attempt to protect their children by sending them away from the Hostage Rescue Team siege promptly resulted in the children being held hostage by the FBI.

Treatment of the children who did leave was, by the Davidians' standards, abusive. The Branch Davidians had, long before Koresh arrived, obeyed the Jewish dietary laws. Koresh kept these, and added new dietary rules. After some of the children were sent out, the FBI sent back a videotape which showed the children were being treated well (by FBI standards); the children were eating candy, jumping on furniture, and watching cartoons. The Davidians were horrified by the possible violations of the dietary laws, annoyed by the unauthorized haircuts (as in Bible days, the boys had long hair), and disturbed by the hyperactive behavior of the children, who were taught to be self-controlled and well-mannered.[53] The FBI viewed rambunctious behavior as "just being normal kids" and "kids being kids," while the Davidians were upset at the children being "very misbehaved, jumping on furniture," and explaining, "Our kids are usually much better behaved than that. Usually."[54]

And the Davidians were upset with public suggestions by psychologists and social workers that the children were abnormal, because they were so well behaved.[55] Indeed, they were upset about the idea of the children being treated by social workers or psychologists at all, leading the FBI falsely to deny the charge, instead falsely claiming that the government was only subjecting the children to medical tests to make sure they were all right.[56] Actually, one of the psychologists treating the children, Dr. Bruce Perry, is closely associated with a "cult awareness" group, leading at least to the suspicion that the "treatment" amounted to deprogramming.[57]

But of all the outside factors impeding negotiations, the greatest factor—in retrospect, the decisive factor—was the Hostage Rescue Team. While the FBI negotiators were in a building miles away from Mount Carmel, at Texas State Technical College, the FBI team (the HRT) was laying siege to the Branch Davidians. FBI sniper teams stared at Mount Carmel, while Branch Davidian sentries stared back. At times, the action-oriented HRT would take action, simply because it could stand the inaction no longer. For example, the HRT temporarily cut off the electricity to the Mount Carmel Center—not for any negotiating or other purpose—but simply to boost the morale of their people, and the rest of law enforcement "out and cold and away from home."[58] As Dr. Alan Stone (an independent reviewer of the Justice Department report on Waco) later observed, some of the tactical measures were mainly used to relieve the action-oriented agents' desire to act.[59]

A modicum of apparent conflict between negotiators and the tactical commanders can be useful—the out-of-custody equivalent of "good cop, bad cop" interrogations[60] —but the conflict between the negotiating and tactical team was much more profound. The negotiating team found itself having to come up with excuses for aggressive tactical actions which the tactical team had not bothered to tell the negotiators about. The tactical team grew increasingly frustrated with the negotiators' allegedly excessive patience with the Branch Davidians. The two FBI teams were often at cross purposes.

For example, when the negotiators finally decided to send in the milk, the tactical team promptly cut off the electricity, making it difficult to store the milk. The electricity cut-off postponed the departure of two Davidians whom the negotiators had convinced to make plans to leave, but would no longer even talk about it.[61]

As the first period of friendly negotiations and numerous exits gave way to a tenser, middle period, the FBI began playing over the loudspeaker tapes from the

Davidians' families, began mocking Koresh aide Stephen Schneider for letting Koresh marry his wife Judy,[62] and started to turn the electricity on and off (leaving it off for good on March 12, the same day that Janet Reno was sworn in is as attorney general). During this intermediate period, letters from sympathetic lawyers were sent in. In this second period, ten people left the Mount Carmel Center.[63] Around March 18, according to the FBI, the FBI and Schneider made tentative plans for up to thirty people to exit together, but Koresh canceled the exodus at the last minute.[64]

March 21 and Thereafter

On March 21 and 22, the fate of the Branch Davidians was inscribed, although its sealing would be delayed until April 17, when Attorney General Reno approved the plan to assault the Mount Carmel Center.[65] In response to the exit of several Branch Davidians, the negotiators demanded more; the tactical team significantly stepped up pressure on the Branch Davidians; and the plan for a tank assault on Mount Carmel began to develop.[66]

Shortly after midnight on March 21, two Davidians left, and later during the day, five more exited. The number of people inside had declined to about 88, from a total of about 127 on the morning of the BATF raid. Schneider told the negotiators that Koresh was all but pushing them out; if the FBI had not cut off electricity on March 12 right after sending in the milk, two-thirds of the Branch Davidians would have left, Schneider said. But the negotiators insisted that five or six exits a day was insufficient.[67] Schneider responded that the numbers might grow, since people who were thinking of leaving were waiting to speak with Koresh. The negotiators and Schneider agreed in general that it had been a very successful day.[68]

That same day, FBI commander Jeff Jamar and HRT leader Dick Rogers decided to increase tactical pressure in order to demonstrate the authority of law enforcement.[69] That evening, a loudspeaker barrage began. Among the items blasted on the loudspeakers were the sounds of dentists' drills, locomotives, helicopters hovering, loud obnoxious music,[70] Christmas songs, Tibetan Buddhist chants, previously recorded negotiations,[71] squawking birds, cows mooing, clocks ticking, telephone busy signals, and the cries of rabbits being killed.[72]

The loudspeakers were used contrary to the negotiators' advice, and the advice of the FBI's psychological experts, who had warned that tactical pressure "would succeed in shutting down negotiations and convince Koresh and his followers that the end was near."[73] FBI psychologist Peter Smerick warned that tactical pressure "might unintentionally make Koresh's vision of a fiery end come true."[74] Commander Jamar later evaded questions at a congressional hearing and from a Justice Department investigator about who, if anyone, advised Jamar that the increased tactical pressure would be wise.[75]

The Davidian response was fury and dismay. Koresh said that no more people would be coming out. In fact, only three more persons did exit, once the increased pressure began. Livingstone Fagan left on March 23 under Koresh's orders to expound the Branch Davidian religious message. The other two exits were persons who had sneaked into the Mount Carmel Center towards the beginning of the siege.[76]

For an exhausted Schneider—he was doing most of the negotiations for his side, while the FBI had teams of negotiators going round-the-clock—it was a reversion to the dark ages of religious persecution, and an abandonment by government of the principles of Lincoln and Jefferson.[77] Schneider stated his belief that the BATF wanted blood, that its "sister agency" the FBI would fabricate incriminating evidence and suppress exculpatory evidence, and that the only place he could prove his innocence would be before God. He told the FBI that the FBI's hostile actions made the people inside less comfortable about surrendering to the FBI.[78]

The FBI asked what Schneider would give as a quid pro quo for shutting off the noise. Schneider replied that he would not give anything, but that the noise made it impossible for him to talk people into leaving.[79] For the next week, the FBI would demand that a certain number of residents leave, Schneider would decline, and the FBI would do further damage to Davidian property with the tanks.[80]

FBI tank drivers destroyed a mobile home, a dozen motorcycles, two dozen children's go-karts (expensive presents, recently acquired), tricycles, and bicycles; knocked out the windshield of a bus; and flattened Paul Fatta's pickup. Cars belonging to the adults were crushed by tanks, or ripped apart with crowbars, with the windows smashed and the tires slashed. The Hostage Rescue Team carried away the fence from Mount Carmel's front yard, flipped a bass fishing boat, and overturned a bulldozer that the community had rented—for some $3,000 per month—from a local building supply house. Some of this damage occurred following the decision to prepare for a second assault, although some, such as cemetery desecration, had occurred during the first week of the siege.[81] During the final week, razor-wire was strung all around the building.[82]

Neither destroying children's toys, nor desecrating the cemetery of highly religious people is apt to facilitate negotiations. Instead, the destruction undermined the FBI negotiators who were promising gentle treatment for children who left the compound. The tactical team's decisions to increase pressure, often undertaken without consulting the negotiating team, made the efforts of the negotiating team to build trust more and more difficult.[83] FBI negotiator Byron Sage later acknowledged that having the tanks flatten the cars was a huge mistake that dramatically changed the course of negotiations.[84]

The Branch Davidians were not only outraged at the unnecessary destruction of their property, they believed that the pattern of bullet holes in the cars would have shown that BATF did most of the shooting, and that shots were fired from the helicopters. The Davidians also believed that the empty shell casings near the cars would have shown the heavy volume of BATF fire.[85] On the other side of the legal fence, Assistant United States Attorney Bill Johnston also objected to the destruction of physical evidence, and complained to Attorney General Reno. Subsequently, the FBI agreed to photograph, graph, and grid the areas surrounding the vehicles, but this promise came too late to prevent the elimination of a large amount of evidence.[86]

The Davidians assert the FBI forces carted off cash, jewels, and other valuables from the cars, never accounting for most of it.[87] The Davidians also allege the FBI looted thousands of dollars worth of specialty tools and air compressors from the Mag Bag garage, and helped themselves to souvenir parts from Koresh's Chevrolet Camaro.[88]

Stadium lights were shined on the house all night long. While the FBI officially asserted the lights were a "purely defensive" response to Branch Davidians pointing guns at federal agents or using night vision sights, other officials admitted that the lights were part of a strategy to "tighten the screws" and disrupt sleep patterns.[89]

The increased pressure had the effect of consolidating and frightening the Davidians, making them fearful that the government wanted to kill them. Indeed, Koresh was able to maintain discipline in the Mount Carmel Center by threatening to force members to leave.[90] For example, Victorine Hollingsworth (a fifty-nine-year-old black woman from Britain), testified that the government tanks were "very frightening" and made her not want to leave, to go out there with those people.[91] Most adults did not want to leave; those who did were allowed to do so.[92] Everything the government was doing, including using flashbangs to keep all Davidians indoors all the time,[93] was simply reinforcing Koresh's control by confirming his prophecies that the Davidians would be attacked by "Babylon." For example, Steve Schneider, Koresh's lieutenant, had (like many Davidians) long grown to dislike Koresh personally, but Schneider, like many others, remained a Davidian because of fear of going to hell. The BATF attack and subsequent siege confirmed for Schneider that everything that Koresh had taught was coming to pass.[94]

The ultimate purpose of the attack and siege, supposedly, was to protect the children. The actions by the FBI were hardly designed to make the children (the purported hostages) safer. Turning off the electricity meant depriving the children of heat, but when Schneider complained, the FBI replied that the Davidians should just send the children out.[95] The loudspeakers and all-night klieg lights, depriving the adult Davidians of sleep, would have been at least as efficacious against the children's sleep. To the extent that the risk of any child abuse might be aggravated if the potential perpetrator is irritable, the FBI psychological warfare had the effect of increasing this risk. Koresh had long had severe mental problems; he had been hearing disembodied voices for years.[96] Sleep deprivation, noise bombardment, and other psychological warfare tactics were well suited to aggravating Koresh's problems, eventually with fatal consequences.[97]

Having caused conditions in the residence to deteriorate by cutting off electricity, by blasting frightening noises all night, by running Bradley Fighting Vehicles at the building, and by shining klieg lights on the house all night, the FBI concluded that "the children were living in a deteriorating environment, and that the prospect of sexual or physical abuse was likely as the standoff continued."[98]

Conditions were, of course, deteriorating as a direct result of the government's siege. The Branch Davidians had to negotiate just to get the FBI to allow the Davidians to eliminate the stench of decomposing dogs by burying them.[99] Among other things, the children had to learn to get used to the constant sound of tanks and helicopters. Still, the children continued with their home schooling, worked at their chores, and attended religious services. Children would often peek out a window or doorway, darting back to the interior of the home when a tank or other armored vehicle approached.[100] Branch Davidian Sheila Martin described life at Mount Carmel during the siege:

> When it rained, we collected water in buckets and brought it back into our rooms to wash our hands and clothes. We stayed close to our rooms and didn't venture down hallways as much. We tried to avoid walking past windows.

> We were in the dark every night. Except for the lights outside, we couldn't see anything. We were glad when the morning came because we felt they weren't going to get us then. We stayed as close as possible to each other for encouragement. We prayed a lot and read our Bibles.[101]

As the FBI knew from statements by Louis Alaniz, who had sneaked into the Mount Carmel Center during the siege and who emerged April 17, the water supply was dangerously low, and rationed at one pint per person daily.[102] This particular deteriorating condition meant that a large number of Branch Davidians would have to come out soon. (And thus, there was no urgent need for an assault on April 19.) But as with many other facts regarding the assault, the attorney general was misinformed. She was told that the Branch Davidians had water enough for an extended stay, despite the imminent end of the rainy season, and despite the irreparable gunshot damage to the water tanks. She was told that rationing was for disciplinary reasons, not due to a shortage, and that one water tank was full.[103] The appendix to the Justice Report blacks out the "Water Intelligence" entries for April 13 and 15.[104]

The FBI's psychological warfare tactics had been successful in past encounters with various criminals. But the FBI could not or would not accept that the Branch Davidians were qualitatively different from branch bank robbers. The Branch Davidians' motives for staying in their home (and for being Branch Davidians in the first place) were nothing like the simple desire for loot and comfort which motivated the criminals the FBI was used to. Ordinary criminals and the FBI both shared a similar "cops and robbers" paradigm, while the Branch Davidians were in an entirely separate mental universe.

The HRT and other law enforcement personnel were "getting tired and their tempers were fraying."[105] This justification, unlike most others offered for the assault, was clearly true. Along with an army of media, huge numbers of law enforcement personnel were staged in Waco: 668 from the FBI, 136 from BATF, 6 from Customs, 15 from the Army, 131 from the Texas Department of Public Safety Patrol; 13 from the Texas National Guard, and 31 from Texas Rangers.[106] The law enforcement and media invasion instantly overwhelmed Waco's hotels, motels, and vacant apartments. The FBI agents, like everyone else, were getting tired of being away from their families after seven weeks, and living on fast food in cramped conditions, and spending the cold nights outside watching the Mount Carmel Center.[107] Dr. Tony Cooper, a University of Texas at Dallas professor who has written extensively on police training and conduct, said that towards the end of the siege, he saw "a lack of patience on the part of the authorities, almost a calculated, acted-out petulance."[108] Complaining about the allegedly excessive patience of FBI negotiator Byron Sage, one of the HRT members wrote "Sage is a Davidian" on a portable toilet.[109]

As the siege wore on, tension remained high. The Branch Davidians had set up sentry posts at the doors and windows,[110] while the Hostage Rescue Team had its own sentries and snipers. Both sides must have been mentally drained by the constant boredom, coupled with the constant fear that the other side might attack at any moment. The mental fatigue on both sides undoubtedly played a role in the very poor decisions that were made on both sides, culminating on April 19.

There was also concern of risks to government personnel from accidents, exemplified by an FBI helicopter accident the week before the final assault.[111]

HAD NEGOTIATIONS REACHED A DEAD END?

The FBI's view was that negotiations were going nowhere, that Koresh never told the truth and would never come out. He had promised to surrender on March 2 in exchange for the broadcast of a radio sermon. Koresh had also said that the group would come out "after Passover," but did not specify when.[112] When the Branch Davidians did not surrender immediately after the end of Passover, the FBI felt that Koresh had lied again. From March 2 onward, Koresh's message was clear: he would lead the Branch Davidians out when God told him to, and nothing the FBI did would change his mind.[113]

Koresh was an unbelievably exasperating negotiation partner. For most of the last decade, he had spent his time with people who regarded him as a divinely inspired Bible teacher, and whose lives were centered on listening to him talk. With the FBI negotiators, he would constantly interrupt, overtalk, and attempt to change the topic to the only issue that really interested him: his analysis of the Bible, especially regarding his role as the "Lamb of God." In addition, the FBI complained that he often feigned illness to get out of serious negotiations.[114]

The FBI must have sometimes wished that Steve Schneider were the prophet, and Koresh the follower, instead of the reverse, since Schneider was so much more open to ordinary conversation and human interaction. For example, on March 11, Schneider told the FBI negotiator that Koresh had heard news reports about major astronomical activity, including a star moving rapidly towards the earth. Koresh thought it was a sign, but was unsure of the meaning. The negotiator responded by summarizing for Schneider a story in the morning's *Houston Chronicle* describing the "Guitar Nebula" —a neutron star moving very rapidly through the Milky Way. The star, only ten miles in diameter, was the fastest-moving star ever found. Schneider was extremely interested, and asked the article be sent in. He took the unusual star as a sure sign of the end times, and of Koresh's prophecies; Koresh was, according to Schneider, an excellent guitar player, and thus the Guitar Nebula was especially meaningful.

Later, Schneider woke Koresh up, and brought him to the phone to listen to the negotiator read the entire *Houston Chronicle* article. According to the article, as the star crashed through interstellar gas clouds of different densities, it gave off a glow which looked like a guitar. This phenomenon is called "bow shock," and the Guitar Nebula gave off the most spectacular bow shock ever observed.

Koresh, however, was not impressed. He started giving a science lesson, using the Bible to illustrate his thoughts about particle physics and astronomy. Koresh touted *Chariots of the Gods?* (a book claiming to have found archeological evidence of alien visits to the earth thousands of years ago), and then discussed Ezekiel's flaming chariot (the Bible prophet saw a flaming ship with strange beings descend from the sky).[115] Koresh segued to a lesson about sea monsters described in the Bible, which he called his "pets." The dialogue degenerated into a monologue, broken only by the negotiator's occasional "uh-umm."[116]

As the negotiations dragged on, Koresh often seemed to be trying to provoke the FBI into starting a gunfight. Based on the prophetic books of the Bible which Koresh was focused on (including Zephaniah, Habukkek, and Nahum), the Branch Davidians may have expected that with divine aid, they would win the firefight, despite the tremendous odds against them; or, if they were all killed, they would be accepting their fate as martyrs as foretold in the Fifth Seal of the Book of Revelation.

Annoying as Koresh could be, the negotiations were still getting results. The theory that Koresh was refusing to negotiate in good faith was based on refusing to credit Koresh with releasing any "hostages." A leader of the FBI's efforts "was convinced that the FBI had not succeeded in getting anyone released from the compound through negotiation. . . . [H]e had never been in any previous situation in which he had experienced such a total impasse."[117] But thirty-five persons had left Mount Carmel during the first weeks of negotiations. The "release" of the "hostages" appeared to be followed by punishment, with the loud noises and lights of psychological warfare, shutting off electricity, and crushing Branch Davidian automobiles.[118] By the time the last "hostages" had left the Mount Carmel Center, plans were already afoot to escalate pressure on the Branch Davidians on the grounds that large-scale releases were unlikely.

Despite all the problems, the "consensus of the negotiation staff" was that "the long-term prospect for a peaceful resolution remains good. . . . However, the short-term prospect for total resolution is not encouraging." Long-term was understood as being months rather than days or weeks.[119]

The FBI negotiators viewed Koresh's monologues as "Bible babble," as he tried to convince them that he was the "Lamb" described in the Book of Revelation. The Justice Department report complains that Koresh "refused to discuss any matters of substance."[120] What the FBI negotiators and the rest of the federal government never understood—then or now—was that to Koresh and the other Branch Davidians, God was the *only* matter of substance.[121] If the Branch Davidians could be convinced that God wanted them to come out, they would come out. If they thought that God wanted them to stay, they would stay. The FBI's preferred topics of negotiation—surrender terms—were meaningless to the Branch Davidians. Thus, when the government decided on March 15 that it would no longer listen to anything Koresh had to say about the Bible, the government shut off the only mode of meaningful communication with Koresh.[122]

There were many experts on religion to whom the FBI could have turned for advice. For example, the faculty of Baylor University Department of Religion (located in the city of Waco) had several scholars who had studied the Branch Davidians. These scholars were rejected by the FBI.[123] Not one person consulted by the FBI had expertise on the Branch Davidians, or even on marginal or apocalyptic religious movements in general.[124] Instead, the FBI relied for advice on the Branch Davidians from the persons closely tied to Cult Awareness Network, an organization with its own set of fanatical beliefs, including that the major reason anyone would belong to a "cult" was that the person was brainwashed.[125]

The government's key outside advisor about "cults" was Rick Ross, who had "deprogrammed" several former Branch Davidians. Although he had no counseling experience, he did have an extensive psychiatric record and a felony conviction as a jewel thief.[126] In 1976, one doctor wrote, "I see Ricky as an individual who has sociopathic inclinations."[127] Ross's specialty was "Bible-based cults."[128] During the post-Waco investigation, an FBI report for the Department of Justice observed that Ross "has a personal hatred for all religious cults" and would help any law enforcement effort "to destroy a cult."[129]

In 1995, a Seattle jury ordered Rick Ross to pay 2.5 million dollars in punitive damages, and the Cult Awareness Network to pay one million dollars in punitive damages, for their conspiracy to kidnap a young man, hold him prisoner, and attempt to force him to renounce his membership in a church affiliated with the United Pentecostal Church.[130] (Ross has recently surfaced as an "expert" on "extremist groups," appearing on programs such as "Nightline" to announce how the government should handle militias.)

Ross was an advisor to BATF before the raid.[131] He knew about the raid well in advance; in early February 1993, Ross urged Steve Schneider's sister to hire him to deprogram (kidnap) Schneider, warning of the need to get Schneider out as soon as possible.[132] Psychiatrist Park Elliot Dietz, whom the FBI also consulted, warned against Ross; Dietz noted a television broadcast in which Ross hoped that Koresh would prove to be a coward who would prefer book and movie rights to death. Calling Koresh a coward for ending the siege could backfire, warned Dietz, if Koresh heard the broadcast.[133]

During the siege, Ross was apparently a major source of advice for the FBI. FBI commander Jeff Jamar later told a congressional committee that "a white paper on cults" (presumably from the Cult Awareness Network) had been "very, very useful to us."[134] Ross advised the FBI to humiliate Koresh, in order to alienate the rest of the Branch Davidians from him. That is what the FBI tried to do.[135]

In situations when a "cult" member has been kidnaped, and is in the custody of a deprogrammer, the deprogrammer will often belittle the "cult" leader. Since the kidnap victim is totally isolated from all support, the belittling often does convince the deprogramming subject to reject the leader. But psychological warfare techniques which are used against an isolated cult member are not necessarily so effective when used against the entire cult, when all the cultists can affirm each other in rejecting the psychological warfare. The FBI efforts to drive a wedge between Koresh and his followers had an opposite effect.

Professor Ammerman complained about the "consensus" among FBI officials that "when they encountered people with strong religious beliefs, those beliefs were usually a convenient cover for criminal activity."[136]

For the FBI's chief negotiator Byron Sage, the key proof that Koresh was a con man was this March 17 exchange:

Koresh: . . . it'll come again according to the Seven Seals.

Sage: Made flesh and dwelt among us.

Koresh: of which you are standing right at the door . . .

Sage: DAVID

Koresh: looking at it right in the face and you know it not.

Sage: DAVID

Koresh: Sir.

Sage: With all due respect, my own personal commitment, my own personal faith, my own personal salvation you are not in a position to attack and I'm not here to debate it with you.

Koresh: You do not know my position to attack.

Sage: Okay, I'm just giving an opinion so you can take it or leave [it]. Obviously you, you'll leave it, but let me please make this, this point you need to realize that we are not here . . . so we that can force a confrontation.[137]

Sage later recalled that Koresh's refusal to challenge Sage's faith in his own Christian salvation proved that Koresh "does not buy off on his own con." Koresh might think himself a prophet, but Koresh was "not delusional" and did not think himself the Messiah.[138]

Based on the transcript, Sage appears to have extracted more meaning from the conversation than it merited. Sage's claim about his personal salvation was met with Koresh's retort that Sage did not know Koresh's position. Sage then defines the matter of Sage's salvation as just "an opinion" that Koresh can take or leave, and Sage then changes the topic. Koresh goes along with the change in topic. If Koresh really did think himself a Christ, he still might have allowed Sage to change the topic, rather than insisting on berating Sage for Sage's allegedly mistaken confidence in his own Christian salvation.[139]

Part of the presumption that Koresh would never surrender was based on his fear of the treatment a child sexual abuser might receive in prison.[140] In addition, he was concerned that his children, by various wives, not only would be taken from him, but custody by their mothers would also be denied; the children would, instead, be placed outside the family in foster care.[141] The FBI believed, in addition, that DNA testing could prove not merely parentage but "that [Koresh] had carnal knowledge of women who were underage. He knew that if he came out of that particular compound, he was not going to prison as a religious martyr who defended his religious faith, he was going to prison as an individual who was a child molester."[142] One of the psychiatrists consulted by the FBI noted Koresh's profound fear of prison.[143] This was confirmed by his attorney, Dick DeGuerin, who noted, in particular, the threat of prison to child molesters. DeGuerin indicated that the sheriff had assured him that Koresh would be segregated in jail, and thus safe while there.[144]

And that, apparently, was known to Koresh and his followers. According to Koresh's attorney, he was confident he would be exonerated in court after the standoff ended,[145] as was Schneider.[146] Even the FBI director emphasized that Koresh was thinking of the future, having been successful in court before, and considering the profits from book and movie rights[147] (although Koresh's only interest in selling book and movie rights was based on his lawyer's suggestion that the revenues could be used to pay legal fees). The model Koresh and his associates had to go on was that of Weaver and Harris. Steve Schneider expressed concern about "what you did with that Weaver case. I mean, that already bothered me and here now I'm involved in something like this. . . . What's happening with the Weaver trial? Let me see how you guys do and what kind of freedom and access he has to defend himself in that case."[148]

Despite the obvious possibility of using the Weaver-Harris trial to suggest that Koresh might win his freedom, the FBI did not use that tactic. According to Deputy Attorney General Philip B. Heymann, such negotiation was unthinkable: "Certain peaceful negotiated outcomes, such as holding out the hope that some suspects might escape prosecution for serious offenses, were necessarily foreclosed. For David Koresh, surrender meant giving up everything, and possibly facing a death sentence. There was little for negotiators to offer him."[149]

The preliminary motions involving Weaver had begun before BATF's assault on the Branch Davidian household. Those preliminary motions were not helping the prosecution's case. The Weaver trial began during the Waco siege. To persons who followed the Weaver trial closely, the government's case was a disaster. After the verdict, the judge would comment that much of the prosecution's evidence had helped the defense. The defense won a speedy acquittal without even bothering to call a single witness. It is unknown—and will probably never be known—whether the poor progress of the Randy Weaver prosecution played any role in encouraging the FBI to terminate the Waco standoff regardless of risks of death or injury to the Davidians—or especially if those deaths might prevent a Texas trial as embarrassing as the Idaho one.

The possibility of Koresh and his followers winning freedom would likely have been an effective negotiating tool. Koresh had been extremely interested in the Weaver case even before the BATF attack at Mount Carmel.[150] However, while the FBI was advised to note the possibility of Koresh being exonerated at trial, and to assure Koresh and his followers of due process of law should they surrender to the authorities, the FBI also always told Koresh he would probably go to jail.[151] Minimizing Koresh's chance of obtaining freedom was contrary to the advice of, among others, forensic psychiatrist Park Dietz.[152] Dietz thought that Koresh would choose death over losing power, and therefore the negotiation strategy should "create the illusion that Koresh would not go to prison but would emerge with more followers than he had before."[153]

Other Davidians were assured by the various negotiators that their legal risks might be minimal; that "even for the worst, people make bond"; that they would get a fair trial where they could say anything they wanted; that if they had not shot anyone, they faced few legal problems; that there was a presumption of innocence; and that merely being in the building during the shootout would not mean they were criminally culpable.[154] They were even told they could claim self-defense.[155] Several of these promises turned out to be false. The trial judge refused to let the Branch Davidians offer evidence about BATF misconduct; several Davidians were convicted of serious charges based on nothing more than the fact that they were seen holding a gun during the BATF assault; and the court refused to allow the jury to consider self-defense in determining the Branch Davidians' guilt of voluntary manslaughter, the most serious charge of which they were convicted.

Dr. Dietz also advised the FBI to distance itself from BATF "and express sympathy with Koresh's anti-BATF views."[156] The negotiators varied in their willingness to criticize BATF. One blamed public statements that the Davidians had fired a .50 caliber rifle in the February 28 shootout—constantly denied by Koresh—on BATF "trying to save face."[157] One negotiator read criticisms of BATF from a newspaper column, while not necessarily agreeing with the criticism, and a negotiator cited cases where police were prosecuted for excessive force, and where cases brought by BATF have resulted in acquittals.[158] One negotiator even suggested the possibility of a civil suit against BATF, at a time when the Davidians were still insisting that a baby had been killed in the shootout.[159] On the other hand, another negotiator noted that while BATF and the FBI were different agencies, "we work . . . under the same general umbrella. We have the same . . . guidelines."[160] And Sherri Jewell was told that Koresh had a large role in the shootout; the negotiator dismissed her opinion that BATF had done wrong.[161]

Regardless of whether Koresh could be convinced to come out, many of the other persons inside might have left. According to David Thibodeau (a Davidian inside the residence, who escaped during the fire), about twenty adults were considering exiting, and bringing all the children with them.[162]

From the start, the FBI precluded what might have been the most effective tactic in drawing people out of the besieged residence: contact with family members. Many relatives of the persons trapped at Mount Carmel begged the FBI for permission to talk to the people inside, either in person or by telephone. The FBI's response was "there is no room for family in this operation." All that was allowed was the occasional exchange of audio- or videotapes. Family members repeatedly implored Attorney General Reno, by fax and by registered mail, to allow direct family contact.[163] Attorney General Reno later testified that she had not been told of the families' attempts to communicate with her.[164]

Other potential negotiators were also excluded. Koresh's former attorney Gary Coker was barred (supposedly because he was just looking for a client).[165] A group of ministers from Koresh's former hometown of Tyler, Texas, asked to go in to "have a prayer with them, see if we could help get the kids out." The FBI told them "Not a chance."[166] FBI Director William Sessions offered to negotiate personally, and was forbidden by Acting Attorney General Stuart Gerson.[167] Koresh's stepfather also offered to negotiate, and was rejected,[168] as were Koresh's mother and his grandmother.[169]

Vietnam war hero Bo Gritz had successfully talked Randy Weaver into surrendering to end the standoff in Idaho. Gritz offered to negotiate at Waco, and was rejected by the FBI.[170]

On March 12, Schneider told the FBI that a lot of people would come out, if led by an intermediary such as radio host Ron Engelman. But, perhaps reluctant to endanger a third party, the FBI did not pursue Schneider's offer.

Koresh asked to talk to Robert Rodriguez (the BATF undercover agent with whom Koresh had shaken hands, as Rodriguez left the Mount Carmel Center just before the attack). He offered to send out six-year-old Melissa Morrison in exchange. The offer was refused, on the grounds Rodriguez was upset and assigned elsewhere.[171] The girl died in the April 19 fire.[172]

The FBI did, however, allow attorneys for Koresh and Schneider to go in. One reason may have been that the attorneys were going to deliver the same message the FBI was sending: the Branch Davidians would be treated fairly if they surrendered, would have their day in court, and might well prevail in court.

Even so, FBI commander Jamar was taking a risk that defense attorneys, once inside, would instruct the Branch Davidians to destroy evidence incriminating them in the shooting of the BATF agents. Jamar let the lawyers go in over the objections of the U.S. Attorneys, the BATF, the Texas Rangers, the negotiators,[173] and most of the rest of FBI except for press spokesperson Bob Ricks.[174] That the lawyers were allowed in is among the most powerful pieces of evidence that the FBI was *not* deliberately trying to sabotage negotiations, as some Davidian supporters have charged.

At one point, a face-to-face meeting was arranged between Sheriff Harwell, lead negotiator Byron Sage, and Davidians Wayne Martin and Steve Schneider. Rapport was established, after which, inexplicably, Sheriff Harwell was no longer involved in the process.[175] Instead, the FBI loudspeakers simply broadcast the previous negotiations involving the sheriff.

The FBI limited all types of communications between Branch Davidians and the outside world. Dallas talk-show host Ron Engelman was sympathetic to the Davidians' plight, and made the standoff the constant topic of his show. According to the Branch Davidians, when the FBI found out the Davidians were listening to Engelman's show, the frequency was jammed, as were all other frequencies, so that the only news the Branch Davidians could get was the FBI daily news briefings (for which jamming was temporarily lifted).[176] The jamming was performed by two civilian employees of the Department of Defense, although the government states that jamming was only for television signals, not radio.[177]

The decision to rely more and more on tactical pressure—capped by the April 19 tank assault, was not supported by the FBI's experts. FBI psychological expert Mark Young worried that the FBI tactical team was too "action-oriented." He maintained that tactical pressure should only be used as a last resort.[178]

In April 1995, Peter Smerick, an employee of the FBI's Behavioral Science Center and the lead criminal investigative analyst at Waco, in charge of profiling Koresh, revealed that he felt pressured to change his recommendations. Between March 3 and March 8, 1993, he wrote four memoranda recommending a cautious, nonconfrontational approach. Aggressive tactics, Smerick warned, "could eventually be counterproductive and could result in a loss of life." Along with Special Agent Mark Young, Smerick recommended that the FBI pull back: "This may appear to be appeasement of his [Koresh's] wishes, but in reality, it is taking power away from him. He has told his followers that an attack is imminent, and this will show them that he was wrong." Smerick was told by senior FBI officials that the memos "were tying their hands," and, feeling pressure from those officials, he wrote a get-tough memo on March 9, and then left Waco in disgust. As Smerick later recalled, the more tactical approach preferred by the HRT was being stymied by

> the tone of my memos . . . they felt it was tying their hands, meaning they were not going to be able to increase any type of pressure within that compound and instead were going to have to rely strictly on negotiations. No one at FBI headquarters, at any time, told me or directed me that, hey, write different memos. But . . . [we] all have a tendency of wanting to please our supervisors. And I believe what I did subconsciously is to tone down my memo . . . to more of less fall in line with what they would want to hear.[179]

Dr. Bruce Perry had been placed in charge of evaluating the twenty-one children who had been sent out at the start of the siege. Based on observations of their play, their drawings, and interviews with them, he rapidly found that the children expected all the Branch Davidians to be killed; shortly thereafter, David Koresh would return from the dead, kill all the bad guys, and reunite all the Branch Davidians in Heaven. When the FBI tactical team began intensifying pressure on Koresh, by blasting noise at Mount Carmel all night, Dr. Perry arranged a meeting with the FBI. He suggested that the tactical pressure was counterproductive, given the mindset of the people inside (which he reasonably assumed would be similar to the children's overall mindset). He predicted that the Branch Davidians would try to set up some kind of abstract suicide resulting from a confrontation with the FBI. But if the FBI de-escalated, many of the Branch Davidians would leave, with a core group of "Mighty Men" and other true believers remaining inside.[180]

The negotiators continued to believe that further negotiations would lead to the surrender of more people. But it is not clear if the attorney general was told their views. Nor is it clear that she was told that the behavioral science and negotiation experts believed that a major reason for the stall in negotiations was the aggressive behavior of the Hostage Rescue Team.[181]

Lead negotiator Byron Sage later recalled a conversation with Webster Hubbell (then the second-in-command at the Department of Justice) not long before the April 19 tank assault: "My conversation with Mr. Hubbell was that the negotiations were at an impasse as far as the possibility of a substantial number or substantial flow of people out of that compound in the near future. . . . I did not then, nor do I now feel that we were at a process where we should abandon negotiations."[182]

Attorney General Reno later approved the FBI's plans for the tank and chemical warfare assault based on her understanding that the FBI experts were "unanimous" in favoring such an approach.[183]

THE SURRENDER LETTER AND THE CLOSING OF NEGOTIATIONS

After the impasse that had begun with the FBI's tactical escalation on March 21, there had been little negotiating progress. But on April 14, 1993, Koresh offered to surrender. Koresh's surrender promise obviously made the FBI's April 19 tank and chemical warfare attack—the plans for which were in motion long before the fourteenth—much more difficult to justify. While the FBI saw the letter as the stall following the lie about coming out after Passover, others saw the letter as fulfilling that promise. The surrender letter was sent out on April 14, the day after Passover, as observed by the Davidians.[184]

James D. Tabor is a professor of Religious Studies at the University of North Carolina at Charlotte. On the evening of February 28, 1993, Tabor saw a CNN report of the failed BATF attack on Mount Carmel; Tabor was intrigued that the leader of the Branch Davidians was named "Koresh," which Tabor recognized to be the Hebrew word for "Cyrus." As Tabor watched the news over the next few days, he concluded that neither the media nor the FBI had the slightest clue about the Branch Davidians' biblically based worldview. Tabor contacted his friend Philip Arnold, a scholar at the Reunion Institute in Houston. (The Reunion Institute is a scholarly institute of religious studies, with what fundamentalists would consider a "liberal" orientation.) Both Tabor and Arnold were specialists in the study of apocalypticism—religious predictions of the events to take place at the end of history.

Arnold and Tabor contacted the FBI and offered to help. They found a situation which was both comical and frightening. Baffled by Koresh's biblical reasoning, FBI agents were frantically reading the Gideon Bibles in their hotel rooms, trying to find out what was going on with "the seven seals" that Koresh kept discussing. At first, some of the agents thought that "the seven seals" were marine mammals.[185]

Professors Arnold and Tabor were allowed to meet at length with Livingstone Fagan, a Davidian who had voluntarily left Mount Carmel, and who was then being held in jail. After talking with Fagan—who had previously been a graduate student at a Seventh-day Adventist seminary—the two professors began to understand the Branch Davidian approach to the seven seals, which were the center of Koresh's theology.[186]

The FBI was not particularly eager to work with Tabor and Arnold: "[W]e received no information, no transcripts of negotiation tapes. We were left in a void and could not therefore give the information that would have helped them [the FBI]. . . . We didn't want to be on the telephone day in and day out with David Koresh. We are not qualified negotiators. . . . But we believe that we should have been given transcripts of those negotiations so that we could evaluate them and explain the religious language. If we had done that, we believe that we could have helped resolve the crisis without further loss of life."[187]

The Book of Revelation, the final book of the Bible, portrays the final conflict between good and evil; the forces of evil cause immense destruction before the final triumph of God. In one part of Revelation, the narrator watches "the Lamb" unseal the seals on seven scrolls one by one. As each seal is removed, progressively more amazing events take place. Since 1985, Koresh had taught and his followers had believed that he was "the Lamb" who alone was privileged to understand the seven seals. The unsealing of the seals leads to the following events:

- first seal: A conquering rider charges forth on a white horse.
- second seal: A rider on a red horse destroys peace; slaughter begins.
- third seal: A rider on a black horse holds a set of scales.
- fourth seal: "And I looked, and behold a pale horse: and his name that sat on him was Death, and Hell followed with him. And power was given unto them over the fourth part of the earth, to kill with sword, and with hunger, and with death, and with the beasts of the earth."[188]
- fifth seal: The souls of the dead martyrs slain for God ask "How long, O Lord," until God avenges their blood on their murderers. The martyrs are told "that they should rest yet for a little season, until their fellowservants also and their brethren, that should be killed as they were, should be fulfilled."[189]
- sixth seal: A great earthquake ushers in the day of wrath.[190]
- seventh seal: The commencement of a fantastic battle in the sky.[191]

As Tabor and Arnold discovered, the Davidians believed that they were currently in the fifth seal. The first seal had been fulfilled in 1985 when Koresh, receiving a vision while on a visit to Israel, was told of his mission to unseal the seven seals, and thereby became the rider on the white horse. Seals two, three, and four had been fulfilled, the Branch Davidians believed, by various events in 1985 through 1992.[192] Accordingly, the time was ready for the fifth seal.

Tabor and Arnold did not believe in the Branch Davidian theology, but they did understand that the Branch Davidians (unlike the professional criminals who are more usual targets of the Hostage Rescue Team) would never surrender simply because the forces of the government were overwhelming. To the contrary, the Branch Davidians, seeing themselves in the fifth seal, were expecting to be massacred.

When the fifth seal is uncovered, dead martyrs (including, from the Davidian viewpoint, the victims of the February 28 BATF assault) ask "How long, O Lord" until God avenges the martyrs. The martyrs find that they must wait "a little season" until all of the true believers "should be killed." Following the deaths of the rest of the believers (namely the people remaining alive in Mount Carmel), the fifth seal would be completed. The sixth seal would commence with a tremendous earthquake; God would punish an unbelieving world, and the end of the world would begin.

The "little season," as the Davidians saw things, would logically be less than a normal three-month season. Presuming that the fifth seal had commenced with the February 28 attack, the Davidians expected to be massacred sometime sooner than three months after February 28.[193]

Tabor and Arnold set out to convince Koresh that an imminent massacre was not foreordained.[194] Unlike the FBI, Tabor and Arnold tried to communicate within Koresh's interpretive framework. They arranged to appear on KRLD radio talk-show host Ron Engelman's program, knowing that the Davidians listened to Engelman's show. Tabor and Arnold explained how the "little season" described in the fifth seal might not necessarily mean a literal three-month season; the time referred to might actually be quite long; "little season" was *chronos* in the original Greek, and could, in the original, refer to a time period as long as a year.

Arnold and Tabor also argued that, thus far, Koresh had not had the opportunity to present his understanding of the seven seals to the world at large. Using Revelation and other biblical texts, Tabor and Arnold suggested that the Bible forecast that before the final destruction of the unbelieving world, the world would have an opportunity to listen to and choose to accept the true word of God—meaning Koresh's interpretation of the seven seals. Revelation forecast that 144,000 faithful would be saved, and Koresh needed to speak to the world at large, so that 144,000 might believe. Koresh's interpretation of the seven seals, rather than being hidden as Koresh had thought it would be, was actually meant to become known to all the world. As Revelation 10:11 states: "And he said unto me, Thou must prophesy again before many peoples, and nations, and tongues, and kings."[195] Arnold and Tabor also pointed out that Paul, generally regarded as the greatest propagator of the Christian faith, had composed much of his writings while held in prison by the Romans.

On March 15, Schneider mentioned Professor Arnold as part of a possible solution to the issue of the seven seals.[196] On March 19, the FBI agreed to send in a tape of Dr.

Arnold. Unfortunately, there were often delays between when the FBI agreed to send something in, and when the agreement was fulfilled. For example, at the same time the FBI agreed to send in a tape from Dr. Arnold, the FBI also agreed to send in a copy of the original search and arrest warrants, which were not actually delivered until March 28.[197]

After the FBI had delivered an initial tape from Dr. Arnold, he and Dr. James Tabor initiated a radio show interview on April 1 geared toward the Branch Davidians and their religious language.[198] With the FBI's consent, a tape of the radio interview was sent in to Mount Carmel on April 4. Passover was coming up—the Davidians celebrated a full Passover lasting eight days—and Koresh and the Davidians were praying for guidance.[199] In the next week, Koresh sent out several hostile letters, threatening in biblical terms to destroy the FBI and everyone else who was confronting him.[200]

But on April 14, Koresh sent out a letter stating that God had told Koresh that Koresh would be "given over into the hands of man." The letter explained that Koresh was writing his analysis of the seven seals in the Book of Revelation, and "Upon completion of this task, I will be freed of my 'waiting period.' I hope to finish this as soon as possible and to stand before man to answer any and all questions regarding my actions."[201]

According to Koresh's attorney, based on conversations with Schneider and, later, some of the survivors, "the mood on the inside had definitely changed on the night of the 13th and the morning of the April 14th."[202] The Davidians were joyful "'because we knew we were coming out, that finally David had got his word of how to do this legally . . . and theologically in terms of his system.'"[203] The Branch Davidians now believed that Koresh "had received his mission, that he was working on writing his interpretation of the seven seals, and that everyone inside was relieved that they didn't have to die now, that the prophecies were not being fulfilled now, and that this would be resolved."[204] The adults knew that they would be going to jail for at least a while, but that was acceptable. Schneider indicated that he was certainly sick of the residence, and he noted that Davidians were talking about "gray walls" (jail) being better than where they were.[205]

Further indicating an intention to stay on earth for a significant while longer, Koresh allowed attorney DeGuerin to meet with New York lawyers regarding book and film rights to the David Koresh story.[206]

The April 14 letter was quite significant for several reasons. Koresh, who thought that he had been chosen by God to be the "Lamb" who would interpret the seven seals, had thought that God wanted the interpretation kept secret from the world at large.[207] But in the April 14 letter he wrote that:

I have been praying so long for this opportunity; to put the Seals in written form. . . . I want the people of this generation to be saved. I am working night and day to complete my final work of the writing of "these Seals." I thank my Father. He has finally granted me the chance to do this. . . . As soon as I can see that people, like Jim Tabor and Phil Arnold have a copy I will come out and then you can do your thing with this Beast.

Yahweh Koresh[208]

DeGuerin, convinced that the letter was an "iron-clad" surrender promise, took the letter and showed it to Jeff Jamar and Bob Ricks. When Ricks expressed disgust at Koresh for not giving a firm date, Jamar cut Ricks off, saying, "No, we've got all the time it takes."[209] Unbeknownst to DeGuerin, the FBI plans for the tank and chemical warfare assault were already well underway.[210]

By the time of the tank attack on April 19, Koresh had finished his writing on the first of the seven seals. (A Davidian fleeing the burning building brought out a computer disk containing the text.) Professor Tabor is "absolutely persuaded" that Koresh would have come out in one or two weeks, after finishing the writing.[211]

The FBI, which had already determined to end the siege with a tank and chemical warfare assault, and was only waiting for permission from the attorney general, displayed little interest in Koresh's surrender letter. The negotiators made it clear that they believed Koresh's seven seals offer was just another stalling tactic.[212] The daily chronology log, in the Department of Justice report, simply states, "Koresh had established a new precondition for his coming out."[213] The Tabor-Arnold tape and Koresh's surrender letter are never even mentioned in the Justice Department report.

The FBI, consistent with its preference for using anticultists to get information about Koresh, sent the Koresh letter of April 14, and four Koresh letters from the previous week, to psycholinguistics professor Murray Miron at Syracuse University.[214] Dr. Miron, who has no academic qualifications in religious studies or the sociology of religion, and who had been involved with the "anticult" Citizens' Freedom Foundation (which later became the Cult Awareness Network) had trouble understanding some of the letters. He apparently thought that the April 14 letter's request that the seven seals manuscript be examined by Professors Arnold and Tabor was some kind of discussion about literary agents named Arnold and Tabor.[215] Even so, Professor Miron recognized the importance of the manuscript:

> It is apparent the muse is upon him [Koresh] and he is feverishly working on the manuscript. . . . He can be expected to value these writings in the highest regard. Their publication/dissemination could be a powerful negotiating tool. Koresh expects the authorities to try to suppress his work. Only he, bringing the manuscript out himself, would insure that it reaches the eyes of the audience he desires. . . .
>
> Although Koresh declares upon completion of his book he will surrender, this reference to divine intervention presided over by an angel may provide an additional condition allowing him further delay, as he has in the past.[216]

Professor Miron's conclusions make common sense. On the one hand, Koresh clearly had a strong interest in coming out so as to disseminate his message. On the other hand, Koresh had changed his mind before, and might do so again.

On April 17, the FBI asked Dr. Park Dietz, a respected forensic psychologist (who had never met or spoken with Koresh) for his opinion. He pronounced that Koresh "would not come out" and that "Koresh would continue to make sexual use of the children who remain inside."[217]

It is possible that the promise to surrender was a lie.[218] In the congressional hearings of July 1995, Rep. Charles Schumer repeatedly summarized himself, or elicited summaries from witnesses, all of the lies Koresh told the FBI regarding his plans to surrender. But as the two lawyers involved in the negotiations pointed out, once the attorneys got involved:

> there was never a promise of a specific date, and there never was a broken promise by Mr. Koresh. . . . Once Dick DeGuerin became his lawyer, Mr. Koresh never made a false promise to do anything that he didn't do. . . . Now, there were some other promises before then, but you [Representative Schumer] have to put it in context. Until there was somebody he trusted, he didn't trust those people out there. But once Mr. DeGuerin became involved, that's when it happened.[219]

If Koresh were lying, that would have become evident by the end of April.

While the FBI would insist that the surrender plan was merely a stall, with no evidence of progress, tapes of the negotiations certainly demonstrate that Koresh was progressing. A few days after the surrender letter was delivered, Koresh had completed his first draft on the first seal, and was using it as a basis for work on the second seal.[220]

After the April 19 fire, the FBI found support for its view that Koresh had no intention of coming out from the fact that, when they "did the crime scene, they still found 40-some automatic weapons that had not been reconverted back to semiautomatic, the very best evidence . . . if they had come out to face trial—in other words, there was no preparation on their part to come out and face a court of law with those weapons still in there."[221] But had the Davidians wished to reconvert any machine guns (discussed in more detail in chapter 5), they still had several days, at least; Koresh had only finished one seal. In addition, of the Branch Davidian gun experts, one, Paul Fatta, had been at a gun show on the morning of the BATF raid, and was not available to do any gunsmithing, and the other, Mike Schroeder, was dead.

From the FBI's point of view, the failure of Koresh to produce parts of his manuscript of the seven seals in the days following the letter of surrender was evidence that Koresh was simply using another stalling tactic. In fact, however, the FBI did not tell Koresh or the attorneys that progress reports were due[222]—at least not until grounds around the Mount Carmel Center were being cleared; by that point, Koresh, in response to the latest increase in tactical pressure, had slowed his work on the seals.[223] The day before the tank attack, the last demand of the negotiators was not that Koresh send out proof of progress, but proof of good faith, in the form of the Koresh-ordered exodus of fifty Davidians; the Branch Davidians responded that the day's hostile FBI actions left them with no interest in leaving.[224]

It is possible that Koresh meant the letter when he wrote it, but might have backed out later. Or it is possible that he might have taken the only step possible to spread his message to a world which contained many people (at least, the 144,000 of the Book of Revelation) who were curious about his message, and interested in hearing or reading it.

After the April 19 fire, FBI officials were asked why they could not have waited for Koresh to finish his manuscript. On April 20, Jeffrey Jamar, the special agent in charge of the Mount Carmel operation, insisted that the FBI has "absolute certain intelligence" that the manuscript promise was "another sham, another stall."[225] Whatever this intelligence was has never been disclosed.

To the contrary, transcripts of the April 16 negotiation tapes quote Steve Schneider: "He [Koresh] said it's between twenty-eight and thirty pages or something like that. I saw the pages all over the place." That same day, Koresh told the FBI that he had completed the first seal, and he asked for a word processor and batteries to speed completion of the remaining six seals. On the morning of the tank attack, FBI surveillance devices heard Schneider say, "Here's the manuscript; the first one is about completed, it was worked on all night." (Koresh had been revising the first seal.) At the 1995 congressional hearings, Jamar testified if there had been any indication that Koresh was really working on a manuscript, Jamar would have called off the tank assault.

Jamar further testified that in a negotiation, Schneider said "I haven't seen the first page." In fact, the transcript has Schneider say "He [Koresh] says he's ready on the second [seal], but I haven't seen the first one." Schneider then said that he had seen pages "all over the place" but had not had the whole first seal document assembled for editing, and Schneider would not release the document until it had been edited.[226] (Schneider edited much of what Koresh wrote, Koresh being a dyslexic with poor spelling and grammar.)

Whatever the significance of the surrender letter, it appears that FBI Director Sessions[227] and Attorney General Reno[228] were not informed about its existence, even as they were being asked to approve a new assault.[229] Jamar eventually testified that there was not enough reason to apprise the attorney general of the surrender letter because the FBI's understanding and judgment of the letter was that "it was not a serious plan. It was just another delaying tactic."[230] Presumably, any reports from Jamar to the attorney general would have reflected Jamar's perception that "the game was constant . . . there is a sameness to it all [the negotiations] after a while."[231] But Jamar remembered making no report himself, believing someone—possibly lead negotiator Byron Sage— had. Sage's recollection was that there was no point in conveying the surrender offer. "We were still in the process of trying to determine through the negotiation process the veracity of the offer."[232]

Ruth Riddle, to whom Koresh had been dictating the manuscript, brought the manuscript out on a computer disk during the fire. The manuscript begins with a poem, "Eden to Eden," about a pair of lovebirds. There is an introduction, followed by chapter 1, discussing the first seal.[233] The third-to-last paragraph of the first chapter quotes the Book of Joel, "Blow the trumpet in Zion, sanctify a fast, call a solemn assembly: Gather the people, sanctify the congregation, assemble the elders, gather the children, and those that suck the breasts: let the bridegroom [Koresh] go forth of his chamber, and the bride [the Branch Davidian church] out of her closet."[234]

Koresh adds the following commentary: "Yes, the bride is definitely going to be revealed for we know that Christ is in the Heavenly Sanctuary anticipating His Marriage of which God has spoken. Should we not eagerly ourselves be ready to accept this truth and come out of our closet and be revealed to the world as those who love Christ in truth and in righteousness."[235]

Thus, it was time for the Branch Davidians to "come out of our closet" and to share their saving message, to "be revealed to the world as those who love Christ in truth and in righteousness." This would be necessary so that the 144,000 believers spoken of in the Book of Revelation could hear the truth about the Lamb, and be saved.

No one will ever know for sure if Koresh would have surrendered after completing the manuscript. But the words that Koresh was dictating only a short time before the FBI assault were clearly a justification for coming out.

CS CHEMICAL WARFARE AGENT

"Any time you start the day by gassing women and children, you have to expect it to end badly." Wesley Pruden, *Washington Times*, April 20, 1993.

The FBI deceived the attorney general regarding the effects of the CS chemical warfare agent, which at Waco was used in the most massive CS assault against civilians in American history.[236] Experts assured the attorney general that CS produced short term discomfort, but had no long term effects and posed no special threat to pregnant women, children, or others. It was, in short, merely to cause tears, coughing, and sneezing, and at worst a feeling of suffocation and mild burns in sensitive people.[237] She was not told those were not the only effects, particularly when the CS agent was used inappropriately—indoors.

And almost no one seemed concerned about using a military riot control agent in a civilian law enforcement environment.[238] Deputy Treasury Secretary Roger Altman was one exception. After being briefed on the FBI plan for the CS attack, even with the assurance that the "gas would not be followed by an assault," he predicted that the attorney general would not approve the plan, since Koresh would eventually "concede" anyway, and "The risks of a tragedy are there."[239]

Nature of CS

Although commonly referred to as "tear gas," CS is actually a fine white crystalline powder. As a powder, CS can plug up gas masks, a feature touted by its manufacturer.[240] CS sticks to everything.[241] A study in the *Journal of the American Medical Association* noted that direct contact with the CS powder (O-chlorobenzalmalononitrile) could cause sustained blistering skin burns, and while recovery is normally rapid (within minutes), side effects lasting up to weeks could include coughing and shortness of breath, and persons with asthma or chronic obstructive lung disease could require hospitalization. In addition to causing crying and temporary blindness, the CS can induce nausea, vomiting, and possibly diarrhea—the building lacked normal bathroom facilities—and headache.[242] The authors of the article questioned its use "under any conditions."[243]

Use of CS gas in war was barred by the Chemical Weapons Convention, which the United States signed at Paris in January 1993, although the treaty has not been ratified by the Senate.[244]

CS Indoors and on Children

There appears to have been no particular consideration given about CS's proposed use indoors. However well expert proponents of CS can defend its intended use, that intended use is not indoors: "When gases are thrown into . . . shelters a condition is obtained which differs completely from that following use in the open air. All the data available for CN, DM, and CS are calculated for low concentrations obtained by dispersion in the open air. But it must be emphasized that when powder is thrown into a closed area much higher concentrations build up."[245]

According to Amnesty International, CS chemical warfare agent is "particularly dangerous when used in massive quantities in heavily built-up or populated areas . . . or when launched directly into homes or other buildings." One manufacturer of CS stopped selling the product to the Israeli government in 1986 because CS was being introduced, with fatal consequences for forty persons (including eighteen babies), into buildings occupied by Palestinians. Amnesty International reports that eighty people worldwide had been killed by CS misuse as of 1992.[246]

The U.S. Army *Manual on Civil Disturbances* notes that although CS and other agents "will not seriously endanger health or cause death when used properly, their use in buildings or other closed areas requires caution to avoid producing excessive concentrations of the agent. . . . The dispersers should not be used to introduce a riot control agent directly into a closed structure except under extreme circumstances."[247] An army field manual explains that CS "causes severe burning of the upper respiratory passages, pain, and involuntary inability to open the eyes."[248]

The FBI plan which the attorney general approved called for a forty-eight-hour gas attack. The government also knew that gas masks were available. But gas masks are not manufactured for small children. (One reason is that they lack the lung capacity to breathe through gas masks.) Thus, the degree of suffering from the CS attack, as the FBI must have known, would be in inverse proportion to the criminal culpability of those exposed to it. As the *Washington Post* later reported, when CS gas is put "into enclosed areas such as rooms or small courtyards . . . such misuse of the gas can be harmful, especially to small children, the elderly, pregnant women and people suffering from heart or lung problems."[249]

As the Hostage Rescue Team began to prepare for the siege at Ruby Ridge, before the killing of Vicki Weaver, one of the plans for action if the Weavers did not comply with FBI demands was that CS "will be deployed into the main house. . . . The deployment of gas into the residence presents a high degree of risk to small children. There may be a one-year-old baby inside."[250]

Dr. Alan Stone, one of the independent reviewers of the Department of Justice Report on Waco in the fall of 1993, noted the case history of a baby suffering a two-to-three-hour exposure to CS gas, the exposure resulting in first-degree burns on the face, severe respiratory distress typical of chemical pneumonia, and an enlarged liver; the baby would have died but for his immediate treatment in an emergency room, followed by twenty-eight days of hospitalization, during which the baby had to be hooked up to a respirator. "The infant's reactions were of a vastly different dimension than the information given the AG suggested," Stone noted. "It certainly makes it more difficult to believe that the health and safety of the children was our primary concern."[251] In another case cited by Dr. Stone, a half-hour of exposure to CS indoors caused the death of an adult.[252]

Incapacitating Effects of CS

With regard to the idea that the CS was supposed to drive the Branch Davidians out of their house, an army field manual explains: "Generally, persons reacting to CS are incapable of executing organized and concerted actions and excessive exposure to CS may make them incapable of vacating the area."[253]

Others have noted that CS, inserted into enclosed places like buildings, may immobilize by causing nausea, vomiting and vertigo; may hamper movement of rioters because of severe onslaught of symptoms; and should not be used "where innocent persons may be affected . . . [or] where fires may start or asphyxiation may occur."[254] (The disorienting effects of CS were believed by the FBI to be an effective means of preventing the coordinated action necessary for a mass suicide.[255])

The use of CS at the Mount Carmel Center was analyzed by retired U.S. Army Colonel Rex Applegate, one of the world's leading authorities on riot control,[256] who helped to develop the ferret round used to deliver CS.

Regarding the effect of CS, Colonel Applegate notes:

> [T]he immediate physical and psychological symptoms are so unpleasant that, during a first time exposure, blind panic usually ensues and most individuals have an immediate and overwhelming desire to exit the area of concentration. In this writer's opinion, no amount of ideology, or devotion to a messiah will materially affect this automatic reaction. This must have certainly been true among the women, children and the elderly in the Davidian compound.
>
> It is reasonable to assume that individuals in the Waco building were subjected to such CS gas concentrations, that they were incapacitated to the point where they were physically unable to exit the gassed areas.[257]
>
> The total amount of CS gas delivered into the compound from the CEV vehicles is estimated to have been from 8–10 projectile loadings. The CEV vehicles made a total of 6 tear gas deliveries. Total estimated amount of CS projected during the 6 hour period was approximately 2,000 grams plus 26,000 grams of methylene chloride.[258]

Assuming an even dispersal of the chemical warfare agent, the amount of CS inserted into the house on April 19 was approximately 2.5 times the effective dosage for a healthy young male, and approximately half the lethal dosage.[259] Colonel Applegate wrote that:

> The degree of CS concentrations undoubtedly varied from room to room depending on the numbers of Ferrets, penetration through windows, doors, thin wood walls, etc. Totally incapacitating CS concentrations had to be present in some areas. . . . Lacking specific "gassing" details, room dimensions, etc. it is impossible to estimate where the major concentrations of CS were present. Aside from later prevailing, cleaning winds, these concentrations at some time had to be excessive, if not lethal, in some locations.[260]

CS Delivery Agents

Apart from the CS itself, the delivery and carrying agents posed additional risks. CS was at first inserted by spraying from the thirty-foot booms on the M-60 tanks.

According to the Justice Report, the FBI used carbon dioxide as the propellant for the CS spray. Carbon dioxide is not, however, the only carrying agent for CS. Acetone and ethanol are also carrying agents, and are more effective at dispersing the CS than is carbon dioxide. They are also highly volatile and flammable. In case of a fire, acetone or ethanol would serve as accelerants[261]; the presence of acetone and ethanol is fully consistent with the extremely rapid speed at which the April 19 fire spread throughout the building. Autopsies of several of the Branch Davidians found ethanol in their blood or urine. (Acetone was not tested.)[262]

A few minutes after spraying began, Bradley Fighting Vehicles (tanks) began shooting in additional CS. The BFVs shot "ferret" rounds (a 40mm canister). During the morning of April 19, about 400 ferret rounds were shot inside.[263] The ferret is fired at such speed that it can penetrate windows and thin walls, such as those at the Branch Davidians' home.[264] The ferrets themselves, at close range, can cause serious injury or death.[265]

The sprayers and the ferret rounds both used methylene chloride as the carrying agent for the CS. Each ounce of CS was suspended in roughly two pounds of $MeCl_2$. Methylene chloride is toxic, and may be metabolized by the body to form carbon monoxide. Its combustion may produce toxic gases, including phosgene, which was used in poison gas warfare during World War I.[266] According to Dow Chemical's Material Safety Data Sheet, methylene chloride forms flammable vapor air mixtures. "In confined or poorly ventilated areas, vapors can readily accumulate and cause unconsciousness and death."[267] Methylene concentrations inside Mount Carmel on April 19 reached 8,000 ppm. This is sixteen times the level which can cause intoxication, and is 80 percent of the fatal dose.[268]

The $MeCl_2$ would not have been spread evenly. Since $MeCl_2$ is heavier than air, it would have accumulated in very high concentrations on the floor of the first story of the building. This is precisely where the women and children were huddling in blankets, in the cold storage room in the middle of the house.

Given the extreme pain which CS can cause, many persons have found it incomprehensible that Branch Davidians did not flee the building. One answer is that many of them were incapacitated by the very high dosage of methylene chloride. The effects would have been cumulative to the carbon dioxide (which reduces oxygen intake) and to CS, which causes fluid to accumulate in the lungs, and which makes breathing difficult, and which is also disorienting and incapacitating.

Although high winds arose after two hours, almost all of the chemical warfare agent had already been delivered when the air was still and toxic concentrations of CS, $MeCl_2$, and other chemicals would have reached their peak.

Hydrogen Cyanide

Disturbing as all of the above information about CS chemical warfare agent is, there is another danger of CS that came to light over a year after the April 19, 1993, inferno. The autopsies of some of the Waco victims included traces of cyanide,[269] a strange fact since there was no evidence that anyone at Mount Carmel took cyanide pills; if the government's numerous listening devices inside Mount Carmel had picked up any evidence that the Branch Davidians had contingencies involving cyanide pills, it is doubtful that the government would have kept secret this damning fact about the Davidians.

Burning CS can sometimes turn into cyanide. If burning CS is sprayed with water, it can form hydrogen cyanide (HCN) fumes.[270] One source of water was the wet towels used by mothers in an effort to protect their children from the CS. At congressional hearings, Attorney General Reno's adviser on CS, Dr. Henry Salem, at first acknowledged only that such wet towels, while protecting the children from the effects of the CS getting into their lungs, would also increase skin irritation. Under cross-examination by Representative Barr, he also indicated that combining the fire with the chemicals could have generated hydrogen cyanide.[271] CS is metabolized in the body to form cyanide and the toxicity of hydrogen cyanide is increased in the presence of carbon dioxide, used as a propellant of the CS at the Mount Carmel Center.[272] Hydrogen cyanide is the active ingredient in Zyklon B, the gas used to exterminate Jews, gypsies, and others in the Nazi death camps.[273] Hydrogen cyanide is also used in some American states where the death penalty is administered by gas.

So, in contrast to the mass suicide with cyanide at Jonestown, this time it was the government that may have forced cyanide on the "cultists." It is possible that a number of people in the compound may have been unable to escape because they were immobilized, either as a direct result of the CS and its toxic carrying agents, or as a result of cyanide poisoning. Forty-four of the Branch Davidian corpses would eventually test positive for cyanide, with at least some with enough to reach the concentration in the blood where a coma or death could result.

The fate of the children at Mount Carmel was not dissimilar to that of the children at Auschwitz: gassing, followed by cremation.

What the Attorney General Was Told

It cannot be known exactly what Attorney General Reno was told about CS, but some clues can be gleaned from the testimony given by Dr. Henry Salem of the U.S. Army Defense Command at the Aberdeen Proving Ground, Edgewood, Maryland, since he was Reno's chemical/biological advisor during the consideration of the FBI's planned April 19th assault, and, basically, her only source of information on CS.[274] His view was that, "According to all of the evidence that is available, there is no difference in the sensitivity for children, adults, or the elderly. . . . There was no difference in sensitivity to the CS by young people, older people, and the infirm."[275] And while some who looked at the CS use discussed the increasing problems with increasing dosage,[276] Salem believed that "after you reach the irritating point, if you increase the concentration, it does not really increase the symptoms."[277]

At the 1995 congressional hearings, Rep. Sonny Bono told Janet Reno that two members of his staff, in one day's research, had found an article in the *Journal of the American Medical Association* (August 4, 1989) which stated that CS could kill children in as little as ten minutes. Representative Bono stated that he found it impossible to believe that the attorney general, with all the resources of the Department of Justice, could not have found out that same information.

During the hearings, testimony explained in detail how Attorney General Reno had been deceived. On April 12, one week before the FBI tank assault, the FBI gave her a briefing book which claimed: "Experience with the effects of CS on children has been extensively investigated. Available reports indicate that, even in high concentrations or enclosed areas, long term complications from CS exposures is extremely rare." But according to the testimony of Department of Defense toxicologist Harry Shaw, there have only been two studies of the effect of CS on children. One study showed that a few hours exposure to CS had put a baby in a hospital for twenty-eight days. The FBI plan was to gas the children for forty-eight hours.[278] When Henry Salem finally detailed the briefing material he had furnished to Attorney General Reno, the only item was a 1971 British study promoting use of CS in open-air crowd-control situations.[279]

After Shaw's testimony, Attorney General Reno testified, and insisted that no one had misled her about the effects of CS, about child abuse, or about anything else: "We didn't suffer from misinformation. I wasn't misled."[280]

Despite the perceived need to end the standoff quickly, the federal government's decision to use chemical warfare was not inevitable. Twenty years before, the American Indian Movement and the federal government were engaged in a standoff at Wounded Knee, South Dakota (the site of the infamous massacre in 1890). The standoff had dragged on for fifty days, and the Justice Department presented President Nixon with a plan for helicopters to blanket Wounded Knee with tear gas, forcing an end to the siege. The briefing on the tear gas plan had barely begun when President Nixon cut it short: "There will be no dead babies at Wounded Knee." The Wounded Knee siege was quietly ended twenty-five days later.[281]

The lives of babies are too important to depend on the contingency of an attorney general or a president having good judgment. Legislation should prohibit the use against American civilians of any chemical, biological, or other warfare item which has been banned from international warfare.[282]

D DAY

The FBI supposedly was merely escalating pressure on Koresh when it began to ram Koresh's house with tanks to pump in CS.[283] The plan was supposedly implemented to allow some Branch Davidians to escape and to encourage serious negotiations with Koresh.[284] The official "plan was to insert gas [*sic*] periodically over a 48-hour period, to then withdraw, and then to wait as large numbers of people left the compound."[285] "It was not law enforcement's intent that this was to be 'D-Day.' "[286] That, at any rate, was the plan as approved by the attorney general, and emphasized in her conversations with the president.[287]

Janet Reno testified:

> I directed that if at any point Koresh or his followers threatened to harm the children, the FBI should cease the action immediately. Likewise, if it appeared that as a result of the initial use of tear gas, Koresh was prepared to negotiate in good faith for his ultimate surrender, the FBI was to cease operation.[288]

In case of risk of harm to the children, she recalled that her exact words were: "Get the hell out of there. Don't take any risks with the children."[289]

Ironically, as Harvard professor and Justice Department reviewer Alan Stone observed, the FBI attack was essentially directed at children, despite Reno's orders. It was known that the children, unlike the adults, would not be protected from the CS by gas masks. It was a "conscious strategy . . . to stir up the maternal instinct of the mothers" by causing their children's suffering, hoping that they would desert their religion for their children.[290] The government gave the mothers a choice: surrender, or watch their children be tortured. As Amnesty International has documented, presenting parents with this type of choice is a tactic used by totalitarian regimes. Never again should it be used in America.

Rep. Henry Hyde pointed out one of the problems with using CS to cause mothers to desert their religion was that the plan incorrectly assumed religious beliefs were lightly held. "Was it reasonable to assume that these parents, who have devoted themselves to this Koresh, evil person, who were taught that the outside world was Babylon and that an FBI attack was the beginning of the apocalyptic end, would pick up their infants and run out into the embrace of the Babylonians? Or is it more reasonable to assume they would pick up their suffering children, put wet rags over their mouths[291] and try to find a remote corner where they could pray and wait? In other words, the question isn't what would you or I do, but—if the gas were coming in, but what would a Branch Davidian do? And I don't think much attention was given to that. . . . The true believer can be approached not through tape recordings of rabbits being slain, but theological approaches."[292]

Part of the FBI's confidence that the children could be safe was inferred from the fact that, on February 28, "during that entire fire fight, not a single child was harmed. . . . Children were probably in some place that was safe. You give them advance warning, they can either bring them out of the compound or they can put the children somewhere that's safe."[293]

In fact, there was a safe place for the children to be hidden. The sprawling Mount Carmel Center included a bus that had been buried underground, for use as a tornado shelter. A trap door in main building led to a hallway which connected the bus with the main building. Even after the 2,000-degree fire on April 19, the air in the school bus was clean and cool.[294]

But during the trial of the Branch Davidians, FBI witnesses admitted that the orders were to use the tanks to direct the CS into the end of the building where the entryway to the bus would be found, in order to prevent people from coming down the hall and getting into the bus. The FBI's Larry Potts explained that the goal of the gradual assault was "to move people toward the center of the compound . . . on an incremental basis. . . . We still held out a lot of hope that even though that area had been gassed that they would go through that area, put the children through the area, and down into the bus, which did have clean air." Representative Barr may not have been alone in wondering how you get people to escape by using gas to herd them toward the center of the building, away from the exit leading to the cool, clean air.[295]

Moreover, on April 19, one of the first actions of the tanks was to deliberately destroy access to the underground bus where it was expected that the children would want to hide (and where they would have survived the fire).[296]

Attorney General Reno authorized return of gunfire, and later praised the FBI's response to Davidians shooting at the tanks; rather than shooting back, the FBI escalated the chemical warfare attack.[297] The FBI only had the attorney general's permission to escalate beyond gradual use of CS if there were a violent response from the Davidians. But the FBI knew, from its expert advisers, that a tank attack would be met with Davidian defensive violence.[298] The FBI field commander, Jeffrey Jamar, indicated that he believed there was a 99 percent likelihood that the Branch Davidians would respond to the CS assault with gunfire;[299] the gunfire would result in an immediate shift from the gradual forty-eight-hour Plan A to the all-at-once Plan B. Webster Hubbell, associate attorney general at the time of Waco, also thought Davidian shooting at the tanks "a likelihood," perhaps more than a likelihood, but not necessarily as likely as Jamar's 99 percent expectation.[300] FBI Assistant Director Larry Potts later said that he thought return fire was possible, but hardly certain. He thought that, between the initial planning in late March, and presentation of the final plan to the attorney general, a plan had been developed which "everybody believed significantly decreased the chances of them firing on us when we inserted the gas."[301]

But of course not "everybody" believed that the modified plan reduced the chance of Davidian gunfire. The FBI commander at Waco, SAC Jeffrey Jamar, still thought return gunfire 99 percent likely. But his opinion was apparently not passed up the chain of command. As a result, the attorney general underestimated the chances that the gradual Plan A would be escalated to the much more aggressive Plan B.

As Colonel Applegate evaluated the situation:

> When Attorney General Reno approved the . . . plan, she relinquished control. This resulted in the Bureau initiating what appears to be a pre-planned escalation of the tear gas attack, instead of the agreed upon, gradual tear gas insertion strategy. Attorney General Reno had also understood that April 19th was not to be considered a final termination or "D" Day. . . . The FBI was aware, from the very first planning stages, that they would encounter gunfire. This was a known factor from the very beginning of negotiations with Attorney General Reno. They counted on this probability (gunfire from the Davidians) to enable them to immediately go into a plan of escalation. Attorney General Reno was probably unaware of this when she "signed off" granting tactical control to the FBI at the scene of operations. Consequently, the FBI, apparently motivated by various pressures and factors, decided to bring the entire matter to an immediate conclusion.[302]

The plan envisioned by the attorney general—insertion of the CS, with no other violent action by the government—lasted only six or eight minutes. Then, the tanks began destroying the building. As Colonel Applegate summarizes:

> Expected gunfire from the Davidians caused and allowed them [the FBI] to escalate the failed plan. After the first two hours of gas attack, a great deal of command frustration took place as no Davidians surrendered. It is estimated the majority of 400 Ferret rounds had been expended. This was a massive concentration of CS, considering the estimated 2 hour time frame. It was prior to reported high winds. . . . It would appear that only a relatively small amount of gas was inserted into the building, still

with no evacuation by the Davidians. Apparently most of the occupants were either not mobile, incapacitated and couldn't evacuate, or were restrained from doing so, maybe both conditions were taking place.[303]

While the FBI at first used a telephone—promptly rendered ineffective by a tank's steel tracks severing the line[304]—and loudspeakers to insist the CS agent was just a slight increment in pressure, everything the FBI did and said to the Branch Davidians indicated the FBI personnel on the scene were treating April 19 as D day.

Consistent with a D day operation (as opposed to an intensification of negotiation pressure), as soon as the Combat Engineering Vehicles began ramming holes in the house and inserting CS, a loudspeaker system announced that everyone was under arrest and should come out immediately: "You are under arrest. This standoff is over."[305] The loudspeaker also said that anyone's going to the tower (perhaps to escape the chemical warfare agent) "will be considered to be an act of aggression and will be dealt with accordingly."[306]

By midmorning, despite pleas from the Branch Davidians to reconnect the telephone—their life-line to the outside world—the FBI refused to reactivate the telephone unless the "Davidians clearly indicated they intended to use the phone to make surrender arrangements."[307]

THE ATTORNEY GENERAL

The FBI did not have an easy time obtaining the attorney general's permission for the tank and chemical warfare attack to end the siege. On April 12, FBI officials, including Director Sessions, asked for approval for a chemical warfare ("tear gas" in their words) attack on April 14, claiming that Koresh was unlikely ever to surrender.[308] On April 14, Director Sessions brought along former commanders of the army's Delta Force and army toxicologist Dr. Harry Salem to tell the attorney general that CS was safe, nonflammable, and would not harm pregnant women or children. HRT head Dick Rogers told her that the HRT would soon have to "stand down" for rest and retraining. When Attorney General Reno asked why SWAT teams could not be used in relief, she was told that the HRT was "essential." Again, permission was refused.[309]

When informed of the attorney general's decision, Director Sessions asked for a personal meeting with her. She asked him instead to prepare a document detailing the plan, the state of negotiations, and conditions inside Mount Carmel. The documentation was delivered on Saturday, the plan was approved, and the assault took place on Monday. The Justice Report states that Attorney General Reno only gave the documentation a cursory overview, although she had testified to Congress that after all the briefings, "Then I started asking the questions . . . asking every question I knew to ask."[310]

Attorney General Reno later explained that her two reasons for approving the assault were the "fatigue" of the Hostage Rescue Team and physical abuse of babies. She explained: "We had information that babies were being beaten. I specifically asked 'You really mean babies?' 'Yes, he's slapping babies around.' These are the concerns that we had."[311] The Justice Report's chronology states that sometime in the week preceding April 19 "someone made a comment in one of the meetings that Koresh was beating the babies." Attorney General Reno asked the person who made the comment if he was sure. She recalls that she was given "the clear impression that, at some point since FBI had assumed command and control for the situation, they had learned that the Branch Davidians were beating the babies."[312]

Who told the attorney general about child abuse? Webster Hubbell, the second-ranking official at Justice at the time, later stated, "I remember it [the comment] specifically, but I can't remember who said it."[313] Justice Department spokesman Carl Stern said, "All I can tell you is, I was personally present when Ms. Reno was told by the FBI that somebody inside the compound had reported that children were being beaten or struck."[314]

Throughout the siege, Attorney General Reno's predominant concern had been the children still inside.[315] The day after all the children had died in the fire, President Clinton echoed Reno's statement about ongoing child abuse, claiming that the FBI "had reason to believe that the children who were still inside the compound were being abused significantly, as well as being forced to live in unsanitary and unsafe conditions."[316] Likewise, White House spokesman George Stephanopoulos asserted that there was "absolutely no question that there was overwhelming evidence of child abuse in the Waco compound."[317]

Child abuse, as the FBI likely knew, was the hottest of hot buttons for Reno; as a state attorney, she had prosecuted several sensational child abuse cases (some of which did not result in a finding of guilt).[318] According to FBI Director Sessions, there was "no contemporaneous evidence" of child abuse; given the many FBI listening devices inside the compound, Sessions's conclusion appears accurate.[319] According to FBI Waco spokesman Bob Ricks, "To say that we had intelligence that that was going on, I can't say that."[320] Several months later, Attorney General Reno said that she might have misunderstood FBI comments, and there was no evidence of ongoing child abuse in the besieged home.[321]

As on other issues related to FBI conduct, Attorney General Reno was being inappropriately generous to the FBI. She had not misunderstood; she had been deceived by an FBI determined to get her approval for the tank attack.

In a May 5, 1995, speech, Attorney General Reno explained her decision not in terms of child abuse, but of child safety:

> They [the FBI] told me that the conditions were deteriorating inside. I was concerned about the safety of the people inside. The behavioral experts were telling me that children—for a siege that could last a year—it would have a lasting effect on them.[322]

In that same speech, she also offered a new primary version for why the April 19 attack was necessary: the "first and foremost" reason was that "law-enforcement agents on the ground concluded that the perimeter had become unstable and posed a risk both to them and to the surrounding homes and farms. Individuals sympathetic to Koresh were threatening to take matters into their own hands to end the stalemate [and] were at various times reportedly on the way."[323]

This "first and foremost" reason of a threat to the perimeter was unsubstantiated. The only example cited by Attorney General Reno was the "Unorganized Militia of the

United States." According to an early April 1993 cable from the FBI field office in Indianapolis, the "Unorganized Militia of the United States" consisted of Indianapolis lawyer Linda Thompson, who had appointed herself "Adjutant General." She was going to "drive a van with other people to Waco, Texas, and stage a protest in support of the constitutional right of assembly and to have weapons." Mrs. Thompson and whoever would join her would "have an assortment of shoulder weapons" which "would be unloaded and used only as a form of protest."[324]

Linda Thompson did eventually play an important role regarding Waco. She made a widely circulated video, aptly titled "The Big Lie," which incorrectly accused the FBI of using flame-throwing tanks to burn the building down. But Ms. Reno's claim that Ms. Thompson's potential presence necessitated an immediate tank assault is no more plausible than Ms. Thompson's claim that Ms. Reno wanted to murder the Branch Davidians.

Conditions in the Mount Carmel Center were unsanitary, but this condition was, of course, the result of the FBI conducting a siege, rather than the desire of the Branch Davidians to live in unsanitary conditions.

As for the long-term condition of the children, according to Reno, "the Bureau, time after time, asked Koresh for some evidence that the children were okay . . . the bureau sent in videotapes, asking Koresh to do something to prove that the children were okay. . . . We did not receive verification that the children were okay."[325] The thought that the children might be dying haunted the attorney general, as she considered the possibility of the siege ending one day in the future, and the discovery of children dead from disease, starvation, or Koresh's assaults.[326] But if Attorney General Reno had these worries, she was grossly misinformed. The *third* Davidian videotape was sent out on March 28. On March 31, 1993, FBI spokesman Bob Ricks announced that Koresh had sent out a videotape showing sixteen of the seventeen children and all four of the teenage girls still inside. News of the video was carried, among other places, in the *Washington Post*, making Attorney General Reno's ignorance of the video—and use of the alleged absence of such a video as the reason for the tank assault—either an indication of fatal carelessness, or a falsehood.[327]

In early March, the Branch Davidians had made other videos with extensive interviews of people at Mount Carmel, including the children, all of whom looked healthy. The tapes were seized by the FBI, and not released to the public until after the April 19 fire. Thus, three tapes were unquestionably sent out during March.[328] How could Attorney General Reno—long after the fact—claim that there were no tapes, when the FBI had told the whole world that there were tapes?

An explanation not related to child abuse was offered by the assistant director of the FBI's criminal enforcement division: Koresh had treated their efforts to negotiate with contempt, and it was not in the nature of law enforcement officials, who had seen the federal officials killed on February 28, to let the group go on with its way of life: "These people had thumbed their noses at law enforcement."[329] Police science scholars Vance McLaughlin and Steve Smith use Waco as an illustration of what they call Rodney King syndrome: "when the police are not successful in their initial attempts to bring a subject under control using the tactics and techniques they have been taught." Having absorbed the lessons of police subculture that the police must always be in control, an officer who cannot control an unusual suspect becomes frustrated, angry, and then violent.[330]

There is perhaps no institution in the United States government with more unchecked power than the Department of Justice. The job of attorney general is therefore one of the most difficult in the entire cabinet. It cannot be performed effectively by an attorney general who looks the other way at misconduct by her own employees. Nor can it be performed effectively by an attorney general who, having been deceived into approving a plan which directly led to the unnecessary deaths of seventy-six persons, fails to discipline a single one of the persons who deceived her.

NOTES

1. U.S. Department of Justice, *Report on the Events at Waco, Texas, February 28 to April 19, 1993* (Redacted Version, Washington, D.C.: October 8, 1993) (hereinafter "Justice Report"), p. 238.

2. On March 2, 1993, two women in their seventies, Margaret Lawson and Catherine Matteson, voluntarily left Mount Carmel. They were promptly arrested and the next day were charged with attempted murder, and held in jail. Charges were dropped a week later, but the women were still held as "material witnesses." The FBI's Jeffrey Jamar noted, "the first two adults . . . were elderly ladies, they were charged with capital murder. I complained to the U.S. Attorney and they changed it to material witness warrants. And it was a horrible message sent back." United States House of Representatives, Subcommittee on Crime of the Committee on the Judiciary and the Subcommittee on National Security, International Affairs, and Criminal Justice of the Committee on Government Reform and Oversight, *Joint Hearings on Activities of Federal Law Enforcement Agencies Toward the Branch Davidians*, 104th Cong., 1st sess., July 19–August 1, 1995 (Washington, D.C.: Government Printing Office, 1996) (hereinafter "Joint Hearings"), part 2, p. 334.

Kathryn Schroeder was held without bail as a "material witness." Steve Schneider told the FBI that Schroeder's incarceration was not the group's "expectation" for what would happen when she surrendered in order to see her children. Lee Hancock, "Agents Use Light Against Sect as Psychological Measure," *Dallas Morning News*, March 15, 1993. Nineteen-year-old Oliver Gyarfas was likewise detained. Christy Hoppe, "Teen-ager Who Left Sect Ordered Held as Material Witness," *Dallas Morning News*, March 18, 1993.

3. Dick DeGuerin, testimony Joint Hearings, part 2, p. 75.

4. Joint Hearings, part 1, p. 917. Chief FBI negotiator Gary Noesner explained that the forces, such as the HRT, are inclined toward the "action imperative" while the negotiators lean toward "active listening," where they try to "find ways to explain to the barricaded subject why it is in his best interest to seek a nonviolent solution." He went on to note: "I do not awake from nightmares or have trouble sleeping at night . . . because everything that I predicted would happen, did happen." United States House of Representatives, Committee on Government Reform and Oversight in conjunction with the Committee on the Judiciary, *Investigation into the Activities of Federal Law Enforcement Agencies Toward the Branch Davidians*, Report 104–179, 104th Cong., 1st sess. (Washington, D.C.: Government Printing Office, August 2, 1996) (hereinafter "Committee Report"), pp. 56–57.

5. FBI negotiator Frederick Lanceley told the internal investigators from the Department of Justice that when he heard Dick Rogers tell the group at the first meeting at Ruby Ridge that it would be "no long siege," he perceived that Rogers did not intend to engage in negotiations, and that Lanceley conveyed this impression to Rogers. Rogers responded, "good," which confirmed Lanceley in his impression. United States Department of Justice, *Department of Justice Report Regarding Internal Investigation of Shootings at Ruby Ridge, Idaho, during Arrest of Randy Weaver* (cited as "DOJ Internal Investigation of Ruby Ridge"), available at http://www.courttv.com/library/government/ruby.html. Rogers's initial plan was, however, rejected by headquarters in Washington precisely because it lacked negotiations.

6. Carol Moore, *The Davidian Massacre* (Frankin, Tenn.: Legacy Communications and Gunowners Foundation, 1995), pp. 222–23.

7. Jeffrey Jamar, Joint Hearings, part 2, p. 299.

8. "I didn't know at the time that there were conflicts between the tactical people and the nego-

tiators." Janet Reno, Joint Hearings, part 3, p. 400. "Smerick notes that the FBI commanders were action oriented. They wanted to treat Koresh not as a negotiating partner, but rather as a psychotic criminal who needed to be caught and punished." Quoted by Representative Hyde, Joint Hearings, part 3, p. 428.

9. Gary Noesner, Joint Hearings, part 2, p. 316. While there had been a deadly shootout on February 28, the Branch Davidians did nothing physically threatening for the next fifty days. They were, however, much better armed than the Weavers had been.

10. Philip B. Heymann, "The Hostage Team is for Hostages," *Washington Post*, October 20, 1995.

11. The HRT's motto is "To save lives," but, as in Idaho, this would turn out to be a particularly cruel version of doublespeak. The hostage-holding Hostage Rescue Team was referred to by the FBI as the "tactical" component at Waco, with the other component being the negotiators. "Tactical" is the word currently used for paramilitary groups like the HRT or SWAT Teams. Members of these groups often belong to the National Tactical Officers Association. The primary meaning of "tactical" is "of or pertaining to military or naval tactics." *The New Shorter Oxford English Dictionary*, vol. 2 (Oxford: Clarendon Press, 1993), pp. 3201–3102. Thus, "tactical" is literally accurate, but lacks the frightening edge of words like "paramilitary" or "militaristic."

12. U.S. House of Representatives, Events Surrounding the Branch Davidian Cult Standoff in Waco, Texas. Hearing before the Committee on the Judiciary, U.S. House of Representatives, 103rd Cong., 1st Sess., April 28, 1993 (hereinafter "Hearing"), p. 14.

13. The rule:

Agents are not to use deadly force against any person except as necessary in self-defense or the defense of another, when they have reason to believe they or another are in danger of death or grievous bodily harm. Whenever feasible, verbal warnings should be given before deadly force is applied.

(FBI *Legal Handbook for Special Agents*, § 3–6.4.)

14. "Reno Approves New Rules on Force," *Washington Times*, October 23–29, 1995 (national weekly edition), p. 5 (Associated Press).

15. Justice Report, p. 42.

16. Justice Report, p. 62.

17. One issue is whether the FBI would have been justified in using sniper fire to kill Koresh in an effort to end the confrontation with minimal additional bloodshed. While killing generally violates the rules of engagement, the FBI insisted that the children in the building were being held and used as hostages. FBI Deputy Director Floyd Clarke told the House Judiciary Committee that the Branch Davidians had used their children as human shields. Hearing, p. 77. In hostage situations, the suspect presumably is such a threat to the lives of others that the rules of engagement would allow sniper fire to remove a hostage holder. Richard J. Davis, one of the outside experts called in by the Justice Department to review the incident, suggested such a killing would only have been appropriate in a true hostage situation, where people were being held against their wills. U.S. Department of Justice, *Recommendations of Experts for Improvements in Federal Law Enforcement After Waco* (Washington, 1993), Davis Recommendations, p. 23.

18. U.S. Department of the Treasury, *Report on the Bureau of Alcohol, Tobacco, and Firearms, Investigation of Vernon Wayne Howell also known as David Koresh* (Washington, D.C.: Government Printing Office, September 1993) (hereinafter "Treasury Report"), p. 59.

19. Justice Report, p. 98.

20. Testimony of Maj. Mark Petree, Joint Hearings, part 1, p. 409.

21. Testimony of FBI Agent Thomas G. Rowan, Trial Transcript, *United States* v. *Brad Branch et al.,* Crim. Action Nol. 2–93–Cr–046 (W.D.Tex., 1994) (hereinafter "Trial Transcript"), p. 5232; Reavis, *The Ashes of Waco*, p. 152. Koresh's attorney testified that after he returned from the house after meeting with his client:

I brought to the FBI agents and showed them a spent grenade. That's what is sometimes euphemistically called a flashbang. It is a grenade. It has an explosive charge in it. It is very dangerous. It can blow your hand off. It can blow your face off. It can kill. I would have brought out some of the unexpended grenades that the ATF threw in, but I was worried about bringing out a live grenade, so I left them there.

(Dick DeGuerin, Joint Hearings, part 2, p. 87.) The Branch Davidian defense called a witness, Sandra Sawyer, to testify that a flashbang had pretty much blown her arm off. Trial Transcript, pp. 6806–6809.

22. 18 U.S.C. § 2332a.

23. Ron Cole, "Davidian Tells Truth about Waco," *Boulder Weekly*, July 27, 1995, p. 8; Moore, *The Davidian Massacre,* pp. 218–19.

24. Negotiation transcript, March 17, 1993, 1:45–2:05 P.M., available at http://www.wgbh. org (Koresh admits that he reneged on his promise to come out, because "My commander in chief told me to wait.")

A compact disc of the sermon (along with two songs written and performed by Koresh) is commercially available. David Koresh, *Voice of Fire* (Otho, Iowa: Junior's). The sermon is also available on the Internet, at http://www.ime.net/~mswett/march2.html.

The government apparently broke its promise that medical care would be provided to the victims of the February 28 attack, by later insisting that medical care would be provided only after surrender. Jack DeVault, *The Waco Whitewash: The Mt. Carmel Episode Told by an Eyewitness to the Trial* (San Antonio: Rescue Press, 1994), pp. 171–72.

25. Dick Reavis, *The Ashes of Waco: An Investigation* (New York: Simon and Schuster, 1995), ch. 24. On March 2, several mothers talked by telephone with their children who had left on February 28. One mother told her child "see you on the other side." Transcripts of BATF Tapes of the Negotiations between Federal Law Enforcement and the Branch Davidians, February 28–April 19, 1993 (hereinafter, "Negot. Tapes"), no. 12B, March 2. The FBI negotiators were justifiably concerned about the implications of her statement.

26. Negot. Tapes nos. 15–16, March 2; no. 53, March 5. Koresh's religious system allowed him to lie: "The Man-child can fulfill the prophecies even to the point of alluring his people deceitfully." The Chosen Vessel, *Seven Seals,* Book One (1996), p. 240.

27. The best rapport was actually established by BATF Agent Jim Cavanaugh, who stayed less than a week. Negot. Tapes no. 84, March 7. Although the Branch Davidians liked him, he was in the horrible position of trying to be friendly with those he held responsible for murdering four of his colleagues.

28. James D. Tabor and Eugene V. Gallagher, *Why Waco? Cults and the Battle for Religious Freedom in America* (Berkeley: University of California Press, 1995), p. 73. Five older girls asked to stay, and were allowed to do so, as were the children of Juliet Martinez. Ibid.

29. Negot. Tape no. 79, March 7; Jamar, Joint Hearings, part 2, pp. 320, 332.

30. Negot. Tape no. 85, March 7. The Davidians, with advance notice and approval from the FBI, left the building briefly to bury Peter Gent near the residence on March 8. To the FBI, the initial agreement to take the bodies referred to known dead, and the body of Gent was not covered by the initial agreement (since the Davidians thought he was missing, but did not then know he was dead until March 5. Negot. Tape no. 55, March 5). But to the Davidians, it appeared the FBI was reneging on a "tit for tat" negotiation. Negot. Tape no. 58, March 5. Curiously, the FBI apparently did not call the Davidians' bluff by asking why they were so concerned about Gent's body but not about the body of the baby they falsely asserted was killed by the BATF raiders, or even about Perry Jones, whom the Davidians got permission to bury two days later. Negot. Tapes no. 101, March 9–10; no. 103, March 10.

31. Negot. Tape no. 85, March 7. Reavis, *The Ashes of Waco,* pp. 227–29, suggests it was the Branch Davidians' idea. The FBI's Jeffrey Jamar, however, suggested that the FBI asked for tapes of children to force the Davidians to clean the children if they were not already clean, to show that the children were healthy. Joint Hearings, part 2, p. 473.

32. Negot. Tapes no. 98, March 9; no. 119, March 12.

33. Negot. Tape no. 124, March 13. At other times, there were simply orders from the FBI with no suggestion of negotiation. This was the case with what the FBI called "rules of safety," dealing with the circumstances under which Davidians could leave the residence, whether they could go to the tower, and the like. E.g., Negot. Tapes no. 96, March 9; no. 242, April 18.

34. Negot. Tape no. 86, March 7.

35. Negot. Tapes no. 50, March 4–5; no. 54, March 5; no. 84, March 7; Joint Hearings, part 2, pp. 331–32.

36. Negot. Tape no. 66, March 6. Those actually were two slightly different options. The Davidians insisted that since the milk was for the children, if they sent the children out, there was no

need for the milk. The FBI's view was that the quid pro quo for Heather Jones was not milk, but photographs and a videotape of the children who had already left. But Kathy Schroeder complained that the Davidians wanted milk and instead were sent photos "to pull on my heartstrings," in an effort to lure her, and other mothers whose children had left, out of the Mount Carmel Center.

37. Negot. Tapes no. 78, March 7; no. 79, March 7; no. 80, March 7. Koresh thought withholding the milk was "cruel" since it related to children, who were "neutral." Negot. Tapes no. 98, March 9; no. 79, March 7.

38. Negot. Tapes no. 66, March 6; no. 78, March 7; no. 79, March 7; no. 80, March 7; no. 84, March 7.

39. Negot. Tape no. 78, March 7.

40. Negot. Tapes no. 93, March 8; no. 96, March 9; no. 98, March 9; no. 155, March 23; Joint Hearings, part 2, p. 319. To the FBI, the Davidians had rejected the milk, since they had rejected the milk as offered, with children as the quid pro quo. Negot. Tapes no. 79, March 7; no. 80, March 7.

41. "[I]t's hard to . . . have this trust relationship when the freedom of the press has been cut off, and there's only one-sided story given by your agencies which is . . . far from factual." Negot. Tape no. 51, March 5.

42. Negot. Tapes no. 67, March 6 (Steve Schneider), and no. 90, March 7–8, 1993 (Sherri Jewell).

43. Negot. Tape no. 93, March 8 (Steve Schneider).

44. Moore, *The Davidian Massacre,* pp. 237–38.

45. Shortly after the siege had begun, former McLennan County District Attorney Vic Feazell (who had unsuccessfully prosecuted Koresh for attempted murder in 1987), noted the mobilization of military equipment. "The feds are preparing to kill them," said Feazell. "That way they can bury their mistakes." Roy Bragg, "Ex-Prosecutor Laments Agents' 'Storm Trooper' Tactics," *Houston Chronicle,* March 2, 1993, p. 7A.

46. Negot. Tapes no. 44, March 4; no.49, March 4; no. 64, March 6; no. 66, March 6; no. 84, March 7; no. 88, March 7. One FBI explanation for the wild driving of tanks was that it was young agents' only chance to drive tanks, so they were acting a bit reckless, like kids. Negot. Tape no. 53, March 5. Larry Potts later explained, with an infelicitous choice of words, "We had to put our hostage rescue people through a crash course on learning to drive those vehicles." Joint Hearings, part 3, p. 68. In response to the suggestion that the Bradley's 25 mm barrels posed a threat, the FBI insisted the tanks had no barrels, just "tubes in a barrel mount." Negot. Tapes no. 84, March 7; no. 85, March 7.

The FBI offered to remove the tanks if the Davidians agreed first to send out four women and four children, and then, once the tanks were removed, if everyone else in the compound came out. According to the negotiator, presumably disappointed that Koresh gave up his plan to come out on March 2 when God allegedly told him it was not yet time to leave, the tanks and surrender proposal was given to Bob Ricks by God. Koresh wondered why God would tell two different things to two different people. "Maybe God's trying to get us to fight, or something." Negot. Tape no. 68, March 6.

47. Negot. Tape no. 95, March 8–9.

48. Negot. Tape no. 88, March 7.

49. "'No Question' Fire was Set by Davidians," *Washington Times,* August 1, 1995 (Federal News Service transcript).

50. Victoria Loe, "FBI's 'A-Team' Plying Varied Skills in Sect Talks," *Dallas Morning News,* March 14, 1993; Moore, *The Davidian Massacre,* p. 233; Justice Report, pp. 123–24. While Steve Schneider complained regularly about the tanks, Koresh was more threatening, saying the Davidians would use something bigger than .50 caliber, something that could incinerate part of a tank, and also saying the Bradleys were not a concern, "that's why we haven't done nothing to them yet." Negot. Tapes no. 49, March 4; no. 53, March 5; no. 68, March 6. It is possible that Koresh contemplated using his grenade launcher to fire homemade grenades, which would have done little damage to the tanks. The FBI, however, leaped to the conclusion that Koresh had light antitank weapons (LAWs) and rockets. The negotiators asked several Davidians why they had LAWs, and insisted to all the Davidians who denied having such weapons that they just did not know about them. Negot. Tapes no.64, March 6; no. 70, March 6; no. 74, March 6–7; no. 87, March 7.

The presence of LAW rockets was inferred by the FBI from Koresh's references to incinerating tanks or blowing them fifty feet in the air, neither of which a LAW rocket would normally accomplish, and despite Koresh's express statement that it was explosives the government kept saying he had which could send the Bradleys forty or fifty feet in the air. Negot. Tapes no. 41, March 4; no. 49, March 4. The FBI paid no attention to the suggestions by Koresh that he might just have BB guns, or that he might have an atomic bomb, or that he might have placed landmines on the property. Negot. Tape no. 26, March 3.

Like BATF, the FBI made extensive use of U.S. military equipment and training. Materials supplied under the Freedom of Information Act make it clear that, unlike BATF, the FBI did not pretend Waco was a drug operation. Therefore, the Defense Department was reimbursed by the Justice Department, military equipment had military markings covered, and military personnel trained FBI personnel but did not themselves use the equipment in operations against Mount Carmel Center. E.g., Justice Report, p. 123. In practical terms, the FBI actions appeared as militaristic as the BATF's: a tank attack looks military even if some markings are covered up, and even if the unseen driver is not a soldier. As the House Committee Report observed, "images of the tanks and other military vehicles gave the impression that the FBI was using excessive force together with military weapons and tactics against U.S. citizens, contrary to our civilian law enforcement tradition." p. 7.

51. Clive Doyle, Joint Hearings, part 3, p. 117. The mooning was condemned by negotiators as unprofessional and unacceptable, and caused by "frustration and anguish," Negot. Tape no. 89, March 7; Reavis, *The Ashes of Waco,* p. 249.

52. One FBI explanation was that the nearest of kin were inside the compound. Negot. Tape no. 88, March 7.

53. Reavis, *The Ashes of Waco,* p. 227; Negot. Tape no. 79, March 7. The videotape which the Davidians sent out to attempt to communicate with the outside world (and which was intercepted and withheld by the FBI), contains numerous complaints about treatment of the children who had been sent out. The photographs showed the children eating hot dogs, leading to the question as to whether that meant the children were being fed pork in violation of their religion. The FBI negotiators insisted they were beef or chicken or turkey hot dogs, eventually settling on beef. Dietary laws often seem petty to outsiders, but of fundamental importance to believers. One of the great tales of Jewish tradition, the story of Eleazer and his seven sons, recounts in horrifying details how a pious old man and his seven sons allowed themselves to be tortured to death rather than profane themselves by eating pork (4 Maccabees. Shorter versions of the story appear in 1 and 2 Maccabees.) As would later be the case with the FBI's actual treatment of the children who were sent out, BATF's plans for the children at the Mount Carmel Center indicated a failure to appreciate or respect the religious views and dietary restrictions of the innocents in the compound. BATF's Bill Buford proudly testified, "if we were successful . . . and were able to neutralize the people on the inside, . . . that's what we were striving for. We even took extraordinary measures to make sure that we had people there to take care of the children after the situation was neutralized, and were even going to bring Happy Meals out for all of the children from McDonald's, once we got them outside the compound." Joint Hearings, part 1, p. 719.

54. Negot. Tapes no. 98, March 9, and no. 99, March 9, views of David Koresh and Kathy Schroeder. While the FBI was attempting to lure children outside with reports of soft drinks and candy, the parents viewing the videotapes complained that the children were "eating candy all day long, drinking soda pop . . . hyper as heck." Negot. Tape no. 99, March 9 (Judy Schneider). And it is not entirely clear that soft drinks and candy were a great lure for some of the children. Asked his favorite food, Cyrus Koresh, responded "healthy food," although he sometimes liked burritos, chips, and Cheetos. Negot. Tape no. 14, March 2.

55. In discussions with one negotiator who admitted to having, like Koresh, been spanked as a child, Koresh warned that the social workers handling the Davidian children were liable to put the negotiator's parents in jail. And shortly before sending Heather Jones out, Koresh said to her, so the negotiator could hear, "are you ready? You scared? Okay. Now, you may need to jump around and scream a bit so you'll be considered normal." Negot. Tape no. 50, March 4–5.

56. Negot. Tapes no. 50, March 4–5; no. 86, March 7.

57. Justice Report, pp. 171–74. Negotiators denied a Koresh accusation that the children were being deprogrammed. Negot. Tape no. 53, March 5.

58. Jeffrey Jamar, Joint Hearings, part 2, p. 320.

59. Committee Report, p. 57.

60. At one point, when a negotiator blamed the commanders, Koresh summarized the com-

manders' viewpoint: "They want patience, and they want it now." Negot. Tape no. 99, March 9. Later, Steve Schneider misheard a negotiator's reference to "commanders" as a reference to "commandos." Negot. Tape no. 124, March 13.

61. Negot. Tapes nos. 122–23, March 13.

62. Moore, *The Davidian Massacre*, p. 264.

63. Justice Report, pp. 21–57, 70–75.

64. Christy Hoppe, "FBI Challenges Koresh to Let Followers Leave," *Dallas Morning News*, March 19, 1993.

65. According to Jewish tradition, one's fate for the coming year is inscribed on the two days (as observed in America; only one day in Israel) of Rosh Hashanah (the Jewish New Year) and sealed on Yom Kippur (the day of atonement), but "repentance, prayer, and righteousness avert the severe decree." E.g., Morris Silverman, ed., *High Holiday Prayer Book* (Hartford: Prayer Book Press, 1951), p. 358.

66. Negot. Tapes nos. 151–52, March 21; Byron Sage, Joint Hearings, part 2, p. 490.

67. Negot. Tape no. 151, March 21.

68. Negot. Tape no. 152, March 21.

69. Justice Report, pp. 134–38.

70. The music included Nancy Sinatra and Andy Williams. The Nancy Sinatra song was "These Boots Are Made for Walking," which includes the taunt: "One of these days these boots are gonna walk all over you," as well as the warning: "and if you play with matches, you know you're gonna get burned." Koresh responded by playing back cassettes of his own music, which one music critic compared to the soft-rock/folk sound popular in Los Angeles in the early 1970s. Eddie Dean, "David Koresh Unplugged," *City Paper*, February 11, 1994; David Koresh, *Voice of Fire* (CD containing two Koresh songs). "Achy Breaky Heart" also made the FBI playlist, as did Mitch Miller. Susan J. Palmer, "Excavating Waco," in *From the Ashes: Making Sense of Waco*, ed. James R. Lewis (Lanham, Md.: Rowman and Littlefield, 1993), p. 105; Jon Pareles, "It's Got a Beat and You Can Surrender to It," *New York Times*, March 28, 1993, section 4, p. 2. Loud music had been successfully used by the United States military in Panama to force Manuel Noriega to come out of an embassy where he had found sanctuary.

71. The theory behind broadcasting previous negotiations was to let the other Branch Davidians know that Koresh saw death as a serious alternative to surrender, with statements such as: "If they want blood, then our blood is here for them to shed. . . . We are not afraid of the government. If we have to die for what we stand for, we're going to. I don't mind if I die." Linedecker, *Massacre at Waco*, p. 221; Victoria Loe and Lee Hancock, "Two Leave Sect Compound," *Dallas Morning News*, March 20, 1993.

72. Justice Report, pp. 78, 82, 88; Edward S. G. Dennis, Jr., *Evaluation of the Handling of the Branch Davidian Stand-Off in Waco, Texas, February 28 to April 19, 1993, Redacted Version* (Washington, D.C.: Department of Justice, October 8, 1993), p. 45; Peter Maas, "None of This Had to Happen," *Parade*, February 27, 1994, p. 5–6; Moore, *The Davidian Massacre*, pp. 266–67. When Koresh responded to the noise by playing his guitar during negotiations, the FBI complained that Koresh was hurting the negotiators' credibility by making the negotiations seem like a game, which they were not. Negot. Tape no. 155, March 23.

73. Dennis, *Evaluation of the Handling*, p. 45; Lee Hancock, "FBI Failed to Weigh Cult's Beliefs, Outside Report Says," *Dallas Morning News*, October 9, 1993. Near the end, when Schneider, seeing a peaceful solution in sight, had his sense of humor back, he jokingly complained about some lights not being on, since, lacking electricity, he had found a couple places where he could use the FBI lights for reading. Negot. Tape no. 239, April 17.

74. Memorandum of March 8, 1993, quoted in Committee Report, pp. 57–58.

75. Moore, *The Davidian Massacre*, p. 269 (citing 1993 House Judiciary hearing); Nancy Ammeran, Reviewer's Comments on Justice Report, p. 2.

76. Reavis, *The Ashes of Waco*, pp. 249–51; Justice Report, pp. 107–108. The two who snuck in were not Branch Davidians; for more, see Appendix D.

77. To Schneider, the change was in the willingness to tolerate differences; "a republic guarantees the rights of minorities. A democracy is where majority rules." Negot. Tape no. 52, March 5.

78. Negot. Tape no. 153, March 21–22.

79. Negot. Tape no. 152, March 21.

80. Justice Report, pp. 81–90.

81. Negot. Tapes 69–70, March 6. "The government's tracked vehicles also planed the surface of the Mt. Carmel cemetery, leaving Anna Hughes, among others, to await Judgment in an unmarked plot." Reavis, *The Ashes of Waco*, p. 224.

82. Negot. Tape no 204, April 10; Moore, *The Davidian Massacre*, p. 267. The wire had several purposes: it prevented people from slipping in; it provided a clear exit path for Davidians if they left; and it prevented a Davidian break-out, with the Davidian mothers holding a child in one arm, and a rifle in another. This fear was unfounded. Committee Report, p. 76. About the closest thing to any such threat in the negotiations with the FBI was Koresh's statement that, "When my father tells me to come out, we'll see what you do." Negot. Tape no. 85, March 7.

83. Peter J. Boyer, "Children of Waco," *The New Yorker*, May 15, 1995, p. 40.

84. Richard Leiby, " 'Frontline': What Went Wrong at Waco?" *Washington Post*, October 17, 1995.

85. Negot. Tapes no. 64, March 6; no. 122, March 13; no. 242, April 18.

86. Justice Report, p. 251; Moore, *The Davidian Massacre*, pp. 256–67.

87. DeVault, *The Waco Whitewash*, p. 68; Ron Cole, *Sinister Twilight* (Longmont, Colo.: self-published, 1994), pp. 57–58.

88. James L. Pate, "We Have Truth on Our Side: Jailhouse Interviews with Branch Davidians," *Soldier of Fortune* (July 1994): 49.

89. Lee Hancock, "Officials Use Secrecy as a Siege Tactic," *Dallas Morning News*, March 16, 1993; Arnold Hamilton, "FBI Meets with Cult Leaders," *Dallas Morning News*, March 17, 1993.

90. JoAnn Zuniga, "Outcome Shocks Compound Visitor," *Houston Chronicle*, April 20, 1993, p. 16A; Moore, *The Davidian Massacre*, p. 268–69. The FBI's no-shades-of-gray approach denied it was possible to strengthen Koresh's grip on his flock. Explained FBI Special-Agent-in-Charge Jeff Jamar: "How do you intensify absolute devotion? This is devotion to a god in their eyes. We didn't drive them to him. . . . The devotion was absolute. There was no way to drive them any closer." Hearing, p. 127.

91. Ken Fawcett, *Blind Justice: A Chronology of the Historic Trial of Eleven Branch Davidians in January 1994,* 2d ed. (Royse City, Tex., Electropress, 1994), p. 23; Trial Transcript, pp. 4169–71, 4193, 4241–42. Ms. Hollingsworth did finally leave on March 21; she was immediately hospitalized because of a heart problem. Ibid.

92. Tabor and Gallagher, *Why Waco?* p. 33.

93. Ben Shalit, *The Psychology of Conflict and Combat* (New York: Praeger Pub., 1988): "All crowding has an intensifying effect. If aggression exists, it will become more so as a result of crowding; if joy exists, it will become intensified by the crowd."

94. Kenneth Samples, Erwin de Castro, Richard Abanes, and Robert Lyle, *Prophets of the Apocalypse: David Koresh and Other American Messiahs* (Grand Rapids, Mich.: Baker, 1994), p. 181 (interview with Schneider's sister).

95. Negot. Tape no. 125, March 13.

96. See Prologue, text at notes 36–39.

97. As Koresh's attorney noted: "Increasing the pressure, rather than drive them away from David Koresh, had the effect of bonding them closer together. Sharing a terrible experience like basic training, for instance, you bond together. People from diverse backgrounds, no matter how different they are, will bond together with that kind of experience, and that's exactly what the FBI was doing. It was wrong." Dick DeGuerin, Joint Hearings, part 2, p. 39.

98. Justice Report, p. 226.

99. Negot. Tape no. 42, March 4.

100. George Robertson, "Suffer the Little Children," in Lewis, *From the Ashes,* p. 176.

101. Gary Null, "Holocaust at Waco," *Penthouse* (April 1994): 34.

102. Reavis, *The Ashes of Waco,* p. 261. When a negotiator told Schneider that Alaniz was thirsty at the debriefing, Schneider confirmed that the Davidians had to ration water. Negot. Tape no. 239, April 17.

103. Reavis, *The Ashes of Waco,* pp. 265–66; Byron Sage, Joint Hearings, part 2, p. 356. "I asked

the FBI to check the water supply again and I was advised the supply was plentiful and it was constantly being replenished." Janet Reno, Joint Hearings, part 3, p. 354.

104. Justice Report, Appendix I, "Intelligence on Water Supply." The FBI was in the uncomfortable position of trying to pressure the Davidians out while trying to provide bare necessities for the children. "I think . . . they had 2 years of food, and if they had told us that they needed water for the children we would have brought water in." Jeffrey Jamar, Joint Hearings, part 3, p. 297.

105. FBI chief negotiator Byron Sage's report to Associate Attorney General Webster Hubbell on April 15, 1993, quoted in Justice Report, p. 271. See also, Justice Report, p. 71.

106. Moore, *The Davidian Massacre*, p. 223. There were also representatives from the Austin Police Department and the Department of Protective Services. Negot. Tape no. 69, March 6.

107. Michael Isikoff and Pierre Thomas, "Reno, FBI Took Fatal Gamble," *Washington Post*, April 21, 1993, p. A15; Richard Leiby, "'Frontline': What Went Wrong at Waco?" *Washington Post*, October 17, 1995. Schneider expressed regret about having to keep the negotiators away from their normal work and family for so long. Negot. Tape no. 239, April 17.

108. Ed Timms, "Sect Members Often Frustrated Agents," *Dallas Morning News*, April 20, 1993.

109. Richard Leiby, "'Frontline': What Went Wrong at Waco?" *Washington Post*, October 17, 1995.

110. "Frontline" interview with Barry Higginbotham, HRT member, October 1, 1995, available at http://www.wgbh.org.

111. Major Alexander S. Wells, April 15, 1993, memorandum on Aircraft Mishap at Waco, Texas: "The aircraft . . . struck a guide wire on takeoff during a routine mission and sustained minor damage. . . . There were no injuries. FBI agents piloted the aircraft and there were no military personnel on board. The FBI will pay for repairs."

112. The Branch Davidians celebrated all Old Testament holy days, and for the Davidians (as for the Hebrews of the Old Testament), the eight-day Passover celebration was the most important of all. The Passover story, of course, celebrates the miraculous liberation of the Hebrews from the mighty Egyptian government.

113. Tabor and Gallagher, *Why Waco?* p. 21.

114. Jeffrey Jamar, Joint Hearings, part 2, p. 298. Not all of this was feigned. Koresh had been shot and seriously wounded on February 28. Many of the negotiations involved the FBI seeking information on Koresh's vital signs. After the Branch Davidians sent out a videotape of themselves, the FBI negotiators told Koresh about a doctor's interpretation of the footage of Koresh which indicated that he had a possible deep-seated infection, which could potentially develop into septicemia. Negot. Tape no. 111, March 11. There is no way of knowing how much negotiation avoidance by Koresh was due to feigned as opposed to real physical suffering. If the FBI exaggerated the danger Koresh was in, in hopes of encouraging his surrendering for medical care, it was simultaneously giving him an excuse for avoiding their telephone calls.

115. Erich Von Däniken, *Chariot of the Gods?* (New York: Bantam, 1971). Ezekiel 1–2. The Grateful Dead song "Estimated Prophet," quoted in the prologue, uses imagery from Ezekiel's vision.

116. Koresh, knowing the Bible so much better than the FBI negotiators, obviously could not be talked out of his theology by them. Even if the FBI had employed Bible experts who could refute Koresh, he probably would not have changed his mind; Marc Breault had convinced most of the Australia and New Zealand Branch Davidians that Koresh was not "the Lamb" by pointing out that "the Lamb" is Jesus. (Breault's interpretation is the standard one among virtually all Christians.) Koresh did not claim to be Jesus, although Koresh did believe that he (like Jesus and Melchizadek) was a "Christ," meaning specially anointed by God.

117. Justice Report, p. 270.

118. Justice Report, p. 140. Understandably, the FBI wanted it both ways, and their response to criticism that they had not taken negotiating seriously was to observe that they managed to get 35 "hostages" out of Mount Carmel Center during the first few weeks of the negotiations. "We saved the lives of thirty-five people during the course of this thing . . . that's lost on the public sometimes. I'm proud of it from a negotiating standpoint." Dick Rogers, Joint Hearings, part 2, p. 496.

119. Byron Sage discussion with Representative McCollum, part 3, pp. 225–26.

120. Justice Report, pp. 54–55.

121. Tabor and Gallagher, *Why Waco?* p. 6.

122. Justice Report, p. 70; Tabor and Gallagher, *Why Waco?* p. 6. The Justice Department assertion that from March 15 onward, the negotiators refused to listen to "Bible babble" was not quite accurate, although the volume of Bible babble declined. E.g., Negot. Tapes no. 139, March 19; no. 142; March 20; no. 145, March 21; no. 204, April 10; nos. 218–19, April 13; nos. 231–32, April 15.

123. Nancy T. Ammerman, "Waco, Law Enforcement, and Scholars of Religion," in Stuart A. Wright, *Armageddon in Waco: Critical Perspectives on the Branch Davidian Conflict* (Chicago: University of Chicago Press, 1995), p. 286.

124. Ammerman, "Waco, Law Enforcement, and Scholars of Religion," p. 287. The one genuine religious scholar whom the FBI consulted was Glenn Hilburn, chair of Baylor's Religion Department. He was used for interpretation of various Bible passages. Ibid., p. 288.

125. In this regard, the Cult Awareness Network shares a common characteristic with advocates of lifestyle intolerance who believe that persons who engage in disapproved behavior (such as smoking cigarettes, or using other drugs) do not actually derive any pleasure from the behavior; they simply engage in the behavior because they are addicted. The no-benefits theory, of course, has trouble explaining why people continue the behavior long enough to get addicted, if the behavior yields no pleasurable benefit to the behaver.

An editorial in the *Journal of Church and State* stated that:

> Government agencies would do well not to rely, as they did in the case of the Branch Davidians, on so-called "cult" experts and deprogrammers whose one purpose is to discredit the religious claims of nonconventional and unpopular religious groups and thereby promote intolerance and discrimination against them. The repeated references in the press and the media at large to members of the Cult Awareness Network (CAN) as "experts" was misleading and unfortunate. The fact is that members of the Cult Awareness Network have a history of persecution of members of groups they deem to be "cults."

(James E. Wood, Jr., "The Branch Davidian Standoff: An American Tragedy," *Journal of Church and State*, vol. 35 [1993], p. 7.) "For those who promised to drive off the fears and disorders of a sick soul were sick themselves with ridiculous fear." Wisdom of Solomon 17:8.

126. James R. Lewis, "Introduction," in Lewis, *From the Ashes*, p. xiv. The word "awareness" appears to be undergoing an Orwellian transformation. In the context of "Cult Awareness Network" or "drug awareness," the word now appears to signify "hatred, bigotry, and misunderstanding."

Indeed, newspeak was omnipresent at Waco. As Dan Cogdell (defense attorney for Clive Doyle) observed in his summation at trial, the torn-up earth of a tank's path is a "ground disturbance"; a flash grenade is a "diversionary device"; an explosion is a "rapid expansion of gasses"; a sniper is a "forward observer," yelling is "announcing our presence," and shooting to kill is "neutralizing a violator." DeVault, *The Waco Whitewash*, p. 159; Trial Transcript, p. 7528. Along those lines, BATF Agent Danny Curtis testified that the goal on February 28 was a "peaceful entry," noting that entry with flashbangs and a battering ram would qualify as peaceful. Trial Transcript, pp. 1902–1907.

127. Sharon Churcher, "Wacko in Waco," *Penthouse* (April 1994): 130.

128. Tabor and Gallagher, *Why Waco?* p. 93.

129. Ammerman, "Waco, Law Enforcement, and Scholars of Religion," p. 289.

130. Ross had been acquitted in a criminal case on charges of unlawful imprisonment. Jennifer Hiorhus, "Man Wins $5 Million in Deprogramming Suit," *Seattle Times*, September 30, 1995; Michael Tarsala, "Cult Deprogrammer Loses Civil-Rights Suit," *Arizona Republic*, October 1, 1995; *Scott v. Ross et al.*, Case no. C94–0079C, Verdict Form (Seattle, Wash.: Western District, 1995).

The Cult Awareness Network has announced that it will disband as a result of the judgment. "Cult Awareness Network to Discontinue Operations," *Washington Post*, June 22, 1996. Deprogrammers associated with CAN have allegedly deprogrammed Baptists, Mormons, Episcopalians, and Sufi Muslims, among others. "CAN Canned," *Liberty* (September/October 1996), p. 5.

131. Anson Shupe and Jeffrey K. Hadden, "Cops, News Copy, and Public Opinion: Legitimacy, and the Social Construction of Evil in Waco," in Wright, *Armageddon in Waco*, p. 195.

132. Marc Breault and Martin King, *Inside the Cult* (New York: Signet, 1993), p. 317. According to a sworn affidavit from a former national director of the Cult Awareness Network, the group has

received kickbacks from fees paid to "deprogrammers." James R. Lewis, "Self-Fulfilling Stereotypes, the Anticult Movement, and the Waco Confrontation," in Wright, *Armageddon in Waco*, p. 97.

133. Justice Report, p. 167.

134. Hearing, p. 137. Denying direct association with the FBI at Waco, the president of the American Family Foundation described his group as "dedicated to educating the public about the dangers destructive cults pose to society . . . and to afford assistance to individuals and families who have been injured by them." Herbert L. Rosedale, "Never Consulted About Waco," *Washington Post,* July 12, 1995, p. A18 (letter to the editor). Also, Joint Hearings, part 1, pp. 248–57.

135. Lewis, "Self-Fulfilling Stereotypes," in Wright, *Armageddon in Waco*, p. 99. The Justice Report maintains that the FBI "did not solicit" or "rely" on advice from anticultists. Justice Report, p. 190.

136. Ammerman, "Waco; Law Enforcement, and Scholars of Religion," p. 5.

137. Negotiation transcript, March 17, 1993, 1:45–2:05 P.M, available at http://www. wgbh.org.

138. "Frontline" interview with Byron Sage, August 8, 1995, available at http://www. wgbh.org.

139. In a sneering response to Davidian complaints about statements made at an FBI press conference, a negotiator asked Koresh if he wanted to be referred to as "the Lamb, as David, as Christ, or as the Lord." Koresh answered that his "name is David Koresh . . . and that's what you need to call me by." Negot. Tape no. 90, March 7–8.

140. Koresh expressed concern that he would be placed in jail with "big guys . . . [t]hat'll poke us in the rear. . . . It's against our religion." The negotiator indicated that Koresh would be respected in jail as "a man of the cloth," to which he responded, "first, they're going to want to bend me over to show that I'm nothing." And he expressed fears that federal prisons are meaner than state facilities. Negot. Tape no. 48, March 4. Koresh said, "there's a lot of rumors that I molest children . . . there's a lot of bubbas [in prison, who] want to molest you if they think you molest children." Negot. Tape no. 33, March 3. When arrested in 1987, Koresh had expressed fears of being raped and getting AIDS. Negot. Tape no. 11B, March 2.

141. "Four Koresh Children Listed as His Heirs," *Washington Times*, September 6, 1993, p. A2 (summary of article from Waco *Tribune-Herald*).

142. Peter Smerick, Joint Hearings, part 2, p. 340. See also Ray Jahn, Joint Hearings, part 1, p. 113. This led some FBI agents to conclude that Koresh was never going to surrender. It is not so clear that they were correct in being similarly confident he would never allow other women and his children to leave. For example, psychiatrist Bruce Perry testified that he advised the FBI two to three weeks prior to the final assault that, while he doubted the "core of the strongest believers (including the Mighty Men)" were likely to leave, "many of the Davidians might leave the compound should the situation be de-escalated." Prepared statement, Joint Hearings, part 1, p. 240.

143. Justice Report, p. 163.

144. Joint Hearings, part 2, p. 22.

145. R.W. Bradford, "There's No Kill Like Overkill," *Liberty* (August 1993): 29. Koresh also knew that he had perpetrated numerous statutory rapes of twelve-year-old girls. Had Koresh ever been tried for the rapes, it is not clear whether any of the girls with whom he had had sex would have testified against him.

146. Andrew Blum, "Waco Tragedy Spawns Litigation," *National Law Journal* (May 17, 1993): 3, 31.

147. Hearing, pp. 82, 85. Schneider, when asked if he too might write a book, replied that he did not think of himself as a writer, but he might have to write a book just to pay his attorneys, based on preliminary estimates that attorneys fees would be about $450,000. Negot. Tapes no. 201, April 9; no. 239, April 17. One of the risks of the Davidians consulting counsel was that earlier efforts by the negotiators to minimize financial concerns were undermined. FBI negotiators had earlier attempted to assuage Schneider's concerns about legal costs; when Schneider recalled that legal defense regarding the 1987 shootout had cost $100,000, the negotiators said that lawyers were lining up for the opportunity to defend the Branch Davidians. Negot. Tape no. 52, March 5.

148. Negot. Tapes, no. 40, March 4; no. 52, March 5; no. 105, March 10. Schneider was assured that Weaver had been allowed to surrender safely, but surrender was only part of Schneider's concern; he wondered about the shootings of Weaver's wife, son, and dog, and whether Weaver would get a fair trial.

149. Phillip B. Heymann, *Lessons of Waco: Proposed Changes in Federal Law Enforcement* (Washington, D.C.: Department of Justice, October 8, 1993), pp. 4–5.

150. Breault and King, *Inside the Cult,* pp. 317–18 (reporting February 18, 1993, diary entry of Sue Schneider, non-Davidian sister of Steve Schneider).

151. Justice Report, pp. 163–64. On at least one occasion, Koresh accepted that: "I have no intention of . . . sitting here rotting and dying. I'd rather live in prison than to have to live here in this cold place." Negot. Tape no. 81, March 7.

152. Dennis, *Evaluation of the Handling,* p. 49.

153. Ibid., p. 43. For more on Dietz, see Joyce Johnson, "Witness for the Prosecution," *New Yorker,* May 16, 1994, p. 42.

154. Negot. Tapes no. 54, March 5; no. 61, March 5; no. 66, March 6; no. 88, March 7; no 95, March 8–9; no. 97, March 9; no. 99, March 9, where Kathy Schroeder is assured that the worst that would happen to her would be being held as a material witness. She was arrested immediately on her departure. She eventually plea-bargained to a major felony carrying several years of prison time in exchange for testifying against some of the surviving Davidians.

Some of the Davidians' concerns involved the inconvenience of the judicial system, as well as its risks. They feared being held for a year, prior to completion of trial, even if eventually acquitted. They noted that being a material witness, with bond required, seemed very similar to arrest and bail. They noted that the trial from the 1987 shootout cost $100,000 and damaged their reputation. Koresh insisted that the prosecutor convinced some jurors to vote guilty simply because Koresh possessed firearms. Negot. Tapes no. 51, March 5; no. 52, March 5; no. 61, March 5; no. 95, March 8–9; no. 97, March 9.

Clive Doyle and Bob Kendrick, who were acquitted of all charges, spent over ten months in jail pending trial, and were released just two days before the anniversary of BATF's initial raid on Mount Carmel Center. DeVault, *The Waco Whitewash,* p. 165.

155. Negot. Tape no. 82, March 7. The negotiators could not cite a case involving the FBI or BATF, but they did point out that self-defense has been successfully invoked in the homicide of a police officer. Negot. Tape no. 39, March 4; no. 104, March 10. The only case of a BATF agent being tried for a violent crime was when an agent murdered his wife. Negot. Tape no. 104, March 10.

156. Dennis, *The Evaluation of the Handling,* p. 43.

157. Negot. Tape no. 98, March 9.

158. Negot. Tapes no. 67, March 6; no. 79, March 7;

159. Negot. Tape no. 99, March 9.

160. Negot. Tape no. 96, March 9.

161. Negot. Tape no. 89, March 7.

162. Samples, pp. 178–79.

163. Balenda Gamen, mother of Davidian David Thibodeau, "Maury Povich Show," November 8, 1993; Linedecker, *The Massacre at Waco,* p. 213; Moore, *The Davidian Massacre,* p. 255.

164. Hearing, p. 29.

165. James L. Pate, "What the Feds Don't Want You to Know about Waco," *Soldier of Fortune* (October 1993): 73; Justice Report, pp. 131–32.

166. Terrence Stutz, "Koresh Preached Violence, Officials, Ex-follower Say," *Dallas Morning News,* March 12, 1993.

167. Justice Report, pp. 239–40. Sessions had graduated from Baylor University, in Waco, and had practiced law in Waco for ten years. Ronald Kessler, *The FBI* (New York: Pocket Books, 1993) , p. 381. According to critics, Sessions had a pattern of arranging business trips to Texas, so he could visit friends and family. Gerson thought Sessions's idea was "stupid" and just a ploy to retain his job as FBI Director, since the Clinton administration was planning to remove him as soon as reasonably possible. Ibid., pp. 423–24. Schneider had said he was impressed with Sessions, Negot. Tape no. 121, March 12–13.

168. Samples, *Prophets of the Apocalypse,* p. 174 (interview with Koresh's mother).

169. Bruce Nichols, "2 Branch Davidians Leave Compound, Are Detained," *Dallas Morning News,* March 13, 1993; Linedecker, *Massacre at Waco,* p. 213.

170. Gritz states that on April 18, 1993, he began making plans to get into Mount Carmel, and negotiate a surrender. Dick J. Reavis, "Remembering Waco, and Stealing It," *New York Times,* May 13, 1995.

171. Justice Report, pp. 54, 321, 325, 327; Negot. Tape no. 68, March 6; Moore, *The Davidian Massacre,* p. 210.

172. Unidentified remains of three five- to six-year-old females were found in the cold storage room near Melissa's mother, Rosemary. Justice Report, pp. 321, 325, 327.

173. Justice Report, p. 144; Committee Report, p. 60.

174. "Frontline" interview with Jeff Jamar, August 7, 1995, http://www.wgbh.org; Joint Hearings, part 2, p. 312.

175. Committee Report, p. 59.

176. Lee Hancock, "Man Who Sneaked into Compound Leaves," *Dallas Morning News,* April 18, 1993; Ron Cole, *Sinister Twilight* (Longmont, Colo., self-published, 1994), p. 55. Cole was not a Davidian during the events leading up to April 19, but he later joined the group.

177. Ambassador H. Allen Holmes, Joint Hearings, part 3, p. 315; Committee Report, p. 50.

178. Boyer, "Children of Waco," p. 40.

179. Peter Smerick, Joint Hearings, part 2, p. 328.

180. Bruce Perry, Joint Hearings, part 1, pp. 239–40.

181. Dr. Alan Stone, reviewer comments on Justice Report, pp. 10–11.

182. Joint Hearings, part 2, p. 343.

183. Dan Freedman, "FBI Analyst Says He Was Ignored on Waco," *Washington Times,* May 1, 1995, p. A1, A20 (Hearst Newspapers); Ammerman, "Waco, Law Enforcement, and Scholars of Religion," pp. 290–91.

184. Joint Hearings, part 2, p. 248.

185. Tabor and Gallagher, *Why Waco?* p. 108. At one point early in negotiations, an FBI negotiator used a Catholic Bible, and Koresh commented, "what a sorry translation." Negot. Tape no. 80, March 7.

186. Fagan's lengthy manuscript on Branch Davidian theology is available on the Internet at http://www.ime.net/~mswett/fagan.html.

187. Philip Arnold, Joint Hearings, part 2, pp. 152–53. The religious experts were not suggesting they should do the negotiating, only that they should be giving advice to professional negotiators after listening to tapes of negotiations. Ibid., and pp. 163–64.

188. *Time* magazine's cover story the week of the Waco inferno showed the burning building, with David Koresh's unshaven, laughing face superimposed. The caption read: "His name was death, and Hell followed with him." The four riders are popularly known as the four horsemen of the apocalypse.

189. Revelation 6:1–11.

190. Some surviving Davidians see this prophecy as being fulfilled by the 1994 Los Angeles earthquakes. Koresh had long taught that an earthquake off Hawaii (the fiftieth state, related, in Koresh's view, to the fifty days of Pentecost) would fulfill this prophecy.

191. Contrary to standard interpretations of the seventh seal, the Branch Davidians believed that entire remainder of the Book of Revelation was encompassed in the seventh seal.

192. J. Philip Arnold, "The Davidian Dilemma: To Obey God or Man?" in Lewis, *From the Ashes,* p. 25.

193. The Davidians saw the "little season" of the siege as also foretold by Isaiah 26:20: "enter thou into thy chambers, and shut thy doors about thee: hide thyself as it were for a little moment [compare "a little season"], until the indignation be overpast." Arnold, "The Davidian Dilemma," p. 26.

194. Either Tabor and Arnold convinced Koresh, or Koresh had always had that position: "His view was a flexible view . . . his view of what was prophesied was not set in concrete. They didn't have to die, and he didn't see that the end of this situation as necessarily being his death and the death of his followers." Dick DeGuerin, Joint Hearings, part 2, p. 23.

195. The King James Bible, the Davidians' text, does not use quotation marks.

196. Negot. Tapes no. 129, March 15; no. 133, March 19.

197. Negot. Tape no. 133, March 19; Justice Report, App. C.

198. Background letter prepared by J. Phillip Arnold, Joint Hearings, part 2, pp. 209–10.

199. James D. Tabor, "The Waco Tragedy: An Autobiographical Account of One Attempt to Avert Disaster," in Lewis, ed., *From the Ashes,* pp. 13–21; Arnold, "The Davidian Dilemma," in Lewis, ed., *From the Ashes,* pp. 21–31.

200. Schneider tried to convince the FBI that Koresh was threatening natural, not man-made dis-

asters, and thus the letters were not a threat. The negotiators viewed the letters as criminal acts, threatening FBI personnel. Negot. Tapes no. 203, April 9; no. 204, April 10. Earlier negotiations would suggest that some of Koresh's threats were supernatural, as when he had Schneider ask, "Do you think this country is too big to be disciplined by God?" Negot. Tape, no. 25, March 3.

201. David Koresh, letter of April 14, 1993, to Dick DeGuerin; Joint Hearings, part 2, p. 249.

202. Dick DeGuerin, Joint Hearings, part 2, p. 30. As further evidence that a surrender was being planned rather than a suicide, DeGuerin noted that his work for Koresh was to include filing a lawsuit to perfect title to the Mount Carmel property.

203. James Tabor, quoting David Thibodeau, Joint Hearings, part 2, p. 173.

204. Dick DeGuerin, Joint Hearings, part 2, p. 30.

205. Negot. Tape no. 239, April 17.

206. Moore, *The Davidian Massacre*, p. 271.

207. David Tammeus, "Religion: The Overlooked Key to the Waco Tragedy," *Boulder Daily Camera*, April 24, 1994, p. 4E (originally published in *Kansas City Star*).

208. David Koresh, letter of April 14, 1993, to Dick DeGuerin, p. 1. Joint Hearings, part 2, p. 249. "Yahweh" is a substitute name of God used by the Hebrews. The true name is a long-lost secret. "Yahweh" is a scholarly extrapolation of YHVH, with the vowels interpolated by guesswork. Many Jews omit the vowels when writing God's name, as a sign of respect. Koresh signed his name in English as "Yahweh Koresh" and in Hebrew as "YHVH KVRSh."

209. Most of the actual surrender plan was proposed by the FBI, with minor changes incorporated at the suggestion of Koresh's and Schneider's attorneys. Schneider's attorney explained:

> The people on the inside were going to tell the FBI the night before [the actual surrender], Dick [DeGuerin, Koresh's attorney] and I were going to be there, we're going to start during daylight, so this is all done during the day, and Dick DeGuerin and David Koresh were going to exit first to show everybody that they weren't going to get executed the minute they stepped outside. And there would be a metal detector set up outside the front door in a bus 100 or so yards away, approximately.
>
> When Mr. DeGuerin and Mr. Koresh went through that metal detector, then Mr. Koresh would have plastic wrist restraints placed on him, be patted down by a male FBI or ATF agent—FBI was our request—and then he and Dick would go to the bus, and then I was supposed to stay in there and see that the other adults came out, keeping a distance so that law enforcement wouldn't get nervous about people bunching up.
>
> It was going to be tape recorded by the FBI, and there was going to be a press representative taping it so that there would be no claims of police brutality and . . . the opposite. In other words, both sides would be protected.
>
> . . . Steve Schneider would be the last Branch Davidian out, and I would bring up the rear. When they saw me coming through there, that was the signal to send in the HRT teams. They'd come in, make sure nobody else was hiding anywhere. Once they cleared that, then that EODT explosive ordinance disposal team, was going to come in and check for booby-traps, and the Feds were gone.
>
> The Texas Rangers were going to take over, and the people that were wounded or needed medical care, go to the hospital. Everybody else goes to the command post where a U.S. magistrate judge was going to be . . . they would be warned, taken into official custody, appointed a lawyer, or released, if they weren't charged with anything.
>
> [T]he only suggestion I remember us making was I said I'm uncomfortable about those little kids walking out by themselves. Can't we just let the kids walk out with the mothers. And they agreed to that. So that was all worked out.
>
> In my judgement, we had a deal, we were going to do it. We told them on the 14th they were coming out. We told them it would take another 10, 12 days. We asked them, "Do you have that much time?" They said, "We have all the time in the world to resolve this peacefully."

(Testimony of Jack Zimmermann, Joint Hearings, part 2, pp. 41–42.)

Representative Schumer and other critics said that during the fifty-one days of negotiations,

Koresh told four lies about coming out. But only the promise to come out March 2 was an unambiguous lie. Koresh's letter of April 14 was a step toward fulfilling his promise to come out after Passover, the fourteenth being the first day after Passover, by Branch Davidian calculations of the calendar. Rep. Henry Hyde, quoting from Dean Kelly of the National Council of Churches, Joint Hearings, part 2, p. 47. He had said that he was not coming out prior to the end of Passover; he had not promised to come out as soon as the holy days were past.

210. Tammeus, "Religion," p. 4E. Jamar, not believing Koresh was in earnest, later equivocated, "when I said there was plenty of time, there was no approval of our plan. . . ." Jeffrey Jamar, Joint Hearings, part 2, p. 297.

211. Tammeus, "Religion," p. 4E.

Arnold and Tabor found Koresh's writing to be a "rather substantial piece of work." They estimated that Koresh would have needed "another two or three weeks" to finish the rest of the Seals. Peter Maas, "None of This Had to Happen," *Parade* (February 27, 1994): 6.

212. Negot. Tapes no. 232, April 15; no. 233, April 15–16. Schneider responded that if the FBI thought it were a stalling tactic, they could get ten of their Abrams tanks "if you'd like, and run through the entire building."

213. Justice Report, p. 105.

214. Justice Report, pp. 174–76.

215. Tabor and Gallagher, *Why Waco?* pp. 17–18, 21 n.40.

216. Larry Witham, "Advisor told Reno Koresh's Manifesto Might Bring Him Out," *Washington Times*, August 1, 1995, p. A10.

217. Justice Report, pp. 167–68.

218. Koresh had also claimed, at first, that a baby had been killed during the BATF attack, although this was not true. According to Branch Davidian survivor Jamie Castillo, Jaydean Wendell's blood splattered on the baby, and Koresh was incorrectly told that the baby had been killed. Carol Moore, "Nightline: Waco Tapes (morning after)" July 6, 1995 (e-mail broadcast).

219. Jack Zimmermann, Joint Hearings, part 2, pp. 61–62.

220. Negot. Tape no. 239, April 17. While Miron may have thought the manuscript could eventually be a negotiating tool, his overall recommendation was that the FBI act sooner rather than later. J. Gordon Melton and Lawrence Criner, "What the Hearings May Tell Us," *Washington Post,* July 2, 1995, p. C3.

221. Dick Rogers, Joint Hearings, part 3, p. 297. Other possible explanations are that the firearms were to be reconverted once the manuscript was nearing completion, by which time the Davidians would be confident the guns would not be needed for protection; or that the Davidians believed the firearms could be suppressed as evidence for some reason; or that the firearms had not been converted to full-auto, evidence for most of the alleged conversions being rather weak. (Evidence of conversion is discussed in chapter 5.)

222. Jeffrey Jamar, Joint Hearings, part 2, p. 333: "I am not going to call Mr. DeGuerin and tell him we have an operational plan we are going to execute on Monday."

223. Negot. Tape no. 242, April 18.

224. Joint Hearings, part 2, p. 537.

225. Lee Hancock, "Koresh Vowed Not to Give In," *Dallas Morning News*, April 21, 1993.

226. Larry Witham, "Transcript Belies Talk of Koresh 'Ploy,' " *Washington Times*, August 7–13, 1995 (national weekly edition), p. 12; Moore, *The Davidian Massacre,* p. 275; Justice Report, p. 107.

227. In congressional testimony, Director Sessions reported that the last time "we were on the verge of having them come out if Mr. Koresh kept his promise" was "in connection with Passover" (Hearing, p. 149), when in fact Passover preceded the April 14 letter.

228. The Justice Report states that "The FBI provided the Attorney General with memoranda prepared by Dr. Miron and Dr. Krofcheck and SSA [Supervisory Special Agent] Van Zandt analyzing Koresh's April 9th letter." Justice Report, p. 274. There is no evidence in the Justice Report, or elsewhere, which suggests that Attorney General Reno was informed of the April 14 letter.

229. Negotiator Byron Sage indicated that, while he may have passed along to Webster Hubbell and others some of the details related to the letter, Sage's communication would have conveyed the same impression the FBI in Waco had, which was that the offer was not genuine, and did not reflect a

change in attitude by Koresh. Joint Hearings, part 2, pp. 507–508. This was confirmed by Hubbell, who indicated that he had been briefed by Sage regarding what DeGuerin had said, but that Sage had indicated that the plan would not work, "that the attorneys were being manipulated by Mr. Koresh . . . to buy more time, and that he wasn't going to come out." Joint Hearings, part 3, pp. 39–40.

230. Joint Hearings, part 2, p. 306.

231. Joint Hearings, part 2, p. 314.

232. Joint Hearings, part 2, p. 357.

233. David Koresh, *The Decoded Message of the Seven Seals of the Book of Revelation* (Axtell, Tex.: General Assoc. of Branch Davidian Seventh-day Adventists, 1994). The manuscript is reproduced as an appendix, with commentary by Phil Arnold and Jim Tabor, in Tabor and Gallagher, *Why Waco?* pp. 191–211. Also available from The Research Center, at http://www.ime.net/~mswett, and Joint Hearings, part 2, pp. 227–45.

234. Joel 2:15–16. Parentheticals added.

235. Koresh, *The Seven Seals*, in Tabor and Gallagher, *Why Waco?* p. 203; Joint Hearings, part 2, p. 242.

236. Justice Report, pp. 277, 292, 294 (400 rounds); "Jury in Sect's Trial Views Photos of FBI Assault," *New York Times*, February 8, 1994; Trial Transcript, p. 5167 (300-round estimate accepted by FBI agent Thomas Rowan who fired 75 ferret rounds of the CS).

237. Stone, pp. 29–30; Justice Report, pp. 105–106, 266–70, Appendix J.

238. Rex Applegate, *Riot Control: Materiel and Techniques* (Boulder, Colo.: Paladin Press; London and Melbourne: Arms and Armour Press, 1969, 1981), pp. 172–75.

The use of an anesthetic gas (to render the Davidians unconscious, rather than drive them from the house in agony) was rejected by the FBI on grounds that it might kill children and weak adults. Kessler, *The FBI,* p. 424.

239. Roger Altman, Memorandum of April 15, 1993, to Secretary Bentsen, with a copy to Treasury Assistant Secretary for Enforcement Ron Noble, discussed in Joint Hearings, part 1, p. 509. Altman was not involved in the decisionmaking process. He was merely keeping his supervisor briefed on what the Justice Department was thinking about doing, as relayed to him by Noble, whose job included overseeing BATF operations. By April, BATF's role in Waco was limited to cooperating with the FBI. Altman later made it clear that neither he nor Bentsen had any role in the FBI's assault decision. Joint Hearings, part 1, pp. 790–91.

240. Jerry Seper, "Reno Faces Questions on Waco Gas Attack," *Washington Times*, June 4, 1995. CS is named for its inventors B.B. Corson and R.W. Stoughton.

241. Laurie Kellman, "Gas Hit Children Hardest, Panel Told," *Washington Times* (national weekly edition), July 31–August 5, 1995, p. 11.

242. "They didn't have a lack of toilet facilities out of design, just they hadn't built them yet. They were in the process of building it. . . . There were shower stalls. There were toilets. . . . They just weren't operating yet. They were in the process of construction, future plans that they had, inconsistent with the world's going to end now." Dick DeGuerin, Joint Hearings, part 2, p. 50.

243. Howard Hu et al., "Tear Gas—Harassing Agent or Toxic Chemical Weapon?" *Journal of the American Medical Association* 262 (August 4, 1989): 660.

244. FBI officials recommending the use of CS at Waco were not aware of the chemical warfare convention. Jerry Seper, "FBI Used Chemical Banned for War," *Washington Times*, April 22, 1993. According to a treaty expert for the U.S. Defense Department, CS would not be considered a chemical weapon under the previous Geneva protocols, and even with the new Convention, "we can use these in other military operations short of actual armed conflict: peacekeeping operations such as Somalia or Haiti, rescue operations, and things like that. So our policy is quite similar to that for law enforcement operations." Hays Parks, Joint Hearings, part 2, p. 429.

245. Robin Clarke and J. Perry Robinson, "United Kingdom," in *CBW: Chemical and Biological Warfare: London Conference on CBW,* ed. Steven Rose (London: George G. Harrap and Co., 1968), pp. 91–92.

246. Amnesty International, *Chemical Report on C.S. Agent #6*; Jerry Seper, "Reno Faces Questions on Waco Gas Attack," *Washington Times*, June 4, 1995. See also Amnesty International, *Israel and the Occupied Territories: The Misuse of Tear Gas by Israeli Army Personnel in Israeli Occupied*

Territories, AI Index: MDE/15/26/88 (June 1988). Defenders of CS insist that the Amnesty International report was imprecise in distinguishing CS from other chemical warfare agents, and some or all of the deaths might have been caused by other riot-control materiel.

247. U.S. Department of the Army, *Civil Disturbances*, FM 19–15. (October 1975), §§ 6–1, 6–3.

248. Ibid.

249. Glenn Frankel, "Israel's Use of Tear Gas Scrutinized," *Washington Post*, May 31, 1993. Environmental Protection Agency toxicologist William L. Marcus said:

> [T]his material [some of the flame retardants used in the injection of CS] causes adults to vomit when it is in high concentration. It also causes children, even young children, to vomit. If they are small and they have been knocked down by the gas, or in this case the powder, the chance of aspirating their own vomit is very high. This causes an aspiration pneumonitis which cannot be differentiated, after all is said and done, from what would have occurred if it was CS alone.

(Joint Hearings, part 2, p. 436.)

The government's interpretation of CS for children was somewhat different. Assistant U.S. Attorney Johnston told the jury: "I submit to you that a child could be around today and say, 'The smell of tear gas, of CS gas, it's the greatest smell in the world, because it's the smell that saved my life.' Because it could have been the smell that saved their lives." He went on to note that, since the adults had gas masks, however, the adults stayed and the children did not have the option to leave and to live. Trial Transcript, p. 7081. The government knew at the time, of course, that the adults had those masks.

250. Unpublished Department of Justice "Crisis Center Log: Degan Incident," August 22, 1992, 4:50 P.M. EDT.

251. Stone, p. 35. The case is described in Park and Giammona, "Toxic Effects of Tear Gas on an Infant," *American Journal of Diseases of Children* 123 (1972): 245.

252. James Bovard, "Convoluted Trail of Waco Explanations," *Washington Times*, April 19, 1995, p. A15.

253. U.S. Army, *Civil Disturbances*, § 6–9a.

254. Army Institute for Professional Development, *MP: Civil Disturbance Operations, Subcourse MP 1005,* 5th ed. (Army Institute for Professional Development, n.d.), p. 129; Robert W. Lee, "Lethal Fumes," *The New American* (June 28, 1993): 38.

255. Linedecker, *Massacre at Waco,* p. 233.

256. Applegate, *Riot Control.*

257. Rex Applegate, *Unpublished Report on FBI Planning and Operations Relating to the CS Gas Assault at Waco, Texas February 28 to April 19, 1993* (Scottsburg, Oregon, 1995) (hereinafter, "Applegate Report"), p. 23.

258. Applegate Report, p. 27.

259. Applegate Report, Appendix D.

260. Applegate Report, p. 24.

261. According to retired Air Force Colonel George F. Uhlig, now a chemistry professor, the acetone and ethanol "liquid aerosol obviously was of the correct particle size, came into contact with a flame, and the flame front traveled from particle to particle rapidly, to create the fireball described by survivors." Dr. George F. Uhlig, letter of July 13, 1994, to Dave Hall, station manager, KPOC television, reprinted in KPOC TV, *Overview and General Information of Criminal Negligence by Agents of Federal Government*, report for U.S. Senate Judiciary Comm., August 1994; James L. Pate, "Wacogate," *Soldier of Fortune* (June 1995): 49.

262. Office of the Chief Medical Examiner, Nizam Peerwani, case no 930008 (Steve Schneider); 930012 (Sherri Jewell); 930018 (adult female); 930027 (female child); 930028 (sixty-year-old black female); 930037 (white male); 930041 (Gregory Allen Summers).

263. Justice Report, p. 277.

264. Justice Report, p. 147.

265. Applegate Report, pp. 9, 63.

266. Reavis, *The Ashes of Waco,* p. 268; Trial transcript, pp. 5735, 5756, 5916, 5921 (testimony of Rick Sherow). Although commonly given a chemical formula MeCl$_2$, methylene chloride is more formally CH$_2$Cl$_2$.

267. James Bovard, "Hearings Show Waco Defense is Wacky," *Wall Street Journal,* August 2, 1995 (congressional testimony of fire expert Rick Sherow).

268. Failure Analysis Associates, *Investigation of the April 19, 1993 Assault on Mt. Carmel Center, Waco, Texas* (Menlo Park, Calif., July 1995); Dow Chemical Material Safety Data Sheet for product code 55572, copy available at http://www.indirect.com/www/dhardy/mecl.txt.

269. Office of the Chief Medical Examiner, Nizam Peerwani, case no 9300005 (unidentified adult female); 930006 (Wayne Martin); 930008 (Steve Schneider); 930012 (Sherri Jewell); 930016 (Adebowale Davies); 930018 (adult female); 930024 (Susan M. Benta); 930027 (female child); 930028 (sixty-year-old black female); 930030 (Beverly Ellist); 930037 (white male); 930041 (Gregory Allen Summers); Glenn F. Bunting, "Use of Tear Gas in Waco Raid under Scrutiny," *Los Angeles Times,* May 30, 1995.

270. Aldrich Chemical Co., *Material Safety Data Sheet* for product no. 37528–4. Alpha-chloro-benzylidenemalononitrile (April 13, 1994) ("Hazardous Combustion or Decomposition Products[:] Toxic Fumes of: Carbon Monoxide, Carbon Dioxide, Hydrogen Cyanide, Nitrogen Oxides, Hydrogen Chloride Gas"); Moore, *The Davidian Massacre,* pp. 295–96.

271. Testimony of Dr. Henry Salem, chief scientist for life sciences at the U.S. Army Chemical Biological Defense Command, Joint Hearings, part 2, pp. 575–76.

272. Failure Analysis Associates, *Investigation of the Assault,* p. 7.

273. After the destruction of the Mount Carmel Center, Steve Schneider's voluble attorney, Jack Zimmermann, reported having had a telephone conversation with the mother of an Israeli citizen who was a Branch Davidian:

> [A]nd then she described for me, an Israeli Jew talking to an American Jewish lawyer, watching that gas be inserted into that building, watching an American tank knock down an American house, and then it burst into flames.
>
> Can you imagine the images in an Israeli's mind with the Holocaust survivors in Israel? I couldn't answer. I think you can tell from today, it is not often that I am without words. But I could not explain to her how that happened. And her answer . . . was, "I thought he would be safe in America."

(Joint Hearings, part 2, p. 43.) Pablo Cohen reportedly died from smoke and carbon monoxide inhalation. Justice Report, p. 319.

274. Janet Reno, discussion with Rep. Sonny Bono, Joint Hearings, part 3, pp. 453–54.

275. Joint Hearings, part 3, pp. 9, 53. Even if the statement were true, gas masks for small children were not available, and Dr. Salem's observation that it causes most people to "flee from that area . . . unless there is an obstruction" glosses over the inability of babies to flee from any area. Ibid., p. 9. As was later noted, had the attorney general read the briefing book—part of which was read into the record by Rep. John Mica—she would have been misled by the assertion that the effects of CS on children, even infants, had been extensively investigated. In fact, to the extent the issue was studied, the studies had been few and largely anecdotal. Joint Hearings, part 3, pp. 334–35.

276. Failure Analysis Associates, *Investigation of the Assault.*

277. Joint Hearings, part 3, p. 48.

278. James Bovard, "Hearings Show Waco Defense is Wacky," *Wall Street Journal,* August 2, 1995.

279. Glenn F. Bunting, "Use of Tear Gas in Waco Raid under Scrutiny," *Los Angeles Times,* May 30, 1995.

280. Janet Reno, "Reno: 'Koresh Chose Death'," *USA Today,* August 1, 1995, p. 11A (op-ed summarizing her testimony).

281. Stanley Pottinger (assistant attorney general for Civil Rights during Nixon administration), "At Wounded Knee" (letter to the editor), *New York Times Book Review,* November 12, 1995, p. 4.

282. Rep. Robert Wise observed that information he received from the FBI indicated that "of 867 State and local law enforcement [agencies] surveyed 688 maintain CS gas in their inventory."

Joint Hearings, part 2, p. 515. "The FBI has used it six times in the last 5 years, not including Waco, three before and three afterwards. . . . So CS gas still seems to be considered by law enforcement to be a viable usage in certain situations." Joint Hearings, part 2, p. 427.

283. FBI spokesman Bob Ricks explained that the FBI just wanted to "up the ante"—perhaps a poor choice of words when the wager was for the Davidians' lives. "The 20th Century" (Arts & Entertainment network), October 2, 1996.

284. Michael Isikoff and Pierre Thomas, "Reno, FBI Took Fatal Gamble," *Washington Post*, April 21, 1993, p. A15.

285. Justice Report, p. 5.

286. Justice Report, p. 267. It was the military consultants' view that April 19 was to be D day. "The military evaluated the plan at length in front of the Attorney General, myself . . . as well as Floyd [Clarke] and others, and Judge Sessions. They had only one slight disagreement with the plan . . . they would go in with the gas totally at first as opposed to a partial insertion into one area . . . they weren't limited by the rules of engagement that the FBI had." Webster Hubbell, Joint Hearings, part 3, p. 30. Asked if that meant that they would have "taken Koresh out," Hubbell continued, "They didn't say that directly, but you certainly had that impression, if they were on foreign soil and these people were being held as hostages." If there were evidence that murder-suicide was being planned, or that the Davidian "Mighty Men" would prevent others from leaving the building, standard American rules of engagement could have allowed such a preemptive killing. FBI Director Sessions would insist, after all, that "Koresh no longer allowed people to come out." Joint Hearings, part 3, p. 31.

287. Justice Report, p. 273.

288. Hearing, p. 16.

289. The Hostage Rescue Team had more mixed feelings, combining fear for the children with fear of the children, seeing them both as hostages and as persons who "could and would take up arms against the agents." Justice Report, p. 147.

290. Joint Hearings, part 2, p. 424. The plan to use the pain of children to encourage the exit of mothers was not uniformly endorsed as practical. A military expert, Allen Holmes, noted that "one of the officers . . . involved, in the context of explaining the different reactions, said something like some mothers might abandon their children" in their efforts personally to escape from the CS-filled building. Joint Hearings, part 3, p. 314.

291. Which exacerbates the skin irritation of the CS. Henry Salem, Joint Hearings, part 2, p. 529.

292. Joint Hearings, part 2, p. 511. Under questioning by Rep. Robert Scott, Jeffrey Jamar acknowledged that their expectation of the response to the CS was based on consultation with behaviorists "who were expert in human behavior not necessarily cults." Joint Hearings, part 3, p. 210. Following up on this notion of misunderstanding, Representative Chabot asked: "Don't you think this reveals a failure on the part of the agents in the field to recognize how differently Davidians would react as a result of their religious beliefs and their devotion to Koresh, even though obviously the rest of us, it is hard to fathom how they had this regard for Koresh . . . ?" The attorney general dismissed the religious issue and insisted that the only reason the Davidians failed to emerge from the building as expected was that the winds had dissipated the CS so that the pressure was not great enough on them to come marching out with their children. Joint Hearings, part 3, p. 455.

293. Larry Potts, Joint Hearings, part 2, p. 486.

294. Hearing, pp. 78–80.

295. Discussion between Representative Barr and Larry Potts, Joint Hearings, part 3, pp. 63–64. One of the tank drivers testified that the goal was to prevent Davidians from reaching the bus: "[T]hese folks are already in an entrenched mind and body . . . in this . . . fortified compound. They want to stay there. If we allow them to get into that bus, . . . then it would be even harder to get them out. . . . So if we pushed them away from that trap door initially, that was our goal." R. J. Craig, Joint Hearings, part 3, p. 219.

296. Floyd Clarke, Hearing, pp. 78–80; Dick Rogers, Joint Hearing, part 2, p. 504; Reavis, *The Ashes of Waco*, p. 275.

297. Hearing, p. 16; Justice Report, pp. 288–89. The praise was excessive. Experts who have watched the government's forward-looking infrared (FLIR) tapes of the later stages of the assault have sworn seeing clear evidence of machine gun fire originating outside the Branch Davidians' house,

which could only have originated with some governmental agents. Affidavit of Edward F. Allard, Ph.D., January 20, 1996.

Even an initial nonshooting response might not warrant excessive praise. Since the attorney general was assured in advance that the only vehicles in firing range would be impervious even to shots from a .50 cal. rifle (Hearing, p. 59), she was essentially giving the FBI the authority to ignore the traditional rules of engagement. Whatever the motives of the Davidians shooting at the tanks, they gave FBI agents no reason "to believe they or another are in danger of death or grievous bodily harm," as the published FBI guidelines require.

HRT Director Dick Rogers disagreed: "Everyone has made the assumption that because we had military armored vehicles, that the agents inside were completely safe. And that's just not true. In order to fire those ferret rounds, there were openings in the sides of those Bradley fighting vehicles that we had actually enlarged from what their original design was for the military." Joint Hearings, part 2, p. 478. Perhaps, but putting a bullet through one of those openings would require an exceedingly lucky shots very difficult even for marksmen, and all the more difficult for amateurs who did not even know the vulnerable spots in the BFVs, and the Davidians had been told the vehicles were bulletproof. Negot. Tape no. 9, March 1.

298. Justice Report, pp. 168–79. Although assault planners thought Davidian gunfire likely (Webster Hubbell, Joint Hearings, part 3, pp. 38–39), perhaps even 99 percent likely (Jeffrey Jamar, Joint Hearings, part 2, p. 484), and HRT head Dick Rogers reported confirmation of Davidian gunfire within minutes of the beginning of the CS assault (Joint Hearings, part 3, p. 208), and "when fired upon, the FBI responded by beginning to insert gas throughout the compound" (Janet Reno, Hearing, p. 16), Branch Davidian David Thibodeau testified that he heard no gunfire from the Branch Davidians during the final assault. He more convincingly observed that the Davidians'.223 rounds would not have penetrated the FBI's tanks, and insisted that the FBI returned gunfire. Joint Hearings, part 1, pp. 182–83.

299. Joint Hearings, part 2, p. 484.

300. Joint Hearings, part 3, pp. 38–39.

301. Larry Potts, Joint Hearings, part 2, p. 577. He also indicated that, otherwise, he would have conveyed Jamar's expectations up the chain of command.

302. Applegate Report, pp. 5–6.

303. Applegate Report, p. 27. When the gradual insertion of CS chemical warfare agent had escalated to an all-out CS attack, but had produced no Davidians in four hours, the attorney general reported to the president that everything appeared to be going well. Justice Report, p. 245. She later told Congress that they had expected more to come out in the morning. Hearing, p. 60.

304. Reavis, The Ashes of Waco, pp. 274–75. The Justice Department erroneously suggested that the telephone connection was permanently cut off because residents threw the telephone outside in response to the final pre-assault notification. Justice Report, pp. 286–93.

305. Justice Report, pp. 110, 286.

306. Justice Report, p. 286.

307. Justice Report, p. 292.

308. Boyer, "Children of Waco," p. 41.

309. Ibid.

310. Justice Report, pp. 272–73; Hearing, p. 19.

311. Sam Howe Verhovek, "Scores Die as Cult Compound Is Set Afire after FBI Sends in Tanks with Tear Gas," New York Times, April 20, 1993; Michael Isikoff and Pierre Thomas, "Reno Says, 'I Made the Decision'," Washington Post, April 20, 1993, p. A9. According to President Clinton, Attorney General Reno told him that the two major reasons she felt the FBI should be allowed to go forward were that the children were being abused and that the inside of the compound was increasingly unsafe. Linedecker, Massacre at Waco, p. 235.

Just before Kathy Schroeder came out, in mid-March, she went to say goodbye to Koresh, and found him in bed with a girl; Schroeder told the FBI about this when she was debriefed while being held in jail. Jamar, Joint Hearings, part 2, p. 324. There is no indication how old the girl was; Koresh's brides ranged from pre-teens to forty-something adults.

312. Boyer, "Children of Waco," p. 42.

313. Ibid., p. 45.

314. Anne Marie Kilday, "Clinton Pledges Probe of Siege," *Dallas Morning News*, April 21, 1993.

315. Barbara Kantrowicz, "The Messiah of Waco," *Newsweek*, March 15, 1993, pp. 56–58 (citing sources close to Reno).

316. Presidential press conference, April 21, 1993.

317. Jerry Seper, "Reviewer Disputes Clinton over Waco," *Washington Times*, April 27, 1995, p. A1.

318. Lawrence Lilliston, "Who Committed Child Abuse at Waco?" in Lewis, p. 170. In one case, outside specialists were enlisted by the Dade County District Attorney's Office to "help" (pester and intimidate) allegedly abused children into "disclosing" what had happened. Under pressure from the investigators, many children finally "disclosed" what the investigators apparently wanted to hear, and told lurid tales of ritual abuse, in which a fourteen-year-old church babysitter killed and ate babies, led naked dances around a campfire, took the children to cemeteries where movie character Freddy Krueger came out of a grave, and introduced them to flying witches. Many of these activities supposedly took place while daytime church services were in progress at the Presbyterian church where Bobby Fijnje was a volunteer babysitter. After spending 20 months in jail awaiting trial, Bobby Fijnje was acquitted on all counts. "It seems clear that in at least some child abuse investigations the chief problems children face are those created by the well-meaning rescuers," observed journalist Peter J. Boyer. Boyer, "Children of Waco," p. 44. Boyer's observation about District Attorney Reno's attempted "rescue" of the non-abused Presbyterian children is equally applicable to her attempted rescue of the Branch Davidian children. See also "Janet Reno's Witch Hunts," *Washington Times* (national weekly edition), November 17, 1996, p. 45.

319. Justice Report, p. 226.

320. Anne Marie Kilday, "Clinton Defends Probe of Siege," *Dallas Morning News*, April 21, 1993.

321. Michael Isikoff, "Waco Siege Prompts Crisis Training for Top Justice Department Officials," *Washington Post*, December 9, 1993.

322. "Reno on Waco: 'I Would Not Do It Again,' " *Washington Post*, May 15, 1995 (Reuters). Similarly, she told "Larry King Live" about her "horrible fear" that "if I delayed, without sanitation or toilets there . . . I could go in and find children dead from any number of things." Christopher G. Ellison and John P. Bartkowski, "'Babies Were Being Beaten'," in Wright, *Armageddon in Waco*, p. 131.

323. James Bovard, "Waco Must Get a Hearing," *Wall Street Journal*, May 15, 1995.

324. Joe Rosenbloom III, "Waco: More than Simple Blunders?" *Wall Street Journal*, October 17, 1995.

325. ABC Nightline, "Waco: What Went Wrong," April 19, 1993 (New York: ABC News).

326. Kessler, *The FBI*, p. 424.

327. Justice Report, p. 201; Lee Hancock, "Koresh, Attorney Meet Again" *Dallas Morning News*, March 31, 1993; Howard Schneider, "Waco Cultists Send out Home Movies," *Washington Post*, March 30, 1993.

328. Reavis, *The Ashes of Waco*, pp. 226–29.

329. "Prophet's Fulfillment," pp. 4, 6; Stephen Labaton, "Death in Waco: The Government's Plan," *New York Times*, April 21, 1993, p. A21. While jailed in Washington (for attempting to dig a grave on the White House lawn as protest against U.S. militarism), the radical priest Daniel Berrigan wrote: "Bellicose, selfish, self-deluded, icy, absurdly resolute—behold the Rome of the Book of Revelation. Behold also America?" Daniel Berrigan, *Nightmare of God*, p. 23, quoted in Paul Boyer, *When Time Shall Be No More: Prophecy Belief in Modern American Culture* (Cambridge, Mass.: Harvard University Press, 1992), p. 261.

330. Vance McLaughlin and Steve Smith, "The Rodney King Syndrome," *Journal on Firearms and Public Policy* 9 (1997, forthcoming).

4

The Great Disappointment

> Some say the world will end in fire
> Some say in ice.
> From what I've tasted of desire
> I hold with those who favor fire.
>
> Robert Frost[1]

"None of us expected them to commit suicide," insisted FBI Director William Sessions.[2] "[E]very single analysis made of his writing, of what he [Koresh] had said, of what he had said to his lawyers, of what the behavioral science people said, what the psychologists thought, the psycholinguists thought, what the psychiatrists believed, was that this man was not suicidal, that he would not take his life."[3] Similarly, Attorney General Reno noted that experts had "advised the Bureau that the chances of suicide were not likely."[4] She added, "Obviously, if I had thought that the chances were great for mass suicide, I never would have approved the plan."[5] Two years later, the attorney general would say just the opposite, justifying the tank assault based on "the fact that he had rehearsed a suicide plan and could, based on what the experts were telling us, based on . . . some of the religious statements, could possibly commit suicide."[6]

The attorney general's 1995 statement was much closer to the truth than what she and the FBI director had claimed in 1993.

Law Enforcement Expectations

Suicide had been a major issue from the outset. One reason BATF adopted the assault method for serving the warrants rather than mounting a siege was the fear of mass suicide.[7]

Concerns about suicide led the FBI in early March to develop an assault plan, sim-

186

ilar to that eventually implemented, as an emergency measure, should mass suicides begin. Then one of the psychologists, Dr. Bruce D. Terry, told the FBI that Koresh would not personally take his own life, but Dr. Terry also warned that Koresh would arrange "an abstract suicide—some way for everyone to die, like setting up a large-scale explosion."[8] Another psychiatrist, Park Dietz, thought Koresh would order a mass suicide. The FBI's Behavioral Sciences Unit suggested Koresh might arrange a "suicide by cop," where someone arranges for law enforcement to take his life.[9] Along with FBI profiler Clinton Van Zandt, psychiatrist Joseph L. Krofcheck concluded that Koresh would never come out, and voiced the concern that Koresh "may have been planning to set his own trap for the FBI, including 'the destruction by fire and explosion' referred to in many of the scriptural references contained in the April 9 letter."[10]

The FBI agents at Waco had always thought there was a very serious possibility of suicide. One month before the April 19 disaster, FBI press spokesman Bob Ricks said: "We're very concerned as part of Koresh's grand scheme that he would like to see a large number of his people die, which would be justification for his pronouncements and the fulfillment of his scriptures. . . . The majority, and it may be the totality of all those inside, they do not express fear of being involved in a firefight of any sort of that nature. Any fear they express is fear of losing their eternal soul."[11] Shortly after April 19, Ricks stated that the FBI expected very high casualties. "We knew that the chances were great that the adults would not come out unharmed."[12]

Commander Jeff Jamar likewise insisted the FBI had expected a mass suicide all along: "This was his plan from the beginning. It's clear to us it would have happened thirty days ago if we had gone in there."[13]

These consistent and accurate predictions from the FBI agents on the ground at Waco were not conveyed to the attorney general. Rather, she was (falsely) told that the FBI behavioral experts were unanimous that mass suicide was very unlikely.

After April 19, FBI Director William Sessions claimed that the FBI thought suicide was unlikely because David Koresh assured the negotiators that suicide would not occur.[14] Yet the FBI's stated reason for abandoning negotiations was that Koresh never told the truth and the FBI could thus no longer negotiate with him in good faith.

Branch Davidian Warnings and Eschatology

There were numerous signs that Koresh expected the siege to end in the death of himself, his followers, and the government agents (as well as much or all of the rest of the world) in a great fire; but since the fire would be a holy one for God's purpose, setting the fire and dying in it would not be a suicide.

When the FBI began to clear the area around the house on April 18, preparatory to the April 19 attack, Koresh warned that "this could be the worst day in law enforcement history."[15] The FBI felt they could ignore such statements. "Day in and day out, David Koresh preached an apocalyptic theology. . . . So it is hard to discern is this his general theological approach to the end of the world or is he specifically talking about a fire."[16] Had the FBI relied more on religious experts, the specific warnings about fires might have been taken more seriously.

The teachings of David Koresh forecast deliverance by fire. Koresh believed that the FBI siege related to the event forecast in Revelation at the opening of the sixth seal:

> And I beheld when he [the Lamb, meaning (to the Davidians) Koresh] had opened the sixth seal, and, lo, there was a great earthquake; and the sun became black as sackcloth of hair and the moon became as blood. . . . For the great day of his [the Lamb's] wrath is come; and who shall be able to stand?[17]

The seven seals were the core of Branch Davidian theology. Koresh's Bible teachings, some of which he included in his letters to the FBI, argued that various Old Testament passages also related to the sixth seal. These passages are suffused with images of God kindling a massive, destructive fire that will destroy sinners and purify the righteous. In Amos, Koresh pointed to the prediction: "The LORD will roar . . . and the top of Carmel shall whither."[18] (The Davidian home was, of course, named Mount Carmel.) That passage is followed by the repeated warning of God: "I will send a fire."[19] Besides destroying the unbelievers, what Koresh called "The fire that will cleanse" was also expected to wash "away the filth of the daughters of Zion . . . by the spirit of burning"[20] which Koresh interpreted as changing the DNA of the Branch Davidians.[21]

According to social worker Joyce Sparks, when she had visited Koresh, he told of a vision he once had: "the enemy will surround the camp, and the saints will die. . . . There will be blood and fire, an explosion at the end." Ms. Sparks informed the FBI about this vision.[22]

Weeks into the siege, Steve Schneider called his family in Wisconsin;[23] and his sister Sue asked him when the Davidians would be coming out. "Very soon," Schneider replied, but adding, "It's a lot more complicated than that, Sue. Read the book of Nahum." Nahum describes a great battle, in which God warns the enemy "Behold, I am against thee, saith the LORD of hosts, and I will burn her chariots in the smoke."[24] Koresh had long taught that the "chariots" in Nahum referred to tanks.[25]

Koresh (whose chosen name was the Hebrew word for "Cyrus") taught that the "Death of Cyrus" would take place pursuant to the Book of Amos: "And it shall come to pass in that day, saith the Lord GOD, that I will cause the sun to go down at noon, and I will darken the earth in the clear day."[26] Notably, the fires of April 19 broke out at about noon.

There were plenty of other Bible prophecies for the Branch Davidians—who rejected the world and immersed themselves in the Bible (as expounded by their prophet)—to see themselves and the world ending in fire. On the "day of the Lord," the earth "shall be burned up," explains 2 Peter.[27]

In a passage with particular resonance for a group about to be conquered by its enemies, Baruch advises "make haste, and take all things, and cast them into the fire . . . and the flame sends them to him who created them, so that the enemies do not take possession of them."[28] Thessalonians foresees "flaming fire" as the instrument of "vengeance on them that know not God."[29] The Book of Isaiah, in passages that Koresh lectured about frequently, warns, "Howl ye; for the day of the LORD is at hand . . . their faces shall be as flames."[30] Koresh also taught other passages forecasting apocalyptic fire: Psalms 50:3 ("a fire shall devour before him, and it shall be very tempestuous round about him"); Isaiah 26:11 ("yea, the fire of thine enemies shall devour them"); and Jeremiah 21:14 ("I will punish you according to the fruit of your doings, saith the LORD: and I will kindle a fire in the forest thereof, and it shall devour all things round about it.").[31]

But later, as Koresh also noted, Isaiah prophesies that God's chosen will be safe: "when though walkest through the fire, thou shalt not be burned; neither shall the flame kindle upon thee."[32] Zechariah, by one reading, speaks of God using fire to protect the true believers: "For I, saith the LORD, will be unto her [Jerusalem] a wall of fire round about, and will be the glory in the midst of her."[33] (Zechariah and the fire around Jerusalem had also been crucial elements in the teachings of Koresh's predecessors Victor Houteff and Lois Roden.[34])The Branch Davidians may have expected that, like Elijah, they would literally be carried off to heaven in a flaming chariot.[35] The flames were for their enemies, not themselves. As the women used to chant during their morning runs:

> We're with Cyrus, he's our man.
> Gonna kill his enemies where they stand.
> If you have the world's desire,
> Gonna throw you in God's holy fire.[36]

And when would the great cleansing fire, which Koresh taught would give "faces of flames" to the Davidians, come? The Davidian eschatology (as interpreted by Koresh) looked for the event shortly after April 18. According to disaffected Davidian Marc Breault, there had been plans for a mass suicide shortly after April 18, 1992, but the plans had been put off, perhaps as a result of an Australian television exposé of Koresh. One analyst of Branch Davidian theology concluded that the Branch Davidians believed that they were experiencing one of the "tribulations" from the Book of Baruch; each tribulation lasts seven weeks, meaning that the current one would end around April 18.[37] As a religious scholar later noted, the FBI attack "delivered to David Koresh the apocalyptic situation that he had predicted and expected for 10 years, and it came on the 19th."[38]

Koresh was not the first Branch Davidian prophet to expect the apocalypse around Passover. Florence Houteff's prediction for the end of the world was for April 22, 1959, the first night of Passover. The failure of the world to end on that date became known among Branch Davidians as the Great Disappointment. Even before the BATF raid, Koresh had been telling the Branch Davidians that the 1993 Passover might be the last one they would spend together.[39]

Branch Davidian theology was always evolving, and perhaps only a few of the Davidians really understood the full implications of what Koresh had been teaching. During the siege, Frank Leahy, the husband of one of the social workers (Joyce Sparks) who had investigated Koresh, studied Koresh's tapes and writings, and then wrote FBI commander Jeff Jamar a letter:

> David Koresh is currently on the fifth seal. . . . In order to progress to the Sixth Seal, David and some of his followers must be killed for their beliefs. The end must be a

fiery conflagration. Suicide is not an option as, according to David, "it is not written in the book." . . . The standoff as it now exists, will end after Sunday, April 18. . . . It must be a fiery ending, and David and a number of his followers must die . . . there will be some aggressive action by the Federal law enforcement officials . . . even if the final conflagration is caused internally, it must be some sort of act of the law enforcement officials.[40]

On April 18, 1993, the Davidians hung a sign in one of their windows, which an FBI sniper saw, reading: "Flames Await."[41] The week before, one of Koresh's letters to the FBI had warned that if FBI agents attacked, they would be "devoured by fire."[42]

Whatever the Davidians were planning, they could not have kept it secret from the FBI, which was using sophisticated electronic devices to monitor everything in the compound. According to a London *Sunday Times* article during the siege:

Aircraft flying overhead can pick up conversations between cult members and pinpoint their position using infra-red devices that lock on to heat sources. The walls, air vents and chimneys are all places where tiny fibre-optic microphones and cameras have been inserted to relay audio and visual images back to the control centre. . . .

Two weeks ago, the FBI requested that a special surveillance plane fly down to Waco. The multi-sensor surveillance aircraft is made by Pilatus Britten-Norman on the Isle of Wight. . . .

Other equipment has been adopted from the hospital operating theatre. Fibre-optic cables which can be inserted into walls and down chimneys are identical to the cameras used to explore patients' arteries and organs. At Waco, they relay a full-colour picture of a whole room from a lens measuring no more than an eighth of an inch.

Even before the raid last month, the compound had been infiltrated by undercover agents. . . . While the agents were inside, normal telephones have been replaced by converted sets which double as microphones to relay all conversation inside a room.[43]

The *Sunday Times* was at least partially in error, since Mount Carmel had no chimneys; if the other parts of the article are true, then BATF began taping the Davidians long before a warrant was obtained, a flagrant violation of the Fourth Amendment, and a violation of federal criminal law.[44] There is no evidence that BATF or the FBI ever obtained a warrant to use remote or local listening devices to spy on the people at Mount Carmel. Once the siege began, a warrant would have been readily granted, but—if this report is accurate—the FBI and BATF apparently considered the Fourth Amendment a technicality which could be brushed aside.

The surveillance devices did pick up important warnings. On April 18, several Branch Davidians were heard discussing the possibility that God would "take us up like flames of fire."[45]

The FBI was well aware the structure was a fire hazard. Steve Schneider mentioned to the FBI negotiators that reading was by candle and Coleman lantern light. Early on, Rachel Jones Koresh confirmed to a negotiator that propane heaters were in use; she worried that if someone fired at the heaters, they could explode.[46] "Bales of hay, brought from storage in the gymnasium, had been stacked against walls which faced outside, as protection against renewed gunfire. Schneider's negotiator recognized a hazard and asked, 'Do you have any fire extinguisher systems?' Schneider wasn't sure how many of the devices were on hand, and at the negotiator's request sent a resident to do a count. Schneider reported that only one extinguisher was found. 'Somebody ought to buy some fire insurance,' his negotiator said."[47]

Most significantly of all, the FBI has admitted that it expected Koresh to start a fire. As the negotiations deteriorated, Koresh kept urging the FBI to "get it on" and launch their big attack. According to FBI spokesman Bob Ricks, "What we think was in his mind was that he expected us to come in and mount a frontal tactical assault against the compound. Once we were inside, he would light it up and burn us up with his own people."[48]

The forty-eight-hour chemical warfare plan that was presented to the attorney general was designed to counter Koresh's strategy. Rather than entering the building, the FBI tanks would stay outside, and, by inserting the chemical warfare agent, make it intolerable for anyone to remain inside.

But the FBI did not execute this plan which they sold to the attorney general. Tanks began entering the building by breaking down the walls. This had precisely the effect that the FBI anticipated. According to Ricks, Koresh ordered the fire lit in order to destroy the tanks in the building; when the tanks began to withdraw, Koresh attempted to abort the murder-suicide, shouting "Don't light it up," but it was too late.[49]

Yet the day after the fire, Ricks claimed that officials in charge of the operation had not expected a fire.[50] Even today, many defenders of the FBI and the Department of Justice continue to insist that the burning of Mount Carmel was an unforeseeable tragedy, and the FBI would never have gone ahead if they had been aware of the risk.

Despite all the indications that the Davidians would set a fire, there was no firefighting equipment present or on call. Despite the attorney general's insistence that "I was concerned about intentional or accidental explosions and ordered that additional resources be provided to ensure that there was an adequate emergency response,"[51] and despite FBI Director Sessions's insistence that there was a "fire contingency plan," this "plan" expressly included deciding not to have fire trucks in the vicinity because the Davidians had rifles which could shoot long distances.[52]

The United States military, which had honored the FBI's requests for the tanks which were used to assault the Mount Carmel Center, has its own heavy-duty firefighting tanks, which could have been used without risk of injury from Davidian bullets.[53] The U.S. military also has aerial firefighting capability.[54] Further, a California company, Flamecheck, had offered to let the FBI use its remote-controlled firefighting tank. The tank, manufactured in the Czech Republic, can shoot six hundred gallons of water or foam per minute.[55] The FBI apparently did not request the loan of any of this equipment.

Commented Ohio Representative Jim Traficant, "When you have one hundred TV crews but not one fire truck, that's not a well-thought-out plan, that's box office."[56]

The FBI was acting, it should be remembered, to save the children, whose morning hours of government-supplied chemical warfare torture were completed with early afternoon death.

APRIL 19

Mary (singing to her baby): "In Heaven there is great joy."

Blacksmith: "It will soon be daylight, but the heat is stifling."

Blacksmith's wife: "I'm so afraid."

Squire: "We feel something will happen to us, but we don't know what."

Knight: "Doomsday perhaps."

Ingmar Bergman, *The Seventh Seal*[57]

The nineteenth of April, 1993, was a strange conjunction of anniversaries of armed peoples and armed governments.

In Massachusetts, April 19 is an official holiday, Patriots' Day, marking the anniversary of Paul Revere's 1775 ride, and the beginning of the American Revolution, when British Redcoats attempted to seize American weapons at Lexington and Concord, and were met at Concord by a militia of farmers with their guns.[58] Starting in 1989 (when the national furor over "assault weapons" broke out), gun rights activists around the country have commemorated April 19 with rallies at state capitals and with legislative phone-ins.

April 19, 1903, was the birthday of the late Elliot Ness, the "Untouchable" federal prohibition agent who was known for enforcing alcohol prohibition laws by breaking into buildings and opening fire. Ness is revered as BATF's greatest hero, and the annual Ness birthday celebration is one of the most important social events on the BATF calendar. On April 19, 1993, 1,500 BATF employees celebrated Ness's ninetieth birthday at a party in Baltimore.[59] It is possible that BATF agents on the scene at Waco made known the significance of the date to their FBI colleagues. It could be that at least part of the reason for choosing April 19 for the final assault was to humor BATF, which was ready to celebrate its conquest of Mount Carmel Center on its patron saint's birthday.[60] A more reasonable date for the FBI assault would have been near the end of the month, since that is when the HRT would have reached the point of needing to stand down.[61] The later date would also have allowed the FBI to determine whether the surrender letter was genuine. On the other hand, April 19 may simply have been the first date that the FBI could bring the matter to a conclusion and go home. The attorney general had ruled out executing the plan on the weekend because of concern about the availability of emergency rooms.

In contrast to the well-known Ness birthday, there is no evidence that the FBI or the Branch Davidians knew that April 19, 1993, marked the fiftieth anniversary of the Nazi assault on the Warsaw ghetto. In January 1943, the Nazis had attempted to begin rounding up the remnants of the Jews in Warsaw. To the Nazis' great surprise, armed Jews drove the Nazis away.[62] The Jews had built bunkers with underground tunnels, and grew increasingly well-armed with rifles, machine guns, handguns, grenades, and other explosives supplied by the Polish resistance, smuggled out of Nazi factories, or taken from dead Nazi soldiers. A major Nazi assault began on April 19, with the expectation that the ghetto would be cleared in time for Hitler's birthday on the twentieth.

The assault was led by a tank and two armored cars; a Jewish unit set the tank on fire twice, forcing a Nazi retreat.

The Nazis returned with artillery, and after April 22, Nazi artillery drove many Jews into the Jewish tunnel system that connected with the sewers. The Nazis used poison gasses to attempt to clear the Jews out of the sewers. Nazi forces could not directly take on the buildings where the Jews had built hidden bunkers, cellars, and attics; room-to-room fighting would have inflicted unacceptably high casualties on the Nazis. So the Nazis began to burn down the Warsaw ghetto, one building at a time. Explosives and artillery were used to smash the buildings that were not flammable. On April 25, the Nazi commanding general recorded in his diary: "this evening one can see a gigantic sea of flames." SS General Stroop wrote: "Over and over, we observed the Jews and the bandits, despite the danger of being burned alive, preferred to return to the flame, rather than being caught by us." The Jewish will to resist never broke. Finally, on May 16, the Warsaw synagogue was blown up, and the battle was over. In contrast to the usual result when the Nazis made an area into a "Jew-free zone" (*Judenrein*), there was nothing of economic value for the Nazis to take; to the contrary, the Nazis had been forced to pay a price in order to take Jewish lives.

Although almost none of the Warsaw ghetto defenders survived, the importance of the Warsaw uprising for Judaism's future was immense. According to Raul Hilberg, a scholar of the Nazi war machine, the Warsaw battle was perhaps the most significant in modern Jewish history: "In Jewish history, the battle is literally a revolution, for after two thousand years of a policy of submission the wheel had been turned and once again Jews were using force."[63]

April 19 was also an anniversary (approximately) of one of the last great Jewish military actions before Warsaw: Masada. In the year 66, a group of Jews known at the Zealots led an uprising to liberate their homeland from the Roman Empire. The revolt failed, and the Zealots took refuge in a mountain fortress city known as Masada. The Romans laid siege, but the Zealots held out in Masada. A few days after Passover in the year 73, the 960 defenders of Masada realized that Roman conquest was at hand. They could surrender and let their wives be raped, their children be enslaved, and themselves be tortured by the Romans. The Zealots were familiar with the Book of Daniel (the Old Testament apocalyptic book which is the foundation for the New Testament's Book of Revelation). Daniel forecast that after a last battle, "And they that understand among the people shall instruct many: yet they shall fall by the sword, and by flame, by captivity, and by spoil, many days."[64] Indeed, the Zealots of Masada would later be held up as role models by many generations of Jews, as well as by Romans and other Gentiles.

According to the Jewish historian Josephus, the Zealot leader Eleazer ben Ya'ir said:

> It is very plain that we shall be taken within a day's time; but it is still an eligible thing to die in a glorious manner, together with our dearest friends. . . . But first let us destroy . . . the fortress by fire.

The Jews cast lots for the order in which the men, women, and children would be killed by the sword. The wooden fortress was ignited; according to Josephus, "once set on fire, its hollowness made that fire spread like a mighty flame."[65]

David Koresh knew about Masada and the Book of Daniel.[66] Masada and Mount Carmel both ended up being destroyed first by siege, then by battering, and finally by fire.[67]

Koresh obviously knew about Jesus as well. In addition to thinking himself to be, like Jesus, God's anointed, Koresh was thirty-three years old, the same age as Jesus when Jesus was executed on the afternoon after the Passover Seder.

There is one other historical event worth keeping in mind, although it has no particular relation to April 19. It is an event that Koresh, as a child in the Texas public school system, had been taught was one of the glorious events in human history. A few hundred armed people, who had declared themselves independent from the government in power, found themselves in a fortified religious center surrounded by an immensely more powerful national army. One of the key disputes between the armed revolutionaries and the central government was the revolutionaries' adherence to a practice of human exploitation (slavery) which was repugnant to the central government at the time, and to the judgement of history. But rather than surrender to the government, the extremists in their religious center decided to fight to death, and every one of them was killed. The defenders of the Alamo are held up to children in Texas and in the United States as exemplars of courage. Yet few people who have passed through the modern American school system appear to understand why willingness to die for one's beliefs is a trait not just of Texan revolutionaries at the Alamo in 1836, but also of the minority of people in the 1990s who think they have beliefs that are worth dying for.[68]

As the sun began to rise on April 19, 1993, the Branch Davidian flag with its flying serpent and Star of David flew above Mount Carmel.[69] Opening ceremonies for the new Holocaust Museum in Washington were scheduled for later that day.[70]

TO RAZE A VILLAGE

"[T]he sun became as black as sackcloth of hair, and the moon became as blood."[71]

On April 18, the FBI telephoned Mount Carmel and told the Branch Davidians that milk and other supplies would be delivered on the nineteenth.[72] Before, the FBI had been obstreperous about allowing milk to be brought in. The sudden change in attitude, according to Dick Reavis, made Koresh suspicious. Koresh said, "They're going to invade us tonight or in the morning."[73] Also on April 18, the FBI began clearing the grounds around the building, preparing for a new assault. In response, the FBI was told that Koresh was slowing his work on the manuscript.[74] According to the FBI, listening devices inside Mount Carmel heard a Branch Davidian say, "David has decided that we are to step out onto the sun . . . it is going to be really bad, but that is what David has decided."[75]

Before the Fire

At about 5 A.M. on the morning of April 19, according to a hospital nurse, an FBI agent contacted the burn unit at Parkland Memorial Hospital to inquire as to its capacity, and its ability to accept a helicopter landing.[76] Two other hospitals were also contacted.[77] FBI agents dressed in fire-retardant Nomex suits, standard for high risk SWAT operations.[78] The FBI had arranged for the military to supply "three CH-47 aircraft—for MEDEVAC in event of a mass casualty. . . . The FBI will give us 12-hour notice prior to initiating operations that may require the CH-47 aircraft."[79]

David Koresh had been wounded in the wrist, in addition to a much more serious wound in the abdomen, during the February 28 attack, and accordingly could not type. His spelling skills had always been weak, partly as a result of his dyslexia. So Koresh did most of his writing by dictation. He spent the night of April 18–19 dictating his manuscript on the seven seals.[80] As detailed in the previous chapter, Koresh's belief was that, to complete the fifth seal, the Branch Davidians would be killed "a little season" after February 28. This expectation was consistent with previous teachings of Koresh about some kind of giant conflagration or explosion that, shortly after Passover, would kill him and perhaps usher in the sixth seal, whereby Koresh (acting as "the Lamb" of Revelation) would unleash his wrath and destroy a wicked world.[81]

Competing with the view just described was the argument that Professors Arnold and Tabor had made to Koresh via a tape delivered to Mount Carmel: the "little season" before the Davidians' destruction might be much longer than a literal season, and Koresh (the Lamb) might be permitted to reveal his knowledge of the seven seals to the whole world, thus allowing more people to believe the message and be saved. The latter view was the basis for Koresh's April 14 offer to surrender after he finished his manuscript on the seven seals, a manuscript he was writing before dawn on April 19.

One of the Branch Davidians who survived the fire recalled seeing Koresh at five in the morning, looking very tired. Koresh said he had been working on his manuscript,[82] although it is also possible that he was making plans or anguishing over the expected FBI attack. He was also probably tired as a result of the FBI's month-long sleep-deprivation and psychological warfare campaign.[83] Koresh's fatigue probably did not put him in the best frame of mind for making decisions.

At about 5:50 A.M., the FBI telephoned to inform the Branch Davidians that unless they surrendered instantly, they would be gassed. As the FBI demanded that Koresh and his followers immediately "come out and surrender to proper authority," Koresh must have concluded that his initial understanding was right, and Tabor and Arnold were wrong: the "little season" had ended, and now was the time the surviving Davidians "should be killed."[84] The fifth seal was being completed, and the end of the world was at hand. To simply surrender now, in a manner that could not possibly be in fulfillment of any interpretation of Revelation, would be to put obedience to the state above obedience to God. David Koresh and his followers had been preparing for years to face such a choice, and there was no doubt which alternative they would choose, now that the FBI had forced a choice.[85]

The first chemical warfare rounds were launched at about 6 A.M., and a fifty-four ton tank, the vanguard of a strike force consisting of over a dozen armored combat vehicles, began punching holes in the building at about 6:04 A.M.[86] One tank deliberately destroyed trapdoor access to an underground bus, which was known to the Davidians and the FBI to be the only place where the Davidians could survive a fire or resist a chemical warfare attack.[87] Koresh walked through the hallways, telling his followers "Get your gas masks on." There were no gas masks which fit the children.[88]

The tank and chemical warfare operations continued throughout the morning. Also throughout the morning, loudspeakers ordered the Davidians to come out, because they were under arrest:[89]

> We are in the process of placing tear gas into the building. This is not an assault. . . . Do not fire your weapons. If you fire, fire will be returned. Do not shoot. This is not an assault. The gas you smell is a non-lethal tear gas. This gas will temporarily render the building uninhabitable. . . .
> The tower is off limits. . . . Anyone observed to be in the tower will be considered to be an act of aggression and will be dealt with accordingly.
> If you come out now, you will not be harmed. . . . Come out with your hands up. Carry nothing. . . . Walk toward the large Red Cross flag.
> Follow all instructions of the FBI agents in the Bradleys. Follow all instructions. You are under arrest. This standoff is over.
> We do not want to hurt anyone. . . . This is not an assault. . . .
> Gas will continue to be delivered until everyone is out of the building.[90]

"The rickety buildings rattled violently with each ram of the tank," summarized the *Dallas Morning News*.[91] Some tanks pumped in CS from huge canisters; others fired in shells containing CS ferret rounds.[92] The tank pumps continued until the CS supply was nearly exhausted, at which point the FBI ordered more to be brought in from Houston.[93]

Meanwhile, the masked adults went on with their chores; some women did laundry or cleaned; others read the Bible.[93] "But there are also places in the bugs where you can hear or read the Branch Davidians knowing the gas was coming in, you heard them say 'Let's pray.' You hear them reading psalms, something like the 23rd Psalm: 'Lo, though I walk through the Valley of the Shadow of Death I will fear no evil.' . . . They gathered to pray, they began to recite these Biblical passages. What were they doing? They were calling upon their God to protect them from this CS gas . . . lives were lost and prayers were unanswered."[95] The FBI listening devices recorded the voices of children calling for their parents,[96] and the Davidians' frantic pleas for negotiations and for an end to the chemical warfare attack.[97]

Before the attack had begun, some FBI agents had breakfasted at a Waco diner. On a paper napkin, they drew a detailed map of the Mount Carmel Center, indicating who was located in which room. (The electronic surveillance was very thorough.) The napkin was left behind when the agents left; a waitress found it, and turned it over to the media. Unless the waitress drew the napkin herself, the tanks deliberately rammed parts of the building where people were known to be located.

"Plan A" had been based on forty-eight hours of gradual chemical warfare. When the Davidians tried shooting at the tanks, Plan B went into effect (Plan A having lasted for eight minutes[98]), and the pace of gassing was greatly accelerated. Later in the morning, in a deviation from Plan B, the tank drivers were ordered to drive all the way into the building to the cold storage room, where it was correctly expected that people would have retreated. All the children and their mothers were found there. The person who gave this order has not yet been identified.[99] (And he probably will never be identified, unless a special prosecutor is appointed.)

When the tank charged the cold storage room, it came as close as possible, until its boom began to catch on the rafters of the ceiling. The tank then fired a large amount of CS straight ahead, at the room where the women and children were hiding.[100]

After hours of bombardment with incapacitating CS chemical warfare agent, some of the Branch Davidians may have been unable to move, let alone flee. According to a study conducted by Failure Analysis Associates, the first four assaults of the Model Five delivery systems (the ones spraying CS from thirty-foot booms) created gas concentrations two to ninety times the concentration needed to deter a soldier. Anyone directly hit by the CS spray could be instantly sent into systemic shock, or killed.

The carrying agent for the CS spray, methylene chloride, achieved concentrations much higher than the level considered immediately dangerous to life and health; concentrations reached about 80 percent of the fatal dose for a healthy adult.

The effects of all the chemicals would have been cumulative. CS interferes with breathing. Methylene chloride (which has an anesthetic effect) lowers the respiration rate. When a person breathes in methylene chloride, the body converts some of it to carbon monoxide; carbon monoxide accumulating in the bloodstream reduces blood's ability to carry oxygen. The carbon dioxide, used as a propellant for the CS spray, would lower the oxygen concentration in the air.

The FBI stated that strong winds dissipated the CS so quickly that there was no pressure to leave. But the winds did not begin to blow until hours after dawn, by which time most of the chemical warfare agent had been inserted, and toxic concentrations of CS and $MeCl_2$ would have reached their peaks. It is entirely possible that a number of Branch Davidians were unconscious, unable to move, or too disoriented to know where to go.

The possibility is especially high for persons in the concrete room in the middle of the building, where all mothers and children had taken refuge. Most of the chemical warfare agent had been inserted before the winds began. The winds would likely not have dissipated the CS and methylene chloride which had accumulated in the cold storage room, for the room had no windows, and its only doorway faced into the wind. The $MeCl_2$, being heavier than air, would have accumulated in greatest quantities on the first story, near the floor, where the mothers and children were huddling.

As the destruction of the building proceeded, communication between different parts of the building was cut off. Clive Doyle (who suffered severe burns) was in the chapel, where it was almost impossible to see. But he could hear the cries of people without gas masks.[101]

At one minute after noon, the loudspeakers taunted Koresh (who disliked being called Vernon, and who was known to be implacably determined to maintain his role as a prophet), in the manner of a person shouting "Jump, coward" to a person on the ledge of a tall building: "David, we are facilitating you leaving the compound by enlarging the door. David, you have had your 15 minutes of fame. . . . Vernon is no longer the Messiah. Leave the building now." Six or seven minutes later, heat sources appear in the southeast portion of the building.[102]

As the fire burned, FBI negotiator Byron Sage had more constructive things to say: "Don't lose control of this, David. Don't lose control of this. Bring your people out safely."[103]

The Fire

Jack Zimmermann, an attorney who entered Mount Carmel during the siege, later testified that Davidian Graeme Craddock had told him that the group planned to set FBI tanks on fire if they invaded the house.[104] Koresh's attorney confirmed that Branch Davidian survivors explained to him "that they were pouring fuel and that they were making Molotov cocktails to throw at the tanks."[105] As FBI negotiator Byron Sage noted, as soon as the CS attack began, "The microphones indicate two things. They immediately donned gas masks and they immediately began to spread fuel."[106]

One of the so-called Mighty Men[107]—one of the males who enforced the will of Koresh—who survived the blaze reported hearing words like "Start the fires," "Light the fire," and "Don't light the fire." He also denied knowledge of any suicide pact.[108]

According to the enhanced tapes played at the trial, the FBI listening device heard someone say, "Pablo, have you poured it yet?" "In the hallway," came the reply. Four minutes later, another voice said, "Don't pour it all out. We may need some later." Ten minutes later, an unidentified voice said, "Start the fire?" The fuel was discussed by various voices the rest of the morning.[109]

The FBI listening devices in the building picked up all this talk about a fire. Two years later, at the House of Representatives hearings, FBI officials contradicted each other about what they had heard on the tapes. Jeffrey Jamar, the commander at Waco, testified that he would not have used the CS chemical warfare agent if he had heard the talk about spreading fuel. Jamar testified that he had no idea what was being said until the tapes were enhanced later.

In contrast, FBI negotiator Byron Sage testified that he heard the Branch Davidians talk about spreading fuel a few minutes after the first CS was inserted.[110]

As one of the attorneys for the Branch Davidians pointed out, prosecutor Ray Jahn

testified very truthfully that he could hear those tapes unenhanced with his ears the first time he listened to them. . . . Now, true, it was garbled; true, you had to listen carefully, and yes . . . every now and then you couldn't distinguish words. . . . But if you take the sum total of it, the whole morning for 6 hours . . . you had to have known that somebody in there was going to start that fire. . . . Let's just say the Davidians did start the fire. Our Government is held to a higher standard than those people in the compound, and they knew for 6 hours that continuing to pound that place and tear down the whole back side of it was going to cause something like this. But, folks, they had been down there too long. . . . And it was going to be over, come hell, high water or holocaust, and what we got was a holocaust.[111]

At about 11:42 A.M., a voice allegedly said, "Let's keep that fire going."[112] A videotape from the government plane using Forward Looking Infrared (FLIR) photography shows a small heat source at 11:42:56 in one of the first-floor rooms; the heat source then disappears.

At about 12:07 P.M., three heat sources become visible in rapid succession. The first is at 12:07:41 on the second floor of the tower, and is very small. It is possible that this first heat source comes from outside the tower window, rather than inside.[113] The second heat source becomes visible at 12:08:11 near the rear window of the dining room, and emits white smoke; and the third appears at 12:09:44, in the second window from the left on the southeast side of the chapel.[114] The heat source is seen ninety seconds after an FBI tank smashed into the nearby gymnasium.[115] At 12:08:32, near the CEV which had been demolishing the gymnasium, there are two bright thermal flashes; twenty seconds later, also near the CEV, there are flashes which appears to be gunfire, moving in the direction of the building.[116]

The Branch Davidians who escaped the building all said that the fire was started by tanks knocking over kerosene lanterns. But none of the fires started near the first-floor areas where the tanks were breaking in.[117] Nor is it likely that the three separate fires, starting within a few minutes of each other shortly after noon, would all be caused by tanks knocking over lanterns.

The Justice Department review states the fires were probably not set by accident by the tanks because the fires started after the tanks had withdrawn.[118]

The near-simultaneous ignition of three fires is strong evidence of arson, rather than an accidental fire. But the FLIR video is designed to observe heat which is escaping from the building, such as through a window or a hole in the roof. Nine thousand feet above the ground, the FLIR plane was circling Mount Carmel, so that any given room would be visible to the FLIR for fifteen seconds, then disappear for a minute or two, then reappear for fifteen seconds. While the heat from a large fire would glow through the walls and roof of the building, a small fire would be visible to the FLIR only if the fire were within two feet of the window. Thus a fire away from a window, especially on the first floor, would not necessarily show up right away on the FLIR.

It is possible that only a single fire was ignited, and that fire spread rapidly, resulting in the three hot spots which show up on the FLIR tape. Thus it is not impossible that the fire started on the second floor when a tank that was knocking down the building caused a burning lantern on the second floor to fall over.

Although the Branch Davidians clearly did expect deliverance by fire, survivor Jamie Castillo explains that they thought the fire would be started by God, not by themselves. Carol Moore, author of *The Massacre of the Branch Davidians*, argues that because the fires do not begin on the first floor near the tanks, the fires were not set by the Branch Davidians, since they would logically have set the fires near the tanks if the fires were intentionally set for defense.[119] Schneider's attorney also suggested that the location of the bodies—with the leaders in one room and the followers spread out elsewhere, many in the concrete room in the middle of the building—was "[n]ot exactly a mass suicide scenario."[120]

On the other hand, a fire that is intended to destroy the building and all the attackers therein does not necessarily have to be lit next to the attackers. And a holy fire, being holy, could accomplish its purposes no matter where it was ignited. Further, many of the rank-and-file Branch Davidians may not have known about any plan by Koresh to light a fire; the plan might have been known only to a few in the inner circle.

While the building was still in flames, a Department of Justice spokesman in Washington claimed the fire had been started by the Davidians; the spokesman stated that an FBI sniper using a rifle scope had seen a male figure, wearing black Ninja-style clothes and a black hood, pour liquid on the floor behind a piano, and then light it.[121]

The day after the fire, the FBI's Jeffrey Jamar said that agents saw a person "get down with cupped hands and then there was a flash of fire."[122]

But at the trial, the testimony and evidence were rather different. FBI Special Agent Jack Morrison said that he could see, through a hole created by a tank, somebody bent or kneeling by an overturned piano. The man appeared to be washing his hands, although the sniper admitted on cross-examination that he could not see the man's hands. The sniper testified that he could not tell if the man were starting a fire, or trying to put out a fire that had started accidentally. The fire did not erupt while the man was in the sniper's sight, but the sniper did see a fire shortly thereafter. However, pictures of the progress of the fire show that the area near the overturned piano (the front door) was not a starting point for any fire.[123] No fire appears there until several minutes after the sniper's observation.[124] Indeed, photographs show no fire in the area when much of the rest of the building is on fire.[125]

One question which has been raised is why the FBI had a Forward Looking Infrared (FLIR) camera overhead, if its primary use is to detect a source of fire. One possibility is that a fire was expected by the FBI, and the purpose was to show that if any fire broke out, the FBI did not ignite it.[126] But if the FBI expected the fire, then the FBI violated Attorney General Reno's orders by proceeding with the attack. The official explanation is that the FLIR was being used because the raid began prior to daylight,[127] which may not explain the flight and filming continuing through noon.[128]

The Government's Role in the Fire

The government may have made important contributions to the fires and the fires' deadliness. First, it is possible the spread of the fire might have been enhanced by spillage of flammables caused by the tanks.[129]

Although the CS had been partially dissipated by the mid-morning winds, the remaining CS could have made the fires spread much faster. An army field manual states, "Warning: When using the dry agent CS-1, do not discharge indoors. Accumulating dust may explode when exposed to spark or open flame."[130]

George Uhlig, a chemistry professor at the College of Eastern Utah and retired air force lieutenant colonel, explained one reason why the fire had grown so quickly:

> [T]he C.S. was diluted with either acetone or ethanol, as the autopsies indicated both solvents were in the lungs of the individuals killed at the Branch Davidian complex. . . . The liquid aerosol . . . came into contact with a flame, and the flame front traveled from particle to particle rapidly to create the "fireball" described by survivors. We used a similar concept in designing fuel-air explosive devices in the Air Force. . . . The structure burned rapidly to the ground, and the C.S. agent was burned in the process. Cyanide radicals were generated in the C.S. burned, combining with normal fluids in the lungs of the people to generate hydrogen-cyanide gas.[131]

Destruction of the walls by the tanks, which let the midday's warm twenty-five-mile-an-hour winds enter the building, contributed to the fire's spread by allowing more oxygen to fuel the fire.[132]

The federal government has not been forthcoming in releasing all of its videotapes from April 19, which has led some persons to suspect that the videos contain evidence that someone from the government provided the spark that started the fire. Only a few minutes of the morning's FLIR videotape have been made available to the public. The FLIR tape shows another plane, at a lower altitude, circling Mount Carmel, but the FBI has never acknowledged the purpose of this plane (which might reasonably be expected to be taking daytime photos or videos, since a FLIR produces poor daylight images). In addition, news footage shows an FBI agent on the ground using a camcorder. This footage has also never been released.

The most reasonable theory for the FBI starting the fire is not that the FBI had a plan to murder all the Branch Davidians. Instead, by noon, the FBI assault plan may have looked like a failure. The attorney general had been deceived; the FBI had violated her orders, and yet after six hours after the most massive chemical warfare assault on civilians in American history, nobody had come out of the building. If so much CS had failed to bring out a single person, it was hard to believe that still more CS would do the trick. What would the FBI do? Pull back, humiliated, and face the possible wrath of the attorney general?

Perhaps a lone FBI agent, or an FBI commander, decided that the only way to ever get the "cultists" out of their "compound" would be to burn it down. In the wooden firetrap, soaked with lantern fuel and full of flammable CS dust, one spark could start the fire that could finally force the Davidians out. The impromptu plan, if there were such a plan, did work. Nine people ran out of the building. The failure of everyone else to come out can be explained by the possibility that some had been rendered incapable of moving or were totally disoriented by the CS and $MeCl_2$, others were trapped by the rubble, and perhaps others were shot by zealots while attempting to flee.

Some evidence is consistent with this hypothesis. Branch Davidian survivors reported that some of the incoming CS came in "ferrets" which landed in the walls and spewed smoke, or which skittered around the floor. A ferret round, however, bursts on impact. What the survivors described appears to be the Federal Laboratories "Flite-Rite" or a similar product. These products are not supposed to be used indoors because they can cause fires.[133]

In addition, some of ferret rounds were shot through M-79 grenade launchers. These same grenade launchers had been used during the siege to shoot flashbang grenades at the Branch Davidians. A flashbang grenade, as the name implies, is pyrotechnic. When it lands, it creates a large flash and three-foot fireball. There were about four hundred ferret rounds shot inside.[134] If just one of the persons firing the ferrets had accidentally or intentionally loaded a flashbang and fired it, the grenade could have given off the spark to start the fire. The Texas Rangers later found a pyrotechnic device in the gymnasium, near where a fire started.[135] Both the FBI and the Branch Davidians had flashbangs on hand the day of the fire.[136]

The question of who started the fire is hard to resolve with finality because there were *two* groups who had the motive, means, and opportunity to start a fire. As previous chapters have detailed, the credibility of some members of both groups is open to serious question.

Until more evidence is developed (perhaps through the civil suits discussed in the next chapter, or through a special prosecutor), the issue of who started the fire cannot be settled. While the evidence is entirely consistent with a fire started by Koresh, and the weight of the evidence points toward his guilt, the evidence does not exclude the possibility of another origin for the fire.

Whatever happened in the final minutes, it seems likely that at least some Branch Davidians were dead before the fire began, killed by the CS.[137] The autopsies were, of course, conducted several days after the fire; by then, any CS in a victim's body would have broken down to simpler molecules.[138] Nevertheless, the autopsy evidence points directly to CS.

Animal studies of CS show that fatal doses of CS cause lung congestion and edema (fluid in the lungs), and sometimes cause bleeding in the lung and throat.[139] In contrast, autopsies of deaths from smoke inhalation reveal a high blood level of carbon monoxide and large amounts of soot in the bronchi. For example, the autopsy of Koresh showed 24 percent carbon monoxide saturation, and "a dense black soot deposition over the mucosa of the tracheobroncial tree extending to the smaller airways."[140]

Contrast Koresh's autopsy with that of Jane Doe, an unknown fifty-five-year-old woman. Although her lungs were too decomposed to be analyzed, her blood showed no carbon monoxide. This suggests that she died before the fire started. The coroner reported nine deaths, including six children, as due to suffocation or asphyxia (which could be caused by CS), rather than by smoke inhalation or by burns (which would be caused by the fire).[141] The FBI chemical warfare may have killed at least six children and three adults.

The FBI assault blocked paths which would have led to safety. As the arson report noted, "It is also possible that the escape route planned included the . . . tunnel system accessible through an opening in the floor at the west end of the building. A significant amount of structural debris was found in this area indicating that the breaching operations could have caused this route to be blocked."[142] The blocked tunnel, reachable by a trap door in the house, led to a buried school bus.

The FBI knew about the buried bus. The first CEV to hit the building carried out instructions to destroy access to the bus. CS was inserted so as to drive people away from the trap door leading to the bus.[143]

After the fire, the FBI checked the bus. The bus remained cool, but it was empty.[144] (Strangely, FBI SAC Jeff Jamar told the *Washington Post* the day after the fire that four bodies had been found in the bus,[145] but this claim was never repeated.) At the Davidians' trial, Dr. Nizam Peerwani, the medical examiner who investigated the dead bodies, reported that seven women were found dead in the hallway that led to the trap door that led to the underground bus. Had they gotten to the underground bus, they would have survived; but they could not open the trap door, because it was covered with debris from a wall that collapsed as a result of the tank attack.[146]

The concrete cold-storage room in the center of the house held the bodies of twenty-six children and sixteen mothers.[147] The mothers had wrapped their children and themselves in sleeping bags, apparently for protection from the flames.[148] At least two of the children died from blunt trauma consistent with being struck by rubble from the two-foot hole in the ceiling.[149]

What were the final conscious hours of the children like? Benjamin C. Garrett, the executive director of the Chemical and Biological Arms Control Institute, states that as a result of the incessant chemical warfare barrage, the CS "would have panicked the children. Their eyes would have involuntarily shut. Their skin would have been burning. They would have been gasping for air and coughing wildly. Eventually, they would have been overcome with vomiting in a final hell."[150]

The fire burned for only about twenty-five minutes, but reached about 2,000 degrees Fahrenheit, "approaching cremation temperature," as a government medical report later put it.[151] The report noted that "Most of the burned bodies were unrecognizable as humans."[152]

It is unclear whether fire equipment would have done any good, but it was not summoned until at least ten minutes after the fire began. The trucks arrived at a checkpoint ten minutes later, and firemen were held up by the FBI for fifteen or sixteen minutes.[153]

According to the FBI, fire equipment had to be delayed "because the exploding ammunition made it too dangerous."[154] Actually, when ammunition burns, it does not explode, although it is possible that the FBI was unaware of this fact.[155] More realistically, the FBI worried the Davidians might shoot the firefighters; there was no guarantee that the Davidians would recognize that the fire crews were not hostile.[156]

Indeed, there were shots fired. Steve Schneider was found with a gunshot wound in the back of his head and David Koresh with a gunshot wound to the front of his head. Koresh and Schneider had last been seen upstairs. The bodies of eighteen other Branch Davidians who died by gunshot were found in a first-floor room next to the cold storage room.

One possibility is that these Branch Davidians, having decided not to surrender, shot themselves, or shot each other, to avoid a painful death by fire. In cases of suicide or voluntary execution, the decedent would be shot in the head, since that shot produces the quickest, least painful death. Several deaths were from gunshot wounds to the head. But other persons were wounded only in the chest or the back.[157] While most of the bodies had some evidence of carbon monoxide inhalation, some had none at all, even though they were relatively well preserved; this suggests that they died before the fire spread.[158] It also suggests that not all of the eighteen died at the same time.

One explanation for the strange wound patterns in a suicide would be that some or all of the Davidians might have stood in a circle and shot each other.

An alternative scenario is some or all tried to flee out the back door, but were shot by one or more of Koresh's "Mighty Men" stationed as guards.

A third possibility is explored in the film *Waco: The Rules of Engagement* (produced by William Gazicki and Mike McNulty), which premiered in January 1997 at the Robert Redford Sundance Film Festival, in Salt Lake City.

The film examines the FLIR videotape, and finds evidence of a heavy volume of automatic weapons fire into the back of the building—the one side which was not visible to the media. The film also shows a lesser volume of gunfire originating inside the building, and directed out. This evidence could be consistent with an attempted breakout by some of the Branch Davidians, resulting in a gun battle which the Branch Davidians lost, or of some other type of combat between government forces and the Branch Davidians. The scenario would not be consistent with FBI statements that nobody in the government fired a single shot during the entire day of April 19.

Exactly what happened in the final hours at the Mount Carmel Center on April 19 remains a mystery.

At the request of BATF, a Texas Ranger mounted the blue "ATF" flag, along with the American and Texas flags, above the wreckage and the smoldering bodies.[159]

That night, Attorney General Reno hit a public relations home run by saying that the buck stopped with her, and she accepted responsibility for the day's events. The next day, the president of the United States called the attorney general, and said, "That-a-girl."[160] At a press conference later that day, the president said: "I do not think the United States government is responsible for the fact that a bunch of religious fanatics decided to kill themselves."[161]

CHILD ABUSE

"The horror, the horror."

Col. Walter E. Kurtz, *Apocalypse Now*[162]

From start to finish, charges of child abuse against Koresh were used as justification for the government's aggressive actions. Attorney General Reno led off her 1995 congressional testimony justifying her 1993 actions by describing an incident of child abuse perpetrated by David Koresh in 1988.[163] Even if Koresh had stood trial and been acquitted of all charges related to the raid and the siege, there is a good chance he would currently be serving a long prison sentence for child abuse.

First of all, Koresh took as wives in his "House of David" girls young as eleven or twelve.[164] While girls of such age have often been brides in other cultures or other eras, Koresh's actions violated the statutory rape laws of Texas.[165] There was at least one 1987 incident in which the rape, besides being a statutory rape, may also have been a forcible rape.[166]

Before the July 1995 congressional hearings, Koresh's guilt of statutory rape was not in dispute. Representative Charles Schumer, the special committee's most ardent defender of governmental actions, nevertheless was allowed to pull a brilliant public relations coup by calling as a witness on the first day of the hearings Kiri Jewell, whose testimony dominated media coverage the next day. Ms. Jewell testified that when she was ten years old, Koresh had climbed on top of her in bed. Although they had not had sexual intercourse,[167] the purpose was to prepare her for having sex with him when she was older. The incident was said to have occurred at a Waco motel.[168] Allegations about Koresh's sexual contact with Ms. Jewell were first made years before the hearings, as part of a child custody dispute.

As is common in child custody cases, evidence is contradictory: Ms. Jewell's mother and grandmother denied the event ever took place; Ms. Jewell had made contradictory statements in the past;[169] and she had refused previously to testify against Koresh.[170] During the siege, she appeared on the "Donahue" show, and claimed that she and other Branch Davidians had been taught how to take cyanide pills. The claim was promptly disputed even by persons who had left the Branch Davidians, and by deprogrammer Rick Ross.[171]

While some persons have questioned the Kiri Jewell story,[172] even if the incident never took place, Koresh unquestionably perpetrated numerous statutory rapes on victims only a couple years older than Kiri Jewell. While some children's rights advocates have questioned the legitimacy of statutory rape laws, the Branch Davidian case illustrates the purpose of such laws to protect vulnerable young people against predatory adults.

The second component of abuse was physical violence against the children. Children were expected to be absolutely obedient; they were spanked often. This would not legally constitute child abuse in some other cultures, or in any generation of Americans before the current one, although many modern Americans would consider it abusive.

There were also reports of several incidents of severe beatings of babies or small children. The dates of these incidents are 1986, 1988 (two incidents), and 1990. There are no allegations of any such events in the two years preceding the BATF raid.[173] Carol Moore, head of the Committee for Waco Justice, was told by surviving Branch Davidians that church members had told Koresh that his discipline methods were becoming excessive, and that Koresh thereafter desisted.[174]

The Texas Department of Children's Protective Services examined the twenty-one children who left Mount Carmel. (Most left on the first night of the siege, and a few others left in the following days. They ranged in age from five months to twelve years.) The department found no evidence of child abuse. Instead, the children were "surprisingly happy, healthy, well adjusted, well educated, and only wanted to return as soon as they could to their friends and relatives in the compound." They were "voracious readers" of children's books and the Bible. Before the children came out of Mount Carmel, noted Joyce Sparks, some parents had lovingly prepared little bags of belongings or notes that listed favorite foods.[175]

The most detailed study of the children was conducted by Dr. Bruce Perry, who has served on the research advisory board of the American Family Foundation, an "anticult" group.[176] While treating the children at a Methodist home, he saw his job as overcoming the "inappropriate psychological practices" to which the children had been exposed.[177] He concluded that the children were physically abused, but not so severely as to warrant state intervention. He also concluded that the children were friendly, happy, likable, and had good interpersonal skills and were open to other people, although none of these traits are necessarily inconsistent with child abuse.[178]

Later, Dr. Perry spoke at the Cult Awareness Network's annual conference, delivering more detailed findings about the state of the Branch Davidian children;[179] a summary of the findings was presented at the House of Representatives hearings in 1995.[180] Some of these findings suggest the sometimes narrow mindset of the anticult movement, while other findings provide additional proof of Koresh's abuse.

"These kids have been terrorized," he said, based on the fact that their heartbeats were 30 to 50 percent faster than normal.[181] Perry blamed the terror in part on the Branch Davidians teaching the children to be afraid of the outside world, in which they were suddenly immersed, although he also acknowledged the effect of government actions on the children.[182] Regardless of prior teachings, it would hardly be abnormal for children to feel terrorized by a massive ground and helicopter assault on their home leading to the deaths of several adults, followed by the home being besieged, followed by the children being sent out of the home and being told that they would be staying with relatives, but instead being held in government custody by professionals determined to undo everything the children had learned. Fear would likely increase once the children found out that their home had burned to the ground, killing almost everyone they knew (including many children), after the same government that was holding them in custody had attacked the home with chemical warfare and tanks. What normal child would not feel afraid of his custodians under such circumstances?

In addition, said Dr. Perry, the children had little sense of traditional nuclear families. They made little distinction between siblings and other children, or between biological parents and other adults. Such a communal orientation is certainly abnormal, but in a society which claims to value diversity, it is hardly clear that unusual, communal social organization is per se child abuse. Indeed, it could be described as being raised by a village.

Dr. Perry reported that the children were limited because they did not recognize coins, but could quote long passages from the Bible.[183] It is difficult to understand why it should be considered harmful for small children to have greater knowledge of the central book of Western civilization than they do about money. Amish children, for example, also lead lives in which they may have little knowledge of common elements of ordinary American culture, but it would be wrong to take their condition as evidence of abuse.

Unlike Amish children, the Branch Davidian children had a very high knowledge of and interest in firearms. While Dr. Perry considered this a sign of abuse,[184] such knowledge has historically been common among children in rural America.

The children organized a boys group and a girls group, and chose a leader for each group by consensus. The leader would speak for the group, and make decisions for the group. Although Dr. Perry thought this method of social organization to be a sign of "cult" maladaption, it might not be a self-evidently bad idea for a group of small children, suddenly alone in a hostile, strange world, to rely for leadership on the boy and the girl who seem by mutual agreement to be the wisest. Adults, after all, rely on a lone person to make all sorts of important decisions for them; many religions have a single leader with great authority over believers' lives.

Perry complained that the children deferred to the boy leader and the girl leader for even simple decisions such as whether to put jelly on a peanut butter sandwich.[185] But what the complaint overlooks is that the Branch Davidian children, like the children of some other religious groups, including Orthodox Jews, had elaborate dietary rules that were a central item of their faith. The question for the Branch Davidian children was not whether jelly and peanut butter taste good together; the question was whether the mixing would violate a dietary law. The Branch Davidian dietary laws were generally hostile to highly processed foods, and had strict rules against eating fruit (e.g., jelly) with other foods.[186]

Given the importance of dietary laws to the children, the children were behaving at a high level of functioning when they recognized that mixing fruit jelly with other foods might violate a dietary restriction, and the children were hardly unreasonable in deferring to the wisest among them for a decision.

Other behavior, though, did show signs that the children had been raised in a poor environment. Many children, when asked to draw a self-portrait, drew a small primitive figure. Many put the figure in a corner of the piece of paper, rather than in the center.[187]

Primitive drawings sometimes reflect only lack of drawing skill. Many of the children were small, and there is no indication that artwork was a major part of their home schooling—certainly not as important as reading. On the other hand, primitive self-portraits by children who have the skills to draw better can be indications of low self-esteem, poorly developed self-awareness, or other problems, as can placement of the self-portrait in a small corner of the piece of paper.

Further, the children, including babies, were subjected to harsh and inappropriate punishments.[188] Koresh would also make arbitrary demands on the children—such as requiring a child to eat only potatoes for three days—which had the effect of reducing their ability to make independent decisions.[189]

None of the children had engaged in sex with Koresh but the girls expected to eventually become his brides. During Koresh's lengthy sermons, attended by the entire group, he sometimes gave graphic descriptions of sexual intercourse and his sexual "technique," a plainly inappropriate topic before an audience including children.[190]

A sexually, physically, and psychologically abused child, David Koresh grew into an abusive adult. As Dr. Perry accurately summarized, "The fact that the name of God and religion were used" to justify Koresh's various abuses made his criminal actions "even more heinous and destructive to the long term development of these children."[191]

The fact that Koresh was abusing the children does not, of course, give anyone else an excuse to abuse them. Now let us consider the actions of the federal government regarding child abuse:

- In order to serve an arrest warrant on one man and search a building, BATF launched an armed attack on the children's home.
- BATF may have used armor-piercing Cyclone ammunition, which carried particularly high risk of penetrating the thin walls of the home and killing or injuring a child.
- BATF helicopters (procured by lying to the military) may have strafed the second floor of the home, where the mothers and children lived. Among the evidence supporting the charge of strafing are pictures drawn by Davidian children showing bullet holes in the roof of their home.
- BATF later claimed that service of the warrant via armed assault was necessary because the children had to be protected from the dangers of the automatic weapons and explosives allegedly possessed by some of the children's parents.
- A siege ensued, and the FBI urged the families to come out. Whenever any families did come out, the parents were immediately jailed. Children who came out were not sent to relatives, but kept under government control under the supervision of persons actively hostile to the children's religious beliefs.
- Koresh offered to send out a six-year-old girl if he could talk to Robert Rodriguez, the BATF undercover agent whom Koresh had almost converted. The offer was refused, and the girl died in the April 19 fire.
- While FBI negotiators were attempting to convince the Branch Davidians that any children who left the residence would be treated well, FBI tanks gratuitously crushed the children's bicycles and go-karts in the yard.
- The FBI cut off electricity, shined lights on the house all night to deprive the res-

idents (including the children) of sleep, and bombarded them with noises such as dentists' drills and rabbits being slaughtered.[192]

- The FBI then convinced the attorney general that a new assault was necessary because of "deteriorating" conditions in the compound—deteriorating conditions that had been caused by the FBI.
- The attorney general also supported the new assault because she believed that Koresh was "slapping the babies." In fact, there was no contemporaneous evidence of child abuse. The FBI may have concealed from her the fact that videotapes had been sent out from the house, and the children interviewed did not appear to be suffering from abuse or deprivation.
- The attorney general authorized a plan which would not be "D day," but rather an incremental increase in pressure. She ordered that the plan be abandoned immediately if there were any risk to the children. The FBI then implemented a plan designed to produce an immediate surrender. FBI listening devices revealed that the adults would light the building on fire if the FBI attacked, and during the attack the listening devices revealed the flammable materials were being spread. The FBI ignored the attorney general's instructions to abandon the attack at the first sign of risk to children.
- The FBI had obtained the attorney general's permission to use CS by telling her that it is a mild form of tear gas. In fact, it is a potent chemical warfare agent whose use in warfare is barred by the Paris Convention. The chemical warfare agent is particularly harmful to children in enclosed areas. The FBI knew that none of the children had protective masks.
- The chemical plan was premised on the assumption that causing horrible suffering in the children would cause the mothers to run out the building with their children, thereby condemning themselves and their children (as the mothers believed) to eternal horrible suffering in hell.
- A tornado shelter underneath the children's home would have provided full protection from the fire; access to this shelter was deliberately destroyed by a tank. The CS was inserted so as to drive people away from the entrance to the tornado shelter.
- From the day of the BATF attack until the present, the federal government has insisted that its primary motive was to protect the children at Mount Carmel.[193]
- While ashes of the dead children were still hot, government flags were victoriously hoisted over the children's home.

Had David Koresh survived, he would have been prosecuted for child abuse, and would likely be serving a sentence of hundreds of years. Which of the various forms of child abuse perpetrated by BATF and the FBI will result in a prosecution?

GROUPTHINK

It would not be an exaggeration to say that the Waco disaster resulted from extremely poor collective decision making by three groups who would be expected to know better.

First, there are the Branch Davidians. As videos of the Branch Davidians illustrate, the followers of Koresh were not brainwashed, nor were they stupid. To the contrary, the adults in this group were by and large people who were successful in their various jobs; some of them were highly educated and articulate. Yet all of them made a decision to follow a self-proclaimed prophet and messiah whose behavior would suggest symptoms of mental illness and sociopathology, rather than divine anointing. The collective pull towards Koresh was so strong that even the undercover BATF agent who was sent to spy on Koresh almost became a Branch Davidian. Despite his training to resist the lures of his undercover targets, and his initial antipathy towards the "cult" he was infiltrating, he might have converted if he had not left the Branch Davidians at the end of every day. How could so many adults place so much faith in a very sinful messiah, ultimately giving up their lives for him?

The Bureau of Alcohol, Tobacco and Firearms made its share of collective, foolish decisions as well. The middle and upper management of BATF knowingly endangered the lives of BATF agents, innocent Branch Davidian adults, and children, in planning a military raid as a high-publicity method of serving a search warrant. The BATF's tunnel visionaries planned in detail how to send faxes to the press announcing the raid's success, but planned nothing at all for what to do if their carefully-scripted dynamic entry did not work. Dozens of agents in the BATF Special Response Teams, supposedly the cream of the BATF crop, raced into the cattle cars and then charged at a house full of people known to be heavily armed—even after their commander told them that the targets of the surprise raid knew they were coming. Four BATF agents and six Branch Davidians died as the result of the BATF's flawed decisions.

The FBI is the élite of American law enforcement. But like the Branch Davidians and the BATF, the FBI ignored huge, obvious risks, and many people died as a result. There were so many good reasons not to precipitously launch the tank and chemical warfare attack on April 19, it is sometimes hard to understand how so many highly intelligent, highly trained FBI officials could make such a bad decision together.[194]

Conspiracy theorists have a ready explanation for all these bad decisions. The BATF and the FBI were part of a vast United Nations conspiracy to enslave the world. There were no mistakes made; everything that the BATF and FBI did was a conscious part of the conspiracy. On the other side of the political fence, the anticult propagandists insist that the Branch Davidians did not make any bad decisions. Being "brainwashed" members of a "cult," they had no free will to exercise.

The more plausible explanation, however, for the high-risk, low-quality decisions of the Branch Davidians, BATF, and FBI is what is known as "groupthink."[195] The term groupthink was created by academics in the early 1970s to describe how groups of intelligent individuals could collectively make decisions much worse than the individuals might have made if they had decided alone. Public policy disasters which have been studied as instances of groupthink include the Bay of Pigs invasion during the Kennedy administration; the Johnson administration's escalation of the Vietnam War; the Carter administration's Iranian hostage rescue mission; the decision of Morton Thiokol managers to proceed with the Space Shuttle Challenger launch in 1986 despite the warnings of engineers, in order not to interfere with NASA's desire for a timely launch which would help NASA politically; and the Reagan administration's Iran-Contra fiasco.

Many of the factors leading to groupthink were present, on all sides, at Waco. First, in groups which are vulnerable to groupthink, group members tend to value the group above everything else. The social isolation of law enforcement officers from the non-police community has been documented by many researchers. Unquestioning adherence to group norms is likely all the higher in special high-prestige law enforcement groups, such as the FBI, its HRT, or the Special Response Teams (the BATF versions of the HRT). The Branch Davidians, of course, explicitly saw their church as the only good thing in a Babylonian world permeated by sin.

Groupthinking groups tend to have certain structural flaws: insularity; no tradition of impartial leadership; no norms requiring methodical decision-making; and a homogeneous background for their members. The militaristic HRT and SRTs, heavily drawn from ex-military personnel, had these flaws, as did the BATF and the FBI. While the Branch Davidians were highly heterogeneous in terms of race, nationality, and social background, they were intensely homogeneous in their ideology.

Groups likely to suffer from groupthink often overestimate their group's morality and invulnerability, while also stereotyping outgroups. The Branch Davidians thought themselves the only righteous people in the world, thought themselves invulnerable if God wanted them to be invulnerable, and stereotyped their adversaries as the Babylonian tools of Satan. Conversely, the FBI and BATF stereotyped their adversaries as "cultists," and acted as if resistance to the armed might of the government were inherently immoral.

Groupthink tends to produce self-censorship among the dissenters, as when FBI behavioral psychologist Peter Smerick changed his memos to support the aggressive "tactical" approach that his superiors wanted.

Groupthink is more likely to occur in a provocative situation with high amounts of external stress. In these situations, groupthink is especially likely when the members of the group have little hope for better solutions than those proposed by the leader. The attractiveness of the Branch Davidians' alternative to Koresh—surrendering to the FBI—was greatly undermined by the government's treatment of the adults and children who did surrender.

One symptom of groupthink is deindividuation, which results in individuals becoming less self-aware, and more inclined to go along with group decisions. Rather than taking personal responsibility for their own actions, de-individuated people see responsibility as diffused and placed on the group as a whole. The diffusion of responsibility leads to more aggressive behavior toward outsiders.

Some social scientists believe that an important factor leading to deindividuation is anonymity, and at least at Waco, the results were consistent with this theory. Except for Koresh, the Branch Davidians were thoroughly anonymized. They were treated—and they acted—as if they were just a mass of indistinguishable followers of Koresh.

Anonymity is intensified when the group all wears the same clothing. The HRT and SRT members not only wore identical "assault" clothing, they even wore identical tactical masks, the most anonymizing piece of clothing possible.[196] The individual members of SRTs never would have shot wildly into a building containing women and children. Nor would the HRT members, as individuals, shoot an unarmed mother carrying a baby, torture children with chemical warfare agents, or destroy someone else's home. It was only in the context of groupthink, of the diffusion of responsibility, that people could collectively perpetrate atrocities they would never perpetrate individually.

Bad decisions tend to breed more bad decisions, "the tendency to become entrapped in a spiral of ineffective policies."[197] In the Iran-Contra cases, the North-McFarlane group made more and more commitments to arm the Iranians "because so much had been invested already and the alleged costs of stopping would be unacceptable."[198] At Waco, the heavy commitment to training for the BATF raid helped create a perceived necessity to go forward with the raid, no matter what. Once four lives of federal agents had been lost, federal law enforcement became entrapped into finding some way to rationalize those four deaths, by achieving a "victory" over the Branch Davidians. The Branch Davidians were even more heavily invested in their previous mistakes. Most had given up their old lives to move to the Mount Carmel Center. Husbands and wives had given up their marriages. To admit that Koresh was a false messiah, not a person who was worth dying for, would be to admit that the Branch Davidians had squandered their careers, their families, and their earlier faiths, for nothing at all.

Groupthink often leads the group to ignore risks which affect only the stereotyped outgroup. While the BATF and the Branch Davidians both exposed themselves, as well as their "enemies," to high risks, the FBI's April 19 assault was a risky decision in which almost all the risks would be borne by the outgroup—even though the outgroup included many innocent children.

The military, with all of its internal pressure for conformity, including adherence to a "can-do" spirit, is especially vulnerable to groupthink. The April 19 assault was planned by the military's Delta Force, and executed by the FBI counterpart to Delta Force, the HRT. The military during peacetime has an institutional overeagerness to take on high-profile missions, while underestimating the risks of failure. Quasi-military units, such as the HRT, likewise spend long periods sitting idle, and may be overeager to contribute their "solution" to a high-profile problem, while underestimating the dangers of their involvement.

How can groupthink, and its resultant risky decisions, be minimized? Three reforms would have been particularly relevant at Waco, and should be implemented by decision-makers in crisis situations. First, every group meeting should have a designated devil's advocate, who will point out potential risks. Second, special care should be taken so that no one agency or coalition of experts can monopolize the flow of incoming information. Janet Reno, by allowing the FBI to monopolize the information coming to her, made it almost inevitable that she would eventually do what the FBI wanted. Finally, the virtues which make the military such an effective international killing force—such as uniformity, obedience, and group cohesion—make it especially susceptible to groupthink. For this reason, the military should have no participation in law enforcement; quasi-military units such as the FBI's HRT and the BATF SRTs should be thoroughly demilitarized, and should play, at most, a very subordinate role in law enforcement decision making.

More generally, American society should consider whether it is a good idea to teach children that obedience[199] and conformity are important virtues. If there were more individualism and iconoclasm, there would be fewer potential followers of disturbed characters like David Koresh.

NOTES

1. Robert Frost, "Fire & Ice," originally published in *Harper's*, December 1920.

2. James L. Pate, "Waco Standoff Ends in Disaster," *Soldier of Fortune* (July 1993): 39.

3. U.S. House of Representatives, *Events Surrounding the Branch Davidian Cult Standoff in Waco, Texas*, Hearing before the Committee on the Judiciary, U.S. House of Representatives, 103rd Cong., 1st Sess., April 28, 1993 (hereinafter "Hearing"), p. 124.

4. Hearing, p. 16.

On the recommendation of Kiri Jewell, her father wrote a letter to the president indicating that it was Koresh's plan

> to instigate an assault by the authorities in which they would be killed. But if the Feds could not be baited, Koresh and his followers would commit suicide. . . . If they attack, people on both sides will die, and the authorities will be blamed. . . . Stand back too long, and the Davidians will simply resort to Plan B, suicide, and then the authorities will be blamed for not stepping in. . . . "Daddy, it's better that some of them die than all of them." . . . Those who are inside are there by choice. America did not create the situation. It was designed by a pedophile with a Bible in one hand and a gun in the other. Please, Mr. President, end it now.

It is unlikely that the letter was ever read by someone in a decision-making position prior to excerpts being read by Rep. Zoe Lofgren. United States House of Representatives, Subcommittee on Crime of the Committee on the Judiciary and the Subcommittee on National Security, International Affairs, and Criminal Justice of the Committee on Government Reform and Oversight, *Joint Hearings on Activities of Federal Law Enforcement Agencies Toward the Branch Davidians*, 104th Cong., 1st sess., July 19–August 1, 1995 (Washington, D.C.: Government Printing Office, 1996) (hereinafter "Joint Hearings"), part 2, pp. 499–50; full text of letter in part 1, pp. 158–60.

5. Clifford L. Linedecker, *The Massacre at Waco, Texas* (New York: St. Martin's, 1993), pp. 248–49.

6. Joint Hearings, part 3, p. 403.

7. U.S. Department of the Treasury, *Report on the Bureau of Alcohol, Tobacco, and Firearms, Investigation of Vernon Wayne Howell also known as David Koresh* (Washington, D.C.: Government Printing Office, September 1993) (hereinafter "Treasury Report"), p. 9.

8. Sara Rimer and Sam Howe Verhovek, "Growing Up under Koresh: Cult Children Tell of Abuses," *New York Times*, May 4, 1993, p. B11.

9. U.S. Department of Justice, *Report on the Events at Waco, Texas, February 28 to April 19, 1993* (Redacted Version, Washington, D.C.: October 8, 1993) (hereinafter "Justice Report"), pp. 161, 184. The FBI's Larry Potts testified, "they [the behavioralists consulted] didn't believe that there was necessarily going to be a mass suicide, but they think that if there is a suicide effort, that it would be . . . suicide by cop, and that there might be some kind of a breakout plan. . . . The Government has their timeframe . . . and David [Koresh] has his own separate one, so he might decide at any time to come out." Joint Hearings, part 3, p. 51.

Thus Jeffrey Jamar testified that, just as the FBI would not sit around for Koresh to abuse the children there, "we do not sit still and let Koresh pick the time to leave the compound at 1 o'clock in the morning with a horde of people, with a child under one arm and a machinegun under the other. . . . So that is why we cleared the stuff out, to make it harder for Koresh to do a breakout. . . . As time passed, the possibility of a breakout increased every day." Joint Hearings, part 2, pp. 346, 351. The joint subcommittees dismissed this explanation since there was no evidence for such a concern on the part of the FBI prior to the April 19 attack, and it was abundantly clear that the Branch Davidians were intensely devoted to their sacred home. United States House of Representatives, Committee on Government Reform and Oversight in conjunction with the Committee on the Judiciary, *Investigation into the Activities of Federal Law Enforcement Agencies Toward the Branch Davidians*, Report 104–79, 104th Cong., 1st sess. (Washington, D.C.: Government Printing Office, August 2, 1996) (hereinafter "Committee Report"), p. 76.

10. Justice Report, pp. 176–77.

11. Christy Hoppe, "FBI Challenges Koresh to Let Followers Leave," *Dallas Morning News*, March 19, 1993.

Some other Ricks quotes: "Some believe that if they leave at this time, they are in fact giving up their beliefs and will be damned forever. A life on this planet may not be as important to them as eternal life." Bruce Tomaso, "Cult Members Refuse Medical Help, FBI Says," *Dallas Morning News*, March 14, 1993. "We believe David Koresh would consider it a substantial achievement to get a large number of his people killed." Victoria Loe, "Agents Warn of Tighter Security after Infiltration of Cult Compound," *Dallas Morning News*, March 28, 1993.

12. Dirk Johnson, "Inside the Cult: Fire and Terror on Final Day; Last Hours in Waco: A Special Report," *New York Times*, April 26, 1993, pp. A1, B10.

13. Quoted in R.W. Bradford, "Who Started the Fires?" in Lewis, *From the Ashes: Making Sense of Waco* (Lanham, Md.: Rowman and Littlefield, 1993), p. 111.

14. The Justice Department review makes it clear that Koresh regularly denied plans for suicide. Justice Report, p. 37, *passim.*

15. Justice Report, pp. 283–84. Attorney General Reno later testified that one of the reasons no one expected suicide was that "Koresh didn't seem to be alarmed at all" by the various activities around the building at Mount Carmel Center on April 18. Hearing, p. 54. Again, the attorney general appears to have been misled by her subordinates.

16. Jeffrey Jamar, Joint Hearings, part 2, p. 348. Note that this is essentially identical to the reasoning of the BATF's raid leaders in ignoring the warning from undercover agent Rodriguez that Koresh knew BATF was coming: that Koresh's statement may just have been a metaphysical assertion. Curiously, about the only bragging from Koresh which the FBI firmly believed must be based on fact, was the conclusion that Koresh had anti-tank weapons in his arsenal, even though there was nothing from the BATF investigation or any specific statement from Koresh to confirm such a belief.

17. Revelation 6:12, 17.

18. Amos 1:2.

19. Amos 1:4, 7, 10, 12, 14; 2:2, 5.

20. Isaiah 4:4.

21. The expectation of a dramatic fire to end the world was hardly unique to the Davidians. In a book widely regarded as one of the classics of Western literature, Baptist author John Bunyan wrote: "This our city will be burned with fire from heaven." *The Pilgrim's Progress from This World to That Which is to Come* (1678). Electronic version available at: http://ccel.wheaton.edu/bunyan/pilgrims_progress/title.html.

22. Joint hearings, part 1, pp. 576, 592.

23. He had circumvented the FBI's cutting of all phone communication by using a battery-powered cellular phone.

24. Nahum 2:13. Other passages of Nahum contain images of burning chariots: "The shield of his mighty men is made . . . the chariots shall be with flaming torches" (Nahum 2:3); "The chariots shall rage in the streets . . . they shall seem like torches" (Nahum 2: 4). Indeed, the scene at Mount Carmel after April 19 parallels the disaster which *Nahum* forecasts for the Assyrian city of Ninevah: "there is a multitude of slain, and a great number of carcases; and there is none end of their corpses; they stumble upon their corpses." Nahum, 3:3.

25. David Koresh, "Shower Head Tape," August 24, 1987 (Wisconsin teaching session; transcript available from The Research Center at http://www.ime.net/~mswett), pp. 4–5. During the March 2 negotiations, Koresh told the FBI negotiator, "It says here—it says here, 'The chariots shall be with flaming torches.' That's what you got out there [tanks which had recently arrived]." Department of Justice negotiation transcript, March 2, 1993, 4 P.M. See also Transcripts of BATF Tapes of the Negotiations between Federal Law Enforcement and the Branch Davidians, February 28–April 19, 1993 (hereinafter "Negot. Tapes"), no. 72, March 6.

26. Amos 8:9. Koresh had followed the scholarly investigation of newly released Dead Sea scrolls. One of the scrolls (according to a possible but not universally accepted translation) discusses a "Branch of David" who is wounded and killed by the government. Tabor, "The Waco Tragedy," in Lewis, *From the Ashes*, p. 21.

27. 2 Peter 3:10.

28. Baruch 10:19, discussed in J. Philip Arnold, "The Davidian Dilemma: To Obey God or Man?" in Lewis, *From the Ashes,* p. 28. Although the Branch Davidians used the King James Version of the Bible, they read the Apocrypha as part of their historical studies of the life Jesus had led; the Apocryphal writings were, among other things, important elements of the theological world of early first-century Judaism. Kopel telephone conversation with Arnold, September 21, 1994. Many passages from the Apocrypha were consistent with the Davidians' expectations of an apocalyptic fire. In 2 Maccabees (a book detailing the successful Jewish revolt against the Seleucid Empire), Judas Maccabeus exhorts his guerrilla warriors not to worry about the powerful army they are facing: "[W]e trust in the Almighty God, who is able with a single nod to strike down those who are coming against us, and even, if necessary, the whole world." 2 Maccabees 8:18.

Second Esdras, an apocalyptic book, details how a hostile army is destroyed by a great fire (13:11), and how later, "a fire went forth from his wrath, and consumed the foundations of the earth and the sinners, like straw" (15:23). Other passages foretell, "Fire will go forth from his wrath, and who is there to quench it? . . . The fire is kindled, and it shall not be put out until it consumes the foundation of the earth . . . the tested quality of my elect shall be manifest, like gold that is tested by fire. Listen, my elect ones says the Lord; the days of tribulation are at hand but I will deliver you from them" (2 Esdras 16:9, 15, 73–74).

29. 2 Thessalonians 1:7.

30. Isaiah 13:6, 8.

31. Victoria Loe, "About 40 Cultists' Bodies Found in Rubble; Report Given to FBI Predicted 'Fiery Ending' to Cult Standoff," *Dallas Morning News,* April 22, 1993.

32. Isaiah 43:2.

33. Zechariah 2:5.

34. James Scott Trimm, *The Role of Fire in Branch Davidian Eschatology* (Hurst, Tex.: 1994), available at The Research Center, http://www.ime.net/~mswett.

35. Trimm, quoting National Public Radio interviews with Janet Kendrick and Janet McBeam.

36. Marc Breault and Martin King, *Inside the Cult* (New York: Signet, 1993), p. 179.

37. Loe, "About 40 Cultists' Bodies Found in Rubble."

38. James Tabor, Joint Hearings, part 2, p. 149.

39. Linedecker, *The Massacre at Waco,* p. 219.

40. Kenneth Samples, Erwin de Castro, Richard Abanes, and Robert Lyle, *Prophets of the Apocalypse: David Koresh and Other American Messiahs* (Grand Rapids, Mich.: Baker, 1994), pp. 79–88; Loe, "About 40 Cultists' Bodies Found in Rubble." Leahy has two felony convictions for con games, which could make him less credible in general, but more reliable in his conclusion that Koresh was not a con artist. Leahy's theory was based on the apocryphal Book of Baruch, which all surviving Davidians deny was part of Koresh's teaching. Leahy's statement was delivered by fax and there is no verification of when it was sent, other than the fax dateline (which can be altered); some have suggested that the fax was sent after the fire.

41. Justice Report, pp. 109, 177, 283–84.

42. Jerry Seper, "House to Probe Reno's Reasoning behind Waco Raid," *Washington Times,* May 31, 1995, p. A6.

43. James Adams, "FBI Brings out Secret Electronic Weapons as Waco Siege Drags On," London *Sunday Times,* March 21, 1993. Listening devices had been sent in concealed among deliveries of milk, magazines, a typewriter, and other requested items. Sam Howe Verhovek, *New York Times,* April 21, 1993, p. A20.

44. 18 U.S.C. § 2511. BATF Director Higgins denied there were any listening devices prior to February 28, 1993. Hearing, pp. 163–64.

45. Carol Moore, *The Davidian Massacre* (Frankin, Tenn.: Legacy Communications and Gunowners Foundation, 1995), p. 307.

46. Negot. Tape no. 38, March 4.

47. Dick Reavis, *The Ashes of Waco: An Investigation* (New York: Simon and Schuster, 1995), p. 271. When Joyce Sparks was briefed by the FBI on possible CS use, a week or more before the actual attack, she wondered whether the existence of "propane tanks in the hallway . . . was going to present a problem." Response to questions by Rep. Ed Bryant, Joint Hearings, part 1, p. 596.

48. Moore, *The Davidian Massacre,* p. 308, citing Associated Press wire story, August 26, 1993.

49. "Koresh Order Comes Too Late," *Washington Post*, August 26, 1993, p. A6. Ricks's chronology is inconsistent, however, with the government's argument at trial that the fire was set while a tank was inside the building. Reavis, *The Ashes of Waco*, p. 292.

50. Sam Howe Verhovek, "Scores Die as Cult Compound is Set on Fire," *New York Times*, April 20, 1993.

That at least one official did not expect a fire, and was not aware that the fire plan was to do nothing, would explain the otherwise puzzling immediate call to the fire department when the fire did break out—even though the fire trucks would then be prevented from reaching the building, once they arrived. Committee Report, p. 88.

51. Hearing, p. 16.

52. Hearing, pp. 80, 84; Justice Report, pp. 302–303.

53. James L. Pate, "Wacogate," *Soldier of Fortune* (June 1995): 51; Moore, *The Davidian Massacre*, p. 324.

54. R.W. Bradford, "Who Started the Fires," in Lewis, *From the Ashes*, p. 113. There is some irony in the government's unwillingness to use military resources in the one instance where it might have prevented tragedy. But for saving Davidians (as opposed to attacking them), only ordinary civilian measures were considered.

55. Pate, "Wacogate," p. 51; Moore, *The Davidian Massacre*, p. 324.

56. Moore, *The Davidian Massacre*, p. 327.

57. 1957: Svenski Filmindustri (campfire scene).

58. David Hackett Fischer, *Paul Revere's Ride* (Oxford University Press, 1994). Carol Moore, author of one of the Waco books, *The Davidian Massacre* (cited in the bibliography), is the great-great-great-great-granddaughter of Col. James Barrett, commander of the Concord militia. The British expedition to Concord was intended to seize militia weapons which were stored at Barrett's farm. At the Concord Bridge, Barrett gave the now-famous order that the Concord militia should return fire if the British shot first. Moore, *The Davidian Massacre*, p. vii.

59. James L. Pate, "No Longer Untouchable," *American Spectator*, August 1993, p. 35. Some sources give Ness's birth year as 1902.

60. Former FBI Deputy Director Floyd Clarke, asked how much longer beyond April 19th the HRT could remain deployed, responded: "I think that we probably had a couple of weeks, maybe a little bit longer. In talking with both Dick Rogers as well as his people . . . , I think they would have told you that they could have continued." Joint Hearings, part 3, p. 73.

61. Justice Report, p. 272.

62. Deborah Kalb, "Warsaw Ghetto," *Intermountain Jewish News*, April 29, 1994; David I. Caplan, "The Warsaw Ghetto: 10 Handguns Against Tyranny," *American Rifleman* 136, no. 2 (February 1988): 31, 75; Yitzhak Zuckerman, *A Surplus of Memory: A Chronicle of the Warsaw Ghetto Uprising* (Berkeley: University of California Press, 1993); Jews for the Preservation of Firearms Ownership, *The Warsaw Ghetto "Uprising": The First Battle to Re-Establish Israel* (Milwaukee: JPFO, 1993).

63. Raul Hilberg, *The Destruction of the European Jews* (Holmes and Meier, 1985), p. 499.

64. Daniel 11:33; J. Philip Arnold, "The Davidian Dilemma: To Obey God or Man?" in Lewis, *From the Ashes*, p. 28.

65. Flavius Josephus, *Wars of the Jews* (c. 73), vol. 7, ch. 8:5–7. Consistent with the practice of Roman historians, Josephus wrote farewell words for Eleazer which meshed with Josephus's judgment of the character of Eleazer and the Zealots.

Masada was not the only time when Jews burned themselves and their home, rather than surrender to attackers. After the coronation of King Richard I in England, anti-Jewish riots broke out. In York, more than a thousand Jews took refuge in a castle, and courageously held out against the rioters. But on March 16, 1190:

Seeing they were in a hopeless position, the defenders decided to kill themselves rather than surrender to the blood-thirsty mobs. They dispatched their wives and children first and then cut their own throats. The small minority who offered to give themselves up were promised terms but were butchered as soon as they opened the gates. The palace had been set on fire by the more resolute ones, and much of their wealth was destroyed by flames.

(Thomas B. Costain, *The Conquering Family* [Buccaneer Books, 1996].) This type of martyrdom is known as *Kadosh HaShem*, meaning "Sanctification of the Name."

In Russia in the late seventeenth and early eighteenth century, there was continuous conflict between the government, which had changed certain traditional portions of Russian Orthodox practice, and the "Old Believers" who opposed any change. Neither side believing in separation of church and state, violence resulted. The Old Believers' militance and political activism led to intense persecution by the Czar, which in turn made the Old Believers all the more frenzied and alienated. The vicious cycle of repression and escalation is termed "deviance-amplification," a process that was clearly in evidence at Waco. Time and again, the Old Believers provoked violent confrontations with the government, which led to hundreds or thousands of Old Believers taking sanctuary in a monastery or hermitage, and then immolating themselves and the property. At least twenty thousand people killed themselves this way. After decades of these mass suicides, the Russian government finally learned to tolerate the Old Believers, and the Old Believers gave up their dream of taking control of the government and returning the state church to traditional practices, although some mass suicides continued well into the nineteenth century. Thomas Robbins, "Religious Mass Suicide before Jonestown: The Russian Old Believers," *Sociological Analysis* 41, no. 1 (1986): 1–20.

66. James D. Tabor, "The Waco Tragedy: An Autobiographical Account of One Attempt to Avert Disaster," in Lewis, *From the Ashes*, p. 21.

67. Susan J. Palmer, "Excavating Waco," in Lewis, *From the Ashes*, pp. 101–102.

68. Martin Luther King, Jr., once said, "A man who is not willing to die for what he believes is already dead." Among the massive crowd that had gathered outside the perimeter at Waco was an organization calling itself the "Common Sense Patrol," which passed out leaflets drawing an express parallel between Mount Carmel and the Alamo. Linedecker, *Massacre at Waco*, p. 196–97.

69. The flag featured a "fiery flying serpent" coming through the center of the star, and was based on Koresh's interpretation of Isaiah 14:29, in which a fiery flying serpent helps inflict God's wrath on the unholy. Ron Cole, *Sinister Twilight* (Longmont, Colo.: self-published, 1994), p. 59.

70. There has been some debate as to whether the events at Waco on April 19 can be described as a "holocaust." The original Greek word from which "holocaust" derives means "burned entirely," and thus April 19 was at least a holocaust in the literal sense.

71. Revelation 6:12 (describing events when the sixth seal is opened).

72. Plaintiffs' Complaint in *Brown et al.* v. *United States et al.* (S.D. Tex., Houston Div., February 25, 1995), ¶ 108.

73. ABC News Nightline, "The Waco Tapes," July 5, 1995.

74. Negot. Tape 242, April 18.

75. Alan Stone, Joint Hearings, part 2, p. 421.

76. Statement of nurse at the hospital, reported in James R. Lewis, "Fanning the Flames of Suspicion: The Case Against Mass Suicide at Waco," in Lewis, *From the Ashes*, p. 115.

77. KPOC television, David Hall, producer, *The Waco Incident*, television documentary, September 19, 1994 (Ponca City, Okla., channel 27).

78. Testimony of FBI Agent James Magee, in Ken Fawcett, *Blind Justice: A Chronology of the Historic Trial of Eleven Branch Davidians in January 1994*, 2d ed. (Royse City, Tex.: Electropress, 1994), p. 30.

79. Maj. Alexander S. Wells, Memorandum for the Record, Subject: FBI Request for Emergency Medical Support in Waco, April 15, 1993. The equipment would come from Fort Hood; since there was no drug nexus, the FBI would reimburse the military for all direct and indirect costs. Because the CH-47 helicopter is more commonly used for transporting troops, how many litters it could carry is uncertain, but three of the helicopters could probably have carried out most of the Davidians at Mount Carmel Center.

80. Tabor, "The Waco Tragedy," in Lewis, *From the Ashes*, p. 20. The manuscript was brought out on a computer disk, and has been reprinted. David Koresh, *The Decoded Message of the Seven Seals of the Book of Revelation* (Axtell, Tex.: General Assoc. of Branch Davidian Seventh-day Adventists, 1994). Also available from The Research Center, at http://www.ime.net/~mswett; and in James D. Tabor and Eugene V. Gallagher, *Why Waco? Cults and the Battle for Religious Freedom in America* (Berkeley: University of California Press, 1995), pp. 191–203.

81. It is not entirely clear whether Koresh thought he would perish in the fire, and then, as "the Lamb," carry out his wrath in some nonhuman form.

82. Tabor, "The Waco Tragedy," in Lewis, *From the Ashes,* p. 20.

83. Schneider had indicated before that one reason Koresh might be looking forward to jail was that he recalled his previous jailing, in 1987, as providing his best sleep in years. Negot. Tape no. 201, April 9.

84. Tabor, Joint Hearings, part 2, p. 201.

85. Tabor, "The Waco Tragedy," in Lewis, *From the Ashes,* p. 20; and Joint Hearings, part 2, p. 201.

86. Dispensing the chemical warfare agent were Combat Engineering Vehicles, a variant of the M-60 tank. Also on the scene were nine Bradley Fighting Vehicles (used to transport agents and to fire 40mm ferret canisters), one M-1 Abrams (battle tank), and M-88 Tank Recovery Vehicles. While the Bradley Fighting Vehicles fired ferret canisters of CS, the Combat Engineering Vehicles carried large containers of CS, which was sprayed by the tanks. Testimony of FBI Special Agent R. J. Craig, in Jack DeVault, *The Waco Whitewash: The Mt. Carmel Episode Told by an Eyewitness to the Trial* (San Antonio: Rescue Press, 1994), pp. 116–17; Plaintiffs' complaint in *Brown* v. *United States,* ¶ 98.

87. Trial testimony of R. J. Craig (driver of first CEV to ram the building) in DeVault, *The Waco Whitewash,* p. 5.

88. It is very difficult to find gas masks which fit children. Jerry Seper, "Reno Faces Questions on Waco Gas Attack," *Washington Times,* June 4, 1995 (quoting senior FBI official). As Harvard's Alan Stone explained, "They [small children] do not have enough ventilatory capacity to pull the air through the mechanism that cleans the air out." Joint Hearings, part 2, p. 425; see also p. 403.

89. Justice Report, pp. 110–11.

90. Committee Report, pp. 79–80. According to Jeffrey Jamar, the message was "we want to talk to you . . . send us out a manuscript . . . if you've got something done, send it out to us. He continuously broadcast our desire to engage in negotiations." Joint Hearings, part 3, p. 213. There is nothing in the reports of Sage's remarks to support Jamar's assertion that anything short of immediate surrender was acceptable. Joint Hearings, part 1, pp. 642–51.

Some of the persons in the building may have been unable to understand the loudspeakers. Clive Doyle, a Branch Davidian who eventually fled, stated that the speakers were out of sync, with one set of speakers a second or two behind the other set, making all the messages incomprehensible. David McLemore, "53 Bodies Found So Far at Cult Site," *Dallas Morning News,* April 25, 1993.

91. George Kuempel and Lee Hancock, "Pathologist Says No Bullet Wounds Found on Cultists," *Dallas Morning News,* April 23, 1993.

92. The plan called for starting with having the CS inserted by the tanks, for fear that sitting back at a distance and "firing [ferrets] on them, they would believe we were shooting at them, shooting bullets at them, ammunition at them, and that would be more provocative than trying to go up and put it in this other way." Larry Potts, Joint Hearings, part 2, p. 560. The ferret or ferret grenade has been described, by one on the receiving end, as being "big as a coke can." David Thibodeau, Joint Hearings, part 1, p. 127.

Just as the FBI kept trying to insist, unsuccessfully, that the morning's activities were not an assault, the FBI sometimes seems quite puzzled about suspects' interpretations of FBI activities. In Ruby Ridge, the Weavers were repeatedly asked to go outside and retrieve a telephone from a shotgun-equipped robot. The FBI seemed uncertain why the Weavers did not trust the robot, since the FBI— but not the Weavers—knew that the shotgun was unloaded.

At Waco, tanks ramming a building were not perceived by the FBI as particularly provocative. Later, Attorney General Reno explained: "With respect to the use of military weapons, these pieces of equipment were unarmed, as I understand it, and were contracted. I mean, it was like a good rent-a-car." Representative Zeliff: "A good rent-a-car? A tank going into a building?" Reno: "These tanks were not armed. They were not military weapons." Joint Hearings, part 3, p. 366.

Rep. William Clinger later commented: "I can appreciate the statement that the tank was used as a defensive means of protecting agents who were involved in that raid, but I think you would agree that if you were on the inside of the compound looking out you might not have had quite such a benign view of that tank, nor would you have been aware that the tank was not armed . . . it would look . . . very, very menacing. . . ." Joint Hearings, part 3, p. 375.

93. Peter J. Boyer, "Children of Waco," *The New Yorker,* May 15, 1995, p. 45.

94. Nancy Gibbs, "Fire Storm in Waco," *Time*, May 3, 1993, p. 30.

95. Phil Arnold, Joint Hearings, part 2, p. 149.

96. Sam Howe Verhovek, "Murder Case Against 11 Cult Members Goes to Jury," *New York Times*, February 24, 1994, p. A-14.

97. Ibid.

98. Plan A began at 5:59 and was replaced by Plan B at 6:07 A.M. Committee Report, pp. 79–80. The Branch Davidians maintain that they did not shoot at the tanks. The FLIR tape shows a tank driver, twenty feet away from the building, removing rubble from the front of the tank. Declaration of Edward F. Allard, *Brown v United States*, civ. no. H-95-587 (S.D. Tex., Houston Div., February 1, 1996).

99. Testimony of FBI Special Agent R.J. Craig, in DeVault, *The Waco Whitewash*, pp. 118–19.

100. David T. Hardy, "Use of CS Gas at Waco," available at http://www.indirect.com/www/ dhardy/CS_Gas_at_Waco.

101. Clive Doyle, Joint Hearings, part 3, p. 113. According to Doyle, not only did children lack masks, so did most of the women. Ibid., p. 111.

102. Justice Report, pp. 111, 294–95 (ellipsis in original).

103. Sue Anne Pressley, "White House Counsel Denounces Representative Zeliff's Remarks on Waco," *Washington Post*, August 1, 1995.

104. "Defense Rests without Calling Cultists," *New York Times*, February 18, 1994, p. A20.

105. But he added, "If you notice . . . , the conversation about [pouring of the fuel] takes place in the early morning. . . . The fire didn't start until right around noon. . . . Now, they never did throw Molotov cocktails at the tanks . . . all of the survivors were unanimous that they did not start the fire and knew of no plan to burn the place down." Dick DeGuerin, Joint Hearings, part 2, p. 55. The FBI had apparently been expecting the Davidians to throw Molotov cocktails at the tanks. Trial testimony of Agent R. J. Craig, reproduced in Joint Hearings, part 3, p. 100.

106. Joint Hearings, part 2, p. 352.

107. Justice Report, Appendix F3.

108. Justice Report, p. 301.

109. Hugh Aynesworth, "Jury Hears Cultists Plot Fire on Tape," *Washington Times*, February 16, 1994.

110. Joint Hearings, part 2, p. 352.

111. Tim Evans, Joint Hearings, part 1, pp. 623–24. In Evans' prepared testimony, he noted that the agent monitoring the tapes should have known by 7 A.M. both that there was CS being inserted and talk by Davidians about setting a fire. Joint Hearings, part 1, p. 630.

112. Hugh Aynesworth, "Jury Hears Cultists Plot Fire on Tape."

113. Allard Declaration, ¶ 10.

114. Failure Analysis Associates, Inc., *Investigation of the April 19, 1993 Assault on the Mt. Carmel Center, Waco, Texas* (Menlo Park, Calif., July 1995), p. 5.

115. "Grisly Testimony in Cultists' Trial," *New York Times*, February 13, 1994.

116. Allard Declaration, ¶¶ 11–12.

117. Moore, *Massacre of the Branch Davidians*, p. 378.

118. Justice Report, pp. 294–95.

119. Moore, *Massacre of the Branch Davidians*, p. 378.

120. Prepared statement of Jack Zimmermann, Joint Hearings, part 2, p. 133.

121. James L. Pate, "Feds Find No Fault with their Handling of Branch Davidian Standoff," *Soldier of Fortune* (February 1994): 57. At the Davidians' trial, FBI agent John Morrison testified that he had seen the man at the piano through his binoculars. Paul McKay, "FBI Agent Defends Use of Gas in Assault on Cult," *Houston Post*, February 8, 1994, p. 6A.

122. Sue Ann Pressley and Mary Jordan, "Cultists May Have Been Forced to Stay," *Washington Post*, April 21, 1993.

123. DeVault, *The Waco Whitewash*, pp. 108–10; Fawcett, *Blind Justice*, p. 29. BATF agents had reported seeing Branch Davidians in similar clothing on the day of the first raid. Linedecker, *Massacred at Waco*, p. 29.

124. Moore, *Massacre of the Branch Davidians*, p. 321, citing news video footage.

125. Trial Transcript, *United States* v. *Brad Branch et al.*, Crim. Action No. W-93-CR-046 (W.D.Tex., 1994) (hereinafter "Trial Transcript"), p. 5433; Moore, *Massacre of the Branch Davidians*, p. 376.

126. Reavis, *The Ashes of Waco*, p. 273.

127. Ray Jahn, Joint Hearings, part 1, pp. 97–98. He also explained why it remained aloft after daybreak: "they were trained observers. What better choice to the FBI than to leave that camera up there, even though it did go into the daylight? Not because they thought a fire was going to start, but merely because they wanted the extra set of eyes that were up above."

That extra pair of eyes would be of little value in daytime. During daylight, a FLIR produces a poor-quality grey-scale image, unless the FLIR is observing something hot.

128. Experts analyzing the FLIR tape have also detected machinegun fire from outside the building during late morning (affidavit of Edward F. Allard, January 20, 1996), which is inconsistent with the FBI's claim that "during that entire time, those 6 hours, and indeed those 51 days, the FBI never fired one shot at the Davidians" (Dick Rogers, Joint Hearings, part 3, p. 225), unless one of the agencies on the scene other than the FBI was responsible for the shots rather than the FBI.

129. Edward S. G. Dennis, Jr., *Evaluation of the Handling of the Branch Davidian Stand-Off in Waco, Texas, February 28 to April 19, 1993, Redacted Version* (Washington, D.C.: Department of Justice, October 8, 1993) , p. 33.

130. *Army Field Manual FM 21–27*, p. 21.

131. Dr. George F. Uhlig, letter of July 13, 1994, to Dave Hall, Station manager, KPOC, reprinted in KPOC TV, *Overview and General Information of Criminal Negligence by Agents of Federal Government*, report for U.S. Senate Judiciary Committee, August 1994. While methylene chloride, the carrying agent for the CS, is flammable, an independent reviewer has determined that the $MeCl_2$ "was not of sufficient quantity to play a significant role in the ignition or spread of the fire." Failure Analysis Associates, p. 5.

132. The Arson Report (discussed in chapter 5) acknowledges that winds from holes punched in the wall intensified the fire. The report also states the extra oxygen would also have lowered the concentration of carbon monoxide, and increased the time a person might have survived if trapped. Justice Report, Appendix D-6. It is not entirely clear what the benefits are of surviving longer while trapped.

133. David T. Hardy, "Use of CS Gas at Waco," available at http://www.indirect.com/www/dhardy/CS_Gas_at_Waco.

134. Justice Report, p. 277.

135. Moore, *Massacre of the Branch Davidians*, p. 373.

136. Koresh's attorney reported that there were some live flashbangs in the residence, which had been dropped by BATF during the February 28 raid. Joint Hearings, Part 2, p. 87. The attorney, not wishing to carry a live grenade, had refused Koresh's request to bring the flashbangs out to the FBI. Koresh had earlier offered to send out to the FBI some handguns which had been dropped by BATF agents during the February 28 raid. Negot. Tape no. 27 (mislabeled no. 29), March 3.

FBI Deputy Director Floyd Clarke testified that if there were "hard evidence that there was a suicide taking place inside, there was a plan . . . immediately totally immerse the place in gas, and throw in flash bangs which would disorient them." Hearing, p. 78.

137. We are indebted to David Hardy for his analysis of the topic. David Hardy's paper analyzing the effects of CS and $MeCl_2$, "Use of CS Gas at Waco," can be found at: http://www.indirect.com/www/dhardy/CS_Gas_at_Waco.

138. Ibid.

139. Ballantyne and Callaway, "Inhalation Toxicology and Pathology of Animals Exposed to O-Chlororbenyliden Malonitrile (CS)," *Medicine, Science and the Law* 12 (1972): 43, 45. See also Chapman and White, "Death Resulting from Lacrimatory Agents," *Journal of Forensic Sciences* 23 (1978): 527.

140. The full autopsy reports, including photos, are available at http://www.mnsinc.com/SkyWriter/WacoMuseum/death/map/d_list00.html.

141. Committee Report, pp. 71, 73. The dead were: Audrey Martinez (age 13); Star Howell (4 to 6 years); unknown child (1 year); Cyrus Howell (8); R. Silvia (13); Mayanna Schneider (1); Judy Schneider Koresh (41); Rachel Howell Koresh (24); Ruth Morrison (29). The coroner's report said that "burial in structural collapse" was the cause of the suffocation or asphyxia. But for the bodies found in the cold storage room, this is impossible. The two-foot hole in the roof did not produce enough debris to cause so many deaths. Hardy, "Use of CS Gas."

142. Justice Report, Appendix, p. D–10.

143. See chapter 3, text at note 296.

144. Hearing, p. 78–80.

145. Sue Ann Pressley and Mary Jordan, "Cultists May Have Been Forced to Stay," *Washington Post*, April 21, 1993.

146. "Grisly Testimony," *New York Times*, February 13, 1994.

147. The room, which was used for storage of Branch Davidian papers and other artifacts, had one-foot concrete walls, reinforced by one-inch steel rods. The FBI, consistent with their calling the rickety Mount Carmel Center the "compound," called the concrete cold-storage vault "the bunker." According to the dictionary, a bunker is "A reinforced underground shelter." *The New Shorter Oxford English Dictionary*, vol. 1 (1993), p. 300. The above-ground room was the base of a four-story tower that was part of the Mount Carmel Center.

Generally excluded from the death count are two otherwise viable fetuses—one term, and one at seven months. "Both are believed to have been born as the result of an evolutionary reflex, instants after their mothers, Aisha Gyarfas and Nicole Gent, expired. Gyarfas was the victim of a gunshot wound; Gent of the crashing concrete. The deaths of their infants, who would have been viable had they experienced normal births, were the omega of the day whose alpha was the seemingly innocuous tear-gas raid." Reavis, *The Ashes of Waco*, p. 277.

148. Nizan Peerwani testimony in DeVault, *The Waco Whitewash*, p. 124.

149. "Grisly Testimony"; Paul McKay, "Witness Claims Davidian Bragged About Shooting," *Houston Chronicle*, February 12, 1994; testimony of Texas Ranger Raymond L. Hoffman, in DeVault, *The Waco Whitewash*, p. 65. Exactly what happened to those women and children is one of the as yet unsolved mysteries of Waco. It may be that the incapacitating effects of the CS and $MeCl_2$ made them so disoriented—or even unconscious—that they were unable to flee the fire. It is possible that the large quantity of rubble brought down by the tanks' destruction of the house prevented them from escaping through the room's single exit.

150. Jerry Seper, "Reno Faces Questions on Waco Gas Attack," *Washington Times*, June 4, 1995. "She watched the flesh of her children being consumed by fire, their toes and fingers scattered on the ground, and the flesh of the head to the chin exposed like masks." 4 Maccabees 15:15.

151. James E. McCarroll, Carol S. Fullerton, Robert J. Ursano, and Joan M. Hermsen, *Psychological Stress of Forensic Dental Examinations: The Waco Disaster* (Washington, D.C.: Walter Reed Army Institute of Research, Div. of Neuropsychiatry, Department of General Psychiatry, August 1, 1994) (hereinafter "Walter Reed Institute, *Dental Examinations*"), p. 1.

152. Walter Reed Institute, *Dental Examinations*, p. 10.

"[O]n ne trouvera que feux, Que charonges, que morts ou visages affreux." ("We found only fire, only corpses, only the dead, or appalling faces.") Agrippa d'Aubigné, "Misères," first book of the poem *Les Tragiques*, ed. A. Garnier and J. Plattard (Paris: 1962–67), quoted in Judy Sproxton, *Violence and Religion: Attitudes towards Militancy in the French Civil Wars and the English Revolution* (New York: Routledge, 1995), p. 34.

153. Phyllis Goldberg, "FBI Uses 'Cults' as Bait," in Lewis, *From the Ashes*, p. 230; Pate, "Waco Stand-off," p. 41.

154. Hearing, p. 81.

155. Regarding ammunition in a fire:

> To put a little more light on the subject of shells exploding in fires, let me add my experience. I am a firefighter who has been in house fires with cartridges of different calibers, and no shell has ever exploded. The lead melts away from the steel or metal casing and the gun powder goes off harmlessly. No danger to anyone.

(Carl Braden, "Cartridges in Fires," *American Rifleman* [August 1994]: 12 [letters to the editor].)

As ammunition is heated in a fire, the primer and the gunpowder will ignite. But because the ammunition is not in the chamber of a gun, the energy is not directed to drive a bullet down a barrel and send it flying; rather, the energy travels in all directions, causing the brass shell to burst harmlessly. The bullet never goes anywhere.

The only real danger from ammunition in a fire is when the ammunition is stored in a sealed tin or other airtight container. Then, the metal container will behave the same way as a can of sealed paint. The flammable material (gunpowder or paint) inside the tin or paint can will heat up; because the container is sealed, there will be no outlet for the heat, and pressure will continue to build until the container (be it ammunition tin or paint can) explodes. This explosion would endanger a person nearby. The danger, however, comes not from flying bullets, but from the exploding metal containers used for bulk storage. Ian Thompson, "Small Arms Cartridges: The Fact and Fiction in Fires," *International Ammunition Association Journal* (September/October 1994): 30–32, reprinted from *Australian Shooters Journal* (July 1992). See also Herman Bockstruck, "Sporting Ammunition in a Fire," *International Ammunition Association Journal* (May/June 1995): 14–15, reprinted from *SHOT Business magazine*.

156. Investigative journalist Gary Null writes:

It was probably a good decision on the part of the federal agents on the scene not to attempt to put out the fire using water. The resulting steam generated by the water coming into contact with the hot structure would further generate hydrogen cyanide, and the resulting cloud of cyanide gas and steam could have been carried by the prevailing winds over populated areas. This could have killed people not even involved in the incident, or at least made them sick.

(Gary Null, "Holocaust at Waco," *Penthouse* [April 1994].)

157. Aisha Summers (entry wound on right side of chest, exit wound on left side, no head wound); Mary Jean E. Borst (gunshot wound in the back, possible head wound); Lorraine Silvia (six back wounds). The autopsy reports can be found at: http://www.mnsinc.com/SkyWriter/WacoMuseum/death/map/d_listOO.html. Two of the nine persons whose bodies were found upstairs, in the room above the cold storage room, were also found dead of gunshot. Novelette Hipsman was shot in the back and the head; Neal Vaega twice in the head. The rest appear to have died from smoke inhalation.

158. Nicole Gent Little. David Jones's body, found in the second-floor room above the concrete room, also showed signs of death from a gunshot wound to the head before inhalation of carbon monoxide.

159. David Byrnes, Trial Transcript, pp. 642–43. Sam Howe Verhovek, "Murder Case Against 11. Cult Members Goes to Jury," *New York Times*, February 24, 1994. Rep. Mark Edward Souder observed "a copy of a picture, we don't know whether it is an FBI or an ATF agent, on top of a tank with an American flag and two guns . . .—it was clearly after the first and before the second event . . . this type of picture doesn't mean that there was any malicious intent by agents, but when people, . . . particularly little children are dying in the background or . . . you are trying to prepare for something that could lead to the death of children, this comes very close to show-boating." Joint Hearings, part 1, p. 618.

160. Lee Hancock, "Reno Testifies on Siege," *Dallas Morning News*, April 29, 1993.

161. Hugh Aynesworth, "President Calls for Investigation," *Washington Post*, April 21, 1993; Anne Marie Kilday, "Clinton Pledges Probe of Siege," *Dallas Morning News*, April 21, 1993.

162. In the movie, the Marlon Brando character is quoting Joseph Conrad's *Heart of Darkness* (1902) (electronic version available at http://etext.lib.virginia.edu/modeng. browse.html).

163. Koresh had spanked an eight-month-old baby for forty minutes because she would not sit on his lap. Justice Report, pp. 224–26.

164. Jeanine Bunds, cited in Davy Aguilera, "Application and Affidavit for Search and Arrest Warrants for Vernon Wayne Howell and the Residence of Vernon Wayne Howell, and others," Waco, Tex., February 25, 1993, pp. 9–10. Although the Bible does not detail Mary's age at the time of the Annunciation, tradition places her between the ages of twelve and sixteen years old. E.g., Sally Cunneen, *In Search of Mary: The Woman and the Symbol* (New York: Ballantine Books, 1996), pp. 32–33 (twelve or thirteen); *Dictionary of Mary* (New York: Catholic Book Pub. Co., 1985), p. 189 (Annunciation took place thirteen to sixteen years after Mary's birth). The Branch Davidian parents were obviously greatly mistaken in their belief that their daughters were like Mary being impregnated with God's holy seed.

165. The age of consent in Texas is seventeen. Before a 1993 amendment to the law, it was a defense to prosecution if the child was at least fourteen years old and had, prior to the time of the offense, promiscuously engaged in sex. 5 *Vernon's Texas Statutes and Codes Annotated* § 21.11(b) (deleted in 1993). Under the old law, which would have been applied to Koresh's actions, Koresh would have had no defense. First, some of the statutory rape victims were less than fourteen years old.

Second, there is no evidence that any of the older Branch Davidian girls were promiscuous. The girls' prior sexual involvement with Koresh would not qualify Koresh for the promiscuity defense, since the defense can only be invoked in cases where there has been indiscriminate grant of physical favor to persons of the opposite sex without any requirement for love. *Connally v. State*, 838 S.W.2d 646 (Texas App. 13 Dist. 1992).

166. Koresh began having sex with Michelle Jones, the twelve-year-old sister of his wife Rachel, in 1987, and, according to Branch Davidian apostates, Koresh later described the sex as non-consensual. Christoper G. Ellison and John P. Bartkowski, " 'Babies Were Being Beaten,' " in *Armageddon in Waco: Critical Perspectives on the Branch Davidian Conflict,* ed. Stuart A. Wright (Chicago: University of Chicago Press, 1995), p. 126.

167. Rep. Charles Schumer described Kiri Jewell as having been "raped" by David Koresh. Joint Hearings, part 1, p. 279. Jewell's testimony, however, did not assert that the sexual assault involved penetration. Joint Hearings, part 1, pp. 151–55. See also the letter from her father to President Clinton, stating the penetration did not occur. Joint Hearings, part 1, p. 159. Sexual contact without penetration can constitute "sexual assault," but it is not "rape," as any first-year law student knows, as should Harvard Law School graduate Schumer.

168. Kiri Jewell, Joint Hearings, part 1, p. 156.

169. Jack Zimmerman, Joint Hearings, part 2, p. 86.

170. BATF's only serious effort to arrest Koresh away from the Mount Carmel Center involved seeing if Kiri Jewell would agree to testify against him, which would have allowed the Texas authorities to call in Koresh for arrest by Texas law enforcement. Treasury Report, Appendix D-12; Joint Hearings, part 1, pp. 576, 585. Ms. Jewell's refusal to testify led to a chain of events resulting in the deaths of several of her close friends, at least one of whom was pregnant. It cannot be determined what, if any, influence the chain of events may have had on her future recollections. Testimony of Kiri Jewell, Joint Hearings, part 1, pp. 151–55; Reavis, *The Ashes of Waco*, p. 277.

171. Christy Hoppe, "FBI Challenges Koresh to Let Followers Leave," *Dallas Morning News*, March 19, 1993.

172. Those who disbelieve the Jewell story do not claim that Koresh was a decent human being; instead, they note (as did a congresswoman who believed Kiri's testimony): "Females, including children as young as 12, were known to be taken by Howell Koresh as his wives. He would impregnate them as soon as possible with his holy seed." Rep. Zoe Lofgren, Joint Hearings, part 2, p. 499 (reading letter from David Jewell). At the time of the alleged incident, the prepubescent Jewell was too young to bear his children.

173. Ellison and Bartkowski, "Babies Were Being Beaten," pp. 120–26.

174. Kopel telephone conversation with Carol Moore, April 1994.

175. George Robertson, "Suffer the Little Children," in Lewis, *From the Ashes*, p. 179; Sam Howe Verhovek, "In Shadow of Texas Siege, Uncertainty for Innocents," *New York Times*, March 8, 1993; Jennifer Nagorka, "Koresh Tells Negotiators He Won't Kill Self, Denies He's Christ," *Dallas Morning News*, March 6, 1993.

176. Perry said that being on the Research Advisory Board was the limit of his connection with the American Family Foundation and the Cult Awareness Network. Joint Hearings, part 1, p. 246. Those groups denied involvement in Waco, denounced the Branch Davidians as a "cult," and criticized some of scholars the Department of Justice asked to evaluate the FBI's activities in Waco. Joint Hearings, part 1, pp. 248–57.

177. Bruce Perry, Joint Hearings, part 1, pp. 234–41; Lynne Lamberg, "Children and Families Need Help After Disasters," *Journal of the American Medical Association* 275 (June 12, 1996): 1714–15; Peggy Kneffel Daniels and Carol A. Schwartz, eds., *Encyclopedia of Associations, 1994,* 28th ed., National Organizations of the United States, vol. 1 (Detroit: Gale Research, Inc., 1993), p. 1762.

178. Lawrence Lilliston, "Who Committed Child Abuse at Waco?" in Lewis, *From the Ashes,* p. 172; Boyer, "Children of Waco," p. 42.

179. Bruce Perry, "Raised in Cults: Brainwashing or Socialization?" lecture delivered at the Cult Awareness Network annual conference, Minnesota, November 1993, summarized in Margaret Thaler Singer, *Cults in Our Midst: The Hidden Menace in our Everyday Lives* (San Francisco: Jossey-Bass, 1995), pp. 252–53.

180. Written testimony of Bruce Perry, Joint Hearings, part 1, pp. 235–41.

181. Singer, *Cults in Our Midst,* p. 252.

182. Ibid.; Joint Hearings, part 1, pp. 238–39. In his congressional testimony, Dr. Perry used the word "traumatized" rather than "terrorized."

183. Singer, *Cults in Our Midst,* p. 253.

184. Joint Hearings, part 1, pp. 236–37.

185. Singer, *Cults in Our Midst,* p. 253.

186. Prologue.

187. Singer, *Cults in Our Midst,* p. 253.

188. Joint Hearings, part 1, p. 237.

189. Ibid., pp. 237–38.

190. Ibid., p. 237.

191. Ibid., p. 241.

192. Many children love rabbits and fear dentists.

193. Commented defense attorney Dan Cogdell in his closing remarks, "ATF said they went in to save the children. And the IRS is here to save you money!" Fawcett, *Blind Justice,* p. 51.

194. "Seemingly intelligent people who pursued a course of insanity and mass murder" is how Edward Dennis characterized the Branch Davidians. Press briefing for release of Justice Report, October 8, 1993, quoted in James D. Tabor and Eugene V. Gallagher, *Why Waco? Cults and the Battle for Religious Freedom in America* (Berkeley: University of California Press, 1995), pp. 111–12. The characterization is not wholly inapt for the BATF and FBI as well.

195. The discussion of groupthink is based on Paul 't Hart, *Groupthink in Government: A Study of Small Groups and Policy Failure* (Amsterdam: Swets and Zeitlinger, 1990), which summarizes previous research on groupthink, while also making substantial original contributions.

196.

> [I]n the repressive and military parts of the state apparatus, there is a large reservoir of the type of highly-cohesive, uniformity-inducing, depersonalizing groups acting under external pressures which most closely fit the deindividuation profile. . . . [P]olice and military are uniformed (compare the appearance of modern anti-riot police, complete with helmets, gas masks—indeed the unrecognizability of individual officers has been a constant source of criticism and claims from protesting groups who claimed this had a disinhibiting effect upon police officers during disturbances, promoting excessively violent behavior). . . . [T]ight discipline and uniformity of conduct are part of the occupational socialization and culture.

(Ibid., p. 156.)

197. Ibid., p. 280.

198. Ibid., p. 281.

199. Obedience in this context means doing what an authority figure says simply because the authority figure said so.

5

The Cover-Up

Of course, those who commit atrocities understand that what they are doing will be considered criminal by the rest of the world, and this is why at the level of nation-states they attempt to control their population and the press.

Still, controlling people and knowledge is only a stopgap measure, particularly as ubiquitous electronic communication becomes widely available.

Lt. Col. Dave Grossman, *On Killing: The Psychological Cost of Learning to Kill in War and Society*[1]

COVER-UP THROUGH THE SIEGE AND IMMEDIATE AFTERMATH

As soon as the raid had ended, BATF spokespersons began telling lies about the raid, including the claim that they had no idea that the element of surprise had been lost. Not one of the dozens of BATF agents came forward to contradict these lies, although some of them apparently spoke to the press on conditions of anonymity, so that the official story about the element of surprise started to unravel by late March, about a month after the raid.

The day after the BATF had attempted to serve its search warrant by shooting its way into Mount Carmel, the BATF approached Koresh's gun dealer, Henry McMahon, and McMahon's common-law wife,[2] Karen Kilpatrick. (Other than BATF agents and Koresh, the pair were the only witnesses to Koresh's invitation to BATF to inspect his guns, the summer before the raid.) The two were told that the Branch Davidians not trapped inside Mount Carmel might try to kill them. The couple then asked to be taken into protective custody. They were taken to Oregon, and then to Waco, constantly admonished not to talk to the press or to the FBI.[3] It is difficult to believe that the safety of McMahon and Kilpatrick was foremost in BATF's collective mind when BATF attempted to prevent the pair from talking with the FBI.

On March 9, in the second week of the siege, the Branch Davidians filmed a two-hour videotape in which they explained themselves to the American people. The FBI refused to make the tape available to the media until after the siege was over. The negotiators in Waco told the Davidians that the video had a major humanizing effect; seeing the Davidians as real people made the negotiators redouble their determination to achieve a peaceful resolution.[4] The negotiators said that while the negotiators could, with the tapes, see Koresh as a person, some people in Washington, D.C., "don't have the same identification process." Koresh responded, reasonably, "Send them a tape."[5] The negotiator's log reveals that the FBI chose to keep the tape secret out of fear that if the American public could see it, there would be great sympathy for the Branch Davidians.[6]

Had the tape been available to the electronic media during the siege, public pressure might have forced the federal government to back off. Public support for the government depended on the perception of the Branch Davidians as a weird bunch of "cultists." The tape, however, portrays dozens of normal-looking men, women, and children. On the tape, the Branch Davidians look like the kind of people one would find at any shopping mall on a Sunday, except that the Branch Davidians are somewhat more clean-cut.[7] As the Department of Justice report later summarized:

> Each person on the video—male and female, young and old—spoke in a calm, assured tone of their desire to remain inside, even after the experience of the ATF raid only a few days earlier. Steve Schneider, who photographed the video and "interviewed" the subjects, also speaks in a thoughtful, articulate manner on the video. The abiding impression is not of a bunch of "lunatics," but rather of a group of people [who], for whatever reason, believed so strongly in Koresh that the notion of leaving the squalid compound was unthinkable. . . .
>
> They also believed that the end of the world was near, that the world would end in a cataclysmic confrontation between themselves and the government, and they would thereafter be resurrected. The February 28 ATF raid only reinforced the truth of Koresh's prophetic pronouncements in the minds of his followers.[8]

But with the tape securely in FBI custody, the Branch Davidians were successfully "otherized" as people with whom ordinary Americans could feel no more identification than with a cadre of Iranian terrorists.

The FBI may also not have disclosed the existence and contents of the tape, and another tape from later in March, to Attorney General Reno. Several hours after the conflagration, she asserted that the FBI had sought a videotape from Koresh showing that the children were all right, but he had refused to provide a tape.[9]

On March 15, BATF agents were ordered not to discuss the raid with the media.[10]

Attorneys for David Koresh and Steven Schneider successfully requested a court order that all BATF audiotapes and videotapes of the raid on Mount Carmel be preserved; the court rejected the attorneys' request that the court, rather than BATF, have custody of the tapes.[11] BATF claimed that it had a tape, taken from the surveillance house, which would prove that the Branch Davidians fired first on February 28. When the Branch Davidians went on trial in January 1994, BATF claimed that the tape was mysteriously blank.

On March 19, as part of the negotiations, Koresh was allowed to see the original search warrant. Accordingly, any law enforcement purpose for keeping the warrant secret from the public vanished. Nevertheless, the warrant remained sealed until after the April 19 fire.[12] Had the warrant been dissected while the siege was in progress, the fact that the warrant was built on falsehoods and distortions might have become an important topic of discussion in the media, and might have created pressure for the federal government to pursue only peaceful outcomes. By the time the warrant was released, Mount Carmel was in ashes, and the warrant was irrelevant.

Although federal courts have agreed that search warrants and supporting affidavits should be open to inspection by the public, a warrant may remain sealed when the government demonstrates a compelling state interest (such as protecting the life of a confidential informant) in maintaining secrecy.[13] Even in such a case, as much of the warrant and affidavit as possible is supposed to be released, while confidential portions can be redacted.[14]

At Waco, once the government voluntarily gave the warrants and warrant application to the Branch Davidians, there was no longer any law enforcement interest in keeping the warrant hidden from the American people and the media. While the magistrate's decision to allow the warrant to be kept secret was grossly inconsistent with established case law, there was nothing that could be done to reverse the decision at a time when reversal could have mattered.

As a prophylactic to future abuse of the sealing process, Congress should amend the Federal Rules of Criminal Procedure to specify that after the service of a search warrant, the warrant and all supporting documents should be made available to the public within twenty-four hours, unless the government (or in rare cases, the warrant target) demonstrates by clear and convincing evidence that there is a substantial risk that specific harm may result from unsealing the warrant. Mere generalized assertions by the government that unsealing the warrant would compromise an investigation should not be sufficient.

As noted in chapter 3, FBI spokesman Bob Ricks consistently misled the press and the American people about what was going on in the negotiations.[15] Of course, the FBI falsehoods about the negotiations, coupled with successful FBI efforts to block any communications by the Branch Davidians with the outside world, massively increased Davidian mistrust of the FBI and substantially undermined the chances of a successful negotiation.

Whatever the government knew about the fire apparently did not leave the government with enough confidence to have the fire independently investigated. Texas state fire marshals were denied access to the scene.[16] The "independent" arson investigator chosen by the U.S. Attorney's Office[17] to head the review, Paul Gray, is married to a BATF secretary,[18] and socialized with his wife's colleagues, including one of the agents killed in the BATF assault on the Mount Carmel Center, Steve Willis, whose funeral he attended. Additionally, Gray's office used to be in BATF offices in Houston. He had also served on BATF's National Arson Response Team. He carried business cards, featuring a Special Agent, U.S. Department of the Treasury shield, giving the BATF address and telephone number.[19]

Asked Jack Zimmermann, attorney for Steve Schneider: "Out of all the independent fire examiners they have in these United States . . . why didn't they pick someone from Chicago, or Philadelphia, New York, Miami, California? . . . Why do they pick a guy from Houston who worked in the ATF office until three years ago, who's married to an ATF employee who, I understand, may have had something to do with typing the warrant? And then went to the funeral of one of the four guys who was killed. How much more partial can you be than that?"[20] According to Dick DeGuerin, there were at least ten other "very qualified" arson experts at the Houston Fire Department who could have been used, rather than an expert with such close ties to BATF.[21] And Gray reportedly sped to release the report early before Branch Davidian attorneys could "reveal that it was really not an independent arson review."[22]

The fire investigators, contrary to normal practice, never interviewed any of the fire survivors.[23]

William Cass, a fire expert with the Los Angeles Fire Department, was one of the members of the four-person "independent" arson investigation team headed by Paul Gray. At the Davidians' trial, Mr. Cass testified that the arson investigation team did not watch the portion of the government tape showing the heat plume rising from near the gymnasium. FBI logs had recorded a fire that began close to the gymnasium; but, testified Mr. Cass, Paul Gray kept the logs from the other investigators.[24]

On April 22, three days after the siege ended, state troopers arrested Associated Press and *Houston Chronicle* reporters and confiscated film they had been shooting of the burned building. "One has to seriously wonder if the Bill of Rights has been suspended in McLennan County," said Tony Pederson, managing editor of the *Chronicle*.[25]

After the fire, the Texas Rangers were not allowed to take control of the property until after the federal government had unrestricted access.[26] Before any defense lawyers could examine the scene, the FBI decided what would be kept as evidence, and what should be thrown away.[27] Forensic evidence, rather than being analyzed by the Texas Rangers, was turned over to BATF and the FBI.[28]

Then the Branch Davidian property was bulldozed. The bulldozing was ostensibly so that the Texas Health Department could begin work at Mount Carmel, although the work did not commence until over a year later. A thorough study of evidence by unbiased parties was made impossible.[29] A lawsuit by some of the Branch Davidian survivors alleges that the FBI's bulldozing and other property destruction

> prevented examination of the blast hole in the ceiling, the scraping and removal of the remains of the building including concrete foundation slabs and dirt which contained thousands of expended bullet slugs from government firearms, evidence of lethal chemicals, accelerants and other dangerous elements used in the assault and other evidence.[30]

As is customary after a military triumph, there was also some reported looting. A church safe containing $50,000 in cash, plus platinum and gold survived the fire and was found in the ashes by the Texas Rangers. The Rangers signed the safe over to the FBI, but the safe did not appear on the FBI's evidence list, and remains missing.[31]

One investigation which was well handled was the identification of the burned bodies by a team of volunteer forensic dentists. Although many of the dentists were understandably repelled by the bodies riddled with maggots and by other horrible sights, the dentists were able to identify conclusively many of the dead at Mount Carmel, including David Koresh. One dentist recalled, "There was a particular instance where all that remained was the arm and hand of a mother clasping a small child's hand and remain of arm. You could see how tightly the child's hand was being squeezed by the mother."[32]

The autopsies, however, conducted by the Tarrant County Medical Examiner were not handled well.[33] Many of the autopsies were careless; for example, an adult woman was identified as a ten-year-old girl. Even worse, the medical examiner made it impossible for independent experts to examine the bodies; the refrigeration system failed, and nobody noticed, apparently, for so long that the bodies disintegrated. Thus it was impossible for the families of the deceased to conduct thorough autopsies which would attempt to identify the caliber and firearm type used in the deaths that occurred from gunshot.[34]

The National Association of Medical Examiners barred the public and news media from part of their September 1993 conference discussion regarding the Branch Davidians on the grounds that some of the information revealed might hinder prosecution of surviving Davidians. It is hard to understand what legitimate prosecution could be hindered by the defendants learning truthful information available to the government.[35]

A federal court had ordered that relevant audio- and videotapes in government custody not be tampered with. At a June 9, 1993, congressional hearing, the FBI provided House Appropriations subcommittee staff with a tape of the 911 call from the Branch Davidians to sheriff's lieutenant Larry Lynch. The segment in which Davidian Wayne Martin shouts that a new helicopter attack has begun was moved to the back of the tape, thus placing it in a time period after the helicopters had withdrawn. The alteration was noticed by a communications specialist with local law enforcement in Waco; the Waco police promptly informed Congress that the FBI alteration had created a "false impression of how the event occurred."[36]

In the coming months and years, the FBI would withhold a significant amount of important Waco evidence from the public. Koresh's manuscript on the seven seals was held by the FBI for months, although there was no law enforcement need to keep secret the Bible analysis of a self-proclaimed prophet. But prompt release of the Koresh manuscript would have undermined FBI claims, made shortly after the April 19 fire, that the FBI had conclusive evidence that the Koresh was not working on the manuscript.

On April 19, an FBI plane using Forward Looking Infrared circled Mount Carmel, starting at dawn, and continuing till the fire was over. The FLIR videotapes have been withheld from the public for years. One tape was finally released, accompanied by government claims that it was the only tape.[37] Then, in response to a Freedom of Information Act lawsuit by attorney David Hardy, a second tape was released, again with the claim that there was only one tape.

Moreover, the FLIR video shows a second plane circling at a lower altitude. Because a FLIR video is good for spotting heat, but produces poor-quality gray-scale images of ordinary objects in the daytime, it would have been sensible to the FBI to have used a second surveillance plane on April 19, with the second plane using a high resolution color camera. But no one in the FBI or the Department of Justice has ever admitted the existence of the second plane (which is visible on the FLIR tape), and no photos from that second plane have been released to the public.

On April 19, a long-distance news camera took a picture of an HRT member using a camcorder to record the action at the Mount Carmel Center. This video also remains unacknowledged and unreleased.

EXECUTIVE BRANCH

The Shooting Review and the Texas Rangers

Less than thirty-six hours after the BATF raid, a formal coverup began. Standard procedure at BATF, like most other law enforcement agencies, is that whenever shots are fired by law enforcement, there is a shooting review, to assess whether the use of deadly force was consistent with official policy.

The shooting review had barely begun when Assistant United States Attorney William Johnston advised BATF Deputy Director for Enforcement Daniel Hartnett to stop the BATF shooting review because it was creating *Brady* material.[38] (Under the *Brady* rule, the government must turn over to defendants exculpatory evidence which is in the government's custody. Statements made by BATF agents during a shooting review would be *Brady* material if, for example, an agent said that he thought BATF fired first.)

In April 1993, the Department of Justice asked the Department of the Treasury (of which BATF is a subordinate bureau) to stop all internal investigations into the Waco fiasco: "DOJ does not want Treasury to conduct *any* interviews or have discussions with *any* of the participants, who may be potential witnesses; the prosecutors do not want us to generate additional *Jencks*, *Brady* or *Giglio* material or oral statements which could be used for impeachment."[39]

The memoranda show that the U.S. Department of Justice was curtailing an investigation of the February 28 shootout due to concerns that some of the information gathered would, when turned over to the defense attorneys, provide exculpatory or explanatory material which would help the defense against murder and related charges. Such information might make it harder to achieve guilty verdicts. Put another way, the Department of Justice wanted to be able to use BATF agents as witnesses in the prosecution of the Branch Davidians. The Department did not want those witnesses to be interviewed in the days and weeks following the shooting, when their memories would be freshest. The Department was afraid that statements made by the agents when their memories were fresh would be inconsistent with the stories that the agents would later tell when testifying against the Branch Davidians. Those inconsistent, earlier statements, could be used to impeach the credibility of the agents at trial.

In fact, this is exactly what happened. While the shooting review was aborted, the Texas Rangers conducted their own investigation. Statements which BATF agents made to the Rangers were used to impeach government witnesses at the trial, who told the jury stories quite different from what they had told the Texas Rangers.

The DOJ evidence suppression memos were revealed during the first days of the 1995 congressional hearings on Waco. The Department of Justice promptly put out a press release claiming, "This is Prosecution 101, and any prosecutor worth his or her salt would know it."[40] Perhaps the deliberate suppression of evidence is a basic tactic at the Department of Justice these days. But the ethical rules which govern prosecutors mandate that the prosecutor's duty is to truth and justice, not to rack up convictions. In contrast to attorneys for private clients, whose primary ethical duty is to represent zealously the client's interests, a prosecutor is subject to a much higher ethical standard.[41]

Before initiating a prosecution, a prosecutor should gather enough evidence to assure himself that there is probable cause to believe the defendants are guilty.[42] The request to terminate the shooting review, one day after the shootout, reveals that Assistant U.S. Attorney Johnston and the Department of Justice had already decided to prosecute the Branch Davidians, without gathering evidence as to whether the Branch Davidians had fired in lawful self-defense. (At trial, the Branch Davidians would be acquitted of all violent crimes for which the jury was allowed to consider self-defense as a justification.)

Within the executive branch of the federal government, the Department of Justice and its United States Attorneys are supposed to serve an important checking function. Rather than blindly accepting the cases which other executive departments bring to the Department of Justice for prosecution, the department must carefully evaluate the cases, in part to see if there really is substantial evidence of the defendant's guilt. But at Waco, the Department of Justice simply assumed—wrongly as it turned out—that in any shootout between federal agents and American citizens, the federal agents must be right, and the citizens wrong. No responsible prosecutor could make such a determination the day after the shooting, *before* any of the witnesses to the shooting had been interviewed.

The "Prosecution 101" that is part of expected behavior at the Department of Justice at present needs to be revised. Apparently there is a need for increased formal training in ethical standards for prosecutors, a topic discussed in more detail in the next chapter.

Apart from suppressing evidence, there could have been plausible reasons for curtailing the shooting review. When testifying before Congress, Assistant U.S. Attorney Johnston pointed out that a standard shooting review would have been redundant, since the Department of the Treasury was eventually going to do a report on the controversial BATF raid.[43] Further, an ordinary shooting review would be conducted by BATF supervisors; but in the Waco situation, regular BATF agents might be reluctant to speak freely with BATF supervisors, since the shooting review could implicate BATF supervisors as partially responsible for the loss of four BATF agents.[44] Rather than have BATF investigate the shooting, Treasury and Justice decided that the Texas Rangers should conduct the investigation.[45] All the rationales are sensible. But the memoranda from the Department of Justice urging that internal Treasury and BATF investigations be shut down do not mention redundancy, or problems of BATF supervisors investigating their own mistakes. Instead, the memos discuss the need to avoid creating material which could be used at trial by defendants. If the BATF agents were expected to tell the truth consistently—both in government investigations and at trial—then there would be little need to worry that the initial interviews would contradict trial testimony. The Texas Rangers who testified before Congress in 1995 said that in over a quarter-century of police work each, they had not seen similar directives to curtail investigations to prevent the production of exculpatory evidence.[46]

The Texas Rangers proceeded to interview over eighty BATF agents involved in the raid, along with Branch Davidians when they left Mount Carmel. After the April 19 fire, the Rangers sought evidence in the ashes of the residence. For a number of reasons, however, the Texas Rangers' shooting investigation was unsatisfactory.

First, the FBI Hostage Rescue Team was so single-minded about tactical maneuvers against the Davidians that the HRT heedlessly destroyed evidence which the Rangers wanted preserved. The evidence included vehicles which the Rangers hoped to investigate for signs of bullet trajectories in an effort to figure out from which windows they came.[47] Such evidence could have helped link specific Davidian shooters to specific BATF deaths. The Rangers complained to Assistant U.S. Attorney Johnston, who complained to the FBI, and eventually wrote to Attorney General Reno. He noted that, soon after trying to assemble an investigative team of Rangers to "work the homicide . . . in conjunction with other agencies and with crime laboratories," the U.S. Attorney, Ronald Ederer, "instructed me to halt any efforts in that regard." He also noted, "The FBI is using tanks to push vehicles away from the compound. This is destroying important trajectory evidence because these vehicles were being used by the agents during the shootout as cover and were riddled with defendant gunfire . . . our concerns about the preservation of evidence go unheard. . . ."[48]

Second, even as the FBI negotiators were assuring the Branch Davidians there would be a thorough investigation to see if there was wrongdoing by BATF,[49] the Texas Rangers viewed the investigation solely as a murder investigation of the Branch Davidians for killing four BATF agents.[50] There is no indication that the Rangers even attempted to investigate Davidian claims that BATF had started the whole thing.[51]

Indeed, while the Texas Rangers complained about the FBI's destruction of evidence, there is no indication they solicited FBI cooperation in obtaining the bodies of dead Davidians to determine whether Davidian complaints they were murdered by BATF had any validity.[52] And the Rangers apparently did not investigate thoroughly complaints about injuries or near-injuries to noncombatants, such as Judy Schneider or children the Davidians insisted were missed only by inches.[53] Such improper shooting at unidentified or misidentified targets could easily have occurred because BATF agents may have entered Mount Carmel believing that men would be separated from women and children at the time of their raid,[54] and massive quantities of empty ammunition casings were found far from the residence, indicating wild shooting.[55] The Texas Rangers reported no concern about these possible misdeeds in the course of their shooting review.

The potential instance of government malfeasance which the Texas Rangers did take seriously was the death of Mike Schroeder. He had been at the Mag Bag when the BATF raid took place. Later in the day, he attempted to sneak into the Mount Carmel Center. The FBI prevented the Texas Rangers from investigating the body and the shooting scene until heavy rains had washed away the footprints around Schroeder's body. Although a picture of Schroeder's body shows a blue cap on his head, the cap—which could contain powder burns from a close-range shot to his head—had disappeared. If it is assumed that coverups only take place when there is something to cover up, it is entirely possible that Mike Schroeder was executed while in custody.[56]

And, finally, the Texas Rangers' investigation failed to lead to prosecution of anyone except Branch Davidians. The Rangers "were commissioned early on in this as deputy U.S. marshals . . . so that we could prosecute federally anyone that lied to us, and we feel real comfortable . . . that we were lied to." But any possible cases—such as against BATF commanders Sarabyn and Chojnacki—were referred to the Department of Justice, which did nothing.[57]

As the Texas Rangers investigation faded away, hopes were raised that comprehensive reports by the Department of the Treasury and the Department of Justice would provide more information.

The Treasury Department wrote a report on the BATF actions, while the Justice Department created a report on the FBI. The Justice team was initially told not to review the actions of April 19,[58] although that quickly changed.[59] The Departments then turned the reports over to outside reviewers. Some of the outside reviewers of the Justice Report offered important insights, although some of the other members of the Treasury[60] and Justice review teams had serious conflicts of interest which may have compromised objectivity. The worst conflict involved the person chosen to head the Justice review, Edward Dennis, Jr., formerly a senior official in the Bush Department of Justice, and currently an attorney with the Philadelphia law firm Morgan, Lewis & Bockius. When Mr. Dennis was selected, he was representing several clients with litigation before the Department of Justice. Because of the potential that the Dennis report might influence the department's attitude in its dealing with Mr. Dennis's clients, some critics complained that the Dennis report was tainted by conflict of interest. More significantly, reports *New York Times* columnist William Safire, Dennis had been in charge of the bungled investigation of Banca Lavoro and its relations to Iraqgate:

> Ms. Reno's Criminal Division directed Atlanta prosecutors to shoot down the explosive case with a plea bargain, avoiding a public trial that would have exposed the machinations of the Bush-Thornburgh-Dennis crowd. How could Ed Dennis not be grateful? His judgment about the Waco fiasco: "there is no place in this evaluation for blame, and I find no fault." One hand whitewashes the other.[61]

As the Treasury Report on BATF's actions neared completion, the Treasury Department created and then implemented an administrative rule to shield a large number of Waco-related documents from normal disclosure pursuant to the Freedom of Information Act.[62] The concealment was criticized not just by the usual BATF critics, but also by Rep. Pat Schroeder, an ardent defender of Janet Reno's Waco performance, and a staunch advocate of federal gun control.

Treasury Report

The Treasury Department report's cover page explained that the report was conducted as a memorial to the four BATF agents who were killed at Waco. The Treasury Department review claimed there was no evidence of religious bias in the investigation[63] and rhetorically referred to David Koresh's firetrap as "fortress-like."[64]

Similarly, at Ruby Ridge, the U.S. Marshals Service regularly referred to the Weavers' property as a "compound," even though it consisted of unfenced acreage, a cabin, and small outbuildings. And long after Weaver's and Harris's acquittals, when FBI Director Louis Freeh was announcing mild punishments for some of the FBI agents involved in the siege, he referred to the construction-grade plywood house as a "fortified cabin."[65]

The Treasury Report about Waco attempts to justify the use of Texas National Guard helicopters based on the false allegation of a drug nexus. The Report suggests that provisions for using the military are not sufficiently clear, but exonerates the agency of any wrongdoing. According to the report, BATF did "not . . . misrepresent the facts concerning the nexus between the proposed raid and the evidence of drug violations."[66] The Treasury Report omits mention of the fact that the United States Army special operations Mobile Tactical Training Team was training BATF agents for the raid during February 1993—training that would violate the Posse Comitatus Act unless drugs were involved, as BATF knew they were not.[67]

With no supporting evidence, and despite substantial contrary evidence, the Report ignored the history of friendly relations between Koresh and law enforcement. Treasury repeatedly asserted Koresh had an overpowering hatred of law enforcement, particularly of BATF.[68]

The Treasury Report's text asserted that probable cause was obtained by December,[69] in conflict with the Treasury Report's chronology which admits that BATF did not believe it had probable cause until February 1993.[70]

Treasury accurately noted that of two explosives experts consulted, one said Koresh was clearly in violation of the law, and the other said otherwise.[71] The expert asserting a violation of the law incorrectly believed that the quantities of blackpowder and igniter cord possessed were "explosives" requiring proper registration and storage.[72] The expert misstated the law, since the quantity of blackpowder was below that requiring conformance with any storage requirement, and neither blackpowder nor igniter cord requires registration. Similarly, the assertion that possession of blackpowder and inert grenade hulls constitutes an explosive grenade because it is possible to make one is misleading. More materials are needed, along with machinery to drill and plug a hole.[73]

And, finally, although it is known that Koresh's gun dealer told the Treasury Department investigators about the invitation Koresh had extended to BATF to visit the Mount Carmel Center, the fact is ignored in the Treasury Department review. Instead, Treasury noted only that the dealer allegedly "lied" about Koresh by referring to him sometimes as Koresh and other times by the name on his driver's license, Vernon Howell.[74]

The report denies allegations of injury or death to BATF agents from friendly fire, although the report fails to provide any specifics with regard to the ammunition involved in the shootings of government agents on February 28. No information was provided about the death of BATF agent Robert Williams. The death of Branch Davidian Mike Schroeder (killed while trying to sneak back into Mount Carmel after the firefight) is also absent from the Treasury Report. The Report claims that Branch Davidian Winston Blake was "killed by cult members" with a close-range gunshot. The Branch Davidians maintain that he was killed at the very beginning of the raid, as he was eating a breakfast roll in his bedroom. Because Blake was a British citizen, a British coroner's office conducted an investigation into the cause of his death. The investigation determined that Blake was killed by a long-range, high-velocity gun shot that penetrated an exterior wall before hitting him in the head.[75] In other words, Blake was probably killed by a rifle shot from a BATF agent who was firing wildly into the building and not aiming at visible targets.

Besides the ballistics evidence regarding BATF casualties, there is quite a lot more that is simply missing from the Treasury Report, including: the fact the Davidians operated a lawful firearms business at gun shows; the possibility that publicity and politics were motives for the BATF raid; and the fact that BATF agents in National Guard helicopters may have strafed the residential tower, catwalk area, and women's dormitory.

Other, misleading, items are inserted uncritically. For example, the report notes the efforts to isolate men from the household guns by timing the raid for when men would be outside working in the swimming pool construction pit.[76] The report buries the fact that an assault plan based on so isolating the men was absurd. They were observed in the pit on fewer than half of BATF's surveillance observation days, with the number of men in the pit never exceeding thirteen.[77]

The Treasury Report did acknowledge that various BATF officials had incompetently planned an armed assault, and had then lied and attempted to cover up their culpability when the assault went awry. BATF Director Stephen Higgins was forced to resign. Deputy Director Daniel Hartnett, Deputy Associate Director of Law Enforcement Conroy, and BATF intelligence head David Troy were suspended with pay pending further discipline.[78] Hartnett and Conroy eventually retired.[79] When Conroy retired in 1993, his work for the year was rated "outstanding" and he received a $10,000 bonus.[80] Troy was given a punitive demotion and removed from the Senior Executive Service (SES). He has since been promoted and returned to SES.[81]

BATF raid commanders Phillip Chojnacki and Charles Sarabyn were placed on paid administrative leave for over a year, eventually fired, and shortly thereafter reinstated with full back pay, and the Waco incident was expunged from their personnel records.[82] Chojnacki's new job includes serving as an expert witness for the government in court cases. Testifying under oath is a curious assignment for a person believed by the Treasury Report to have prevaricated repeatedly, and who the Texas Rangers asked the Department of Justice to prosecute for lying to them under oath.[83] According to an unnamed Treasury official, Chojnacki and Sarabyn, during negotiations over job status, had threatened to spill the beans about high-ranking BATF managers.[84]

The major criticism voiced in the Treasury Report was continuation of the assault on the Mount Carmel Center after the element of surprise was lost. There has been considerable dispute since then, both in law enforcement circles and in congressional hearings, as to the importance of surprise. Phillip Chojnacki and Chuck Sarabyn did not believe they were wrong to proceed after being told by Rodriguez that Koresh was expecting BATF and the National Guard.[85] And BATF's Associate Director for Law Enforcement, Dan Hartnett, noted that discussion of the loss of surprise occurred more after the raid than in planning for it.[86]

The most serious criticism of BATF in the Treasury Report is for going ahead with the raid despite alleged orders to halt if surprise were lost; but it is not clear that Chojnacki and Sarabyn were ever given such orders. According to the National Association of Treasury Agents, the final order to proceed was given by someone higher-ranking than Chojnacki and Sarabyn.[87]

Chojnacki and Sarabyn were punished—although much of the punishment was rescinded—for going forward with the raid despite Rodriguez's telephone call. And BATF Director Higgins was forced to retire early because he had assured his superiors that such a mistake would not happen, that "if anything unusual or out of the ordinary occurred, the raid would not proceed," such as "when you plan a raid to surprise someone and you learn 45 minutes in advance they know you're coming."[88]

Most of the remaining basis for punishment was for covering up the loss of the element of surprise. Thus, the Treasury Report blamed particular individuals for mistakes or lies about surprise, but glossed over the more serious problems manifested by BATF's conduct at Waco. The Treasury Report paid little attention to BATF's decision to arrest Koresh with a massive armed assault on his house despite the more peaceful options that were available.

Because the Treasury Report did directly lead to the punishment of certain BATF employees, the report was generally praised by the media as hard-hitting. If the purpose of the report was to ensure that future BATF attacks are more competent, the report made an important contribution. But to persons who wondered about why attacks as unnecessary at the February 28 assault on Mount Carmel were to be allowed in the first place, the report had nothing to say.[89] Dan Hartnett (who was criticized in the report), later told Congress that the Treasury Report was deliberately distorted, and he blamed the distortion on Treasury Undersecretary Ron Noble.[90]

Justice Report

The Treasury Department, investigating its subordinate bureau, BATF, did not use BATF personnel to conduct the investigation. In contrast, the Justice Department, investigating its own subordinate bureau, the FBI, used the FBI to interview witnesses. Henry Ruth, one of the independent Treasury reviewers, expressed concerns about the credibility of an FBI review conducted by the FBI.[91]

The Justice Department's report included various conflicting recommendations which were obtained over the fifty-one days of the standoff. The conclusion was that no one was to blame for anything which went wrong except for Koresh; mistakes were made, but no one except for Koresh was responsible for any of them.[92] The short summary review accompanying the report included such false statements as: "The Attorney General was adequately briefed on the tear gassing plan, was fully informed of the options, and was given a realistic appraisal of the risks."[93]

Some of the "facts" in the Justice Report were simply false. Contrary to Justice Department claims that the arson report stated that all the Davidians could have escaped if they wanted to,[94] the arson report had only stated that a "great many of the occupants could have escaped to the outside of the compound even as the building burned."[95]

The Justice Report also omitted significant information, especially information which suggested the standoff could have been brought to a peaceful resolution. Missing from the Justice Report is the fact that Koresh, on April 4, received a tape from two religious scholars who interpreted Revelation to suggest to Koresh that the apocalypse was not imminent, and that Koresh could honorably continue his religious writings in prison.[96] Nor does the report even mention Koresh's April 14 surrender letter, except to dismiss it as psychotic. The chronology likewise omits events related to Koresh's writing of his interpretation of the seven seals (such as the requests for typewriter ribbons), which Koresh in his April 14 letter called the only condition precedent to his surrender.

The outside reviewers whom the Justice Department had chosen to comment on the report had a difficult time obtaining information. The surrender letter was apparently shown to none of the seven independent reviewers. One outside reviewer, Nancy Ammerman, finally obtained a copy of the letter from Dr. Tabor, the religion professor who had established the religious dialogue with Koresh.[97]

Harvard professor Alan Stone, another of independent reviewers, complained that the FBI "stone-walled" his requests for information about CS chemical warfare agent, supplying him instead with "ambiguous and irrelevant material."[98]

The written comments from the outside reviewers were particularly critical of the FBI's repeated refusal to consult religious experts who might perceive the views of religious devotees as something other than brainwashing or a cover for criminal activity.[99]

The news media were more skeptical of the "no fault" Justice Report than of the Treasury Report. After all, while the Treasury Department ignored questions regarding why the raid was planned, it did severely criticize how it was carried out and the coverup which followed.

The FBI carried out an internal investigation of the Ruby Ridge shootout. According to FBI agent Eugene Glenn (one of the subjects of the investigation), "The leader of the Weaver inquiry said this is not going to be a whitewash like Waco was."[100] The FBI report remains secret. During the Senate investigation of the Weaver case, the FBI allowed one Republican and one Democratic staff member to look at the report; no senator was allowed to see it.

The Justice Department's Office of Professional Responsibility carried out its own investigation of the Randy Weaver case in Idaho. The report concluded that federal agents had violated both statutory law and the Constitution, and recommended criminal prosecution. Deval Patrick, a Justice Department official, overruled the call for prosecution. The federal government refused to release the report to the public, although the report has been leaked, and posted on the Internet.[101]

Internal discipline was meted out to various FBI officials for conduct related to the Weaver case, conduct which, according to the judge who presided over Weaver's trial, included the deliberate falsification of evidence. The most serious punishment was a fifteen day suspension without pay. Larry Potts, the FBI supervisor of the Ruby Ridge siege who had allegedly authorized the shoot-to-kill orders, and who had been a key planner of the April 19 Waco assault, was given a letter of censure for his conduct in Idaho—the same punishment given to FBI Director Louis Freeh for losing his portable phone in an unrelated incident. Potts was later promoted to the number two position at the FBI.[102]

Dick Rogers, commander of the HRT at both Waco and Ruby Ridge, was replaced in late 1993.[103]

The White House

White House handling of Waco consistently considered political advantage, to the exclusion of virtually everything else. At the press conference the evening of the fire, the president's press secretary repeatedly stated that while President Clinton had ultimate responsibility, the decision had been made by Janet Reno. The White House tried to create the impression that Clinton had only learned about the assault plan the day before it was executed.[104] Actually, Clinton had first been told about it on April 13, six days before.[105] *Washington Times* columnist Wesley Pruden observed, "He gave the order, but didn't inhale."[106]

At about the same time, Janet Reno, clearly anguished, said that the responsibility was hers. Like President Kennedy's acceptance of responsibility for the Bay of Pigs fiasco, Attorney General Reno's taking the blame was a public relations bonanza. Her maturity in accepting responsibility for her bad judgment rapidly erased any problems about the quality of her judgment.

The president, seeing what was happening, promptly announced that he was the most responsible person of all.[107] The Chairman of the Democratic National Committee attended a White House strategy session (along with the president, First Lady, vice president, chief of staff, and six assistants) to discuss if President Clinton should go to Waco.[108]

For the next several months, Attorney General Reno bathed in favorable press attention, her popularity far outstripping the president's. This in turn led to further strains in the already tense relationship between the attorney general and the White House.

Two weeks after the fire, FBI Director William Sessions headed to Waco to present a plaque to the mayor on May 5, 1993. Attorney General Reno was disgusted by the grandstanding; Waco had put a temporary impediment in her long-standing plan to fire Sessions, since the White House did not want it to appear that he was being fired for Waco. Sessions's performance related to Waco reinforced Reno's plans to dismiss him, which she did several weeks later.[109]

JUDICIAL BRANCH: THE TRIAL

> [T]hey may have been gunmen. They may have tried to murder. But they were not cowards. . . . [E]leven of them go into a house, gentlemen, with no police protection, in the face of a mob, and the hatred of a community, and take guns and ammunition and fight for their rights, and for your rights and for mine, and for the rights of every other human being that lives.
>
> > Clarence Darrow's summation from the trial of Doctor Ossian Sweet,
> > a black man who shot at a white mob that was attacking his home
> > after he moved into a white neighborhood[110]

The pattern of deception continued when the Davidians were put on trial for allegedly ambushing the BATF raiders.

The Prosecutors

One problem was the initial involvement of the prosecutor in the preraid investigation, giving him a special animus; part of what was being prosecuted was the result of his own failure to help conclude a successful initial investigation and arrest.

Assistant U.S. Attorney Bill Johnston had been involved in the investigation of David Koresh for months before the original search warrant—procured with the sloppy, mistake-filled affidavit which he helped write—was obtained. According to the Treasury Report, Johnston had been the one who insisted that the search warrant be served by "dynamic entry."[111] In an effort to disqualify Johnston as a prosecutor—since he would have a personal motive to cover his own mistakes—defense attorneys attempted to introduce the Treasury Department Report into evidence. The prosecution successfully objected. Mr. Johnston told the court that "The Treasury Review is a book that was written for newspapers and the public to read, but is not intended for the ATF or the government to use."[112] In other words, the Treasury Report was propaganda, not truth, he thought.

The lead prosecutor, Ray Jahn, also had been personally involved in the disaster; the Justice Department had consulted with him about the chemical warfare plans. A motion to remove him from the case was also denied. (After Waco, Jahn became one of the attorneys assisting the Whitewater special prosecutor.)

There was a similar problem at Ruby Ridge, where Assistant U.S. Attorney Ron Howen took a special interest in the investigation of the Aryan Nations, which led to the entrapment of Randy Weaver. When Weaver refused to become an informer for Howen, Howen insisted on prosecuting Weaver as if Weaver were a dangerous member of the Aryan Nations. Howen added the charge that Weaver had failed to show up for his trial on February 20, 1991, even before Weaver had missed the March 20 trial date Howen knew Weaver had mistakenly been given. Howen inappropriately terminated negotiations the marshals were having with Weaver, which might have brought a peaceful end to Weaver's self-imposed house arrest at the cabin, on the grounds that such negotiations could only be done through Weaver's assigned attorney, with whom Weaver was not in contact. Howen insisted that negotiations would be acceptable only if Weaver would plead guilty to a crime. Howen then went on to prosecute Weaver— yet with so much of himself at stake that his judgement may have been jeopardized, as was his personal health.[113]

The Judge

The judge, Walter S. Smith, was known to Waco attorneys as intelligent and vindictive, and extremely intolerant of criticism. He was generally regarded as biased in favor of government litigants.[114]

Judge Smith declared that he would "not allow the government to be put on trial." True to his word, he suppressed defense attorneys' efforts to introduce self-defense evidence. For example, the judge refused to allow defense attorneys to call BATF agents Chojnacki, Royster, or Aguilera (all of whom had been in the Blackhawk helicopters during the raid) to determine whether shots had been fired from the helicopters. The defense attorneys were allowed to raise self-defense in their closing arguments, but not to present evidence regarding self-defense during the trial.[115] Judge Smith did exclude other material as prejudicial to the defendants. For example, he stated that the prosecution could not call the Mount Carmel Center "Ranch Apocalypse" (a name which had been used on two occasions by Perry Jones). But while the prosecution lost nothing essential to their case, the defense was deprived of the essence of their case: self-defense.

At the trial, pictures of the four dead BATF agents were displayed for long periods of time, but the judge refused to let the jurors see pictures of the dead children.[116]

The judge played a major role in selecting a pro-prosecution jury. The three hundred jurors in the initial jury pool were sent an extensive juror screening questionnaire demanded detailed revelations of the potential juror's political beliefs, including about gun control. Judge Smith used the questionnaire to eliminate 216 jurors, leaving the attorneys with 84 potential jurors from which to choose the panel. While explaining the concept of self-defense to the jury, Judge Smith revealed his attitudes by stating that he hoped no one on the jury would ever carry a gun on the street.[117]

When BATF had launched its dynamic entry, Branch Davidian Wayne Martin and Koresh had dialed 911 and begged the local sheriff's office to arrange a ceasefire. The hour-long tape was played for the jury, but the judge excised two brief statements in which Martin and Koresh each said that BATF had fired first.[118] The judge called these statements "self-serving," but it is properly the function of the jury to evaluate whether statements are self-serving or truthful. The jury forewoman, Sarah Bain, later stated that if the jury had heard the tapes and other evidence which the judge excluded, the Branch Davidians would have been acquitted on all counts.

Missing and Altered Evidence

Evidence seemed to disappear. The front door to the house, which could have provided physical evidence that the Branch Davidians did not fire first, mysteriously vanished, although the steel door was known to have survived the fire. After the first raid, BATF had claimed to have a videotape proving that the Branch Davidians fired first. Later, BATF claimed that the camera at the BATF undercover house had malfunctioned on the day of the raid. All eleven listening devices inside Mount Carmel were announced to have been destroyed or to have started malfunctioning so that no records were available for the five minutes before the fire started.

Under cross-examination, the prosecution's audio expert admitted he had altered the tape transcript in half a dozen places, at the request of the prosecutor, for what he called technical reasons. For example, the jury was presented with a transcript which read: "So we only light 'em as they come in." The words had been altered from the original "So we only light 'em as soon as they tell me it's the last chance, right?"[119] Even with enhancement, the tapes were extremely difficult to understand, and jury forewoman Sarah Bain said that the jury gave the tapes little credibility.[120] The judge refused to let the jury see the original transcripts which had been made on the day of the fire.[121]

According to Texas Ranger Ray Cano, all of their interview materials had been turned over to the United States Attorney's office, and the original notes destroyed.[122] The destruction removed a vast body of evidence would could have been used to challenge BATF witnesses at trial, if the BATF witnesses told one story at trial, but had told a different story to the Rangers.

Even though the Rangers' notes were destroyed, the Rangers remembered enough to undermine BATF testimony. For example, at trial, BATF agents Eric Evers and Gary Orchowski pointed out defendant Livingstone Fagan, who is black, as the man who had shot them on February 28. Yet when interviewed by the Texas Rangers, both agents had identified the man who shot them as simply a black man. (Fagan was one of nine black males at Mount Carmel.[123])

A Bunch of Brady *Material*

The government illegally withheld several items of *Brady* material. (In *Brady* v. *Maryland*, the Supreme Court established a rule that a prosecution must show the defendant exculpatory evidence which is in the government's possession.[124]) One item which the prosecution failed to give to the defense, as legally required, was the fact that a BATF agent who in court identified defendant Livingstone Fagan as the man who shot him had earlier picked Fagan out of a photo line-up but had written "unsure if identified from shooting or TV."

Other *Brady* material was withheld for ten months from defendant Norman Allison's attorney, finally released only on the eve of trial. Allison, a Branch Davidian who had been away from Mount Carmel during the BATF raid, had tried to sneak inside on the evening of February 28. He had been captured peacefully, but was charged with attempted homicide. Ballistics tests on his handgun proved that he did not fire the gun; but these tests were illegally kept from him for ten months. Allison, who was acquitted of all offenses, spent ten months in jail awaiting trial in large part because exculpatory evidence was withheld from the bail hearing.[125]

Similar tactics had characterized the prosecution of Randy Weaver in Idaho. Background information about FBI sniper Lon Horiuchi, and Horiuchi's initial reports, were required to be turned over to the defense, but were mailed fourth-class from Washington, arriving the day after Horiuchi testified.

The problem of government concealment of *Brady* material is hardly unique to sensational cases. For example, in one unpublicized case, a man was convicted of counterfeiting, and spent three years in prison for the offense, before discovering (through a Freedom of Information Act request) that the FBI had a fingerprint report showing the fingerprints of sixty-eight different persons on the counterfeit bills, and not one of the fingerprints belonged to the convicted man. At a second trial, the man was acquitted.[126]

One of the reasons that *Brady* material is too often withheld is the lack of the practical sanction. If the defendant/victim can prove that a government agent acted in bad faith, the agent can be sued. But even when bad faith is undisputed, the government gets a second chance to try the defendant again, this time allowing use of evidence which the government illegally withheld at the first trial. Thus, the defendant is forced to go through two trials (and if he is not indigent, to pay a second round of very expensive legal fees). The situation violates at least the spirit of the double jeopardy clause.[127] In some cases, courts will not overturn a conviction after *Brady* material was illegally withheld if the court can be convinced that the defendant was guilty anyway, and so the withholding was "harmless error."

An improved deterrent to *Brady* violations would be to state that whenever it is discovered that *Brady* material has been withheld, the conviction should automatically be voided, and the prosecution should not be allowed to put the defendant on trial again. The sanction of barring a second prosecution is not too severe, because it is impossible for a prosecutor to commit a "good faith" *Brady* violation. The *Brady* rule is violated only if the prosecutor knows about the evidence, yet deliberately withholds it.

More generally, Federal Rule of Criminal Procedure 16 should be amended to conform with recommendations of American Bar Association "Standard on Criminal Discovery." Both sides of a criminal trial should be allowed to take statements from the other side's witness before a criminal trial, as is currently allowed in civil trials. The current system of concealing evidence until trial—in effect, trial by ambush—is a relic of the Cold War, and a statute known as the Jencks Act is designed to protect government information from Communist defendants.[128] The purposes of the Jencks Act have no modern relevance, certainly not in criminal cases not involving espionage.

The FBI Lab and the Machine Guns

James Cadigan was the firearms expert testifying on the alleged machine guns possessed by the Branch Davidians. At Ruby Ridge, according to the Department of Justice Internal Investigation of Ruby Ridge, Cadigan was on the scene when bullets were found, and took a photograph which another agent believed insufficient for evidentiary purposes. So the bullet was moved and rephotographed, in what amounted to staging of evidence.

Staging of evidence was not the the only thing that Cadigan did wrong at Ruby Ridge. A diagram of the shooting of Vicki Weaver, made by Cadigan, was determined to be erroneous because sniper Horiuchi's position at the time the shots were fired was not correctly identified.

More serious complaints were voiced regarding the work of the FBI Laboratory under Agent Cadigan. Some blood evidence was ignored, returned, and eventually spoiled. Outside experts had to be hired because of the lab's apparent unwillingness or inability to provide assistance in certain areas of expertise. At first the lab indicated it could not reconstruct a shooting, although Cadigan later indicated that it could, and Cadigan was the FBI's expert in the area. The prosecutors nonetheless found the private expert they hired to be more knowledgeable. Some ballistics evidence was provided so slowly that the trial was delayed and discovery problems were created. Overall, the Justice Department investigation of Ruby Ridge found some of the lab work of Cadigan to result in problems caused by delays and lack of initiative.

When FBI Director Louis Freeh announced the mild punishments meted out for misbehavior at Ruby Ridge, one paragraph focused on censures and reprimands associated with the problems with preserving crime scenes and evidence. It is quite likely that the week before he testified against the Branch Davidians in San Antonio, Jim Cadigan was the one referred to in the press release statement that "One FBI Laboratory employee has been reprimanded for failing to accurately prepare a crime scene depiction."[129]

Cadigan was the firearms expert used in the trial of the Branch Davidians. Again, there seemed to be a problem with his lack of initiative and thoroughness. Although he testified that at least forty-six firearms had been converted to machine guns, he had actually tested only one AR-15 which had been converted to full auto. And that one was "damaged beyond repair," so he supplied his own upper receiver and barrel and then test fired it.[130] The rest he simply looked at, using a magnifying glass, perhaps, but no x-ray equipment and no test-firing.

Just as a firearm is a device capable of expelling a projectile, a machine gun is one capable of expelling more than one projectile with a single pull of the trigger. And conversion kits are only unlawful if someone can put them on a gun and then fire it full-auto; if someone attempts to install a conversion kit and does it so incompetently that the gun will not fire automatically, or will not fire at all, there is no illegal machine gun. If the gun cannot be fired, it is broken; it is not a machine gun; it is not even a gun.[131]

The defense's gun expert was not allowed to examine the guns. Instead, he was only permitted to view the guns through a plastic covering, supposedly because the guns still had such a heavy stench.[132] Changing a semiautomatic to full automatic involves complex modifications of small internal components; depriving the defense expert of an opportunity to examine the guns in detail and to disassemble them made it impossible to verify if the guns had been converted at all, or, if the guns had been converted, whether the conversions were the kind that could have been accomplished with equipment the Davidians owned.

The lackadaisical Cadigan was the only person allowed to examine the evidence that would establish whether the crimes for which a warrant was issued for David Koresh (illegal conversion of semiautomatics into machine guns) was actually committed.

Of course, if a search warrant is based on genuine probable cause, the warrant does not become wrongful if it turns out that the warrant target was innocent. Machine guns were what the Waco affair was all about; they were the pretext for the search warrant and its dynamic entry and they were (as will be detailed below) the basis for imposing thirty-year sentence enhancements on several Branch Davidians. If the federal government believed that machine guns were a good reason for a seventy-six-person armed assault, and also a good reason to put people in prison for thirty extra years, it is hardly asking too much for the government to make a better effort to determine if more than one of the alleged machine guns actually were machine guns. Later, as will be discussed in the section on the congressional hearings, the Department of Justice successfully blocked plans to have outside experts examine the alleged machine guns.

The Verdict

The Fully Informed Jury Association (FIJA) and Judge Walter Smith carried out a low-grade war over FIJA's efforts to make sure the jurors knew they had the right to vote an acquittal if their consciences so dictated, even if the Davidians were technically guilty. The judge closed public access to the entire jury pool wheel (the list from which potential jurors are drawn) for the Western District of Texas. He explained that his motive was not fear that anyone might harm the jurors, but concern that the jurors might be told about their ability to acquit in defiance of the judge's instructions. The FIJA activists apparently won the war. While the jurors were being transported, FIJA arranged for them to see a FIJA banner and to hear FIJA activists shout in unison "Vote your conscience. Restore the Bill of Rights." FIJA sympathizers with telephoto lens and binoculars noted the license plate numbers of cars in the court parking lot which might belong to jurors. FIJA then searched public records at the Texas Department of Motor Vehicles to obtain the addresses of the owners. FIJA brochures and cards were mailed; the judge found out and demanded that all jurors surrender the FIJA materials without reading them.[133]

Judge Smith did eventually give jury instructions which outlined self-defense as a lawful justification for what would otherwise be a crime. Notably, the only serious charge for which most Branch Davidians were convicted, aiding and abetting voluntary manslaughter, was the one for which the judge had failed to give a self-defense instruction.[134]

According to jury forewoman Sarah Bain's subsequent statement, in the jury room the jurors agreed that "The federal government was absolutely out of control there. We spoke in the jury room about the fact that the wrong people were on trial, that it should have been the ones that planned the raid and orchestrated it and insisted on carrying out this plan who should have been on trial."[135]

The defendants were acquitted of murder of a federal officer, of aiding and abetting murder of a federal officer, and of conspiracy to murder a federal officer. When the verdicts were announced, prosecutor Bill Johnston burst into tears.[136] Several defendants were convicted of aiding and abetting the voluntary manslaughter of a federal officer. The charge of carrying a firearm during the course of a crime was tied to only charge one (the murder charge), and not to the aiding and abetting voluntary manslaughter charge. Confused, the jurors convicted on the weapons count under the belief that it was tied to the manslaughter charge.

In addition, Graeme Craddock was found guilty of possession of a grenade and Paul Fatta of two charges of manufacturing machine guns.

When the jury brought in the inconsistent verdict, Judge Smith had the option of reinstructing the jury, and sending them back to reconsider. Indeed, Ray Jahn, the lead prosecutor, asked the court to "Send them back." Instead, the judge stated that the guilty verdict for using a firearm during a crime would simply have to be set aside.[137]

The judge did then throw out the convictions which were inconsistent with the rest of the verdict. The prosecution then moved for reinstatement of those convictions, on the grounds that the jury might have arrived at the convictions as a compromise verdict. (For example, if half the jurors wanted a murder conviction, and half wanted complete acquittal, the jury might have split the difference by agreeing to a conviction to an intermediate charge.) The jurors (who after rendering their verdict no longer had a formal role in the proceeding) filed a document stating that the inconsistent convictions were not the result of a compromise. The convictions were a mistake, the jurors said in sworn affidavits; the mistake resulted from the jury's inability to fully digest all sixty pages of the court's jury instructions. The judge reinstated the convictions.[138]

Ruth Riddle, who had been about to return home to Canada, was re-arrested following the judge's decision.[139]

Sentencing

The convictions were for carrying a firearm during a crime—not for carrying an automatic weapon. But under the federal sentencing guidelines, judges must use a procedure called "real offense sentencing." Under real offense sentencing, a defendant is sentenced not for the crimes for which he was found guilty beyond a reasonable doubt, but for the "conduct" which the judge considers to have been proven by a preponderance of the evidence.[140]

In the Waco trial, it was the judge, not the jury, who found that the defendants were using machine guns. Rather than the prosecutor having to convince the jury beyond a reasonable doubt that every individual defendant used an automatic weapon, the judge needed only to convince himself by a "preponderance of the evidence" (51 percent) that the defendants had used machine guns.

Five Branch Davidians were sentenced to the maximum possible term of forty years, while three others received lesser terms.[141] The total sentences amounted to 243 years. At the sentencing, Judge Smith stated that the severe sentences were being imposed because he believed the defendants were guilty of attempting to murder the federal agents—the crime for which they had been acquitted by the jury.[142]

Sarah Bain, the jury forewoman, later stated that she felt the trial was not fair and impartial.[143] Like other jurors, she stated that she had never intended for the Branch Davidians to be sentenced to anything more than "time served."

Before sentencing, the Branch Davidians were allowed to make a statement. Livingstone Fagan did not ask for mercy:

> Let me also state for myself personally, never, at any point, have I sought to distance myself from David Koresh, his teachings, or from the actions of the residents of Mount Carmel during February 28th through April 19th. There is no doubt in my mind that the actions that we were forced to take were justified, given the circumstances that we were placed in by the actions of the agents of the Government. . . .
>
> Appeal doesn't mean nothing to me. It doesn't mean nothing to us, nothing short of the lives of the people that were lost is of any benefit. But we are comforted in the thought that we entered into this whole situation on the basis of a faith that has been proven true inasmuch as that we endured the circumstances we did. We don't particularly care what you want to do. You're going to do it anyway.

Judicial System Reforms

Judge Smith's performance in the Waco trial was disgraceful. One reform, to protect people from judicial malfeasance, would be for the federal courts to allow peremptory challenge to a judge, as sixteen states currently do. (The American Bar Association supports such a reform.) A litigant would be allowed, one time only, to ask that his case be assigned to a different judge. The case would be assigned at random to a different judge. No second challenge would be allowed.

Unlike state judges, federal judges are not subject to democratic control through contested elections or retention elections. In general, the insulation of the federal judiciary from popular pressure helps give federal judges the courage to enforce the Constitution, even when such enforcement may be unpopular. But the huge growth of the federal criminal docket, accompanied by a large increase in the number of federal judges, as led to quality control problems, of which Judge Smith is a prime example. The peremptory challenge would be embarrassing to the judge (particularly one as prickly and self-important as Judge Smith), and might encourage behavioral improvement. Peremptory challenges, unlike almost all of the rest of right-wing agenda for reducing the power of the federal judges, run no risk of diminishing the judiciary's institutional ability to enforce the Constitution.

The National Rifle Association has expressed opposition to the persecution of the Branch Davidians—a proper stance for a group whose charter commits it to defense of the entire Bill of Rights, including of course the right to keep and bear arms. But, ironically, it was an NRA-backed law which allowed the judge to impose the draconian sentences.

After nearly a decade of intense work, the NRA in 1986 pushed through Congress the McClure-Volkmer Firearms Owners' Protection Act, which reduced BATF search and seizure powers. While reducing what NRA saw as BATF's ability to terrorize law-abiding gun owners and gun dealers, the 1986 law fulfilled another NRA goal, by significantly increasing the severity of punishment for use of a firearm during a crime. The law contained a five-year sentence enhancement for use of a gun during a crime of violence or a drug crime, and a thirty-year enhancement for use of a machine gun.

The NRA obviously never intended the law to be used against people whose only crime was to use a gun while defending themselves against an unjustifiable BATF attack. Yet it is an incongruous aspect of federal criminal law that the offense of carrying a machine gun while aiding and abetting a voluntary manslaughter carries a much more severe sentence (thirty years) than does voluntary manslaughter itself (ten years).

Pushing for "tougher sentences" on convicted criminals as an alternative to restricting the Second Amendment rights of law-abiding citizens has proven to be an effective political strategy. And at the highest level of abstraction, it makes obvious common sense. But Congress and many state legislatures have so long been at the game of "cracking down" on criminals that the only remaining ways to "crack down" are to make already draconian punishments even more severe. Thus, we have the absurd result that if Livingstone Fagan had perpetrated the voluntary manslaughter of three federal agents by stabbing them to death, he would have received a shorter sentence (three consecutive ten-year terms) than he did for merely "aiding and abetting" the voluntary manslaughter of one agent while he was carrying an alleged machine gun.

As the Washington State Supreme Court recognized, in declaring unconstitutional a statute which allowed a defendant's use of an AR-15-type semiautomatic rifle in a homicide to be used as a factor in determining whether the defendant should receive the death penalty, there comes a point at which "tough-on-crime" statutes chill the non-criminal exercise of firearms rights.[144]

Even after Waco, the NRA—as part of its generally worthwhile "CrimeStrike" program to increase punishment for violent criminals—continues to push for expansion of real offense sentencing in state and federal courts. NRA Executive Vice President Wayne LaPierre argues that all courts should be able to apply sentence enhancements for use of a gun in a crime simply based on a judge's finding regarding the preponderance of the evidence—rather than as a result of a jury's finding of proof beyond a reasonable doubt.[145] The better approach would be to abolish real offense sentencing as inconsistent with the fundamental standard that guilt must be proven beyond a reasonable doubt.

Of all the institutions involved in Waco, the one that performed best was the jury. It recognized government lies for what they were. When the jury made mistakes, the jury admitted them. Compared to the injudicious behavior of Judge Smith, the Waco jury performed especially admirably.

The reforms that are appropriate for juries are reforms which can help the jury function more effectively. Given the jury's function as a check on governmental over-reaching, a strong jury system is more important today than ever. Thus, all states should enact constitutional amendments like those in Maryland and Indiana which explicitly affirm the jury's right to judge the law, and to acquit a technically guilty defendant in cases where the jury's conscience so demands. By constitution or statute, juries should be explicitly informed of this aspect of their duty.

At the same time, proposals to weaken the jury should be vigorously resisted. The most prominent such proposal is that jury verdicts should not be required to be unanimous. The typical case cited by proponents of non-unanimous juries is the O.J. Simpson criminal case—although in that case it was easy for the jury to conclude unanimously that they had reasonable doubts about a case which was undermined by the presentation of obviously perjured testimony by the prosecution.

As law professor and former prosecutor Bennett L. Gershman observes, "The prosecutor's power to institute criminal charges is the broadest and least regulated power in American law."[146] One important check on this prosecutorial power is the grand jury, which can refuse to indict. But today, prosecutors can present a selective version of the facts in order to win an indictment. Congress should enact a statute over-turning the 5-4 Supreme Court decision holding that prosecutor's failure to provide exculpatory evidence to grand jury can never be cause for dismissing an indictment.[147] Instead, prosecutors should be required to present to the grand jury exculpatory evidence of which the prosecutor is aware, if that evidence is known to be reliable and obviously exculpatory.[148]

The grand jury is supposed to serve as a gateway, and a checkpoint, in the criminal justice system. But the grand jury's role is evaded when prosecutors can ask that a defendant be sentenced based on a so-called real offense for which the defendant was never indicted, let alone convicted. Thus, as part of the abolition of real offense sentencing, defendants should only be sentenced to crimes of which they are convicted, and they should only be convicted of crimes which are named in the indictment. At Waco, most of the time the defendants are serving is for possessing a machine gun during a violent crime, even though the indictment never charged them with using a machine gun in a crime.[149]

Appeal

All of the Branch Davidians except for Livingstone Fagan appealed their sentences to a three-judge panel of the Fifth Circuit Court of Appeals. Most of convicted Davidians had received thirty-year extra sentences for "use" of a machine gun in a crime of violence. Pursuant to the 1993 Supreme Court decision *United States* v. *Bailey*, the federal statute authorizing the sentencing enhancement can only be applied to people who actively employ a gun in a crime.[150] Merely possessing the gun (i.e., having the gun unloaded in an upstairs closet while the crime takes place) does not authorize the sentence enhancement. Accordingly, the Court of Appeals ordered Judge Smith to reconsider the sentences after making a determination whether the defendants had actively employed machine guns.[151]

On the rest of the key legal issues, the appeals court split two-to-one. The two members voting to affirm the convictions were Judges Higginbotham, who wrote the opinion, and Duh, both conservative Reagan appointees. The dissenter was Judge Schwarzer, a Clinton appointee from California who was sitting by designation.[152]

The first key issue on appeal was the federal statute that declares that if a defendant is found guilty of using a "firearm" as part of a crime of violence, he may be sentenced to an extra five years. If he is found guilty of using a machine gun, he may be sentenced to an additional thirty years.[153] Several Branch Davidians were convicted or using a "firearm." The indictment did not accuse them of using machine guns, and the machine gun issue was never presented to the jury for a verdict. The Davidians were sentenced to thirty additional years because the judge believed that they had been carrying machine guns. The imposition of such sentences based solely on the determination of a judge, with no role for a grand or petit jury to evaluate the machine gun issue, was upheld.

The second question was if the defendant is acquitted of the underlying crime of violence (murder), but is convicted of carrying a firearm to facilitate the crime (the murder he did not commit), can the firearm offense be allowed to stand, or must the trial judge throw it out as inconsistent? The court ruled that the trial judge had acted properly in reinstating the inconsistent conviction after he had initially said he would throw it out.

Third, should the trial judge have instructed the jury that they could acquit the Branch Davidians of aiding and abetting homicide if the jury believed that the Davidians had acted in self-defense? The court had given a self-defense instruction for murder, and the defendants were acquitted of murder. The appellate majority ruled that no self-defense instruction was required for the manslaughter count, since there was no real evidence of self-defense.

The majority's holding on the self-defense issue was ludicrous. The evidence suggesting self defense had been so strong that self-defense was the reason the Davidians were acquitted of murder. The jury could hardly have acquitted on the grounds that the BATF agents died of natural causes, or that somebody other than armed Branch Davidians killed them all, or that the Branch Davidians did not mean to kill the people they were shooting at.

The majority, however, ruled that the evidence of self-defense was so insubstantial that the trial court had no obligation to give a self-defense instruction. For example, the majority said that there was no evidence that helicopters had strafed the roof. But of course Judge Smith had prevented the defendants from introducing evidence of self-defense, including evidence of a helicopter gunfire attack.

Despite the judge's ruling, some evidence of self-defense had come in anyway though the examination of witnesses. The majority consistently mischaracterized this evidence, in order to maintain the argument that there was no genuine evidence of self-defense. For example, attorney Jack Zimmermann, while in Mount Carmel during the siege, said that he had seen incoming bullet holes in the front door and in the roof. The holes in the roof, of course, were evidence of gunfire from the helicopters. The holes in the front door, as discussed in chapter two, contradicted BATF's trial testimony that the Davidians fired first, through the front door. The incoming bullet holes also provided evidence that BATF agents were firing wildly near where Koresh and several of the defendants were standing. Zimmermann's testimony, by itself, was sufficient to make self-defense a proper issue for jury consideration. But the majority brushed aside Zimmermann's testimony; without mentioning the obvious inferences to be drawn from the testimony, the majority claimed that Zimmermann's testimony simply showed that gunfire was exchanged in both directions.

Kathryn Schroeder, a Davidian testifying for the prosecution as part of a plea bargain, had testified that she hid under her bed during the gunfight, and that shots were fired into her window. The majority acknowledged that these facts, if the jury believed them, would constitute adequate grounds for self-defense on her part. But the majority said that Schroeder's testimony provided no evidence which the other Davidians could use to claim self-defense, since there was no proof that she had talked to the other Davidians while the firefight was going on, and told them about the unprovoked shots through her window.

Again, the majority was deliberately obtuse. A reasonable juror could conclude that if BATF was firing wildly at unarmed victims in one room, BATF might be doing the same at other rooms, and the defendants would be aware of this.

The fourth issue was whether the government could use select portions of a defendant's statement, or whether the jury had to be allowed to find out about the whole statement. Davidian Jamie Castillo had told the Texas Rangers that after the gun battle broke out, he tried to chamber a round, but the gun jammed. He then ran to his room to get a pistol, and went to the front of the house. While admitting these inculpatory parts of Castillo's statement (as Castillo gave it to a Texas Ranger when Castillo had left Mount Carmel in March), the trial judge had refused to let the jury hear about the rest of the statement, in which Castillo said that he took cover during the battle and never fired a shot, that no one in the room he was in fired a gun, and that he only picked up the rifle after he saw one of his friends shot through the head by BATF.

In rejecting the Davidians' claim that BATF had used excessive force to effect the warrants, the majority sneered that the defendants were complaining that the government had sent too many agents to arrest them. The dissent noted that under the majority's "sweeping rationale, it would have made no difference if the agents had been supported by armored personnel carriers, or by tanks, or by suppression fire from aircraft." (Indeed, there probably was suppression fire from aircraft.)

The majority's unjust affirmation of the Davidian convictions suggests several reforms. First, Congress should clarify the sentence enhancement statute to make it clear that a person may be sentenced for using a machine gun in a violent crime only if he has been indicted for the crime, and a jury has convicted him of using a machine gun.

Second, Congress should make it clear that a person cannot be sentenced in federal court for an auxiliary act (such as carrying a gun in a crime) if he is found innocent of the underlying crime.

Third, Congress should specify that a defendant is entitled to have the jury consider self-defense (or other justifications or excuses) if there is "any evidence" regarding self-defense. The Fifth Circuit majority had rejected prior precedent using the "any evidence" standard in favor of a higher threshold of evidence.

Fourth, Congress should amend the Federal Rules of Evidence to prevent the prosecution from picking and choosing only certain items of a defendant's statement to introduce as evidence. If the prosecution wants to use a statement, the jury should be allowed to see the entire context in which the statement was made.

Finally, Patrick Higginbotham frequently makes the list of possible Supreme Court nominees in a Republican administration. No president who cares about due process should nominate him, and if he is nominated, his nomination should be rejected by both liberal and conservative senators who support the Bill of Rights. Civil liberties organizations from the whole political spectrum should make it clear that they will vigorously oppose the nomination of Judge Higginbotham to the Supreme Court.

Civil Suits

As is the American custom, lawsuits have broken out all over. Several BATF agents sued an ambulance company, TV station KWTX, and the Waco *Tribune-Herald* for allegedly blowing the cover on the BATF's secret raid.[154] In 1996, all three defendants settled out of court for undisclosed sums. Cox Newspapers, Inc., the parent company of the newspaper, said that the decision to settle had been made by Cox's insurance company, over Cox's strong objection to settling a case which Cox believes it would have won at trial.[155]

Firearms dealer Henry McMahon and his wife, Karen Kilpatrick, have sued BATF for false imprisonment.[156]

The families of some of the deceased Branch Davidians have filed wrongful death lawsuits against the federal government; among the lawyers representing the plaintiffs is former United States Attorney General Ramsey Clark (an ardent gun control supporter).[157] The Clark lawsuit alleges that a secret squad from the Hostage Rescue Team, wearing special breathing gear, entered the Mount Carmel Center during the fire, and shot Branch Davidians who were disabled or who were attempting to escape out the back (which was not visible to television cameras). The suit further alleges that the fireball which erupted well after the fire had begun was not caused by a propane cylinder, but instead was the product of an incendiary bomb intended to kill everyone in the concrete cold-storage room.

Norman Allison, a Branch Davidian who was at the Mag Bag during the raid, tried to sneak into Mount Carmel later on the day of the raid, but was intercepted by federal agents, and surrendered nonviolently. He was indicted, prosecuted, and acquitted of attempting to murder federal agents. He spent ten months in pretrial detention for a crime he did not commit. He is suing BATF for withholding evidence which proved that Allison had never fired his gun.[158]

Of all the federal employees being sued by the Branch Davidians, only one is not being defended by the United States Department of Justice at taxpayer expense. That lone employee is Robert Rodriguez, the undercover agent who warned the BATF raiders that Koresh knew they were coming.[159]

In regards to Waco, the lawsuits all around are probably a good thing, since the civil discovery process offers at least the opportunity for a fuller accounting of facts than did the Treasury and Justice Department internal investigations, and the less-than-fair criminal prosecution of the Waco survivors. Unfortunately, lawsuits after the fact, however just the eventual outcomes, are slow and costly to all involved—including the innocent taxpayers. As one report on the plethora of lawsuits summarized the situation: "Get ready for Jarndyce vs. Jarndyce, Western style."[160]

LEGISLATIVE BRANCH: CONGRESSIONAL OVERSIGHT

From the earliest days of the American Republic, one of the most important duties of Congress has been investigating the operations of the executive branch of government. This duty's roots extend deep into Anglo-American history; the primary function of the English institution which eventually became known as the Parliament was to control and to prevent the abuses of England's chief executive, the king.

Immediately following the destruction of the Mount Carmel Center, Congress showed some interest in oversight. Congress was, however, quickly satisfied that the executive branch intended to investigate thoroughly the actions of BATF and the FBI. Thus, Congress could legitimately defer investigating until it could see the results of the administration's self-analyses and the trial of the Branch Davidian survivors by the judicial branch. The Branch Davidian trial and the Treasury and Justice Reports satisfied few skeptics of the executive branch's actions near Waco, and there was considerable pressure for Congress to exercise oversight—particularly when the Republicans won control of both houses of Congress in the 1994 elections.

On the second anniversary of the burning of the Branch Davidians' home, a federal building in Oklahoma City was blown up, killing 168 people. The Branch Davidian survivors were horrified at the wanton murders.[161]

One effect of the bombing was to reawaken national attention about Waco, a subject for which the Republican leadership had already promised there would be congressional hearings. Some proponents of Waco hearings—including NRA Executive Vice President Wayne LaPierre—called for hearings on Waco and on the militia movement,[162] although there was no evidence that any militia members participated in the Oklahoma City bombing.

The primary congressional hearing was set for late July by a joint subcommittee, comprised of the House Judiciary Subcommittee on Crime and the House Government Reform and Oversight Subcommittee on National Security, International Affairs and Criminal Justice. Some of the reasons for the hearings were stated by one of the attorneys who attempted to negotiate the surrender of David Koresh:

> I can tell you what the American public does not buy, that they [BATF] changed the leadership, . . . because nobody has been disciplined in a meaningful way. There has been no criminal prosecutions, and people have committed felony offenses. . . . There has been no one disciplined because of Waco in the entire U.S. Department of Justice chain of command. That is horrible. Ten people died on February 28th, 80 people died on April 19, and no one has been disciplined. No policies have been changed. The only thing they have done is, they have asked for more money to double the hostage rescue team size. That is ridiculous.[163]

In an opening statement, committee cochair Bill Zeliff emphasized that the hearings were about constitutional oversight, not gun control, the militias, or any other issue.[164] In retrospect, the hearings were frequently more about partisanship—Republican and Democratic—than about constitutional or other issues. For example, during the short congressional hearings on Waco in 1993, Democratic Rep. John Conyers had told Attorney General Reno that she should have resigned. But in the 1995 hearings, Representative Conyers extended warm greetings to the attorney general.[165] In general, progun Democrats united with antigun Democrats to defend the executive branch, while pro- and antigun Republicans teamed up to look for fault. Unfortunately, for several reasons, the hearings achieved only limited success.

Obstruction

First, the Clinton administration, to the best of its abilities, impeded the investigation by refusing to cooperate with the Republicans on the joint committees. Even in times of "congressional government,"[166] the power of Congress is limited by administration intransigence. Congress can publicize things it knows about, but Congress has relatively little practical power—other than to encourage media criticism—to force the executive to divulge information the executive wants to secrete.

The day after Waco, the president had promised to cooperate fully with all congressional investigations. But that promise was operative only as long as Congress was controlled by Democrats. The Clinton administration made the 1995 Congress struggle for every bit of information.

The congressmen could complain that the administration would give information only to Democrats, but these complaints elicited little media attention. What the administration did provide the Republicans was often provided late, so that committee members and their staffs lacked time to evaluate the material.

Thus, Representative Zeliff (R-N.H.) thanked Representative Schumer (D-N.Y.) for his announcement that the Treasury Department would supply documents the Republicans had requested, but Zeliff noted that the request was made on June 8, 1995, and the announcement of compliance on July 20, the second day of the hearings. Zeliff further complained that while Treasury materials were finally being turned over, documents in the possession of the White House and the Justice Department were not. When documents were provided, they were provided in a manner designed to obfuscate, and to prevent committee staff from discovering incriminating papers. As Representative Zeliff recounted, "We received at one point 13,000 loosened, unindexed pieces of paper from the initial Treasury production."[167] Like hostile litigants in a corporate takeover case, the administration disassembled key documents, and scattered them among mountains of irrelevant papers.[168]

Representative Zeliff would later complain: "the majority shared all available documents, set up a document room accessible to all staff, and shared all indexes received to those documents; by contrast the majority subsequently learned that the minority staff received and intentionally withheld from majority staff the key Treasury Department index to tens of thousands of documents. . . . Two Democrat staffers apparently met secretly with the Texas Rangers and told them that they should not or did not need to honor subpoenas issued by the majority. . . . In a further example of unjustifiable manipulation, the Treasury Department also flew the Texas Rangers who were going to testify to Washington ahead of time and at taxpayer expense—to brief them for 2 days on what they should say."[169]

Rep. Howard Coble complained that the subcommittee's request for a report on damage done to the tanks the FBI used was unfilled after seven weeks. Since there was no gunfire prior to April 19, the damage report would provide evidence of Branch Davidian gunfire during the final assault.[170] The fourth day of hearings concluded with complaints about how it takes days or weeks for the Republicans to get access to documents, firearms, and the like, while "Mr. Schumer has some miracle power to get anything he wants."[171]

The administration was similarly obstructionist regarding the Senate Ruby Ridge hearings. The FBI would not even allow senators to examine the FBI 300-page internal report on Ruby Ridge; only one Republican and one Democratic staffer were allowed to look at it, and then only under FBI supervision, with no copying allowed.[172] Just before the Senate hearings began, the Department of Justice announced that it was conducting a criminal investigation of the FBI agents involved in shooting, and that the Senate hearings, if held, might interfere with the investigation.[173]

Besides refusing to produce documents in good faith for the Waco hearing, the administration set up a "war room" in the White House to coordinate media and congressional Democrat strategies to undermine the hearings. The operation was run by White House aide Rahm Emanuel, who brags about the fact that both the American Civil Liberties Union and the National Rifle Association think that the Clinton administration has a miserable record on civil liberties.[174] Republicans complained about the "damage control" efforts by the White House,[175] but could not stop them.[176]

Although it was not known at the time, the Clinton administration was collecting a large number of confidential FBI files on government employees. Among the persons whose FBI files were sent over the White House were "a number of Hill staffers responsible for investigations into such natty problems as the Waco fiasco."[177]

Some of the White House effort to frustrate the hearings backfired, as when one progun Democrat, Bill Brewster of Oklahoma, publicly complained about pressure from the Secretary of the Treasury not to embarrass the administration in the hearing process.

The Clinton administration spin machine was in high gear. When a toxicologist for the Environmental Protection Agency testified critically regarding the use of CS, the EPA almost immediately sent word indicating that he was not testifying as an EPA employee. As Representative Shadegg observed with some sarcasm, the EPA quickly reported to the media "on their own because they happen to be sitting back watching TV, watching these hearings, glued to the TV 19 minutes past 7 P.M. in the evening, and they flash over here a letter. They've got a typist on the staff. . . . I am impressed. I will never criticize a Government official again for not working hard, because, clearly, when the Clinton administration. . . . The Clinton administration has apparently everyone so scared of the results of this hearing. . . ."[178]

Structure of the Hearings

Most congressional hearings are "dog and pony shows." They are presented for public consumption, rather than for Congress to learn anything. The Joint Committee could have conducted a lengthy investigation of Waco, and then presented the results at a typical Potemkin hearing. Commendably,

> rather than using the hearings as a forum for presenting the results of a lengthy and completed investigation, it was decided that the hearings would consist of an exhaustive public airing of the issues associated with Waco. These "discovery hearings," rather than "presentation hearings, would afford members of the joint subcommittees, . . . the media, and C-SPAN audiences an opportunity to hear from the people directly involved in the Waco matter."[179]

While the discovery hearings might have been fruitful, the committee chairs made the terrible mistake of adopting Democratic demands for the format, so that each committee member had only five minutes to question each panel of witnesses.[180] (Panels included as many as eleven witnesses.) This prevented any consistent line of questioning from being followed. Shortly after a congressman began questioning, it was someone else's turn to question, generally someone with at least different, and often opposing, interests. As one columnist noted, "five minutes gives the advantage to liars, even when rigorously questioned. To get the truth you need lengthy, systematic and knowledgeable questioning."[181]

In addition, unlike some hearings, only the congresspersons could question, not staffers who might have had more knowledge and a greater ability to ask appropriate follow-up questions. Staff questioning is particularly important when some witnesses may not tell the truth, and only detailed, expert probing will expose their lies.

The NRA Distraction

As is commonplace on Capitol Hill, the committee members and their staffs were not working insulated from the outside world. Traditionally, public interest groups have actively assisted in the hearing process, including suggesting and briefing witnesses, proposing lines of questioning, and the like. Outside groups have an expertise generally lacking among congresspersons and staffers, who usually have broad knowledge of many subjects, rather than expertise in any one. Among the most active of such interest groups are the White House and federal departments apt to be affected by a congressional hearing. While the Democrats on the joint subcommittees were ably assisted by the White House and representatives from the Departments of Treasury and of Justice, the complaints against other assistance impeded the effectiveness of Republican members.

At the outset, the National Rifle Association (which employs one of us, Paul H. Blackman) attempted to assist the subcommittees and their staffs with expertise and even with the offer to hire outside experts who could not otherwise be afforded by the limited budgets of congressional subcommittees. In addition, the NRA coalesced outside experts with its own staff into a task force to research possible witnesses and information which might prove useful to the subcommittees.[182]

This is normal for Capitol Hill hearings, with both sides in most controversial issues assisting their allies on relevant committees and subcommittees. Rare is the congressperson who is so familiar with an area that he can arrange hearings without the assistance of outside interest groups or from other branches of government. Similarly rare is the congressperson who discusses the matter. Congresspersons, their staffs, and the various lobbyists all prefer not to acknowledge too publicly the role of interest groups in arranging hearings.

Sociology professor Fran Haga was spending her summer working, without pay, as part of the NRA's task force investigating Waco and assisting the subcommittees. As part of her interviewing of witnesses, she called social worker Joyce Sparks, and identified herself as part of the "Waco hearing team." While the identification was accurate, Sparks believed that Haga was misrepresenting herself as being on a congressional staff, and she complained about Haga to the media.[183]

Representative Conyers asserted that Haga might have violated U.S. Code, Title 18, Section 1512, which prohibits the use of misleading conduct to influence witnesses before an official hearing, including a congressional hearing. It is unclear how finding out what a potential witness might know and/or be willing to testify to would constitute an effort to "influence" witnesses.[184] Rep. Steve Buyer suggested a better case of witness tampering could be made against Treasury Secretary Robert Rubin for telephoning Rep. Bill Brewster and asking he refrain from asking questions at the hearing which might embarrass the administration.[185] Sparks acknowledged that the NRA's activity, while annoying, "has not affected my testimony."[186]

Nothing in the Sparks-Haga affair affected the information that was presented to the committee, but another NRA-related issue did. The NRA contracted with Failure Analysis Associates, Inc. (FaAA), the nation's largest engineering firm dedicated to the analysis and investigation of failures of an engineering or scientific nature. FaAA had previously investigated the grounding of the *Exxon Valdez,* the explosion of the *Challenger* space shuttle, and the "Dateline NBC" episode concerning gas tanks in General Motors pickup trucks. In areas related to violence, some involving firearms, FaAA was involved in some research on the Oklahoma City bombing, the assassination of John F. Kennedy, and the murders of Nicole Simpson and Ronald Goldman,[187] and José and Kitty Menendez.

Failure Analysis Associates asked to examine the Branch Davidian firearms, currently stored in Texas by the Department of Justice, to see if they were automatics. (The trial testimony that the Branch Davidians had almost four dozen automatics came from one FBI lab employee who had rebuilt one gun to make it fire, and who had not tested any of the other alleged automatics. Defense experts had been forbidden to examine the alleged automatics.) The Justice Department refused to let Failure Analysis Associates examine the firearms, unless FaAA disclosed who it was working for. (FaAA normally keeps its clients confidential.)

When FaAA finally said that the NRA was its client (after the NRA gave permission), the Department of Justice refused to allow an inspection. Instead, committee Democrats promptly began criticizing the Republicans for allowing the NRA to pay for the investigation.[188] The Failure Analysis Associates investigation, with NRA funding, had actually been authorized in advance by the House Ethics Committee, but the Democrats went on the offensive anyway.[189] Instead of noting the universality of interest-group assistance, the Republican response was embarrassed withdrawal of contact with the NRA. FaAA had also conducted studies of the effects of the CS and the way the fire spread, but the Republicans now refused to look at this evidence.[190]

The Democrats ignored, as did the media, Republican countercomplaints that the White House "war room" on Waco was being run by a political consultant with close ties to Handgun Control, Inc.[191]

Forgotten in all the charges and countercharges were the machine guns themselves. To head off the FaAA investigation, the Department of Justice agreed to conduct the tests itself, and present the findings to the joint subcommittees. It was then decided that the tests were too expensive, and none were performed.[192]

The committee Democrats, of course, were receiving massive assistance, not from an organization with an abstract ideological interest, but from organizations with a very direct interest in covering up their own misconduct: the Departments of Justice and Treasury. As a result, the Democrats were often much better prepared in their questions than were the Republicans, who were relying exclusively on their paid staff, with no outside assistance.

The NRA contretemps not only cowed the Republicans into unilateral disarmament in terms of outside assistance, it also gave the administration's defenders something to talk about so as to take attention off what happened at Waco. White House Press Secretary Mike McCurry asserted that "The NRA bought and paid for the congressional investigation that's under way here," and seconded the call for an investigation of the NRA's involvement, and for the Republicans to "cut out this cancer that now surrounds this hearing as a result of the NRA hijacking the proceedings and choreographing the testimony that some key witnesses are to give."[193]

For the first few days of the hearings, each morning began with some Democratic complaint of how the hearings had been tainted by the evil NRA.[194] The morning clash gave the news media—which prefer morning and early afternoon news for meeting deadlines, particularly for broadcast media—a story of controversy without substance regarding the Waco disaster.

Representative Schumer indicated that he was "very troubled" that the NRA may have been involved in the planning and organization of the hearing, and called for an investigation, including questioning NRA employees under oath, because the NRA's "hatred of the ATF so distorts their view . . . that this hearing runs the danger of missing the broader point. One man bears the ultimate burden for the horrible scar on American history of Waco. This man is David Koresh . . . no matter how others seek to twist and revise history."[195] Rep. Cardiss Collins went on to suggest, erroneously, that "this is an unprecedented case of an outside advocacy group using Congressional hearings to further their own agenda and at the same time potentially tampering with Congressional witnesses."[196] The various Democrats took up most of the first morning's session complaining about possible tainting of the hearings by the NRA, so that there was almost no substantive testimony prior to the lunch break.[197]

The second day of hearings began with Rep. Tom Lantos demanding "NRA officials come here under oath and testify." Describing "the monstrous character of this demon [Koresh]. We need to know what the NRA did for the preparation of this hearing."[198] By Day Two, however, there was more of a Republican response, with Rep. John Mica bringing up reports of involvement in the hearings by a White House aide, Rahm Emanuel, various Treasury Department aides, and John Podesta, from the private sector,[199] who, as it happens, had ties to Handgun Control, Inc., a lobbying organization at odds with the NRA.

The second day's first panel included law enforcement experts, including Robert Sanders, a former BATF deputy director for enforcement. Sanders, in response to questioning by Representative Schumer, acknowledged: "I have met Ms. Metaksa [Executive Director of the NRA's lobbying arm, the Institute for Legislative Action]. I do not know her. . . . I have not been with her [in the last four or five months], but in a setting where she had been present . . . on probably three occasions."[200] The next day, Schumer proclaimed that Sanders "admitted yesterday he meets regularly with NRA leader Tanya Metaksa."[201]

The third day began with Representative Lantos again suggesting there was a coverup involving Waco, namely "the coverup of the involvement of the National Rifle Association in the preparation of this hearing."[202] Rep. Cardiss Collins chimed in, attacking the "taint" of the hearings by the NRA, and complaining about the committees' refusal to "investigate the role of the NRA in these hearings."[203] Again, on the fourth day, Representative Schumer began the morning's activities with more calls for an investigation into the NRA's involvement in the hearings.[204]

On the sixth day of testimony, with some of the strongest criticism of the FBI's actions of April 19 coming from Harvard professor Alan Stone, Representative Schumer asked all of a panel testifying—including some defending the use of CS—whether they had been contacted by the National Rifle Association. Dr. Stone was the only member of that panel who acknowledged having talked to anyone from that organization. Schumer noted, "I will come back to that in a little bit."[205]

The Republican defenders of the hearings, aided by some pro-NRA Democrats, had a two-pronged response. Led by Henry Hyde and others, some congressmen insisted that the NRA's activities, or attempted activities, were not the issue, that the hearing dealt with what the government did at Mount Carmel, and that if there were serious complaints about the NRA, they should be dealt with at other hearings, geared toward that topic.

Rep. Ileana Ros-Lehtinen denounced the Democrats for trying "to divert attention from the real issues of the hearing," noting that "the liberal press may plan along with this 'bashing the NRA' hysteria," but insisting that the Republicans would continue to seek out the truth so that "Government agents will no longer . . . be in harm's way ever again." She first "confirmed this morning that my NRA rating was D-minus last year. I don't think that the NRA considers me exactly to be a sterling legislator on their issues," and explained her failure to achieve an F on a procedural vote.[206]

David Koresh

The hearings had been called to investigate the conduct of the Department of Treasury and the Department of Justice, which was the subject of controversy. The hearings were not called to inquire as to whether David Koresh was a good person; it was uncontroversial to almost all Americans that Koresh was a scurrilous character. Nevertheless, the committee Democrats managed to shift a substantial amount of attention away from the topic of the hearings, and onto David Koresh's many sins.

The most successful effort occurred on the first afternoon of the hearings when some congresswomen insisted that Kiri Jewell be allowed to give sexually explicit and detailed testimony regarding a sexual assault on her, and of other actions and comments by David Koresh.[207] Her testimony was carefully orchestrated. Even though she was perfectly willing to testify without a subpoena,[208] she was subpoenaed in order that her father might accompany her to the witness table. (Her father, a talk-show host, had previously tried to sell her story to tabloid television programs.[209])

The next day the president said: "There is no moral equivalency between the disgusting acts which took place inside that compound in Waco and the efforts that law enforcement officers made to enforce the law and protect the lives of innocent people."[210]

The testimony was effective in dominating the day's headlines in television and in the next morning's newspapers. The news media focused almost exclusively on Miss Jewell's testimony, rather than on any other events of the first day of the hearings.[211]

Thus, what most Americans got out of the first day of the hearings was confirmation that their earlier judgment that Koresh was a vile person and a child molester was correct. But what was obscured by the near-exclusive focus on Koresh was all the other information that came out on the first day of the hearing—information of which the American public had not been aware.

Commenting on one of the issues from the first day of testimony which had been overshadowed by the sensational sex testimony, Rep. Steve Schiff complained "that a Government agent does not know the United States Code under which he's proposing to arrest people is far more significant" than a sex story.[212] Republicans like Rep. Fred Heineman opined that there was no question that Koresh was a pervert, but the issue was the investigation of why four BATF agents died, a topic unrelated to Koresh's warped sex life.[213]

Pursuant to rules for congressional testimony, Miss Jewell's testimony had been submitted in writing beforehand. Arizona Republican John Shadegg had read the testimony, and attempted to warn committee cochairs Bill McCollum and Bill Zeliff of the consequences of allowing Miss Jewell to testify on the first day. The cochairs never read her testimony, and ignored Representative Shadegg's warning.[214]

Another way to demonize Koresh was to make it unthinkable to seriously consider that he could have been more violent. One common observation regarding the alleged ambush by the Branch Davidians on BATF was that a true ambush would not have allowed the officers to leave their trailers; instead, the Branch Davidians would have massacred them while they were in the cattle trailers, before BATF could return fire. When raised at the hearings this observation was not answered, but instead dismissed as hideously offensive.[215] Most witnesses refused to confront the fact that Koresh could have killed all federal agents but deliberately avoided doing so; such a notion would be inconsistent with the presentation of Koresh as pure evil.[216]

Along the same lines, Rep. Gene Taylor (D-Miss.) often used his five minutes for one of two basic questions: whether anything which had been reported at the hearing could justify the murder of four BATF agents on February 28, 1993.[217] Occasionally, a witness would remind the joint subcommittees that there was serious question whether the agents had been murdered, since no one was convicted of that offense, partly because there was considerable evidence of self-defense.[218]

Representative Taylor also repeatedly wondered about the absence of such witnesses as the reporters who were working on the exposé of Koresh which began the day before the BATF raid. He noted that they left town, and the newspaper took extra security precautions as soon as the articles began to appear in the Waco newspaper. Representative Taylor doubtless believed that the reporters' and the newspaper's fears demonstrated how villainous a man David Koresh was, justifying extreme federal government behavior. But as noted in chapter two, Koresh had no response, violent or otherwise, to the exposé. The Branch Davidians correctly identified the newspaper series as just another set of accusations coming from Marc Breault.[219] During the negotiation, Steve Schneider mentioned that the BATF agent "brought over Sunday's paper that morning . . . and we all looked at it, so he . . . saw the reaction . . . it was not a big deal."[220]

Defending the Feds

A number of Democrats adopted the policy of defending the federal government at all costs. Rep. Charles Schumer announced that he would not let "this become a show trial with law enforcement the defendant. These Waco hearings must not degenerate into a kangaroo court."[221] At times, some of the Democrats attacked like defense attorneys for the federal agencies, rather than like investigators.[222]

For example, some Democrats tried to establish that the Branch Davidians fired first on February 28. Rep. Karen Thurman, for example, began the fifth day of the hearings—the first which would investigate matters once the siege began—by concluding that this "important fact that is now established."[223] In fact, no one had established such a fact. It had been repeatedly asserted by several witnesses, but with little supporting evidence.[224]

Perhaps in no area was more effort expended in defending the actions of federal law enforcement than in the decision to use CS in an enclosed area with a many children, including some babies. British experts—perhaps less concerned with civil liberties because much CS use in the United Kingdom is in response to domestic terrorism—testified that the accumulated dosage of CS would not have caused serious harm.[225] Representative Conyers admitted that he had changed his mind since the 1993 congressional hearings on the topic, when he vehemently criticized the use of CS. He explained: "I have learned a lot about CS gas and tear gas and all of its variations on the theme," concluding that it is safe to use even in enclosed spaces.[226]

An American expert, chemistry professor George Uhlig, testified that there was a 60 percent or greater probability that the CS itself, or the substances associated with it, may have directly caused suffocation of some children. He further indicated that two to five times more CS was used "than you need to incapacitate a person, even with the winds."[227] Dr. Uhlig was disputed by an FBI expert, who noted no documented deaths "unequivocally attributable to CS" and asserted that the calculations were based on "low ventilation [which] was unrealistic."[228]

The defense of the CS as a mild "tear gas" was made more difficult by the intended use, which is to have such an intense painful effect as to overcome a person's entire way of thinking. According to the FBI, "the gas [CS] is designed to make you want to leave that room. It removes all the fear of Babylonia or Babylonians, fear of Koresh. And the instinct we were hoping for is mothers to say, 'I have got to get out of here, and I have got to get my child out of here. I'm reclaiming my child from Koresh.' "[229]

The determination to defend the federal government on every front sometimes grew ridiculous. Rep. Louise Slaughter responded to the suggestion that infants were killed, by asserting, "I want to point out that the only infant that I am aware of on this list [of Mount Carmel Center decedents] was one that came out 5 months old."[230] Actually, there were five one-year-olds and two younger infants among the deceased.[231]

On some issues, the Republicans simply gave up. Despite the substantial evidence that BATF agents in helicopters strafed the second story of the Branch Davidian home (see chapter 2), the joint subcommittees made no inquiry into this issue. According to Carol Moore, "one committee staffer has told me several times that agents have confessed to doing so in 'self-defense,' but that staffers or Zeliff/McCollum believe they will all lie if asked so it is not worthwhile doing so."[232]

Partisanship

The GOP effort to get at the truth regarding the tragedies of Waco was undermined by a different Republican agenda, an agenda which helped encourage the Democrats' circle-the-wagons response to the hearings:[233] The Republicans wanted to embarrass the Clinton administration rather than to find and correct law enforcement failings. While most of the mistakes at Waco were made by career law enforcement personnel, the Republican effort was to embarrass political appointees, even to tie the problems to the First Family.

As a result, House Republicans preferred to attack the administration rather than the FBI for the chemical warfare attack plan. They spent a huge amount of time mentioning and asking questions about a memorandum that Deputy Treasury Secretary Roger Altman had sent his boss, Lloyd Bentsen. The April 15, 1993, memo noted the FBI's desire to end the standoff with gas, because the FBI had "concluded that the outlook for a negotiated end to the standoff is poor." Altman's prediction was that Attorney General Reno would not approve the plan: "The risks of a tragedy are there. And, if the FBI waits indefinitely, Mr. Koresh eventually will concede."

Altman's memo might have been a starting point for questions as to why the FBI wanted to risk tragedy with the CS, or why the FBI believed negotiations could never succeed while Mr. Altman was certain that eventually Koresh would surrender. Instead, the memo served as a basis for questioning and attacking Secretary Bentsen, despite his quite correct insistence, "The decision belonged to the Attorney General, not to me."[234] Both Bentsen and Altman were out of the decision-making loop regarding FBI actions. The FBI was merely keeping Altman apprised as a courtesy.

Bentsen was also criticized for failing adequately to supervise the BATF with regard to the initial raid, even though he was engaged in important international economic events at the time, and even though proper control should have been exercised by the BATF director, who was a Ronald Reagan appointee.[235]

In response to Republican efforts to blame the White House for the April 19 assault on the Mount Carmel Center, Representative Schumer elicited testimony from higher-ranking Justice Department personnel that they had no contact with the White House.[236]

It is certainly possible that Bill or Hillary Clinton may have influenced, directly or indirectly, some of the decision making at the Justice Department, but a congressional hearing was an unlikely place to find proof, simply by asking a variety of the Clintons' friends and appointees. Suspicions are likely to continue along those lines for years, although there is no hard evidence yet, and none should be expected any time soon, either to exonerate the President and First Lady or to clearly tie them to aggressive law-enforcement decisions.

Possible wrongdoing by the White House is not the important issue for persons genuinely concerned about Waco, Ruby Ridge, or other law enforcement excesses. These excesses have occurred regardless of which party controlled the White House and therefore controlled the executive departments and agencies. Ruby Ridge took place entirely under the Bush administration, while part of the coverup was during the Clinton administration. The planning for Waco likewise took place during the Bush years. Almost everything that went wrong at Waco and Ruby Ridge was the result of acts by career federal employees. Of the misfeasance by political appointees, most was committed by Reagan or Bush appointees. The only significant exceptions are FBI Director Louis Freeh's role in abetting the Ruby Ridge coverup, and Janet Reno's and Ron Noble's handling of Waco.

While all of the evidence suggests that Attorney General Reno had been misled—often deliberately—by the FBI agents in Waco and their supervisors in Washington, she repeatedly denied it, asserting, "We didn't misunderstand Koresh. We didn't suffer from misinformation. I wasn't misled."[237] The effect was that the attorney general had changed her mind between April 1993 when she acknowledged that her decision was wrong, to a conclusion that the decision was right and Koresh entirely to blame.[238]

Attorney General Reno insisted that "they had reached an impasse in negotiations in terms of anybody coming out voluntarily. And I don't think there's any doubt about that." In fact, as detailed in chapter 3, the FBI's own behavioral experts had considerable doubt about that.

Similarly, rather than admit she was misled about the plan for a 48-hour gradual escalation (which would immediately intensify into an all-out attack if the Branch Davidians fired their guns, as the FBI thought likely), she testified that the chemical warfare plan was really not expected to be gradual. Contrary to everything she had said before on the subject, she testified that the FBI "expected them to fire perhaps in certain instances. [Otherwise w]e wouldn't have had the people in those armored vehicles."[239]

In addition, contrary to testimony from the previous day, Attorney General Reno denied that debris was bulldozed over the trap door leading to the school bus. She claimed that the tank driver had testified that he "immediately started to push the burning debris away from the bus area."[240] In fact, there was no burning debris until about noon; the door to school bus had been deliberately blocked six hours earlier.

Her defense of FBI conduct was often implausible. When asked by Representative Shadegg about tanks repeatedly smashing into the gymnasium, demolishing about a quarter of the Davidians' residence, she referred to the "inadvertent crushing of a back support." One of the congressman's aides explained his boss's laughter, noting "that FBI tanks had 'inadvertently' smashed into the compound eight different times."[241]

As one columnist accurately summarized:

> What the Republicans cared about was trying to pin the whole boondoggle on President Clinton and thereby chalking up yet another cheap point to score against him in next year's presidential campaign.
>
> By avoiding the real and important issues raised by Waco and wrapping themselves and their investigation in their own petty partisan political ambitions, the Republicans lumped it. By doing so, they not only made themselves look like fools but also may have destroyed the usefulness of Waco as Exhibit No. 1 for what is wrong with federal intrusion into law enforcement. . . .
>
> For all the trumpet-blowing about equal rights for all, the federal police regiments know full well that there are some people on the fringes of American society to whom it can do pretty much anything they want. That is the real lesson of Waco and Randy Weaver, a lesson no Republican and no Democrat has ever learned or even shown much interest in learning. Until that lesson is learned, all the hearings and investigations in the world will be as useless as the ones just concluded.[242]

The Committee Report

The joint subcommittees produced a report representing the views of all twenty-eight Republicans, six of the twenty-three Democrats, and the one independent on the House Committee on Government Reform and Oversight. The report was directed more toward problems with the Democratic political hierarchy than with the flaws of BATF and the FBI staff.

Even though BATF oversight is a small and ancillary part of the duties of the Secretary of the Treasury and his Deputy Secretary, the House Republicans placed significant portions of the blame on Secretary Bentsen and Deputy Secretary Altman for failing to meet with, and be briefed by, BATF leaders regarding a raid they had not been told about.[243]

Similarly, the Republicans blamed Attorney General Reno for endangering the lives of the children by approving the raid. They attacked the timing, the use of CS, and the entire plan as fatally flawed. While the criticism had partisan roots, Reno had invited it by refusing to admit that she had been misled by her subordinates.[244] If she did know as much as she now says she did, she acted with wanton and reckless disregard for the lives of the children.

The majority held the attorney general responsible for being misinformed about perimeter control and the alleged need for the HRT to "stand down," and the ability of SWAT teams to take the HRT's place, since she either did not ask the right questions prior to the assault or failed to discipline responsible parties after, making her negligent either way.[245]

In efforts to minimize the responsibility of career law enforcement, the Committee Report blamed "fatigue and frustration" of the negotiators for failing to take Koresh's surrender letter more seriously.[246]

Also reflecting a bias toward career law enforcement just as strong as the bias against Democratic appointees, the Committee Report inaccurately asserted that the Davidians "lay in ambush, waiting for the arrival of the ATF agents," and that staging a massive assault with no plans to "knock and announce" was perfectly appropriate given the Branch Davidians' "possession of illegal automatic weapons."[247] The Committee Report, ignoring its own findings on the disabling and possibly asphyxiating affects of the CS and the tank damage, asserted that almost all the Branch Davidians could have escaped the fire, had they wanted to.[248]

The committee also offered some useful recommendations, although they are far short of the comprehensive reforms needed to renew citizen trust in federal law enforcement. One recommendation was that the Department of Justice actually enforce existing laws against making false statements in support of search and arrest warrants. Second, search warrant information should be "fresh and unbiased," although the Report offered no standards for how to implement this platitude.[249] Some clarification of the Posse Comitatus Act and the restriction of the National Guard for drug-nexus law enforcement was suggested. Better negotiation practices were recommended, including the use of outside experts, such as religious experts for religiously motivated groups like the Branch Davidians. The committee recommended further study on the appropriateness of CS when children, pregnant women, the elderly, or persons with respiratory problems were present. And the committee report recommended increasing the size of the HRT, a dubious proposition unless the HRT is first reformed so that it no longer holds people hostage.

The committee had been successful at uncovering some new evidence (such as the Department of Justice memos urging Treasury not to conduct an investigation), and had provided an opportunity for many issues to be fleshed out in much more detail than in the Treasury and Justice Department Reports. But the Democrats had so thoroughly dominated media coverage of the hearings that many people concerned about Waco thought the hearings were a failure.

Cochair Bill McCollum (R-Fla.) issued his own summary, with an even sharper attack on the mistakes of Attorney General Reno:[250]

> If the attorney general had taken the time to talk with outside experts, she would have quickly discovered the situation was not as dire as the FBI was painting it. She would have realized the lack of merit in the reasons given to her for proceeding with the high-risk gas assault plan.
>
> Ironically, Miss Reno testified she thought it was probable the Davidians would open fire on the tanks when the assault began. She also knew the plan called for rapid acceleration of the gas insertion, and it was likely the women and children would panic and stay inside, allowing Davidian leaders to react more violently and self-destructively.[251]

Representative McCollum then proceeded to debunk the various reasons given for having the attack on April 19, with most of the blame falling on Janet Reno, and concluding: "With Waco, Americans got rationalizations instead of accountability. President Clinton should have accepted Janet Reno's resignation."[252] Much of his criticism of Janet Reno made sense, but the criticism applies all the more to the FBI, for which Representative McCollum spent much of the 104th Congress helping to get a bigger appropriation and greater surveillance powers.[253]

Ruby Ridge Hearing

Soon after the hearings on Waco were completed, the Senate ended some of the coverup of Ruby Ridge, with hearings conducted by Sen. Arlen Specter's Judiciary Subcommittee on Terrorism, Technology and Government Information.

The administration attempted to stall the investigation; Deputy Attorney General Jamie Gorelick warned shortly before the hearings began that Senate hearings might "undermine the integrity and confidentiality of [the Justice Department] investigation" into Ruby Ridge. Apparently the Justice Department had suddenly decided, nearly three years after the FBI assault on the Weavers' cabin, that a criminal investigation should be started, and this new investigation would justify asking the Senate not to inquire.

The FBI limited Senate access to an FBI internal report on Ruby Ridge, as if the FBI were a coequal branch of government, and the senators just a bunch of meddlesome interlopers.[254] But Senator Specter continued with his scheduled hearings. There were no allegations of undue NRA influence on the hearings, partly because Senator Specter and his staff were sharply restricting any assistance from the NRA to receiving some documents, and partly because Randy Weaver's attorney, Gerry Spence, disliked the NRA and would not let his client near NRA staff. By having a hearing on the militia movement several weeks earlier, Senator Specter forestalled assertions that his subcommittee was just picking on law enforcement.[255]

In contrast to the House hearings, there were fewer time constraints on senators, with each senator allotted fifteen rather than five minutes per panel, and so more effective questioning was possible. Still, the questioning was certainly inexpert at times, with large holes in the testimony of some witnesses left unexplored.[256]

One of the main limitations on the Senate hearing was that so many witnesses would not testify. FBI sniper Lon Horiuchi (who killed Vicki Weaver), Dick Rogers (HRT commander at Ruby Ridge and Waco), and three other FBI agents refused to testify on Fifth Amendment grounds of possible self-incrimination.[257]

The BATF witnesses were willing to testify, but they often did so implausibly. BATF Agent Herb Byerly had lied about Randy Weaver's criminal record, inventing one. Before the Senate, he described the invention as a "typographical error." And, although Weaver had been acquitted on the weapons charges because the jury found he had been entrapped, BATF Director John Magaw defended the charges, and denied the entrapment. When pushed by Senator Specter, he replied: "Do you believe Randy Weaver—or do you believe the federal agents who have sworn to tell the truth and are carrying out a career in this government?"[258]

It would be difficult to exaggerate how much *less* partisan the Senate hearings were. On the House side, the House's leading gun prohibition advocate, Rep. Charles Schumer, executed a brilliant strategy of disrupting the agenda and shifting the attention away from misconduct by federal officials and onto politics. In contrast, one of the Senate's leading gun prohibition advocates, Sen. Dianne Feinstein (D-Calif.), skeptically questioned government witnesses and criticized the government's disproportionate reaction to the "threat" posed by Randy Weaver.

In the long term, Senator Feinstein did the antigun cause more good than did Representative Schumer, for it is unlikely that the kinds of controls they both favor will be enacted unless Americans are convinced that the federal gun control agencies will enforce the gun laws in a responsible, conscientious manner.

Following the Senate Weaver hearings, Senator Specter's subcommittee issued a report which called the Treasury Department's review of the Ruby Ridge incident "inadequate," agreed with the jury in finding BATF guilty of entrapping Randy Weaver into a technical gun law violation, called BATF Director John Magaw's testimony not credible, and recommended that BATF be abolished as a separate bureau. We address this recommendation in the next chapter.

The cynical lies which pervaded the government's involvement in Waco (and Ruby Ridge)—from the deceit to procure the initial warrant, through the lies at congressional hearings—might be seen by some persons as simply government business as usual. Even if deceit were usual (and it really is not) deceit in the context of law enforcement is particularly corrosive to society. As police ethicist John Kleinig explains,

> There is a deep and dangerous irony in police cynicism, for one of the major functions of police as social peacekeepers is to safeguard and foster social conditions that will be sustained and characterized by trust. True, police are needed in part because that trust is fragile and has been compromised. Nevertheless, theirs is the task of preventing its further erosion, and helping to restore it.[259]

THE FOURTH BRANCH: THE NEWS MEDIA

While the three official branches of government—executive, judiciary, legislative—may commit wrongdoings and cover them up, there is still the "fourth estate." But the media's feistiness is somewhat muted when the victims of government aggression are "cults" or "gun nuts," or especially "gun-nut cults."

The FBI forbade the media from coming closer than three miles to Mount Carmel, because of the alleged risk that reporters would be shot with the Davidians' .50 caliber rifles. The media were cleared even further away on the morning of the tank and chemical warfare assault.

After some radio time and a CNN interview on February 28, Koresh was forbidden to speak to the media. FBI and BATF agents were forbidden to speak to the press as well, except as part of official daily briefings held at the convention center in Waco. As a result, while Waco developed into a media circus, the only act the media was allowed to cover was the government's daily press briefing. With few exceptions, the national media accepted the government's making itself into the only source of information, much as the media had accepted similar treatment by covering the Gulf War through the single lens of daily press briefings in a room in Saudi Arabia.

Shelly Katz, a photographer for *Time*, stated that "in over thirty years, twenty-seven of which have been with Time-Life, I have covered everything from wars to riots—you name it. I have never been restrained as I was at Waco, and I will say needlessly and senselessly."[260]

After KRLD radio host Ron Engelman began broadcasting sympathetic coverage of the Branch Davidians, FBI Special Agent in Charge Jeff Jamar pointedly reminded KRLD management that the Federal Communications Commission licenses radio stations.[261] Engelman was eventually squeezed out when he refused to stop talking about the siege.

To reduce the opportunity for the kind of coverup that occurred at Waco, newspaper and television reporters should not be prohibited from covering law enforcement actions "up close," if the reporters are willing to assume the risk of injury, and if they do not invade private property. At the same time, government officials should not be encouraged to invite news crews along to trespass on private property to provide publicity for a raid.

The Davidians were appalled at the lack of news media access, correctly fearing that when they eventually got it, after the end of the siege, they would already have been permanently tainted as "a bunch of loonies . . . and cultists."[262] But they were begging for coverage, and fearful of the press being kept so far away and only hearing one side: "The press are so far back, you guys could come and blow us away . . . and you could . . . give any kind of a story you wanted."[263] Steve Schneider repeatedly made it clear he wanted the press to be part of the negotiation process.[264] With the misinformation being fed to the media, the Davidians feared, "We're toast."

When told that the news media had to be kept away because of Koresh's weaponry, Rita Riddle denied the Branch Davidians were a threat, but added, "All we need is a telephone line." "Well, you're not going to get it."[265] The FBI repeatedly told the Davidians they would have access to the media as soon as they came out and not before, citing such odd reasons as, "We have to do a crime scene investigation . . . to begin with." When one of the negotiators sneeringly asked, in response to one of the repeated complaints about the tanks, did Kathy Schroeder just want the Bradleys, the FBI agents, and the press to leave, she responded, "No, I'd like to have some open communication with the press. That would be nice."[266]

All the FBI would promise was access to the news media when the Branch Davidians surrendered; Koresh could have a press conference or interview, not with all the hundreds of reporters who would be interested, but with a pool.[267] Whether such a press interview would actually have been allowed or was merely part of the effort peacefully to end the standoff cannot be known.

The FBI had some basis for fearing that media access would just make Koresh all the more self-important. During the negotiations, he repeatedly asked for recent issues of *Time* and *Newsweek* which had long stories about him. But once the negotiations had stalled, it would not have been unreasonable to try using media access, or a certain amount of media access, as a bargaining chip.

Ms. Katz excepted, much of the media acted as a lapdog rather than a watchdog. They uncritically accepted the federal government's framing of the event as a confrontation between hard-working law enforcement officers and cultists. The over-whelming majority of media stories used the pejorative word "cult," rather than the more neutral "sect." Most of the media also heavily used other FBI propaganda words, such as "fortified bunker."

Over the course of the siege, much of the media did begin to pick apart BATF's lies about not having lost the element of surprise. (As a result of the questions, BATF stopped participating in the daily press briefing.[268]) But this discovery excepted, the media remained remarkably uninterested in scrutinizing government actions, and usu-ally accepted government statements at face value.

Most of the news media simply presumed the propriety of the federal operation in Waco, criticizing its planning and performance but not its motivation, and accepting sharp limitations on their right to know which normally would have inspired editorials denouncing government-in-secret.[269]

The self-inflicted blindness produced by the "cult" stereotype was illustrated in a March 10, 1993, story in the *Dallas Morning News*. The afternoon before, the Branch Davidians hung out a banner which read "God help us. We want the press." News pho-tographers and camera crews rushed to take pictures with their telephoto lenses. "No one," wrote the *Dallas Morning News*, "including FBI officials at the negotiating head-quarters near the compound, could explain what it meant."[270] Was there really no one in the horde of reporters from the top news organizations in the world who might ven-ture a guess that maybe the Branch Davidians wanted to talk to the press?

In addition to suffering from anticult bias, much of the media were just plain lazy.[271] The Branch Davidians sent out more than one videotape, and the media knew about the tapes, since the FBI mentioned them in the daily press briefings. But no one in the media attempted to obtain copies of the tapes, despite their obvious news value. The enterprise displayed by CNN's Wolf Blitzer—who presented a Baghdad viewpoint on incoming American missiles during the Gulf War—was absent from most of the mainstream media.

The 1995 joint subcommittee hearings gave the media a new chance to demon-strate that they would work to expose a coverup. But hard-hitting journalism was sadly wanting. During those ten days of hearings, there was limited television coverage—nothing compared to the coverage of the trial of O. J. Simpson. Even cable television devoted to the operations of Congress, C-SPAN, offered only partial coverage of the hearings into the deaths of over eighty persons on American soil, including four law enforcement officers and over two dozen children. Happily, just months later, greater media coverage was devoted to the Senate hearings on Ruby Ridge.

The news media did give attention to possibly racist and sexist activities by off-duty federal law enforcement personnel at annual weekend gatherings originated by a former BATF agent, the so-called Good O' Boys Roundups. Although no one died at the roundups, the news media, as well as Congress, were attracted by the appeal of stories of racism and sexism, even including some suggestions of drug use, rape, and other sexual misconduct, which became known just prior to the commencement of the joint subcommittee hearings on Waco.[272] That reporting produced the most extensive re-porting really critical of federal law enforcement during the month of July 1995, as most of the major media chose not to focus on the criticisms from the congressional hearings.

The *Washington Post* gave greater attention on July 25, 1995, to its exposé of the fact that an NRA employee (Blackman) wrote letters to the editor under a pen name[273] than to the revelations in the joint hearings that the BATF initial raiding party had not bothered to bring along the search or arrest warrants, and that on the day after the raid, BATF officials suppressed the normal shooting review for fear of what evidence would be produced.

NBC News demonstrated as well as any media outlet how the fourth estate essentially became part of the government cover-up. On July 25, 1995, there was extensive and dramatic testimony from two attorneys who believed they had worked out a negotiated settlement under which no assault by the FBI was necessary, including a report that they felt "betrayed" by the FBI when they learned of the CS attack.[274] NBC's evening news show that night found it more important—measured by broadcast time— to report that an NRA employee who writes for a living has a pen name than that the government-spurred deaths of seventy-six persons were unnecessary.

Columnists such as Paul Greenberg, and newspapers such as the *New York Times* editorial page, which had long been criticizing the government actions at Waco, did cover the hearings. Some writers bemoaned the perceived failure of the hearings,[275] while others highlighted the best parts as evidence of a collapsing cover-up.[276]

According to the nonpartisan Center for Media and Public Affairs, media coverage of the hearings ignored "broader civil liberties issues such as those involving probable cause for obtaining warrants and the rights of unorthodox religious groups."[277] In general, media coverage of everyone who had anything to do with the hearings was negative. Media coverage of David Koresh was 93 percent negative; of the Branch Davidians 88 percent negative; of the NRA, 86 percent; of Congress, 79 percent; of the BATF, 74 percent; of the FBI, 65 percent; and of the Treasury Department, 59 percent. This means that the Waco victims fared worst in media coverage; those who wanted to investigate Waco the next worst; and the perpetrators fared relatively best.

The one entity that received majority positive coverage was the Justice Department (61 percent positive), with Janet Reno gaining 67 percent favorable coverage.[278] She handled the media beautifully. The week before she was to testify, she called a press conference to discuss the hearings, said nothing new or significant, and dominated the day's Waco coverage, taking attention away from the hearings themselves.

When she did testify, she began with a story about David Koresh beating a baby in 1988. Her testimony revealed that, two years after the disaster of April 19, she either never learned the facts, or had decided to lie about them.

The most Orwellian moment came when General Reno claimed that it was wrong to call the Bradley Fighting Vehicles and Abrams armored units "tanks" since they did not have guns attached. They were merely "a very good rent-a-car." It is difficult, though, to rent a car which can be used to fire over a hundred ferret canisters containing chemical warfare agents banned from international warfare. Indeed, few cars can be used to demolish a two-story building.

Dan Quayle's spelling mistake (thinking that since the plural is "potatoes," the singular is "potatoe") was the subject of endless media ridicule. But Attorney General Reno's calling a tank "a rent-a-car," and her other statements which were far out of line with the truth, elicited a thunder of media applause. Because she had not broken down under hostile questioning, or deviated from her implausible version of the facts, she was reported as having "won" her confrontation with Congress.

Overall, observed *Washington Post* reporter Richard Leiby, "From the very start, much of the media coverage of Waco has been superficial. Investigative hearings this summer devolved into political sideshows."[279]

AFTERMATH

In August 1993, Amo Bishop Roden—George Roden's ex-wife—and her companion moved onto the Mount Carmel property.[280] They have set up a small museum, and give five-dollar tours to the many people who come to visit Mount Carmel.[281] A court battle has again begun between Mrs. Roden and the rest of the Branch Davidians over who really owns the seventy-seven acres.[282]

Crepe myrtle trees (of special symbolism to the Branch Davidians) have been planted in memory of the dead, and wooden crosses and marble markers have been placed on the ground.[283]

Rachel Jones (Vernon Howell's first wife) and twenty-seven other Branch Davidians were buried in unmarked paupers' graves in Waco, on a gray, rainy day in October 1994.[284]

Although Koresh's prophecy about the end of the world was not fulfilled, the Branch Davidian religion survived, and reinterpreted its analysis of the Bible, as have various other religions (including the Millerites, the early Christians, and the 1959 Branch Davidians) to adapt to current events. The majority of the Branch Davidians died at Waco. Within the remnant, there was a dispute over leadership between Clive Doyle (an Australian, and long-time Branch Davidian, acquitted in the Waco trial) and Ron Cole, a young man who had come to Waco during the siege and become interested in "the message."[285]

As Cole sees things, the events of April 19, 1993, were the fulfillment of Isaiah 64:11: "Our holy and our beautiful house, where our fathers praised thee, is burned up with fire: and all our pleasant things are laid waste." One day, the Branch Davidians will have a new leader and a new home, as prophesied in Isaiah 65:9.[286] Koresh was the seventh and final Angel anointed by God. Although Koresh had the true message, "He was a man and he blew it, just as the Bible prophesied he would," Cole believes, finding Koresh's downfall foretold in Psalm 89.[287] As of December 1995, Cole was looking for a site in New Mexico, and planning on keeping it heavily armed.[288]

From federal prison, Jaime Castillo and Livingstone Fagan dictate religious tracts which are circulated on the Internet. An unnamed Davidian prisoner, writing as the "Chosen Vessel," points to passages of Revelation and other parts of the Bible which forecast all that has come to pass. It is now the duty of the "remnant" of "the Bride" (the Branch Davidian church) to "prophesy again." Like previous Branch Davidian theology, the Chosen Vessel's is authoritarian. Readers are welcomed to find out more about the message, but its authority is not subject to question.[289]

Based on prophecies in the Book of Daniel, the Branch Davidians expect David Koresh to return within the next few years, although different prophecies point to different dates.[290]

It is not unheard of for religions to thrive, in the long run, as an unforeseen result for a disaster. For example, after Jerusalem was destroyed and the Jews taken into the Babylonian captivity, Judaism became stronger, as it was isolated from the syncretist threat of the Canaanite nature religions. In many respects, the Branch Davidians may be better off without Koresh. The events at Waco were apocalyptic enough to fit into an evolving analysis of Revelation, even if things after the fire did not happen as Koresh had predicted. Freed from the direct influence of Koresh's malignant personality, the Branch Davidians may be able to retain the traditional core elements of their faith, without having those elements distorted by the predatory lusts of a sociopath.

Certainly the Branch Davidians are now preaching to a far wider audience than ever before. Even while confined in prison, a Branch Davidian can reach an audience through the World-Wide Web and other media that dwarfs the audience which heard the Branch Davidian message before 1993.

The eight Branch Davidian convicts are scattered in various federal prisons. The main locus of the Branch Davidians is the city of Waco, since it is centrally located among the various federal prisons housing the Waco Eight.[291]

From prison, Livingstone Fagan writes: "The government overstepped its mark in asking us to surrender our souls to it. . . . In truth, the government's action was a late and last-ditch effort to hold onto power. The deaths of those who died at Mt. Carmel merely sealed God's victory. Those of us who remain alive in faith are an open show of that victory. The Kingdom of God can now be made manifest in the earth, the next event to shortly come to pass."[292]

Fagan has adopted a stance of peaceful noncooperation with the authorities, resulting in his confinement in progressively harsher environments.

INDEPENDENT COUNSEL

The federal executive branch does not police itself well enough. In December 1993, FBI Director Louis Freeh called indictments against some of the FBI agents in Idaho a "virtual certainty."[293] And while some BATF officials have been forced to resign for mounting an incompetent assault and then lying about it, no BATF or FBI official has been prosecuted for any of the deaths at Waco that resulted from the BATF's and FBI's dishonest, malicious, and illegal conduct.

On July 19, 1993, Sen. Dennis DeConcini asked Attorney General Reno for an investigation regarding the tape of the Branch Davidians' February 28 911 phone call, which had been given to a congressional committee. The tape was resequenced and edited, but the committee believed that it was listening to a real-time tape. To date, there has been no report to the public or to Congress regarding the tampering.[294]

Many commentators have offered cogent criticisms of the special prosecutors who have been empowered in recent years. But whatever the problems of special prosecutors, greater problems are created when large groups of people, armed with tanks, grenades, automatic weapons, and chemical warfare agents can break the law, violate their superiors' orders, and use those weapons with impunity. The fact that there has been no prosecution by state or federal prosecutors for the events at Ruby Ridge and Waco—and the generally poor performance by Congress in its oversight of the executive branch regarding Waco, except for pointing out the failures of the Democratic attorney general—suggest the need to appoint a special prosecutor for Waco and Ruby Ridge.

Jim Jorgensen, the deputy executive director of the National Association of Treasury Agents, an employee organization for Treasury Department law enforcement employees (including BATF staff), has taken the lead in calling for a special prosecutor to investigate government misconduct at Waco. Jorgensen argues that BATF's purported post-Waco reforms have been cosmetic, and the bureau has done nothing to reduce the possibility of future disasters.[295]

As an alternative, Rep. James Traficant (D-Ohio) has urged the McLennan county prosecutor to convene a grand jury.[296]

For the long term, it is appropriate to begin considering how to create a permanent prosecutor who would focus on cases involving crimes of violence perpetrated by federal officials under color of law.[297] The prosecutor might also take up cases of federal agents who violate the law by telling deliberate lies in order to obtain search warrants; this variety of criminal has been at the bottom of the Department of Justice's prosecution priorities. The prosecutor's office would have to be structured so that it would be immune to political pressure from the Department of Justice or the White House.

Following is a list of some of the possible crimes at Waco a special prosecutor or a county prosecutor might investigate. The prosecutor might conclude that other crimes occurred, and might conclude that some of the items listed below did not occur or were not in fact criminal. But it is hard to believe that *none* of the items below would be found to be criminal. And since the Department of Justice will not prosecute these crimes, a special prosecutor is amply merited to investigate:

- Lying in an affidavit on a search warrant affidavit application, as detailed in chapter 1.
- Conspiracy of two or more persons to "injure, oppress, threaten, or intimidate" a person because of the person's exercise of constitutional rights. Targeting the Branch Davidians for a BATF raid because of their unusual religious beliefs and because Koresh played a videotape criticizing BATF to an undercover BATF agent; BATF's chronology of events shows that BATF considered the critical videotape to be an element creating probable cause for the raid.
- Civil rights violations and interference with United States mail. BATF's warrantless searches of incoming mail and UPS packages for the Branch Davidians, months before the raid.
- Civil rights and wiretapping offenses related to warrantless insertion of phone taps months before the raid.
- Homicide and lesser included offenses. National Guard helicopters (carrying BATF commanders) strafing the second story (known to be the residence of women and children) at the Mount Carmel Center at the outset of the raid.[298]
- Homicide and lesser charges, based on conduct evincing reckless indifference to human life, based on the decision to use armor-piercing ammunition (capable of penetrating walls) during the raid (thereby endangering children), and the use of an armed assault to serve an arrest warrant for one person in a group home where about 125 other persons lived.

- Posse Comitatus Act violations growing out of the use of Ft. Hood and military personnel as a training center for the BATF raid. Related violations involving use of National Guard helicopters and personnel during the raid.
- Obstruction of justice and related charges for destruction of front door of the Mount Carmel Center, other property at Mount Carmel, and the BATF videotape of the raid, which could demonstrate that BATF fired first.
- Obstruction of justice and related charges for destruction of Mike Schroeder's wool cap, and for interference with Texas Ranger investigation of Schroeder's death.
- Homicide for shooting Mike Schroeder twice, inches from his skull, as he lay wounded.
- Making false statements to a federal official. The Texas Rangers (who had been specially deputized as federal agents) recommended that the Department of Justice prosecute Chojnacki and Sarabyn for lying to them during the Rangers' investigation of the February 28 shootings. The Department of Justice took no action.
- Property destruction and vandalism offenses related to destruction of the Mag Bag (an off-property garage owned by a non-Davidian under no personal suspicion), and tanks' crushing of Davidian automobiles and children's go-karts.
- Theft of $50,000 in cash, plus gold and platinum, found in a safe which survived the fire. Texas Rangers signed the safe and its contents over to the FBI, but the safe and contents are now unaccounted for.
- Homicide and lesser charges, based on conduct evincing reckless indifference to human life, related to the final FBI assault on Mount Carmel. Evidence of the offense includes: the FBI concealing from Attorney General Reno the opinion of FBI behavioral experts and negotiators that further negotiations were *not* hopeless; concealing from Attorney General Reno the April 14 surrender offer from Koresh; telling General Reno that CS is a mild tear gas, when in fact it is a potentially lethal chemical warfare agent which army manuals specify should not be used in enclosed spaces or against children; telling General Reno that there was no risk of suicide, when FBI behavioral experts had stated that an attack would probably provoke some kind of mass suicide; intentionally blocking access to the tornado shelter, thereby preventing some people from escaping the fire; intentionally ramming and spraying the central cold storage room (in violation of all operational plans); intentionally destroying rooms known to contain people, and thereby killing several people with falling rubble; and disobeying General Reno's orders to desist if there was any risk to the children.
- Tampering with evidence, contempt of court, and related charges based on the alteration of the 911 tape recording of the Branch Davidians calling the sheriff's office to plead for a cease-fire.
- Perjury. The conflicting tales told to Congress—all under oath, with it being a crime for federal employees to lie to congressional committees—mean that at least some federal employees committed perjury, apparently without any fear of prosecution.
- Civil rights offenses related to the harassment of investigative reporters, including the confiscation of reporters' pictures of the burned building.
- Obstruction of justice and related offenses, based on BATF's taking Henry

McMahon and Karen Kilpatrick into "protective custody" and attempting to prevent them from talking with the FBI.

* Interference with a federal investigation, based on the concealment of Koresh's April 14 surrender letter from the independent review team studying the Department of Justice report on Waco.
* Obstruction of justice and related offenses, based on the Department of Justice whitewashing Iraqgate in exchange for an Iraqgate perpetrator (Edward Dennis, Jr.) conducting an "investigation" of FBI conduct at Waco.

In regard to the homicide and other violent offenses listed above, a thirty-year additional sentence may be imposed under federal law for crimes of violence in which a machine gun was used.[299] If a "weapon of mass destruction" (such as a flashbang grenade) was used, a life sentence may be imposed.[300]

The 1994 Clinton administration crime bill contained a provision granting federal employees immunity from state prosecution for crimes which they perpetrated on the job. This proposal brings to mind George Mason's concern that an abusive federal government could use the federal capitol (an area not under the jurisdiction of any state) as a base from which to oppress the people, while remaining immune from state law.[301] Happily, the immunity provision was removed from the final bill. But unless a prosecutor moves forward, the effect will be the same as if the perpetrators of many of the crimes at Ruby Ridge and Waco were above the law.

NOTES

1. Dave Grossman, *On Killing: The Psychological Cost of Learning to Kill in War and Society* (Boston: Little, Brown and Co., 1995), p. 215.

2. Ken Fawcett, *Blind Justice: A Chronology of the Historic Trial of Eleven Branch Davidians in January 1994,* 2d ed. (Royse City, Tex.: Electropress, 1994), p. 26.

3. Henry Stanley McMahon, Jr., and Karen J. Kilpatrick, *In re: Interviews of Henry Stanley McMahon, Jr. and Karen J. Kilpatrick,* deposition taken May 25, 1993, pp. 93–199, 205; James L. Pate, "Waco: Behind the Cover-Up," *Soldier of Fortune* (November 1993): 39–40.

4. Transcripts of BATF Tapes of the Negotiations between Federal Law Enforcement and the Branch Davidians, February 28-April 19, 1993 (hereinafter "Negot. Tapes"), no. 93, March 8; no. 96, March 9.

5. Negot. Tape no. 98, March 9.

6. Dick Reavis, *The Ashes of Waco: An Investigation* (New York: Simon and Schuster, 1995), p. 228.

7. KPOC television, David Hall, producer, *The Waco Incident,* television documentary, September 19 1994 (Ponca City, Okla., channel 27).

8. U.S. Department of Justice, *Report on the Events at Waco, Texas, February 28 to April 19, 1993* (Redacted Version, Washington, D.C.: October 8, 1993), pp. 205–206 (hereinafter "Justice Report"). The Justice Report uses the tape *not* to argue that the "thoughtful, articulate" people at Mount Carmel should have been left alone, but to demonstrate that they were unlikely to surrender, and that therefore the government was correct in attempting to force them out.

9. ABC News Nightline, April 19, 1993.

10. Moorman Oliver, Jr., "Killed by Semantics: Or Was It a Keystone Kop Kaleidoscope Kaper?" in *From the Ashes: Making Sense of Waco,* ed. James R. Lewis (Lanham, Md.: Rowman and Littlefield, 1993), p. 84.

Randy Weaver and his children Rachel, Sara, and Elisheba play in a park in Grand Junction, Iowa, August 18, 1995. (AP/Wide World Photos)

Aerial view of the Branch Davidian compound at Waco, Texas, before the April 19, 1993 assault. (AP/Wide World Photos)

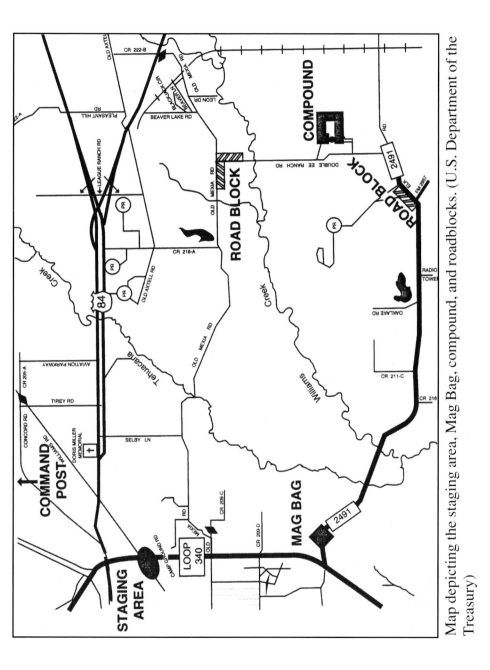

Map depicting the staging area, Mag Bag, compound, and roadblocks. (U.S. Department of the Treasury)

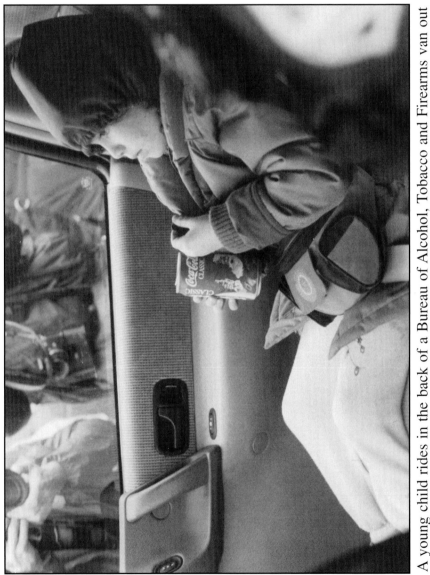

A young child rides in the back of a Bureau of Alcohol, Tobacco and Firearms van out of the Mount Carmel Center in March 1993; the child was one of several sent out after FBI negotiations with the Branch Davidians began. (AP/Wide World Photos)

David Koresh's wife, Rachel (*left*), and his mother, Bonnie Haldeman (*right*), hold two of his children in this undated photo. (AP/Wide World Photos)

An aerial view of the left side of the Mount Carmel Center during the fourth tank assault. At this time, approximately half of the gymnasium had been demolished and a tank was penetrating deep into the center of the front of the structure. (Failure Analysis Associates)

FBI aerial photograph of the Mount Carmel Center, approximately six minutes after the first fire was detected. Rapidly spreading fire is observed in the southeast tower, the dining room, and the chapel/gymnasium. (Failure Analysis Associates)

FBI aerial photograph of the Mount Carmel Center, prior to arrival of fire fighting equipment. Nearly complete destruction of the center is evident. (Failure Analysis Associates)

11. Order, *United States* v. *Vernon Wayne Howell* (W.D.Tex, Waco Div., April 20, 1993).

12. Edward S. G. Dennis, Jr., *Evaluation of the Handling of the Branch Davidian Stand-Off in Waco, Texas, February 28 to April 19, 1993, Redacted Version* (Washington, D.C.: Department of Justice, October 8, 1993), p. 15.

13. *In re Search Warrant for Secretarial Area outside the Office of Gunn*, 855 F.2d 569, 573 (8th Cir. 1988), *cert. denied*, 488 U.S. 1009 (1989).

14. *Baltimore Sun*, 886 F.2d 60, 66 (4th Cir. 1989). For a good overview, see James E. Phillips, David F. Axelrod, and Kevin G. Matthews, "Litigating Sealed Search Warrants," *The Champion* (March 1996): 7–11.

15. Dick Reavis, private communication with Carol Moore, cited in Carol Moore, *The Davidian Massacre* (Frankin, Tenn.: Legacy Communications and Gunowners Foundation, 1995), p. 237.

16. Gary Null, "Holocaust at Waco," *Penthouse* (April 1994).

17. Trial Transcript, *United States* v. *Brad Branch*, Crim. No. W-93-CR-046 (W.D.Tex., 1994) (hereinafter "Trial Transcript"), pp. 5811, 5816, 5834.

18. Lee Hancock and Enrique Rangel, "Remains May Be Those of Koresh, Sheriff Says," *Dallas Morning News*, May 1, 1993.

19. Jack Zimmermann introduced the card at United States House of Representatives, Subcommittee on Crime of the Committee on the Judiciary and the Subcommittee on National Security, International Affairs, and Criminal Justice of the Committee on Government Reform and Oversight, *Joint Hearings on Activities of Federal Law Enforcement Agencies Toward the Branch Davidians*, 104th Cong., 1st sess., July 19–August 1, 1995 (Washington, D.C.: Government Printing Office, 1996) (hereinafter "Joint Hearings"), part 2, p. 141.

20. "Grisly Testimony in Cultists' Trial," *New York Times*, February 13, 1994; James L. Pate, "What the Feds Don't Want You to Know about Waco," *Soldier of Fortune* (October 1993): 74–75; Jack DeVault, *The Waco Whitewash: The Mt. Carmel Episode Told by an Eyewitness to the Trial* (San Antonio: Rescue Press, 1994), p. 80.

21. Dick DeGuerin, Joint Hearings, part 2, p. 81.

22. Ibid., p. 52.

23. Trial Transcript, p. 5951.

24. "Grisly Testimony"; Trial Transcript, pp. 5836–37, 5847, 5859–62, 5869.

25. Paul McKay, "Photographers for Chronicle, AP Arrested," *Houston Chronicle*, April 22, 1993. The McLennan County district attorney's office dropped the charges. Lee Hancock and Bruce Nichols, "Four Bodies Found in Tunnels," *Dallas Morning News*, May 5, 1993.

26. Testimony of Texas Ranger Fred Cummings, in DeVault, *The Waco Whitewash*, p. 67.

27. Testimony of Texas Ranger Fred Cummings, Trial Transcript, p. 1081; Moore, *The Davidian Massacre*, p. 416.

28. Testimony of Texas Ranger Marshall Brown, in DeVault, *The Waco Whitewash*, p. 120; Moore, *The Davidian Massacre*, p. 417.

29. Moore, *The Davidian Massacre*, p. 418. The Mount Carmel Center was in disgusting shape. Large amounts of human waste had built up over the course of the siege, since the Branch Davidians, forbidden to leave the building to carry waste outside, had resorted to throwing it out the window. There was also rotting food and pools of stagnant water. "Cultist's Lawyer Calls Bulldozing of Site a Cover-up," *Washington Times*, May 13, 1993; Lee Hancock, "Doctors Says at Least 22 in Cult were Shot," *Dallas Morning News*, May 14, 1993. But since the Mount Carmel Center was not going to be open for human habitation anytime in the near future, there was no real health risk, and certainly no risk which justified such a massive destruction of possible evidence.

30. Plaintiffs' Complaint in *Brown et al.* v. *United States et al.* (S.D. Tex., Houston Div., February 25, 1995), ¶ 109.

31. Trial Transcript, p. 6847; James L. Pate, "We Have Truth on Our Side: Jailhouse Interviews with Branch Davidians," *Soldier of Fortune* (July 1994): 49.

32. Walter Reed Institute, James E. McCarroll, Carol S. Fullerton, Robert J. Ursano, and Joan M. Hermsen, *Psychological Stress of Forensic Dental Examinations: The Waco Disaster* (Washington, D.C.: Walter Reed Army Institute of Research, Division of Neuropsychiatry, Department of General Psychiatry, August 1, 1994), pp. 25–26.

33. The examiner explained that, rather than the McLennan County Medical Examiner, he did the autopsies because his lab had superior facilities. Testimony of Dr. Nizam Peerwani, Trial Transcript, pp. 5961, 5965.

34. Plaintiffs' Complaint in *Brown et al. v. United States et al.* (S.D. Tex., Houston Div., February 25, 1995), ¶ 109.

35. Bob Mahlburg, "Secrecy Shrouds Coroners' Talks on Waco Deaths," *Washington Times*, September 13, 1993, p. A3.

36. "FBI Tape of Waco Talks Probed," *Washington Times*, June 17, 1993. No one has ever been punished for violating the federal court order or for attempting to introduce fraudulent evidence for the congressional committee.

37. James Bovard, "Convoluted Trail of Waco Explanations," *Washington Times*, April 19, 1995, p. A15.

38. Sarah Elizabeth Jones, memorandum of September 17, 1993, for Ronald K. Noble, Asst. Secretary for Enforcement (description of events of March 1, 1993). Joint Hearings, part 1, p. 436: Rep. Bob Barr read from a memorandum dated March 1, 1993: "Johnston at this point advised Hartnett to stop the ATF shooting review because ATF was creating Brady material. Because Chojnacki had not yet been interviewed, Johnston authorized that interview, but no notes were created." Reprinted in Joint Hearings, part 1, p. 657.

39. Robert M. McNamara, Assistant General Counsel for Enforcement, Department of the Treasury, April 14, 1993 memorandum to John P. Simpson, Michael D. Langan, p. 2. Referred to in Joint Hearings, part 1, p. 893; reprinted in Joint Hearings, part 1, pp. 555–57 (emphasis in original). As Rep. Henry Hyde summarized the situation: "The prosecutors don't want us to generate additional Jencks, Brady or Giglio material. In other words, exculpatory material that might prove one of these 11 who were locked up, one at least for a year, might help them prove their innocence. So let's not discover anything, let's not take statements, even though it would be helpful in this comprehensive review of what happened and what went wrong, but for God sake, we can't help prove anybody's innocent." Joint Hearings, part 1, p. 892. Since Justice and Treasury are coequal cabinet departments, Justice did not attempt to order Treasury to stop the internal investigation. The Department of Justice simply knew that its attorneys would be prosecuting the Branch Davidians, and calling Treasury employees (BATF agents) as witnesses.

40. Department of Justice, "Justice Department Statement on Law Enforcement Procedures," July 21, 1995 (no. 95-409), reprinted in Joint Hearings, part 1, p. 608.

41. "A prosecutor has the responsibility to see that justice is done, and not simply to be an advocate." First line of the Comment to Texas Disciplinary Rules of Professional Conduct, Rule 3.09, Special Responsibilities of a Prosecutor.

42. In fact, this is the very first rule for prosecutors. Texas Disciplinary Rule 3.09: "The prosecutor in a criminal case shall: (a) refrain from prosecuting or threatening to prosecute a charge that the prosecutor knows is not supported by probable cause."

43. Assistant U.S. Attorney William Johnston, Joint Hearings, part 1, p. 208.

44. Ibid., part 1, p. 209.

45. Ibid., part 1, pp. 208–209.

46. Maurice Cook and David Byrnes, Joint Hearings, part 2, p. 186.

47. Capt. David Byrnes, Joint Hearings, part 2, pp. 148, 159. After the fire, the Rangers' investigation was supported by the FBI, and "we did get 100 percent cooperation from the FBI laboratory." Ibid., p. 161.

48. William Johnston, letter of March 23, 1993, to Attorney General Janet Reno, reprinted in Joint Hearings, part 2, pp. 166–68. Justice Report, pp. 228–30. A Texas Ranger complained about the lack of communication between the FBI, in particular the HRT, and the rest of law enforcement. "It got to the point where we couldn't even talk to them on the phone. They were destroying the outside of the compound, especially moving the vehicles, which we thought had critical evidence for the trajectory. We were hopeful we could put people shooting out of those windows, and from that window, maybe, do some trajectory things with ballistics and charge someone specifically with murdering some of those four agents. . . . We were told that we would be able to urge our concerns before that [destruction of evidence] happened. That was not done. We found out about it on CNN, as a matter of fact." Texas Ranger David Byrnes, Joint Hearings, part 2, p. 148.

49. Negot. Tapes no. 29, March 3; no. 38, March 4; no. 66, March 6.

50. Texas Ranger Capt. Maurice Cook, Joint Hearings, part 2, p. 147.

51. Negot. Tapes no. 64, March 6; no. 242, April 18.

52. Most of the claims by Branch Davidians were bogus, but more prompt examination of their bodies would have confirmed this more convincingly than autopsies conducted seven weeks after their deaths and casual burials. The Davidians, for example, claimed that Jaydean Wendell had been killed by a round from a helicopter through the top of her head as she handed her baby to another woman (James L. Pate, "What the Feds Don't Want You to Know about Waco," *Soldier of Fortune* [October 1993]: 101–102; Negot. Tape no. 204, April 10), a wound eventually determined to have been received while she was shooting at BATF agents from the prone position. Reavis, *The Ashes of Waco,* p. 166. And the Davidians said Peter Gent was killed by a round to the back of the head. Negot. Tape no. 58, March 5. But instead of welcoming the opportunity to put to rest such assertions, the FBI, with no apparent objections from the Rangers, refused to take Gent's body without a quid pro quo release of at least one adult hostage, and, instead, allowed the burials of Gent and Jones. Negot. Tapes no. 63, March 6; no. 79, March 7; no. 86, March 7; no. 101, March 9–10.

53. Negot. Tapes no. 64, March 6; no. 100, March 9.

54. Ron Noble, Joint Hearings, part 1, pp. 885, 889.

55. Chapter 2, p. 127. BATF's initial testimony was that about 1,500 rounds had been fired at the Mount Carmel Center on February 28. U.S. House of Representatives, *Events Surrounding the Branch Davidian Cult Standoff* in Waco, Texas. Hearing before the Committee on the Judiciary, U.S. House of Representatives, 103rd Cong., 1st sess., April 28, 1993 (hereinafter "Hearing"), p. 130.

56. Reavis, *The Ashes of Waco,* pp. 197–99.

57. Maurice Cook, Joint Hearings, part 2, p. 181; David Byrnes, Joint Hearings, part 2, pp. 186–87. While the congressional hearing exposed the shooting review cover-up, and while representatives asked numerous questions about documents related to the cover-up, the Committee Report is silent about the shooting review and the efforts by Justice to limit interviews and the creation of evidence which might benefit the defendants. United States House of Representatives, Committee on Government Reform and Oversight in conjunction with the Committee on the Judiciary, *Investigation into the Activities of Federal Law Enforcement Agencies Toward the Branch Davidians,* Report 104–79, 104th Cong., 1st sess. (Washington, D.C.: Government Printing Office, August 2, 1996) (hereinafter "Committee Report").

58. Stephen Labaton, "Inquiry Won't Look at Final Waco Raid," *New York Times,* May 16, 1993.

59. Stephen Labaton, "Justice Inquiry Will Now Examine Assault on Cult," *New York Times,* May 18, 1993.

60. The Treasury report team was headed by Assistant Secretary of the Treasury for Law Enforcement Ronald K. Noble. Noble, while still awaiting official Senate confirmation in his post, had approved the raid. Moore, *The Davidian Massacre,* pp. 192, 199. Among the three independent panelists chosen by President Clinton to review the Treasury Report was Willie Williams, currently police chief of Los Angeles and formerly police chief of Philadelphia. As police chief of Philadelphia, Mr. Williams had run a department whose informal slogan was "Death from Above," as a result of the disastrous bombing of the MOVE home, which resulted in the burning of a neighborhood. James L. Pate, "One Hand Whitewashes the Other," *Soldier of Fortune* (February 1994): 60. Rep. Barney Frank had mentioned MOVE as a disaster comparable to Waco. Hearing, p. 50.

61. William Safire, "Waco, Reno, Iraq-gate," *New York Times,* October 14, 1993. A *Washington Post* columnist contrasted candidate Bill Clinton's indignant demands that the truth about Iraqgate be uncovered, with President Clinton's "deep incuriousity," and the Justice Department's acceptance of "in-house whitewash" about Iraq issues. Mary McGrory, "Clinton Closes the Iraqgate," *Washington Post,* November 14, 1993.

62. 58 Fed. Reg. 43312 (August 16, 1993).

63. U.S. Department of the Treasury, *Report on the Bureau of Alcohol, Tobacco, and Firearms, Investigation of Vernon Wayne Howell also known as David Koresh* (Washington, D.C.: Government Printing Office, September 1993) (hereinafter, "Treasury Report"), p. 121. Both the Treasury and Justice reports found themselves unable even to spell correctly the name of the book that was central to the Davidians. The reports refer to the book of "Revelations" (properly, "Revelation"), which one re-

porter likened to "trying to explain Hitler by saying you've read 'Mine Camp.'" David Tammeus, "Religion: The Overlooked Key to the Waco Tragedy," *Boulder Daily Camera*, April 24, 1994 (originally published in *Kansas City Star*), p. 1E.

64. Treasury Report, p. 9.

65. FBI National Press Office Release, January 6, 1995.

66. Treasury Report, pp. 16, 213.

67. James L. Pate, "Special Forces Involved in Waco Raid," *Soldier of Fortune* (May 1994): 34.

68. Treasury Report, pp. 8, 172. Indeed, the Justice Department review noted: "Koresh's hatred of the government did not always seem apparent. The tapes of the negotiations between Koresh and the FBI contain many lighthearted moments, and many hours of calm, peaceful conversations between Koresh and negotiators. Koresh even proclaimed his admiration for law enforcement during some of the conversations." Justice Report, pp. 209.

69. Treasury Report, pp. 8, 122.

70. Treasury Report, Appendix D-3–6.

71. Treasury Report, pp. 31, 124, Appendix D-7–8.

72. Treasury Report, pp. 31, 124.

73. Treasury Report, pp. Appendix B-156; 18 U.S.C. § 921; 26 U.S.C. § 5845.

74. Treasury Report, pp. 26, 218, Appendix A-7.

75. The British official was Detective Chief Superintendent Albert Yates, who testified at a Coroner's hearing in Manchester, England, in January 1995.

76. Treasury Report, pp. 46, 51, 56.

77. Reavis, *The Ashes of Waco,* p. 182; Treasury Report, pp. 145–46.

78. Stephen Labaton, "Report on Initial Raid on Cult Finds Officials Erred and Lied," *New York Times*, October 1, 1993, pp. A1, A20.

79. Mark England, "One Year Later: The Branch Davidian Raid," *Atlanta Constitution*, February 27, 1994, p. A12 (story from Waco *Tribune-Herald*).

80. Bob Lesmeister, "Bad Influence: Corruption within the Ranks of BATF," *American Firearms Industry* (June 1995): 57.

81. Mark Smith, "Agent Testified ATF Misled Public; Officer Says He Gave Warning that Cult Had Been Tipped Off," *Houston Chronicle*, January 29, 1994, p. A1; James L. Pate, "Troy Trounces Truth," *Soldier of Fortune* (January 1997): 52.

82. "ATF Rehires 2 Agents Fired over Waco Case," *Washington Times*, December 22, 1994. The administrative cases were *Chojnacki* v. *United States*, DA 0752-95-0126-1-1 (Merit Systems Protection Board); *Sarabyn* v. *United States*, DA 0752-95-0127-1-1 (Merit Systems Protection Board).

83. James Bovard, "Clues to a Collapsing Coverup on Waco?" *Washington Times*, August 16, 1995.

84. James L. Pate, "Wacogate," *Soldier of Fortune* (June 1995): 48

85. Joint Hearings, part 1, pp 428–29.

86. Ibid., pp. 230, 264–65, 271–72, 755.

87. "The Agents' Forum," *The Agent,* National Association of Treasury Agents, Fall 1996, p. 36. Davy Aguilera, Joint Hearings, part 1, p. 272: "I didn't recall quite clearly, but I do believe that the element of surprise was asked by Mr. Higgins. If the element of surprise was going to be lost, don't continue the raid." If all of this is true, then one of the few persons held most responsible for the raid continuing despite the loss of the element of surprise, BATF Director Stephen Higgins, was the only person using the words "element of surprise," the loss of which was to cause the raid to be canceled. The best justification for Higgins's punishment is that, as director, he is properly held responsible for such poor leadership that his subordinates managed such a bungled operation, regardless of the details. Further, he set the general tone of the Bureau, which during his tenure became increasingly violent and enamored of dynamic entries.

88. Ron Noble, in discussion with Representative McCollum, Joint Hearings, part 1, p. 926. Higgins and his deputy, Hartnett, were blamed for failure "to become significantly involved in the planning for it," and "they share some blame for not instilling in the senior raid commanders an understanding of the need to ensure that secrecy was maintained in an operation of this type." Committee Report, p. 23.

89. The two men most criticized in the Report, Sarabyn and Chojnacki, each testified that they thought the report about 70 percent accurate, with some of the remainder split evenly between true but misleading, and false. Joint Hearings, part 1, pp. 419, 449. To Ron Noble, responsible for what was admittedly a "self-examination," "where no one other than people criticized challenge it [the Treasury Report], in the core accuracies it contains . . . we [should] get a pat on the back instead of having our parents listen on television or see on television where someone says there was a cover-up or I engaged in a 'coverup,' or the Department engaged in a coverup without showing what fact was missing or not disclosed." Joint Hearings, part 1, p. 953. Contrary to Noble's declaration, core inaccuracies were attacked, generally with documentation, by persons other than Sarabyn and Chojnacki. This included such issues as the basis for the warrant, with false statements from the warrant which were repeated in the report, the apparent willingness of Koresh to cooperate, and the importance of arresting Koresh away from the Branch Davidians.

90. Daniel Hartnett, Joint Hearings, part 1, p. 755.

91. Lee Hancock, "Report on FBI Actions in Raid on Cult Delayed," *Dallas Morning News*, October 2, 1993.

92. Justice Report. As Benjamin Franklin put it, "The absent are never without fault, nor the present without excuse." Franklin was creating an American version of the French saying "Les absents ont toujours tort" ("Those not present are always in the wrong"). Philippe Néricault, *L'Obstacle Imprévu* (1717), Act I, scene 6.

93. Dennis, *Evaluation of the Handling*, p. 4.

94. "The arson team also concluded that the Davidians could have escaped the fire if they had wanted," notes the Justice Report. Justice Report, p. 113. Another Justice reviewer asserted that all who died were there voluntarily, held against their will, or shot to prevent their escape. Dennis, *Evaluation of the Handling*, p. 2.

95. Justice Report, Appendix F-9.

96. James D. Tabor, "The Waco Tragedy: An Autobiographical Account of One Attempt to Avert Disaster," in Lewis, *The Davidian Massacre*, p. 8.

97. Justice Report, p. 105; Moore, *The Davidian Massacre*, p. 431.

98. Jerry Seper, "Reviewer Disputes Clinton over Waco, Says Agents Share Blame for Deaths," *Washington Times*, April 27, 1995, p. A1; Moore, *The Davidian Massacre*, p. 431.

99. U.S. Department of Justice, *Recommendations of Experts for Improvements in Federal Law Enforcement After Waco* (Washington, 1993).

100. Testimony of Eugene Glenn, before the Senate Judiciary Committee, Subcommittee on Terrorism, Technology, and Government Information, *Federal Raid in Idaho Hearings*, September 19, 1995.

101. Editorial, Spokane *Spokesman-Review*, July 7, 1994; United States Department of Justice, *Department of Justice Report Regarding Internal Investigation of Shootings at Ruby Ridge, Idaho, during Arrest of Randy Weaver* (hereinafter, "DOJ Internal Investigation of Ruby Ridge"). In June 1995, *Legal Times* obtained a copy of the report, and posted it on the Internet. The URL is http://www.courttv.com/library/government/ruby.html.

102. Jerry Seper, "Agents Split over New Deputy Director," *Washington Times*, May 11, 1995, p. A6; Ruth Marcus, "FBI Chief Gets His Man for No. 2 Post," *Washington Post*, May 7, 1995, p. A6; Richard Cohen, "Censured by the FBI—and Then Promoted," *Washington Post*, May 9, 1995.

103. Moore, *The Davidian Massacre*, p. 434.

104. The press conference the evening of the fire:

Dee Dee Myers: "He stands by the Justice Department and the Fbi [*sic*]. They made a difficult decision . . . I think, again, the President today—the Justice Department and the Fbi made these decisions. The President was briefed on them last night and didn't raise any objections, but did not micromanage the situation." . . .

Q. "Dee Dee, one more Waco question. Has the President had any briefings on this prior to this weekend, do you know? Has he had any personal involvement—"

Ms. Myers: "He's been kept current of the situation there and is briefed regularly on the outcome, but not in terms of the specific—this specific plan."

(Press Briefing By Dee Dee Myers, The Briefing Room, April 19, 1993, 6:20 P.M. EDT.)

105. Elizabeth Drew, *On the Edge: The Clinton Presidency* (New York: Simon and Schuster, 1994), p. 131.

106. Wesley Pruden, "A Fatigued Excuse for a Holocaust," *Washington Times*, April 20, 1993, p. A4.

107. "She is not ultimately responsible to the American people; I am." Remarks by the president in question-and-answer session with the press, the Rose Garden, April 20, 1993, 1:36 P.M. EDT.

108. Jeffrey H. Birnbaum, *Madhouse: The Private Turmoil of Working for the President* (New York: Random House, 1996), p. 203.

109. Ronald Kessler, *The FBI* (New York: Pocket Books, 1993), p. 429.

110. Arthur Weinberg, ed., *Attorney for the Damned: Clarence Darrow in the Courtroom* (New York: Simon and Schuster, 1957), pp. 241–42. Dr. Sweet was acquitted, although the case moved the Michigan legislature to enact a handgun licensing law. Don B. Kates, "Handgun Prohibition in the United States," in *Restricting Handguns: The Liberal Skeptics Speak Out,* ed. Don B. Kates (North River Press: Croton-on-Hudson, 1979), p. 19.

111. Treasury Report, p. 38n16.

112. Quoted in Fawcett, *Blind Justice,* p. 18.

113. Department of Justice Internal Investigation of Ruby Ridge.

114. Hugh Aynesworth, "Waco Judge: 'Smart' and 'Vindictive,'" *Washington Times*, January 30, 1994, p. A1.

115. Moore, *The Davidian Massacre,* p. 440.

116. DeVault, *The Waco Whitewash,* p. 45.

117. Fawcett, *Blind Justice,* p. 8.

118. DeVault, *The Waco Whitewash,* pp. 208–35.

119. "Prosecution Completes Case Against 11 Koresh Followers," *New York Times*, February 16, 1994.

120. Moore, *The Davidian Massacre,* p. 381.

121. Ibid., p. 382.

122. Testimony of Lt. Ray Cano, Trial Transcript, pp. 783–84; DeVault, *The Waco Whitewash,* p. 63.

123. DeVault, *The Waco Whitewash,* p. 90.

124. 373 U.S. 83 (1963). The Brady rule is an application of the Fifth Amendment guarantee of Due Process in criminal trials.

125. Written testimony of Tim Evans, Joint Hearings, part 1, pp. 628–29, 641–41.

126. *Ware* v. *Barr*, 883 F.Supp. 654 (M.D.Fla. 1995).

127. U.S. Constitution, Fifth Amendment ("nor shall any person be subject for the same offense to be twice put in jeopardy of life or limb"). Courts will often reverse a conviction because of a prosecutor's failure to disclose Brady material, but will not bar a second prosecution.

128. 18 U.S. Code § 3500.

129. FBI National Press Office, January 6, 1995.

130. DeVault, *The Waco Whitewash,* p. 70; Trial Transcript, pp. 1177–92, 1209–16. An undamaged full-auto AK-47 was identified by Kathy Schroeder (but it had come from her late husband's van, and was not used by anyone on February 28). Trial Transcript, p. 4501.

131. If the gun is broken but can "readily" be restored using parts in the possession of the defendant, the broken gun still counts as a real gun.

> The term "machinegun" means any weapon which shoots, is designed to shoot, or can be readily restored to shoot, automatically more than one shot, without manual reloading, by a single function of the trigger. The term shall also include the frame or receiver of any such weapon, any part designed and intended solely and exclusively, or combination of parts designed and intended, for use in converting a weapon into a machinegun, and any combination of parts from which a machinegun can be assembled if such parts are in the possession or under the control of a person.

(26 U.S. Code § 5845[b].) The Davidians' broken machine guns, however, were not shown to be readily restorable with parts that they owned. Cadigan did the restoration using his own parts. More-

over, his lengthy efforts to make the gun fire automatically may be so involved that the gun could not be considered "readily" restorable. That the destruction of the guns could deprive the prosecution of essential evidence was understood by the FBI, however much the fact was ignored at trial. Observing the fire, Danny O. Coulson, the FBI deputy assistant director of the Criminal Investigation Division, worried that Koresh was "burning the arms . . . and he'll walk out and say, 'Prove I had automatic weapons.'" Nancy Gibbs, "Fire Storm in Waco," *Time* (May 3, 1993): 30.

132. Paul H. Blackman, June 29, 1995 personal communication with journalist James L. Pate, who attended the trial.

133. Sam Howe Verhovek, "Letter to Jurors Leads to Inquiry," *New York Times*, February 25, 1994; Larry Dodge, "The Branch Davidian Trial: Was the Jury Fully Informed?" *FIJA Activist* (Spring 1994): 1, 10–11, 16–17.

134. The jury instructions are available at http://i2i.org/SuptDocs/Waco/wajuryin.htm.

135. Paul Greenberg, "Unanswered Questions at Waco," *Washington Times* (weekly ed.), May 22, 1995, p. 21.

136. James Bovard, "Waco Must Get a Hearing," *Wall Street Journal*, May 15, 1995.

137. Transcript excerpts reprinted in *AID & ABET Police Newsletter*, April 1994, pp. 14–15.

138. Judge Smith's memorandum explaining the reinstatement of the convictions is available at http://i2i.org/SuptDocs/Waco/wasmith.htm.

139. DeVault, *The Waco Whitewash*, p. 166.

140. Sentencing Guidelines, § 1B1.3 (relevant conduct). For more, see Kevin R. Reitz, "Sentencing Facts: Travesties of Real-Offense Sentencing," 45 *Stanford Law Review* 523 (1993).

141. Hugh Aynesworth, "5 Koresh Followers Handed 40 Years," *Washington Times*, June 18, 1994, p. A3.

142. Judge Smith's sentencing memorandum is available at http://i2i.org/SuptDocs/Waco/wasentmm.htm

143. "Sarah Bain, Branch Davidian Trial Forewoman," *FIJActivist* (Summer 1994): 18.

144. *State* v. *Rupe*, 101 Wash.2d 664, 683 P.2d 571 (1984)

145. Wayne LaPierre, *Guns, Crime and Freedom* (Washington, D.C.: Regnery, 1994), p. 223.

146. Bennett L. Gershman, "A Moral Standard for the Prosecutor's Exercise of Charging Discretion," 20 *Fordham Urban Law Journal* 513 (no. 3, 1993).

147. *United States* v. *Williams*, 112 S.Ct. 1735 (1992).

148 This is the rule in New Jersey. *State* v. *Hogan*, No. A-83-1995 (N.J.S.Ct., May 23, 1995).

149. The indictment is available at http://i2i.org/SuptDocs/Waco/waindict.htm.

150. 116 S.Ct. 501 (1995).

151. *United States* v. *Branch*, 91 F.3d 699 (5th Cir.), *rehearing denied*, —91 F.3d 752— (5th Cir. 1996) (per curiam), available at http://www.ljextra.com/cgi-bin/f_c/ljextra/data/external/9608002.c05.

152. Sometimes a court of appeals panel will include district (trial) judge, or a judge from another circuit. The judge is said to be sitting by designation.

153. 18 U.S.C. § 924(c)(1).

154. The allegation is that employees of American Medical Transport, which was on standby for the attack, tipped off the newspaper or the television station, which in turn tipped off the Branch Davidians. A different set of BATF agents and the families of three of the agents killed in the raid sued the TV station and the newspaper, but not the ambulance company. See *Risenhoover* v. *Cox*, W93-CA-138 (W.D. Texas); *McKeehan* v. *Cox Texas Pubs., Inc.*, CAW-94-CA-082 (W.D. Texas); *Curtis* v. *Cox Texas Pubs., Inc.*, W94CA-196 (W.D. Texas); *Rodriguez* v. *Cox*, W94-CA-157 (W.D Texas); Janet Elliot, "Suit by ATF Agents Says Media Tipped Off Koresh," *Legal Times*, February 20, 1995; Associated Press, "Federal Agents: Media and Ambulance Co. Caused Shootout at Davidian Compound," Associate Press Wire, July 19, 1993.

155. Lee Hancock, "Lawsuit over Waco Raid Is Settled," *Washington Post*, October 18, 1996, p. A3 (originally published in *Dallas Morning News*).

156. *McMahon and Kilpatrick* v. *Aguilera*, no. W-95-CA-087 (W.D. Tex., Waco Div.).

157. E.g., *Brown* v. *United States*, (S.D. Texas, Houston Division)(Ramsey Clark case); *Andrade* v. *Chojnacki*, 1194-0923 (S.D. Texas); *Gyarfas* v. *United States*, CAW93-CA334 (W.D. Texas, Waco Division); *Holub* v. *Reno*, H94-2153 (W.D. Texas) (estates of three of Koresh's children); Janet Elliot,

"Suit by ATF Agents Says Media Tipped Off Koresh," *Legal Times* (February 20, 1995); Gary Taylor, "Fire and Death in Waco Spark a Legal Slow Burn," *National Law Journal* (December 12, 1994): A1.

158. *Allison* v. *Meyer*, no. W-95-CA-073 (W.D. Tex., Waco Div.).

159. *The Agent* (National Association of Treasury Agents), March 1996, p. 1. The Department of Justice has refused to represent Rodriguez because he has filed a separate lawsuit against Chojnacki and Sarabyn for defamation, and this suit is said to create a conflict of interest making it impossible for the Department to represent Rodriguez in the Branch Davidians' suit. "The Agents' Forum," *The Agent* (National Association of Treasury Agents) (June 1996): 17.

160. Hugh Aynesworth, "Waco's Long Siege Begets a Longer Drama in Court," *Washington Times,* June 23, 1996, p. A1. In Charles Dickens's novel *Bleak House* (1853), the case of *Jarndyce* v. *Jarndyce* was a dispute over rights of inheritance. The suit continued for decades, until all the money on the original estate had been spent on legal fees.

161. Stuart A. Wright, "Preface," in *Armageddon in Waco: Critical Perspectives on the Branch Davidian Conflict,* ed. Stuart A. Wright (Chicago: University of Chicago Press, 1995), p. xi; Sue Anne Pressley, "Waco, the Rise of a Symbol," *Washington Post,* May 28, 1995.

162. The suspected Oklahoma City bomber was not a member of the militia movement, which consists of groups generally fearful of government and armed defensively against government, but not interested in initiating confrontation with the government. Analogies could include investigating socialists out of fear of communism or honeybees out of fear of African killer bees.

163. Jack Zimmermann, Joint Hearings, part 2, p. 41.

164. Joint Hearings, part 1, pp. 3–5.

165. Joint Hearings, part 3, pp. 348–49; Hearing, pp. 25–26.

166. Woodrow Wilson, *Congressional Government: A Study in American Politics* (Cleveland and New York: World Publishing Co., [1885,] 1956, 1963), pp. 179–80.

167. Joint Hearings, part 1, p. 322. He probably said "loose and unindexed."

168. James Bovard, "Hear No Evil," *American Spectator* (January 1996): 43.

169. Additional Views, Committee Report, p. 92. See also the Discussion between Ron Noble and Representative McCollum, Joint Hearings, part 1, 883.

170. Joint Hearings, part 3, p. 325.

171. Rep. John Shadegg, Joint Hearings, part 1, p. 955. Representative Schumer's jovial response was, "Hey, if you're nice, I may tell you what it [the miracle power] is." Ibid.

172. James Bovard, "Hear No Evil," *American Spectator* (January 1996): 43.

173. Jerry Seper, "FBI Probe of Killing Drags On," *Washington Times,* October 8, 1996, p. A7. Initial charges have dealt only with the cover-up, not with the actual wrongdoing at Ruby Ridge.

174. Which is not to say that the Clinton administration is worse than its predecessor. One person (David Kopel) involved in the coalition of groups seeking improvements in the way the administration's law enforcement agencies operated was quoted at the time of the hearings, saying: "The problems really escalated under George Bush. Probably the worst you could say about Clinton is that things haven't gotten any better." Charles Oliver, "Is Waco the Tip of the Iceberg?: Federal Law Enforcement Tagged with Abuses," *Investor's Business Daily,* July 19, 1995.

175. Rep. Bill McCollum, Joint Hearings, part 1, p. 8.

176. The efforts of the White House, in conjunction with House Democrats, were summarized in a complaint by Rep. Bill McCollum. Listening to the president's chief of staff, Leon Panetta:

> I realized how trivialized these hearings are in danger of becoming as a result of the administration's overreaction to this.
>
> The events of Waco in 1993 were tragic; 90 Americans, including 22 children and 4 ATF officers, were killed, and many more wounded. . . . These hearings were and are designed to allow our Nation to fully vent the pent-up feelings of sorrow, dismay, and anger that arose from the ashes of Waco; to do the first and only comprehensive congressional review of what happened at Waco; to debunk outlandish conspiracy theories, but at the same time hold all of those responsible publicly accountable; and to begin the process of healing necessary to restore confidence and credibility in two of our key Federal law enforcement agencies.

Apparently out of fear that revelations in these hearings could damage the Clinton Presidency, the White House, Congressman Schumer, and some at Treasury and Justice set out this past week to ridicule, trivialize, and discredit these hearings.

First, a political operative was hired by the White House just for Waco political damage control. Then the line was put forward that these hearings were being held just to please the National Rifle Association, that somehow they were tainted. By the end of the week, the President's press spokesman, Mike McCurry, said quote, the NRA bought and paid for these congressional hearings, unquote. Whatever one thinks of the NRA, this is just plain political hogwash.

. . . Along with that came the effort to focus the public's entire attention on the child abuse committed at the Davidian compound by David Koresh, with both Mr. Schumer and the President implying that these moral atrocities alone justify the ATF raid and perhaps even excused all of the tragic mistakes. . . .

Of course this conveniently ignores the fact that Federal law enforcement has no jurisdiction over child abuse. . . .

So determined has the administration been to derail these hearings that it was revealed last week that Treasury Secretary Rubin called Congressman Brewster requesting that he not ask questions that could embarrass the administration, and it was learned that the Justice Department is considering bringing up all of the guns from Mount Carmel to Washington just to give Mr. Schumer a convenient . . . publicity prop. . . .

[O]ne could logically ask, why go to all of this trouble if the administration has nothing to hide? . . .

Today I will be sending a letter, along with Cochairman Bill Zeliff to President Clinton asking him to order his staff to stop this mass public relations and damage control campaign. The American people deserve an opportunity to hear the unadulterated truth about what went wrong at Waco and who is responsible.

(Joint Hearings, part 1, pp. 684–86.)

177. Frank Gaffney, Jr., "Real 'Snafu' of the File Scandal," *Washington Times*, June 18, 1996, p. A12.

178. Rep. John Shadegg, Joint Hearings, part 2, p. 441, expanding on a point made by Rep. Steven Schiff. Ibid., p. 435.

179. Committee Report, p. 8.

180. Joint Hearings, part 1, p. 29.

181. Llewellyn Rockwell, Jr., "Waco Mission . . . Unaccomplished," *Washington Times,* August 10, 1995, p. A17.

182. Coauthor Blackman was an NRA employee assigned to the task force preparing for hearings to be held later on the Ruby Ridge incident. A third task force was assigned to prepare, along with various other interest groups (including the American Civil Liberties Union), for general hearings to be held on federal law enforcement abuses by a variety of federal law enforcement agencies, including the Immigration and Naturalization Service, the Customs Service, the Bureau of Indian Affairs, the Drug Enforcement Administration, as well as by BATF and the FBI.

183. Part of the problem may have been confusion due to the nature of the relationship of Prof. Fran Haga to the NRA, and the wording of Mrs. Sparks's questions, which were geared toward eliciting where Haga was employed. Joint Hearings, part 1, pp. 581–82. Haga was on vacation from her teaching job, and working as a volunteer for the NRA's task force dealing with Waco. She was not employed or paid by the NRA, except for living expenses while in the Washington, D.C., area.

184. Joint Hearings, part 1, p. 585.

185. Ibid., p. 591.

186. Ibid., p. 583.

187. Failure Analysis Associates, Inc. *Investigation of the April 19, 1993 Assault on the Mt. Carmel Center, Waco, Texas* (Menlo Park, Calif., July 1995), p. 1.

188. "The instances of the National Rifle Association providing valuable services to the subcommittee may have violated the law and the Rules of the House." Additional Views of Hon. Tom Lantos, Committee Report, p. 97.

While it is unusual for an advocacy group to hire a research or consulting firm to work directly for a committee, contracting a report specifically for committee hearings is not unusual. The law firm of Wilmer, Cutler & Pickering provided Handgun Control, Inc., with a legal analysis of S. 1030 for Hearings on "The Firearms Owner Protection Act," December 9 and 11, 1981, and February 8, 1982, the Committee on the Judiciary, United States Senate, 97th Cong., 1st and 2d sess. (Washington, D.C.: U.S. Government Printing Office, 1982), pp. 143–61.

Examples of private organizations helping committees arrange testimony abound. In the 1970s, the Equal Rights Amendment Extension hearings were accomplished because of the prodding, guidance, written statements, and questions for senators and representatives from such lobbying organizations as the National Organization for Women, Women's Equity Action League, the Women's Legal Defense Fund, the National Women's Party, and the National Federation of Business and Professional Women's Clubs, Inc.

The Children's Defense Fund conducted research, wrote testimony, questions and answers, and assisted and provided witnesses for Senate hearings on the civil rights of institutionalized persons in 1977. The Business Roundtable did it for hearings on Superfund. It is not uncommon for lobbyist/ lawyers to provide wording of both proposed legislation and legal explanations and defenses of it for a congressman to use as his own. (Personal communications to Blackman from lobbyists and congressional committee staffers.)

Sometimes lobbyists not only help with research, they help draft proposed legislation. During the 104th Congress, it was reported that bill sponsors and a group of lobbyists "worked side by side on the bill, inserting one provision after another to satisfy industry groups like the Chemical Manufacturers Association, companies like International Paper, and organizations of the cities and states covered by the law." John H. Cushman, Jr., "Lobbyists Helped the G.O.P. in Revising Clean Water Act," *New York Times*, March 22, 1995, pp. 1, C19; Stephen Engelberg, "Business Leaves the Lobby and Sits at Congress's Table," *New York Times*, March 31, 1995, pp. A1, A10; Micheal E. Kraft and Diana Wuertz, "Environmental Advocacy in the Corridors of Government," in *The Symbolic Earth: Discourse and Our Creation of the Environment*, ed. James G. Cantrill and Christine L. Oravec (Lexington: University Press of Kentucky, 1996), pp. 105–106. When environmental groups criticized the Republicans for letting lobbyists help them draft legislation, the Republicans correctly responded that the environmental groups themselves, which are also lobbies, had helped to draft legislation when the Democrats controlled Congress.

In a thorough academic study of interest group activity, Kay Kehman Schlozman and John T. Tierney report, based on interviews with a large sample of interest group leaders whose groups actively engaged in lobbying in Washington, D.C., that about 85 percent of Washington-based advocacy organizations help to draft legislation, and 92 percent present research results or technical information. *Organized Interests and American Democracy* (New York: Harper and Row, 1986), p. 150.

Certainly, outside groups have paid for research which could be used by friendly congressmen. For example, the Nuclear Energy Institute has supported research on public attitudes toward nuclear power; and the Edison Electric Power Institute for years had funded risk assessment research that documents the relatively low risks of relying on nuclear power as a power source. Private communication to Paul H. Blackman from environmental policy professor Michael E. Kraft.

"[L]egislators demand information to reduce uncertainty and lobbyists supply it. . . . The special role that interest groups play in the acquisition and transmission of information is recognized by representatives, lobbyists, and academics alike." John R. Wright, *Interest Groups and Congress: Lobbying, Contributions, and Influence* (Boston: Allyn Bacon, 1996), p. 88. For oversight of administrative agencies, congressional committees tend to rely on interest groups for complaints or criticisms in particular, and information in general. Joel Aberbach, *Keeping a Watchful Eye: The Politics of Congressional Oversight* (Washington, D.C.: Brookings, 1990).

And congressional committees tend to rely upon interest groups in preparing hearings, so that staff sometimes borrow ideas from interest groups. John Kingdon, *Agendas, Alternatives, and Public Policies,* 2d ed. (New York: HarperCollins, 1995), pp. 45–53. Lobbies encourage their "champions" on committees to encourage favorite witnesses to testify, and "a private organization will bring in grass roots witnesses to add freshness and variety to a committee hearing." Edward V. Schneier and Bertram Gross, *Legislative Strategy: Shaping Public Policy* (New York: St. Martin's, 1993), p. 163; Roger H.

Davidson and Walter J. Oleszek, *Congress and Its Members*, 5th ed. (Washington, D.C.: Congressional Quarterly Press, 1996).

What was unusual regarding the Waco hearings was all the attention to the fact that the NRA was acting like other lobbying organizations.

189.   Prior to the attempt by FaAA to study the firearms, the Chairman and Ranking Democratic member of the House Committee on Standards of Official Conduct, Nancy L. Johnson and Jim Mc-Dermott, wrote to a subcommittee staff member, Robert B. Charles, June 16, 1995: "You have also obtained permission for employees of Failure Analysis Associates, Inc. to examine the evidence. This organization has been retained by an advocacy group and no subcommittee funds will be used by/for this company . . . the Committee finds no legal or ethical objections to your allowing Failure Analysis Associates, Inc., to examine the physical evidence under the control of the Department of Justice."

190.   Part of the FaAA report could have proved useful to the Democratic defenders of the FBI. FaAA found nothing inconsistent with the allegation that the Branch Davidians started the fire. FaAA also found that the methylene chloride used as a carrier for the CS was not of sufficient quantity to have played a role in the ignition or spread of the fire. Failure Analysis Associates, *Investigation of the April 19, 1993 Assault on the Mt. Carmel Center.*

191.   The White House took advantage of HCI expertise on the NRA by employing an outside consultant with ties to HCI, John Podesta.

At the same time, one progun group (Gun Owners of America) was preparing to publish a book on Waco by Carol Moore, *The Davidian Massacre,* and an NRA employee (Blackman) had coauthored a monograph on the issue (an earlier version of this book) which was distributed to Congress at the time of the hearings.

In addition, NRA staff attorneys had assisted the Branch Davidians' attorneys, particularly in efforts to explain the technicalities of federal firearms laws.

192.   Committee Report, p. 9.

193.   Afternoon press briefing, July 20, 1995. Nicholas von Hoffman observed that "the NRA has had as much to do with these hearings as the NRA's enemies had to do with the previous hearings . . . in which gov-love came out on top . . . the NRA wants to impose gun control on the government." "America's Sects Problem: Demonizing the Davidians and Other Oddball Religionists," *Washington Post,* July 30, 1995.

194.   To demonize the NRA requires attacking as extremist and out of the mainstream an organization generally supported by gun owners, who, in turn, constitute about half of American households. Gary Kleck, "Bad Data and the 'Evil Empire': Interpreting Poll Data on Gun Control," *Violence and Victims* 8 (1993): 367–75.

195.   Joint Hearings, part 1, p. 12.

196.   Ibid., p. 25.

197.   A less successful effort came later when Representative Conyers sought "yes or no" answers as to whether witnesses critical of the government had been contacted by the NRA. Koresh's gun dealer, Henry McMahon, replied, "Yes, sir. Those were the only people that wished to hear the truth." Joint Hearings, part 1, 197.

198.   Joint Hearings, part 1, pp. 282–83. Representative Lantos's denunciation of the NRA was followed by similar denunciations by Representatives Schumer and Conyers. Koresh might have found the demonization of the NRA amusing. According to undercover agent Rodriguez: "He [Koresh] denounced the Government many times, denounced the NRA, called it as corrupt as our Government." Joint Hearings, part 1, p. 802.

199.   Joint Hearings, part 1, p. 288.

200.   Ibid., p. 294.

201.   Ibid., p. 506.

202.   Ibid., p. 498.

203.   Ibid., p. 505.

204.   Ibid., p. 688.

205.   Joint Hearings, part 2, p. 431. Representative Schumer did not get back to the witness's contacts with the NRA. Professor Stone's report to the Justice Department preceded any contacts by the NRA. As soon as his report was announced to the press, Blackman wrote to him requesting a copy

of his report. The request was ignored. The attack on the Republicans for holding the hearings culminated on the final day with Representative Lantos asserting, "I must say that, in part, these hearings are eerily reminiscent of the McCarthy hearings or the 1950's." Joint Hearings, part 3, p. 377.

The same day, Rep. Louise Slaughter called for the Democratic attorney general to investigate how the Republican Congress held its hearing into how the Democratic Justice Department operated.

> [I]t seems to me that the Constitution and the rules under this House are very clear on how we conduct hearings. . . . We have not, as you know, had an opportunity on our side to call a lot of witnesses we would like to hear from. If you have jurisdiction over this, I would like to know . . . if you plan to look into it, what kind of request you need. And certainly I would like to have your opinion on that, because I think in the history of this country and of this Congress that this is a very serious breach that I don't ever want to see happen again in any hearing at any time.

The attorney general assured Representative Slaughter that she was sure Congress would take any actions "appropriate under the rules of this great institution." Joint Hearings, part 3, p. 392.

206. Ibid., p. 523. Similarly, Rep. Peter Blute (R-Mass.), while criticizing the administration, insisted "the NRA is not a friend of mine. I have a zero rating from them." Ibid., p. 441.

207. Interestingly, Representative Schumer expressly declined to ask religious experts about the credibility of Kiri Jewell's testimony. Joint Hearings, part 2, p. 151. It is unclear whether Schumer feared that the experts would find reasons in Koresh's theology for doubting her story, or whether Schumer thought that the religious experts, like the attorneys DeGuerin and Zimmermann, would doubt Kiri Jewell's veracity, or whether Schumer simply wanted to talk about other topics. Some of Koresh's religious teachings could be seen as inconsistent with Miss Jewell's testimony. Koresh denounced lesbianism "because it's nonproductive" (Negot. Tape no. 50, March 4–5), something which would also be true of heterosexual relations with a prepubescent girl. On the other hand, Koresh was fully able to modify his religion to let him indulge in his personal temptations. Koresh also recalled having been described as a child molester because of his marrying twelve-year-old Michelle Jones, a relationship he denied having when she was that young. Negot. Tape no. 48, March 4. Steve Schneider confirmed that Koresh had a relationship with a fourteen-year-old, but denied any younger wives. Justice Report, p. 222. While Dr. Tabor was uncertain about Miss Jewell's story, he was more concerned with explaining that Koresh did not have dictatorial control over his followers. Joint Hearings, part 2, pp. 162–63.

208. Response to questioning by Representative Zeliff, Joint Hearings, part 1, p. 187.

209. James Bovard, "Hear No Evil," *American Spectator* (January 1996): 44. The Davidians expressed some concern about her father influencing her public statements. Sherri Jewell, through Schneider, requested a copy of a television show on which Kiri was reported to have appeared, because Sherri was "very curious to know . . . what the ex-husband pumped into her mind and what she had to say." Negot. Tape no. 118, March 12. Marc Breault was correctly seen by the Davidians as being behind Kiri's father's legal efforts to gain custody of her. Negot. Tape no. 96, March 9.

210. Remarks by the president at Federal Law Enforcement Meeting, Blair House, July 20, 1995. The sex crime was perpetrated in a motel room, not at the Mount Carmel Center. Different persons might evaluate differently the "moral equivalency" of statutory sexual assault and staging a needless violent raid on a home with the expectation, according to military personnel involved with planning for the raid, "medical personnel potentially would be treating gunshot wounds of children." Committee Report, p. 40.

211. While most news media decline to identify victims of sexual assaults, Kiri Jewell's coming forward to so public a forum was understood to waive any such privacy. With her name and face all over the nation's print and broadcast media on July 19–20, one television news giant, CNN, stuck with tradition and refused to identify her.

212. Joint Hearings, part 1, p. 297.

213. Ibid., p. 329.

214. James Bovard, "Hear No Evil," *American Spectator* (January 1996): 44.

215. E.g., Vance McLaughlin, "Operation Trojan Horse: The Effects of Access to Information," a paper delivered at the annual meeting of the Academy of Criminal Justice Sciences, Boston, March 1995.

216. The only persons who attempted to make a rational response were some BATF commanders; they said that the Davidians did not fire on the cattle trailers because the Davidians thought trailers really were just a farmer's trailers which unintentionally strayed onto private property. The Davidians, expecting an invading force of federal agents, would have to be extremely stupid to believe that the trailers, at the head of a long convoy of BATF vehicles, just happened to have made a wrong turn at the same time the BATF invasion force was coming.

217. In his effort to demonize Koresh, Representative Taylor even harkened back to the Cold War: "So you are talking about a group that was supposed to be a religious group, has more firepower than the Vietcong who was supplied by the Soviet Union and the Communist Chinese." BATF Agent Buford: "That is correct." Joint Hearings, part 1, p. 459. Representative Taylor may have simply meant that Buford's service in Vietnam may have included ambushes by enemy who outgunned Buford and his colleagues at particular moments. Overall, of course, Koresh was estimated to have hundreds of firearms, dozens of which were said to be capable of automatic fire. The Viet Cong, at their peak, numbered over 75,000 men under arms, including some automatic rifles and semiautomatic rifles, but also mortars and other artillery. Office of the Assistant Secretary of Defense (Systems Analysis), *The Vietnam Conflict, 1965–1972 (Selected Charts)* (February 1973); personal communication from former military visitors to South Vietnam and vacationers in the "Hanoi Hilton" and from the U.S. Army Center of Military History.

218. A jury might have found Koresh and some of his lieutenants guilty of murder, or the jury might have acquitted them on grounds of self-defense, as the jury did for the Branch Davidians who were put on trial. (The Branch Davidians were convicted of aiding and abetting manslaughter, but the judge did not allow the jury to consider self-defense in relation to this charge.)

219. Committee Report, p. 15. The Davidians just saw the exposé as more of the work of Marc Breault, and said, "Here we go again." Negot. Tape no. 56, March 5. Koresh recalled lots of prior negative publicity, including three reports the prior year they were planning a mass suicide, and allegations that he was a child molester. Negot. Tape no. 48, March 4. Joyce Sparks recalled one rumor of mass suicide, and Koresh's denial. Joint Hearings, part 1, p. 578.

220. Negot. Tape no. 141, March 20.

221. Joint Hearings, part 1, p. 11.

222. Although virtually everyone agreed it would have been best to arrest Koresh away from the Mount Carmel Center, Representative Schumer insisted, instead, that BATF should not have been expected to attempt to arrest him elsewhere, since there was, in addition to an arrest warrant for Koresh, a search warrant for the Mount Carmel Center: "you don't usually go serve somebody or arrest them off the premises, since you don't want . . . the place to have destroyed the evidence. . . . The proper procedure when you do a search warrant is to serve it at the place you're searching. . . . Not when someone's jogging or getting ice cream or visiting another place. You serve the place." He elicited agreement from Robert Deschamps of the National District Attorneys Association. Joint Hearings, part 1, p. 173. When Steve Schneider's and David Koresh's attorneys testified that they had seen the front door to the house, and that most of the bullets appeared to be coming in from the outside, the attorneys viewed the bullet patterns as evidence that BATF had fired first. Representative Schumer defended BATF by suggesting that of course most of the shots came from the outside, BATF was responding to shooting from inside. The reply, however, would have meant that the federal agents were unlawfully firing at a closed door, into a house where innocent women and children were known to be, without having any idea whether their guns were aimed at the suspects or the innocents. Joint Hearings, part 2, pp. 32, 44; part 3, p. 88.

223. Joint Hearings, part 2, p. 3. Reportedly, however, the jury did not decide which side fired first because the evidence was in conflict. Jack Zimmermann, Joint Hearings, part 2, p. 29.

224. Regarding the conflict—which some congressmen simply pretended did not exist—about who fired the first shots, Representative Schumer defended BATF: "If you really back up law enforcement, you don't say that two defense lawyers who were not on the scene are more credible than 20 law enforcement officers and several reporters who were on the scene." Representative Schumer, Joint Hearings, part 2, p. 470. In one sense, of course, the defense lawyers were on the scene: No law enforcement officer was able to inspect the inside of the Mount Carmel Center prior to its destruction by fire. And the reporters to whom Representative Schumer was referring were kept hundreds of yards

from the raid. They were not "on the scene" in the sense of being able to determine who fired the first shots on February 28, 1993.

225. David Upshall, accompanied by Paul Rice, Joint Hearings, part 2, p. 389. Rep. Steve Schiff observed that when he asked the British experts

> upon whom Mr. Schumer said we should place the most reliance, to their knowledge has the British Government . . . ever come up with a plan to insert CS gas into a building where they knew were children and infants, they both said no. So I think it is extremely interesting that the experts that we are told are the superior experts on this subject, can't cite an example where their Government did exactly what our Government did in this particular situation.

(Joint Hearings, part 2, p. 471.)

226. Joint Hearings, part 2, p. 330. Rep. Mark Edward Souder quickly got the Los Angeles police officer testifying on the safety of CS also to admit that none of the experiences involved children in a confined area. Ibid., p. 331.

227. Joint Hearings, part 2, p. 398. He noted specifically the irrelevance of winds in the unventilated, windowless concrete room, where all the mothers and children were.

228. Anthony Betz, Joint Hearings, part 2, pp. 473–74. Representative Schumer attempted further to undermine such attacks on CS the next morning by summarizing the testimony:

> CS teargas is what I am attempting to call it, because CS gas has sort of a nefarious ring to it, and this is the mildest form of teargas table [?] available. . . . Anyway, we had two of the world's experts, who spent their lives studying this issue. They come from Britain. And they said unequivocally, that the gas was not harmful the way it was used for children. . . . If you look at the autopsy reports, . . . there is not a trace found of this gas on any of them. . . .
>
> Then we had two other people. One was a professor of chemistry at a 2-year college in eastern Utah, who has done no papers, has no expertise, on this kind of gas. The other was an employee in the drinking water section of EPA, who also had no expertise, and they of course painted more dramatic and dire pictures about what the gas is like. . . . And then there was a fifth witness, who was a very credible witness, Dr. Stone, he is not an expert on CS gas. . . . But the four witnesses who were experts on the gas were not comparable at all.

(Representative Schumer, Joint Hearings, part 2, pp. 468–69.) It is difficult to reconcile such statements with others: "CS and CR are both more potent than either DM or CN. . . . Consideration must be given to the effects of these agents on the very young, the elderly, and the infirm. These uncertainties highlight the need to understand fully the possible toxic effects of riot-control agents, just as one would investigate any pharmacologic drug or workplace hazard." Satu M. Somani, *Chemical Warfare Agents* (San Diego: Academic Press, 1992), p. 277. CS is not mild. Because CS is so potent, the effective dose is much less than the lethal dose. Thus, CS is relatively safe, because there is generally little risk of hitting a person with a lethal dose while merely attempting to give him an effective dose. In Waco, however, the total amount of CS used was close to the lethal dose.

229. Jeffrey Jamar, Joint Hearings, part 2, p. 564.

230. Joint Hearings, part 2, p. 455.

231. Justice Report, pp. 326–28.

232. Carol Moore, *The Davidian Massacre,* "Waco Hearings Update," July 25, 1995, e-mail broadcast.

233. One example of this is the dramatic change in attitude of Democratic Rep. John Conyers between the April 1993 and the July 1995 hearings. He was the congressman most critical of the attorney general during the first set of hearings, but could only claim in the later set that his earlier criticism helped to justify his "great reservations about the purpose of these hearings," suggesting they should be about the NRA, the militias, and other groups, not "the law enforcement agencies and Waco." Joint Hearings, part 1, pp. 21–22.

234. Joint Hearings, part 1, p. 509 (reprinting Altman memo, and containing Bentsen quote).

235. Joint Hearings, part 1, p. 510; Reps. Bill Zeliff and Bill McCollum, *Summary of the Find-*

ings and Recommendations on Waco as Proposed to Members of the Committee on Government Reform and Oversight and the Committee on the Judiciary, July 1996. While BATF is in the Treasury Department, supervision of BATF has not traditionally been seen as an important duty by previous Treasury Secretaries. It was unfair to attack Secretary Bentsen for following the policies of his predecessors, including the Treasury Secretaries under Presidents Reagan and Bush who had stood idle while BATF degenerated to its current state. Committee Report, p. 16.

236. Joint Hearings, part 3, pp. 20–21.

237. Janet Reno, "Reno: 'Koresh Chose Death,'" *USA Today,* August 1, 1995, p. 11A. Reno also argued that she risked criticism regardless of what she did: "We will never know whether waiting longer would have produced a different result. Had Koresh fulfilled his prophecies by later initiating a sudden and violent finish, such as the Davidians had rehearsed, I would justifiably be asked why I had not done something sooner." It is true that high-profile office holders are often criticized no matter what they do. But if the Davidians had killed themselves while the siege dragged on, the deaths would not have been directly provoked by employees under her command, as the deaths of April 19 were. Second, she could have pointed out that many of the behavioral experts and negotiators advised a waiting game as the less risky path.

238. Paul Greenberg, "Report from the General of Waco," *Washington Times,* August 7, 1995, p. A17.

239. Joint Hearings, part 3, p. 422.

240. Janet Reno, responding to Representative Chabot, Joint Hearings, part 3, p. 456. Representative Chabot was remembering prior testimony; Attorney General Reno said she would check it out. Representative Chabot added "we should probably follow up." Joint Hearings, part 3, pp. 455–56. The published hearing transcripts, produced fourteen months later, state: "[Information not received by time of printing.]" Joint Hearings, part 3, p. 456.

241. James Bovard, "Hear No Evil," *American Spectator* (January 1996): 44. General Reno interrupted her testimony to interject, "don't laugh at me please." Joint Hearings, part 3, p. 408.

242. Samuel Francis, "Why Was the Waco Inquiry a Washout?" *Washington Times,* August 11, 1995.

243. Committee Report, pp. 3, 14, 16–17.

244. Ibid., pp. 75–81. Rep. Ileana Ros-Lehtinen (R-Fla.) issued additional views indicating agreement with the Waco-specific conclusions of the report but praising Janet Reno for her career prior to and since Waco. Committee Report, p. 91.

245. Committee Report, p. 78.

246. Ibid., p. 76. The dissenting Democrats responded that there was no evidence the negotiators "were adversely affected by physical or emotional fatigue." Dissenting views, p. 105.

247. Committee Report, pp. 14, 18, 26, 29.

248. Ibid., p. 87. Such statements were disputed in the Submission by Hon. Steven Schiff, Committee Report, pp. 94–95.

249. Ibid., p. 14.

250. Bill McCollum, "Riveting Portrait of a Grim Disaster," *Washington Times,* July 26, 1996, p. A15.

251. In her testimony, Reno insisted that but for the winds, the accelerated gas attack would have caused the Davidian women and children to leave the building. Her testimony ignores the fact that no winds were blowing into the unventilated concrete room in the middle of the building, where all the women and children were.

252. She had offered it immediately after the April 19, 1993, assault and fire.

253. See the discussion of the FBI and terrorism legislation in chapter 6.

254. James Bovard, "Hear No Evil," *American Spectator* (January 1996):43.

255. The hearing witnesses included an African-American militia member denying the militia were racist, and Senator Specter holding up a document which he believed was suggestive of Nazi sympathies in some of the militia. The document turned out to be from the fiercely anti-Nazi and progun Jews for the Preservation of Firearms Ownership, a national lobbying and educational organization which is not a militia. JPFO materials sometimes contain swastikas because JPFO believes that gun control laws are Nazi laws, either because the laws are derivative of the Nazi gun laws, or because the laws reflect the same desire to leave the people defenseless against the government.

256. For example, after Deputy Marshal Degan was killed, three of the remaining marshals stayed at Ruby Ridge, ostensibly with the body. In the course of the day, the Weavers and Kevin Harris came, loudly wailing and cursing, to retrieve Sammy Weaver's body. Had the marshals actually been where they said they were, the Weavers and Harris could easily have been arrested, either without any further violence, or with no further harm to federal law enforcement. The marshals' story, however, was unquestioned.

257. The other three were William D. Gore, special agent-in-charge of the Seattle FBI office, who provided management assistance to Eugene Glenn; Stephen P. McGavin, deputy commander of the HRT; and Lester B. Hazen, sniper/observer coordinator.

258. James Bovard, "Hear No Evil," p. 44.

259. John Kleinig, *The Ethics of Policing* (Cambridge, England: Cambridge University Press, 1996), p. 78.

260. Freedom of Information Foundation Conference, "Mount Carmel: What Should the Public Know?" (Austin: September 10–11, 1993), p. 7, quoted in James T. Richardson, "Manufacturing Consent about Koresh: A Structural Analysis of the Role of the Media in the Waco Tragedy," in *Armageddon in Waco: Critical Perspectives on the Branch Davidian Conflict,* ed. Stuart A. Wright (Chicago: University of Chicago Press, 1995), p. 165.

261. Moore, *The Davidian Massacre,* p. 236.

262. Steve Schneider, Negot. Tape no. 132, March 18–19.

263. Negot. Tape no. 40, March 4.

264. Negot. Tape no. 67, March 6.

265. Negot. Tape no. 73, March 6.

266. Negot. Tape no. 66, March 6. Steve Schneider asked an FBI negotiator, "Does it bother you in any degree at all that the FBI and/or the government can control and have such power over the press . . . ? . . . I'm talking about how they've not been allowed to cover the story and they're all basically saying the same thing." Negot. Tape no. 132, March 18–19.

267. Negot. Tape no. 62, March 5–6.

268. Victoria Loe, "Koresh Threatens in Letter to Smite His Enemies, Agents Say," *Dallas Morning News,* April 11, 1993.

269. William P. Cheshire, "Looking beyond the Waco Smoke," *Arizona Republican,* August 22, 1993. A Pensacola television station thought an interview with Koresh's gun dealer, in which he repeated over and over that Koresh would have let BATF visit the compound peacefully and without a warrant, was headline-making news. And so the show "Lawline" announced that there were other media filming the show behind their regular cameras, and that the station was planning to send tapes of the show to major media outlets around the nation, certain that the media and Congress would be interested in pursuing the investigation. The April 21, 1993, program—entitled "Fiasco in Waco"—has remained unknown to most of the American public. If the news media received copies of a tape providing important evidence that no raid was needed, no lives had to be lost, they ignored them.

270. David McLemore, "Cryptic Sign at Compound Asks for Help," *Dallas Morning News,* March 10, 1993.

271. Three exceptions were the *New York Times,* the *Wall Street Journal,* and the *Washington Times.*

272. While there were occasional racist and lewd activities at the Good O' Boys Roundups, the racist incidents were few and clearly violative of the rules of the organizers of the events. The sexual shenanigans were mostly puerile incidents of exposure of males, primarily with other males, with improper behavior toward females largely limited to the sorts which might occur at a singles bar. And BATF personnel were not as responsible as some other agencies for any racist or sexual improprieties which took place at the rural weekend camping parties. Michael R. Bromwich, *Allegations of Racial and Criminal Misconduct at the Good O' Boy [sic] Roundup* (Washington, D.C.: Office of the Inspector General, U.S. Department of Justice, March 1996); Department of the Treasury, *Good O' Boys Roundup Policy Review* (Washington, D.C.: U.S. Government Printing Office, April 1996).

273. NRA Research Coordinator Blackman began writing letters under the pen name Theodore H. Fiddleman in the early 1980s, as a way to express views on controversial issues without involving his employer. (The NRA does not take policy stands on issues unrelated to Second Amendment and the rest of the Bill of Rights.) The pseudonym was discovered, with the aid of some Johns Hopkins University researchers, by the *Journal of the American Medical Association (JAMA)* in January 1995,

regarding a letter that Fiddleman/Blackman wrote on the tobacco issue. (Tobacco regulation is one of the many issues on which the NRA takes no stand; besides being outside the scope of NRA's charter, controversial non-gun issues such as tobacco inevitably have many NRA members with passionate stands on both sides of the issue. Coming down on one side or the other would unnecessarily alienate members.) Having discovered that Fiddleman was really Blackman, *JAMA* promptly notified the *Washington Post*. The *Post* did not deem the fact newsworthy for six months, until the Joint Subcommittee hearings were under way. A little while after "breaking" the Fiddleman scandal, the *Washington Post* again made "news" out of something half a year old. An August 1, 1995, story reported a January 27, 1995, letter from Speaker Newt Gingrich to NRA leader Tanya Metaksa in which Gingrich promised no gun control legislation would move in the House of Representatives. "A copy of the 'Dear Tanya' note was obtained by The Washington Post." George Lardner, Jr., "Gingrich Promised NRA No Gun Control Legislation," *Washington Post*, August 1, 1995. While the article left the impression that a *Post* reporter had uncovered secret correspondence, the Gingrich letter had been posted on the NRA's world-wide web site since January, and repeatedly cited by NRA spokesmen in subsequent months. The *Post*'s "discovery" of the letter while the Waco hearings were in progress showed that the *Post* was used, perhaps unwittingly, by persons who had an interest in changing the focus of news coverage from the federal law enforcement misconduct and onto the NRA.

Fiddleman and Kopel had coauthored three newspaper op-eds on Waco in 1993. One editorial critiqued the original warrant; one criticized the Treasury Report; and one criticized the Department of Justice Report. None of these articles were consistent with NRA policy, since NRA Waco policy during 1993 was limited to calling for further investigation.

It may seem surprising to some that NRA had such a timid policy on Waco during 1993, but one should remember the political context. The gun prohibition movement was at the peak of its strength in Washington. NRA leadership correctly recognized that it would be impossible to defeat the Brady Bill, and that defeating the "assault weapon" ban would take every available resource. (The ban eventually passed the House of Representatives 216–214, after the White House also threw in the kitchen sink in its lobbying efforts.) For good or ill, the NRA leadership had made a determination that Waco was not going to be a major part of the NRA's agenda.

But Waco was, of course, a very important part of Blackman's personal agenda. After all, that is why he wrote a book about it. Using the Fiddleman pen name gave Blackman a chance to speak out on an issue that was extremely important to him personally, but without involving his employer. Fiddleman's letters were written without the knowledge or consent of his supervisors, and thus "Fiddleman" did not need to get his letters to the editor approved in advance by the NRA bureaucracy. Even after 1993, Fiddleman continued not only to write on subjects foreign to the NRA, but to contradict NRA policy. His final letter, for example, opined that a congressional investigation of what the federal government had done at Waco was justified, but that similar hearings into the militias would threaten First Amendment rights; this position was contrary to NRA policy that Congress should hold hearings on the militias.

The Fiddleman letters, of course, meant an expert on the gun issue was writing progun views without his affiliation being announced, but was substantively no different from private citizens writing views with the expert assistance of public-interest groups. Handgun Control, Inc.; U.S. Term Limits; the NRA; and many other public-interest groups provide their activists with prewritten "letters to the editor," with the suggestion that members modify the prewritten letters for their local newspapers. Yet the *Washington Post* has never found such an ordinary practice to be worth a front-page story researched by three reporters.

The use of pen names for a certain amount of anonymity has been common in American letters-to-the-editor since colonial days. If one reads the pro and con articles written during the debate over ratification of the Constitution, one finds pervasive use of pen names. The Federalist Papers (written by James Madison, Alexander Hamilton, and John Jay) were newspaper op-eds published under the pen name "Publius." Authors on the other side of the issue took names such as "A Federal Farmer" (probably Richard Henry Lee). One of the best-known political novels in American history (*Democracy*) was written anonymously, the moral equivalent of a pen name.

Blackman prides himself that all purportedly factual statements in his letters—except for the name Theodore Fiddleman, to which he is apparently the only American claimant—could be documented.

The following month, after breaking the Fiddleman scandal, the *Washington Post* did a profile on media critic Reed Irvine. The fact that Irvine often writes letters-to-the-editor under pseudonyms was revealed in a parenthetical sentence fragment in the middle of a long article; Irvine reportedly writes hundreds or thousands of letters. Irvine's pseudonyms were presented as barely worth mentioning. Perhaps if Blackman had worked for any organization other than the *Washington Post*'s public enemy number one, his pen name would not have been worth a front-page story. To be sure, the exposure of the author of the best-selling *Primary Colors*, whose identity had been the subject of media speculation for months, appeared on page one of the *Washington Post*, but below the fold. July 18, 1996. The exposure of the author of letters to the editor appeared above the fold. July 25, 1995.

274. Jack Zimmermann and Dick DeGuerin, part 2, pp. 19–141 (feeling of betrayal noted on p. 100).

275. Editorial, "Waco's Unlearned Lessons," *New York Times*, July 31, 1995; Samuel Francis, "Waco Inquisition Turned into El Floppo Grande," *Arizona Republic*, August 17, 1995, p. B5; Llewellyn Rockwell, Jr., "Waco Mission . . . Unaccomplished," *Washington Times*, August 10, 1995 (featuring a cartoon showing Janet Reno wearing an "I survived Waco" t-shirt); Paul Greenberg, "Report from the General of Waco," *Washington Times,* August 7, 1995, p. A17.

276. E.g., James Bovard, "Hearings Show Waco Defense is Wacky," *Wall Street Journal*, August 2, 1995, p. A10; "Clues to a Collapsing Coverup on Waco?" *Washington Times,* August 16, 1995, p. A15.

277. Print media coverage was more extensive and less progovernment; the weakest television coverage was from NBC news, which devoted about half as much air time to the issue as did ABC and CBS.

278. "Watching the Waco Hearings," *Media Monitor* (Center for Media and Public Affairs, Washington) (July/August 1995).

279. Richard Leiby, "'Frontline': What Went Wrong at Waco?" *Washington Post*, October 17, 1995.

280. Lee Hancock, "Tragic Spectacle," *Dallas Morning News*, August 29, 1993. For George Roden, see prologue and chapter 2.

281. Sue Anne Pressley, "Waco, the Rise of a Symbol," *Washington Post*, May 28, 1995.

282. Sam Howe Verhovek, "On Anniversary, Sect's Members Commemorate a Fatal Fire," *New York Times*, April 20, 1996, p. A1.

283. Ibid. For biblical references to myrtle trees, see Nehemiah 8:15 ("myrtle branches"); Isaiah 41:19; Isaiah 55:13 ("the myrtle tree: and it shall be to the LORD for a name, for an everlasting sign *that* shall not not be cut off."); Zechariah 1:8, 1:10, 1:11 ("behold a man riding upon a red horse" [note Rev. 6:4], and he stood among the myrtle trees. . . . And the man that stood among the myrtle trees answered and said, These *are they* whom the LORD hath sent to walk to and fro through the earth. And they answered the angel of the LORD that stood among the myrtle trees, and said, We have walked to and fro through the earth, and, behold, all the earth sitteth still, and is at rest.")

284. Associated Press, October 15, 1994, 22:04 EDT, V0047.

285. Wayne Laugesen, "Longmont Man Works to Resurrect Branch Davidians," *Boulder Weekly*, available at http://www.tesser.com/bwoe/waco/story.html.

286. "And I will bring forth a seed out of Jacob and out of Judah an inheritor of my mountains [the Branch Davidian message]: and mine elect shall inherit it, and my servants shall dwell there." Quoted in Ron Cole, "Waco: History Repeats Itself," *Boulder Weekly*, January 11, 1996, p. 9. Cole states that he was thrown out of the Branch Davidian Association for telling embarrassing truths about David Koresh. Ron Cole, "Davidian Tells Truth about Waco," *Boulder Weekly*, July 27, 1995, p. 8.

287. Psalm 89: . . . I have made a covenant with my chosen, I have sworn unto David my servant, Thy seed will I establish for ever, and build up thy throne to all generations. . . . I have found David my servant: with my holy oil have I anointed him: With whom my hand shall be established: mine arm also shall strengthen him. The enemy shall not exact upon him: nor the son of wickedness afflict him. And I will beat down his foes before his face, and plague them that hate him. But my faithfulness and my mercy *shall be* with him: and in my name shall his horn be exalted. I will set his hand also in the sea, and his right hand in the rivers. He shall cry unto me, Thou *art* my father, my God, and the rock of my salvation. Also I will make him *my* firstborn, higher than the kings of the earth. My mercy will I keep for him for evermore, and my covenant shall stand fast with him. His seed also will I make *to endure* for ever, and his throne as the days of heaven. If his children forsake my law, and walk not in my judgments; If they break my statutes, and keep not my commandments; Then will I visit their transgression with the rod, and their iniquity with stripes. Nevertheless my lovingkindness will I

not utterly take from him, nor suffer my faithfulness to fail. My covenant will I not break, nor alter the thing that is gone out of my lips. Once have I sworn by my holiness that I will not lie unto David. His seed shall endure for ever, and his throne as the sun before me. It shall be established for ever as the moon, and *as* a faithful witness in heaven. Selah. But thou hast cast off and abhorred, thou hast been wroth with thine anointed. Thou hast made void the covenant of thy servant: thou hast profaned his crown by *casting it* to the ground. Thou hast broken down all his hedges; thou hast brought his strong holds to ruin. All that pass by the way spoil him: he is a reproach to his neighbours. Thou hast set up the right hand of his adversaries: thou hast made all his enemies to rejoice. Thou hast also turned the edge of his sword, and hast not made him to stand in the battle. Thou hast made his glory to cease, and cast his throne down to the ground. The days of his youth hast thou shortened: thou hast covered him with shame. Selah. How long, LORD? wilt thou hide thyself for ever? shall thy wrath burn like fire? Remember how short my time is: wherefore hast thou made all men in vain? . . . LORD, where *are* thy former lovingkindnesses, *which* thou swarest unto David in thy truth? Remember, LORD, the reproach of thy servants; *how* I do bear in my bosom *the reproach of* all the mighty people; Wherewith thine enemies have reproached, O LORD; wherewith they have reproached the footsteps of thine anointed.

288. Wayne Laugesen, "Waco II," *Boulder Weekly*, December 14, 1995, p. 11.

289. The Chosen Vessel's work is found at *Hidden Manna* at http://www.sevenseals.com. Fagan and Castillo writings are available at http://www.ime.net/~mswett/.

290. James D. Tabor and Eugene V. Gallagher, *Why Waco? Cults and the Battle for Religious Freedom in America* (Berkeley: University of California Press, 1995), p. 79. For Marc Breault's discussion of various prophecies in Daniel as relating to Koresh's expected return, see The Research Center web page at http://www.ime.net/~mswett.

291. Sue Anne Pressley, "Waco, the Rise of a Symbol," *Washington Post*, May 28, 1995.

292. Livingstone Fagan, *Mt. Carmel: The Unseen Reality Part 2*, p. 8. Available from The Research Center, http://www.ime.net/~mswett.

293. Jerry Seper, "FBI Agents Likely to Face Charges in Deadly Siege," *Washington Times*, December 14, 1993, p. A14.

294. There was a separate mini-controversy about why the tape had been released in the first place. Oliver "Buck" Revell, a senior FBI official was then the special agent in charge of the Dallas FBI office, was revealed as the person who had released the tape. Lee Hancock, "Waco Dispatch Chief Assails 911 Tape of Cult Talks," *Dallas Morning News*, June 15, 1993; Lee Hancock, "FBI Set to Reveal Today Whether Release of Koresh Tape Violated Policy," *Dallas Morning News*, June 17, 1993; Lee Hancock, "FBI Agent Criticized for Releasing Cult 911 Tape," *Dallas Morning News*, June 30, 1993 ("The Justice Department letter does not address whether the committee's investigators were told that the tape had been edited. . . ."); Lee Hancock, "12 Branch Davidians Indicted in February 28 Shootout," *Dallas Morning News*, August 7, 1993.

295. Jim Jorgensen, "Special Prosecutor Needed for ATF," *The Agent* (March 1996): 3.

296. Congressional Record, August 2, 1995, p. H8180.

297. Paul Craig Roberts, "Special Inquiry in Order?" *Washington Times*, March 3, 1994.

298. Former BATF Director Stephen Higgins, while denying that any shots were fired from helicopters, has stated that if the helicopters did fire on the building, murder charges should be filed. Stephen Higgins, appearing on "Mitchells in the Morning," *National Empowerment Television*, May 31, 1995.

299. 18 U.S.C. § 924(c)(1).

300. 18 U.S.C. § 2332a.

301. Virginia Ratifying Convention, June 16, 1788; *Elliot's Debates*, vol. III, p. 431; David E. Young, ed., *The Origin of the Second Amendment* (Ontonagon, Mich.: Golden Oak Books, 1991), p. 433.

6

Policy Lessons

No free man shall be taken or imprisoned or dispossessed, or outlawed, or banished, or in any way destroyed, nor will we go upon him, nor send upon him, except by the legal judgement of his peers or by the law of the land.

Magna Carta, para. 39[1]

Let us set for ourselves a standard so high that it will be a glory to live up to it, and then let us live up to it and add a new laurel to the crown of America.

Woodrow Wilson

We can do better.

John F. Kennedy

The United States can do much better. The National Association of Treasury Agents (NATA) is a voluntary organization of Treasury Department law enforcement employees, including BATF agents. NATA has often been highly critical of BATF management, including management's performance at Waco. NATA offers its members a jacket patch which says "Never Again. 2-28-93. Waco, Texas." The American people have the power to make "Never Again" a reality. They have the power to make sure that federal law enforcement lives by the first principles of American government, by the commands of the Constitution, and by the spirit of Magna Carta. When we restore law enforcement to full lawful control, then we will not only protect the lives and property of American citizens, we will restore America to its rightful place as exemplar of ordered liberty to the peoples of the world.

Attorney General Reno told the ABC News program "20/20" in July 1993 that she would approve the same actions, that there is nothing she would do differently,[2] although the next year she stated, "Obviously, I saw what happened, and knowing what had happened, I wouldn't do it again."[3] Yet she continued to maintain that nobody in the government had done anything wrong: "There is much to be angry about when we talk about Waco—and the government's conduct is not the reason. David Koresh is the reason."[4]

While Reno may perhaps lack 20/20 hindsight, others in the FBI and BATF were appalled at the actions undertaken by their organizations. That is one of the reasons information came out, but it is also one of the reasons much of the information first came from unusual sources, as agents spoke (or leaked) to friends who write for conservative publications or the gun press, or who work for progun organizations.[5]

The reluctance of many law enforcement professionals to approve of unconstitutionally aggressive federal law enforcement was also demonstrated at Ruby Ridge. There, the SWAT team from Denver interpreted the modified rules of engagement as being "If you see 'em, shoot 'em." Their response was, "You've got to be kidding," and they decided to ignore the unconstitutional order, and instead to abide by the traditional, and constitutional, FBI rules on the use of deadly force.[6] Indeed, when HRT sniper Lon Horiuchi started shooting at the Weavers and Kevin Harris, he expected the rest of the FBI snipers to open fire too. Not one of them did, although one was preparing to.

MORE GUN CONTROL?

In *Armageddon at Waco*, an excellent collection of scholarly essays on Waco, with a particular focus on issues of religious deviance and tolerance, Stuart Wright points out that if the Branch Davidians had not possessed any guns, there would have been no shootout at Waco.[7] He suggests that more gun laws are one way to prevent future Wacos. Indeed, if there were no guns, there might not be a need for a federal firearms bureau. It is certainly true that in Japan, where gun controls on ordinary citizens are very strict (shotguns can be owned after a rigorous licensing process, but rifles and handguns are prohibited) as are gun controls on the police, fatal violence between police and dissidents is extremely rare.[8] In English-speaking nations such as Canada, New Zealand, or Great Britain, the population is more submissive to the government than in the United States, and the government is less violent toward even the nonsubmissive part of the population. The stricter gun laws in these nations reflect and reinforce more restrictive attitudes toward both private and governmental violence, even when that violence is legally justifiable.[9] American law enforcement officers kill people at a much higher rate than do officers in most other democracies, and they carry far more weaponry. The American gun culture is not the only cause of this phenomenon, but it is a very important factor.

If there were a magic magnet that could collect and destroy all the firearms, including police firearms, in the United States, and if there were some other magic device which could change the attitudes of everyone in the United States, including law enforcement officers, toward firearms and violence, then future Wacos would be much, much more unlikely.[10]

The policy question for the United States in the late twentieth century is rather different. How do we reduce the potential for future Wacos in a society where there are currently more firearms than adults, where millions of people already defy restrictive gun laws, and millions more will defy more restrictive laws, and huge numbers of Americans, both inside and outside law enforcement, will fiercely resist any attempt to disarm them?

The pretext for the BATF attack was that Koresh owned guns without the proper federal license. Thus, columnist Paul Craig Roberts noted that Waco

> happened precisely because of federal laws regulating gun ownership. The Branch Davidians hadn't assaulted anything. They lived peacefully in the community. Except for the federal gun laws, they would all still be alive. It wasn't the state of Texas that provoked the confrontation. . . . The . . . premise that gun ownership should be illegal, or at least heavily regulated, has created the atmosphere in which the ATF, like an unthinking bully, feels compelled to increasingly and brazenly show its presence.[11]

Accordingly, whatever the other merits of prohibition of so-called assault weapons, the new federal prohibition of about two hundred semiautomatic firearms models and all new ammunition magazines holding more than ten rounds could subject many millions of Americans to Waco-style attacks by the BATF, although enforcement of the ban has so far involved little effort to confiscate illegal items from individual owners.[12]

An even larger group of Americans could become subject to BATF attack if the Brady II legislation from Handgun Control, Inc. (HCI), were enacted. The proposal claims to "treat guns like cars," although it goes considerably further than that.[13] Of particular relevance here is HCI's proposed arsenal license; HCI uses the Branch Davidians in its fundraising letters as proof of the need for an federal arsenal licensing system.

Under the HCI plan, anyone who owned at least twenty guns or 1,000 rounds of ammunition would be required to obtain a federal "arsenal" license. Licensees would be subject to three unannounced police inspections per year. Persons who were required to have a license but did not obtain one would of course be subject to whatever enforcement action BATF deemed appropriate. For purposes of defining an "arsenal," firearms, firearms parts, and ammunition magazines would all count as a "firearm." In other words, if a person owned three rifles, three handguns, two magazines for each gun, and set of disassembled spare parts for the rifles and the handguns, he would have an "arsenal" consisting of at least twenty "guns." Even if the enactment of the arsenal law were widely publicized, it is doubtful that someone who owned six real guns would realize that he was the keeper of a federally defined "arsenal" of twenty statutory guns.

Rimfire ammunition (the kind used in .22 rifles) is commonly sold in bricks consisting of five hundred rounds. Many target shooters use rimfire ammunition because it is so inexpensive compared to centerfire ammunition; rimfire ammunition costs less than two cents per round. And thus, the hundreds of thousands (or millions) of target shooters who are accustomed to picking up a couple bricks of rimfire ammunition for twenty dollars every few months would also become the owners of "arsenals."

In addition, Brady II would bring all magazines holding seven or more rounds under the federal licensing system applicable to machine guns. Magazines of seven or more rounds are standard for almost every semiautomatic handgun in the world.[14] Hence, a person who owned a Colt .45 pistol and a single magazine for the pistol would need to get a federal machine-gun-type license for the magazine. Failure to obtain the license would again authorize BATF intervention.

In assessing the costs and benefits of gun controls such as those proposed by HCI, it would seem appropriate to factor in the potential loss of life, destruction of property, and terrorization of nonviolent citizens that could result from bringing tens of millions of additional American families under the jurisdiction of the Bureau of Alcohol, Tobacco and Firearms.

Because of Waco, many Americans have concluded that armed resistance to a tyrannical federal government might one day be necessary.[15] Small militias have formed all over the United States, and are actively training. If Waco was intended to deter the stockpiling of firearms and ammunition, the effect has been the opposite.

Why BATF Should Not Be Abolished, Even Though It Deserves to Be

Some of BATF's Other Notorious Raids

The Waco raid was the most spectacular, but hardly the only instance of abuse of power by BATF, although nothing ever approached the mass violence of the raid on the Mount Carmel Center.[16]

On September 5, 1991, sixty agents from the BATF, DEA, U.S. Forest Service, and National Guard—wearing painted faces and camouflage—joined by twenty more National Guard troops in a light armored vehicle, raided the homes of Sina Brush and two neighbors in Mountainair, New Mexico. The door was kicked in, and Ms. Brush and her daughter were handcuffed in their underwear and forced to kneel in the middle of a room while agents ransacked their home. No drugs were found. The warrant had been based on a tip from an unreliable informant. (BATF's involvement was predicated on the federal law barring gun possession by persons who sell or use drugs.)

On December 16, 1991 (the first day of the third century of the Bill of Rights), sixty BATF agents, accompanied by two television crews, broke into the Oklahoma home of John Lawmaster. Acting on a tip (suspected to be from Lawmaster's ex-wife) that Lawmaster had illegally converted a semiautomatic to full automatic, BATF worked with the ex-wife to lure Lawmaster away from his home before the raid. With Lawmaster absent, BATF knocked down his front door with a battering ram. While some agents stood guard with weapons drawn, other agents broke open Lawmaster's gun safe, scattered his personal papers, spilled boxes of ammunition onto the floor, and broke into a small, locked box that contained precious coins. To move some ceiling tiles, one agent stood on a table, breaking the table in the process.

Neighbors who asked what BATF was doing were threatened with arrest. Having found nothing illegal, BATF left weapons and ammunition strewn about the home, and departed. They closed the doors, but since BATF had broken the doors on the way in, the doors could not be latched or locked. Upon returning to the shambles that remained of his home, Lawmaster found a note from BATF: "Nothing found." Utility company representatives arrived, and informed Lawmaster that they had been told to shut off all his utilities.[17]

One of the commanders of the Waco raid was Ted Royster, head of BATF operations for Texas, Oklahoma, and New Mexico. Royster also supervised the Lawmaster raid, watching the operation from a parked vehicle with tinted windows.[18] He was subsequently made head of Operation Alliance, a multiagency drug task force along the Mexican border.[19] (It has been suggested that Timothy McVeigh targeted the Alfred P. Murrah Building in Oklahoma City because Royster had an office there.[20])

When Lawmaster asked for a court order to unseal the search warrant application—and reveal the identify of the informant who had made such obviously false, malicious, and harmful charges against him—the Tenth Circuit Court of Appeals refused. Although there was no assertion that Lawmaster intended to cause any harm to the informant—other than a civil suit to recovery monetary damages caused by the informant's deceit—the court refused to unseal the warrant.[21] By thereby stifling Lawmaster's lawsuit, the court failed to protect the integrity of the courts and of the executive branch, both of which have apparently been used by a *mis*informant to cause unjustified harm to a personal enemy. Failure to sanction such an informant fails to create any deterrent to future liars who contemplate tricking law enforcement and the courts for their own malign ends.

On February 5, 1993—twenty-three days before the Waco raid—BATF ransacked the home of a black woman in Portland, Oregon, terrorizing her for hours and refusing to allow her to call an attorney, until BATF discovered that there was a case of mistaken identity.

Of all the post-Waco BATF incidents, the one that has gotten the most attention was a raid on a married couple who were gun show promoters. As promoters, they did not personally sell guns, but they arranged large weekend gun shows at which both individuals and gun stores would set up tables to sell firearms. According to a report from Gun Owners of America:

> The lives of Harry and Theresa Lamplugh were turned upside down on the morning of May 25, 1994. Early that day, 15-to-20 armed men and women burst into their rural Pennsylvania home. Under the threat of violence, the Lamplughs cooperated completely with the intruders as they opened safes, locks and cabinets. In spite of their compliance, however, Harry and Theresa were treated with contempt. Throughout the ordeal, a fully automatic machine gun was intermittently thrust in both their faces.
>
> The Lamplughs watched in horror as the thugs literally trashed their home. Furniture was overturned or smashed and papers were scattered everywhere. Three pet cats were ruthlessly killed—one literally stomped to death. The gang ransacked their home for more than six hours. When they finally left, Harry and Theresa stood confused and angry in the midst of their demolished home.
>
> The brutal and inhumane events that you have just read about are not fiction. They were taken from the testimony of Harry and Theresa Lamplugh. Only the intruders were not some violent street gang members or foreign terrorists; they were agents of the Bureau of Alcohol, Tobacco and Firearms (BATF) and the Internal Revenue Service (IRS).[22]
>
> On Wednesday, May 25, 1994, the search warrant was executed. At about eight in the morning, Harry answered a knock on the front door and was instantly surrounded by agents. His wife was in the bathroom at the time. He had been sitting at the kitchen table in a pair of pajama bottoms, having his morning coffee. "Unto this day I don't know exactly how many there were, but they had my house secured in seconds," Harry said.

According to Lamplugh, there were a total of six cars full of agents. They were not dressed in any uniform, and only two had the identifying ATF vests on. All firearms were drawn. An MP-5 machine gun was stuck in Harry's face. They did not announce who they were or why they were there, and no search warrants were displayed. "When I asked if they had a search warrant, their first reply was 'shut the fuck up mother fucker; do you want more trouble than you already have?' with the machine gun stuck in my face." Harry said. "They then proceeded to tear my house apart."

The Lamplughs were not permitted to dress all day. "We couldn't even go to the bathroom without an armed guard, as if we were prisoners in our own home," says Mrs. Lamplugh. Then, like a slap in the face, the agents stopped everything to eat lunch. "They gave no thought to what we were going through. Some agents went out for pizza, and they had a little party. It was like a room full of kindergartners with no chaperone. They threw half-emptied soda cans, pizza and pizza boxes everywhere. To some people, maybe it sounds like we're complaining about a small thing, but this is our home and they trashed it."[23]

The agents' reckless conduct at the "pizza party" characterized their behavior throughout the raid. "Because I have cancer, I usually have about 20 bottles of prescription drugs on top of my bureau. For some unknown reason, they thought it necessary to open the bottles and scatter the contents all over the floor. Consequently, two of our cats got into the medication and died horrible deaths."

The agents continued their aimless search. "Where's the machine gun?" one of the agents asked. Finally, an indication they were looking for something in particular. "At first I didn't know what he meant," Harry said. "Then I recalled that I once owned a Vietnam commemorative Thompson, inlaid in 22 karat gold, but that was a semiautomatic. One of the agents then responded, 'That must be what they're talking about.'" The agents were apparently looking for something that wasn't even there, or illegal to possess.

However, they were very thorough in sifting through what was there. But for what reason did the agents take marriage and birth certificates, school records, insurance information, vehicle registrations and titles? Harry points out that "they were so thorough that for about two weeks we would have had a hard time proving who we were. They took all of our contacts with newspapers (over 600), all friends and family phone numbers, and even my medical records." There were 61 firearms and assorted ammo seized in the raid, valued at over $15,000. The agents took about 70,000 names and addresses of exhibitors and also gun show contracts through the year 2000. A stack of mail was opened, read and also confiscated. . . .

For reasons unknown to the Lamplughs, the affidavits were sealed by a local federal judge. An Assistant United States Attorney was asked by the Lamplughs' attorney to unseal the document, but he has steadfastly refused to do so.

. . . The BATF has refused to return any property, even medical records and other personal documents and possessions.[24]

When the Lamplughs asked if they were under arrest, they were told that they were not. Yet they were held in their kitchen at gunpoint, and forbidden to call their attorney, as even persons under arrest have a constitutional right to do. When they asked to see a search warrant, they were told (falsely) that no warrant had to be shown until the search was over.[25]

A simultaneous raid was carried out at the nearby home of the Lamplugh's eldest son, John. After the end of that raid, John Lamplugh asked for the two thousand dollars in currency that BATF and IRS agents had taken from his wallet and car. Correctly stating the effect of federal forfeiture laws, IRS Agent John Bittenbender allegedly replied, "You'll have to fuckin' prove its yours."[26]

Eighteen thousand dollars worth of forfeitures were effected at Mr. and Mrs. Lamplugh's home.[27] Thirty dollars and a grocery list were taken from Mrs. Lamplugh's coat pocket. When she asked for the money back, the agent grinned and told her she could have it if she could give the serial numbers of the bills. Mr. Lamplugh says he planned to purchase a truck that morning; ten thousand dollars in cash and supporting paperwork were taken from his dresser. Agent Bittenbender found $1,500 that Mrs. Lamplugh had hidden in her pantyhose drawer, for, she said, cosmetic surgery. When she complained about the money being taken, Agent Bittenbender allegedly replied, "We'll see how cooperative you are when we throw you in a jail full of lesbians."[28]

The Lamplugh incident was widely reported in gun rights publications, including *Soldier of Fortune*. The Lamplughs appeared on the G. Gordon Liddy radio talk show, and when their story was reported in *Washington Times*, it came to the attention of congressional aides and other persons charged with supervising BATF. The Lamplughs allege that after appearing on the Gordon Liddy radio show, the Lamplughs were awakened by a three A.M. phone call warning, "Don't fuck with the feds. You have to learn to button your lips or else you're dead." In October 1994, Mrs. Lamplugh says, as she was leaving a drug store where she was picking up her husband's cancer medication, a man came up to her and said, "Don't fuck with the bureau." He walked away and said, "Check out what's in your van." The van contained a dead black cat, its neck broken.[29]

Charges were eventually filed based on allegations that Harry Lamplugh, a gun show promoter, illegally bought and sold firearms. His wife has a federal firearms license but he does not, because of a disputed burglary conviction from 1964.[30] (The license is needed in order to conduct the business of firearms sales, but is not necessary to promote a gun show at which other people sell firearms.) Assuming that every single charge against the Mr. Lamplugh is true, why was it necessary for the search to be conducted is such a brutal manner?

Are charges against BATF reported in ideological publications such as the *Washington Times* or *Soldier of Fortune* simply a pack of right-wing lies? If the complaints about BATF are really just a conspiracy, as BATF spokespersons have claimed, then the conspiracy must be immense, for the conspiracy even extends to such innocuous publications as the *Ely Daily Times* in Ely, Nevada. Dr. Jed Cserna, a forty-three-year-old physician with sixteen years of service in the Air National Guard, was arrested by BATF for weapons violations. Although there is no evidence that Dr. Cserna would not have appeared in court if BATF had simply sent him a registered letter, the arrest proceeded rather differently:

> "I was in my office talking on the telephone. They told me someone hit my car. As soon as I walked outside the clinic they put a shotgun to my head, handcuffed me, took me to their car and drove me to Reno." [Reno is in far western Nevada, near the California border; Ely is in far eastern Nevada, about 300 miles away.]
>
> The physician wears a back brace and walks on crutches due to injuries sustained in a March 13 traffic accident. His back is broken in two places and his ankle is broken.

Cserna said that when he was arrested, federal agents forced him to walk about 10 feet to their car, but he wasn't allowed to use his crutches.

"I told them I could only sit about an hour because of my back, but they didn't pay any attention," he said.

They did stop in Austin, where Cserna said he had to walk to a restroom without the aid of his crutches.

. . . [In Reno], he had to spend the night in jail. He said he was never given a chance to eat or drink all day Thursday, although he was served breakfast in jail Friday morning.

The magistrate released him on $50,000 unsecured bond, meaning he doesn't have to put up any money. . . .

After the hearing, he said, federal agents dropped him off in Reno and left him to find his own way back to Ely. . . .

[Dr. Kendall Jones who works in the clinic with Dr. Cserna, complained that] the arrest was "one of the most gross displays of police power that I could ever imagine . . . I have not understood all the hype and folderol about militias against the government, but after witnessing this display, I more fully understand."[31]

In contrast to the Lamplugh or Waco cases, there are many other instances of BATF abuse which never get reported beyond the city where they occurred. According to a report in the Pittsburgh *Tribune-Review,* in 1993 in Pittsburgh the BATF, along with the FBI and the IRS, was conducting an investigation of David Costa, who was later sentenced to probation for fencing stolen property. A search warrant was obtained for David Costa's home. On April 26, 1993, twenty-five men screaming threats and orders, and brandishing weapons, pulled into the driveway of Costa's sister, Sandra Chan, who was not a suspect, and whose home is an entirely different address from David Costa's. At gunpoint, the Chan family was ordered to allow the BATF and the other agencies to search their home without a warrant, despite the Chans' protestations that their home's address was obviously different from the address listed on the warrant. According to a lawsuit filed by the Chans, one of their children developed a stutter and other speech difficulties as a result of the invasion and search.[32]

On November 21, 1995, fifteen BATF agents held the six employees of Sierra Vista Guns (in Sierra Vista, Arizona) at gunpoint for six hours while they conducted a search for export licenses. No charges have been filed.[33]

According to the *St. Louis Post-Dispatch,* on April 30, 1996, in a suburb of St. Louis, the Bureau of Alcohol, Tobacco and Firearms assisted in a search of the quiet suburban home of Paul and Patty Mueller, which an informant (hoping for leniency in the criminal charges pending against him) had falsely claimed was a distribution center for illegal weapons. At 9:30 P.M., thirteen local law enforcement officers and one BATF agent, all wearing black, kicked open an unlocked door, breaking its frame. A gun was held three inches from Patty Mueller's head. Her husband was handcuffed, and the intruders threatened to kill the family dog. An hour later, the intruders showed the Muellers the search warrant, and explained what they were looking for. No illegal weapons were found (the Muellers do not even own a BB gun), and the agents left.

A BATF supervisor admitted that the local police were wrong in their failure to attempt to corroborate independently some of the information supplied by the criminal informant. What little checking had been done had already shown that the informant was, at the least, entirely misinformed. The informant had claimed that a particular man alleged to be a gunrunner lived in the Mueller's home. When the police found that the home was owned by the Muellers, rather than the gunrunner, the informant claimed that the gunrunner was living with the Muellers. No effort was made to observe the Muellers' home to see if the gunrunner ever came or went.

The special agent in charge of the St. Louis BATF office offered an apology, and also said that BATF would pay to clean the Muellers' carpet (the searchers had tracked mud all over it).[34] This official show of remorse, while rather minimal, still represented a step forward in BATF behavior toward innocent victims of its searches. Although pointing a gun at someone's head and threatening her without a legitimate need to do so would normally constitute felony menacing, no one suggested that the intruders should be prosecuted for the offense.

A lying informant played a central role in the first of BATF's notorious raids, when on June 7, 1971, BATF agents broke into the Maryland home of Kenyon Ballew.[35] A burglar had told the police that Ballew owned grenades. Ballew did own empty grenade hulls, which are entirely legal and unregulated. Wearing ski masks and displaying no identification, BATF agents broke down Ballew's door with a battering ram. Responding to his girlfriend's screams, Ballew took out an antique blackpowder pistol, and was promptly shot by BATF. Nothing illegal was found. He remains confined to a wheelchair as a result of the shooting, and now subsists on welfare.[36]

The cases described in this book are far from the sum of all of BATF's misguided enforcement efforts. BATF abuses could literally supply the material for an entire book. Since that book has already been written by attorney David Hardy, we will not attempt to duplicate it.[37]

Improving Civil Remedies for Law Enforcement Misconduct

Two defenses can be offered for BATF. The first is that the large majority of BATF agents are good people who enforce the law in a reasonable manner. The incidents of abuse which come to public attention are a small fraction of the total BATF caseload. The fact that a high percentage of news reports about BATF involve BATF abuse does not prove that most BATF agents are abusive. By analogy, most newspaper stories about guns involve gun crime, but far less than 1 percent of gun owners are gun criminals.

BATF has a large number of honorable, admirable employees who have quietly gone about their work for years, enforcing federal regulations applicable to gun dealers, and enforcing federal laws against possession of guns by persons with felony convictions for violent crime. Misbehavior of some BATF staff (and some BATF leadership) should not be taken as proof that all BATF employees are bad. Indeed, many of the agents who participated in the Waco raid may have been misled by false statements from supervisors that several people in the "cult compound" wanted to be rescued.[38]

A second defense of BATF is to point to a 1995 General Accounting Office report of BATF activity. In the period covered by the report, there were 46,930 suspects arrested, thirty-nine shooting incidents, and twenty-five allegations of excessive force. In none of these cases did BATF end up being held civilly liable for excessive force.

BATF management points to its record in tort cases as proof that the Bureau is just about perfect in terms of not using excessive force. But what the record really shows is the need for strengthening the ability of victims of law enforcement violence to recover damages.

One important reason why so few excessive force claims are brought against BATF is that some BATF agents use threats of criminal prosecution to deter complaints and lawsuits. Even without explicit threats, most people who have been subjected to illegal or gratuitously violent searches will prefer to put the incident behind them, rather than invest years in suing the federal government.

In 1971, the Supreme Court said that the Constitution created an implicit right for persons to sue the federal government for violations of the Fourth or Fifth Amendments. But this *Bivens* action cannot be used to recover damages in cases where there are other possible remedies, or where damages might impair effective functioning of government. From the time the *Bivens* action was created in 1971 until 1986, only five federal agents have had to pay damages under *Bivens*.[39] For all practical purposes, *Bivens* offers no deterrent to law enforcement misconduct.

As an alternative to a *Bivens* action, a victim can file suit under the Federal Tort Claims Act. But in practice, the remedy is practically worthless. First of all, the victim can only recover if he can prove that the law enforcement officers were deliberately acting in bad faith. Gross neglect of proper standards is not bad faith. Thus, even Kenyon Ballew was not able to recover anything from BATF in his civil suit.[40] Similarly, Randy Weaver never sued BATF for spending three years trying to entrap him into committing a crime, then libeling him by claiming he was a violent felon, and if he had sued, he probably would not have won.

The Weaver family did settle out of court with the Department of Justice for 3.1 million dollars for claims involving the FBI sniper's killing of Vicki Weaver. But that was a rare case, involving a death rather than merely the wanton destruction of property and people being roughed up. Further, the possibility of a drawn-out trial created a risk of disastrous publicity for the Department of Justice and the FBI, a risk that only can exist in the very rare abuse case which becomes a major national news topic.

In the case of someone like Kenyon Ballew (crippled for life) or Vicki Weaver (dead), there will be a need to bring a suit. But in the more typical situation—a family is terrorized at gunpoint for several hours while their home is ransacked, but no one is injured—the victims will not bring suit. To file a suit would mean to pay years of litigation expenses against the most powerful defendant in the world, the United States government, which has, for all practical purposes, unlimited resources when compared to a lone family. Many families understandably decide just to put the incident behind them, rather than spend years trying to prove bad faith on the part of the government. Thus, BATF's claim that it has not been found civilly liable in any search and arrest incidents is hardly proof that BATF is a law-abiding bureau which always tries to minimize use of unnecessary force.

Rather than being required to go to federal court (where civil cases move very slowly, due to the huge volume of criminal drug cases), victims of federal law enforcement violence should be able to bring an expedited action to recover actual (not punitive) damages that result from any wrongful search. The case would be heard before an administrative law judge. In order to recover personal injury and property damages, the victim would not have to prove bad faith. Rather, the plaintiff would need to prove that he was the victim of law enforcement behavior which fell below reasonable standards of law enforcement conduct. Thus, if a BATF agent did not attempt to corroborate information from an informant's tip, BATF would be liable for damage from the resulting search, even if the failure to corroborate were the result of laziness or bad training, rather than malice. The administrative remedy should be available for all federal law enforcement abuses, not only BATF, although the remedy could be phased in through a pilot program that initially applied only to BATF.

The realistic potential of civil damages will incline searchers to be less wanton in destroying property. If wrongful searches are a necessary cost of law enforcement, then the cost should be borne by entire community (i.e., the community's taxes should be used to compensate the individual victims). It is not fair that the cost of wrongful property destruction by law enforcement be borne solely by the random group of unlucky victims.[41]

Preventing Informant Abuse

To prevent the need for lawsuits in the first place, Congress or the Supreme Court should give better guidance to law enforcement personnel and lower courts in the use of informants. Until 1984, the Supreme Court required that warrants based on tips from informants must pass a two-prong test, as set forth in the case of *Aguilar* v. *Texas*.[42] The first prong was the informant's basis of knowledge. For example, if the informant claimed that somebody possessed unregistered machine guns, how did the informant know about the machine guns? Had he gone shooting with the gun-owner and actually fired the machine guns (a very strong basis of knowledge) or had he just heard somebody else say that the gun owner had expressed interest in machine guns (a very weak basis of knowledge, used in the Waco warrant). If illegal activity, such as drug sales, was allegedly going on inside someone's home, had the informant been inside the home and seen activity (strong basis of knowledge), or seen a suspicious pattern of people coming and going to the home (a moderate basis of knowledge) or just heard a rumor about the drug sales (weak basis of knowledge)?

The second prong of the two-part test was the informant's veracity. Was there reason to believe that the informant, even if he had a good basis of knowledge, was telling the truth? The veracity prong was frequently examined for two factors: credibility, and reliability. Regarding credibility, was the informant someone with a strong personal motive to lie—such as a criminal who was working as an informant in order to receive more lenient treatment for his own crimes? Conversely, did the informant have nothing personal to gain by conveying the information?

The reliability factor examined whether the informant, even without a motive to lie, was a good observer of events. One way to test reliability would be for the police to corroborate some of what the informant had said. For example, if the informant said that a suspect lived at a particular address, the police could verify the information, either by using a phone book, or by observing who came and went at the particular address (as they did not do in the St. Louis raid discussed above).

Verification of suspicious activity would be more important than verification of innocent activity. For example, if an informant said that someone ran a crack house at a particular address, the police could corroborate the tip by observing many persons coming and going from the house at unusual hours, but only spending a few minutes, and coming out with a glassy look in their eyes; this corroboration would be much stronger than merely corroborating that the suspect happened to live at the house in question.

The Supreme Court's two-part test provided structured guidance to magistrates who were asked to issue warrants based on informant tips. The two-part test likewise guided law enforcement officers who were seeking to obtain a search warrant. They knew that they should investigate the informant's basis of knowledge and veracity, and that corroborating incriminating information from the tip would be especially important.

The net effect was that informant tips would rarely be the only basis for a search warrant. Instead, informant data would be the starting point for a more thorough investigation to build probable cause. The two-prong test promoted good police work.

But like many other civil liberties protections, the *Aguilar* two-prong test fell victim to the drug war. In 1983, the Supreme Court heard a case involving a search warrant which three lower courts had ruled clearly failed the two-part test. Someone had written an anonymous poison-pen letter accusing a married couple of being drug dealers. The letter indicated no basis of knowledge. The writer did not even know the couple's address. The police did attempt to corroborate some information from the tip, but the only information corroborated was of innocent conduct. The husband flew down to Florida where he met his wife, and the two were observed driving north, in the direction of Disneyworld.

Issuing a search warrant for the couple's home was plainly wrong under the *Aguilar* two-prong test, as a trial court, intermediate court of appeals, and the Illinois Supreme Court all found. The United States Supreme Court did not disagree. Instead, the Court majority, in an opinion written by Justice Rehnquist, scrapped the two-prong *Aguilar* test (without actually overruling *Aguilar*), and replaced it with a "totality of the circumstances" test.[43]

In contrast to the structured *Aguilar* test, the amorphous "totality of the circumstances" test allows search warrants even if there is no evidence regarding the informant's basis of knowledge, or demonstration of the informant's veracity. In theory, magistrates should still consider basis of knowledge and veracity in assessing the totality of the circumstances. If all magistrates were as conscientious as Justice Rehnquist, replacing the two-part test with the totality test would not make a major difference. But in real-world law enforcement, where many magistrates are inclined to rubber-stamp warrant applications, the totality standard means that magistrates are less likely to take a serious look at the informant's basis of knowledge and reliability.

For example, in the Waco warrant application, the magistrate made no inquiry into the credibility or reliability of the BATF agent Aguilera's informants. If the magistrate had, he might have discovered that Aguilera's principal informant, Marc Breault, had very poor credibility (he was a self-described "cult buster" with what he called a "vendetta" against Koresh) and even worse reliability (he was legally blind).

An example of the kind of searches which the *Gates* standard (which has been adopted by many state courts) encourages was the search that led to the death of Rev.

Accelyne Williams. The Reverend Williams was a substance abuse counselor in a poor neighborhood in Boston. One evening he was visited in his apartment by a substance abuser who also happened to be an undercover informant in the pay of the Boston police. Later, the informant, obviously drunk, gave the police the address of a drug dealer, except the informant mistakenly gave the police the address of the Reverend Williams. Freed, by *Gates*, from any requirement to corroborate anything the informant said, the police promptly obtained a search warrant. Of course, if the police had attempted corroboration, they would have found that the apartment in question belonged to a seventy-year-old retired Methodist minister, and there were no signs of drug activity at the apartment.

Armed with the search warrant and plenty of firearms, the Boston police executed a dynamic entry, breaking into the Reverend Williams's apartment, chasing him into his bedroom, shoving him to the floor, and handcuffing him while pointing guns at his head. He promptly died of a heart attack.[44]

Given the real-world impact of *Gates*'s lowering of standards for police work, including in the many BATF cases built on informants, the United States Supreme Court should overrule *Illinois* v. *Gates*. Further, Congress should exercise its power to set standards for federal courts, and should enact a statute mandating that the two-prong test be used when magistrates are asked to issue warrants based on informants. Congress should bar the use of evidence in federal courts which is obtained in violation of the two-prong test.

The harm done by informants is not limited to providing false information used to obtain search warrants. The whole Ruby Ridge disaster started when a BATF undercover informant spent three years trying to get Randy Weaver to sell him a sawed-off shotgun. But the BATF is still using undercover informants to encourage, rather than uncover, violent crime. After the much-publicized arrest of the dozen-man "Viper Team" in Arizona, it turned out that while there may have been violations of federal weapons licensing laws, the only proposals for violence came from the BATF infiltrator. He suggested that they start robbing banks, and they all refused.[45]

The Viper case appears to be the pattern for BATF's newfound interest in militias. A huge press conference announces an arrest, and a terrible crime narrowly averted. Then, at pretrial hearings, it turns out that all the talk about committing crimes came from BATF informants, and whatever technical violations of federal weapons laws took place were also instigated by the informants. For example, the Blue Ridge Hunt Club case, the subject of a high-publicity attention in 1995, by 1996 had turned out to involve nobody who wanted to do anything violent except for the BATF informant, and the only crimes perpetrated were nonviolent violations of federal gun sale laws, also at the behest of the informant.[46]

For all the big talk of some militia folk, BATF has had a very hard time finding a militiaman who can be talked into agreeing to commit a violent crime. Perhaps this suggests that the militias are not the great threat which BATF and the media have made them appear to be. But if BATF continues to use undercover informants who get paid for encouraging violent crime, sooner or later somebody may actually go along with the informant, and hurt an innocent person.

It's Still Showtime

Even after the Waco disaster showed the dangers of staging huge raids as publicity stunts, the BATF planned a March 22, 1995, attack by two hundred agents on the Kelly Miller public housing project in Washington, D.C., using military equipment from Bolling Air Force Base. Although the raid was intended to search for drugs and guns, the nation's primary drug law enforcer, the Drug Enforcement Administration, was not asked to participate in the preraid investigation or the raid itself.

To state the obvious, such a raid would have netted mostly the smallest fish in the drug distribution chain, raising questions about why BATF felt a need to get involved in a project that used every BATF agent from Baltimore to Richmond. The dangers to the hundreds of innocent children and adults in the housing project posed by a massive assault were also obvious, or should have been.

Fortunately, BATF canceled the raid when the special agent in charge of the Washington office discovered that a press release announcing the raid had been sent out at least twelve hours *before* the raid began.[47] Waco appears to have taught BATF not to launch surprise attacks when surprise is lost; no lessons about the advisability of attacking group homes with large numbers of innocent people appear to have been learned.

As a reform, Congress should require that any raid involving more than twenty BATF agents be personally approved by the secretary of the Treasury. Similar-sized raids by the FBI or the Drug Enforcement Administration should require the personal approval of the attorney general. Massive military-style raids ought to be for purposes important enough to merit the attention of cabinet officers. They should not be allowed merely because a bureau wants to make work for itself and capture media attention.

BATF Regulatory Enforcement

Violent dynamic entries and informant abuse are not BATF's only problems. Fierce as BATF can sometimes be, the fierceness is frequently directed at gun owners suspected of unintentional technical violations, rather than against armed violent criminals. In 1982, the Senate Subcommittee on the Constitution investigated the BATF and unanimously concluded that the agency had habitually engaged in:

> conduct which borders on the criminal.... [E]nforcement tactics made possible by current firearms laws are constitutionally, legally and practically reprehensible.... [A]pproximately 75 percent of BATF gun prosecutions were aimed at ordinary citizens who had neither criminal intent nor knowledge, but were enticed by agents into unknowing technical violations.[48]

For example, if the sear (the catch that holds the hammer at cock) on a semiautomatic rifle wears out, the rifle may malfunction and repeat fire. The BATF arrested and prosecuted a small town Tennessee police chief for possession of an automatic weapon (actually a semiautomatic with a worn-out sear), even though the BATF conceded that the police chief had not deliberately altered the weapon.[49] In March and April of 1988, BATF pressed similar charges for a worn-out sear against a Pennsylvania state police sergeant. After a twelve-day trial, the federal district judge directed a verdict of not guilty and called the prosecution "a severe miscarriage of justice."[50]

Part of the problem is that while the employees of regulatory agencies do not normally hate the object of their regulation (employees of the Department of Transportation often *like* cars; Department of Agriculture employees think farming is a good idea), the BATF is increasingly manned by younger recruits who dislike the idea of civilian gun ownership per se.[51]

The Treasury Department defends the Waco attack on the basis that "the raid fit within an historic, well-established and well-defended government interest in prohibiting and breaking up all organized groups that sought to arm or defend themselves."[52] The candid admission of BATF's objective, however, conflicts with the fact that nothing in existing law makes it illegal for persons, alone or in groups, to collect large number of weapons and to defend themselves. To the contrary, the ownership of large numbers of weapons is protected by the Second Amendment, just as the First Amendment protects the ownership of books, without regard to quantity.[53]

BATF publishes a book summarizing federal firearms regulations every year, to provide guidance to Federal Firearms Licensees (licensed gun dealers). The 1995 update contains twenty-three different errors and misstatements; all but one of the errors falls on the side of overstating the scope of federal gun laws and of describing various legal acts as criminal.[54]

While BATF insists that all firearms dealers strictly account for every firearm, BATF itself cannot keep track of the seized weapons in its own inventory. According to a report by the Treasury Department Inspector General, "Officials have accepted the practice of 'writing off' hundreds of firearms that could not be accounted for during annual physical inventories." When 152 guns were lost in 1991, they were simply erased from BATF inventory records, with no effort made to find where they had gone.[55] A firearms wholesaler guilty of such sloppiness would likely be put out of business by BATF, and perhaps criminally prosecuted.

BATF's history of negligent, sloppy maintenance of the National Firearms Registration and Transfer Record (NFR&TR), the list of registered machinegun owners and their guns, was detailed in chapter 1. BATF has presented false testimony in court, asserting that the database is 100 percent accurate, while knowing that the error rate is as high as 50 percent. Innocent owners of registered machine guns have been convicted of not having registered their guns, because BATF lost or destroyed the registration record. In some cases, BATF employees shredded firearms transfer records which had been submitted to them, in order to avoid the work of entering the information on the database.[56]

As part of a course of conduct which BATF knew would substantially reduce the number of licensed firearms dealers, BATF began requiring that applicants for new or renewal licenses provide a copy of their leases and a security plan for storage of their inventories. But the relevant statute only gives BATF authority to see if the applicant is eligible to be given a license, not to require information about the details of the business.[57] The law requires that BATF act on licenses within sixty days,[58] but some applicants have been forced to wait several months, while their businesses hang in limbo. BATF is authorized to deny licenses to applicants whose businesses do not conform to local zoning ordinances, but in some cases BATF has encouraged local governments to enact ordinances to drive gun licensees out of business. Federal law imposes no minimum number of sales that a federally licensed gun dealer must make during a given year. But BATF has coerced tens of thousands of small-time dealers, who sold a few guns a year to themselves and their friends and family, to surrender their licenses.

The Bureau of Alcohol, Tobacco and Firearms (a descendant of the Bureau of Prohibition) also enforces the federal alcohol laws in a manner characterized by administrative abuse, overreaching its statutory power, and selective enforcement against persons or companies who dare to criticize BATF.[59] For example, BATF takes the position that alcohol companies may not disseminate information about the health benefits of wine or other alcohol, "regardless of their truthfulness."[60]

Unfortunately, the Clinton administration takes pride in being the most aggressively antigun administration in American history, and in not restraining itself with the civil liberties squeamishness that characterized some previous Democratic administrations. It seems doubtful the administration will lead BATF in the direction that its quieter, more law-abiding employees might prefer.

BATF misapplication of the law, and BATF prosecution of persons for purported technical violations of federal gun laws used to be the major complaints about BATF. That these complaints are now overshadowed by complaints about BATF's violent raids, and BATF informants who foment violence, is a sad result of the last decade's trend toward more violent federal law enforcement.

Reforming BATF

Under BATF Director John Magaw, who replaced Stephen Higgins in late 1993, several worthwhile reforms have been implemented. First of all, all new recruits are required to read the Treasury Report on the Waco fiasco. While the report (discussed in the previous chapter) covers up important elements of BATF culpability, the report still serves as a reminder of what can go wrong when agents look at a mission with blinders on.

Second, Magaw has set up peer groups for various agents (including white males) to discuss grievances and, ideally, to head off the kind of frustration that led to the race and sex harassment lawsuits which set the stage for Waco. As detailed in chapter 1, BATF revived the dormant Waco investigation when BATF learned that "60 Minutes" was preparing a story on racial and sexual harassment at BATF.

Mr. Magaw's effort to improve the climate for female and minority agents is laudable. But some critics—including the National Association of Treasury Agents—would argue that the problem is not discrimination against women and minorities, but discrimination against anyone who is not part of the "good old boys" network. Until the Gun Control Act of 1968, the BATF had been mainly an alcohol enforcement bureau, and preferred to hire white male agents from the Southeast who could penetrate moonshining networks.[61] As a result of seniority, these agents rose to top management during the 1970s (even as BATF was becoming mainly a gun bureau), and they hired today's senior management. Not surprisingly, they tended to promote people who seemed like younger versions of themselves.[62]

One reform is especially commendable, and should be adopted by every other federal law enforcement agency, as well as required by statute. Starting in October 1995, BATF plans dynamic entries only after all other options have been considered.[63]

Other reforms are less significant. Testifying at the Senate Waco hearings, Mr. Magaw and Mr. Noble stated that in the future, any BATF operation as large as the Waco assault would be carefully monitored and controlled by headquarters. But this is no solution at all. The Waco raid was closely monitored and controlled by headquarters. After the summer 1992 investigation of Koresh had been closed, headquarters ordered that it be reopened. Undercover agent Robert Rodriguez testified that headquarters imposed intense pressure to go ahead with the raid in February 1993, even though Rodriguez argued that the investigation had not progressed far enough yet.[64]

One approach to improving BATF's conduct would be incremental reforms of the statutes governing BATF. Such an approach was attempted by the Firearms Owners' Protection Act, signed into law in 1986. The 1986 reforms, pushed by the National Rifle Association and other progun organizations, reduced BATF search and seizure powers, and reduced some paperwork offenses from felonies to misdemeanors. The Act also imposed draconian penalties on convicted felons found in possession of a gun, and on persons who use guns in drug or violent crimes. (It was these provisions which were used to give the Branch Davidians their thirty-year sentence enhancements.)

But BATF does not always obey the act. The Firearms Owners' Protection Act specifically allows BATF to copy the information from firearms purchaser registration forms (which are maintained by gun dealers) only in conjunction with a specific criminal investigation.[65] Yet in Operation Forward Trace, BATF copies all of a dealer's record of sales for a particular gun type (such as small handguns, or semiautomatics), and then follows up by finding out what each purchaser did with the gun. Federal law specifically forbids gun registration records being used for this kind of proactive, random investigation, yet BATF does it anyway.[66] While conducting a Forward Trace in a Kansas gun store, BATF agents allegedly told the owner, a volunteer in the campaign against pro-gun-control Rep. Jim Slattery, "If you don't lay off Congressman Slattery, you won't have a firearms license."[67]

BATF is also computerizing 800,000 gun purchase records from Massachusetts, where state government firearms records are far out of date.[68]

Given the limited success of statutory reform, it is not surprising that one columnist responded to the BATF's long reputation of abusing rights by calling for the bureau's abolition.[69] After the Ruby Ridge hearings, Sen. Arlen Specter, dismayed by BATF Director Magaw's refusal to admit that BATF had done anything wrong, also called for abolishing the Bureau.

But simply abolishing BATF would leave in place the federal alcohol, tobacco, and firearms laws, and transfer their enforcement responsibility to some other bureau. The FBI is frequently suggested as the new federal gun law enforcer. The performance of the FBI and its parent, the Department of Justice, at Waco and in general during the 1990s (discussed in the next part of this chapter) hardly inspires confidence that moving gun law enforcement to a different spot on the federal organization chart will result in improved performance.

For the same reason, proposals to restructure BATF by making part of a consolidated Treasury Department superpolice (also comprising Customs, Secret Service, and

IRS enforcement) should be rejected. The Clinton administration has taken the first major step toward such consolidation, by creation of the office of Undersecretary for Treasury Enforcement. The first appointee to this office, Ron Noble, played a leading role in the Waco coverup. While BATF should not be abolished, the new Undersecretary office should be.

The strongest argument in favor of transferring BATF functions to another agency, such as the FBI, is that if BATF were just part of another bureau, "mission creep" or "empire building" (looking for new areas to get involved in, to justify greater funding) would not occur. Lacking a separate institutional identity, the firearms enforcement officers would not be constantly looking for additional fields of enforcement activity, and spectacular publicity events like Waco.

The point has some validity, since a distinct bureau may have more institutional incentives, and more freedom to respond to those incentives, in favor of mission creep than would a mere component of another bureau.

On the other hand, an FBI that swallowed BATF would be a huge law enforcement agency, all the more difficult for the FBI director to control. Many fiefdoms can spring up within a single bureau, and each of these fiefdoms would have at least some incentive to magnify its importance.

The benefits of shoving BATF to a new position on the federal organizational chart are, at best, tiny, especially when compared the high political cost of accomplishing such a move.

James Simpson, a former analyst at the Office of Management and Budget, who oversaw the BATF budget from 1990 to 1993, writes that Waco and Ruby Ridge

> are only the most egregious examples of an increasingly widespread pattern of federal law enforcement abuse of U.S. citizens, whose crimes, if any, have not warranted the massive force leveled against them. . . .
>
> Most [BATF] field agents want to go after criminals, but to win in the budget process, managers want statistical results. The number of arrests is much more important than the quality of arrests—big numbers impress members of Congress.[70] Furthermore, the national media and the Washington political class, including most Democrats on the appropriations committees, are hostile to gun owners. . . . [Y]ounger agents increasingly reflect the liberal bias of criminal justice programs at American universities. . . . All these factors conspire to make gun owners an easy target for hostile law enforcement action, regardless of which agency has the mission. . . .
>
> This Congress should bite the bullet and reform the gun laws so that they focus on criminal behavior, rather than serving to demonize gun owners, as they do now. If they don't, Waco and Ruby Ridge will be just the beginning.[71]

It is the very nature of the victimless crimes—such as laws criminalizing the peaceful possession or manufacture of alcohol or firearms—which lead to enforcement abuses. When a violent crime is perpetrated, there is a victim who will often complain to the police, and help them investigate. But with victimless crimes, law enforcement is necessarily forced to rely on paid informants with built-in motives to lie. As long as the consensual offense laws remain in the U.S. Code, abusive enforcement is likely, as has been the historical norm since the enactment of such laws. Removing most firearm (and alcohol and tobacco) laws from the federal statutes does not imply that alcohol, tobacco, and firearms should be subject to no legal controls. Perhaps the control of those objects can continue to be achieved at the state level, without a redundant layer of federal control and the manifold temptations of federal abuse.

Absent getting rid of the body of firearms laws which do not regulate interstate gun sales, and thus reducing the need for an large, oppressive BATF, the next best solution is to keep BATF at a reasonable size. Like the rest of federal law enforcement, BATF has enjoyed huge budget and personnel increases, much larger than the overall rate of growth in many other federal programs.

Since 1985, BATF's size has increased nearly 50 percent, from 2,900 employees to 4,300.[72] In the last two decades, BATF's budget has increased 299 percent, while the number of personnel rose 20 percent.[73] From 1972 to 1992—a period in which BATF's jurisdiction remained relatively constant—the number of staff in a typical urban BATF office has risen from six to twenty-five.[74] In a time of vast budget deficits, simply restoring BATF to its former size might save both taxpayer dollars and taxpayer lives.

BATF's budget should be reset to its 1984 level, with appropriate adjustments for inflation. If BATF discovers that Congress is determined to keep BATF's funding constant, then BATF will have much less incentive to pull stunts like Waco (or to try to entice militia members into committing violent crimes) for budgetary purposes.

FBI

The ancestor of the FBI, the Bureau of Investigation, was created in 1908 by the attorney general as a small investigative branch of the Department of Justice. The FBI was not created by act of Congress, which until recently has been afraid of the civil liberties threat of a national police force.

As Communists took over the Soviet Union following the end of the war, American fears of violent foreign radicals intensified. In August 1919, Attorney General A. Mitchell Palmer established the immediate predecessor of the FBI, the General Intelligence Division of the Department of Justice. The Division was headed by J. Edgar Hoover, and charged with gathering information on radicals. Over the next year, six thousand people were seized in the "Palmer Raids," many of them innocent of any crime and unconnected to radical politics. Many suspects were held in filthy jails and beaten into false confessions. Even people who came to visit these victims in jail were arrested, on the theory of guilt by association.

While Attorney General Palmer was well on his way to using the hysteria he helped create as a stepping-stone to the Democratic presidential nomination, he overplayed his hand. His prediction of a major terrorist attack on May Day 1920 failed to materialize, and the national panic subsided. In September, an anarchist's bomb killed thirty-three people on Wall Street, and the nation correctly recognized the crime as the work of a lone perpetrator, rather than a manifestation of some immense conspiracy.[75]

President Warren Harding commendably ended the Palmer raids. But in 1922, an obscure publisher began door-to-door sales of a book, *A Review of the Facts*, that compiled various rumors about President Harding, including the claim that Harding was actually

"Our first Negro President," who used cosmetics to make himself appear white. The Bureau of Investigation promptly raided the publisher, got a list of purchasers, and scoured the country to retrieve every book that had been sold. (Only a handful escaped.[76])

During the Eisenhower administration, the FBI provided the president with reports about the social activities of Eleanor Roosevelt, Bernard Baruch, and Justice William O. Douglas.[77] During the Kennedy administration, the FBI was ordered to wiretap (without court authorization) a congressional staff member, three executive branch employees, a lobbyist, and a Washington law firm.[78]

Victims of the FBI surveillance abuses have included Dr. Martin Luther King, Jr., the Ku Klux Klan, the Congress of Racial Equality, Barry Goldwater,[79] Cesar Chavez,[80] and the civil rights movement. The Counter-Intelligence Programs (COINTELPRO) invaded the constitutional rights of American people who simply were expressing in public what Secretary of Defense Robert McNamara had concluded in private: that America should get out of Vietnam. The targets of illegal FBI surveillance have included civil rights workers, antiwar protesters, underground newspaper publishers, and homosexuals.[81] Among the tools of surveillance were illegal "black-bag jobs" (break-ins to plant bugs without a court order) against persons suspected of involvement in the Weather Underground.[82] Some of these led to felony convictions of the agents involved.

Not all targets of FBI surveillance have been political activists or even controversial. The FBI spied on radio host Arthur Godfrey and his wife for years, coming up with intelligence gems such as the observation that Mr. Godfrey was an extrovert, while his wife was an introvert. The FBI file on Helen Keller is over a hundred pages long; three-quarters of it remains classified, although she has been dead since 1968.

Far from being confined to a single type of dissident, or to a few years of excess, FBI abuses date back to the 1940s and were pervasive until brought to light by fifteen months of hearings before Sen. Frank Church's special committee in 1975–76. Altogether, there were 675 FBI operations against civil rights, white supremacist, or antiwar groups, which led to only four convictions.[83]

These political investigations are not confined to the "bad old days" of J. Edgar Hoover. Even after all the public hearings, and the implementation of guidelines, the FBI continued to abuse the rights of dissident Americans, through a massive surveillance of people in CISPES (Committee in Solidarity with the People of El Salvador) who opposed President Reagan's policy in El Salvador in the mid-1980s.[84] The CISPES investigation was conducted with the knowledge of Oliver "Buck" Revell, then the number two official at the FBI.[85] The CISPES investigation, justifiably regarded today as shameful, would have been lawful under the Clinton/Dole terrorism bill which became law in 1996.

Beginning in 1972, but continuing through 1992, the FBI and the U.S. Attorney's Office conducted an intensive undercover campaign against civil rights activist and Birmingham Mayor Richard Arrington.[86]

A General Accounting Office investigation of FBI terrorism investigations from 1982 to 1988 found that only 12 percent were predicated on information that the target was involved with, or planning, a terrorist act, or was raising money for terrorist purposes. Seventy-four percent of investigations were predicated simply on an individual's belonging to a lawful group, or some other tenuous association with political activity of which the FBI was suspicious.[87]

Right up to the present, FBI infiltrators have frequently served as agents provocateurs, inciting and directing murders and other violent crimes.[88] During the 1960s, paid informants would try, sometimes successfully, to convince antiwar radicals or Klansmen to blow up a building or to kill someone. In one of the most notorious recent cases, an FBI informant solicited the murder of Louis Farrakhan by a dissident family of Black Muslims. The *New York Times* wrote that the case "reeked of entrapment" by an FBI informant "clearly motivated by money and the need to please the government." The informant, who was working for the FBI in order to escape cocaine charges, was the one who initiated the idea of trying to assassinate Farrakhan. FBI agents later violated the Constitution in order to obtain an invalid "confession" from Qubilah Shabazz. The suspected FBI objective, promoting division between followers of Malcolm X (Shabazz's late father) and pro-Farrakhan forces, was totally inappropriate for a federal law enforcement agency [89]

As with BATF abuses, a few cases of FBI abuses get national attention every year. But there are other cases for which the victim's story is never told nationally. In 1990, the FBI was investigating letter bombs which had been sent to federal judges. Leroy Moody, who was eventually convicted of the bombing, wrote a note that accompanied the bombs on a used typewriter his wife had bought from Robert O'Ferrell. When the FBI discovered that O'Ferrell was connected to the typewriter, the FBI was fully justified in investigating O'Ferrell intensively. But the FBI did much more than that.

One day, FBI agents showed up at the school attended by O'Ferrell's teenage daughter. They removed her from school, and asked her if she knew her father was a bomber. They also asked her if her parents had sex.

Mr. O'Ferrell was told by the FBI that if he did not confess, he would be executed in the electric chair. According to his attorney, the FBI with its 175 agents on the case was responsible for the leaks naming O'Ferrell as the major suspect, leaks which destroyed O'Ferrell's marriage and business, and put him in the hospital with a bleeding ulcer. After ten months, the FBI arrested the actual perpetrator, never bothering to apologize to O'Ferrell for ruining his life, much less pay his medical expenses.[90] More recently, the FBI did have the decency to announce eventually that Olympic bombing suspect Richard Jewell was no longer a suspect, after a leak from the bureau had made him one of the most notorious people in the United States for several months.

In 1989, an FBI agent interrogated Virginia Bernard, a seventy-three-year-old parochial school teacher in Phoenix, because of "national security" concerns. The agent explained the two reasons for suspicion about Mrs. Bernard: first, she subscribed to *Soviet Life*, a glossy magazine produced by the Soviet government for American readers, under a 1956 cultural exchange agreement. Second, she had written a letter to the Soviet embassy (commending the Soviets for having sent an icebreaker to free two whales who were trapped by ice off the coast of Alaska).[91]

If the FBI currently keeps enough records on Americans to match subscriber lists for particular magazines with the names of persons who write to foreign embassies, what can be expected in coming years, as the FBI engages in "data mining" programs to conduct computer analysis of the huge databases of consumer information owned by credit card companies, credit bureaus, and others? Legislation enacted in 1996 now allows the FBI to access certain credit bureau information on individuals without first obtaining a court order.[92]

During the first Clinton administration, the pace of FBI scandals and the pace of FBI demands for new powers to spy on American citizens both accelerated.[93]

In the "Filegate" matter, the FBI delivered more than nine hundred highly confidential background investigation files to political operatives at the White House. According to a high-ranking, anonymous FBI official, the files could not possibly have been turned over to the White House without authorization from a high-ranking FBI administrator.[94] In a response which took chutzpah to new limits, FBI Director Freeh claimed that Filegate was a case of "victimization"of the FBI.

Filegate is not an exception, but rather part of a pattern of the FBI allowing itself to be used for political purposes. In 1993, the FBI cooperated with the Clinton administration's efforts to get rid of the White House travel staff. At the request of the White House, the investigation of alleged financial misconduct by the travel staff was conducted by FBI headquarters, rather than by the Washington, D.C., branch office. The FBI public relations office worked closely with the White House public relations office to create a press release to justify the firings of the travel staff. And the FBI left travel office files unsecured for three weeks, during which (according to witnesses), Clinton White House staff removed documents, including, perhaps, exculpatory ones.

Pursuant to FBI rules, former FBI Agent Gary Aldrich gave the FBI an advance copy of his manuscript detailing his experiences in the Clinton White House. The FBI is supposed to review ex-agent manuscripts for security concerns, not for political advantage. But FBI General Counsel Howard Shapiro hand-delivered the manuscript to the Clinton White House, giving the Clinton administration months of lead times to prepare a well-organized spin campaign against Aldrich's book, *Unlimited Access*.

In 1995, FBI agents were sent to lobby firearms companies to support a ban on the production of full-jacketed ammunition and a ban on the importation of foreign surplus ammunition. This activity appears to violate federal law against the use of appropriated funds for lobbying.[95]

In short, FBI spying on and harassment of Americans for exercising their constitutional rights are not isolated problems from a single period in the bureau's history. They have been common bureau practice at all times, right up to the present. The FBI is and always been has a serious threat to American civil liberties. Various institutional reforms, such as term limits for the FBI director, have failed to stop FBI abuses.

Wiretapping

The FBI should not be given additional powers before fundamental reforms have taken root. Yet at a time when Filegate and other FBI scandals might make one cautious about handing the FBI more authority, the FBI has been fighting, largely successfully, to obtain vast new surveillance powers over American citizens. A case in point is wiretapping.

Federal wiretaps are currently at record levels. The overwhelming majority of wiretaps are not for violent crime, let alone for terrorism. Instead, they are for vice offenses, principally drugs and gambling. According to the Administrative Office of the United States Courts, wiretappers intercepted two million innocent conversations in 1995; 80 percent of intercepted conversations are innocent.

The FBI has announced plans to raise the number of wiretaps 130 percent by 2004.[96] Under the "Digital telephony" legislation enacted by Congress in 1994, the phone companies of the United States are to be paid to reconfigure their operating systems to make them wiretap-friendly. This will allow FBI agents (or the DEA, or other federal agencies) to listen in on phone conversations without having to leave their office. The FBI has stated that phone companies in urban areas must reconfigure their systems so that the federal government can listen to 1 percent of all conversations at any given time.[97]

The Clinton/Dole terrorism bill, enacted in April 1996, opened up a whole new class of data transmission to warrantless surveillance. The Electronic Communications Privacy Act outlaws wiretapping by the government or by private parties, with certain exceptions (such as when a warrant is obtained). The terrorism bill narrowed the type of communication interceptions which are considered to be wiretapping, and thereby greatly expanded the scope of communications which can legally be intercepted by private persons, as well as by government officials who lack probable cause and a search warrant. Wireless transmission of computer data (such as from a radio modem, or a cellular phone connected to a modem) is now subject to search at will, with no need for court authorization.[98]

The FBI's success in getting the authority to intercept radio modem communications without the need for a warrant is consistent with the FBI's efforts to exempt other wiretaps from the Fourth Amendment's warrant requirement. For example, most court-ordered wiretaps are for the interception of particular speakers on particular phone lines. If the interception target keeps switching telephones (as by using several pay phones), the government may ask the court for a roving wiretap, authorizing interception of any phone line the target is using. Yet while roving wiretaps are currently available when the government shows the court a need, the FBI, with strong support from the Clinton administration, has pressed for legislation allowing roving wiretaps for whatever an FBI agent, in his own opinion, calls a terrorism investigation, *without* court order.[99]

Similarly, proposals have been offered to require credit card companies, financial reporting services, hotels, airlines, and bus companies to turn over customer information whenever demanded by the federal government.[100] Document subpoenas are currently available whenever the government wishes to coerce a company into disclosing private customer information. Thus, the proposals do not increase the type of private information that the government can obtain; the proposals simply allow the government to obtain the information even when the government cannot show a court that there is probable cause to believe that the documents contain evidence of illegal activity.

Confrontations

While the FBI administration worked overtime to avoid taking responsibility for Waco and Ruby Ridge, it is undeniable that, at least in highly publicized standoff situations, the FBI has become "kinder and gentler." In February 1996, the FBI negotiated a peaceful end to a standoff with an armed physician in Louisiana who had refused to make child support payments.[101] (Whether the FBI should be enforcing child support laws at all is discussed below.)

In Montana in 1996, the FBI handled the "Freemen" siege with patience and skill.

Unlike the Branch Davidians, who just wanted to be left alone, the Freemen were appropriate targets for federal law enforcement even under a strict reading of the Constitution, since they were running a multistate bank fraud operation. They had also, unlike the Branch Davidians, made violent threats against their neighbors and other innocent people.

In contrast to Waco, the FBI brought in a huge variety of third-party negotiators. Tactical pressure, such as shutting off electricity, was not done just to keep the tactical people busy. The pressure was used carefully, and appropriately, and integrated into the overall negotiation strategy. Coming on the heels of Ruby Ridge and Waco, the Freemen siege gave the FBI an opportunity to show it had learned something from those disasters, and the FBI rose to the challenge.

The question for the future is how to guarantee similar good behavior on the part of the FBI in the future, when Waco and Ruby Ridge will seem as distant as *Saturday Night Fever* and Watergate do today. What kind of institutional reforms can help ensure that the FBI performs appropriately even when not under intense public pressure because of recent incidents of excessive force?

Reforms

Throughout the J. Edgar Hoover era, many critics of the FBI naïvely assumed that the only thing wrong with the FBI was the director-for-life. When he went, the FBI would become a good bureau. But in fact the scandals, the violations of the Constitution, the obstruction of justice, and the lying to the public have continued in each new regime. When Republican appointee William Sessions was forced out of office and replaced by Democratic appointee Louis Freeh, the FBI continued to obstruct justice and cover up the murders at Ruby Ridge; the FBI's architect of Waco and Ruby Ridge (Larry Potts) was appointed second-in-command; personal files on nearly a thousand people were shipped to political operatives at the White House with no justification; and the FBI continued its incessant demands for greater surveillance powers, more wiretaps, and more money. Perhaps the problem is not that we need a new FBI director. We need a new FBI.

As at BATF, there are many good, law-abiding agents at the FBI who do good work. Wanting to reform the FBI should not be construed as attacking the character of the majority of FBI personnel.

During the Justice Department investigation of Ruby Ridge, the FBI refused to allow Justice investigators to see certain documents, or only allowed them to see redacted versions. The FBI is a subordinate division of the Department of Justice, but it would not (until political pressure became too great) cooperate with a Department of Justice investigation of Ruby Ridge. Such defiance smacks of an effort to have the FBI treated as an agency independent from the control of the attorney general.[102] This was always J. Edgar Hoover's dream, but it is utterly unlawful. The FBI has no statutory basis for its existence. It was set up by the attorney general for the use of the Justice Department. In contrast to a genuine independent agency—such as the Environmental Protection Agency—the FBI was never established by an act of Congress. The FBI is the creation of the attorney general, and a real law-and-order attorney general would make it clear that the FBI—unlike the old KGB—is not an independent branch of government.

The FBI's internal checks and balances are ineffective. As journalist Ronald Kessler, author of a generally laudatory book about the FBI, observes, the FBI's inspection division has failed to raise questions about any of the FBI's most serious civil liberties problems in the post-Hoover era, such as the Library Awareness Program (collecting lists of people who checked out suspicious books from libraries),[103] the CISPES investigation, or prejudice directed at minority agents.[104]

The most important reform is to keep the FBI from growing into a de facto national police agency. When the precursor of the Bureau of Investigation was created in 1908, it had jurisdiction over bankruptcy fraud, antitrust offenses, neutrality law violations, and compulsory servitude (holding persons as slaves or peons in violation of the Thirteenth Amendment). Now the FBI claims jurisdiction over 271 federal crimes.[105] FBI jurisdiction should be sharply curtailed, to cases for which a national agency is truly necessary, and which will not duplicate other law enforcement. Thus, the FBI should get out of the business of child support enforcement, which is a state and local matter. The FBI should get out of drug cases, since there already is a separate Drug Enforcement Administration.[106]

After years of solid growth in the Reagan-Bush administrations, the FBI budget has ballooned under the Clinton administration, rising 53 percent from 1993 to 1996, with requests for more large increases in coming years.[107] Like the BATF budget, the FBI budget should be reset to its 1984 levels, adjusted for inflation. Budgetary restraint would encourage the FBI to prioritize criminal law areas for which FBI expertise is essential, and which are not duplicative of state, local, or other federal agencies.

The 1996 scandals over the FBI sending confidential files to political operatives at the Clinton White House are, obviously, indications of serious institutional problems at the FBI and at the White House. But the broader question is why any government agency should have such files in the first place. Simply because a person has a job as a third-tier policy analyst at the White House does not mean that the FBI ought to be conducting investigations into the person's past sex life. Background checks are appropriate to make sure that the individual is not in the pay of a foreign intelligence service, but they are not appropriate simply to collect all the dirt that can be dug up—based on unverifiable, unrebuttable accusations from old acquaintances—about an individual who wants to work in government.

OTHER LAW ENFORCEMENT AGENCIES

In many of the cases for which the BATF draws the heat, there are several agencies involved. For example, state wildlife departments have long operated gamecheck stations to quickly examine the cars of people returning from a hunt, to ensure that the hunters have not exceeded their limits or bagged any illegal game. But in Nebraska (and perhaps other states as well), it is alleged that the BATF, the Drug Enforcement Administration, and the Immigration and Naturalization Service have started piggybacking on game checks, and used the checks to remove door panels from cars, search baggage by scattering the contents on the ground, and subject the vehicles to dog-sniff searches.[108]

At times, the BATF has helped undo the damage caused by irresponsible conduct by other federal agencies. For example, in May 1995, the United States Customs Service pulled off a very highly publicized raid on ammunition importer Eagle Exim, in Santa Clara, California, and seized 75 million rounds of Russian ammunition. A joint Customs-BATF task force, clad in combat jumpsuits, first went to the wrong address to serve the warrant, then, after finding the Eagle Exim warehouse, grabbed every paper or document they could find, and carried off ten truckloads of ammunition.

The raid was based on what turned out to be an entirely false tip from an informant, which law enforcement officials made little effort to verify. Customs officials told the media that the Russian ammunition was Chinese-made (and hence subject to a 1994 embargo), and then falsely claimed that Eagle Exim's import license for the Russian ammunition had expired. An Assistant United States Attorney asserted, without offering any supporting evidence, that Eagle Exim was suspected of selling the ammunition to militia groups; even if this were true, there would be nothing illegal about it.

Every round of ammunition was eventually returned, and Eagle Exim's president praised the BATF agents for playing a constructive role in convincing Customs to undo its mistake.[109]

Department of Justice

The number of federal prosecutors (Assistant United States Attorneys) per capita rose 114 percent from 1980 to 1992.[110] This expansion has been fueled primarily by the increasing intrusion of federal law enforcement into state and local matters. As federal appellate judge Richard Posner observes, "The increase in the number of federal prosecutors in recent years has brought with it problems of quality control."[111] The DOJ budget grew from 2.3 billion dollars in 1981 to 9.8 billion in 1993. With 100,000 total employees, the Department of Justice should be subjected to an immediate hiring freeze, while attrition shrinks the department down to the size necessary to handle federal matters.

While the number of federal attorneys sets new records every year, making control of attorney quality all the more difficult, Attorney General Reno is attempting to exempt her attorneys from ethics laws. Every attorney who practices in federal court (such as, for example, the federal district court for Colorado) must be licensed to practice law in state courts in the relevant state. As members of state bars, Department of Justice employees are subject to the ethical laws which apply to all members of a given state's bar. But the Department of Justice promulgated the "Reno Regulation" which purports to exempt federal prosecutors from ethics rule in the states where the prosecutors practice.[112]

This power grab was unanimously condemned by the United States Conference of Chief Justices, who announced that they considered state ethics rules still binding on federal prosecutors admitted to practice law in their state courts; prosecutors who violated ethical rules would be subject to the full range of sanctions, including disbarment. (The Reno Regulation echoes the Clinton administration's efforts, discussed in chapter 5, to exempt federal agents from state criminal laws.[113])

Although the Department of Justice asserts that the flouting of state ethical standards is permitted by the Constitution's Supremacy Clause (which declares that federal law is supreme over contradictory state law), that theory was rejected in federal court, upholding the authority of the New Mexico Attorney Disciplinary Board over a federal prosecutor:

> The idea of placing the discretion for a rule's interpretation and enforcement solely in the hands of those governed by it not only renders the rule meaningless, but the notion of such an idea coming from the country's highest law enforcement official displays an arrogant disregard for and irresponsibly undermines ethics in the legal profession.[114]

Attorney General Reno should resign—not because the Waco tank assault plan failed—but because her unwillingness to discipline people and organizations which flagrantly deceived her, and whose deceptions directly led to the deaths of seventy-six people, is incapable of providing the control and leadership that is necessary for the Department of Justice.[115]

The failures of Attorney General Reno regarding Waco are representative of her general failure to ensure that the Department of Justice operates in the pursuit of justice, rather than for the political advantage of the current president. While she has, appropriately, appointed special prosecutors in some cases, those appointments have been clearly mandated by the special prosecutor statute. In cases where she has the discretion to prosecute, she has often shied away. For example, some high-level Clinton officials obtained personnel files of former political appointees at the State Department who had served during the Bush administration. Information from two of these files was leaked to the *Washington Post*, and the State Department's inspector general found that there had likely been a violation of the Privacy Act. But Attorney General Reno declined to pursue the matter.

When Mrs. Clinton's health care task force was sued for holding secret meetings in violation of federal law, Judge Royce Lamberth found Department of Justice tactics in defense of Mrs. Clinton and her associates so far out of bounds that he asked for an investigation by the United States Attorney (who works for Attorney General Reno, and who never conducted the investigation) to see if the Department of Justice had presented perjured testimony by top Clinton officials.

Breaking with long-standing rules of propriety for attorneys general, Ms. Reno campaigned publicly for the reelection of Democratic Governor Jim Florio of New Jersey in the fall of 1993.[116]

The FBI under General Reno has been allowed to degenerate into an increasingly lawless bureau which poses an imminent threat to civil liberty. As detailed in chapter 5, she participated in and abetted the federal government cover-up of Waco.

Janet Reno appears to be a good person with honorable intentions, but she has proved herself unfit as attorney general. She should resign. She has proved herself incapable of functioning as the ethical rudder which the Department of Justice so desperately needs. The best argument for her staying in office is that the Clinton administration would probably name an even worse replacement.

Other Federal Agencies

After the botched St. Louis raid described above, involving local police and the BATF, the *St. Louis Post-Dispatch* observed that the raid received massive coverage only because the victims were "a nice white, middle-class family."[117] Neither the Weaver family nor the Branch Davidians were ordinary middle-class families. But because the attacks on the Weavers and the Davidians were predicated on federal gun control laws, there was a large, politically potent group of Americans who were inclined to consider the claims of excessive force with some sympathy.

While the BATF does have a bad record of targeting innocent people who are somehow associated with guns (and then getting the FBI involved if things go wrong), one should not assume that the BATF and FBI are necessarily more violent or lawless than other federal law enforcement agencies. BATF and FBI have simply made the mistake of picking on people who arouse sympathy among America's millions of gun rights activists.

BATF has the handicap of having victims—gun store owners and gun collectors—who are middle class, highly informed about their rights, and often not afraid to assert those rights. Further, one of the most powerful interest groups in the United States, the National Rifle Association, makes a point of keeping an eye on and exposing BATF abuses. Thus, by comparison to other federal law enforcement agencies, BATF sometimes appears substantially worse. Likewise, the Internal Revenue Service (IRS) is frequently criticized, and IRS reform bills are enacted every few years, because IRS abuses fall disproportionately on wealthy people, a group with even more political clout than the NRA.

In contrast, other federal agencies may act just as, or more, lawlessly, but pay no political price, because their targets have so few political allies. For example, the Border Patrol is the subject of more complaints to the Department of Justice than any other Justice agency. Unlike BATF or FBI, the Border Patrol has been specifically criticized by the international human rights organization Americas Watch, in a report (April 1995) detailing allegations of sex abuse, unjustified shootings, racism, and torture.

The Bureau of Indian Affairs, one of the smaller federal police agencies, racks up the highest per-officer complaint rate. According to a 1993 investigation by the Associated Press, "BIA police officers routinely use force when arresting suspects and are rarely disciplined for assaulting them."[118]

Similarly, the Immigration and Naturalization Service and the Drug Enforcement Administration both have the luxury of targeting groups with almost no political influence. Unnecessary violence and contempt for civil liberties are at least as prevalent at INS[119] and DEA as at BATF or the FBI.

One of the most outrageous DEA raids began just after midnight on August 25, 1992, in Poway, California. A notoriously unreliable informant had told the DEA that the garage next to the home of businessman Donald Carlson contained several tons of cocaine, which were protected by four armed guards. As Mr. Carlson returned home, he used an automatic garage door opener which automatically turned on a garage light. The DEA agents could easily see that the garage did not contain tons of cocaine, and had no armed guards. Nevertheless, the agents went ahead with the raid, which they commenced by breaking into Mr. Carlson's home in the middle of the night. Afraid that he was being robbed, Mr. Carlson grabbed his pistol and dialed 911. The DEA shot Mr. Carlson again and again, even as he lay wounded on the floor. He spent seven weeks in intensive care. The objective of the raid was to forfeit Mr. Carlson's house and other property.[120]

In the Carlson case, unlike almost every other case discussed in this chapter, the Department of Justice paid Mr. Carlson compensatory damages after he sued them.

Even the Food and Drug Administration has taken to acting like a paramilitary force, with armed agents in flak jackets staging raids on vitamin manufacturers and health food stores. Asked about one controversial raid, an FDA spokesman explained, "We had to play a little rough to send a message to the whole industry."[121] The IRS has also begun serving search warrants by force, and brandishing loaded weapons at people.[122]

Local and state

While the focus of this book is on federal agencies, it cannot be denied that state and local law enforcement agencies have also engaged in their own share of jackbooted thuggery and homicide. For example, according to the *National Review*:

> On the night of April 17 [1995], sheriff's deputies raided the trailer home of Scott W. Bryant in Beaver Dam, Wisconsin to execute a search warrant as part of a drug investigation. Moments after the deputies burst into the trailer, one of them fired a shot that fatally wounded Bryant. The 29-year-old man, who was unarmed and offered no resistance, died in front of his 7-year-old son. The police found three grams of marijuana in the trailer.[123]

Bryant was shot by a detective who had repeatedly made headline-grabbing drug busts. Although the district attorney found the shooting "not in any way justified," no criminal charges were filed, and the detective was returned to active duty.

Hundreds of drug convictions in Philadelphia are being overturned following revelations that police officers planted evidence, beat suspects into confessing, perpetrated robberies, and conspired to convict defendants illegally.[124] The Philadelphia police department had previously received national attention on Mother's Day in 1985, when it dropped a bomb on a row house occupied by a gang of provocative radical criminals known as MOVE. The bomb not only killed all but one of the children in the house, it started a fire which burned down sixty-one row houses in the black, working-class neighborhood.[125]

According to the *New York Times*, "Richard Pennington, the newest chief of police in New Orleans, has to deal with organized drug rings, execution-style murders, bank robbers and rapists. And that's just the cops."[126]

The Los Angeles Police Department has been a leader in militarization and aggression among major urban police departments. Violent break-ins to homes under the pretext of drug law enforcement became routine in the 1980s. In 1989, for example, LAPD officers, including the gang task force, broke into and destroyed four apartments on Dalton Avenue; the apartments were suspected as crack dens, but in fact were not. This did not stop LAPD officers from spray painting on an apartment wall, "Gang Task Force Rules."[127] The officers who participated in the raid were promoted.[128] To many people of color in major cities, the distinction between the bad elements in a police gang task force and a nongovernmental gang is increasingly blurry. Both are likely to perpetrate criminal assaults against persons and property based on weak pretexts, and both are unlikely to be punished for their offenses.

In the small, rural town of Rocky Comfort, Missouri, in 1995, a young mother in her living room grabbed a revolver to frighten away a trespasser on her lawn who had previously made violent threats against her children. (The trespasser was a racist neighbor who had wanted to buy their property, and who claimed that he was good friends with the local sheriff.) Two days later, six men dressed all in black, sporting mirrored sunglasses and assault rifles, barreled through the family's front door and pointed the rifles at the mother and her small children. (The husband, a truck driver, was not at home.) When the terrified six-year-old tried to jump out of her chair and run to her mother, the men pointed guns at the child's face and screamed at her to get down. After another man, wearing a police badge, arrived, the family realized that the intruders were police officers. Executing a search warrant to look for explosives, the police broke rafters and sheet rock while tearing the house apart.

Nothing illegal was found, but the police confiscated the family's guns, arrested the mother (for brandishing the revolver), and took the children into custody, threatening to put them in foster care.

The police ordered her to leave her back door unlocked, because the BATF agents who would be arriving would break down a locked door. BATF agents did arrive later, conducting a second search which again found nothing illegal. The family's small dog, Jeremiah, had its tail broken, apparently during the BATF search. The search warrant was sealed by court order.

The sheriff denied that the officers had been dressed in black, and denied that his officers pointed their weapons at anyone. A judge dismissed the firearms brandishing charge against the mother.[129]

Virtually all the federal law enforcement reforms suggested in the book would also make sense at the state level. This book's focus on federal law enforcement should *not* be taken as suggesting that local law enforcement does not have its own problems. But the more that local law enforcement comes under federal influence, the worse those problems will get. As will be discussed below in the section on law enforcement militarization, the federal government has already played a major role in encouraging local law enforcement militarization, a role that should be immediately terminated. More federal control of state and local law enforcement will make matters worse. As Patrick Henry observed, while local control is far from perfect at keeping law enforcement offices within the confines of the law, controlling law enforcement is all the more difficult when law enforcement officers are answerable only to a distant national capital.[130]

Canada

Traditionally, the Canadian people have taken pride in Canadian law enforcement being less violent and more orderly than its American cousin. But increasingly, Canadian police are behaving like an army of occupation rather than peace officers.

In the middle of the night on January 19, 1996, heavily-armed Royal Canadian Mounted Police officers invaded a middle-class home in suburban Vancouver, yanked the startled occupants out of bed, forced them to the floor, and handcuffed them, while pointing guns at their heads. The RCMP had the wrong address.

Early in the morning of February 19, 1996, in Caledonia, Ontario, two dozen Ontario Provincial Police Tactical and Rescue Unit officers broke through the front door of a home where fifty-seven-year-old John Goddard and his wife, Jean, lived, forced them to the floor at gunpoint, and tied their hands behind their backs with a plastic rope. When Mr. Goddard asked the invaders for identification, he was ordered to keep his face down. The raid was based on the uncorroborated statement of an informant who claimed that the Goddards had blocks of hashish and weapons in their house.[131]

Two days before, the Ontario Provincial Police had broken through the front and back doors of a home in rural Orangeville, Ontario, and tied up the terrified family, including a seventy-year-old grandfather, and held them at gunpoint on the floor. The police mistakenly believed that the family was harboring a man wanted for murders in Toronto. While the raid was going on, Toronto police were in Florida, preparing to arrest the murderer there. The family says that they were warned they would be charged with criminal offenses if they discussed the raid with anyone. After the family notified the media, they were charged with possession of a small amount of marijuana, and unsafe storage of a rifle.[132]

Thirty Canadian national police, from the Royal Canadian Mounted Police and from Customs, were just about to use a battering ram and stun grenades to enter Marstar Trading, a rural firearms store, to conduct a search, when an accompanying officer from the Ontario Provincial Police tactical unit convinced them to ring the doorbell first. They did, and were admitted peacefully. As they conducted a search for evidence of violations of customs laws, they refused to identify themselves, marched the store's staff around at submachine-gunpoint, and, after their seven-hour search, left the premises a shambles. Months later, the government acknowledged that it would not charge anyone with a crime. In November 1995, the offices of Marstar's attorney were burglarized. The only item taken was the hard disk from his computer.

Canadian dynamic entries may increase as a result of the new Canadian gun law, effusively praised by President Clinton, which allows warrantless searches of homes thought to contain guns or gun registration records.[133]

The trend toward violent law enforcement is not the result of a few bad appointments by the Clinton administration. It is a trend that transcends personnel and political parties. Halting and then reversing that trend in America can, at least by example, perhaps help other nations as well.

OTHER LAW ENFORCEMENT IMPROVEMENTS

Quis costodiet ipsos custodes?[134]

Sensitivity Training

One reform to reduce abuses at the BATF, the FBI, and other federal law enforcement agencies would be mandatory sensitivity training. Law enforcement officers, especially members of élite units, should be reminded that loyalty to the unit should be subordinate to respect for the law and for constitutional rights. Officers should be aware that American law justifies the use of force for self-defense by civilians, and that such force may lawfully be used against law enforcement officers, depending on the civilian's reasonable beliefs, such as when a law enforcement officer attacks a person without appropriately identifying himself or uses excessive force. The sixteen-week course at the FBI National Academy in Quantico, Virginia (which also trains DEA agents), currently includes four hours of ethics, and five hours of ethnic/racial sensitivity training. This compares to 198 hours for "Hogan's Alley" (dealing with crimes in progress, in a mock-up town) and emergency vehicle operations, 113 hours for firearms, 76 hours for legal training, and 73 hours of physical fitness and defensive training.[135] There surely are a few hours in the sixteen weeks which can be used for constitutional sensitivity. Judging by results, the current training program is inadequate in this regard.

Nancy Ammerman, one of the independent reviewers of the Department of Justice report, suggests that training for all Justice and Treasury agents should

> include units in the behavioral sciences and units that give attention to the nature of political and religious groups. These units should emphasize both the rights of such groups to exist unhindered and the characteristics of high-commitment groups that may be relevant to future efforts at law enforcement. Such units should be aimed not so much at making every agent an expert as at sensitizing agents to the complex human dimensions of the situations in which they may find themselves. When they hear behavioral scientists advising them later, it will not be the first time they have heard such voices in the law enforcement community.[136]

An afternoon of constitutional sensitivity training might not be a bad idea for other parts of the federal government as well. Perhaps it could help cure the hubris displayed on a Washington talk show, "The Capital Gang," when Waco was discussed. On that show, journalist Robert Novak asked Labor Secretary Robert Reich if federal actions at Waco constituted terrorism.

"We're talking about acts of violence, Americans against Americans," Reich responded.

"Wasn't that an act of violence?" Novak continued.

"We're talking about acts of violence that are not sanctioned by the government, that are not official," explained Reich.[137]

Reich was apparently unaware that the word "terrorist" was first used to describe government officials who created terror.[138] Like the feminist theoretician who argued that a particular woman who had intentionally killed many men over a long period of time could not be a "serial killer" because serial killers are male,[139] some people fail to recognize that government officials, acting in their official capacities, can perpetrate serious violent crimes, including terrorism.[140]

Besides protecting American civilians from illegal or unjustifiable use of force, the suggested reforms might also save the lives of law enforcement agents. Since the law authorizes use of deadly force in self-defense, the less frequently that federal agents use illegal force in a raid, the less frequently they will be subjected to lawful return fire from citizen victims.

Law Enforcement Commissions

Another important way to prevent federal law enforcement violence from escalating to deadly levels would be to create a federal law enforcement review commission, similar to the police review commissions which now exist in 60 percent of major American cities. The permanent, independent commission would review controversial shooting incidents, excessive force allegations, and the like.

With one exception, every scholar who has studied the Second Amendment—including the small minority of scholars who conclude that the Second Amendment was not intended to guarantee an individual right—agrees that one of the most important objectives of the framers of the Second Amendment was to prevent a federal standing army from tyrannizing America.[141] The Second Amendment was one of several ways in which the authors of the Constitution tried to ensure that federal military power would remain subordinate to the American people. As federal law enforcement grows increasingly larger, more militarized, and more lawless, creation of a federal law enforcement review commission would be consistent with the spirit which animated much of the Constitution, including the Second Amendment.

In addition to a commission to review specific incidents, a separate commission should be created to focus on civil liberties policy issues relevant to law enforcement. Criminal Justice Professor James Fyfe suggests a permanent civilian advisory commission for law enforcement, analogous to U.S. Civil Rights Commission.[142] The Civil Rights Commission helps keep civil rights issues visible to federal policymakers, and conducts studies of important civil rights questions.

The FBI does an excellent job collecting data and reports on law enforcement officers killed in the line of duty.[143] The same effort should be put into gathering data about persons killed by the police.[144] The 1994 Clinton crime bill, while deeply flawed in many respects, did take the positive step of ordering the attorney general to collect statistics on police misconduct. The attorney general was also given power to seek injunctions against misconduct, although this power has not yet been exercised.

Rights of Law Enforcement Employees

Bureaucracies that violate the rights of the American people often violate the rights of their own employees. A bureaucratic structure in which employees can be fired arbitrarily, and dissenters can have their careers destroyed, is precisely the kind of structure which is most vulnerable to the kind of groupthink and callousness toward constitutional rights which characterizes too much of federal law enforcement today. Accordingly, one important component of a law enforcement reform strategy is protection of the rights of employees in the federal law enforcement organizations.

Libertarians in particular should not make the mistake of assuming that everyone who works for the federal government is "the enemy." In fact, there are many hardworking federal law enforcement employees who believe that law and order starts with obeying the Constitution. Some of these employees belong to independent organizations such as the National Association of Treasury Agents. NATA works to protect whistle blowers within BATF and other Treasury bureaus and agencies.[145] NATA

Deputy Executive Director Jim Jorgensen has spoken out repeatedly against civil liberties intrusions such as expanded wire-tapping, the evisceration of habeas corpus, and gun prohibition. BATF's alleged post-Waco "reforms" have been critiqued by NATA as window-dressing which fails to address BATF's dysfunctional management culture—a culture in which being part of the "good old boys" network and keeping one's shoes shined is far more important than competence.[146]

The genius of the United States Constitution is its incorporation of the balance of power on numerous levels. Not only is there a division of power among the three branches of government, but there are many other checks and balances, including the division of power between the federal government and the states, the existence of a free press, and so on. Important elements in a modern system of checks and balances are the ability of federal employees to speak out against federal wrongdoing, and the ability of organizations such as NATA to work on behalf of the rights of all law enforcement employees.

Unsurprisingly, the federal law enforcement bureaucracy is hostile to such a system of checks and balances. Treasury Secretary Robert Rubin has issued rules which regulate the speech of Treasury employees *off* the job. Attorney General Reno has issued a legal opinion which claims that federal employees have no right to belong to independent organizations such as NATA; happily, Congress subsequently enacted legislation protecting such groups. When BATF employees attempted to unionize in the 1970s, President Carter issued an executive order, still in force, to prohibit unionization. When two Secret Service agents testified to Congress about how the White House obtained confidential FBI files, the two agents were placed under criminal investigation at the request of the White House.[147] In flagrant violation of a court order, the Drug Enforcement Administration maintains personnel disciplinary records on agents even when agents have been found innocent and a court has ordered DEA to expunge the disciplinary record.[148]

Things are even worse at the FBI. There, in internal disciplinary situations, agents have no right to confront the evidence against them, no right to know who has accused them, no right to an attorney, no right to compel evidence on their behalf, not even a right to a hearing, and no right to an appeal.[149] With such rules in effect, it is easy for high-ranking officials to intimidate lower-level employees, and to cover up misconduct, for any potential whistle blower knows that his career can be destroyed with impunity.

All of these violations of employee rights should be corrected by congressional statute which provides for due process in disciplinary cases, with specific protections for whistle-blowers and others who refuse to acquiesce in the misconduct of higher-ranking officials. As Paul 't Hart points out in *Groupthink in Government*, whistle blowing may be especially when other mechanisms to prevent groupthink have failed, and dissenters have no other mechanism to protect the public from illegal and dangerous government actions.[150]

FORFEITURE REFORM

On October 12, 1992, a multitude of federal and state agencies (including the National Park Service, the Forest Service, the Drug Enforcement Administration, and the National Guard) broke into the home of southern California millionaire Donald Scott. The no-knock, late night raid was supposedly designed to serve a warrant to look for marijuana plants growing on Mr. Scott's estate, although there was no realistic possibility that Mr. Scott could have destroyed the marijuana plants (alleged to be hidden in trees far from his home) during the time it would have taken the police to knock at his door and demand entry. When Mr. Scott, awakened by the noise of people breaking into his home at night, ran to the living room with his legally owned .38 revolver, he was shot dead. The search yielded no evidence of drugs or illegal activity.

An investigation by Ventura County, California, District Attorney Michael Bradbury found that the basis of the warrant—a drug agent's claim that while in a surveillance plane 1,000 feet above the ground, the agent could see individual marijuana plants concealed in leafy trees—was fabricated. The district attorney also noted that the sheriff's department which participated in the raid had conducted an appraisal of the five-million-dollar Scott ranch before the raid, apparently with the expectation that the ranch would be forfeited to the government.

Most forfeitures do not involve violence or death. When the law enforcement officers point their guns at someone and announce they are taking away the property, most property owners do not resist. Similarly, in most robberies perpetrated by criminals with guns, the victim does not resist, and no one gets hurt.

In practice, forfeiture has increasingly become a form of legalized robbery. When the property of an innocent person is taken away at gunpoint, the effect on the victim is the same, whether the perpetrator was an individual criminal with a handgun, or several federal agents with machine guns. For example, two Kansas City police drug squad members, wearing ski masks "to conceal their identity," handed forfeiture papers to the owner of a Corvette car, and then drove the vehicle away. The man was not charged with any crimes.[151] Except for getting a receipt, the man experienced the functional equivalent of a carjacking.

Forfeiture is a huge, profitable business for law enforcement. In 1993 alone, the Department of Justice took in more than half a billion dollars through forfeitures.[152] Since 1990, the federal government has raked in 2.7 billion dollars in forfeitures.[153]

In 1989, Acting Deputy Attorney General Edward S. G. Dennis (who would later oversee the Department of Justice's whitewash of FBI conduct at Waco[154]) ordered the nation's United States Attorneys to do everything possible to keep their forfeiture cases going, even if that meant that other matters would have to be dropped, and attorneys reassigned from criminal cases to forfeiture cases.[155] The next year, Attorney General Thornburgh issued a memorandum which frankly discussed forfeiture as if it were a corporate profit center (although corporations make money though voluntary sales of goods or services, rather than taking things by force):

> We must significantly increase production to reach our budget target. . . .Failure to achieve the $470 million projection would expose the Department's forfeiture program to criticism and undermine confidence in our budget projections. Every effort must be made to increase forfeiture income during the remaining three months of [fiscal year] 1990.[156]

When forfeiture laws are challenged in court, courts will frequently point out the ancient nature of forfeiture, in order to show that forfeiture is a time-honored law enforcement tool. Forfeiture is indeed ancient, but it belongs in the category of ancient law enforcement tools such as trial by ordeal and the rack which were banished from the United States as relics of a barbaric time. From the First Congress until 1970, there was no criminal forfeiture provision in federal law.[157]

But as Randolph Bourne observed, war is the health of the state. The drug war has done more to expand the predatory power of government at all levels than any other policy in the twentieth century, with the exception of the income tax. Although forfeiture laws are not usually limited to drug cases, the drug war provided the opportunity for government agencies to get legislatures to enact broad forfeiture laws, often with little consideration for the details. Many legislators might never have voted for forfeiture laws had they understood how the laws would really work.

Imagine, for example, a proposed forfeiture law that looked like this:

(1) Whenever a police officer is permitted, with or without judicial approval, to conduct a search to investigate a potential crime, the officer may seize and keep as much property associated with the alleged criminal as the police officer considers appropriate.

(2) For purposes of subsection (1), the amount of proof necessary to authorize a forfeiture shall be the same amount of proof necessary to procure a search warrant.

(3) Although forfeiture is predicated on the property being used in a crime, there shall be no requirement that the owner be convicted of a crime. It shall be irrelevant that the person was acquitted of the crime on which the seizure was based, or was never charged with any offense.[158]

(4) Normal procedural protections of the Rules of Civil Procedure shall not be applicable.

(5) Although this section is intended for the punishment of criminals, none of the constitutional protections relevant to criminal cases shall be applicable.

(6) After the property is seized, the burden of proof shall be on the owner seeking to have his property returned.[159]

Does the above statute seem more appropriate to North Korea than the United States? The above statute is *currently* law, for federal seizures, and for most states. In the 1980s, almost every state enacted forfeiture laws along the model above. Although the actual phrasing of the statutes is a little more elegant, the effect is the same as the "model" statute above.

Under existing laws, prior court approval is not necessary for a forfeiture. All that is required is that the police officer seize the property pursuant to a lawful search, and all that is necessary for a lawful search is probable cause.[160]

Probable cause is an extremely easy standard to meet. (Recall the slender evidence that created probable cause for the Waco search warrant, in chapter 1.) Probable cause is not proof "beyond a reasonable doubt," which is the burden of proof the government must meet in a criminal case. It is not proof by "a preponderance of the evidence" (51 percent) that must be met in a civil case. Rather, probable cause is the far lower standard; it merely means that there must be enough tentative evidence of possible criminal activity to justify the issuance of a search warrant. Probable cause, including the probable cause used for forfeiture, can be based on an informant's tip.[161]

Because there are many situations where searches without a warrant are lawful, there are just as many situations where forfeiture without prior court approval is lawful.

In cases when the government does seek prior approval for a forfeiture, the only party presenting evidence is the government. There is no requirement that the property owner be notified, or have an opportunity to present his own evidence to the court. Notification comes only *after* the court has determined that there is probable cause. At that point—when the property is already in the government's hands—the property owner is finally notified and given an opportunity to ask for his property back; the owner is ordered to "show cause" why the property should not be forfeited.[162]

Many persons may believe that since they do not engage in illegal conduct with their property, and do not knowingly allow anyone else to use their property illegally, the property is safe from forfeiture. Those persons are wrong.

First of all, while forfeiture is based on property's alleged connection to a crime, the fact that the owner may be found not guilty is no bar to forfeiture.[163] Indeed, nowhere in forfeiture laws is there a requirement that any person even be charged with the criminal offenses which are the pretext for the seizure of property. The federal Comprehensive Forfeiture Act of 1984 includes no innocent owner defense, so even if a property owner can prove beyond a reasonable doubt that the property associated with a crime was used without his consent and against his best efforts to prevent its use, the property is still forfeitable.

It is true that there may be special situations where a criminal conviction cannot be obtained (as when the defendant flees the jurisdiction). Provisions can be made to allow forfeiture without conviction when the government proves that a special situation exists. But in the vast majority of cases, it is unfair for persons to lose their property for supposedly criminal conduct when they have never been found guilty of criminal conduct.

The implication of allowing forfeiture without conviction is that property rights are unimportant. While the government must secure a criminal conviction to punish a person by depriving him of his liberty (by putting him in prison), the government need not obtain any conviction to punish him by depriving him of his property. The disrespectful treatment of property—as being less deserving of protection than liberty—ignores the United States Constitution, which insists that "life, liberty, *and property*," all deserve the full spectrum of protection from arbitrary government action.[164] As Justice Potter Stewart noted:

> The dichotomy between personal liberties and property rights is a false one. Property does not have rights. People have rights. The right to enjoy property without lawful deprivation, no less than the right to speak or the right to travel, is in truth a "personal" right, whether the "property" in question be a welfare check, a home, or a savings account. In fact, a fundamental interdependence exists between the personal right to liberty and the personal right in property. Neither could exist without the other.[165]

In earlier days, carrying a large roll of cash was considered nothing more than a crime against good taste if the money were flashed ostentatiously. But today, many persons are legitimately afraid of carrying large sums of money through transportation hubs, or on automobile trips. They know that if they are stopped by the police, a police dog may sniff them, and "discover" that their money is "tainted" by drugs. The mere fact that currency contains drug residues is usually sufficient, by itself, for the currency to be forfeited. In fact, one study found that 96 percent of currency in ten major cities in the United States bore traces of cocaine residue.[166] Incredibly, the forfeited "tainted" money is put back into circulation—perhaps to be seized and forfeited again one day![167]

Although forfeiture laws amount to severe, drastic punishments for criminal offenses, forfeiture cases are labeled as "civil." As a result, constitutional protections required in criminal prosecutions are not applicable.[168] There is no right to counsel for persons who cannot afford an attorney, no rules against the introduction of illegally seized evidence or coerced confessions or hearsay evidence or anonymous denunciations, no right to confront government witnesses, and no protection against compelled self-incrimination.

Stripped of the constitutional protections applicable to criminal cases, property owners in forfeiture cases are not even allowed the normal protections granted to litigants in civil cases. A defendant in a slip-and-fall case enjoys broader protections of his property rights than does a person whose property has been seized by the government.

In civil cases, each side is allowed to engage in broad "discovery"—to interview the other side's witnesses,[169] and to review documents possessed by the other side.[170] In contrast, discovery rights in criminal cases are much narrower; for example, there is no right to take the deposition of an adverse criminal witness.[171] The forfeiture laws typically specify that for discovery, the rules of criminal procedure shall apply.[172] So having made forfeiture into a civil action—to deprive the property owner of the constitutional provisions applicable to criminal cases, the forfeiture law turns around and declares that discovery shall be according to the rules of criminal procedure—to deprive the property owner of the discovery rights applicable to all civil cases.

Contesting a forfeiture obviously requires a heavy legal expenditure on the part of the property owner. Thus, a poor person whose car is worth $3,000 may find it economically impossible to spend the necessary money (several thousand dollars at least) in legal fees to get his property back. This problem could be remedied by allowing persons whose property has been improperly taken to recover reasonable attorney's fees. The statutory language might state, "If the owner of property contests a forfeiture action, and the court determines that none of the property belonging to the owner is subject to forfeiture, the owner may recover his or her reasonable attorney's fees for contesting the forfeiture action."

The attorney's fees could be paid from the revenues which the seizing agency has garnered from other forfeitures. The attorney's fee provision would also help deter bad-faith seizures, just as laws allowing attorney's fee awards for frivolous lawsuits help deter bad-faith litigation.

Notably, under current law, when seizing agencies win a forfeiture, they get *their* attorney's fees paid.[173] It is hardly unreasonable that seizing agencies make whole the innocent people whose property has been improperly taken.

Whatever procedural protections are provided by state law or state constitutions have been deliberately subverted by the federal government. When local law enforcement officials perform a forfeiture, they can turn processing of the case over to federal officials. This federal "adoption" means that the forfeiture will only need to meet the lenient federal rules, not the sometimes stricter state rules. And while state law may specify that the seizing law enforcement agency may have to turn over all, or almost all forfeiture revenues to the general fund, or to drug rehabilitation programs, once the federal government has "adopted" the forfeiture, it can give the seizing state agency much more of the forfeiture revenue than the state agency would have been entitled to under state law.[174]

This adoption provision is the key to much of the drug "war." As economists Bruce Benson and David Rasmussen have demonstrated, in 1984 state law enforcement agencies made a massive shift in priorities, away from violent and property crime enforcement, and in favor of drug law enforcement geared to producing forfeiture revenues. The shift was the direct result of the 1984 federal law which allowed use of the adoption tactic as a means for state and local law enforcement to evade state and local laws governing forfeiture.[175] In January 1996, the Clinton administration further expanded forfeiture incentives, by allowing the local share from federal forfeitures to be used to pay police salaries. Thus, a local police officer might have his own salary, or that of his comrades, directly dependent on large forfeiture revenues. The administration has also provided adding the highly complex set of federal environmental laws to the offenses authorizing forfeiture.

Oppressive as the procedural rules for a forfeiture case can be, they are not the limit of what the government can accomplish with forfeiture. For example, undercover Drug Enforcement Administration (DEA) agents went to a gardening store, to buy supplies which they told the proprietor would be used to cultivate marijuana. The store refused to sell to them. The agents then went to the store's landlord, and told him that his building would be forfeited unless the gardening store were evicted, because the gardening store sold grow lights, which could be used in marijuana cultivation (as well, of course, as cultivation of any other indoor plant). The frightened landlord evicted the gardening store.[176]

In August 1994, the California legislature passed, and Governor Pete Wilson (not generally considered soft on crime) signed a forfeiture reform bill which included the following provisions:

- Except in special circumstances, the government cannot take property until it proves that the property is subject to forfeiture.
- Real property (land and buildings) can be forfeited only after a contested hearing in which the property owner can take part. If real property is owned by two or more individuals, the property is not forfeitable if one person "had no knowledge of its unlawful use."
- Family homes and family cars may not be seized.
- Any government agency which wishes to engage in forfeiture must have a department forfeiture practice manual; government employees performing forfeitures must receive special training.
- Vehicles may not be forfeited simply because they contained drugs. Vehicles carrying drugs for sale (or for possession for sale) may be forfeited if they contained more than 10 pounds of marijuana, peyote, or mushrooms, or 14.25 grams of heroin or cocaine.

• Government agencies which seize property may not keep it; the property must be sold. Of the revenues, 50 percent goes to the seizing agency, 15 percent to community antidrug or antigang programs, 24 percent to the state general fund, and 1 percent to a special fund to train government employees in the "ethics and proper use" of forfeiture.

These reforms are a good first step, but do not go far enough. (And besides that, they can be evaded through the federal adoption trick discussed above.) Likewise, the federal forfeiture reforms proposed by Reps. John Conyers and Henry Hyde are well-intentioned, but they merely tinker at the margins. Two more fundamental reforms are needed.

First, it should be recognized that as long as the seizing agency keeps a share of the revenues from the seizure, there will also be immense incentives to forfeiture abuse. All forfeiture revenues should be turned over to the general fund of the relevant government body (i.e., the Treasury of the United States), and none of them should be kept by the law enforcement agency. Any state agency which uses federal adoption to avoid this rule should have its appropriations reduced appropriately.

The second reform is to follow the logic of the 1886 case *Boyd* v. *United States*, in which Justice Bradley declared a civil forfeiture statute unconstitutional, writing, "We are . . . clearly of the opinion that proceedings instituted for the purpose of declaring the forfeiture of a man's property by reason of offenses committed by him, though they may be civil in form, are in their nature criminal."[177] Following the logic of *Boyd*, Congress—and every state legislature—should simply abolish civil forfeiture. Property should only be taken after the government has met the proper constitutional burden of proving guilt beyond a reasonable doubt in a criminal trial.

REVIVE AMERICAN AND MEDIA SUPPORT FOR FREEDOM OF RELIGION

> I am drawn irresistibly
> into a flame that means my death
> the flame of God
> that consumes everything
> Nothing can remain in its presence
>
> The only escape
> lies in changing course,
> veering free from the magnetic draw
> the heart cannot defy.
>
> The decision is mine
> in the split second I have left
> as I circle closer and closer
> Escape or immolation?
> Self or God?
> What will it be?

From Jasmin Lee Cori, "Flame of God," in *Freefall to the Beloved: Mystical Poetry for God's Lovers* (Boulder, Colo.: Golden Reed, 1996)

Because the Branch Davidian religion was a "cult," a large number of Americans apparently concluded that the "cultists" got what they deserved. In May 1993, several religious and civil liberties organizations issued a statement condemning the government's singling out the Davidians for attack because of religious nonorthodoxy.[178] The BATF, meanwhile, has reiterated its determination not to let other "cults" become "armed compounds," as if BATF had the legal authority to prevent the simultaneous exercise of First and Second Amendment rights.[179]

Perhaps the people who benefitted most from the fact that the Branch Davidians were able to repel the February 1993 BATF attack were members of the Hare Krishna sect. Former BATF agent Kay Kubicki told a reporter that BATF had long been interested in the Krishnas: "They thought they were just like the Waco thing: they were storing guns in the big temple that's in West Virginia." Kubicki suggested that if the Waco raid had succeeded, the Hare Krishnas would have been the next target.[180]

The Potential for More Wacos

According to the Cult Awareness Network, there are two to three thousand "destructive cults" in the United States.[181] That is quite a large number of future Wacos, if groups like the Cult Awareness Network can convince governments to take harsh action against these "destructive cults."

With the approach of the millennium, there will almost certainly be a surge in the numbers of people belonging to "cults" and esoteric religions, just as there was in the years leading up to 1000 C.E.[182] In secular media, it is easy to underestimate how widespread apocalyptic sentiments are in the United States. Hal Lindsey's *The Late Great Planet Earth*, a mass-market paperback which suggests that events forecast in Revelation are taking place right now, is one of the biggest-selling books of all time.

What Is a Cult?

What constitutes a cult is in the eye of the beholder. In the 1940s, books about "cults" included descriptions of Christian Scientists, Mormons, Jehovah's Witnesses, and Seventh-day Adventists, groups which are rarely described as cults today.[183] Other religions which have been derided as cults include Hasidic Judaism,[184] Pentecostal Christianity, Shi'ite Islam, Baha'i, and Wicca.[185] One columnist noted: "It has been said that a 'cult' is what we call a religion that we don't like. Perhaps the Branch Davidians were so unlikable that they blinded federal authorities and, for that matter, most of the rest of us to common sense."[186]

Historically, the United States has become a center for religious growth because of its tolerance of offbeat religions derisively called cults. Puritans, Baptists, Quakers,[187] Adventists, Methodists, Mormons, Moravians, Mennonites, Jehovah's Witnesses, Assemblies of God, the Theosophical Society, and Christian Scientists are just a few of the religions which have flourished in America's climate of freedom, and which are or were considered "cults" in other nations. America has hosted some of history's most notable separatist religious communities with behavior at odds with modern life; such communities have included Oneida (communal marriage, belief in imminent millennium),[188] Shakers (communal property, celibacy, and led by a woman who thought she was the reincarnation of Jesus Christ), Oberlin, Amana colonies, the vegetarian communities of Sylvester Graham (a Presbyterian minister, and creator of the Graham cracker), and the Amish.

In the United States today there are about nine hundred religious groups with roots in the Judeo-Christian tradition, and about six hundred others of various origins.[189] This diversity ought to be a source of national pride.

In earlier days, members of nontraditional religions were called "heretics" and often persecuted for their unorthodox beliefs. Today, as religious belief has diminished among opinion élites (particularly in the media and academia), "heresy" seems a quaint word, with its implication that there is a true religious doctrine. Thus, the new condemnation word for the religiously unusual is "cult."

The premise of the word "cult" as used in modern America is that "cultists" are brainwashed. In fact, the evidence for brainwashing is exceedingly thin. The one federal court to rule on the subject has concluded that evidence about "cult brainwashing" is inadmissible because such evidence is not generally accepted by the reputable scientific community.[190]

The court's decision is consistent with real-world evidence that brainwashing is not particularly effective. During the Korean War, the North Korean government made intense efforts to convert American prisoners of war to the Communist side.[191] Yet of the 3,500 American prisoners of war, only fifty made pro-Communist statements, and only twenty-five refused repatriation at the end of the war.[192]

If modern American "cults" were any better at brainwashing, then few people would ever leave cults, except when "liberated" by kidnappers bent on deprogramming. In fact, the defection rate is about 20 percent per year, a rate approximately equal to the defection rate from most other communal living arrangements.[193]

It is not just the federal law enforcement establishment that has found itself incapable of understanding the sincerity and intensity of extreme religious devotion. To many Americans today, the notion of "cults" is repugnant. How many people would have strong objections to violent government action against a "cult" such as this one:

> Numbering a few hundred members, this cult comprised the most extreme religious zealots of its age. Every member was required to sell his possessions and give them to the cult leaders.[194] The founder of the cult told audiences that only persons who hated their families could join the cult.[195] Written documents which the cult held to be sacred celebrated genocide perpetrated in God's name,[196] and recommended that parents beat their children frequently with sticks.[197] Notably, this group bore what Jerry Falwell (and other "anti-cult" spokespersons) consider to be the true mark of a cult; the members of the cult followed a man, rather than a doctrine. The cult's leader stated that he was "the truth" and that he was the exclusive pathway to God.[198]

The cult just described was early Christianity, although most of the elements of the description were shared by the Branch Davidians (except the requirement for sale of all possessions).[199]

The religious group to which the largest number of Americans belong, Protestant sects, takes its name from the "protest" its members raised against the religious ortho-doxy of the sixteenth and seventeenth centuries. The revered European settlers of America, the Puritans whom we celebrate at Thanksgiving, were a "cult" in their day, and had their own prophetic beliefs in the imminent destruction of the wicked world.[200] The Davidians' belief that the world would be destroyed by a giant catastrophe, with the entire human race, except for one righteous family, is, after all, simply an updated version of Noah and the great flood.

The Branch Davidians appear to have been confronted with a choice. On the one hand, they could submit to what they considered a wicked government which wanted them to renounce their God in favor of the government's supremacy. On the other hand, they could face a tremendous inferno; God would rescue them or not rescue them, as He chose, but in any case the believers would not submit to the false god of the government.[201] The alternatives facing the Branch Davidians were, at least from the Da-vidian viewpoint, precisely the same alternatives faced by Shadrach, Meshach, and Abednego in the Book of Daniel, when Babylonian King Nebuchadnezzar threatened to throw the three Jews into a "a burning fiery furnace" unless the Jews would worship the king's statue of gold. As countless Sunday school (and synagogue) teachers have taught their classes, Meshach, Shadrach, and Abednego did the right thing, and defied the government, telling the king, "[O]ur God whom we serve is able to deliver from the burning fiery furnace, and he will deliver us out of thine hand, O king. But if not, be it known unto thee, O king, that we will not serve thy gods, nor worship the golden image which thou hast set up."[202]

Christianity, the professed religion of a large majority of Americans, takes as its Messiah a man who was executed for blasphemy and who was reported by his fol-lowers to have performed numerous supernatural miracles. American Christians revere courageous men and women, from Jesus to the countless Christian martyrs, who pre-ferred death to tempering their sincere religious beliefs to meet the demands of the state. American churchgoers every Sunday sing hymns promising to follow God at all costs.[203] But the reverence for people who are willing to uphold their beliefs at any cost vanishes when the "fanatics" are no longer separated from us by time or geographical distance. Modern Americans, on the whole, sometimes have little more tolerance for their own generation's "religious fanatics" and martyrs than the Roman crowds at the Coliseum had for the early Christian fanatics and martyrs.

Tolerance

The mainstream American media are now heavily committed to diversity and tolerance regarding race and sexual preference. But tolerance is sometimes absent for religious mi-norities, as the word "cult" is bandied freely, and there are no rules at all against ridiculing conservative Christians, much less against taking Mencken-like shots at newer religions.

The general public approval of the attacks on the Branch Davidians suggests that America's religious tolerance has limits. As one scholar observes:

> By "making nice" and profoundly exchanging platitudes like "all religions have the same goal," we bury our conflicts and true differences. Only when someone like the

Branch Davidians comes along, drawing and enforcing a boundary between themselves and the larger society does the mask come off. . . .

Our desire for superficial unity dovetails with an underlying political principle: the State distrusts all loyalties other than to itself. Let a religion generally accede to the state's goals and it will flourish; let it run crossways to them, however innocently, and its adherents, like Antigone, will find they have committed "the crime of piety." So the nonviolent, essentially Christian Sioux Ghost Dancers died at Wounded Knee for the crime of believing the messiah had come and changing their lives (in defiance of government policy) as a result. . . .

I have no . . . great sympathy for David Koresh's apocalyptic doctrine. . . . What we all must do, however, is regard the dead Davidians as martyrs in the long struggle against State-sponsored religious conformity.[204]

During and after the Waco siege, the media frequently referred to Koresh's teachings as "incomprehensible." Religion scholar Nancy Ammeran explained how the "cult" label became a substitute for serious thinking:

I was sufficiently influenced by this widespread assessment of Koresh as incomprehensible that I was surprised when I first began to listen to and read his teachings. They are but a variant on what could be found in many fundamentalist and millennialist churches. The methods of study and exegesis he used would be familiar to many conservative students of the Bible, even if they would disagree with his particular interpretations. The assessment of these beliefs as "incomprehensible" reflects both the biblical ignorance of many public officials and news reporters and the power of the term "cult" to render all other attempts at understanding unnecessary.[205]

An Oliphant cartoon depicts a Koresh-type character marching with a sign reading, "The end of the world is coming." On the back of the sign, it reads: "We gratefully acknowledge the kind assistance of the FBI, the ATF, and the Department of Justice in the production of this prophecy." That is not the job of the federal government, and it is appalling that the American public so quickly accepted the revised job description.

Reforms

One step to reduce persecution of religious dissidents was suggested by Justice Department reviewers Lawrence Sullivan and Richard Davis: the president should issue an executive order requiring the approval of the president or the attorney general before major law enforcement actions (such as raids) are taken against nontraditional religious groups.

Along the same lines, civil and criminal statutes should be enacted to forbid government spying on peaceful religious groups. Groups which discover themselves to be under surveillance should have a right to seek a court order barring further surveillance. The point of these reforms is not that religious groups are entitled to special rights; rather, nonmainstream religious groups are such an attractive target for law enforcement persecution that additional safeguards are appropriate.

In chapter 5, it was suggested that Rep. Charles Schumer (D-N.Y.) had not played a constructive role in encouraging law enforcement reforms to prevent future Wacos. Nevertheless, Representative Schumer did make a major contribution when, in November 1993, his Religious Freedom Restoration Act was signed into law. The act specifies that religious behavior (such as use of communion wine by Catholics, or peyote by American Indians) can be criminalized only when the government demonstrates a compelling state interest. Representative Schumer's bill restores the ordinary standard for protection of religion in America; that standard had been upset by a 1990 Supreme Court case which held that laws infringing the free exercise of religion were constitutional so long as the law was not specially targeted at religion (i.e., wine was made illegal for everyone, not just for people receiving communion).[206]

Finally, all Americans, at least all Americans who revere the First Amendment, ought to drop the word "cult" from their vocabulary as a description of religions to which they do not approve. The word "cult" is as pejorative as the word "nigger" or "kike." All of these hate words create an atmosphere which can (as at Waco) lead directly to mass violence against innocent people. The phrases "sect" or "new religious movements" are more accurate, and less likely to inspire hate crimes. The Nazi Holocaust did not start with Zyklon B gas chambers; it started with words. All people of conscience, especially journalists, might consider whether the word "cult" has already helped cause the death of innocents, and may cause more deaths.

Many sociologists have used the word "cult" without any pejorative intent. But sociology will be little diminished by a small change in vocabulary that could, over the long run, save many lives.

While members of odd religions are the primary victims of "cult" labeling, they are not the only victims. The speakers of hate speech ultimately victimize themselves. As Livingstone Fagan put it, the federal authorities "called us a cult, demonizing us," but "They became victims of their own propaganda."[207] The cult stereotype was integral to BATF's targeting the Branch Davidians, and the decision to execute a massive dynamic entry; the attack on the "cult" not only cost the lives of four BATF agents, it severely damaged the Bureau's reputation. The FBI's cult propaganda, which the FBI itself apparently believed, helped prevent the FBI from trying to engage in a serious religious dialogue with the Branch Davidians, and helped convince the FBI that the "cultists" were so strange that the FBI's only real option was a tank and chemical warfare attack.

The Waco disaster was simply one incident in a long train of collective hysteria and persecution that have characterized American political life. Religious "nuts" who live by themselves, gun collectors who possess machine guns for target shooting, and health "nuts" who take large quantities of vitamins are only a few of the deviant groups who have been persecuted by the federal government in the last decade, for the most part with the active support of a media and public which reflect more the heritage of Cotton Mather than of Thomas Jefferson. As one sociologist observed, "a community will commence to ritually persecute imaginary enemies—conduct a witch-hunt—to manufacture moral deviants as a means of ritually reaffirming the group's problematical values and collective purposes."[208]

Modern Americans tend to think themselves far more civilized than their ancestors of three hundred years ago, who tried, convicted, and executed twenty-two "witches" and "wizards" during the Salem witch hunt. But it is far from certain that historians in the year 2293 will find 1993 to be much more enlightened than was 1693. The victims of ritual persecution are now cultists rather than witches, but the underlying mechanism of hysteria, unreflective hatred against imagined enemies, and popular demands that the government "do something" remain the same.

There is one difference, though, between Salem and Waco. In 1703, the Massachusetts legislature granted retroactive amnesties to the victims of the hysteria. In 1711, the Massachusetts Bay Colony became one of the first governments in world history to pay restitution to the families of the victims of the government's malfeasance. Whether the collective conscience of the modern United States will ever prompt the federal government to apologize and pay damages to the victims of Waco remains to be seen.

DEMILITARIZING LAW ENFORCEMENT

Although it might be hoped that the Ruby Ridge and Waco disasters would prompt a cutback in federal military-style strike forces intended for use against Americans, the opposite has happened.

The Proliferation of Federal Paramilitary Units

The United States Marshals Service now has a one-hundred-man special operations group which is "ready to go anywhere in the world at a moment's notice." The SOG is located at the William F. Degan Memorial Special Operations Center in Louisiana, which is named after the marshal killed in the senseless shootout in which nonsuspect fourteen-year-old Sammy Weaver was shot in the back as he attempted to flee to his cabin.

Attorney General Reno has stated that one reason for the April 19 tank and chemical warfare attack on Mount Carmel was that the FBI Hostage Rescue Team was tired. So the HRT is now expanded to 91 men, although there is no indication that the Hostage Rescue Team's mission has been narrowed to rescuing rather than holding hostages. The only reforms are that FBI Director Freeh promises that before the HRT is deployed in nonemergency situations, he will make the decision personally, and that negotiators and the HRT will henceforth be placed under the same command.[209]

The proliferation of BATF squads whose names imply violence continues: tactical response teams, high-risk warrant teams, forced entry teams, entry control teams, and special response teams (SRTs). In fiscal years 1993 through 1995, the SRTs were used 523 times, carrying out a dynamic entry about half of those times.[210]

BATF continues to recruit the SRTs, in the words of one ex-BATF agent, "handpicking these superhormone guys."[211] As Jim Jorgenson, of the National Association of Treasury Agents, points out, this means that SRTs are composed of people who may run 300 yards and shoot faster than anyone else, but who lack the maturity and judgment to think where they are running. Absolute discipline and obedience to orders may be virtues in the military, but not in civilian law enforcement. Perhaps if the three SRTs that were used in the Waco raid included a larger share of older, slower, and wiser agents, someone would have spoken up when the raid commanders yelled "He knows we're coming" and "Let's go." Rank-and-file defiance of the order to launch a surprise attack with no element of surprise would have saved the lives of the four BATF agents, and of the Branch Davidians.

BATF has stepped up the training of its field commanders in military tactics, under the supervision of the army.[212] In 1994, the army's Joint Task Force Six oversaw BATF training in the use of Bradley Infantry Fighting Vehicles, including the 25mm machine guns on the BFVs. This training was necessitated by BATF planning to use BFVs in future operations such as Waco, to avoid government casualties.[213]

In 1994, BATF acquired three OV-10 light attack aircraft, a type of plane used in the Gulf War and for counterinsurgency, which is commonly equipped with rockets, although machine guns and chain guns can also be attached. Twenty-two such planes had been acquired in 1993. None of the planes are registered to BATF, but at least seven are registered to American Warbirds in Maryland. No company named "American Warbirds" has ever acquired a license to do business in Maryland, and thus, to the extent that American Warbirds actually exists, its operations are a criminal misdemeanor. Aircraft title records indicate that American Warbirds acquired the planes from Mid-Air Salvage, a company with a New Jersey address, but which (like American War Birds) does not exist in the Federal Aviation Administration database. Mid-Air acquired the planes from the federal government's General Services Administration. It is not clear why the transfer of aircraft from the military to the BATF needed to be laundered through two civilian corporations.[214]

According to BATF Director John W. Magaw, the BATF's OV-10 aircraft have their weapons removed. Mr. Magaw describes the OV-10's capabilities as "reconnaissance" and "command and control and insertion of troops." He states that the forward-looking infrared system on the OV-10, which can be used to identify objects at night or under poor visibility conditions, will be used "to enhance the safety of ATF special agents and other law enforcement officers working to combat firearms trafficking and other violent street crime."[215] In 1996, Congress defunded the BATF air force.

Beginning in 1973, the FBI set off a national trend in law enforcement by creating a SWAT (Special Weapons and Tactics) team. Now, every one of the FBI's fifty-six field offices has its own SWAT team.[216] (The 400 FBI satellite offices do not.) Abandoning former Director J. Edgar Hoover's principle that FBI agents should be well-trained generalists, the new FBI SWAT units specialize in confrontation, rather than investigation, even though investigation was, after all, the very purpose of the Federal Bureau of *Investigation*. Whereas Hoover's agents wore suits, and typically had a background in law or accounting, SWAT teams wore camouflage or black ninja clothing, and came from a military background.[217] They were trained killers, not trained investigators. In the early 1980s, an FBI super-SWAT team was invented: the Hostage Rescue Team.[218] Like the SWAT team, it received military training, carried military weapons, and was composed mostly of former military personnel. But rather than rescuing hostages, the Hostage Rescue Team has become notorious for two incidents in which it held hostage people who only wanted to be left alone: at Ruby Ridge, and at Waco.[219] "The swashbucklers are in control," laments Iowa Sen. Charles Grassley.[220] Even the National Park Service and the Department of Health and Human Services now have their own SWAT teams.

Direct Military Intervention

In addition to federal law enforcement agencies becoming more militarized, the military itself has become increasingly involved in domestic law enforcement. On any given day, more than five thousand troops conduct law enforcement operations within the United States.[221] This figure does not include the much larger number of National Guard troops involved in law enforcement every day.

Like other military assets, the National Guard is something which many state officials would like to use, but are reluctant to pay for. They know that their constituents may want a "drug war" in the abstract, but they may not be willing to pay higher taxes for it. In contrast to most state governments, the federal government has no balanced budget requirement, and thus can spend money on all sorts of wish-list programs, without having to pay for them.

Federal deficit financing provides a major source of funding for use of the National Guard in law enforcement. The huge federal subsidies provided by the federal government to the state National Guards are what allows Guard units to participate heavily in the drug war.

The National Guard has begun to lobby for even broader law enforcement privileges. For example, in Rhode Island the National Guard proposed that it be allowed to share profits from asset forfeiture operations.[222]

As illegal immigration has become an increasingly important political issue, the United States Army and Marines have been deployed along the Mexican border to assist federal and local border patrol. These deployments have led to strong protests from the Mexican government, for militarizing the border of a nation with which the United States is at peace.[223]

The Clinton administration is hard at work to remove the remaining restrictions on use of the military in law enforcement. An administration terrorism bill pushed by the president in 1995 defined all property offenses, and all violent crimes more serious than an assault as "terrorism," and authorized the Army, Navy, and Air Force to enforce "terrorism" laws. A bill proposed by Senate Majority Leader Robert Dole did the same thing.[224]

State and local militarization

The federal government actively works to militarize local law enforcement. For example, Mark Lonsdale, the Director of the federal government's Special Tactical Training Unit writes that there are various governmental programs, including those run by the federal Drug Enforcement Administration "available to local law enforcement" for marijuana control. "The thrust of this training is towards developing more of a military approach to tactics along with the study of the methodology of the growers."[225]

The Navy Seals and the Army Rangers both conduct extensive training of paramilitary units such as local police SWAT teams. The United States Marshals Service and the Joint Task Forces (e.g., JTF-6, which helped provide military training to BATF for the Waco raid) act as liaisons between the police departments and the military trainers.[226]

One morning the residents of Cass Corridor (a poor neighborhood in Detroit) were startled by the sounds of explosives and massive gunfire. While many residents hid, the few who dared to look outside found an eighty-person Detroit police department practice assault in progress on a vacant four-story building in the neighborhood. The deputy police chief in charge of the practice assault explained that such drills are routinely performed by police agencies in conjunction with the U.S. Army and other federal agencies.[227] In June 1996, two hundred soldiers from Fort Bragg conducted urban warfare exercises in Pittsburgh and McKeesport, Pennsylvania, in conjunction with the Pittsburgh and Allegheny County SWAT teams. The noise from small explosives and the low-hovering helicopters (dropping troops practicing a nighttime invasion of an urban area) frightened many civilians, who had no warning of what was happening.[228] (SWAT exercises near the Mount Carmel Center in 1992 played a major role in convincing Koresh that an attack was imminent, and in spurring Koresh's paranoia and arms acquisition, although the exercises had nothing to do with him.[229])

The federal government's Advanced Research Projects Agency supervises a joint program steering group for operations other than war/law enforcement which brings Defense Department and Justice Department officials together in order to find civilian law enforcement applications for military technology.[230] The United States Army Aviation & Troop Command (ATCOM) is selling surplus OH6-A helicopters to state and local governments for use in drug law enforcement. Rep. Ed Royce (R-Calif.) has proposed that Congress give states the cash with which to buy more helicopters from the army.[231]

As a result of both federal and local actions, America is moving toward the normalization of paramilitary forces in law enforcement. For example, the police in Fresno, California, have taken the next step toward militarization of local law enforcement. The Fresno SWAT team, in full battle gear, now deploys a full-time patrol unit in the city. Deeming the SWAT patrol an "unqualified success," the Fresno police department "is encouraging other police agencies to follow suit."[232] About 20 percent of police departments in cities over 50,000 have already put their own paramilitary units into street police work. In many cases, funding for street deployment of paramilitary units is funded by "community policing" grants from the federal government. The majority of police departments use their paramilitary units to serve "dynamic entry" search warrants.[233]

SWAT teams also get deployed in missions very foreign to ordinary police work:

> The SWAT Team in Chapel Hill, NC conducted a large-scale crack raid of an entire block in a predominantly African-American neighborhood. The Raid, termed "Operation Redi-Rock," resulted in the detention and search of up to 100 people, all of whom were African-Americans. (Whites were allowed to leave the area.) No one was ever prosecuted for a crime.[234]

The "Drug War"

The major cause of the militarization of American law enforcement has been the "drug war."

In 1981 and 1988, Congress created massive exceptions to the Posse Comitatus

Act, to allow use of the armed services, including the National Guard, in drug law enforcement.[235]

Because of drug war exceptions created in the Posse Comitatus Act, every region of the United States now has a Joint Task Force staff in charge of coordinating military involvement in domestic law enforcement. In region six, the JTF's *Operational Support Planning Guide*, in the edition current in 1993, enthused, accurately, that "Innovative approaches to providing new and more effective support to law enforcement agencies are constantly sought, and legal and policy barriers to the application of military capabilities are gradually being eliminated." Consistent with the trend noted by the JTF, the 1995 session of Congress saw a proposal (H.R. 97) to create a 2,500-member federal rapid deployment force for the attorney general to deploy at her discretion to assist local law enforcement.

The collapse of the Soviet Union has, unfortunately, led many military officials to seek out a new enemy to justify continued funding. Often, that new military enemy turns out to be American citizens. The North American Aerospace Defense Command (NORAD) admits that it is no longer capable of protecting Americans from incoming nuclear missiles. Yet NORAD enjoys hundreds of millions of dollars in annual funding, as part of a 1.8 billion dollar systems upgrade, having convinced Congress to assign NORAD the mission of tracking planes and ships that might be carrying drugs.[236]

Many other federal military programs have hitched themselves to the antidrug bandwagon. For example, when President Clinton in April 1996 requested 250 million dollars in extra funding for antidrug programs, over half that money was earmarked for the military.[237]

The results of such programs are evident not only at Waco, but in Puerto Rico. There, the National Guard provides a large part of the manpower and the heavy military equipment for police-Guard assaults on public housing apartments.[238]

In 1987, the secretary of defense and the attorney general were ordered to provide annual briefings to local law enforcement about available Department of Defense assistance, to set up a special office to assist civilian law enforcement, and even to provide a toll-free number for law enforcement inquiries.[239] In 1993, Congress ordered the Department of Defense to sell military surplus to state and local law enforcement for use in counter-drug activities.[240]

Many "patriot" organizations are comprised of members who have been terrified by the appearance of unmarked black helicopters over nearby rural property. These helicopters (which are actually a very dark green) have played a major role in intensifying fear of the federal government. The helicopters are not from the United Nations, but are part of the National Guard's marijuana eradication program. They are flying over rural property as a result of 1981 and 1989 congressional amendments which created a partial drug exception to the Posse Comitatus Act. In conjunction with the Supreme Court decision in *Oliver* v. *United States*, which allows law enforcement officials to trespass on "open fields" without probable cause or a search warrant—even when the owner has taken all possible steps to exclude trespassers—many rural areas are subjected to low-level overflights and landings of dark helicopters carrying men in military uniforms with automatic weapons. Who would not be frightened by the sudden invasion of an unmarked helicopter and men with machine guns on private property?

Every fall, Humboldt County, California, is invaded by National Guard forces as part of the Campaign Against Marijuana Production (CAMP). In a typical year, one hundred harassment complaints are logged against airborne and ground activities of CAMP personnel.[241]

Tanks, helicopters, and men pointing automatic rifles at children have no place in a free society. Neither the push to make America a drug-free society nor desire to "do something" about terrorism should be accomplished at the expense of losing our freedom.

The incentives for lawless violence and militarization do not come entirely from law enforcement itself. As sociologist Phillip Jenkins observes, "Media images can also frame the expectation and behavior of individual agents and administrators."[242] Sensationalistic "reality television" shows which glorify violent, illegal police conduct play a role in legitimating violence in the mind of law enforcement officers who watch the program.[243] So do movies such as *Dirty Harry*, *Lethal Weapon*, and many others.[244]

Another cause is the use of military rhetoric by politicians. Political talk about a "war on drugs" or a "war on crime" confuses the objectives and methods of war (destruction of a foreign enemy, with little regard for proper procedure) with law enforcement in a free society, involving suspects who are American citizens, and entitled to the full protection of the Bill of Rights. As New York University law professor Paul Chevigny explains:

> Armies are organized and trained for killing an enemy, usually more or less well-defined, and not for service and law-enforcement among a civilian population to which they themselves belong, in situations for which they have to make fine-grained legal and social distinctions about what action is required. . . .
>
> [The results of "war on crime" rhetoric] distort and poison police relations with citizens. The police think of themselves as an occupying army, and the public comes to think the same. The police lose the connection with the public that is the principal advantage to local policing, and their job becomes progressively more difficult, while they become more unpopular.[245]

One can be in favor of drugs being illegal, and still oppose "the war on drugs," just as one can want food stamp fraud to be illegal without wanting a "war on welfare cheaters," because to have "a war" is to make it likely that the military will become involved. As police studies professor Peter B. Kraska writes:

> [T]he militaristic nature of the discourse on crime and drug control—wars on crime and wars on drugs—constitutes more than ineffectual media/political rhetoric. Filtering solutions to the complex social problems of crime and substance abuse through the "war" metaphor helps to structure our values in use, our theories, and most important, our actions. . . . A metaphor and associated discourse materialized, for example, into urban police departments deploying paramilitary police groups to patrol U.S. neighborhoods.[246]

The drug war has been the health of the military state, and may in the long run be the death of the Constitution.

Reform

The military operates on principles of authoritarian control, with no room for dissent, for waiting for a consensus to form, or for democracy. Most members of the armed forces live in enclaves separate from the rest of society—enclaves which are orderly and authoritarian, often quite different from the chaotic civilian world.[247] The military lifestyle and military housing enclaves are ill-fitted to building the values of due process, democracy, and diversity on which civilian law enforcement must be founded.

Reforms to reduce the trend to militarization of domestic law enforcement would include:

Tighten the Posse Comitatus Act so that it proscribes all use of military personnel and equipment, not just use of the Army and Air Force, and not just unreimbursed use.[248] (Currently exempt from Posse Comitatus, the Navy's Seal Team Six has allegedly participated in several "take-downs" of crack houses in the Los Angeles area.[249]) In particular, eliminate the loophole that exempts the National Guard from the act.[250]

Repeal the drug exceptions and other exceptions to the Posse Comitatus Act, expressly making the only exceptions those involved with law enforcement in international waters or requiring unique military expertise related to nuclear weapons.[251]

Make knowing violation of the Posse Comitatus Act a predicate felony for felony murder.

Forbid federal courts and federal law enforcement personnel to use evidence obtained in violation of the Posse Comitatus Act.[252]

Create a civil cause of action for persons injured by Posse Comitatus Act violations.

In the years before the Posse Comitatus Act, any soldier who did engage in police activity was deemed to be acting as a private citizen, rather than as a soldier. Under this Mansfield Doctrine, the individual, since he was not acting as a soldier, could be personally sued or criminally prosecuted for any wrongs he did.[253] Courts should revive the Mansfield Doctrine at once, and allow injured victims to bring lawsuits against individual "law enforcement" soldiers who perpetrate civil torts.

Repeal 10 U.S.C. § 372, which authorized the Secretary of Defense to make "any" Department of Defense equipment available to "any Federal, State, or local civilian law enforcement personnel for law enforcement purposes." Like previous steps to militarize domestic law enforcement, this provision grew out of the "drug war." But the language does not restrict the military equipment to drug enforcement purposes.

Even in the case of drug law enforcement, military equipment—such as tanks—has no legitimate role. The type of equipment which is used to attack hostile nations is not the type of equipment which should be used against Americans, even Americans who are suspected of violating a law. A 1968 law had allowed the military to sell, "at fair market value," surplus firearms and ammunition to local law enforcement.[254] Selling the police ordinary firearms and ammunition is one thing; giving them tanks and other equipment which they could never justify purchasing on their own is quite another.

Compel full disclosure of all military equipment being used or available to civilian law enforcement.

End the Department of Justice/Department of Defense "Troops to Cops" conversion program, which provides local police departments a large federal subsidy for employing ex-military personnel.[255] Of course, any person who has served honorably in the military should be allowed to apply for any civilian job, including law enforcement. But the federal government should not use subsidies to bias police departments into hiring persons with a military background, as opposed to a background in civil society. A good deal of the training which makes a good soldier is contradictory to the training necessary to be a peace officer.

Abolish the federal-state multiagency law enforcement task forces.

Require that all international warfare treaties signed by the United States be binding on domestic operations of the federal government. If the United States is willing to agree not to use certain particularly deadly types of chemical or biological weapons against foreign troops, the U.S. government should also be willing to foreswear use of those same weapons against American citizens.[256]

Various federal statutes authorize different federal agencies to allow their employees to carry firearms. Certainly there are many federal employees with a legitimate need to carry firearms. Sensibly, the statute authorizing forest service employees to carry firearms states that no more than one thousand employees shall be so authorized.[257] Similar caps should be extended to all other agencies with gun-carrying employees, with a view to reducing gun-toting by federal employees to cases of genuine need. The right to keep and bear arms, after all, is for "the People," not the government.

To the extent that nondiscriminatory state laws authorize ordinary persons to obtain firearms carry permits and to carry firearms while at work, there is nothing wrong with federal employees within that state obtaining such permits for themselves. But cases of federal employees carrying firearms in contravention of relevant state law, as if the federal employees were some kind of superior class, should be kept to an absolute minimum.

Law enforcement use of masks in the service of search or arrest warrants should be prohibited, except when specifically authorized by a court when granting the warrant, based on compelling need. Masks not only make peace officers look inappropriately terrifying, they prevent identification of rogue officers so that they cannot be sued later for criminal acts.

As an important symbolic step, federal law enforcement should give up its black or near-black uniforms and replace them with a color (such as ordinary blue) more consistent with law enforcement in a democracy.[258] Rutgers University professor Michael Solomon, a scholar of the psychology of clothing, explains that black law enforcement uniforms tap "into associations between the color black and authority, invincibility, the power to violate laws with impunity."[259]

At all levels of policing, it is time to bring back the honored title peace officer. As police ethicist John Kleinig puts it, "Were police to see themselves primarily as social peacekeepers, they would be less inclined to 'overkill' in their dealings with both ordinary citizens and those whose disruptive activities require their intervention."[260]

DEFEDERALIZING LAW ENFORCEMENT

Former Attorney General Edwin Meese writes:

In recent years, two tragic events have fundamentally changed the way many Americans view federal law-enforcement agencies and jeopardized public confidence in the federal government itself. . . .

Since Ruby Ridge . . . [e]ven those normally supportive of the police ask: Should the federal government have risked this loss of life and expended $10 million to capture a hermit whose only alleged crime was selling two sawed-off shotguns to an undercover federal agent?[261]

After summarizing Waco, Meese wrote:

Both these tragedies are the direct result of federal jurisdiction in crimes once considered wholly within the province of state and local police agencies. In neither incident did the underlying crime involve interstate activity or pose a threat to the federal government. Without the federalization of law regulating firearms, a matter left to the states during most of our country's history, neither the BATF or FBI would have had jurisdiction at Ruby Ridge and Waco, and any law-enforcement would have been handled locally, if at all. . . .

Federal law-enforcement authorities are not as attuned to the priorities and customs of local communities as state and local law enforcement. In the Ruby Ridge tragedy, for example, would the local Idaho authorities have tried to apprehend Weaver in such an aggressive fashion? . . . More fundamentally, would Idaho officials have cared about two sawed-off shotguns? In the Waco situation, would the local sheriff's department have stormed the compound, or instead have waited to arrest David Koresh when he ventured into town for supplies, as he did frequently?[262]

As Meese explains, there are now more than 3,000 federal crimes, and new ones are added in every Congress. Overfederalization is a bipartisan sin. President Johnson and a Democratic Congress federalized laws regarding the simple possession of firearms with the Gun Control Act of 1968, while President Nixon and a Democratic Congress federalized even the most trivial drug crimes with the Controlled Substances Act in 1970.

Currently, New York Sen. Alfonse D'Amato is pushing legislation to federalize all violent gun crimes if the gun were at some point, no matter how many years before the crime, moved across state lines. Approved almost unanimously by the U.S. Senate in 1991, the measure is supported by the congressional Republican leadership, which claims to be in favor of the Tenth Amendment and getting the federal government out of state and local affairs.

There are now more than fifty different federal law enforcement agencies, and 200 federal agencies with some law enforcement authority.[263] Guns and drugs (two non-federal concerns, except for illegal interstate or international sales) have been the primary engines for a massive expansion of federal law enforcement. From 1980 to 1992, the number of criminal cases filed in federal courts rose 70 percent; drug cases and firearms cases both quadrupled.[264]

The federal judiciary is drowning under this increased burden. In many districts, the criminal caseload overwhelms the court's docket.[265] In 1970, there were 500 federal judges. In 1994, there were more than 800. According to the Long Range Planning

Committee of the U.S. Judicial Conference, by the year 2020, there may be 4,000.[266] Such increases in the number of federal judges make it difficult to maintain the high quality of the federal bench, and make uniformity of law in federal courts almost impossible to achieve.

The federal criminal expansion, ironically, occurred during the administrations of Ronald Reagan and George Bush, who were both elected on campaigns promising fealty to states' rights and limited federal government.

The Constitutional System

The practical benefits of decentralized law enforcement were not unknown to the creators of our Constitution. The Constitution specifically authorizes federal enforcement of only three types of laws, all of which involve uniquely federal concerns. The first authorized federal criminal law enforcement is based on the congressional power "To provide for the punishment of counterfeiting the securities and current coin of the United States." The counterfeiting enforcement power immediately follows the delegation of congressional power "To coin money, regulate the value thereof, and of foreign coin."[267]

The second congressional criminal power involves the power "To define and punish piracies and felonies committed on the high seas, and offenses against the law of nations." The third is that "Congress shall have Power to declare Punishment of Treason." Although currency, treason, and the high seas clearly involve areas of federal, and not state concern, it is notable that, even in those cases, the authors of the Constitution felt a need specifically to authorize congressional law enforcement regarding these matters.

While the body of the Constitution grants only narrow criminal law enforcement powers to the federal government, the Bill of Rights, in the Tenth Amendment, specifically reserves to the states all powers not granted to the federal government.[268]

Even the Federalist Papers, which were, after all, an argument for increased federal power, made it clear that criminal law enforcement would not come under the federal sphere under the new Constitution. James Madison wrote that federal powers "will be exercised principally on external objects, as war, peace, negotiation, and foreign commerce. . . . The powers reserved to the several states will extend to all objects which, in the ordinary course of affairs, concern the lives, liberties, and property of the people, and the internal order, improvement, and prosperity of the state."[269]

Likewise, Alexander Hamilton, the most determined nationalist of his era, explained that state governments, not the federal government, would have the power of law enforcement, and that power would play a major role in assuring that the states were not overwhelmed by the federal government:

> The variety of more minute interests, which will necessarily fall under the superintendence of the local administrations and which will form so many rivulets of influence, running through every part of the society, cannot be particularized without involving a detail too tedious and uninteresting to compensate for the instruction it might afford.
>
> There is one transcendent advantage belonging to the province of the State governments, which alone suffices to place the matter in a clear and satisfactory light—I

mean the ordinary administration of criminal and civil justice. This, of all others, is the most powerful, most universal, and most attractive source of popular obedience and attachment. . . . This great cement of society, which will diffuse itself almost wholly through the channels of the particular governments, independent of all other causes of influence, would insure them so decided an empire over their respective citizens as to render them at all times a complete counterpoise, and, not unfrequently, dangerous rivals to the power of the Union.[270]

In contrast to the constitutional system created by Madison, Hamilton, and the other founders, and ratified by the American people, an entirely different system has come into being over the course of this century. The enumerated powers of Congress "to lay and collect taxes" and "To regulate Commerce . . . among the several States" have been turned by specious judicial interpretation into congressional powers over issues that have nothing to do with taxes or with interstate commerce. In the field of criminal law, the result has been a disaster, of which Waco and Ruby Ridge are only among the most visible incidents.

Almost without exception, every single federal law enforcement misdeed which has been detailed in this book has been made possible by the illegitimate expansion of the taxation and interstate commerce powers into criminal law. In the model reform legislation presented in Appendix A of this book, most of the specific reforms would become superfluous if federal jurisdiction over criminal law were returned to its constitutional boundaries.

The United States Supreme Court took a tiny step in that direction in 1995, when in the case of *United States* v. *Lopez*, the court struck down a federal law against possession of a gun within a thousand feet of a school. The Court noted "States possess primary authority for defining and enforcing the criminal law."[271]

But President Clinton, with the acquiescence of the Republican leadership in Congress, soon showed that *Lopez* is a slender barrier against further federalization of state criminal law. Without the knowledge of most members of Congress—but with the knowledge of the leadership of both parties—the Continuing Resolution (to fund the government) which Congress passed in the fall of 1996 contained a new version of the federal Gun-Free School Zones law.[272] The new version contained a number of congressional findings about the need for the new law, such as the invented fact that states are unable to effectively enforce their own state-level school zone laws. The new version also required that the gun must move in or "affect" interstate commerce. In other words, if the gun was manufactured in Connecticut in 1965, sold to a Texas gun store and resold to a Texas citizen, and remained in Texas ever since, the gun's 1965 sale in interstate commerce would be the basis for federal jurisdiction over carrying the gun in the wrong place in 1998.

An optimist might hope that the Supreme Court will eventually declare the new law unconstitutional. After all, the new law is in no substantive way different from the old law. The congressional "findings" about the effects on interstate commerce of guns near schools are a collection of platitudes and assertions. That the gun once moved in interstate commerce does not give the present carrying of that gun any real connection with interstate commerce.

Furthermore, the new law intrudes into two traditional areas of state control: education, and criminal law. The federal law is much stricter than the school zone laws that most states have enacted. The federal law outlaws activity which states have specifically decided should be legal—such as carrying a gun in one's glove compartment for protection, an activity for which many states do not require a permit.[273]

Finally, the law is overbroad. Whatever federal interest there might be in regulating guns on school property, that interest cannot support setting up a thousand-foot radius around every school, turning half of most urban areas into "school zones" in which federal rules about gun transportation negate local regulation.

But it is not clear that the Supreme Court will strike down the new school zone law. After all, if the above paragraphs prove that the new school zone law is invalid, then almost identical arguments prove that most of the rest of the federal criminal code is invalid. If the Supreme Court acknowledges that the school zone emperor is not clothed with constitutional authority, then it must be admitted that most of the rest of federal criminal law is naked as well.

Some constitutional theorists have suggested that judicial enforcement of specifically enumerated civil liberties (such as freedom of speech) is more important than judicial enforcement of constitutional limits on the scope of federal power. As University of Tennessee law professor Glenn Harlan Reynolds points out, this is a false dichotomy.[274] The framers understood that limitations on the power of government are an essential part of the structure of ordered liberty.

As many civil libertarians from both the left and the right sides of the political spectrum increasingly agree, perhaps the most important issue in the next twenty years for defense of civil liberty is to contain and roll back the federal government's expansion beyond its constitutional boundaries. The 1994 crime bill, with provisions for federal funding of local police, unfortunately moves the United States even further along the path of centralizing law enforcement authority in Washington, as did the terrorism bill enacted in 1996.

Critics of the Clinton administration's claim that the 1994 crime bill would put "100,000" police on the streets have pointed out that the 100,000 figure is fraudulent. First, the bill requires large matching payments by local law enforcement; the bill itself provides funding for the equivalent of only 20,000 police officers, and then only for a few years.[275] In addition, administration claims about new police in particular cities appear to be based on some very generous assumptions. For example, the administration claimed that it had added two new police officers in a particular city by giving the city enough money to buy a single personal computer. Supposedly, the computer reduced paperwork so much that two new officers could be put on the streets.

But these criticisms ignore the more fundamental question of whether we should be centralizing funding (and, inevitably, control) of local police from Washington, D.C. As discussed in the previous section, community policing money is being used to finance deployment of paramilitary SWAT units into street patrol. A national police force has been justifiably resisted by civil libertarians. Local police forces controlled by Washington could become a de facto national police.

Frauds and Panics

One important step in keeping federal law enforcement powers within constitutional limits would be for the American public to become more aware of the practice of the FBI (as well as other agencies) fomenting panics in order to be given greater funding and more power.

This chapter has already discussed how Attorney General Palmer used the FBI's predecessor in 1920 to stir up hatred of immigrants and create a panic over alien subversives. During the 1930s, FBI Director Hoover told the American people that an unprecedented wave of child kidnappings was in progress, and the FBI was rewarded with substantial attention and funding. In coming years, whatever type of criminal happened to be the object of highly visible public concern—bank robbers such as John Dillinger, Nazi spies, Communist spies, the Ku Klux Klan, serial killers of children, divorced fathers who fail to pay child support, and now terrorists—also happened to be precisely the kind of devious, interjurisdictional criminal which the FBI, and only the FBI, had the expertise to protect the American people from—provided, of course, that more public funds were provided, and more civil liberties sacrificed.[276]

In 1919, Congress enacted the Dyer Act, which made interstate commercial car theft a federal crime. In future years, the FBI, eager to expand its role, began a program of boosting its Dyer Act enforcement data at all costs. FBI reports would claim FBI Dyer Act recoveries in cases for which a car had simply been taken for a joyride (and hence the Dyer Act was inapplicable, since there was no commercial motive), or in which the car had never been taken across state lines, or in which local law enforcement had solved the case with no FBI assistance. Grossly exaggerated figures for FBI auto recoveries were then used to "prove" to congressmen that the FBI was actually a cost-effective law enforcement agency; there was, in the FBI's words in a 1963 report, "a return to the government of $1.37" for every dollar appropriated to the FBI. As one Department of Justice whistle blower pointed out (to no avail), the FBI's claim was true only if every car which the FBI "recovered" under the Dyer Act had been stolen from the federal government.[277]

Nazi spies and Communist spies were a genuine national security threat, but too much of the FBI and federal law enforcement's jurisdiction expanding has been based on fraud and fiction. Foreign subversives were not remotely as dangerous as Attorney General Palmer insisted. The child serial killer scare of the 1980s turned out to be largely based on false data and dishonest sound bites fed to a credulous media by the FBI.[278]

Americans are at no greater risk of being murdered today than they were twenty years ago (1 in 10,500 in 1993; 1 in 10,200 in 1973). Yet in 1995 when the FBI announced a further drop in the crime rate, based on 1993 data, it claimed that for the first time ever, all Americans had a "realistic" chance of being murdered. The FBI's frightening claim was based on its calculation that 53 percent of homicides were perpetrated by strangers—the first time that strangers had ever accounted for the majority of homicides. This statistic was manufactured by using the implausible assumption that every unsolved homicide in the U.S.—including every single drug-related homicide—was perpetrated by a stranger.[279] FBI and Department of Justice statisticians are not stupid. But quite often, their work is perverted for the benefit of political supervisors who understand that the only route to increased funding is through a new crime crisis, even if one has to be invented.

The BATF is also heavily statistics-driven, with management periodically inventing new programs designed to increase some statistic which it is believed will win more congressional funding. For example, in Operation Big Bird, BATF agents were assigned to accompany local police around the clock, recording every violation of federal firearms laws. Of course, this took the BATF agents away from investigating the kinds of major firearms trafficking cases worthy of federal attention.[280]

More recently, federal powers were vastly expanded to cope with a new terrorism "crisis," even though State Department data showed that international terrorist attacks were at their lowest level in twenty-three years.[281] In the United States in the previous eleven years, according to FBI data, there have been only two international terrorist incidents. (One was the World Trade Center bombing; the other was a trespassing incident at the Iranian mission to the United Nations, in which five critics of the Iranian regime took over the mission's offices, and refused to leave.[282]) As for incidents of domestic terrorism, there were none in the United States in 1994, nor were there any preventions of terrorist incidents. In 1993, there were eleven incidents classified by the FBI as "terrorist." Nine of those eleven incidents took place one night in Chicago when animal rights activists set off small incendiary devices in four department stores that sell fur.[283] The Oklahoma City bombing was one of the most terrible single crimes in American history, but it was just that: an isolated, single crime.

In 1996, an organization named the Center for Democratic Renewal began making claims about an alleged wave of white-supremacist arsons aimed at black churches in the South. As journalist Michael Fumento documented in the *Wall Street Journal*, some of the "arsons" never took place, other "arsons" were accidental fires, and many white churches in the South have also been burned. Of the more than 90 fires at black churches, three were set by racists. But the CDR's exaggerations of a vast racist crime wave fit the media's preconceptions about white racism, and so the "fact" of widespread racist church arsons became the pretext for yet more federal criminal power.[284] The federal law against arson (already illegal, and vigorously prosecuted in every state under state law) was expanded even more.[285]

The asserted basis for federal arson law is the power of Congress "to regulate Commerce . . . among the several States,"[286] as if burning a building in one state had anything substantial to do with the buying and selling of goods across state lines.

We know in retrospect that the Marihuana Tax Act of 1937 was the result of racist campaign of disinformation about the use of marijuana by Hispanic criminals.[287] We know in retrospect that the late 1980s panic over crack cocaine mistook a serious problem in a small number of large cities for an immense national crisis. This last mistake led to widening the drug exception to the Posse Comitatus Act, which in turn set the stage for the use of military equipment at Waco against a group of people who consumed no drugs except alcohol.

Reforms

"There are a thousand hacking at the branches of evil," said Henry David Thoreau, "to one who is striking at the root."[288] In this book, there are over a hundred suggestions for federal criminal reform, but there is one reform that gets to the root of the problem: federal criminal jurisdiction should be restored to constitutional limits. The federal power over interstate commerce should be used only to regulate interstate commerce: the purchase and sale of goods across state lines. The interstate commerce power should be not applied to activity that takes place within the boundaries of a single state.[289]

Similarly, the federal tax power should be used to raise revenues for the federal government—not to impose backdoor regulation on the private possession of machine guns or other items.

The best way to proceed would be to go through the federal criminal statutes line by line, and cut out the portions which are not based on a reasonable construction of the specific, limited powers which the Constitution grants the federal government. In Appendix A of this book, the model federal law enforcement reform statute shows how to do this with regard to some of the federal gun and drug laws. The same thing should be done with all the rest of the federal criminal laws.

Even without a line-by-line repeal of all instances of overreaching by prior Congresses, a new Congress could make a huge step toward restoring constitutional limits by enacting a statute which declared that all funds appropriated to federal departments could only be used to investigate or prosecute crime which takes place in more than one state, or on federal property, or against federal employees.

Appropriate exceptions could be made for the few areas which the Constitution gives separate authority to Congress. For example, Congress is given power to declare uniform rules of bankruptcy; federal law does and should continue to punish bankruptcy fraud, even when perpetrated within a single state. The interstate commerce power should likewise be used for genuinely interstate crimes, such as hijacking. The Leviathan of federal criminal law was not created by the exercise of congressional authority over specific subjects which the Constitution entrusts to the federal government—such as patents and copyright, the post office, or international diplomacy. Rather, the overgrowth of federal criminal law is based almost entirely on overreaching of the interstate commerce and tax powers.

One reform which is far less sweeping than the above suggestions, but which also might save lives, would be to require permission of the local police chief or sheriff before service of federal search or arrest warrant. The Montana legislature passed such a bill in 1995, but it was vetoed by Governor Marc Racicot.

Internationalization

The serious problems caused by the nationalization of law enforcement pale in comparison to the dangers of the internationalization of law enforcement. Internationalization of law enforcement is still in an embryonic stage—no larger than the militarization of law enforcement was in 1981. It would be much easier to stop the internationalization before it grows, rather than to try to make it shrink once it has been put into place.

The first step is for Congress to order the closure of the twenty-three new foreign FBI offices created in 1996. American law enforcement, of course, has a legitimate interest in the apprehension of criminals who have perpetrated crimes in the United States and then fled abroad, or who are planning crimes against the United States. But there is no evidence that friendly nations are refusing to use their own law enforcement resources against such criminals. If there is suspicion that someone in the United States is plotting a crime against the French, American law enforcement will investigate. There is no need for the French to establish gendarmes in the United States. Conversely, there is no need for American FBI agents to do the work of the French police in France. In some cases, overseas FBI agents have proposed violations of local laws, such as agents provocateurs statutes.

The establishment of overseas FBI offices paves the way, in the long term, to the reciprocal establishment of foreign police forces in the United States.

Also, Congress and the president should firmly resist any proposed international treaty which would undermine constitutional protections for American citizens, or allow the operation of non-American law enforcement forces on American soil. For example, the Chemical Weapons Treaty which is currently pending Senate ratification would allow foreign governments to demand the inspection of any American business or home (not just a chemical factory) based on the unsupported allegation that the place was part of a covert chemical manufacturing scheme. Upon the allegation, an international team of inspectors would be authorized—without procuring a search warrant—to enter the property, and seize whatever they wanted as evidence.

Proposals to create a United Nations police force should likewise be resisted. A body whose majority is comprised of kleptocracies with no respect for the human rights of their own people is not likely to set up a police force which respects American constitutional norms.

Global crime is a problem, but Americans should remember that throughout human history, and especially in the twentieth century, the biggest global murderers and thieves have been governments. Governments have killed tens of millions of their own people in the twentieth century.[290] In most nations of the world, the government is the greatest threat to personal security.

Oka

The Waco disaster did not have to turn out the way it did. A few years before Waco, Canada went through a siege of its own, in Québec Province. Although Canadian law enforcement has been growing more violent, the attitude of the Canadian government and the Canadian people in dealing with the siege was instructive.

During the spring and summer of 1990, Mohawk Indians led by the Mohawk Warrior Society seized and held part of the town of Oka, near Montréal, to prevent the expansion of a golf course and housing project onto a pine forest which was Mohawk ancestral land and onto the Mohawks' Pine Tree Cemetery. Besides Kalashnikov rifles, the Mohawks had Fabrique Nationale semiautomatics, high-powered hunting rifles, shotguns, a variety of handguns, RPK machine guns, Molotov cocktails and other homemade explosives, and a large number of booby traps. Canada's gun control laws being stricter than American ones, the Mohawk arsenal was much further out of compliance with Canadian law than were the weapons which the BATF warrant alleged that the Branch Davidians possessed.

After the Mohawks repulsed a raid by the tactical squad of the Sûreté de Québec (the provincial police), Québec Premier Robert Bourassa asked the Canadian army to intervene because his provincial force was outgunned by the warriors. The Mohawks, like the Branch Davidians, saw themselves as the legitimate armed forces of a sovereign nation, defending their territory from attack.[291]

Yet Oka did not end in bloodshed. Although the Waco siege did not involve any unwilling third parties, the Oka standoff, taking place near Montréal, caused massive commuter traffic jams for over two months. And yet, patience prevailed. After some skirmishes, the federal government agreed to buy the golf course and give it to the Mohawks, and the Mohawks surrendered, ending the seventy-seven-day siege.[292] The Canadian government, although subject to greater provocation, displayed far more patience and willingness to compromise than did the United States government.

About a year after Waco, the Israeli government ended a siege with a heavily armed group of religious extremists, again without bloodshed.[293]

Americans have a government which behaves much more aggressively than the Canadian government because that is what Americans want. Suggested one commentator:

> Of all the troubling questions raised by the tragedy at the Branch Davidian compound near Waco, Texas, perhaps the most disturbing arose . . . [when] several national public opinion polls reported that an overwhelming majority of Americans found no fault with the way law-enforcement authorities had brought the standoff to a head. . . . Such enthusiasm for an exercise that was botched from the beginning, that ended in a horrible blood bath, and that continues to pose agonizing questions, ought to dismay all of us: We have allowed our national zeal for "law and order" to carry us beyond the bounds of reason.[294]

By 1995, polls showed the public was about evenly divided on the government's handling of Waco.[295] Perhaps the public, or at least a large part of the public, really does not support lawless law enforcement, once the public learns the truth.

What was perhaps the most important factor in the federal government's decision to launch the tank and chemical warfare attack was the government's unwillingness to tolerate any longer a challenge to its authority. And it is the federal government's increasing insistence on militarized dominance over the populace that is the greatest civil liberties danger for which Waco should be a wake-up call.

THE GOD THAT ANSWERETH BY FIRE

> Thank you, Mr. President, Janet Reno too.
> We musn't forget the ATF, the FBI, all the men in blue.
> How well did you sleep last night?
> Did you toss and turn?
> I myself didn't get much sleep.

Did you know I saw my father burn?
. . .
The day will come we'll all be judged
as we stand before the Lord.
Koresh may have thought himself as Christ,
But you thought yourself as God.

> The Family of Floyd Houtman,
> *We Love and Miss You, Dad*

The poem above was written by a child of one of the adults who died at Mount Carmel on April 19, 1993.[296]

What an absolute classic tragedy. What a total indictment of mankind's inability to communicate and relate, even though we have different religious or personal philosophies . . . this is how wars start, because people can't communicate and don't or won't understand each other . . . this was simply a microcosm of every conflict that man ever had.

> FBI negotiator Clint Van Zandt, explaining his thoughts at seeing the fire[297]

"Mount Carmel" was famous long before Branch Davidians gave the name to their property in Texas in 1935. As the Davidians' prophet Victor Houteff knew when he chose the name, the original Mount Carmel is in northwest Israel. It is mentioned in the Books of Isaiah[298] and Amos.[299] Mount Carmel later became the dwelling of a group of Christian hermits, and the foundation of the Carmelite Order, a group of intensely mystical Catholic men and women who live in communities shut off from the rest of the world. In the most famous biblical event at Mount Carmel, an event which must have been present in the thoughts of the Branch Davidians, persecuted believers witnessed a miraculous fire, followed by a massacre.

In the Book of Kings, the long-standing conflict between the followers of YHVH and the priests of Baal (a Canaanite nature religion) had been going badly for the followers of YHVH. Persecuted by the foreign queen Jezebel, the remaining "prophets of the LORD" were forced to hide in a cave, but were discovered and massacred. The only one who survived was Elijah the prophet. Elijah challenged the Baalists to a contest:

> Now therefore send, and gather to me all Israel unto mount Carmel, and the prophets of Baal four hundred and fifty, and the prophets of the groves [referring to prophets of Asherah, a Baal nature goddess] four hundred.[300]

At Elijah's suggestion, King Ahab ordered the whole Israelite nation to gather at Mount Carmel. Elijah told the Israelites that they must choose between the Baals and YHVH. He then set up a contest to determine who is the true god:

> Let them therefore give us two bullocks; and let them [the Baalists] choose one bullock for themselves, and cut it in pieces, and lay it on wood, and put no fire under; and I will dress the other bullock, and lay it on wood, and put no fire under:
> And call ye on the name of your gods, and I will call on the name of the LORD: and the God that answereth by fire, let him be God.[301]

The Baal priests spent hours importuning their gods to start a fire under their ox, while Elijah taunted them. In the evening, Elijah built his own altar, and instructed the Israelites to build a trench around the altar and fill it with water. Elijah called on YHVH to make Himself known. "Then the fire of the LORD fell, and consumed the burnt sacrifice, and the wood, and the stones, and the dust, and licked up the water that was in the trench." The Israelites immediately recognized YHVH, "the God that answereth by fire," as the true God; at Elijah's instructions, the hundreds of Baal priests were immediately executed.[302]

The Branch Davidians, by the way, saw their church as the typological fulfillment of Elijah.[303] It is possible that the Davidians saw calling down fire on April 19 as the typological fulfillment of Elijah's calling down fire at the first Mount Carmel.[304]

The duel by fire at the first Mount Carmel seems barely more than mythology to many secular Americans. But no less than Elijah—the lone, persecuted prophet of YHVH—America's modern federal law enforcement agencies behave as if they too were under constant attack from a dark, vast empire. One critic of the siege mentality of federal law enforcement argues:

> It's an exaggerated concern that they are facing a nationwide conspiracy and that somehow this will get out of control unless it is stamped out at a very early stage. . . . the formation of a curious crusading mentality among certain law enforcement agencies to stamp out what they see as a threat to government generally.[305]

"You have conspiracy theorists and you have weapons," an Anti-Defamation League spokesperson observed about militia groups.[306] The observation is equally applicable to much of federal law enforcement.

In *Every Knee Shall Bow: The Truth and Tragedy of Ruby Ridge and the Randy Weaver Family*, Jess Walter wisely suggests that the most important lesson of Ruby Ridge is the danger of conspiracy thinking. The Weavers deluded themselves with a harsh conspiratorial worldview which looked on most other people, especially people of other races and religions, as the enemy. The federal government likewise deluded itself by demonizing a pathetic family in a remote, plywood cabin.[307]

The Branch Davidians victimized themselves with their Manichean worldview, in which they and their leader were of God, and the rest of the world was satanic. Their groupthink and their conspiratorialism blinded them so that they failed to see that their messiah was in reality a sick, deluded, evil, and pitiful man.

In this book we cannot offer solutions for the blindness that led the Branch Davidians to follow such a terrible messiah. These solutions lie beyond the realm of public policy.

The federal government, on the other hand, is something that ought to be within the reach of public policy reforms. There is perhaps a serious threat to the security of the American people, and it is a threat that has progressed beyond a very early stage. But it is a threat different from the one imagined by the federal law enforcement agencies.

Dr. Alan Stone's review of the Justice Department report on Waco suggested that the most important reason for the fatal assault on April 19 was that the government ultimately felt a need to demonstrate its authority:

What went wrong at Waco was not that the FBI lacked expertise in behavior science or in the understanding of unconventional religious groups. Rather, the commander on the ground and others committed to tactical-aggressive, traditional law enforcement practices disregarded those experts and tried to assert control and demonstrate to Koresh that they were in charge. . . . [T]he FBI's own experts recognized and predicted in memoranda that there was a risk that the active aggressive law enforcement mentality of the FBI—the so-called "action imperative"—would prevail in the face of frustration and delay.[308]

It would be a great mistake to attribute the disaster at Waco mainly to various BATF and FBI employees who appear to have acted dishonestly, maliciously, and/or illegally. The malignancy at Waco is more than the sum of its parts.

The United States is a country founded on the premise that government is the servant, the people the master, and inalienable rights the foundation of civilization. But federal law enforcement has come a long way from that philosophy.

Spurred by the "drug war," law enforcement in the United States, particularly federal law enforcement, has become increasingly militarized. No-knock raids with battering rams, agents dressed like ninjas and wielding machine guns, the fabrication of information in warrant applications, the forfeiture and confiscation of property without a trial, and a steadily blurring distinction between the standards appropriate for law enforcement in a free society and the practices typical of military occupation of a conquered nation have been the most important law enforcement trend of the last decade.[309] The cancer of militaristic, violent domestic law enforcement can be traced back at least as far as Elliot Ness and the old Bureau of Prohibition, but today that cancer has spread much further than ever before.

In January 1994, the American Civil Liberties Union, the National Rifle Association, the Independence Institute, and seven other civil liberties organizations sent a joint letter to President Clinton asking for the appointment of a commission to study the militarization of federal law enforcement, and the suffering that such militarization has already caused. The letter noted that federal police officers now constitute 10 percent of total national law enforcement, and fifty separate federal agencies have the authority to carry firearms and make arrests.[310] The Clinton administration's most notable initiatives regarding law enforcement militarization, however, have been to seek more of it.[311]

The American public was right to recognize that David Koresh was a false god. But in the fifty-one days at Mount Carmel, the Koresh god contended with another god. This god, like Koresh, was a violent bully, a liar, and was ready to do anything, including take actions which the god knew would cause the death of innocent children, to assert its supremacy. The god is not generally loved by the American public, but it has their fear and they—unlike the Branch Davidians—acknowledge its authority.

Most Americans pride themselves on a degree of contempt for the federal government, which they consider inefficient and sometimes corrupt. But what was revealed at Waco was something far worse than the waste of tax dollars. To see Waco for what it is is to see a nation with a press that foments hatred against unpopular religions; an increasingly lawless and militaristic set of national police agencies; and a generally indifferent public.

Should America one day find itself, like so many unhappy nations of history, a country which had a thriving republic at one time, and a militaristic dictatorship a few decades later, historians may mark the American public's response to the government's actions at Waco as an important turning point. If the current generation of Americans is unwilling to begin to restrain the federal government, then how much more dangerous a country will they leave to the next generation? It is time for the American people to use the ballot box, the jury box, and all other peaceful means to tame their federal government's law enforcement agencies, which have now become a god that answereth by fire.

NOTES

1. Magna Carta, 1215, available at http://www.ecst.csuchico.edu/~rodmur/docs/Magna. html.

2. *Washington Times*, July 9, 1993, p. A2.

3. Jerry Seper, "House to Probe Reno's Reasoning behind Waco Raid," *Washington Times*, May 31, 1995, at p. 6 (quoting Reno's appearance on "60 Minutes").

4. James Bovard, "Waco Must Get a Hearing," *Wall Street Journal*, May 15, 1995 (Reno's remarks of May 5, 1995).

5. Sample federal law enforcement comment: "Have you seen the affidavit? There was no probable cause! And all those children. . . ."

6. United States Department of Justice, *Department of Justice Report Regarding Internal Investigation of Shootings at Ruby Ridge, Idaho, during Arrest of Randy Weaver* (hereinafter, "DOJ Internal Investigation of Ruby Ridge"), available at http://www.courttv.com/library/government/ruby.html.

7. Stuart A. Wright, ed. *Armageddon in Waco: Critical Perspectives on the Branch Davidian Conflict* (Chicago: University of Chicago Press, 1995). See also Molly Ivins, "Ban the Things. Ban Them All," *Washington Post*, March 16, 1993.

8. David B. Kopel, *The Samurai, the Mountie, and the Cowboy: Should America Adopt the Gun Controls of Other Democracies?* (Amherst, N.Y.: Prometheus Books, 1992), ch. 1; David B. Kopel, "Japanese Gun Control," 2 *Asia-Pacific Law Review* 26 (1993).

9. Kopel, *Samurai*, chs. 2, 3, 5; David B. Kopel, *Gun Control in Great Britain: Saving Lives or Constricting Liberty?* (Chicago: University of Illinois at Chicago Office of International Criminal Justice, 1992); David B. Kopel, "Canadian Gun Control: Should America Look North for a Solution to its Firearms Problem?" 5 *Temple Journal of International and Comparative Law* 1 (1991).

10. Since this book is titled *No More Wacos*, we do not address the other implications of total disarmament, such as the suggestion that guns are used to prevent crime more often to commit it, which would imply that successful gun prohibition would be a net loss to public safety. E.g., Gary Kleck and Marc Gertz, "Armed Resistance to Crime: The Prevalence and Nature of Self-Defense with a Gun," 86 *Journal of Criminal Law & Criminology* 150 (1995).

11. Paul Craig Roberts, "Above the Smoke and Stir," *Washington Times*, April 22, 1993.

12. Guns and magazines which are currently lawfully owned need not be registered, and may be transferred without registration. The absence of a registration provision will reduce the grounds for BATF assault on owners of these firearms and components. Assembly of new "assault weapons," however, is banned. Based on BATF interpretation of existing laws regarding assembly of "assault weapons," a person who made cosmetic alterations (such as changing the stock) or repairs (such as replacing a worn-out barrel) might be considered to be engaged in the illegal "assembly" of a new "assault weapon." And of course BATF would need only suspicion, not proof, of illegal assembly, for a raid.

13. The legislation which actually does treat guns like cars is the concealed handgun carry legislation which has been enacted in thirty-one states. If one passes a background check and a safety class, one may obtain a permit to carry a concealed handgun for protection. The process is similar to, although somewhat more expensive and restrictive than, obtaining a driver's license.

14. Such magazines are not standard for .25 caliber handguns, which are usually too small to accommodate a seven-round magazine. Firearms in the .25 caliber would be outlawed under another provision of "Brady II," which would ban small handguns by dubbing them "Saturday Night Specials."

15. The St. Bartholomew's Day Massacre in 1572, in which thousands of French Huguenots were murdered, had a similar radicalizing effect. The massacre led many Huguenots to abandon Calvin's doctrines of obedience to government, and to embrace theories of the right to resist oppression. As the French historian Agrippa d'Aubigné observed, "You will find that the burnings and massacres which flouted all legal rule gave rise to the taking up of arms, and the taking up of arms formed the Party...." Agrippa d'Aubigné, *Oeuvres Complètes,* E. Reaume and J. de Caussade, eds., vol. 2 (Geneva: 1967), p. 86.

16. That raid was intended to be a model for future mass national activations of the BATF paramilitary units, the Special Response Teams; fortunately, no such mass activations have occurred, although one was planned in 1995, and called off at the last minute (discussed below).

17. James L. Pate, "No Longer Untouchable," *American Spectator* (August 1993): 35; James R. Lewis, "Showdown at the Waco Corral: ATF Cowboys Shoot Themselves in the Foot," in *From the Ashes: Making Sense of Waco,* ed. James R. Lewis (Lanham, Md.: Rowman and Littlefield, 1993), p. 89.

18. James L. Pate, "Gun Gestapo's Day of Infamy," *Soldier of Fortune* (June 1993): 50.

19. Carol Moore, *The Davidian Massacre* (Frankin, Tenn.: Legacy Communications and Gunowners Foundation, 1995), p. 204.

20. Brandon M. Stickney, *All-American Monster: The Unauthorized Biography of Timothy McVeigh* (Amherst, N.Y.: Prometheus Books, 1996).

21. *Lawmaster* v. *United States,* 993 F.2d 773 (10th Cir.), *cert. denied,* 114 S.Ct. 196 (1993). The U.S. Attorney's office had given Lawmaster a redacted copy, which concealed all information about the informant's identity. Ibid.

22. According to the Lamplugh's court motion for the return of their property, BATF Special Agent Seiler stated, "We don't mind you selling guns to niggers because they are only killing each other." James L. Pate, "Lamplugh Raid a New Low in BATF Terror Tactics," *Soldier of Fortune* (July 1995): 58.

23. Cigarette butts were tossed on the carpet, scorching it. Ibid., p. 57.

24. "BATF Thugs Strike Again," *The Gun Owners,* December 1996: 6–7, available at http://nspace.cts.com/pub/Firearms/Government/BATF/Harry%20and%20Theresa%20Lamplugh/Gun%20Owners%20of%20America%20Report.

25. Ibid.

26. Ibid., p. 58.

27. Andy Thibault, "ATF Accused of Waging 'War' against Gun Owners," *Washington Times* (national weekly edition), April 1–7, 1996, p. 12 (U.S. Attorney's estimate of property seizure). The cases are *United States* v. *A Quantity of Miscellaneous Firearms, Assorted Ammunition and Other Property,* nos. 3:MI–94–88–01 and 3:MI–94–88–02 (D. Penn. Middle District).

28. Pate, "Lamplugh Raid," p. 58.

29. Ibid., p. 72.

30. Roger Parloff, "How the Gun Lobby is Rescuing the Bill of Rights," *American Lawyer* (November 1995): 74. Mr. Lamplugh's son was charged with one count of possession of a sawed-off shotgun. His attorney claims that the "shotgun" was assembled by BATF from junk and broken gun parts found in the garage. James L. Pate, "Lamplugh Family Charged," *Soldier of Fortune* (February 1996): 6.

31. Steve Collins, "Cserna Questions his Treatment by ATF," *Ely Daily Times,* May 11, 1995. On November 1, 1995, Cserna was found guilty by a jury of possession of a machine gun and a short-barreled rifle without a permit. Our point is not that BATF uses excessive force only against people who are innocent. Gratuitous violence and abuse—unrelated to any need to protect officer safety—do not somehow become appropriate when the victim is convicted of a crime months later.

32. Joe Mandak, "Three Federal Agencies Sued for Raid," Pittsburgh *Tribune-Review,* April 2, 1996, p. B1.

33. August R. Jaxel, "'Gestapo Tactics' Unacceptable" (letter to the editor), *Bisbee Daily Review* (Bisbee, Arizona), January 7, 1996.

34. Michael D. Sorkin, "Raid Deserves Little More than Apology," *St. Louis Post-Dispatch,*

May 3, 1996, p. 1; Michael D. Sorkin, "Federal Agents Raid St. Charles Home by Mistake," *St. Louis Post-Dispatch*, May 2, 1996; "Love, Fear and the ATF," *Potomac News*, May 5, 1996.

35. At the time, BATF was the Alcohol, Tobacco and Firearms Division of the Internal Revenue Service. The Division was separated from IRS, and given status as a Treasury Bureau in 1972. Christi Harlan, "Bureau of Alcohol, Tobacco and Firearms Gains New Attention Following Waco, Texas, Disaster," *Wall Street Journal*, April 26, 1993.

36. David Hardy, *The B.A.T.F.'s War on Civil Liberties* (Bellevue, Wash.: Second Amendment Foundation, 1979) (the Hardy report contains numerous other stories of abuse); Lewis, "Showdown," pp. 90–91.

37. The book is David Hardy, *The B.A.T.F.'s War on Civil Liberties* (Bellevue, Wash.: Second Amendment Foundation, 1979). For some more recent cases, see Carol Vinzant, "ATF-Troop," *Spy* (March 1994): 14, 46–49; Gun Owners of America, *Breaking the Law . . . in the Name of the Law: The BATF Story* (Springfield, Va.: Gun Owners of America, 1989)(videotape); list of BATF incidents at http://www.access.digex.net/%7Ecroaker/individ.html.

38. Trial testimony of Special Agent Eric Evers, describing a briefing pursuant to a pre-raid rehearsal, in Ken Fawcett, *Blind Justice: A Chronology of the Historic Trial of Eleven Branch Davidians in January 1994*, 2d ed. (Royse City, Tex.: Electropress, 1994), p. 12.

39. Department of Justice, Office of Legal Policy, "Report to the Attorney General on the Search and Seizure Exclusionary Rule," *Truth in Criminal Justice Series* report no. 2 (1986), reprinted in 22 *University of Michigan Journal of Law Reform* 573, 626 (1989).

40. Ballew was partly to blame for the failure of his suit, since he and his girlfriend did not honestly testify about their sexual activity at the time of the raid.

41. *Pennsylvania Coal Co. v. Mahon*, 260 U.S. 393 (1922)

42. *Aguilar v. Texas*, 378 U.S. 108 (1963).

43. *Illinois v. Gates*, 113 S.Ct. 2317 (1983).

44. *New York Times*, March 28, 1994, pp. A1, A9.

45. Alan W. Bock, "Raiding the Vipers' Nest," *Reason* (December 1996): 30–34; Vin Suprynowicz, "The Real Viper Conspiracy," *Liberty* (September 1996): 15. A different version of the article is available at http://www.nguworld.com/vindex/071796vs.htm. (Note: the source cited here, *Liberty* magazine, is a libertarian publication. It is not the same magazine as *Liberty* magazine, the Seventhday Adventist publication cited in the Prologue.)

46. Peter Carlson, "A Call to Arms," *Washington Post Magazine*, October 13, 1996: 10–15, 31–38. See generally, Robert Suro, "Preventing Terrorism: Where to Draw the Line?" *Washington Post*, November 11, 1996, pp. A1, A13–14.

47. Brian Reilly, "Loose Lips Sink Drug Raid," *Washington Times*, March 23, 1995, p. A1; Vernon Loeb, "Public Relations Blunder Scotches D.C. Drug Raid," *Washington Post*, March 23, 1995, p. A1; Bob Sanders, "Fighting for Respectability," *Soldier of Fortune* (July 1995): 19.

48. Senate Committee on the Judiciary, Subcommittee on the Constitution, *The Right to Keep and Bear Arms*, 97th Cong., 2d sess., Senate Doc. 2807 (February 1982), pp. 20–23. The Senate Subcommittee's conclusion was based on testimony to that effect by Mike Acree, who had retired from his position as Commission of Customs. Acree had been hired to do a study of BATF law enforcement practices in Virginia and Maryland. Later, Acree said that the Maryland and Virginia data were not necessarily applicable to the country as a whole, which he had never studied.

49. James J. Baker, "Assault on Semi-Autos," *American Rifleman* (April 1987): 42.

50. *United States v. Corcoran*, Crim. no. 88–11 (W.D. Pa., April 6, 1988) (Ziegler, J.).

51. Rick Sherrow, United States House of Representatives, Subcommittee on Crime of the Committee on the Judiciary and the Subcommittee on National Security, International Affairs, and Criminal Justice of the Committee on Government Reform and Oversight, *Joint Hearings on Activities of Federal Law Enforcement Agencies Toward the Branch Davidians*, 104th Cong., 1st sess., July 19–August 1, 1995 (Washington, D.C.: Government Printing Office, 1996) (hereinafter "Joint Hearings"), part 3, p. 164.

52. Frederick C. Calhoun, Federal Law Enforcement Training Center, "A Brief History of Federal Firearms Enforcement," appendix G to U.S. Department of the Treasury, *Report on the Bureau of Alcohol, Tobacco, and Firearms, Investigation of Vernon Wayne Howell also known as David Koresh*

(Washington, D.C.: Government Printing Office, September 1993) (hereinafter "Treasury Report"), Appendix G–7.

53. One possible BATF reform would be for the bureau to adopt internal guidelines similar to those at the Department of Justice which prohibit investigating groups "based solely on activities protected by the First Amendment or on the lawful exercise of any other rights secured by the constitution or laws of the United States." *Attorney General's Guidelines on General Crimes, Racketeering Enterprise and Domestic Security/Terrorism Investigations* (1976). Such guidelines would be unlikely to have much effect. The 1986 Firearms Owners' Protection Act was a statutory attempt to stop BATF from violating constitutional rights; if a legally binding statute has had only limited success, it is doubtful that internal guidelines would accomplish a great deal.

54. Bureau of Alcohol, Tobacco and Firearms, *Federal Firearms Regulation Guide*, ATF P 5300.4 (October 1995); Mark Barnes, letter of March 8, 1996 to William T. Earle, deputy associate director for regulatory enforcement programs, BATF (describing alleged errors).

55. Chris Collins, "ATF 'Writing Off' Hundreds of Its Firearms, Report Says," *Detroit News*, July 3, 1994, p. 10.

56. See chapter 1, text at note 30. According to the agenda for a BATF "Firearms and Explosives Data Integration Meeting" held in Martinsburg, West Virginia, November 9–10, 1994, two months before, an NFR&TR error rate was found to be 50 percent; that rate had been reduced to 2 percent for common errors. http://www.cs.cmu.edu./afs/cs.cmu.edu/user/wbardwel/public/nfalist/rip/doc3.txt.

For a full transcript of Busey's remarks, as well as BATF statements that the database is now reliable, see "Corrections by Gary N. Schaible Concerning Transcript of Roll Call Training by Tom Busey, Chief, National Firearms Act Branch October 18, 1995," available at http://www.cs.cmu.edu./afs/cs.cmu.edu/user/wbardwel/public/nfalist/rip/doc1.txt.

57. 18 U.S.C. § 923(a).

58. 18 U.S.C. § 923(d)(2).

59. Jacob Sullum, "B.A.T.F. Out of Hell," *Reason* (May 1994): 25.

60. Ben Lieberman, "The Power of Positive Drinking," *CEI Update* (November 1996): 1, 8–9 (more available at http://www.cei.org); Carrie Dolan, "Wineries and Government Clash over Ads that Toast Health Benefits of Drinking," *Wall Street Journal*, October 19, 1992, p. B1; John A. Hinman, "BATF Restriction of Truthful Health Claims in Wine Advertising Violates First Amendment," *Legal Backgrounder* (Washington Legal Foundation), vol. 7, no. 25; September 11, 1992.

61. In those days, BATF considered purchase of large amounts of sugar as suspicious as purchase of large numbers of firearms is considered today.

62. Erik Larson, "ATF Under Siege," *Time* (July 24, 1995): 28.

63. General Accounting Office, *Use of Force: ATF Policy, Training and Review Process are Comparable to DEA's and FBI's*, GAO/GGD–96–17 (Washington, D.C.: General Accounting Office, March 1996) (report to the Chairman, Subcommittee On Treasury, Postal Service, and General Government, Committee on Appropriations, U.S. House of Representatives).

64. James L. Pate, "Ask Us No Questions, We'll Tell You No Lies," *Soldier of Fortune* (March 1996): 44–45.

65. 18 U.S.C. § 926(a)(3).

66. A lawsuit pending in federal court in Ohio seeks to have Forward Trace declared illegal.

67. "Time for Congress to Rein in BATF," *American Rifleman* (April 1995): 39.

68. David Arnold and Frank Philips, "US to Help State on Gun-files Snarl," *Boston Globe*, May 10, 1996, p. 5.

69. Charley Reese, "Waco Mess is Reason to Ax Alcohol, Tobacco and Firearms Bureau," *Orlando Sentinel*, March 16, 1993, p. A8.

70. According to Kay Kubicki, currently legal counsel to the National Association of Treasury Agents, and before that a BATF agent for twelve years, BATF management is far more interested in numbers of cases than in quality. James L. Pate, "ATF's Constitutional Conscience," *Soldier of Fortune* (April 1996): 63.

71. James Simpson, "Waco and Ruby Ridge: the Real Story," *Washington Times*, September 13, 1995, p. A21.

72. *U.S. News & World Report*, March 15, 1993.

73. Sara Sun Beale, "Federalizing Crime: Assessing the Impact on the Federal Courts," *Annals of the American Academy of Political and Social Science* 543 (January 1996): 44–45.

74. "NATA Notes," *The Agent* (June 1995): 34.

75. John A. Garraty, *The American Nation* (New York: HarperCollins, 1995). See generally, David Burnham, *Above the Law* (New York: Scribner, 1996), pp. 296–301.

76. Bill Kauffman, "Our First Negro President?" *The American Enterprise* (July/August 1996): 80.

77. Burnham, *Above the Law,* p. 375, citing Senate Select Committee to Study Governmental Operations with Respect to Intelligence Activities, *Final Report: Intelligence Activities and the Rights of Americans*, Book II (Washington, D.C.: 1976), p. 9.

78. Ibid.

79. Lee Edwards, *Goldwater: The Man Who Made a Revolution* (Washington, D.C.: Regnery, 1995)(bugging of Goldwater campaign at President Johnson's request during 1964 presidential election); Burnham, *Above the Law,* pp. 48–49.

80. "F.B.I. Discloses It Monitored Cesar Chavez," *New York Times*, May 31, 1995, p. A19 (Associated Press report of story originally published in *Los Angeles Times*). The FBI spied on farmworker organizer Chavez for seven years, compiling a 1,434-page dossier, none of which supported the FBI's hypothesis that Chavez was a Communist or a subversive. Ibid.

81. Chas S. Clifton, "The Crime of Piety: Wounded Knee to Waco," in Lewis, *From the Ashes,* p. 3.

82. Ronald Kessler, *The FBI* (New York: Pocket Books, 1993), p. 344. We have no objection to electronic surveillance of the Weather Underground, which was a terrorist organization. We simply think that such surveillance should be done legally, after obtaining a warrant.

83. Michael Shanahan and Miles Benson, "Civil Liberties Threatened by Bombing," *Rocky Mountain News*, April 28, 1995, p. 48A (Newhouse News Service).

84. Kessler, *The FBI,* pp. 149–51.

85. Burnham, *Above the Law,* p. 310; Ross Gelbspan, *Break-ins, Death Threats and the FBI: The Covert War Against the Central American Movement* (Boston: South End Press, 1991), pp. 215–16.

86. Burnham, *Above the Law,* pp. 247–53.

87. General Accounting Office, *International Terrorism: FBI Investigates Domestic Activities to Identify Terrorists* (GGD–90–112) (Washington, D.C.: September 1990).

88. E.g., Selwyn Raab, "7 Suspects Says F.B.I. Agent Helped Incite Mob Murders," *New York Times*, May 10, 1995 (organized crime investigation in early 1990s).

89. Monroe Freedman, "Keystone Kops in Jackboots," *Legal Times*, June 12, 1995, p. 27; James Bovard, "The New J. Edgar Hoover," *American Spectator* (August 1995): 29–30. At the outset, FBI Director Freeh assumed a high profile on the case, disappearing from media coverage as the case unraveled. Freeh is said to have approved of the knowing use of perjured testimony in the Wedtech prosecution when he was serving as United States Attorney. Bovard, "The New J. Edgar Hoover," p. 29.

90. Andy Thibault, "FBI Not Ready to Apologize to Jewell," *Washington Times*, August 20, 1996, p. A6.

91. Burnham, *Above the Law,* p. 311.

92. The new law allows the FBI to obtain name, address, and employment information from credit reporting bureaus simply by asserting that the consumer has been "in contact" with a foreign government. "In contact" can include almost anything, such as requesting a visa, or writing a letter of protest to the government's embassy complaining about human rights violations. H.R. 1655, 104th Cong., § 601, amending 15 U.S.C. § 1681(f).

93. For a good overview of the subject, see Burnham, *Above the Law,* pp. 131–71. For regular updates on the issue, see the Electronic Privacy Center's world-wide web site, at: http://www.epic.org.

94. George Archibald, "FBI Broke Its Own Rules in Giving Files to White House," *Washington Times*, June 12, 1996, p. A1.

95. Bob Lesmeister, "Observations," *American Firearms Industry* (January 1996): 30, available at http://www.amfire.com/AFIjan/Page30.html; 18 U.S. Code § 1913.

96. Jim McGee, "Wiretapping Rises Sharply Under Clinton," *Washington Post*, July 7, 1996, p. A4.

97. Obviously there are not enough FBI agents to monitor every single conversation in that 1 percent. Computers could monitor most conversations, alerting human operators when key words—such as "guns," "drug," or "bomb"—were used.

98. Public Law no. 104–32 (became law April 24, 1996), § 731(2), amending 18 U.S.C. § 2510(16). Such transmissions would include the transmission of data from a portable computer over cellular phone lines, and transmission over a local area network that communicates by radio rather than by wire. One can make a reasonable argument that no form of radio communication should be protected by anti-wiretapping laws, since radio communication, by definition, does not involve wire communication. But the point of anti-wiretapping laws such as the Electronic Communications Privacy Act is not, after all, the sanctity of the wire, but the sanctity of privacy.

99. H.R. 896, 104th Congress, § 101(e).

100. E.g., S. 735, 104th Cong., §§ 502 (authorizing FBI to obtain unilaterally certain information, and authorizing court orders for the FBI to obtain a full credit report), 503 (giving FBI unilateral authority to issue administrative summons to "a common carrier or innkeeper").

101. Richard Leiby, "Potential Flash Point Defused in Louisiana," *Washington Post*, March 2, 1996.

102. Dan Thomasson, "Ruby Ridge's Chilling Fallout," *Washington Times*, August 27, 1995, p. B1.

103. Kessler, *The FBI*, p. 71.

104. Ibid., p. 125.

105. Ibid., p. 37.

106. The FBI had steered clear of drug cases until 1982, and did not make drugs a priority until 1987, at which point the FBI, like BATF and other federal agencies, noticed that getting in on the drug war was a good tactic for increased funding. A Department of Justice Office of Inspector General audit gave the FBI the lowest grade possible for its efficiency in handling drug cases. "Maybe Hoover Was Right: FBI Doesn't Belong in Drug Cases," *Law Enforcement News*, February 14, 1996, p. 5.

107. Jim McGee, "Wiretapping Rises Sharply Under Clinton," *Washington Post*, July 7, 1996, p. A4.

108. Bruce Kollar, "Voice of the People" (letter to the editor), *Chicago Tribune*, November 9, 1995.

109. Pamela Burdman and Charles Buress, "75 Million Ammo Rounds Seized in Santa Clara," *San Francisco Chronicle*, May 4, 1995, p. A1; "All Seized Ammo Returned to Eagle Exim," *Firearms Business*, July 1, 1995. Eagle Exim lost $250,000 in sales as a result of the wrongful seizure. Ibid.; "Importer Charges Abuse in Publicized Ammo Seizure," *Gun Week*, June 9, 1995, p. 3.

110. Burnham, *Above the Law*, p. 31.

111. *United States* v. *Van Engel*, 15 F.3d 623, 626 (1993), cert. denied, 114 S.Ct. 2163 (1994).

112. 28 C.F.R. 77.2(a). The omnibus Republican crime bill from the 104th Congress, which was never enacted, included a provision making the attorney general the sole ethical arbiter of her attorney's conduct. S.3, 104th Cong., § 502 (Hatch crime bill).

113. Chapter 5, text at note 306.

114. See p. 272.

115. Unfortunately, her actions have set an example for cabinet members to claim mock "political courage" for taking "responsibility" for a disaster with absolutely no repercussions. For example, rather than hold anyone responsible for providing a situation where lax security made it easy to bomb American military quarters in Saudi Arabia, Defense Secretary William Perry acted as if he were politically courageous by accepting responsibility himself. This did not mean he had to leave office, or suffer personally, financially, professionally, or in any other way. It merely meant he did not have to punish anyone else. Bradley Graham, "Perry Accepts Blame in Dhahran Bombing, Secretary Defends Military Commanders," *Washington Post,* September 19, 1996, p. A18. It certainly did not mean he was really accepting responsibility since he simultaneously—and correctly—denied that anyone could reasonably have expected the Secretary of Defense to know how many feet from residential quarters a perimeter fence was located. NBC Evening News, September 18, 1996. Attorney General Reno has set a standard for lax management to march arrogantly forth as political courage.

116. Mark Levin, "Why Janet Reno Must Resign," *Washington Times* (national weekly edition),

June 30, 1996, p. 32. For more on the decline of ethical standards at the Department of Justice, see Jim McGee and Brian Duffy, *Main Justice* (New York: Simon and Schuster, 1996).

117. Stephen M. Ryals, "Mistaken Raid Wasn't So Unusual," *St. Louis Post-Dispatch*, May 12, 1996): 3B.

118. Roger Parloff, "How the Gun Lobby Is Rescuing the Bill of Rights," *American Lawyer* (November 1995): 73. Human Rights Watch/Americas Watch, *United States: Crossing the Line: Human Rights Abuses Along the U.S. Border with Mexico Persist Amid Climate of Impunity*, vol. 7, no. 4 (April 1995).

119. Burnham, *Above the Law*, pp. 100–102.

120. Leonard Levy, *A License to Steal: The Forfeiture of Property* (Chapel Hill: University of North Carolina Press, 1996), p. 143; Richard Lawrence Miller, *Drug Warriors and Their Prey: From Police Power to Police State* (Westport, Conn.: Praeger, 1996), p. 105.

121. "Word about Government Tactics," *Washington Times*, May 21, 1995, p. B2.

122. Kathryn Keneally, "Increased Use of Search Warrants by the IRS," *The Champion* (January/February 1996): 41–43.

123. *National Review* (June 12, 1995): 14.

124. Debbie Goldberg, "Police Scandal Creates Storm in Philadelphia," *Washington Post*, August 17, 1995, p. A3.

125. Don Terry, "Philadelphia Held Liable in Calamitous MOVE Fire," *New York Times*, June 25, 1996; Vance McLaughlin, "The Fire Sermon (Ashes to Ashes, Dust to Dust): Waco, SLA, MOVE and the Law Enforcement Response," *Police Forum* (July 1995).

126. Paul Keegan, "The Thinnest Blue Line," *New York Times Magazine*, March 31, 1996, p. 32.

127. Paul Chevigny, *Edge of the Knife: Police Violence in the Americas* (New York: The New Press, 1995), p. 45.

128. Ibid., p. 51.

129. Judy Thomas, "Charges Dismissed to End Firearms Case," *Kansas City Star*, May 30, 1996; Carolyn D. Hart, "Neighbor Squabble Escalates into Tale of Police Abuse," *Women & Guns*, May 1996: 10–11, 42–43.

130.

The Federal Sheriff may commit what oppression, make what distresses he pleases, and ruin you with impunity: For how are you to tie his hands? . . . Our State Sheriffs, those unfeeling blood-suckers, have, under watchful eye of our Legislature, committed the most horrid and barbarous ravages on our people: It has required the most constant vigilance of the Legislature to keep them from totally ruining the people. A repeated successions of law have been made . . . and often have their nefarious ingenuity devised methods of evading the forces of those laws: In the struggle they have generally triumphed over the Legislature. . . . If Sheriffs thus immediately under the eye of our State Legislature and Judiciary, have dared to commit these outrages, what would they have done if their masters had been at Philadelphia or New-York? If they perpetrate the most unwarrantable outrage on your persons or property, you cannot get redress on this side of Philadelphia or New-York: And how can you get it there?

(Speech at Virginia Ratifying Convention, June 7, 1788.)

131. *The Spectator* (February 21, 1996); Canadian Firearms Digest, available at http://www.mae.carleton.ca/cgi-bin/mfs/01/Digests/v01n430.

132. Toronto *Globe & Mail*, February 22, 1996; "Ontario Suffering Home Invasions by Police," *Edmonton Journal*, February 22, 1996, p. A–3 (also noting a similar incident the previous month in British Columbia, in which RCMP searching for drugs burst into the home of an innocent middle-aged married couple).

133. Sherri Davis-Barron, "Criminal Charges Dropped against Hawkesbury Arms Dealer," *Ottawa Citizen*, July 25, 1996. Bill C-68, *An Act Respecting Firearms and Other Weapons*, First Session, Thirty-fifth Parliament, 42–43–44 Elizabeth 11, 1994–95, as Passed by the House of Commons, June 13, 1995, §§ 102, 104.

134. Juvenal, *Satires*, 6, line 347 ("Who then shall guard the guardians?").

135. Kessler, *The FBI*, pp. 176–78.

136. Nancy Ammerman, "Waco, Law Enforcement, and Scholars of Religion," in *Armageddon in Waco: Critical Perspectives on the Branch Davidian Conflict*, ed. Stuart A. Wright (Chicago: University of Chicago Press, 1995), p. 293.

137. Virginia Postrel, "Reawakening to Waco," *Washington Post*, April 30, 1995.

138. The first definition of "terrorist" is: "In the French Revolution, an adherent or supporter of the Jacobins, who advocated and practiced methods of partisan repression and bloodshed in the propagation of the principles of democracy and equality." *The New Shorter Oxford English Dictionary* (1993), p. 3258.

139. Phyllis Chesler, "A Double Standard for Murder?" *New York Times*, January 8, 1992.

140. "There is a curious clause in the laws of the Ine of Wessex which seeks to define the various types of forcible attack to which a householder and his property might be subjected: if fewer than seven men are involved, they are thieves; if between seven and thirty-five, they form a gang; if more than thirty-five, they are a military expedition." Carlo M. Cipola, *Before the Industrial Revolution: European Society and Economy 1000–1700*, 3d ed. (New York: W. W. Norton and Co., 1993), p. 20.

141. For scholarship in the last decades supportive of the individual rights view of the original intent of the Second Amendment, see, for example, Thomas McAfee and Michael J. Quinlan, "Bringing Forward the Right to Keep and Bear Arms: Do Text, History or Precedent Stand in the Way?" 75 *North Carolina Law Review* (1997); L. A. Scott Powe, "Guns, Words, and Interpretation," 38 *William & Mary Law Review* (1997) Randy Barnett and Don Kates, "Under Fire: The New Consensus on the Second Amendment," *Emory Law Journal* (1996); David B. Kopel and Christopher Little, "Communitarians, Neorepublicans, and Guns: Assessing the Case for Firearms Prohibition," *Maryland Law Review* (1996); Inge Larish, "Why Annie Can't Get a Gun: A Feminist Appraisal of the Second Amendment," 1996 *University of Illinois Law Forum* 467; Szepanski, "Searching for the Plain Meaning of the Second Amendment," 44 *Buffalo Law Review* 197 (1996); Robert Cottrol and Ray Diamond, "The Fifth Auxiliary Right," 104 *Yale Law Journal* 995 (1995); Glenn Harlan Reynolds and Don Kates, "The Second Amendment: A Thought Experiment," 36 *William & Mary Law Review* 1737 (1995); Glenn Harlan Reynolds, "A Critical Guide to the Second Amendment," 62 *Tennessee Law Review* 461 (1995); David B. Kopel, "It Isn't about Duck Hunting: The British Origins of the Right to Arms" (book review), 96 *Michigan Law Review* 1333 (1995); Stephen Halbrook, "Congress Interprets the Second Amendment: Declarations by a Co-Equal Branch on the Individual Right to Keep and Bear Arms," 62 *Tennessee Law Review* 595 (1995); William Van Alstyne, "The Second Amendment and the Personal Right to Arms," 43 *Duke Law Journal* 1236 (1994); David Vandercoy, "The History of the Second Amendment," 28 *Valparaiso University Law Review* 1007 (1994); Quinlan, "Is There a Neutral Justification for Refusing to Implement the Second Amendment or Is the Supreme Court Just 'Gun Shy'?" 22 *Capital University Law Review* 641 (1993); Martire, "In Defense of the Second Amendment: Constitutional and Historical Perspectives," 21 *Lincoln Law Review* 23 (1993); Don Kates, "The Second Amendment and the Ideology of Self-Protection," 9 *Constitutional Committee* 87 (1992); Akhil Amar, "The Bill of Rights and Fourteenth Amendment," 101 *Yale Law Journal* 1193 (1992); Akhil Amar, "The Bill of Rights as a Constitution," 100 *Yale Law Journal* 1131, 1164ff (1991); Elaine Scarry, "War and the Social Contract: Nuclear Policy, Distribution, and the Right to Bear Arms," 139 *University of Pennsylvania Law Review* 1257 (1991); Robert J. Cottrol and Raymond T. Diamond, "The Second Amendment: Toward an Afro-Americanist Reconsideration," 80 *Georgetown Law Journal* 309 (1991), shorter version in David B. Kopel, ed., *Guns: Who Should Have Them?* (Amherst, N.Y.: Prometheus Books, 1995); Stephen P. Halbrook, "The Right of the People or the Power of the State: Bearing Arms, Arming Militias, and the Second Amendment," 26 *Valparaiso University Law Review* 131 (1991); Sanford Levinson, "The Embarrassing Second Amendment," 99 *Yale Law Journal* 637 (1989); Stephen Halbrook, *A Right to Bear Arms: State and Federal Bills of Rights and Constitutional Guarantees* (1989); Stephen Halbrook, "Encroachments of the Crown on the Liberty of the Subject: Pre-Revolutionary Origins of the Second Amendment," 15 *Dayton Law Review* 91 (1989); Leonard Levy, *Original Intent and the Framers' Constitution* 341 (1988); David Hardy, "The Second Amendment and the Historiography of the Bill of Rights," 4 *Journal of Law and Policy* 1 (1987); Nelson Lund, "The Second Amendment, Political Liberty and the Right to Self-Preservation," 39 *Alabama Law Review* 103 (1987); Robert Shalhope, "The Armed Citizen in the Early Republic," 49 *Law & Contemporary Problems* 125 (1986); Don B. Kates, Jr., "A Dialogue on the Right to Keep and Bear Arms," 49 *Law & Contemporary Problems* 143 (1986); *Encyclopedia of the American Constitution*, vol. 4 (Karst and

Levi, eds., 1986), pp. 1639–40; David Hardy, "Armed Citizens, Citizen Armies: Toward a Jurisprudence of the Second Amendment," 9 *Harvard Journal of Law & Public Policy* 559 (1986).

See also Andrew Herz, "Gun Crazy: Constitutional False Consciousness and the Dereliction of Dialogic Responsibility," 75 *Boston University Law Review* 57 (1995)(individual right to participate in a militia); David C. Williams, "Civic Republicanism and the Citizen Militia: The Terrifying Second Amendment," 101 *Yale Law Journal* 551 (1991) (Second Amendment intended to guarantee an individual rights; since state governments have neglected their duties to promote responsible gun use through drill in a "well-regulated militia," the right to arms is no longer valid); Beschle, "Reconsidering the Second Amendment: Constitutional Protection for a Right of Security," 9 *Hamline Law Review* 69 (1986)(Amendment guarantees an individual right of personal security, which can be protected by confiscating all guns).

Against the individual right: Michael A. Bellesîles, "The Origins of Gun Culture in the United States," 83 *Journal of American History* 425 (1996); Anastaplo, "Amendments to the Constitution of the United States: A Commentary," 23 *Loyola-Chicago Law Journal* 631, 688–93 (1992); Dennis A. Henigan, "Arms, Anarchy and the Second Amendment," 26 *Valparaiso University Law Review* 107 (1991); Keith A. Ehrman & Dennis A. Henigan, "The Second Amendment in the Twentieth Century: Have You Seen Your Militia Lately?" 15 *Dayton Law Review* 5 (1989).

The one major scholar who deviates from this consensus is Garry Wills. He argues that the Second Amendment means nothing at all. It was a conscious fraud by James Madison, used to trick gullible congressmen, state legislators, and American citizens into accepting the federal Constitution. The amendment has no legal meaning at all. Garry Wills, "To Keep and Bear Arms," *New York Review of Books*, September 21, 1995: 62–72.

142. Laurie Kellman, "Waco Lessons Learned, Feds Say," *Washington Times*, November 1, 1995, p. A4.

143. E.g., FBI Uniform Crime Reports, *Law Enforcement Officers Killed and Assaulted, 1994* (Washington, D.C.: Government Printing Office, 1996).

144. Chevigny, *Edge of the Knife*, p. 111. On the lack of such hard data, see, e.g., Lawrence W. Sherman and Robert H. Langworthy, "Measuring Homicide by Police Officers," *Journal of Criminal Law and Criminology* 70 (1979): 546–60; William A. Geller and Michael S. Scott, *Deadly Force: What We Know: A Desk Reference on Police-Involved Shootings* (Washington, D.C.: Police Executive Research Forum, 1992).

145. Based in the Chicago BATF office (the largest one in the nation), Diane Klipfel was a three-time finalist for agent of the year. Her husband Mike Casali had won an award for heroism. Mr. Casali and Ms. Klipfel blew the whistle: on people working with BATF who were selling machine guns and silencers to Chicago street gangs, on a BATF gang task force that stole tens of thousands of dollars of property and which sold confiscated cocaine to drug dealers, and on two top agents who accepted illegal favors from an alleged Mafia member. The accusations were confirmed in a report by the Department of the Treasury's Office of Inspector General. While the two whistle-blowers were not fired, they were stripped of their guns and their badges. Erik Larson, "ATF Under Siege," *Time* (July 24, 1995): 22, 26–27; James L. Pate, "Rise and Fall of the ATF," *Soldier of Fortune* (May 1996): 62–67, 82.

For another incident of harassment of a whistle-blower, see Bob Lesmeister, "Vendetta," *American Firearms Industry* (December 1995): 40, 56–57 (police officer reported cover-up by Customs and Treasury of large illegal arms deal; BATF harassed officer regarding his Federal Firearms License).

146. James L. Pate, "ATF's Constitutional Conscience," *Soldier of Fortune* (April 1996): 63.

147. Paul Finer, "Do Agents Have Any Rights?" *The Agent* (NATA publication) (June 1996): 4; "FBI Whistleblowers Beware," *Washington Times* (national weekly edition), November 10, 1996, p. 37.

148. "DEA Faces Court Quiz About Secret Files on Agents," *The Agent* (June 1996): 13–14.

149. Christopher Kerr, "Flawed Process that Led FBI's Ruby Ridge Inquiry Astray," *Washington Times*, September 15, 1995.

150. Paul 't Hart, *Groupthink in Government: A Study of Small Groups and Policy Failure* (Amsterdam: Swets and Zeitlinger, 1990), pp. 291–92.

151. Miller, *Drug Warriors,* p. 119, citing *Kansas City Star*, April 6, 1991, pp. C1, C8.

152. $556 million, to be precise. Burnham, *Above the Law,* p. 190.

153. Don Van Natta, Jr., " Forfeiture for Fun and Profit," *New York Times*, June 30, 1996.

154. See chapter 5, text at note 61.

155. Executive Office for U.S. Attorneys, Department of Justice, *U.S. Attorney's Bulletin* 214, July 15, 1989, discussed in Burnham, *Above the Law,* p. 191.

156. Executive Office for U.S. Attorneys, Department of Justice, *U.S. Attorney's Bulletin* 180, August 15, 1990, discussed in Burnham, *Above the Law,* p. 191.

157. Senate Rep. No. 225, 98th Cong., 2d sess. 82 (1983), cited in Norman Abrams and Sara Sun Beale, *Federal Criminal Law,* 2d ed. (St. Paul: West, 1993), p. 878 note a.

158. *United States* v. *Sandini,* 816 F.2d 869, 872–73 (3d Cir. 1987)("The innocence of the owner is irrelevant—it is enough that the property was involved in a violation to which forfeiture attaches").

159. *Sandini,* 816 F.2d at 872 ("the burden of proof rests on the party alleging ownership").

160. For example, Colorado Revised Statutes, § 16-13–504(1); *United States* v. *$250,000,* 808 F.2d 895, 897 (1st Cir., 1987); *United States* v. *A Single Family Residence,* 803 F.2d 625, 628 (11th Cir. 1986); *One Blue 1977 AMC Jeep* v. *United States,* 783 F.2d 759, 761 (8th Cir. 1986). See also Levy, *License to Steal,* p. 48.

161. Harry L. Myers and Joseph P. Brzotowski, "Drug Agents' Guide to Forfeiture of Assets," SuDocs J24.8:D84/6/987, revised by William M. Leuck (Washington, D.C.: Department of Justice, 1987), p. 15, quoted in Miller, *Drug Warriors,* p. 92.

162. For example, Colo. Revised Statutes § 16-13–505(2)(b),: "If the court finds from the petition and the supporting affidavit that probable cause exists to believe that the seized property is contraband property as defined in this part 5, it shall, without delay, issue a citation directed to interested parties to show cause why the property should not be forfeited."

163. *One Assortment of 89 Firearms,* 465 U.S. 354, 362–66 (1984); *United States* v. *Dunn,* 802 F.2d 646 (2d Cir. 1986); *People* v. *Milton,* 732 P.2d 1199, 1203–1204 (Colo. 1989).

164. U.S. Const., Amend. XIV ("nor shall any state deprive any person of life, liberty, or property without due process of law")(italics added).

165. *Lynch* v. *Household Finance,* 405 U.S. 538, 552 (1971).

166. "Nosy, Drug-sniffing Pooch Can Land an Innocent Person in the Doghouse," *Rocky Mountain News,* August 12, 1996; Miller, *Drug Warriors,* p. 117. Then-Attorney General Richard Thornburgh stated that over 90 percent of American paper currency has drug residues. *St. Louis Post-Dispatch,* October 7, 1991, p. 6, cited in Miller, *Drug Warriors,* p. 117.

167. Ibid.

168. E.g., *People* v. *Allen,* 767 P.2d 798, 799 (Colo. App. 1988).

169. Fed. Rules of Civ. Procedure 30(a) (depositions allowed by any party, for any reason; no need for court approval).

170. Fed. R. of Civil Procedure 34(a).

171. Fed. R. Crim. Pro. 15 (depositions allowed only after court order finding that special circumstances exist).

172. E.g., Colo. Rev. Stat. § 16-13–505(4): "The discovery phase of such action shall be governed by the Colorado rules of criminal procedure."

173. Colo. Rev. Stat. § 16-13–311(3)(A)(III).

174. Levy, *License to Steal,* pp. 144–60.

175. David W. Rasmussen and Bruce L. Benson, *The Economic Anatomy of a Drug War* (Lanham, Md.: Rowman and Littlefield, 1994), pp. 135–39.

176. Miller, *Drug Warriors,* p. 112.

177. 116 U.S. 616, 633–34 (1886). More recently, Justice Arthur Goldberg made the same observation: "A forfeiture proceeding is quasi-criminal in character. Its object, like a criminal proceeding, is to penalize for the commission of an offense against the law." *One 1958 Plymouth* v. *Pennsylvania,* 380 U.S. 693, 700 (1965).

178.

We are shocked and saddened by the recent events in Waco. . . . Under the religious liberty provision of the First Amendment, the government has no business declaring what is orthodox or heretical, or what is a true or false religion. It should steer clear of inflammatory and misleading labels. History teaches that today's "cults" may be tomorrow's mainstream religion.

Signers included the American Baptist Churches, U.S.A.; American Civil Liberties Union; American Conference on Religious Movements; Americans United for Separation of Church and State; Association of Christian Schools International; Church of Scientology International; Churches' Center for Theology and Public Policy; Episcopal Church; First Liberty Institute; General Conference of Seventh-day Adventists; Greater Grace World Outreach; National Presbyterian Church (U.S.A.); and the Union of American Hebrew Congregations. Lewis, *From the Ashes*, p. 222.

179. Scott Shepard, "ATF Chief Vows to Keep an Eye on Religious Cults," *Washington Times*, November 2, 1993, p. A2. People who exercise their First Amendment rights are not the only persons looked down on by some elements in law enforcement. "Gun fag" is the derisive law enforcement slang for gun collectors.

180. Vinzant, "ATF-Troop," 47–48. Now an attorney, Ms. Kubicki often represents BATF employees in personnel grievances. Bob Lesmeister, "Bad Influence: Corruption within the Ranks of BATF," *American Firearms Industry* (June 1995): 53.

181. Victoria Loe, "Upheaval Feeds Cults, Experts Say," *Dallas Morning News*, March 7, 1993.

182. Belief in an imminent apocalypse, the destruction of the faithless, and the vindication of believers in the true religion has marked Christianity since the early days of Roman persecution. Many Americans, including many members of the Jehovah's Witnesses, Seventh-day Adventists, Church of Jesus Christ of Latter-Day Saints, and Herbert W. Armstrong's Worldwide Church of God share a strong interest in end-time prophecy. Paul Boyer, *When Time Shall Be No More: Prophecy Belief in Modern American Culture* (Cambridge, Mass.: Harvard University Press, 1992), p. 4.

Waco (sometimes dubbed "Jerusalem on the Brazos" by conservative Baptists) hosts one of the largest evangelical prophecy publishing houses, Word Books. Ibid.

183. Michael Barkun, "Reflections After Waco," in Lewis, *From the Ashes*, p. 43.

184. The Lubavitcher Hasidim, in Brooklyn, New York, expect the imminent return of their Moshiach, the late Rebbe Schneerson. For more, gopher://lubavitch.chabad.org:70/1.

185. Frank L. Flinn, "Church, Denomination, Sect, Cult," *Liberty* (July/August 1994): 25.

186. Clarence Page, "Costly Impatience in Waco," *Washington Times*, April 27, 1993, pp. F1, F4.

187. In the first fifty years of European settlement in the New England, the Quakers were frequently persecuted, and sometimes executed, because of their intense opposition to the existing government. Carla Gardina Pestana, "The Quaker Executions as Myth and History," *Journal of American History* 80 (1993): 441–69.

188. In the Oneida's "complex marriage," all the men were married to all the women, but no particular couple was allowed to become excessively attached to each other. A committee determined who would mate with whom, based on estimated genetic compatibility.

189. David G. Bromley, "The Mythology of Cults," in Lewis, *From the Ashes*, p. 122.

190. *United States* v. *Fishman*, 745 F. Supp. 713, 719 (N.D. Cal., 1990).

191. Part of the motivation was the international embarrassment suffered by both the North Korean and Chinese Communist governments as a result of the desire of huge numbers of Communist POWs to escape communism. The United States' refusal to involuntarily repatriate ex-Communist POWs was a major issue of dispute during peace negotiations.

192. Bromley, "Mythology of Cults," in Lewis, *From the Ashes*, p. 121.

193. Ibid., p. 123.

194. Luke 14:33; Acts 4:31–32, 5:1–10 (surrender of all possessions; God kills two converts who surrender only half their property).

195. Luke 14:26 ("If any man come to me, and hate not his father, and mother, and wife, and children, and brethren, and sisters, yea, and his own life also, he cannot be my disciple").

196. Joshua 6:21 (after destroying the walls of Jericho, the Israelites "utterly destroyed all that was in the city, both man and woman, young and old, and ox, and sheep, and ass, with the edge of the sword"); Joshua 8:22–26 (Israelites kill all the soldiers defending the town of Ai, and set the town on fire; as the inhabitants flee the burning town, the Israelites "smote them, so that they let none of them remain or escape [except for the king, who is taken prisoner]. And it came to pass, when Israel had made an end of slaying all the inhabitants of Ai in the field, in the wilderness . . . all the Israelites returned unto Ai, and smote it with the edge of the sword. And so it was, that all that fell that day, both

of men and women, were twelve thousand."); Joshua 11:10–23 (similar treatment for conquered cities of Eglon, Hebron, Debir, Hazor, and other conquered areas, leaving "no survivor").

197. Proverbs: 13:24, 22:15, 23:13–14, 29:15 ("Foolishness is bound in the heart of a child; The rod of correction shall drive it far from him. . . . Withhold not correction from the child. . . . Thou shalt beat him with the rod.") Many of these passages, particularly the one about disciples separating themselves from their families, were emphasized by Koresh.

198. John, 14:6 ("Jesus saith unto him I am the way, the truth, and the life: no man cometh unto the Father, but by me").

199. Americans purport to revere the Bible, but, in part as a result of declining interest in serious reading, have little concept of what the Bible contains. The religion of gentleness and forgiveness followed by many Americans is contained in some parts of the Bible. But so is holy genocide, destruction of unbelievers by fire, absolute commands for blind faith and slavish obedience, prophets who demand that the nation and the world change everything based on the prophet's insistent but unverifiable claim to have direct communication with God, a fantastic apocalypse marked by mass death, and the certitude that everything in the Bible is literally true, and that doubters condemn themselves to eternal torture in Hell. The harsher side of the Bible is the one that has dominated Western history, from Augustine's sanction of torture for religious dissidents to the Catholic church's imposition of a stifling orthodoxy that endured for nearly a thousand years, to the rigid lives inflicted on so many children by parents who emphasize the biblical virtues of submission and unquestioning obedience.

200. Boyer, *When Time Shall Be No More*, p. 68.

201. See chapter 4, text at notes 17–42. (Branch Davidians expected a great holy fire would save them, and destroy their attackers.)

202. Daniel 3:17–18.

203. Compare Sirach 4:28, "Fight to the death for truth, and the Lord God will fight for you."

204. Charles A. Clifton, "The Crime of Piety: Wounded Knee to Waco," in Lewis, ed., *From the Ashes*, pp. 3–5. The Ghost Dance was created in Nevada by a Paiute named Wovoka. It spread faster than any religion in history, reaching as far as the upper midwest and the south central region. It incorporated visions of an Indian Messiah, probably derived from Mormon missionaries. The concept of a ghost shirt that would make the wearer immune from bullets was confined almost entirely to the Sioux and other midwest tribes.

Faith in the ghost dance's vision of the imminent destruction of the whites led many Sioux to abandon the reservations and head for the Badlands of South Dakota. They lived outside of federal authority for several months, until starvation forced them to return to reservation life and meager rations from the whites. At Wounded Knee, the Seventh Cavalry disarmed one group as cavalry Colonel Forsyth ordered, "Now you tell Big Foot [a chief] he need have no fear in giving up the weapons I know his people have, as I wish to treat them with nothing but kindness." As the Sioux were surrendering their guns, the Seventh Cavalry opened fire, massacring men, women, and children. The failure of the ghost shirts to provide protection destroyed faith in the ghost dance. Several thousand other Sioux, seeing the massacre, kept up an armed resistance for several weeks longer, but eventually surrendered from starvation. The Sioux rebellion was the last effort at armed resistance to the white invasion. David Humphreys Miller, *Ghost Dance* (Lincoln: University of Nebraska Press, 1959). See also Pierre Berton, *The Invasion of Canada: 1812–1813* (Ontario: Penguin, 1988), pp. 65, 69.

205. Ammerman, "Waco, Law Enforcement, and Scholars of Religion," p. 295.

206. *Employment Division of Oregon* v. *Smith*, 494 U.S. 872 (1990).

207. Livingstone Fagan, "Waco: The Unseen Reality," available from The Research Center, at http://www.ime.net/~mswett.

208. Albert Bergesen, *The Sacred and the Subversive: Political Witch-Hunts as National Rituals* (Storrs, Conn.: SSSR Monograph Series, 1984), p. vii.

209. David Johnston, "F.B.I. Chief Clamps Down on Unit Involved in Idaho Standoff," *New York Times*, September 16, 1995; testimony of Larry Potts, Joint Hearings, part 2, p. 494; James L. Pate, "Ask Us No Questions, We'll Tell You No Lies," *Soldier of Fortune* (March 1996): 45.

210. General Accounting Office, *Use of Force*, p. 7.

211. Vinzant, "ATF-Troop," p. 49.

212. According to a memo written by BATF Director John Magaw, "ATF has contacted the U.S.

Army Training and Doctrine Command regarding its need for command post training. . . . This training would include Tactical Operations Center (TOC) functions, stress/crisis management, and decision making. ATF was notified in January 1994 that the Army Military Police is developing a tactical commanders course and would provide this training to ATF at no cost. This course would be mandatory for those SACs/ASACs [Special-Agent-in-Charge, Assistant-Special-Agent-in-Charge] who are currently being identified to serve as future 'Incident Commanders' or 'Tactical Coordinators' of major operations." Quoted in Bob Lesmeister, "Bad Influence: Corruption within the Ranks of BATF," *American Firearms Industry,* June 1995, p. 73.

213. "BATF Goes Mechanized," *The Resister* (Winter 1995); Bob Lesmeister, "Bad Influence: Corruption within the Ranks of BATF," *American Firearms Industry,* June 1995, p. 107.

214. At least some of the planes were put through Service Life Extension Program (SLEP), which upgraded the engines from 750 horsepower to 1,040 hp, replaced all of the electronics in the plane, put in the latest military cockpit electronics, and inserted the same FLIR/video system as the Apache helicopter has (allowing surveillance of a target or object from two to three miles away). After the expensive SLEP reconditioning, the planes were immediately decommissioned (in some cases before the SLEP process was completed), and transferred to BATF. James L. Pate, "ATF's Shadow Air Force," *Soldier of Fortune* (September 1995).

215. John W. Magaw, Director BATF, letter of September 5, 1995, to Rep. C. W. (Bill) Young.

216. Kessler, *The FBI,* p. 282.

217. One SWAT team head observed, "Most of the agents who try out for SWAT are former police or people with military backgrounds. . . . Their psychological makeup is they like to go out and do things." Kessler, *The FBI,* p. 154.

218. The creator was Oliver "Buck" Revell, who also started the FBI's air force. Kessler, *The FBI,* p. 159.

219. Mark Levin, "What Became of the FBI?" *National Review,* October 9, 1995, p. 20.

220. Sam Vincent Meddis, "Survivalist Tells his Side of Idaho Raid," *USA Today,* September 7, 1995, p. 3A.

221. Charles J. Dunlap, Jr., "Welcome to the Junta: The Erosion of Civilian Control of the U.S. Military," 29 *Wake Forest Law Review* 341, 359 (1994)(citing Center for Defense Information broadcast of April 11, 1993).

222. 1995 Rhode Island General Assembly, bill 95-S 1096 (not enacted).

223. "World Sitrep," *Soldier of Fortune* (May 1996): 17.

224. H.R. 896 § 101(b)(1); S. 735 § 102(b)(1); H.R. 896, § 101(f); S. 735, § 102(f).

225. Mark V. Lonsdale, *Raids: A Tactical Guide to High Risk Warrant Service* (Los Angeles: S.T.T.U., Training Division, 1991), p. 194.

226. Peter B. Kraska and Victor E. Kappeler, "Militarizing American Police: The Rise and Normalization of U.S. Police Paramilitary Units, *Social Problems* 44, no. 1 (1997, forthcoming).

227. "Detroit Residents Alarmed by Backyard Police 'Raids,' " *Gun Week* (January 13, 1995): 2.

228. "Army War Games are Night Fright," *Pittsburgh Post-Gazette,* June 5, 1996, pp. A–1, A–16; "Military Retreats in Face of Anger," *Pittsburgh Post-Gazette,* June 6, 1996, pp. B–1, B–6.

229. Henry Stanley McMahon, Jr., and Karen J. Kilpatrick, *In re: Interviews of Henry Stanley McMahon, Jr., and Karen J. Kilpatrick,* deposition taken May 25, 1993, pp. 31–33.

230. "Police to Benefit from Defense Gadgetry," *Law Enforcement News* (November 30, 1994): 9.

231. "Crime Fighting Bargain: Army Surplus Helicopters," *American Legislative Exchange Council,* February 23, 1995, p. 5.

232. Peter Kraska, "Enjoying Militarism: Political/Personal Dilemmas in Studying U.S. Police Paramilitary Units," *Justice Quarterly* 13, no. 3 (September 1996): 417.

233. Kraska and Kappeler, "Militarizing American Police."

234. Kraska, "Enjoying Militarism," p. 418, citing *Barnett* v. *Karpinos* (1995).

235. 10 United States Code, §§ 371–79.

236. Jim Malloy, "These days, NORAD Key Player in Drug War," *Denver Post,* April 23, 1996.

237. Specifically: $98 million to modify two Navy P-3B aircraft into "specialized radar warning aircraft" which would be transferred to the U.S. Customs Service; $15 million to install a TPS-70 ground-based radar system in an unspecified foreign country; $6 million for "non-intrusive" inspec-

tion systems along the Mexican border; $3 million more for National Guard marijuana eradication; and $10 million for "classified" Department of Defense drug activities.

238. For a favorable view of these assaults, see Jerry D. Fitz, "Taking Back the Projects," *Police* (May 1996): 56–61. At the end of the article, the following "Editor's Note" appears: "*Police* does not necessarily endorse the methods used to enforce the 'Mano Dura' program. We are merely reporting on the logistics of the takeovers." Ibid., p. 61. It is very rare for *Police* to attach editorial disclaimers to its articles.

239. 10 U.S.C. § 380; 101 Stat. 1163 and 102 Stat. 2046.

240. 10 U.S. Code § 381; Pub. Law 103–60, Div. A, Title XI, §1122(a)(1), November 30, 1993; 107 Stat. 1754.

241. "Trouble in the Fields: Residents Fed Up with Anti-Marijuana Drive," *Law Enforcement News*, October 31, 1994, p. 5; Micheal Dorgan, "California Loses War on Weed," *Denver Post*, November 19, 1995, p. 30A (Knight-Ridder). Use of the National Guard for marijuana eradication is typically preceded by a declaration from the governor that marijuana cultivation represents an "emergency" which necessitates the use of the Guard. While most persons think of an "emergency" as a spontaneous and unexpected event (such as a flood), the Orwellian military use of "emergency" means "something that the governor thinks is a serious problem, even if the problem has persisted at endemic levels for many years."

242. Philip Jenkins, *Using Murder: The Social Construction of Serial Homicide* (New York: Aldine de Gruyter, 1994), p. 233.

243. The very first episode of the supposedly realistic "N.Y.P.D. Blue" involved the police protagonist publicly beating up a man he believed to have been guilty of a crime for which he had just been acquitted by a jury, resulting in only minimal sanction threatened against the officer.

244. While the effects of violent television on children have received a great deal of attention, the effects of violent entertainment on adults, including adults in law enforcement, have rarely been analyzed.

245. Chevigny, *Edge of the Knife,* p. 124.

246. Kraska, "Enjoying Militarism," p. 420. Of course the United States had a "war on poverty" in the 1960s without sending in the army. But the "war on poverty" rhetoric, along with President Carter's assertion that energy crisis was "the moral equivalent of war," helped pave the way for "war on crime" and "war on drugs" rhetoric, rhetoric that has led to military intervention.

247. Dunlap, "Welcome to the Junta," p. 388.

248. Contrast *United States* v. *Yunis*, 924 F.2d 1086, 1093 (D.C.Cir. 1991)(interpreting statutory language literally, so that the Posse Comitatus Act does not apply to the Navy) with 32 Code of Federal Regulations § 213.10(c) (Department of Defense regulation applying Posse Comitatus Act to the Navy and Marine Corps, while allowing Secretary of the Navy to make exceptions on a case-by-case basis). The act does not currently apply to the Coast Guard, which in peacetime is considered part of the Department of Transportation. 14 U.S.C. § 1.

249. "Total Hogwash," *The Resister* 1, no. 3 (Winter 1995) available at http://www.accessone. com/~rivero/POLITICS/ARCHIVE/resister_3.html. See also John P. Coffey, Note, "The Navy's Role in Interdicting Narcotics Traffic: War on Drugs or Ambush on the Constitution," 75 *Georgia Law Journal* 1947 (1987)(criticizing loophole that allows use of navy ships firing artillery in drug law enforcement, under pretext of having the ship fly Coast Guard colors when it begins aggressive activities).

250. While the Guard is almost entirely funded by the federal government, it is exempt from Posse Comitatus when it is in "state status," under the immediate command of state officials, as opposed to "federal status," when the Guard is commanded by federal officers.

251. Besides the drug exceptions, there are various Posse Comitatus exceptions for matters which are well within the competence for civilian federal, state, and local law enforcement: civil disorders (10 U.S.C. §§ 331–34); protection of federal parks (16 U.S.C. §§ 23, 78); protection of foreign officials and other foreign guests (18 U.S.C. §§ 112[f]); crimes against members of Congress (18 U.S.C. § 351); crimes against the president (18 U.S.C. §§ 1751, 3056); neutrality laws (22 U.S.C. §§ 461–62); execution of certain civil rights warrants (42 U.S.C. § 1989); removing unlawful fences from public lands (43 U.S.C. § 1065); and customs laws (50 U.S.C. § 220). We are not suggesting that the substantive laws in question be repealed. Rather, these laws should be enforced by civilian law enforcement.

252. Note, "Fourth Amendment and Posse Comitatus Act Restrictions on Military Involvement in Civilian Law Enforcement," 54 *George Washington Law Review* 404 (1986).

253. Allan R. Millett, "The Constitution and the Citizen-Soldier," in Richard H. Kohn, ed., *The United States Military under the Constitution of the United States, 1789–1989* (New York: New York University Press, 1991), p. 103.

254. 10 U.S.C. § 2576.

255. "Justice, Defense Announce 'Troops to Cops' Conversion Program," *Crime Control Digest* (May 5, 1995): 1.

256. One exception to this last rule should be made for expanding ammunition, which is banned from international warfare. Expanding ammunition is less likely to exit a target's body and endanger a bystander. Expanding ammunition is also more likely to end the gunfight, by incapacitating the target. Accordingly, expanding ammunition is entirely legitimate for defensive use by the government and by civilians. A need for the other exceptions may be found, but the presumption should be: If it is inhumane to use against enemy soldiers, it is inhumane to use against American civilians.

257. 16 U.S.C. § 559c.

258. The BATF's outfits, including their Ninja clothes, are actually blue, but the color is so dark that the clothes are almost always described as black. Moorman Oliver, Jr., "Killed by Semantics: Or Was It a Keystone Kop Kaleidoscope Kaper?" in Lewis, *From the Ashes,* p. 75.

259. William F. Powers, "Dressed to Kill?" *Washington Post,* May 4, 1995.

260. John Kleinig, *The Ethics of Policing* (Cambridge, England: Cambridge University Press, 1996), p. 102.

261. Edwin Meese, III, and Rhett DeHart, "How Washington Subverts Your Local Sheriff," *Policy Review* (January/February 1996): 49, available at http://www.townhall.com/heritage/p_review/jan96/meese.html.

262. Ibid., pp. 49, 52.

263. Abrams and Beale, *Federal Criminal Law,* p. 6.

264. Sara Sun Beale, "Federalizing Crime: Assessing the Impact on the Federal Courts," *Annals of the American Academy of Political and Social Science* 543 (January 1996): 45.

265. Thomas M. Mengler, "The Sad Refrain of Tough on Crime: Some Thoughts on Saving the Federal Judiciary from the Federalization of State Crime," 43 *University of Kansas Law Review* 503 (1995).

266. Ibid.

267. U.S. Constitution, Article I, § 8.

268. Some federal law enforcement spokesmen, on the other hand, seem to think federal action is warranted if state and local officials, in the opinion of the federal officials, do not enforce their own laws adequately. One defender of federal behavior at Waco denounced Texas officials for not stopping Koresh from abusing children, having a firetrap with propane tanks in the building, having a building with inadequate sanitation, and home-schooling most of the children. Victor G. Oboyski, Federal Law Enforcement Officers Association, "Waco: Where Were the State Officials?" letter to the editor, *Washington Post,* August 17, 1995, p. A28. The federal government is not supposed to step in with federal law enforcement merely because appropriate jurisdictions have failed to meet what some federal officials deem appropriate standards.

269. Federalist Papers, no. 45 (James Madison).

270. Federalist Papers, no. 51 (Alexander Hamilton).

271. *United States* v. *Lopez,* 115 S.Ct. 1624, 1631 n.3 (1995).

272. H.R. 3610, 104th Congress; P.L. 104–208.

273. The federal law exempts permit holders, but not persons who do not need a permit.

274. Glenn Harlan Reynolds, *Kids, Guns, and the Commerce Clause: Is the Court Ready for Constitutional Government?* Cato Institute Policy Analysis no. 216 (Washington, D.C., 1994).

275. E.g., Scott A. Hodge, *The Crime Bill: Few Cops, Many Social Workers,* Issue Bulletin no. 201 (Washington, D.C.: Heritage Foundation, August 2, 1994), available at http://www.townhall.com/heritage/library/categories/crimelaw/ib201.html.

276. Ernest K. Alix, *Ransom Kidnapping in America 1874–1974: The Creation of a Capital Crime* (Carbondale: Southern Illinois University Press, 1978); Raymond Kessler, *The FBI* (New York: Pocket Books, 1993); Richard Gid Powers, *G-Men: Hoover's FBI in American Popular Culture* (Car-

bondale: Southern Illinois University Press, 1983); Harold Schechter, *Deranged* (New York: Pocket, 1990); Sanford J. Ungar, *FBI* (Boston: Little, Brown, 1976).

277. Burnham, *Above the Law,* pp. 86–87, discussing Harry Subin, *Review of Departmental Policy on Dyer Act (18 U.S.C. 2312) Prosecutions* (Department of Justice, Office of Criminal Justice: January 27, 1965).

278. Philip Jenkins, *Using Murder: The Social Construction of Serial Homicide* (New York: Aldine de Gruyter, 1994).

279. Richard Moran, "F.B.I. Scare Tactics," *New York Times,* May 7, 1996; FBI Uniform Crime Reports, *Crime in the United States, 1993* (Washington, D.C.: Government Printing Office, 1994), p. 283.

280. The agents were also upset that they were not paid overtime for the routine, long hours required by Operation Big Bird. After they won an administrative action to recover the overtime pay to which they were entitled, many agents were given retaliatory transfers to undesirable cities. William J. Burgess, *Piercing the Shields of Justice: Inside the ATF* (Lawrenceville, Va.: Brunswick, 1996).

281. Associated Press, April 28, 1995 (Washington, D.C.).

282. Center for National Security Studies, *Misleading "Findings" in Clinton Terrorism Bill* (Washington, February 22, 1995), p. 1.

283. *Misleading "Findings,"* pp. 1–2.

284. Michael Fumento, "A Church Arson Epidemic? It's Smoke and Mirrors," *Wall Street Journal,* July 5, 1996; Michael Fumento, "Is Civil Rights Commission Blowing Smoke on Church Fires?" *Sacramento Bee,* October 27, 1996, p. F3, available at http://www.townhall.org/columnists/ Fumento.

285. H.R. 3525, 104th Congress (extending federal arson law to cases which "affect" interstate commerce). Despite the fact that the Mount Carmel Center was a church, nobody in Congress seemed to find any irony in the FBI being told to investigate church fires. For that matter, few people commented when a new award was created for persons who expand opportunities for women and minorities in the legal profession: the Janet Reno Torchbearer Award. "National," Cleveland *Plain-Dealer,* May 28, 1996, p. 2A (award created by Women's Bar Association of the District of Columbia).

286. U.S. Constitution, art. I, § 8.

287. E.g., Gregg A. Bilz, "The Medical Use of Marijuana: The Politics of Medicine," 13 *Hamline Journal of Public Law and Policy* 117, 119 (1992).

288. Henry David Thoreau, *Walden* (1854), ch. 1, available at http://www.inform.umd. edu:8080/EdRes/ReadingRoom/HistoryPhilosophy/OnWaldenPond/.

289. Nor should the interstate commerce power be used to impede the free flow of goods and services between the states. The intent of the interstate commerce clause was to give Congress power to remove state barriers to commerce, not to give Congress the power to erect its own barriers. The Gun Control Act of 1968 makes it illegal for a Colorado resident to buy a handgun from a Kansas gun store. Why should Congress block a commercial transaction of which the Kansas and Colorado legislatures both approve?

290. R. J. Rummel, *Death by Government* (New Brunswick, N.J.: Transaction, 1994); Paul Johnson, *Modern Times: The World from the Twenties to the Nineties,* rev. ed. (New York: Harper-Collins, 1991).

291. E.g., Dick Reavis, *The Ashes of Waco: An Investigation* (New York: Simon and Schuster, 1995).

292. "Rough Justice," *Maclean's* (August 6, 1990): 17–20; "A Ravaged Town," *Maclean's* (August 6, 1990): 21; "An Ancient Warrior Code," *Maclean's* (August 6, 1990): 22–23; "Fury in the Ranks," *Maclean's* (August 6, 1990): 24–25; John Coleman, "Canada's Civil War," *Soldier of Fortune* (December 1990): 38–47; "Mohawk Refugees Pelted," New York *Daily News,* August 29, 1990, p. 15; "Canadian Troops Move on Mohawk Settlement," *Washington Post,* September 2, 1990, p. A38 (Associated Press); "Canada on Brink of War with Indians," *Rocky Mountain News,* September 21, 1990, p. 4; "Mohawk Surrender Turns into One Last Brawl," *Toronto Globe and Mail,* reprinted in *Rocky Mountain News,* September 27, 1990, p. 33.

On July 10, 1995, New York National Guard commanders circulated a "warning order" creating plans for a military-style assault on three New York State Mohawk Indian reservations, which had been resisting state efforts to collect taxes from casinos and other enterprises on reservation property.

The plans were withdrawn within a day. "NY National Guard Planned Assault on Indian Reservations," *Gun Week,* January 1, 1996; Utica *Observer-Dispatch,* November 5, 1995.

293. Dvoorah Getzler, "Cult Standoff Ends," *Intermountain Jewish News,* April 1, 1994, p. 7.

294. Erwin Knoll, "The Tragedy After Waco—Public Response," *Christian Science Monitor,* April 27, 1993, p. 19.

295. According to ABC News/Washington Post polling, the "approve/disapprove" poll results for federal handling of Waco were 70/27 in April 1993, falling to 56/38 in May 1995, falling further to 45/50 in July 1995. "Poll Update ABC/W. Post: Waco Hearings More Legit Than Whitewater," *The Hotline* 8, no. 205 (American Political Network) (July 19, 1995).

As the hearings began, 46 percent of Americans thought the hearings were a good idea, while 51 percent thought them unnecessary. "CBS This Morning," 1995 Westlaw 322026, July 27, 1995 (results of CBS News-*New York Times* survey). After the hearings, a Harris poll found that 52 percent believed that the federal bureaus had behaved reasonably; 36 percent thought they were grossly incompetent, and 9 percent said the bureaus deliberately chose policies which they knew would result in a large number of deaths. Seventy-one percent thought Koresh and the Branch Davidians were mostly to blame, while 24 percent blamed mainly the federal government. "Poll Shows Divisions over Waco," *Salt Lake Tribune,* August 10, 1995, p. A8 (Gannett News Service); Humphrey Taylor, "Sharp Divisions over Waco," Gannett News Service, 1995 Westlaw 2903446, August 9, 1995 (men, blacks, and Hispanics more likely to blame the government; Reno's handling was rated negatively by a 49 to 46 percent vote).

A Kentucky poll found that 38 percent of the state's residents thought the federal bureaus did a good job at Waco, and 44 percent a poor job. Deborah Yetter, "Majority Finds Fault with Way Government Handled Ruby Ridge," Louisville *Courier-Journal,* October 22, 1995, p. 1A.

In an Arizona poll, 28 percent said it was very likely, and 48 percent said somewhat likely, that the government had covered up the truth about Waco. Michael Murphey, "Media, Government Distrust High," *Phoenix Gazette,* August 2, 1995, p. B1.

296. The poem is reprinted in Lewis, *From the Ashes,* pp. 215–16.

297. "Frontline" interview with Clinton Van Zandt, August 17, 1995, available at http://www.wgbh.org.

298. 35:2: "the excellency of Carmel and Sharon."

299. 9:3: "And though they hide themselves in the top of Carmel, I will search and take them out thence."

300. 1 Kings 18:19.

301. 1 Kings 18:23–24.

302. 1 Kings 18:13–40.

303. Catholics see their church in a similar relation to Mary. *Dictionary of Mary* (New York: Catholic Book Publishing Co., 1985), p. 48 ("Mary is prototype of the Church").

304. Arnold, "The Davidian Dilemma," in Lewis, *From the Ashes,* p. 28.

305. Louis Sahagun and Doug Conner, "Pair Acquitted of Murder in Idaho Mountain Shootout," *Washington Post,* July 9, 1993, quoting University of Dallas professor Tony Cooper.

306. Myrna Shinbaum quoted in Mitch Lipka, "Frustration Mobilizes N.Y. Militias," *Standard-Star* (Gannett), April 30, 1995.

307. Jess Walter, *Every Knee Shall Bow: The Truth and Tragedy of Ruby Ridge and the Randy Weaver Family* (New York: HarperCollins, ReganBooks, 1995).

308. Dr. Alan Stone, reviewer comments on Justice Report, pp. 14–15.

309. The militarization of American law enforcement is, sadly, supported by many self-styled liberals. For example, *Washington Post* columnist Mary McGrory suggests that the tactics used by the United States army in Somalia for mass disarmament of the civilian population be used in the United States. *Washington Post,* February 16, 1993, p. A2. Ms. McGrory's call for military enforcement of gun laws during the Somalia incursion came only two weeks before the BATF attacked Mount Carmel. Should Ms. McGrory be considered accountable for having used extreme rhetoric which helped create a climate of violence that led to the deaths of innocent Americans? If not, should persons who advocate peaceful political action in support of the Second Amendment be considered responsible for mentally disturbed individuals who blow up buildings?

310. Other signers included the Citizens Committee for the Right to Keep and Bear Arms, the

Criminal Justice Policy Foundation, the Drug Policy Foundation, the International Association for Civilian Oversight of Law Enforcement, the National Association of Criminal Defense Lawyers, the National Legal Aid and Defender Association, and the Second Amendment Foundation.

311. For more detail, see David B. Kopel and Joseph Olson, "Preventing a Reign of Terror: Civil Liberties Implications of Terrorism Legislation," 21 *Oklahoma City Law Review* (no. 2, 1996): 1–101.

Appendix A

The Comprehensive Public Safety and Federal Law Enforcement Improvement Act, and Other Law Enforcement Reforms

This appendix provides specific statutory language to implement many of the reforms suggested in the text of this book. While the reforms are presented as part of a comprehensive bill, the language for any particular reform can easily be placed in separate legislation. The proposed legal reforms are for federal law, contained in the United States Code, but most are readily adaptable to state codes as well.

Commentary in [brackets] offers explanations where appropriate, and is not part of the proposed statutory language.

This appendix was drafted by Richard E. Gardiner, an attorney in private practice in Fairfax, Virginia, who specializes in constitutional litigation and criminal defense work, and by David Kopel. As with the rest of the book, nothing in this appendix represents the official view of the National Rifle Association, the Independence Institute, or any other organization.

The proposed statutory reform language is offered as a starting point. There may be appropriate exceptions or other modifications which could be added.

The indention and paragraphing used below are slightly different from the style used in congressional bill drafting; changes were made in the interest of readability. Also in the interest of readability, when striking one item in a list (e.g., repealing the fourth item in a list of seven items), the proposed act does not include the language specifying the renumbering of the subsequent items (i.e., item "(5)" should be renumbered as "(4)"; item "(6)" should be renumbered as "(5)" and so on).

1. THE COMPREHENSIVE PUBLIC SAFETY AND
FEDERAL LAW ENFORCEMENT IMPROVEMENT ACT

Be it enacted by the Senate and House of Representatives of the United States of America in Congress assembled,

Section 1. Short title, congressional findings, and construction

(a) Short title. This Act shall be cited as the "Comprehensive Public Safety and Federal Law Enforcement Improvement Act."

(b) The Congress finds that:

(i) federal law enforcement agencies have sometimes conducted their enforcement activities in a manner that infringes constitutional rights;

(ii) federal law enforcement activities have often exceeded the authority granted to the federal government by the Constitution;

(iii) the federal courts have not always ensured the protection of the rights of citizens nor have federal courts ensured that federal law enforcement activities remain within constitutional limits;

(iv) as the body charged with making laws Congress can correct the failures of federal law enforcement agencies and courts by clarifying the laws under which such agencies and courts operate.

(c) Congress intends that this act be broadly and liberally construed. Congress further intends that in case of express or implicit conflict between this law and any other law, this law shall prevail.

Section 2. Enforcement of civil rights

[This section improves the ability of victims of law enforcement abuse to sue the perpetrators.]

Chapter 171 of title 28, United States Code, is amended by adding the following new section:

"§ 2674A. Civil action for deprivation of rights.

(a) Every person who, under color of any statute, regulation, custom, or usage, of the United States, subjects, or causes to be subjected, any person within the jurisdiction of the United States to the deprivation of any rights, privileges, or immunities secured by the Constitution or laws, shall be liable to the party injured in an action at law, suit in equity, or other proper proceeding for redress.

(b) In any action or proceeding to enforce this section, the court shall allow the plaintiff, if he is the prevailing party, a reasonable attorney's fee and expert fees."

Section 3. Use of Tax Power for Non-tax Purposes

[This section and the next section modify the major federal laws regarding guns and drugs so that the laws apply only to interstate activities, and not the possession or sale of items within a single state. The sections serve as models for similar modifications of other federal criminal statutes which overuse the interstate commerce power or use the tax power for non-tax purposes. Section 3 repeals the federal machine gun tax.]

(a) Subsection 922(o) of title 18, United States Code, is repealed.

(b) Section 5845 of title 26, United States Code, is amended —

(i) in subsection (a), by striking "a machinegun; (7)" and by striking out "(8)" and inserting in lieu thereof "(7)"; and

(ii) by striking subsection (b).

Section 4. Interstate or foreign commerce

[Subsection (a) inserts a general definition, applicable to all federal statutes, narrowing the application of the interstate commerce power.]

(a) Chapter 1 of title 1 of the United States Code is amended by adding the following new sections:

§ 7. "'Interstate commerce' and 'foreign commerce' do not include commercial or other activity that takes place solely within the boundaries of a single state."

§ 8. "Commerce" means the purchase and sale of goods or services. "Commerce" does not include the possession of an item.

§ 9. To "affect" or "affecting" interstate or foreign commerce means to have a very substantial and direct effect.

[The following subsections remove language from the federal gun and drug laws which pertain to intrastate activity. They also remove language about "affecting" interstate commerce, since the interstate commerce power should not properly be construed to apply to things which "affect" interstate commerce, any more than the congressional postal power should be construed to apply to things that "affect" the mail. The section 9 clarification of the "affect" language, above, is still useful, pending the repeal of all "affecting interstate commerce" language in all federal statutes.]

(b) Paragraph (a)(2) of section 921 of title 18, United States Code, is amended by inserting: "'Interstate commerce' and 'foreign commerce' do not include commercial or other activity that takes place solely within the boundaries of a single state."

(c) Section 922 of title 18, United States Code, is amended:

(i) in subparagraph (a)(1)(A), by striking "manufacturing," and by inserting "in interstate or foreign commerce" after "firearms";

(ii) in subparagraph (a)(1)(B), by striking "or manufacturing";

(iii) in paragraph (a)(5), by inserting "does not reside in (or if the person is a corporation or other business entity, does not maintain a place of business in) the State in which the transferor resides if" after "who" and by inserting "such person" after "believe";

(iv) in paragraph (a)(7), by striking "manufacture or" and by striking subparagraph (a)(7)(A);

(v) in paragraph (a)(8), by inserting "in interstate or foreign commerce" after "ammunition" the first time it appears and by striking subparagraph (a)(8)(A);

(vi) in subsection (b), by inserting ", in interstate or foreign commerce," after "deliver";

(vii) in paragraph (b)(3), by inserting "does not reside in (or if the person is a corporation or other business entity, does not maintain a place of business in) the State in which the transferor resides if" after "who" and by inserting "such person" after "believe";

(viii) in subsection (d), by inserting ", in interstate or foreign commerce," after "ammunition";

(ix) in subsection (g), by striking ", or possess in or affecting commerce," and by striking "which has been shipped or transported";

(x) in paragraph (h)(1), by striking ", possess," and by striking "or affecting"; and in paragraph (h)(2), by striking "which has been shipped or transported";

(xi) in subsection (j), by striking "or which has been shipped or transported in,";

(xii) in subsection (n), by striking "which has been shipped or transported";

(xiii) in paragraph (p)(1), by striking "manufacture," and "possess," and inserting "in interstate or foreign commerce" after "firearm";

(xiv) by striking paragraph (p)(5);

(xv) in paragraph (r), by striking "assemble from imported parts any semiautomatic rifle or any shotgun" and inserting in lieu thereof "ship or transport in interstate or foreign commerce any semiautomatic rifle or any shotgun which was assembled from imported parts and"; and

(xvi) by striking subsections (s), (v), (w), and (x).

(d) Section 841(a) of title 21, United States Code, is amended in paragraph (1), by striking "manufacture," and "to manufacture," and inserting after "dispense" the words "in interstate or foreign commerce or within the special maritime or territorial jurisdiction of the United States," and in paragraph (2), by striking "create," and inserting after "dispense" the words "in interstate or foreign commerce or within the special maritime or territorial jurisdiction of the United States," and by inserting as a new paragraph, after the end of paragraph (2), "'Interstate or foreign commerce' does not include commercial or other activity that takes place solely within the boundaries of a single state."

(e) Section 848(a) of title 21, United States Code, is amended by inserting "in interstate or foreign commerce" after "enterprise".

(f) Section 848(b) of title 21, United States Code, is amended by inserting "in interstate or foreign commerce" after "enterprise" the first time it appears.

Section 5. Media Standards for Law Enforcement

[This section prohibits the federal government from inviting the news media to cover a raid, as BATF apparently did at Waco, and reduces the ability of the government to impose a news blackout on law enforcement actions, as the FBI did at Waco.]

Chapter 205 of title 18, United States Code, is amended by adding the following new section:

"§ 3109A. Presence of news media.

(a) No officer or other agent of the United States may notify, or cause to be notified, an employee of the news media that a search or arrest warrant is to be executed.

(b) No officer or other agent of the United States may prohibit an employee of the news media from observing the execution of a search warrant or other law enforcement activity from a location accessible to the public, unless United States has obtained an order from court of the United States based on a showing of compelling state interest and no less restrictive alternative."

Section 6. Firearms Law Clarifications and Improvements

[Clarifies that enhanced sentencing for weapons used in a crime must be predicated on: (1) A finding of guilt for the underlying crime; and (2) an indictment charging the person with the specific type of weapon (e.g., with a machine gun) and a finding of guilt for the specific type of indicted weapon. Repeals the portions of the federal ban on armor-piercing ammunition and the federal assault weapons ban which exempt the government from those laws.]

    (a) Paragraph 924(c)(1) of title 18, United States Code, is amended:

    (i) By striking "for which he may be prosecuted" and inserting "for which he has been found guilty."

    (ii) By inserting after "thirty years": "No person shall be sentenced under this subparagraph unless he is indicted for violation of this subparagraph with an indictment that specifies the particular type of weapon used, and is found guilty of use of the particular type of weapon specified in the indictment."

    (b) Subparagraphs 922(a)(7)(A) and 922(a)(8)(B), and paragraph 925(a)(1) of title 18, United States Code, are repealed.

    (c) Subparagraphs (A),(B), and (C) of section 922(v)(4), and subparagraphs (A),(B), and (C) of section 922(w)(4) of title 18, United States Code, are repealed.

Section 7. Fourth Amendment Enforcement

[The proposed § 3104A tightens the procedure for issuance of search warrants, to address the problems discussed in chapters 1 and 6.]

    (a) Chapter 205 of title 18, United States Code, is amended by adding the following new section:

"§ 3104A. Issuance of Search Warrants

    (a) Notwithstanding the provisions of Title 28, Section 2072 or any other law or rule, no warrant for search and seizure shall issue:

    (1) unless the application for such warrant and affidavit has been reviewed, approved, and signed by an attorney for the government and, in the case of a warrant based upon sworn oral testimony, unless the attorney for the government:

    (A) is a party to any telephonic or other communication between the magistrate or state judge and each person whose testimony forms a basis for the warrant and each person applying for the warrant, and

    (B) verifies to the magistrate or state judge that such attorney approves the issuance of the warrant;

    (2) unless supported by affidavit or sworn oral testimony of one or more credible and reliable persons with personal knowledge of the facts set forth in the affidavit or sworn oral testimony and such affidavit or sworn oral testimony establishes the factual basis for the person's or persons' knowledge and veracity and reliability;

    (3) based in any part upon hearsay evidence which would not be admissible under the Federal Rules of Evidence;

    (4) unless the facts establishing probable cause became known or are verified not more than thirty days prior to the issuance of the warrant, except where an offense is to be committed at a specific future time;

(5) unless the law enforcement officer applying for the warrant provides, as part of the application, an affidavit or sworn oral testimony containing any known evidence which would tend to support denial of the application;

(6) unless the affidavit or sworn oral testimony of a person who qualifies as an expert sets forth such person's qualifications and the basis of his conclusions, if the evidence upon which the application is based involves scientific, technical, or other specialized knowledge regarding whether an item or items is a firearm or other item as defined in 18 U.S.C. § 921(a) or 26 U.S.C. § 5845;

(7) unless prior consent has been obtained from the chief law enforcement officer of the county or city where the warrant is to be executed if the warrant is not to be executed within the special maritime and territorial jurisdiction of the United States.

(8) unless, if the warrant is to be served by dynamic entry, the warrant application has specifically noted the intent to serve by dynamic entry, and the warrant application has, by clear and convincing evidence, demonstrated both the need for dynamic entry and the unsuitability of other methods of service.

(9) if based in any part on information supplied from an informant who is paid by any government, and whose payments are contingent on a conviction, arrest, or indictment.

(b) An order to seal a warrant, affidavit, record of testimony, related papers, or voice recording shall not extend beyond the shorter of: thirty (30) days from the date of entry of such order, or the execution of the warrant. Such order may be renewed upon a showing of good cause. An order to seal may only be based on a demonstration, by clear and convincing evidence, that there is a substantial risk of injury to persons or property if an order to seal is not granted.

(c) Notwithstanding any other law or rule, evidence which is obtained as a result of the execution of a warrant, but which was issued without compliance with all provisions of subsection (a) shall not be admissible in any court of the United States and shall not be used by the United States for any purpose."

[The proposed § 2675A creates an administrative remedy for victims of law enforcement abuse, as an alternative to bringing suit in federal court.]

(b) Chapter 171 of title 28, United States Code, is amended by adding the following new section:

"§ 2675A. Administrative remedy.

(a) Any person who is unlawfully injured as a result of a search and seizure or arrest by the United States may file a claim for damages with the Attorney General.

(b) Within 60 days of receiving a claim filed pursuant to subsection (a), the Attorney General shall either approve the claim and so notify the claimant in writing or deny the claim in whole or in part and notify the claimant in writing, stating the specific grounds for such denial.

(c) If the Attorney General denies a claim in whole or in part, he shall, upon written request of the claimant sent by certified mail within 30 days of receiving notice from the Attorney General, promptly hold a hearing to review his denial. The hearing shall be held at a location convenient to the claimant.

(d) If after a hearing, the Attorney General decides not to reverse his denial of the claim, he shall give written notice of his decision to the claimant. The claimant may, within 60 days after receipt of the notice from the Attorney General, file an action for damages against the United States in the United States district court in the district where he resides or where the search and seizure or arrest were executed."

[The amendments to sections 3109 and 3105 reinforce existing law requiring that officers "knock and announce" before breaking into a building to serve a warrant, and limit the use of mass raids to cases approved by the attorney general.]

(c) Section 3109 of title 18, United States Code, is amended:

(i) by designating the existing language as subsection (a); and

(ii) by inserting "has waited two minutes (unless his life or the life of another is in imminent peril) and" after "he";

(iii) by adding the following new subsection:

"(b) Nothing herein shall be construed to authorize an officer to break open an outer or inner door or window of a house, or any part of a house, or anything therein, if another officer involved in the execution of the warrant complied with subsection (a)."

(d) Section 3105 of title 18, United States Code, is amended by inserting "; provided that no search warrant may be executed by more than 20 persons unless the Attorney General (or, in the case of Treasury employees, the Secretary of the Treasury) shall have personally authorized such execution in writing and such written authorization is provided to the judicial officer issuing the search warrant prior to the issuance of the search warrant."

[Repeal of the "good-faith" exception to the exclusionary rule, created by the Supreme Court.]

(e) Federal Rule of Criminal Procedure 41(f) of title 18, United States Code, is amended by adding: "Evidence that would otherwise be suppressed may not be admitted based on a government official's good faith in conducting the search and seizure or in obtaining or relying on the warrant."

[Repeal the 1996 Clinton/Dole terrorism law, which gave the FBI additional search and seizure powers, as well as infringing many other parts of the Constitution.]

(f) Public Law no. 104-132 is repealed, except for Title XII.

Section 8. Fifth Amendment Enforcement

[Reforms federal forfeiture laws. Abolishes civil forfeiture, so that forfeitures may only be imposed after a criminal conviction. The abolition of civil forfeiture obviates the need for some of the interstitial reforms of civil forfeiture suggested in chapter 6, such as allowing recovery of attorney's fees by persons who have been wrongfully deprived of their property. There are a variety of other civil forfeiture statutes, attached to various criminal offenses, which should also be repealed. Subsection (a) takes care of the main ones.]

(a) Section 881 of title 21, United States Code, is amended:

(i) in subsection (a), by inserting "pursuant to section 853 of this title" after "forfeiture";

(ii) in subsection (b), by striking "civil";

(iii) by striking subsection (d);

(iv) in subsection (e), by striking "civilly or criminally";

(v) by striking subsections (i) and (j).

(b) Section 853 of title 21, United States Code, is amended:

(i) by striking subsection (j);

(ii) by striking subsection (o), and inserting a new subsection: "(o) The provisions of this section shall be carefully and narrowly construed so as to protect the private ownership of property."

(c) Paragraph (d)(1) of section 924 of title 18, United States Code, is amended by striking "subject to seizure and forfeiture, and all provisions of the Internal Revenue Code of 1954 relating to the seizure, forfeiture, and disposition of firearms, as defined in section 5845(a) of that Code, shall, so far as applicable, extend to seizures and forfeitures under the provisions of this chapter" and inserting "forfeited to the United States upon conviction of such violation".

(d) Section 981 of title 18, United States Code, is repealed.

[Reinforces the Fifth Amendment's mandate that no person may be prosecuted without a grand jury indictment, by requiring that relevant evidence be presented to the grand jury, as it was not in the Waco case.]

(e) Federal Rule of Criminal Procedure 6 of title 18, United States Code, is amended by adding a new section:

"(h) Exculpatory Evidence.

The attorney for the government shall present reliable exculpatory evidence of which he is aware to the grand jury. Upon motion of the defendant, the district court in which a defendant was indicted shall dismiss the indictment with prejudice if the defendant establishes by a preponderance of the evidence that the attorney for the government failed to present exculpatory evidence of which he was aware and which was within his power to present."

[Enforces the due process clause of the Fifth Amendment by prohibiting undercover agents from soliciting the commission of crimes, as opposed to gathering information about crimes that other persons are intending to commit.]

(e) Section 553 of title 28 of the United States Code is amended by adding the following subsection:

"(4) It shall be a defense to any crime that the crime was originally solicited by a government agent, even if such solicitation does not amount to entrapment."

Section 9. Fair Trials

[Imposes a meaningful deterrent for *Brady* violations, such as occurred in the Waco and Ruby Ridge trials.]

(a) Title 28, United States Code, is amended by adding a new chapter 154 and a new section 2256:

"§ 2256. Exculpatory evidence.

Upon motion of the defendant, the district court in which he was convicted shall set aside the conviction and dismiss the indictment or information, with prejudice, if, following conviction, the defendant establishes by a preponderance of the evidence, that the United States, after being requested to do so, failed to provide exculpatory evidence to the defendant."

[Allows a one-time motion to disqualify a judge, such as Walter Smith, whom the defendant knows to be biased and unjudicial.]

(b) The Federal Rules of Criminal Procedure are amended by adding a new Rule 10.1:

"Rule 10.1. Selection of judge.

Upon motion of the defendant made at any time prior to the date which is 30 days prior to trial, the court shall order that another judge preside over the proceedings. Such motion may be made only once by a defendant in a criminal proceeding."

[Abolishes real offense sentencing, and requires that sentences only be imposed based on offenses for which the defendant was convicted.]

(c) Section 994(f) of title 28, United States Code, is amended:

(i) by inserting "(1)" after "shall" and

(ii) inserting "and (2) ensure that the guidelines are based only upon the conduct that constitutes the elements of the offense of which the defendant was convicted" before the period.

[Allows pretrial discovery of statements or reports made by prospective government witnesses in criminal cases.]

(d) Section 3500 of title 18, United States Code, is amended:

(i) in subsection (a), by striking "no" and inserting "a"; by striking "the subject of subpena, discovery, or inspection until said witness has testified on direct examination in" and inserting ", upon request of a defendant, produced by the United States not later than 5 business days prior to";

(ii) by striking "subsections (b), (c), and (d) of" from subsection (e); and

(iii) by striking subsections (b), (c), and (d) and designating subsection (e) as subsection (b).

[Prevents courts from keeping a factual issue from the jury, because of hostility to defendants, as when Judge Smith refused to allow a self-defense instruction for the voluntary manslaughter charge.]

(e) The Federal Rules of Criminal Procedure are amended by adding to the end of Rule 30:

"The court shall instruct the jury to consider any claim or defense raised by the defendant if there is a scintilla of evidence in support of such claim or defense. Failure to give such an instruction shall constitute reversible error."

[Removes the court's ability to allow only selective use of a defendant's statement, as when the court allowed use of the portion of Jamie Castillo's statement to the Texas Rangers that he carried a gun during the BATF raid, but refused to allow introduction of the part of the statement where Castillo said he never fired a shot.]

(f) The Federal Rules of Evidence are amended by adding to the end of Rule 106:

"In a criminal trial, the defendant shall have the absolute right to introduce the entirety of any statement by him a part of which has been introduced by the United States."

[Requires that juries be fully informed of their power to return a verdict according to conscience. The language is a modification of a proposal from the Fully Informed Jury Association.]

(g) The Federal Rules of Criminal Procedure are amended by adding the following new Rule:

"Rule 24.1

(1) A defendant's right to trial by jury includes the right, if he requests, to have the

jurors instructed both at the opening of trial and in the instructions at the close of evidence, of their power to judge the law as well as the evidence, and to vote on the verdict according to conscience.

(2) This right shall not be infringed by any juror oath, court order, or procedure or practice of the court, including the use of any method of jury selection which could preclude or limit the empanelment of jurors willing to exercise this power, including jurors who object to the penalty which could be imposed on the defendant or to the law which the defendant is being accused of violating.

(3) Nor shall this right be infringed by preventing the defendant from presenting arguments to the jury which may pertain to issues of law and conscience, including the merit, intent, constitutionality or applicability of the law in the instant case; the motives, moral perspective, or circumstances of the defendant; the culpability of the defendant or any other person; the actual harm done; or the sanctions which may be applied to the defendant.

(4) Failure to allow the court to conduct the trial in accordance with this rule shall be grounds for mistrial and another trial by jury."

[Clarifies that federal attorneys are not exempt from ethical standards. The language is a modification of the proposed "Ethical Standards for Federal Prosecutors Act of 1996."]

(h) Chapter 31 of Title 28, United States Code is amended by adding the new section:

"Section 530B. Ethical standards for attorneys for the United States Government.

An attorney for the government shall be subject to the ethical rules governing attorneys in each State in which the attorney practices law, to the same extent as other attorneys in that State. Section 77.2 of title 28, Code of Federal Regulations (commonly known as the "Reno Regulation"), is repealed."

Section 10. Protection of law enforcement from militarism and excessive use of force

[Abolishes provisions encouraging use of the military and military equipment in domestic law enforcement.]

(a) Sections 371 through 379 of title 10, United States Code, are repealed.

[Tightens Posse Comitatus Act and closes all loopholes.]

(b) Section 1835 of title 18 of the United States Code is amended to read as follows:

"Use of military as posse comitatus

(1) Whoever, except as provided in subsection (8), willfully uses any part of the military, including the Army, Navy, Air Force, Coast Guard, National Guard of the United States, or National Guard of any state or territory, as a posse comitatus or otherwise to execute the laws shall be fined not more than $100,000 or imprisoned not more than five years, or both.

(2) This section applies to both military personnel and military equipment.

(3) This section does not apply to military assistance regarding nuclear weapons.

(4) A violation of this section which results in death shall be considered an intentional homicide, and shall be punished with a term of imprisonment up to twenty years.

(5) Evidence obtained as a result of violation of this act shall not be admissible in any court of the United States, nor shall the evidence be used by the government of the United States for any purpose.

(6) A person injured as a result of a violation of this section may bring an action for actual and punitive damages in a court of the United States. Sovereign immunity is waived for any such action. A prevailing plaintiff shall be awarded reasonable attorney's fees and expert fees.

(7) Congress finds that the Attorney General has failed to enforce the criminal sanctions of this section. To effectuate enforcement of this section, all citizens of the United States are designated as private attorneys general, and authorized to bring suit in a court of the United States to enjoin violation of this section. A prevailing plaintiff shall be awarded reasonable attorney's fees and expert fees.

(8) This section shall not apply to use of the military pursuant to sections 461 and 462 of title 22, and section 2576 of title 10."

[Repeals various exceptions to the Posse Comitatus Act]

(c) The United States Code is amended:

(i) by striking ", and use such of the armed forces," from section 331 of title 10;

(ii) by striking "and armed forces" and ", and use such of the armed forces," from section 332 of title 10;

(iii) by striking "or the armed forces, or both, or by any other means," from section 333 of title 10;

(iv) by striking "or the armed forces" from section 334 of title 10;

(v) by repealing sections 23 and 78 of title 16;

(vi) by inserting "but not" before "including" in subsection (f) of section 112 of title 18, in subsection (g) of section 351 of title 18, and in subsection (i) of section 1751 of title 18;

(vii) by repealing section 408 of title 22;

(viii) by striking "or military" from section 1065 of title 43; and

(ix) by striking "Army or Navy or" from section 220 of title 50.

[Bans use of chemical or biological weapons against American citizens, if use is banned in international warfare. CS would be banned, since the United States is a party to the Paris Convention, even though the related treaty has not been ratified.]

(d) Section 5602 to title 22, United States Code, is amended by adding the following subsection:

(c) Notwithstanding any other law, rule, treaty, or convention, no officer of the United States may use a chemical or biological weapon against a person within the United States, if the United States is party to a treaty or convention prohibiting the use of such chemical or biological weapon in warfare. A knowing violation of this subsection shall be a felony punishable by a term of up to five years in prison.

[Amends the Ku Klux Klan Act to forbid law enforcement officers from wearing masks.]

(e) Chapter 13 of title 18, United States Code, is amended by the creation of a new section:

"Section 241.1 No employee of the United States shall wear a mask while performing a law enforcement function. This provision shall not apply to gas masks or similar devices worn to protect the respiratory system or the skin of the wearer. No evidence resulting from a search or seizure in which any employee violated this section shall be admissible in a court of the United States, or used by the United States for any purpose. Violation of this section shall be a misdemeanor punishable by a fine of no more than two thousand dollars, and up to six months incarceration."

[Reduces extent of federal employees carrying firearms without complying with state law.]

(f) Chapter 44 of title 18, United States Code, is amended by addition of the following section:

"Section 930A.

(1) Except for the Department of Defense, Department of Justice, and Department of the Treasury, no cabinet department may authorize more than one thousand employees to carry firearms. No independent agency may authorize more than two hundred and fifty employees to carry firearms.

(2) An employee shall not be counted against the limits in subsection (1) if the employee carries the firearm

(A) in a state which does not require a permit to carry a firearm; or

(B) pursuant to a permit to carry a firearm, if the permit is issued by a state or a subdivision of a state which issues permits in a non-discriminatory manner and without a requirement to prove special need."

[Using language from the Civil Rights Act, this section forbids government agents to deliberately harm children in order to make their parents do something. For example, agents could not use CS chemical warfare agent to make a child suffer so much that the parent brings the child out of a building.]

(g) Chapter 21 of title 42, United States Code, is amended by the addition of the following new section:

"Section 1996A.

Every person who, under color of any statute, ordinance, regulation, custom, or usage, of any State or Territory or the District of Columbia, knowingly tortures or otherwise knowingly inflicts severe physical suffering on any child in the United States under the age of ten years, for the purpose of coercing that child's parent or guardian or custodian to perform an act or to refrain from the performance of an act, shall be liable to the child in an action at law, suit in equity, or other proper proceeding for redress. Further, the person shall be guilty of a felony, and shall be imprisoned for a term of up to ten years."

Section 11. Law Enforcement Commissions

[Restores subpoena power to the Bartlett Commission, a temporary commission, which is charged with investigating and reporting on federal law enforcement practices.]

(a) Section 1205 of Public Law no. 104-132 is amended by addition of the following subsection:

"(e) Subpoena power—

(1) In general—The Commission may issue subpoenas requiring the attendance and testimony of witnesses and the production of any evidence relating to any matter under investigation by the Commission. The attendance of witnesses and the produc-

tion of evidence may be required from any place within the United States at any designated place of hearing within the United States.

(2) Failure to obey subpoena—If a person refuses to obey a subpoena issued under paragraph (1), the Commission may apply to the United States district court for an order requiring that person to appear before the Commission to give testimony, produce evidence, or both, relating to the matter under investigation."

[To supplement the temporary Bartlett Commission, a permanent federal Law Enforcement Review Commission, similar to the federal Civil Rights Commission, should be created. The language creating the Commission should closely follow the statutory language for the Civil Rights Commission, 42 U.S.C. § 1975 et seq. To save space, all the relevant language from the Civil Rights Commission statute which would be reproduced to create the Law Enforcement Review Commission is not quoted in full. Instead, the major Law Enforcement Review Commission language which would be different from the Civil Rights Commission—namely, the duties of the Commission—is specified. The Law Enforcement Review Commission would be created as section 1976 of title 42, United States Code, following the section 1975 through 1975f, which deal with the Civil Rights Commission.]

"Subsection (2). Duties of the Law Enforcement Review Commission.

The Law Enforcement Review Commission shall:

(1) investigate allegations in writing under oath or affirmation that certain persons are being or have been deprived of their constitutional rights by the activities of federal law enforcement; which writing, under oath or affirmation, shall set forth the facts upon which such belief or beliefs are based;

(2) study and collect information concerning legal developments which facilitate or encourage constitutional rights violations by federal law enforcement;

(3) appraise the laws and policies of the federal government with respect to constitutional rights violations by federal law enforcement;

(4) serve as a national clearinghouse for information in respect to constitutional rights violations by federal law enforcement; and

(5) investigate allegations, made in writing and under oath or affirmation, that the rights of citizens of the United States or persons in the United States are being violated by federal law enforcement."

Section 12. Protection of Federal Employees

[This section addresses the due process problems for federal employees, discussed in chapter 6, which make many employees reluctant to challenge law enforcement actions they know to be improper. The proposal offers due process protections to all federal employees, not only law enforcement ones, to avoid creating an incentive for regular employees to get their jobs or missions reclassified as law enforcement. Besides, the protections make sense for all employees. The proposed language is derivative of the proposed law enforcement officers Bill of Rights, but with significant changes. First, the proposal below does not regulate state and local law enforcement agencies, which are outside the constitutional jurisdiction of Congress. Second, the protections apply to all federal employees, not just law enforcement officers, since law enforcement officers should not be treated as a privileged class. There are probably federal employees—such as high-level White House staff—who should be exempted from this section, but since this entire comprehensive proposal is intended only as a starting point, the following section does not itemize the job classifications which should be exempt from the section.]

Title 42 of the United States Code is amended by adding the following new section: "Section 819.

(a) Definitions—In this section:

'disciplinary action' means the suspension, demotion, reduction in pay or other employment benefit, dismissal, transfer, or similar action taken against a federal employee as punishment for misconduct.

'disciplinary hearing' means an administrative hearing initiated by a federal agency against a federal employee, based on probable cause to believe that the employee has violated or is violating a rule, regulation, or procedure related to service as an employee and is subject to disciplinary action.

'emergency suspension' means temporary action imposed by the head of the federal agency when that official determines that there is probable cause to believe that a federal employee

(A) has committed a felony in the course of his employment; or

(B) poses an immediate threat to the safety of himself or others or to the property of others.

'federal agency' means any part of the Government of the United States other than the military.

'federal employee' means a full-time employee of a federal agency.

'investigation'

(A) means the action of a federal agency, acting alone or in cooperation with another agency, or a division or unit within an agency, or the action of an individual federal employee, taken with regard to another federal employee, if such action is based on reasonable suspicion that the federal employee has violated, is violating, or will in the future violate a statute or ordinance, or administrative rule, regulation, or procedure relating to service as a federal employee; and

(B) includes—

(i) asking questions of other persons;

(ii) conducting observations;

(iii) evaluating reports, records, or other documents; and

(iv) examining physical evidence.

'summary punishment' means punishment imposed for a minor violation of a federal agency's rules and regulations that does not result in suspension, demotion, reduction in pay or other employment benefit, dismissal, or transfer.

(b) Application of section—

(1) In general—This section sets forth rights that shall be afforded a federal employee who is the subject of an investigation.

(2) Nonapplicability—This section does not apply in the case of—

(A) a criminal investigation of a federal employees conduct; or

(B) a nondisciplinary action taken in good faith on the basis of a federal employees's employment-related performance.

(c) First Amendment activity—Except when on duty or acting in an official capacity, no federal employee shall be prohibited from engaging in political activity or be denied the right to refrain from engaging in such activity. No employee shall be prohibited from belonging to an employee organization or union.

(d) Rights of federal employees while under investigation—When a federal employee is under investigation that could lead to disciplinary action, the following minimum standards shall apply:

(1) Notice of investigation—A federal employee shall be notified of the investigation prior to being interviewed. Notice shall include the general nature and scope of the investigation and all violations for which reasonable suspicion exists.

(2) Notice of proposed findings and recommendation—At the conclusion of the investigation, the person in charge of the investigation shall inform the federal employee under investigation, in writing, of the investigative findings and any recommendation for disciplinary action that the person intends to make.

(e) Rights of federal employees prior to and during questioning—When a federal employee is subjected to questioning that could lead to disciplinary action, the following minimum standards shall apply:

(1) Reasonable hours—Questioning of a federal employee shall be conducted at a reasonable hour, preferably when the federal employee is on duty, unless exigent circumstances otherwise require.

(2) Place of questioning—Questioning of the federal employee shall take place at the offices of the persons who are conducting the investigation or the place where the federal employee reports for duty, unless the federal employee consents in writing to being questioned elsewhere.

(3) Identification of questioner—The federal employee under investigation shall be informed, at the commencement of any questioning, of the name and position of the person conducting the questioning.

(4) Notice of nature of investigation—The federal employee under investigation shall be informed in writing of the nature of the investigation prior to any questioning.

(5) Reasonable time period—Any questioning of a federal employee in connection with an investigation shall be for a reasonable period of time and shall allow for reasonable periods for the rest and personal necessities of the federal employee.

(6) Counsel—The federal employee under investigation shall be entitled to counsel (or any other one person of the employee's choice) at any questioning, unless the employee consents in writing to being questioned outside the presence of counsel. The United States is not required to pay the federal employee's counsel fees.

(f) Disciplinary hearing—

(1) Notice of opportunity for hearing—Except in a case of summary punishment or emergency suspension described in subsection (h), if an investigation of a federal employee results in a recommendation of disciplinary action, the federal agency shall notify the federal employee that the federal employee is entitled to a hearing on the issues by a hearing officer or board prior to the imposition of any disciplinary action.

(2) Requirement of determination of violation—No disciplinary action may be taken unless a hearing officer or board determines, pursuant to a fairly conducted dis-

ciplinary hearing, that the federal employee violated a statute, ordinance, or published administrative rule, regulation, or procedure.

(3) Time limit—No disciplinary charges may be brought against federal employee unless filed within 90 days after the commencement of an investigation, except for good cause shown.

(4) Notice of filing of charges—The federal agency shall provide written, actual notification to the federal employee, not later than 30 days after the filing of disciplinary charges, of the following:

(A) The date, time, and location of the disciplinary hearing;

(B) The name and mailing address of the hearing officer;

(C) The name, position, and mailing address of the prosecutor.

(5) Representation—During a disciplinary hearing a federal employee shall be entitled to be represented by counsel or nonattorney representative.

(6) Hearing board and procedure—The federal agency shall promulgate regulations determining the composition of a disciplinary hearing board and the procedures for a disciplinary hearing.

(7) Access to evidence—A federal employee who is brought before a disciplinary hearing board shall be provided access to all transcripts, records, written statements, written reports, analyses, and electronically recorded information pertinent to the case that:

(A) contain exculpatory information;

(B) are intended to support any disciplinary action; or

(C) are to be introduced in the disciplinary hearing.

(8) Identification of witnesses—The disciplinary advocate for the law enforcement agency of which the officer who is the subject of the hearing is a member shall notify the federal employee, or his attorney if he is represented by counsel, not later than 15 days prior to the hearing, of the name and addresses of all witnesses for the law enforcement agency.

(9) Copy of investigative file—The federal agency shall provide to the federal employee, at the federal employee's request, not later than 15 days prior to the hearing, a copy of the investigative file, including all exculpatory and inculpatory information but excluding confidential sources.

(10) Examination of physical evidence—The federal agency shall notify the federal employee, at the employee's request, not later than 15 days prior to the hearing, of all physical, nondocumentary evidence, and provide reasonable date, time, place, and manner for the employee to examine such evidence at least 10 days prior to the hearing.

(11) Summonses—The hearing board shall have the power to issue summonses to compel testimony of witnesses and production of documentary evidence. If confronted with a failure to comply with a summons, the hearing officer or board may petition a court to issue an order, with failure to comply being subject to contempt of court.

(12) Recordation—All aspects of a disciplinary hearing, including prehearing motions, shall be recorded by audio tape, video tape, or transcription.

(13) Sequestration of witnesses—Either side in a disciplinary hearing may move for and be entitled to sequestration of witnesses.

(14) Testimony under oath—The hearing officer or board shall administer an oath or affirmation to each witness, who shall testify subject to the applicable laws of perjury.

(15) Verdict on each charge—At the conclusion of all the evidence, and after oral argument from both sides, the hearing officer or board shall deliberate and render a verdict on each charge.

(16) Burden of persuasion—The federal agency's burden of persuasion shall be by clear and convincing evidence as to each charge involving false representation, fraud, dishonesty, deceit, or criminal behavior and by a preponderance of the evidence as to all other charges.

(17) Finding of not guilty—If the federal employee is found not guilty of the disciplinary violations, the matter is concluded and no disciplinary action may be taken.

(18) Finding of guilty—If the federal employee is found guilty, the hearing officer or board shall make a written recommendation of a penalty. The federal agency may not impose greater than the penalty recommended by the hearing officer or board.

(19) Appeal—A federal employee may appeal from a final decision, in accordance with the Administrative Procedure Act.

(g) Waiver of rights—A federal employee may waive any of the rights guaranteed by this section subsequent to the time that the employee has been notified that the officer is under investigation. Such a waiver shall be in writing and signed by the employee.

(h) Summary punishment and emergency suspension—

(1) In general—This section does not preclude a federal agency from providing for summary punishment or emergency suspension.

(2) Health benefits—An emergency suspension shall not affect or infringe on the health benefits of a federal employee or his dependents.

(i) Retaliation for exercising rights—There shall be no penalty or threat of penalty against a federal employee for the exercise of the employee's rights under this section.

(j) Other remedies not impaired—Nothing in this section shall be construed to impair any other legal right or remedy that a federal employee may have as a result of the Constitution, statute, ordinance, regulation, collective bargaining agreement or other sources of rights.

(k) Declaratory or injunctive relief—A federal employee who is being denied any right afforded by this section may petition a federal court for declaratory or injunctive relief to prohibit the federal agency from violating such right."

APPROPRIATIONS LEGISLATION

In addition to the reforms in the Comprehensive Public Safety and Law Enforcement Improvement Act, further reforms could be enacted through appropriations legislation.

The following provisions should be inserted in an appropriation bill for the Department of Justice:

• "No part of any amount appropriated in this Act shall be used for law enforcement activity based on the interstate commerce power to investigate or prosecute an alleged crime which occurs solely within the boundaries of a single state."

• "No part of any amount appropriated in this Act shall be used for the COPS Program (Community Oriented Policing Services)." [This program funds "troops-to-cops" to encourage local police to give preferential hiring treatment to ex-military, and also funds deployment of police paramilitary units into street patrol.]

• "No part of any amount appropriated in this Act shall be used for the Hostage Rescue Team."

• "No part of any amount appropriated in this Act shall be used for the operation of any FBI office not in the United States which was not operating on January 1, 1993."

• "No part of any amount appropriated in this Act shall be used for FBI background checks involving non-criminal activity, including sexual activity, unless the activity clearly subjects the subject of the background check to a high risk of blackmail."

• "No part of any amount appropriated in this Act shall be used for the hiring of new Department of Justice employees until the Department of Justice total workforce has fallen to 50,000 or less. No part of any amount appropriated in this Act shall be used for hiring of new Department of Justice employees whose hiring would bring Department of Justice staffing levels above 50,000."

• "All new employees hired in law enforcement positions shall be trained for at least six hours in constitutional sensitivity, including laws relating to the use of deadly force, and the right of persons to resist improper use of force by law enforcement."

• FBI appropriations should be reset to 1984 level, adjusted for inflation.

• Finally, the Bartlett Commission, created in 1996 to investigate federal law enforcement practices, but never funded, should be fully funded, and its term extended by two years, to allow thorough investigation, and to make up for the period in 1996–97 in which it had no funding.

The following provisions should be inserted in the next Department of the Treasury appropriation bill:

• "No part of any amount appropriated in this Act shall be used for the Office of Undersecretary for Enforcement."

• "No part of any amount appropriated in this Act shall be used for law enforcement activity based on the interstate commerce power to investigate or prosecute an alleged crime which occurs solely within the boundaries of a single state."

• "All new employees hired in law enforcement positions shall be trained for at least six hours in constitutional sensitivity, including laws relating to the use of deadly force, and the right of persons to resist improper use of force by law enforcement."

Finally, BATF appropriations should be reset to 1984 levels, adjusted for inflation.

The following provisions should be inserted in the Department of Defense appropriation bill.

• "No part of any amount appropriated in this Act shall be used for the Joint Task Forces."

• "No part of any amount appropriated in this Act shall be used for civil law enforcement."

SPECIAL PROSECUTOR

In addition to the statutory reforms suggested above, the following request should be submitted in writing to the Attorney General. If such a request is submitted by the Judiciary Committees of the House and Senate, or a majority of the members of either party's members on the Judiciary Committee, the Attorney General has a legal duty to undertake a preliminary investigation.

Request for the Attorney General to investigate the appointment of an independent counsel for Waco.

Dear Attorney General Reno:

Congressional hearings and other investigations have produced substantial evidence of criminal activity by high-ranking federal employees in regards to law enforcement activities against the Branch Davidians.

The authors of this letter hereby request, pursuant to 28 U.S.C. § 592(g), that an investigation be begun into the appointment of an independent counsel regarding the possible crimes against the Branch Davidians.

We further request that you recuse yourself because of your direct conflict of interest in this matter, and assign the preliminary investigation to the next most senior officer in the Department of Justice who does not have a conflict of interest, pursuant to 28 U.S.C. § 591(e).

Appendix B
Chronology

1935   Shepherd's Rod Church near Waco, Texas, is founded by Victor Houteff.

1942   Houteff's group is incorporated as Davidian Seventh-day Adventists.

1955   Houteff dies, and he is succeeded by his wife, Florence.

1959   "The Great Disappointment," when Mrs. Houteff's prediction of the Second Coming fails to materialize, leading to split in Branch Davidians, with Ben Roden heading the largest group. Vernon Wayne Howell is born.

1978   Ben Roden dies, and is succeeded by his wife, Lois Roden, as leader of the Branch Davidians.

1981   Vernon Wayne Howell joins the Branch Davidian community at the Mount Carmel Center, outside Waco.

1985   Lois Roden dies, with her son George Roden claiming control of Mount Carmel, while Howell, already driven out at gunpoint, sets up a separate community near Palestine, Texas. Howell visits Israel, claims to hear the voice of God instruct him to study and fulfill the prophecies of the seven seals of the Book of Revelation.

1987–88   Competition between Howell's group and George Roden's group culminates in a shootout. Howell and his followers are tried for attempted murder. The jury hangs regarding Howell, and acquits the rest. Six month later, Roden is committed to an institution for the criminally insane, after perpetrating an unrelated homicide. Howell's group pays back taxes on the Mount Carmel Center, and is granted contingent title by a court.

1989   Marc Breault rejects Koresh's "New Light" that all Branch Davidian marriages are void, and that all the wives should become Koresh's wives.

Breault leaves to join his new wife in Australia, from where he will lead cult-busting effort against Branch Davidians.

1988–90 Most verified incidents of physical child abuse by Koresh occur in this period. The building in which Roden's methamphetamine lab had been housed burns down.

1990 Vernon Wayne Howell legally changes his name to David Koresh.

1992 *First Quarter:* With Marc Breault as a consultant, an Australian television program films a sensational exposé of Koresh. Non-Davidian David Jewell wins custody of his daughter Kiri Jewell. Kiri's mother, Sherri Jewell, remains at Mount Carmel.

Second Quarter: Texas Child Protective Services ends its investigation into alleged child abuse at Mount Carmel. BATF investigation of Koresh begins, based on a report from a UPS deliveryman about suspicious packages.

Third Quarter: BATF investigation continues with an interview with Koresh's gun dealer, Henry McMahon. BATF declines Koresh's invitation to come inspect his guns. The investigation becomes dormant.

The United States Marshals Service shootout with Weaver family at Ruby Ridge, Idaho, leads to an FBI siege. Three persons are killed, and two wounded, raising concerns about overly aggressive law enforcement.

Fourth Quarter: BATF investigation of Koresh perks up when "60 Minutes" begins looking into racial and sexual discrimination complaints against BATF. Plans for raid begin, with siege approach considered, along with assault. Discussions with the Department of Defense suggest possibility of free military assistance if a drug nexus can be found. Aguilera's assignment is expanded to finding both probable cause and a drug nexus, with the assistance of cult-buster Marc Breault.

1993 *January:* Aguilera interviews additional witnesses, all of whose relations with the Branch Davidians had ended by early 1992. Surveillance is briefly set up in the house across the road from Mount Carmel. BATF Agent Robert Rodriguez pretends to be a Bible student, and begins visiting the Davidians. Koresh almost converts him. Assault is definitively chosen over siege as a means to serve the search warrant.

Early to mid-February: Investigation proceeds with no new information beyond that from Rodriguez who witnesses nothing illegal during his undercover work. Koresh makes frequent trips away from the residence, into town or jogging down the road. Under military supervision, plans and training for the raid are completed at Fort Hood.

Late February: Koresh shows Aguilera a videotape from Gun Owners of America, *Breaking the Law in the Name of the Law,* which details various BATF misdeeds. BATF believes that there is now probable cause to obtain a warrant.

22: Kiri Jewell tells her story to local and federal authorities but says she will not testify against Koresh. Plans to arrest Koresh away from Mount Carmel Center by ordering him to appear in court for child sexual abuse charges are abandoned.

25: An arrest warrant for David Koresh and a search warrant for the Mount Carmel Center are issued.

27: The Waco *Tribune-Herald* newspaper begins exposé of "The Sinful Messiah." Undercover agent Rodriguez finds the Branch Davidians unconcerned.

28: Rodriguez visits Mount Carmel with second installment of Waco newspaper exposé. A TV cameraman tells a mailman that BATF and the National Guard are going to have "a shootout" with "the religious nuts." The mailman is David Jones, a Branch Davidian. He promptly heads back to the Mount Carmel Center. Koresh tells Rodriguez, shakes his hand, and wishes him good luck as Rodriguez leaves. Rodriguez telephones the raid commander and tells him that Koresh knows BATF is coming.

Late morning: BATF raids the Mount Carmel Center. After four BATF agents and five Branch Davidians are killed, a cease-fire is arranged.

Late afternoon: Michael Schroeder and two other Branch Davidians, who had been away from the property in the morning, try to sneak into Mount Carmel. Schroeder is killed, and the other two captured, one then and one several days later. The media is told that the three burst out of the Mount Carmel Center in an armed assault.

BATF Agent Jim Cavanaugh becomes first and favorite negotiator, and a few children leave the residence.

March

1: FBI takes over the operations at Mount Carmel with assistance from other federal, state, and local law enforcement agencies. Davidians are prevented from any contact with the outside world except for FBI negotiators. A plan is arranged for everyone to surrender following the radio broadcast of a Koresh sermon. Several children depart the residence.

2: The radio tape is brought out by two elderly women and more children. The women are promptly arrested. The Koresh tape is played, but Koresh reneges on promise that he and all others will leave Mount Carmel. He claims God told him to wait.

2–6: Cordial negotiations continue. More children leave. Charges against the old ladies are dropped, but they remain in custody as material witnesses.

7–12: Negotiations grow more tense, as each side accuses the other of failing to abide by prior agreements. Shortly after milk is delivered, pursuant to an agreement made by the negotiators, the FBI Hostage Rescue Team shuts off the electricity for a while. On the day that Janet Reno is sworn in as attorney general, electricity is shut off permanently.

12–21: Davidian negotiator Steve Schneider and the FBI negotiators attempt to reestablish trust. Schneider and Wayne Martin meet with Sheriff Jack Harwell and FBI chief negotiator once. Schneider says that more rapid departure of residents is about to occur. Two departures on the nineteenth are the first since electricity was cut off, and are followed by seven departures on the twenty-first. Koresh still awaits consent of God for his own surrender.

21–27: FBI tactical pressure is increased, bringing negotiations to a standstill. The last Davidian departure takes place on the twenty-third. Negotiators and tactical personnel agree March 21–22 to prepare CS assault plan, which is sent to Washington on March 27.

28–April 4: Effort is made to jump-start stalled negotiations by allowing attorneys to visit Koresh and Schneider. At the request of Schneider, a tape from religious scholars Jim Tabor and Phil Arnold is sent in. Tabor and Arnold analyze the seven seals to suggest that the standoff does not necessarily have to end in the death of all the Branch Davidians. God may want Koresh to "prophesy again" to a larger audience.

April

5–13: Davidians observe the full eight days of Passover. There is no progress in negotiations. Koresh sends out threatening letters.

14–17: The day after Passover, Koresh sends out a letter promising to surrender as soon as he writes his interpretation of the seven seals. Koresh begins work, completing drafts for an introduction and the first seal, and beginning on the second seal. His lawyer expects work to be completed in roughly two weeks. FBI perceives a stall and continues efforts to persuade the reluctant attorney general to approve proposed forty-eight-hour gradual CS attack. The FBI tells her that negotiations are going nowhere and there is no hope for a voluntary surrender. She is not told about the Koresh surrender letter.

17–18: Attorney General Reno approves the gradual CS insertion plan. The Hostage Rescue Team clears the area around the Mount Carmel residence, making a clear path for the tanks. Koresh and Davidians believe that an assault is imminent.

19: Just before 6 A.M., the FBI CS chemical warfare attack on Mount Carmel begins. The gradual plan is abandoned within minutes, and the largest chemical warfare assault against civilians in American history commences. After six hours, a fire breaks out and quickly engulfs the building. Less than an hour later, all remaining Davidian children and mothers are dead, as are all but nine other adults. A BATF flag is raised above the property. BATF celebrates the late Elliot Ness's ninetieth birthday in Baltimore. The attorney general takes responsibility for the disaster, and is praised for her political courage.

28: First congressional hearings held, with criticism largely diffused by the attorney general's performance.

June: Randy Weaver and Kevin Harris are acquitted of all charges of criminal violence.

September 30: Treasury Department review of BATF is released. Several Washington BATF officials are forced to retire. The two on-scene raid commanders are suspended with pay.

October 8: Justice Department review of FBI released. No one except Koresh is held to blame for any mistake. Some outside reviewers are more critical.

December: The firing of BATF raid commanders Chojnacki and Sarabyn is rescinded, although they are reassigned to different jobs. Both are granted full back pay, and the Waco incident is expunged from their personnel records.

1994   *January–February:* Trial of most of the surviving Branch Davidians. Some Branch Davidians are acquitted of all charges. The judge allows self-defense to be considered a defense to murder charges, and all Branch Davidians are acquitted of murder. Self-defense is not allowed a defense to voluntary manslaughter, and several Branch Davidians are convicted of that crime. Some Branch Davidians are convicted of violating federal weapons laws.

June: Most convicted Branch Davidians are given the heaviest sentence possible. All except Livingstone Fagan file notices of appeal.

1995   *April 19:* Federal building in Oklahoma City is blown up killing 168 persons, with the primary suspect a person upset by Waco.

July–August: Extensive congressional hearings held on Waco.

1996   *August:* House Committee on Government Reform and Oversight releases its report on the investigation into federal law enforcement activities in Waco, with some severe criticisms, especially of the military involvement, and some suggestions for other law enforcement improvements.

September. By a 2-1 vote, the Fifth Circuit Court of Appeals rejects most issues raised by the Branch Davidians on appeal. One issue is remanded to the trial judge for further factual analysis.

October. The Fifth Circuit Court of Appeals rejects a petition for the appeal to be reheard by the full court.

December. Attorneys for Branch Davidian prisoners file petitions for a writ of certiorari from the Supreme Court.

Appendix C

AGUILERA, DAVY, BATF agent. Responsible for initial investigation of Koresh.

ALANIZ, LOUIS, a young man who managed to enter Mount Carmel during the siege on March 24, staying until April 17.

ALLISON, NORMAN (a/k/a DELROY NASH), black British musician who associated with the Branch Davidians, but did not convert. Arrested attempting to enter Mount Carmel on afternoon of February 28 with unfired pistol; acquitted of all charges a year later.

ALTMAN, ROGER, then deputy secretary of Treasury. Involved after initial BATF assault in Treasury's role in supporting FBI during siege.

AMEN, JESSE, second person to enter Mount Carmel during siege, on March 26, leaving April 4.

APPLEGATE, REX, retired army colonel; leading authority on riot control and materiel, who helped to develop ferret round for delivering CS; critically reviewed CS use at Mount Carmel.

ARNOLD, J. PHILIP, professor, Reunion Institute, Houston, Texas. Established religious liaison with Branch Davidians.

BAIN, SARAH, jury forewoman at trial of Branch Davidians. Generally critical of government's role.

BALLESTEROS, ROLAND, BATF agent. In lead approaching the front door of the Mount Carmel Center to effect arrest and search.

BARR, BOB (R-Ga.), member, House Judiciary Subcommittee on Crime.

BENTSEN, LLOYD, then secretary of the Treasury. Duties included overseeing the operations of BATF.

BLUTE, PETER (R-Mass.), member, House Government Reform and Oversight Subcommittee on National Security, International Affairs, and Criminal Justice.

BONO, SONNY (R-Calif.), member, House Judiciary Committee but not its Subcommittee on Crime. Present for questioning of Janet Reno.

BRANCH, BRAD, Branch Davidian. Left the Mount Carmel Center in March, although departure was set back several days by FBI tactical pressure. Currently in prison.

BREAULT, MARC, disaffected Branch Davidian. Became a cult buster devoted to destroying Koresh and his Branch Davidians.

BREWSTER, BILL (D-Okla.), member, House Government Reform and Oversight Subcommittee on National Security, International Affairs, and Criminal Justice.

BRYANT, ED (R-Tenn.), member, House Judiciary Subcommittee on Crime.

BUFORD, WILLIAM, BATF resident agent in charge, Little Rock. With other agents from New Orleans, helped lead two-pronged BATF assault on the roof of the Mount Carmel Center, aimed at the gun room.

BUNDS, DAVID, former Davidian, brother of Robyn Bunds. Allegedly identified something owned by Koresh in Los Angeles as possibly being a conversion kit. Not reported interviewed by BATF.

BUNDS, DEBORAH SUE, former Davidian. Provided some information to BATF during investigation of Koresh.

BUNDS, JEANNINE, former Davidian. Provided some information during BATF investigation of Koresh.

BUNDS, ROBYN, former Davidian (daughter of Deborah Sue Bunds). Provided some information to BATF during investigation of Koresh.

BUYER, STEPHEN E. (R-Ind.), member, House Judiciary Subcommittee on Crime.

BYERLY, HERB, BATF agent. His informant entrapped Randy Weaver into selling sawed-off shotguns. Without supporting evidence, Byerly told other law enforcement officials that Weaver was an exceedingly dangerous violent criminal.

BYRNES, DAVID, captain, Texas Rangers. Primary on-scene Ranger.

CADIGAN, JAMES, FBI firearms expert in both Ruby Ridge and Waco incidents. Disciplined for poor performance at Ruby Ridge.

CAVANAUGH, JIM, BATF agent. Involved in initial raid, then in arranging the cease-fire, and finally in the first week's negotiations with Koresh and Steve Schneider.

CHABOT, STEVE (R-Ohio), member, House Judiciary Subcommittee on Crime.

CHOJNACKI, PHILLIP, then special agent in charge of BATF's Houston office. Commander of BATF's initial assault on Mount Carmel. Disciplined (but discipline later rescinded) after Treasury Report for continuing with the raid after the element of surprise had been lost and then lying about it.

CLARKE, FLOYD, then deputy director, FBI. Involved in siege and planning for final assault.

CLINGER, WILLIAM F., Jr. (R-Penn.), chairman, House Committee on Government Reform and Oversight, ex-officio member, House Government Reform and Oversight Subcommittee on National Security, International Affairs, and Criminal Justice.

CLINTON, WILLIAM J., elected president at the same time BATF was being criticized for racial and sexual discrimination. Took office during the planning of BATF's assault on Mount Carmel.

COBLE, HOWARD (R-N.C.), member, House Judiciary Subcommittee on Crime.

COHEN, PABLO, Jewish Branch Davidian, killed on April 19.

COLLINS, CARDISS (D-Ill.), ranking minority member, House Committee on Government Reform and Oversight, ex-officio member, House Government Reform and Oversight Subcommittee on National Security, International Affairs, and Criminal Justice.

CONYERS, JOHN, Jr. (D-Mich.), ranking minority member, House Committee on the Judiciary, ex-officio member, House Judiciary Subcommittee on Crime.

COOK, MAURICE, captain, Texas Rangers, senior state Ranger.

COOPER, LARRY, deputy U.S. marshal. Involved in initial shootout at Ruby Ridge. Generally believed to have killed Sammy Weaver with a shot to the back.

COX, JOHN, FBI negotiator. Among the most active of all the various negotiators.

DEGAN, WILLIAM F., deputy U.S. marshal. Killed at Ruby Ridge by Kevin Harris, in response to Degan's firing at Sammy Weaver.

DeGUERIN, DICK, attorney for David Koresh. Allowed to visit Koresh during the siege, he observed physical evidence supporting Davidian claims that BATF fired first and strafed the building from helicopters.

DENNIS, EDWARD S.G., Jr., in the Bush administration, assistant attorney general, Criminal Division, Department of Justice. While a lawyer in private practice, chosen as chief reviewer of FBI's role in Waco.

DIETZ, PARK ELLIOTT, forensic psychiatrist. Advised FBI during siege, suggesting FBI build on Koresh's dislike of BATF.

DOYLE, CLIVE, one of the surviving Branch Davidians. Acquitted on all charges.

DUNAGAN, EARL, then acting special agent in charge of BATF's Austin office, the home base for Aguilera's initial investigation of Koresh. Involved in follow-up search warrant affidavits.

EHRLICH, ROBERT L., Jr. (R-Md.), member, House Government Reform and Oversight Subcommittee on National Security, International Affairs, and Criminal Justice.

EMANUEL, RAHM, White House aide in charge of Waco damage control during joint hearings.

ENGELMAN, RON, Dallas talk-show host sympathetic to the Davidians.

EVANS, TIM, attorney for Branch Davidian Norman Allison (a/k/a Delroy Nash).

FAGAN, LIVINGSTONE, last Davidian to leave Mount Carmel (March 23) before FBI assault. Currently in prison.

FATTA, PAUL, Branch Davidian. Sold his successful business in order to move to Mount Carmel. Involved in Koresh's gun trade. Was at a gun show during February 28 raid, and arrested later. Currently in prison.

FREEH, LOUIS, became director of the FBI in 1993, months after Waco and Ruby Ridge. Consistently defended FBI actions at Waco and Ruby Ridge.

FRITTS, STEVE, army sergeant involved with drug law enforcement. Produced a paper on methamphetamine labs for BATF.

GARNER, RICHARD L., BATF chief of special operations. Helped procure military aid for raid on Mount Carmel.

GENT, PETER, Branch Davidian. Fatally shot while standing on the Mount Carmel Center water tower on February 28. Body was discovered days later. Branch Davidians claim he was killed by shots from a helicopter, while the federal government says he was killed by BATF agents on the ground.

GOLDSTEIN, GERALD H., president, National Association of Criminal Defense Lawyers. Testified to joint hearings about Aguilera's search warrant application.

GRAY, PAUL C., assistant chief, Houston Fire Department. Leader of the arson investigation at Waco.

GREEN, DENNIS G., U.S. magistrate. Issued initial and follow-up search and arrest warrants for Koresh, Mount Carmel, and the Mag Bag, and agreed to seal them.

GRITZ, "BO," Vietnam war hero and right-wing political figure. Negotiated end to Ruby Ridge siege and offered to attempt the same at Waco.

GYARFAS, AISHA (a/k/a Aisha Summers), Branch Davidian teenage "wife" of Koresh. Remained at Mount Carmel during the siege, near-term pregnant with her second child. The child was born shortly after Aisha's death on April 19, through an evolutionary reflex which expels a child in utero upon maternal demise. The child did not survive the fire.

GYARFAS, OLIVER, Branch Davidian teenager, brother of Aisha. Came out from the siege in March.

HAGA, FRAN, sociology professor. Volunteer member of NRA's Waco hearing team.

HARRIS, KEVIN, close friend of the Weavers. Engaged in shootout with U.S. marshals in which he killed a deputy marshal. Injured by the round which killed Vicki Weaver. Charged with capital murder, and acquitted of all charges by a federal jury.

HARTNETT, DANIEL, then deputy director for enforcement, BATF. Pressured to retire following release of Treasury Report, whose findings he challenges, for alleged cover-up of BATF failings.

HARWELL, JACK, sheriff of McLennan County, where Mount Carmel is located. Got along moderately well with Koresh and was briefly used as a mediator during the siege.

HEINEMAN, FRED (R-N.C.), member, House Judiciary Subcommittee on Crime.

HEYMANN, PHILIP B., then deputy attorney general of the United States.

HIGGINS, STEPHEN, then director, BATF. Retirement was announced just prior to release of critical Treasury Report.

HOLMES, H. ALLEN, assistant secretary for defense for special operations and low intensity conflict. Testified to joint hearings about Defense Department assistance to BATF and the FBI at Waco.

HORIUCHI, LON, FBI HRT sniper. Killed Vicki Weaver and injured Kevin Harris and Randy Weaver at Ruby Ridge; also on-scene at Waco.

HOUTEFF, VICTOR, founded Branch Davidians in 1935, died in 1955.

HOWELL, VERNON, birth name of David Koresh, Branch Davidian prophet.

HOWEN, RON, Assistant U.S. Attorney in Idaho. In charge of prosecuting Randy Weaver after Weaver refused to go undercover against Aryan Nations members.

HUBBELL, WEBSTER, then associate attorney general. With Janet Reno not yet confirmed as attorney general, Hubbell was highest ranking Justice Department official at the start of Waco siege. Prior to that appointment, he was associated with the Rose Law Firm in Little Rock. Served a prison term, on charges unrelated to Waco.

HUFFMAN, WALTER B., brigadier general, assistant judge advocate general for military law and operations. Testified at the Joint Hearings regarding Posse Comitatus Act and military involvement in domestic law enforcement.

HYDE, HENRY J. (R-Ill.), chair, House Committee on the Judiciary, ex-officio member, House Judiciary Subcommittee on Crime.

ISHIMOTO, WADE, technical manager, Sandia National Laboratories, U.S. Defense Department. Reviewer of the 1993 Treasury Report. Also testified at the 1995 joint hearings, where he was more critical than he had been before.

JAHN, RAY, Assistant U.S. Attorney. Prosecuted the surviving Branch Davidians, and some Whitewater defendants.

JAMAR, JEFFREY, then FBI special agent in charge, San Antonio. On-scene head of FBI operations in Waco.

JEWELL, DAVID, former husband of Branch Davidian Sherri Jewell. Engaged in custody battle for their daughter, Kiri, which he won one year before assault on Mount Carmel. Encouraged daughter to testify about alleged child sexual abuse, and the FBI to end the standoff by force.

JEWELL, KIRI, ex-Davidian teenager. At age ten, victim of a sexual assault by Koresh. Refused to testify against Koresh.

JEWELL, SHERRI, former school teacher, Branch Davidian. Mother of Kiri, whose story she denied, insisting it was invented for custody battle. Killed in April 19 assault/fire.

JOHNSTON, BILL, Assistant U.S. Attorney. Helped prepare Aguilera's affidavit for arrest and search warrants. Involved in planning of February 28 raid. Upset by FBI destruction of evidence during the standoff. Helped to prosecute most of the surviving adult Branch Davidians.

JONES, DAVID, Branch Davidian. Son of Perry Jones, brother-in-law of Koresh. Worked for U.S. Postal Service. Estranged husband of Kathy Kendrick, daughter of Woodrow Kendrick.

JONES, HEATHER, daughter of David Jones and Kathy Kendrick Jones, who left Mount Carmel early, in exchange for milk being sent in.

JONES, PERRY, long-time Branch Davidian. Vice president of the Branch Davidian Seventh-day Adventist Association. Father of Koresh's legal wife Rachel. Died on February 28.

JONES, RACHEL. See Koresh.

KENDRICK, WOODROW ("BOB"), Branch Davidian mechanic. At Mag Bag at time of BATF raid, thwarted in effort to get in, arrested later and acquitted of all charges.

KILLORIN, JACK, long-time BATF spokesman working out of D.C. headquarters. Currently special agent in charge of the Washington, D.C., BATF regional office.

KILPATRICK, KAREN, partner and common-law wife of gun dealer Henry McMahon. Occasional visitor to the Davidian residence.

KING, KENNETH, BATF agent from New Orleans. Part of two teams attempting entry on roof; injured as two colleagues were killed.

KORESH, CYRUS, oldest son of David Koresh, by Rachel, his only legal wife.

KORESH, DAVID (a/k/a VERNON HOWELL), Branch Davidian leader from mid-1980s. Self-proclaimed Lamb of God, with excessive fondness for extramarital sex, particularly with teenagers, and enforcer of strict religious practices from which he was exempt. His apocalyptic teachings included the prediction of a deadly government assault on Mount Carmel, as fulfillment of the fifth seal in the Book of Revelation.

KORESH, RACHEL JONES, daughter of Perry Jones, sister of David Jones, first (and only legal) wife of David Koresh.

LANTOS, TOM (D-Calif.), member, House Government Reform and Oversight Subcommittee on National Security, International Affairs, and Criminal Justice.

LaPIERRE, WAYNE L., executive vice president (CEO) of National Rifle Association.

LOFGREN, ZOE (D-Calif.), member, House Judiciary Subcommittee on Crime.

LYNCH, LARRY, deputy sheriff in McLennan County. Recipient of initial 911 call from Mount Carmel on February 28.

McCOLLUM, BILL (R-Fla.), chairman, House Judiciary Subcommittee on Crime.

McCURRY, MIKE, presidential press secretary. Involved in spin control for Waco hearings.

McMAHON, HENRY, owner of Hewitt Handguns. Investments in firearms with David Koresh were subject of BATF investigation.

MAGAW, JOHN W., former director of Secret Service, chosen in fall 1993 to succeed Steve Higgins as BATF director. At congressional hearings, admitted tactical mistakes at Waco, while defending BATF actions involving Randy Weaver.

MARTIN, DOUGLAS WAYNE, Branch Davidian attorney. Harvard Law School graduate. Made initial 911 call during February 28 raid. All references to Wayne Martin in the text and the appendices are to this person, not to his son, Wayne Martin.

MARTIN, SHEILA, Branch Davidian and wife of Wayne Martin. One of last Davidians to leave Mount Carmel during siege. Not to be confused with her daughter, Sheila, who died during the fire.

MARTINEZ, JULLIETE ("JULIE"), Branch Davidian. Daughter and mother of other Branch Davidians. Considered leaving, wanted to speak to her brother by telephone. FBI only allowed her to receive a taped message, which did not persuade her and her family to leave.

MICA, JOHN L. (R-Fla.), member, House Government Reform and Oversight Subcommittee on National Security, International Affairs, and Criminal Justice.

MIRON, MURRAY, psycholinguist. Adviser to FBI analyzing letters of David Koresh.

MORRISON, MELISSA, six-year-old. Koresh offered to send her out if he could talk by telephone with BATF agent Robert Rodriguez. The offer was refused, and she died with her mother in the fire.

MORRISON, ROSEMARY ("ROSE"), Branch Davidian, mother of Melissa.

NESS, ELLIOT, legendary agent in BATF's ancestor, the Bureau of Prohibition. Birthday falls on April 19.

NOBLE, RON, served as Treasury Department assistant secretary, then as the first-ever undersecretary for enforcement in the Treasury Department. Oversaw work of BATF, and oversaw Treasury Report reviewing BATF activities in Waco. The then-leading voice for gun control within the Treasury Department.

NOESNER, GARY, chief FBI negotiator. On-scene only early during Waco siege.

PEERWANI, NIZAM, Tarrant County medical examiner. Had primary responsibility for autopsies of Davidian dead.

PERRY, BRUCE D., psychiatrist with ties to anticult groups. Treated the Branch Davidian children released during the standoff.

PETREE, MARK, Fort Bragg army major involved with drug-law enforcement. Delivered paper to BATF on methamphetamine labs.

PICKLER, JOHN M., general then in command of Joint Task Force 6. Involved with military enforcement of drug laws.

PODESTA, JOHN, political consultant. Formerly associated with Handgun Control, Inc. Worked for White House on Waco damage control during joint hearings.

POTTS, LARRY A., former assistant director, FBI criminal investigative division. Supervised FBI operations at Waco and Ruby Ridge from headquarters in Washington.

RENO, JANET, confirmed March 12, 1993, as attorney general of the United States, in the midst of the Waco siege.

RICHARDS, ANN, governor of Texas. Her permission was needed but not obtained for National Guard use in Waco.

RICKS, BOB, FBI spokesman in Waco. Now Oklahoma Secretary of Public Safety.

RIDDLE, RITA, among the last Branch Davidians to leave the residence in March; sister of Jimmy Riddle, who died on April 19, and sister-in-law of Ruth Riddle.

RIDDLE, RUTH, Branch Davidian. Escaped burning structure and was prevented from returning by FBI agents. Carried out the computer disk with the completed portion of Koresh's seven seals interpretation.

RODEN, BEN, Branch Davidian prophet. Led the Waco Branch Davidians after 1959.

RODEN, GEORGE, son of Ben and Lois Roden. Drove Vernon Howell away from Mount Carmel at gunpoint before Roden's mother's death. For a few years, led Branch Davidians remaining at Mount Carmel. Currently confined to an institution for the criminally insane as the result of a homicide.

RODEN, LOIS, wife of Ben Roden. Took over Branch Davidians on his death in 1978, serving until her death in 1985. Had a sexual relationship with Vernon Howell.

RODERICK, ARTHUR, deputy U.S. marshal. One of the six marshals involved in the shootout with the Weavers. Generally believed to have shot the Weavers' dog, Striker, initiating the gunfight.

RODRIGUEZ, ROBERT (a/k/a Robert Garcia and Robert Gonzalez), BATF undercover agent. Visited Koresh repeatedly in January–February 1993. Tried to warn BATF to call off the raid.

ROGERS, DICK, then head of FBI Hostage Rescue Team, at both Ruby Ridge and Waco. Voluntarily reassigned afterward.

ROS-LEHTINEN, ILEANA (R-Fla.), member, House Government Reform and Oversight Subcommittee on National Security, International Affairs, and Criminal Justice.

ROSS, RICK, anticult activist and deprogrammer. Reportedly advised BATF and FBI.

SAGE, BYRON, chief on-scene FBI negotiator at Waco.

SALEM, HARRY, chief scientist for life sciences, U.S. Army Chemical Biological Defense Command. Gave Attorney General Reno information about CS.

SANDERS, ROBERT E., former deputy director for enforcement, BATF. At joint hearings, criticized BATF raid on Mount Carmel.

SARABYN, CHUCK, then assistant special agent in charge at BATF's Houston office. Second in command for raid on Mount Carmel. Punished (but punishment later rescinded) following Treasury Report investigation, for proceeding after element of surprise was lost, and for lying about it.

SCHIFF, STEVEN (R-N. Mex.), member, House Government Reform and Oversight Subcommittee on National Security, International Affairs, and Criminal Justice.

SCHNEIDER, JUDY, Branch Davidian wife of Steve Schneider and later "wife" of David Koresh. Injured in February 28 raid, killed on April 19.

SCHNEIDER, STEVE, Branch Davidian, former religion teacher. Chief negotiator during the siege. Koresh's main aide. Killed by gunshot on April 19.

SCHROEDER, KATHY, Branch Davidian. Left Mount Carmel during the siege. Widow of Michael Schroeder. Testified against surviving Davidians as part of a plea bargain.

SCHROEDER, MICHAEL, Branch Davidian. Involved with the gun trade. At Mag Bag during initial raid, then killed attempting to get into Mount Carmel on the afternoon of February 28, although the Branch Davidians did not learn of his death for several days.

SCHUMER, CHUCK (D-N.Y.), member, House Judiciary Subcommittee on Crime.

SCOTT, ROBERT C. (D-Va.), member, House Judiciary Subcommittee on Crime.

SESSIONS, WILLIAM, then director, FBI.

SHADEGG, JOHN B. (R-Ariz.), member, House Government Reform and Oversight Subcommittee on National Security, International Affairs, and Criminal Justice.

SLAUGHTER, LOUISE M. (D-N.Y.), member, House Government Reform and Oversight Subcommittee on National Security, International Affairs, and Criminal Justice.

SMERICK, PETER, former FBI investigative analyst, Investigative Support Unit, National Center for the Analysis of Violent Crime, FBI Academy. Initial pro-negotiation memoranda were finally toned toward greater support of more tactical approach.

SMITH, WALTER S., federal district court judge. Presided over trial of surviving Davidians with apparent pro-prosecution bias.

SONOBE, FLORACITA ("SITA"), Branch Davidian. Wife of Scott Sonobe. At start of siege, escorted children, including her own, out to the FBI and then returned to Mount Carmel.

SONOBE, SCOTT, Branch Davidian. Wounded in the initial shootout. Husband of Sita.

SOUDER, MARK EDWARD (R-Ind.), member, House Government Reform and Oversight Subcommittee on National Security, International Affairs, and Criminal Justice.

SPARKS, JOYCE, social worker, Texas Child Protective Services. Investigated allegations of child physical and sexual abuse by Koresh, finding enough to convince her of his guilt but not enough to convince her supervisors to pursue the case.

SPECTER, ARLEN (R-Penn.), U.S. senator, chair of the Subcommittee on Terrorism, Technology, and Government Information of the Senate Judiciary Committee. His subcommittee held hearings on the Ruby Ridge incident after the House joint hearings on Waco.

SPENCE, GERRY, famed defense attorney. Defended Randy Weaver, along with local attorney Chuck Peterson, who focused on the defense on the gun-law charges.

STONE, ALAN A., professor of psychiatry and law, Harvard University. One of the seven outside reviewers for the Justice Department report on Waco. Critical of FBI actions at Waco.

TABOR, JAMES D., associate professor of Religious Studies, University of North Carolina at Charlotte. Helped to establish religious liaison with Branch Davidians.

TAYLOR, GENE (D-Miss.), member, House Government Reform and Oversight Subcommittee on National Security, International Affairs, and Criminal Justice.

THIBODEAU, DAVID, surviving Branch Davidian. Drummer in Koresh's band. Hid in the underground bus during most of the BATF raid. Not charged with any offenses.

THOMPSON, LINDA, self-proclaimed militia leader. Staged unarmed demonstrations at Waco. Produced two conspiracy-laden films about Waco afterward.

THURMAN, KAREN L. (D-Fla.), member, House Government Reform and Oversight Subcommittee on National Security, International Affairs, and Criminal Justice.

TRAFICANT, JAMES A., Jr. (D-Ohio). Former sheriff. Congressional critic of federal law enforcement excesses.

UHLIG, GEORGE, chemistry professor at College of Eastern Utah. Critical of use of CS.

WEAVER, RANDY, white separatist. Entrapped into selling sawed-off shotguns to BATF, then became target of USMS on fugitive warrant for avoiding trial. Engaged in standoff with FBI following Ruby Ridge shootout with USMS.

WEAVER, SAMMY, teenage son of Randy and Vicki Weaver. Shot in back fleeing from shootout with U.S. marshals in August 1992.

WEAVER, SARA, teenage daughter of Randy and Vicki Weaver. Ran interference as Randy Weaver fled back to the cabin following his shooting by Horiuchi.

WEAVER, VICKI, white separatist wife of Randy Weaver. Killed by FBI sniper Lon Horiuchi.

WENDELL, JAYDEAN, Branch Davidian. Former policewoman. Killed with shot through head during February 28 BATF assault, a shot Davidians say came from a helicopter but others conclude came while she was shooting at BATF from prone position.

WHEELER, SHARON, BATF agent and press liaison for Waco.

WHITECLIFF, KEVIN, Branch Davidian. Came out during the siege, although departure was set back several days by FBI tactical pressure. Currently in prison.

WISE, ROBERT E., Jr. (D-W.Va.), member, House Government Reform and Oversight Subcommittee on National Security, International Affairs, and Criminal Justice.

ZELIFF, BILL (R-N.H.), chair, House Government Reform and Oversight Subcommittee on National Security, International Affairs, and Criminal Justice.

ZIMMERMANN, JACK, criminal defense attorney. Represented Branch Davidian Steve Schneider.

PART 2. MOUNT CARMEL'S DEAD

(The following is a list of the persons who died at the Mount Carmel Center on February 28 and April 19, 1993. *Deaths from February 28 are italicized.* BATF agents are identified with an asterisk [*].)

Andrade, Chanel, 1, white, American
Andrade, Jennifer, 19, white, Canadian
Andrade, Katherine, 24, white, Canadian
Bennett, George, 35, black, British
Benta, Susan, 31, black, British
Blake, Winston, 28, black, British
Borst, Mary Jean, 49, white, American
Cohen, Pablo, 38, white, Israeli or Argentine
Davies, Abedowalo, 30, black, British
Doyle, Shari, 18, white, American
Elliot, Beverly, 30, black, British
Fagan, Doris, 51, black, British
Fagan, Yvette, 32, black, British
Farris, Lisa Marie, 24, white, American
Friesen, Raymond, 76, white, Canadian

Gent, Dayland, 3, white, American
Gent, Page, 1, white, American
Gent, Peter, 24, white, American
Hardial, Sandra, 27, black, British
Henry, Diana, 28, black, British
Henry, Paulina, 24, black, British
Henry, Phillip, 22, black, British
Henry, Stephen, 26, black, British
Henry, Vanessa, 19, black, British
Henry, Zilla, 55, black, British
Hipsman, Novellette, 36, black, British (American?)
Hipsman, Peter, 28, white, American
Houtman, Floyd, 61, black, American
Jewell, Sherri, 43, Asian, American
Jones, Chica, 2, white, American
Jones, David, 38, white, American
Jones, Little One, 2, white, American
Jones, Perry, 64, white, American
Jones, Serenity, 4, white, American
Koresh, Bobbie Lane, 2, white, American
Koresh, Cyrus, 8, white, American
Koresh, David, 33, white, American
Koresh, Rachel Jones, 24, white, American
Koresh, Star, 6, white, American
*LeBleu, Conway, 30, white, American
Little, Jeffery, 32, white, American
Little, Nicole Gent, 24, white, Australian
Little, newborn of Nicole
McBean, John-Mark, 27, black, British
*McKeehan, Todd, 28, white, American
Malcolm, Livingston, 26, black, British
Martin, Anita, 18, black, American
Martin, Diane, 41, black, British
Martin, Douglas Wayne, 42, black, American
Martin, Lisa, 13, black, American
Martin, Sheila, 15, black, American
Martin, Wayne, 20, black, American
Martinez, Abigail, 11, Hispanic, American
Martinez, Audrey, 13, Hispanic, American
Martinez, Crystal, 3, Hispanic, American
Martinez, Isaiah, 4, Hispanic, American
Martinez, Joseph, 8, Hispanic, American
Martinez, Julliete, 30, Hispanic, American
Monbelly, Bernadette, 31, black, British
Morrison, Melissa, 6, black, British

Morrison, Rosemary, 29, black, British
Murray, Sonia, 29, black, British
Norbrega, Theresa, 48, black, American
Riddle, James, 32, white, American
Saipaia, Rebecca, 24, Asian, Filipino
Schneider, Judy, 41, white, American
Schneider, Mayanah, 2, white, American
Schneider, Steve, 43, white, American
Schroeder, Michael, 29, white, American
Sellors, Clifford, 33, white, British
Sonobe, Floracita, 34, Asian, Filipino
Sonobe, Scott Kojiro, 35, Asian, American
Summers, Aisha Gyarfas, 17, white, Australian
Summers, newborn of Aisha
Summers, Gregory, 28, white, American
Summers, Startle, 1, white, American
Sylvia, Hollywood, 1, white, American
Sylvia, Lorraine, 40, white, American
Sylvia, Rachel, 12, white, American
Thibodeau, Michelle Jones, 18, white, American
Vaega, Margarida, 47, Asian, New Zealander
Vaega, Neal, 38, Asian, New Zealander
Wendell, Jaydean, 34, Asian, American
Wendell, Mark, 40, Asian, American
Williams, Robert, 26, white, American
Willis, Steven, 32, white, American

N.B.: These identifications may err occasionally as different sources give different spellings of some names, and some children are identified by their mothers' maiden rather than married name; in addition, there are conflicts in the various sources regarding age, ethnicity, and nationality.

(Sources: Carol Moore, *The Davidian Massacre,* pp. xii–xiv; Clive Doyle's "Complete List of Mt. Carmel Deaths," and autopsy report identification summary, in Carol A. Valentine's Waco Holocaust Electronic Museum, http://www. Public-Action.com/Sky-Writer/WacoMuseum; Justice Report, pp. 313–21; Treasury Report, pp. v, 102, 104; BATF, *1993 Explosives Incidents Report* [Washington, D.C.: U.S. Department of the Treasury, 1994], p. i.)

Appendix D
Negotiation Tape Summaries

INTRODUCTION

During the fifty-one-day siege, there were over 240 tapes made of discussions between federal law enforcement and the Branch Davidians. A partial summary of what was happening at different times can aid in understanding how the FBI and the Branch Davidians negotiated.

Although primarily involving FBI negotiators, the tapes are labeled as being BATF transcriptions. We have identified the tapes the same way they are identified, which generally includes times but sometimes only dates. The times listed for a given tape do not mean that people were conversing the whole time. There were many stretches when there were no phone negotiations, and the tape recorder was turned off.

It is sometimes clear from the tapes who the negotiator is and often it is not. There were several negotiators named John and Dick, whom the Davidians generally just numbered in the course of their discussions (i.e., "John 3").

We follow the FBI-inspired shorthand, referring to biblical exegesis as "Bible babble"; and we identify Steve Schneider as "Steve" or as "Schneider" and David Koresh as "Koresh." Most of the negotiators are identified by first name.

A few tape transcripts not summarized here were not obtained in time to be included in this book. A summary of those tapes is available at the Independence Institute world-wide web site: http///i2i.org.

Nos. 1–3. February 28.

BATF's Jim Cavanaugh asks Koresh about his medical condition, and the condition of the children. Koresh dictates to Cavanaugh a two-paragraph message (that Koresh has the key to the seven seals mystery) to be broadcast on the radio. Koresh promises to send out the children as soon as the message is broadcast, but he also wants some religious scholars to call him and discuss the seals, before the children are sent out.

412

The sound of a gunshot interrupts the dialogue, and a few minutes later, more gun-fire is heard; Koresh and Cavanaugh both say that nobody on their side fired a shot. The shots appear to be coming from near a barn. [The shots may be from the confrontation between the FBI and three Branch Davidians who, having been at the Mag Bag earlier in the day, were trying to sneak back into the Mount Carmel Center, and were inter-cepted. One of the three, Mike Schroeder, died from several gunshot wounds.]

Koresh wants to talk on the phone to "Robert Gonzalez," the BATF undercover agent whom Koresh was working on converting. Cavanaugh says that Gonzalez is not around.

Cavanaugh asks for at least one person to be sent out in exchange for broadcasting the two-paragraph statement. Koresh agrees.

Koresh worries that BATF will attack again: "you're going to smoke bomb us or you're going to burn our—," Cavanaugh interrupts, "No."

Koresh continues, "building down or whatever."

Cavanaugh insists, "I'm not going to let them do it."

Angelica and Crystal Sonobe (ages six and three) will be sent out once the short Koresh message is broadcast. Koresh says that each time the message is broadcast, two more children will be sent out.

Throughout the dialogue, Cavanaugh and Koresh are friendly, expressing their mutual admiration.

As the car pulls up to take the two children away, Koresh asks that the children be sent to their grandparents in Hawaii, and Cavanaugh says, "Okay." Koresh supplies the grandparents' (non-Davidians) name, address, and telephone number.

No. 4. March 1.

The Davidians claim that a two-year-old girl was killed by BATF during the initial shootout, and recount the start, with "bang, bang, bang," and Koresh saying "we've got women and children." Steve expresses his and Koresh's respect for law enforcement.

Fair amount of Bible babble from Steve to Gary [Noesner?].

They agree to send out some more kids, but there is some issue of dealing with Gary, since Koresh promised Jim Cavanaugh he'd deal only with Jim.

Koresh complains about encroachments on the Mount Carmel property despite promises, as part of the cease-fire, that the feds would stay off.

Throughout the tapes, Steve says he realizes that the negotiators are using psy-chology and the negotiators deny it. Gary says there has been some sighting of Davidians outside the building, which Steve denies, suggesting the spotters might have seen dogs.

Eight kids have been sent out, which media see as a good sign; Gary asks for more.

Koresh really formed a friendship with BATF negotiator Jim Cavanaugh, Steve tells Gary. [Cavanaugh, whose participation ended after several days, was the only BATF negotiator; almost all the rest were from the FBI.]

No. 5. March 1.

Steve mentions the Weaver case; Gary notes "in the Weaver case from the moment ne-gotiations started there wasn't a single shot fired and there wasn't a single person hurt after that point in time."

There is more discussion of why they can't just negotiate with Jim. Gary says he wants to be able to go to his bosses and tell about a couple of more children being sent out. Koresh makes reference to Gonzalez [undercover agent Robert Rodriguez] and to doing everything he could to avoid BATF coming as it did. Koresh says he will continue to send out children as long as Jim is communicating. Gary: "Yeah, yeah. See, what they don't understand, David, is, is, is why you're, you're wrapping everything into one person, because Jim is just a voice for, for the authorities here." Koresh: "No, Jim is a person." Koresh insists that they should stick with the original agreement, which is that he deals with Cavanaugh. Koresh mentions the dead BATF agents and bemoans that in other circumstances they could have been friends.

No. 6. March 1 [Misdated February 28].

Bible babble. Koresh predicts, "You are all going to kill us." Cavanaugh talks with Sita Sonobe about having two more of her children sent out. He takes down information about the relatives the children are to be taken to. Friendly tone throughout.

No. 7. March 1.

Koresh talks about his relationships with Lois and George Roden.

Scott and Chrissie (Kathy Schroeder's children by a previous marriage) are sent out. The Davidians also send out $1,000, without explicit statement of what it's for.

Steve complains about camouflaged guys being on their property.

Koresh complains of the treatment during his arrest related to the Roden shootout.

No. 8. March 1.

Jake Mabb and Bryan Schroeder are coming out, according to Kathy. The children are being taken out by Sita (Floracita) Sonobe, who then returns.

There is discussion of phone troubles, with Koresh threatening violence if the phone line to the outside world is not reconnected. [The FBI has rigged the phone line so that it can only connect to the FBI negotiators.]

Jim notes lots of folks around—FBI coming in, National Guard, state police. He assures the Davidians that the tanks have no gun barrels and are there for tactical reasons only, no assault. He presses Koresh for time frame but they deny there is one.

No. 9. March 1.

Jim observes that the tanks are bulletproof but have no guns. "They took their guns off . . . it's strictly bullet-proof shield."

Koresh agrees on getting children out, but negotiating after that is a problem, because of malignant characterizations of him to the press, suggesting he is responsible for the deaths, calling him a "cult leader." Koresh says he is sending children out, and that women can leave if they want to, but Jim doubts Koresh is encouraging them. Jim asks for a woman to accompany the children and then to stay out. Koresh agrees. Steve objects to media's slanderous tie of this case to the Roden shootout—suggesting how violent the Davidians are—since the Davidians were mostly acquitted. Jim suggests to

Steve the possibility of getting major media coverage for Koresh, possibly even Ted Koppel, for coming out.

No. 10A. March 1.

Steve again complains about camouflaged guys on the Mount Carmel property and they discuss phone problems. Davidians fear a nighttime assault by government.
Bible babble.
"Did Jim Jones ever get this kind of slander?" Koresh asks in response to media reports.

No. 10B. March 1.

Koresh insists the Davidians are not terrorists and they have no hostages—except, in a sense, the children because they're too young to make up their own minds.
Henry says Koresh should ignore the media. The FBI is not telling the media what they're up to, so reports of an FBI attack are unwarranted. Koresh agrees to send out kids, but not all of them, in exchange for a national radio broadcast, after which everybody leaves. Koresh recalls shootout in 1988, when they first tried to get the sheriff to act, but the sheriff insisted that the Davidians needed to act first to get evidence, and that they were dealing with dangerous men in Roden and his followers.
Koresh says he will send out a couple of kids, and probably a couple of women, when he finishes making the tape for the radio broadcast.

No. 11A. March 2.

Koresh complains that lines of communication have all been cut. He agrees to come out if given time on radio to talk of two seals. He is asked for two more kids while working on it, and agrees to send out Jamie and Joshua, along with a paper specifying their closest kin outside the residence. Regarding the radio show, negotiators offer, "If you're not happy with the National Christian Broadcasting Network, we can go to KRLD [a Dallas station]." Koresh notes that to this point sixteen kids are out.
Joshua's mother, Lorraine, emphasizes that he isn't supposed to have any pork.

No. 11B. March 2.

Koresh points out that Moses killed a man, too [Exodus 2:12], and sends out a couple of elderly ladies.
He recalls the fear he expressed prior to the 1988 trial stemming from the Roden shootout of going to jail, getting raped, and getting AIDS; and that the prosecutor said he should have thought of that before he went to Mt. Carmel. Koresh: "We trusted, we trusted—I always trusted law enforcement too."

No. 12A. [March 2.]

They discuss the one-hour radio broadcast, which is to be on Christian Broadcast Network without editing. The negotiators insist on one change, to make it explicit the Davidians are coming out peacefully and immediately, since his original vague wording would have been fulfilled by a mass suicide. Koresh agrees. The guys are to come out not wearing anything bulky; a stretcher is okay for Koresh. In response to requests for a head count, Koresh tells them forty-three men, forty-seven women, twenty children.

No. 12B. March 2.

Several mothers talk with children who have been sent out. Planning for broadcast of Koresh's radio tape nationally, followed by mass exit. "See you on the other side," one mother says to a child.

No. 13. March 2.

Discussion of Koresh's medical condition. He recalls that after his 1985 meeting with God in Israel, he never stuttered again.

No. 14. March 2.

The Davidians are concerned that the four vehicles to pick surrendering Davidians up after the broadcast are on their property, in violation of previous agreements.

As Koresh's son Cyrus, preparatory to coming out, is asked his favorite food, he responds "healthy food," although he sometimes has burritos, chips, and Cheetos.

The Davidians again complain about tanks, but Jim insists the barrels have been removed so they can't be fired.

No. 15. March 2.

With Tape 14, this tape includes the broadcast tape.

Davidians reconfirm that everything is ready for surrender. Four men are to carry Koresh on a stretcher, with some children, if they like. And Steve is to stay back to deal with the FBI. Any kids who need to be carried are to be carried by women.

No. 16. March 2.

Jim and Steve again discuss arrangements, with Koresh to be carried by four able-bodied men, and then set down; women and children will walk (carried if necessary), with men walking single file, to buses.

No. 17. March 2.

Discussion with various Branch Davidians about impending exit. Koresh will be carried on a stretcher to a nearby ambulance. Children's request to bring their newborn puppies with them is refused, but negotiator offers assurance that someone will take care of the puppies.

No 18. March 2

Scott Sonobe asks Jim Cavanaugh if relatives have called. Lots did.

No. 19. March 2.

The broadcast failing to have produced the promised surrender, some of the talk suggests the stalling may be related to Koresh's pain. Steve hints that a higher power spoke to Koresh even after he had given his word. Steve: "He says his God says that he is to wait because that which was played on the air is given for everyone to hear."

No. 20. March 2.

Koresh is asleep, and FBI negotiator Henry is worried that he may die. He asks Rachel Koresh if she can step forward and be a "secondary leader," in light of David's condition. Later, he makes the same request of Scott Sonobe.

Koresh wakes up, but Rachel says he can't come to the phone: "He's weeping right now."

No. 21. March 2.

The same God that revealed to Koresh the seven seals has told him to wait, according to Rachel Jones Koresh. Bible babble.

No. 22. March 2.

Steve cites the Weaver case again, while noting that Henry personally is a fine fellow as are most of the federal agents.

FBI starts to suggest perhaps resuming sending children out.

No. 23. [No date given, but March 2–3.]

According to the FBI negotiators' bosses, Koresh reneged. Steve understands the negotiators' problem, but Koresh had to obey his God, as does Steve. Henry wants something. How about some more kids?

Rachel Koresh says that they were all ready to leave, but not unhappy about not leaving, more neutral, she says, speaking for herself. Rachel expresses some concern about possible criminal consequences, without incriminating herself, but denies Koresh is worried for himself. Rachel complains that the tape was broadcast, but then the FBI cut the Davidians off from the media. Henry asks for kids, even if waiting for God's word on others. Steve temporarily misunderstands Henry's statement regarding after they "take him [Koresh] out."

No. 24. March 3.

Phone problems are noted by the Davidians.

Steve insists they didn't keep their word about surrendering because of God speaking to Koresh, but does note concern about press reports on a conspiracy to murder charge against two elderly women. Jim says that press reports are not totally accurate; it's really just protective custody but courts insist on a reason; no indictment is being sought. He notes that the Davidians can tell their story only when they come out, in court and in the media.

He warns them that vehicle movements will occur with shift changes every few hours, and the Davidians shouldn't be alarmed. Steve notes that he's different from Jim because safety is not his key issue, being right with God is; safety is just not the number one thing with him.

Steve voices concern about Big Brother, the Trilateral Commission, and the Council on Foreign Relations (CFR).

BATF negotiator Jim Cavanaugh denies that the FBI is taking over; BATF, the FBI, and local police are all working together. Jim suggests sending out some kids, to keep the commanders happy; he suggests that the departure of some kids might make commanders feel better about sending in a better phone. Steve replies that that's not a real good bargain since the communication benefits both, the FBI wants it as much as the Davidians.

No. 25. March 3.

Jim wants them to work stuff out for the sake of the children. Steve: "Well, let's hang in there for all of us . . . I mean, I don't choose to die anymore than the children do. I still love life as much as I did when I was five or ten."

Jim acknowledges the two elderly ladies were being charged, but insists the negotiators raised hell, and got it cleared up; the ladies are being held as material witnesses, for their safety.

Steve: Koresh "wanted me to ask you. . . . 'Do you think that you should ask yourself and the other agents do you think this country is too big to be disciplined by God?' "

Steve thinks there must have been a missed signal between them and Robert Rodriguez or between Robert and BATF.

Jim hypothesizes that the Davidians may have enemies, and Steve notes Marc Breault.

Koresh would like to speak with Robert Rodriguez [a/k/a Gonzalez]. Feels sorry for Robert.

Why do the Davidians own all those guns, the negotiator implicitly asks? Two swords, the military weapons of the time, were brought to Gethsemane. Bible babble.

No. 26. March 3.

Bible babble.

Koresh sneers at teeny tiny GI Joes and their tanks and land rovers.

Jim mentions court and Koresh notes that he's been there before. Jim argues that it looks worse to the media and prospective jurors when Koresh avoids coming out.

BATF supposedly had document for arrest but never made that clear.

Koresh points out that Robert knew Koresh jogged regularly and could have been arrested then. He asserts that the Davidians have made it clear BATF can't push butt around Mount Carmel. The government doesn't know what Koresh has, he says. He might just have a BB gun; he might have an atomic bomb; he might have the place landmined; he's been planning for their coming longer than they have.

Koresh agrees to send out more kids, while requesting Robert.

Jim says they got the money over to the Human Services guys for the kids. Koresh suggests that the money is for the phone too.

No. 27 [LABELED 29]. MARCH 3.

Mark is coming out. Koresh tries to figure out how to send out, as well, a couple of guns BATF left behind; "we don't need them here."

There are more complaints about the tanks. Jeff worries that they are coming over to blow us up. Jim insists it's just shift changes. Koresh complains they drive all over the property, to which Jim notes they're disarmed.

Bible babble.

No. 28. MARCH 3.

Bible babble.

Mark Anthony Jones and the puppies are being sent out; the feds shot the dogs' mother. The puppies are in a box, but don't worry about a puppy bomb.

Sita misses the kids, she tells Jim. She recalls that the raid involved guys getting out of trailers and just starting shooting, damaging bunk beds where her kids had just been.

No. 29. MARCH 3.

Mark and puppies finally out. Koresh says Sita can leave, but she won't. How could BATF just come and shoot, knowing there were children? Jim says there'll be an investigation.

No. 30. MARCH 3.

Mark tells his father, David Jones, they gave him soda, a candy bar, and a ride in a tank. Mark speaks to sister Heather, still in residence, and invites her out.

Rachel Jones Koresh suggests, since folks were wondering why Koresh still didn't come out, letting him do talk radio and answer their questions. Jim doesn't agree.

Steve complains about the stench of the dead dogs.

Steve complains about the treatment of Mark, searching him and his stuff. Jim expresses embarrassment.

Steve asks what's going on with the Davidian property in California, where folks are taking care of it, but aren't Davidians.

No. 31. MARCH 3.

(Jim Cavanaugh talking with radio interviewer Charlie Seraphin.)[The tapes sometimes record conversation snippets in the negotiation room.]

Steve complains about National Guard-like tanks, and a plane flying over real low.

Some Bible babble from Steve, along with autobiographical recollections.

He requests again that Koresh be allowed to speak to Rodriguez on the phone.

Jim complains that the FBI spotters, using night-vision, spotted five Davidians in the trees. Sita Sonobe will be sent to check it out, but Steve notes that the five can't be the guys from the Mag Bag, since there aren't five of them around.

Operator interrupts with an "emergency . . . from 'A Current Affair.'" Koresh takes the call. Jim is puzzled and upset.

Nos. 31A–32. March 2.

Blank except for the cover sheet.

No. 33. March 3, 9:53–10:35 P.M.

Koresh notes loss of lots of innocent lives of BATF agents, and "you're going to have to take a look at some of the pictures of the little ones that ended up perishing. . . ."

Koresh suggests that maybe he should have taken Robert hostage, but then he would have been in trouble for that.

Bible babble.

Koresh notes that Henry and Jim are his favorite negotiators.

Koresh assumes he'll have a long time—implying long prison sentence. "[I]f I'm notorious, they won't dump me with no bubbas, huh? . . . you know, there's a lot of rumors that I molest children . . . there's a lot of bubbas [who] want to molest you if they think you molest children."

Nos. 34–35. March 3.

Bible babble.

When BATF undercover agent "Robert Gonzalez" was attending the Bible studies, Koresh could see him counting the number of people present. Koresh also thought Robert's attempt to act inexperienced around guns very unconvincing.

No. 36. March 4.

Bible babble.

Koresh on his guns: "I'm just a temporal cult leader out here, in the middle of nowhere. . . . But I guarantee you what, if we didn't have them, you all sure would have come into here and flared . . . yours around, and busted me around and I'd never be able to say nothing."

Koresh retells story of the 1987–88 shootout background and trial.

No. 37. March 4.

Koresh speaks more on the Roden shootout, and complains a bit of treatment on arrest, mainly harsh treatment of hands when taking his fingerprints, despite his being a guitar player.

No. 38. March 4.

Kevin Jones comes out. He got a donut and soft drink. Rachel, jokingly, says that's a real healthy meal, eh? Jim apologizes and says they'll try to do better, but there's not much else in the hangar [FBI used an airport hangar near Texas State Technical College as headquarters], and asks for suggestions for food for the future. Fresh fruit, juices, and hot dogs are suggested by Rachel. Jim says he understands that means "no pork."

Rachel complains that they still haven't gotten the phone for which they sent out $1,000.

Jim wonders if the Davidians have propane heaters, and Rachel expresses concern that if someone fires at the heaters, they could explode.

Rachel insists she heard BATF agents on the radio confirm that they fired first, accidentally, after hearing Koresh warn about women and children. Rachel: a BATF spokesperson "said that the women and children were all in one place."

Jim: "Right. Yeah, I heard him say that and I know that's not right."

Rachel: "No, it's not true. They were scattered all over the whole building."

Jim indicates the Davidians have a story that has to be heard in court.

Koresh is upset BATF said untrue things about where women and children were, and wants it corrected. Jim promises a big investigation. Koresh says BATF agents were shooting their mouths off at a bar the night before the raid.

Koresh complains about being cut off from press; complains about government oppression and one-sided government, and requests again a call from Robert. He talks more on the Roden shootout.

NO. 39. MARCH 4, 11:00–11:45 A.M.

Jim suggests to Rachel this might be God's way to test Koresh's resolve to spread word beyond Mount Carmel, to the broader world. Heather is mentioned as possible next kid. Jim says they have a good chance to have a convincing story in court and to the media, when they come out, noting that Secretary Bentsen has promised a review. Rachel expresses concerns about kids going to foster homes, and adults who come out being held. Jim replies that he thinks that may happen until they all come out. Initially, all will probably be held, and some will be charged and some won't. He agrees with Rachel on the possibility of a self-defense defense, even citing a California case where a cop-killer got off on grounds of self-defense. Rachel says she is concerned because of court experiences in 1988.

NO. 40. MARCH 4, 11:45 A.M.–12:30 P.M.

Jim Cavanaugh tells seven-year-old Cyrus Koresh that if he comes out, "moms and stuff and everybody can stay together." [Not true; the moms go to jail.] He tells Cyrus regarding his cousins (Kevin and Mark Jones) who had come out, "we gave them some Coke and candy and they got to ride in that tank." He suggests Cyrus can go to his grandmother in Chandler, Oklahoma, if he comes out.

Steve denies Koresh ever saying he was Jesus.

Steve complains: "The press are so far back you guys could come and blow us away . . . and you could . . . give any kind of a story you wanted." Steve recalls various threats to freedom: "But what you guys have already showed me, what you did with that Weaver case. I mean, that already bothered me and here now I'm involved in something like this."

Steve notes he doesn't like the Trilateral Commission.

Steve says that if anyone were watching the initial raid from the air or ground, they know that the government fired first.

Steve: "What about Weaver? What's happening with the Weaver trial? Let me see how you guys do and what kind of freedom and access he has to defend himself of that case." Cavanaugh says that Weaver came out safely. Steve mentions Weaver's wife, who was killed. Jim mentions the dead marshal. Steve counters with mention of the dead kid and the dog.

Jim notes that some people provide wrong information to the government. Steve: "I know that Marc Breault has. I know that he's been an adversary since . . . about six months after he left."

No. 41. March 4, 12:30–3:15 p.m.

There is some discussion about kids going to next of kin. Planning the kids' custody upon exit is hard because Davidians don't know which adults will be held and which will be released once they come out of the building.

The negotiator notes that a body was picked up from the ravine, from the gunfight Sunday, but he has not been identified yet.

Koresh complains about agents sneaking around, and warns he's got night infrared for aiming. He also claims to have explosives: "you know, on one hand, you all are saying we have explosives here . . . which you know could turn one of those vehicles up 40 or 50 feet in the air."

Jim: "Well, we, we realize that."

Koresh: "what happens when, when this all gets heated and you get somebody mad and, and these cars go flying, you know, 40, 50 feet in the air out towards the lake?"

The Davidians get permission to bury the dogs killed in the initial raid.

Steve complains about the lack of media access.

Koresh again tells of standing in the door at the time of the initial shootout, claims BATF admits it shot first, and says that it seems there's some video to support that statement.

No. 42. March 4, 3:45–4:48 p.m.

Jim asks Koresh to think about sending kids out after burying the dogs. Koresh agrees. Time for the daily FBI/BATF press conference. Negotiations stop so the Davidians can watch it on television.

Jim calls with an emergency; three guys are out of the house with guns. The Davidians investigate, and explain that the men are just carrying shovels to bury the dogs, but Jim notes there were three men when only two were expected.

Steve wonders when they will get media lines? As soon as you come out, Jim responds.

Steve complains about Bradleys, "perimeter . . . encroachment," destroying guard shack without advance notice, etc. The perimeter incursions are in violation of the initial agreement and preceded Koresh's false promise to come out. Jim denies any encroachment before Koresh failed to come out. Steve disagrees, noting he complained before.

Koresh discusses helicopter fire into his room during the raid, and expresses fear of being shot when he leaves, because that's the way BATF has treated others.

Jim suggests there were outcoming rounds through the walls, recorded on tape. Steve asks for a copy of that tape. Jim says he can see it when he comes out. Jim denies there were guns on choppers. Koresh calls Jim a damned liar. Tempers flare a bit. They then calmly agree that agents on the choppers had guns but that there were no guns mounted on the helicopters themselves.

Bible babble.

No. 43. MARCH 4.

Jim reports that the U.S. Attorney called him to deny an AP story that all Davidian women would be charged with murder.

Bible babble.

No. 44. MARCH 4, 5:40–7:45 P.M.

Steve complains about Bradleys.

Pablo Cohen says he's Jewish.

Nine-year-old Heather Jones doesn't respond to question regarding the kind of soft drink she'd like when she comes out the next morning.

No. 45. MARCH 4, 7:45–8:32 P.M.

Koresh didn't like drugs and pot in seventies, since he was into athletics; even beer's not good for that. He discusses autobiographical stuff.

No. 46. MARCH 4, 8:30–9:19 P.M.

More autobiographical stuff from Koresh.

To judge the world, Jesus has to know where the world's coming from—like druggies make the best drug-busters. So God must know good and evil. "God's become as one of us, knowing good and evil."

Koresh named his first son Cyrus, English for Koresh.

Bible babble.

No. 47. MARCH 4, 9:19–10:05 P.M.

Koresh recounts more of his early life.

He insists he knew Robert was with ATF, and that the warning Koresh received about the raid was not by phone call. Regarding Rodriguez, "I'm pretty sure that he's going to realize, you know, to hold this thing off. . . . I thought for sure that he understood that . . . what I was asking from him was for him to go out and say, look, guys, let's hold off on this. Let's deal with it a different way. . . . I actually think there was a mess-up."

No. 48. MARCH 4, 10:05–10:50 P.M.

Koresh talks of hoping to persuade Robert. He suggests that not everything said about him is true, noting that the media say he says he's Jesus, and "I'm a child molester and all that kind of stuff." Koresh says it was reported last year three times the Davidians were going to commit suicide. He notes that he was called a child molester because of alleged relations with then-twelve-year-old Michelle Jones, which he [falsely] denies.

Koresh notes talk-shows callers recalling Saturday night seeing BATF agents drinking in local bars and "talking about coming out here to Mount Carmel and . . . busting us up real good in the morning . . . and they were laughing about it. . . ."

Koresh expresses some concern about being stuck in jail with "big guys. . . . That'll poke us in the rear. . . . It's against our religion." Henry says that in jail Koresh would be respected as "a man of the cloth," but Koresh says "first, they're going to want to bend me over to show that I'm nothing." He fears federal prisons are meaner than state.

No. 49. March 4.

Koresh threatens tanks with projectiles that can incinerate part of a tank.

He also insists no .50 cal. firearms were used on the twenty-eighth.

There are more complaints of tank drivers rolling over outbuildings and other outside stuff.

Heather Jones is coming out in the morning, and the negotiator suggests perhaps sending some suturing materials in for Koresh.

No. 50. March 4–5, 11:30 p.m.–8:20 a.m.

Rachel tells Henry she wants the released kids sent to their relatives and that they need six gallons of milk in the residence. Steve complains about FBI sending kids to foster homes instead of to relatives. The relatives were not Davidians, so Schneider didn't envision a problem. He complains of a woman psychologist saying the kids are abnormal because they're well behaved. Henry offers to provide videotapes of released kids. Koresh says that his VCR was shot up by the helicopters. We need milk.

Koresh criticizes lesbianism "because it's nonproductive."

Koresh speaks to Heather Jones while on the phone to the negotiators: "are you ready? You scared? Okay. Now, you may need to jump around and scream a bit so you'll be considered normal."

Koresh indicates that he could have been arrested when he came to town as part of the child abuse investigation.

No. 51. March 5, 8:20–10:05 a.m.

Jim Cavanaugh not able to come on the phone. Instead, Dick is on the line.

Due to 1987–88 experience, Davy Jones is not reassured about coming out and getting justice in a trial, since the trial cost money and trust and people still look down on the Davidians because of that trial. He notes that he's always been on the side of law and order.

Milk is requested again.

Steve notes prior cooperation. The authorities could have phoned, or knocked. The sheriff's been here before; we've been there. There's been no problem. Sometimes the Davidians went down to the sheriff's office when they just heard through the grapevine of possible legal issues.

Steve complains that "there's no way for us to talk to the media. You've cut us off from that. . . . It's hard to . . . have this trust relationship when the freedom of the press has been cut off, and there's only one-sided story given by your agencies which is . . . far from factual."

No. 52. March 5, 10:05–11:44 a.m.

Dick denies to Steve knowing if the body found in the ravine is Mike Schroeder's. Steve is concerned since the story is that the shootout involved people breaking out, but Schroeder and the others weren't here; they may have been trying to get in.

Steve again wonders "what ever happened with this Weaver case? . . . the press, were they held back or did they choose not to report the case?" Dick says the Weaver incident took place in the outback, so to speak, so there was no press. But Weaver walked out and the case will get resolved; the case is pending with motions filed.

Steve recalls that the guys were roughed up during the 1987 arrest, and there they had sought sheriff's aid in advance, and were roughed up while being arrested after doing what the sheriff's office advised. It cost $100,000 for legal defense. Dick says it won't cost that much this time; folks are lining up to defend them.

Steve recalls that the Davidians suspected the folks across the street were agents; they were too old to be students, they had nice cars, and they were too articulate.

Steve says America is now a democracy, not a republic, since "a republic guarantees the rights of minorities. A democracy is where the majority rules."

Koresh claims he was always open regarding his firearms, filling out yellow forms [BATF form 4473, the registration form created for all retail gun purchases].

No. 53. March 5, 11:44 a.m.–12:30 p.m.

Koresh threatens tank with something bigger than .50 cal. while Dick explains that drivers are just like kids; it's their only chance to drive tanks, so they're a bit reckless.

After the radio sermon—which Koresh was told to keep short (58–60 minutes)—was played, the message from God came to wait, "once the light is given . . . then our work is finished."

Koresh complains that the kids were to go out first, and be sent to specific addresses—and they weren't. He accuses the authorities of deprogramming the kids, which Dick denies.

No. 54. March 5, 12:31–2:46 p.m.

More autobiographical material.

Again, Koresh asks for milk, since mothers stopped lactating from stress.

Steve complains about Bradleys close to the building on their property; the Bradleys ran over a shack (former guardhouse) first.

Steve wants press coverage of their side, to which Dick says the press and Congress and the courts are all anxious to hear their side—after they come out.

Dick asks whether the videotape of the kids which was sent in lessens Sherri's concerns a little bit? "A little. But . . . the tape seems to be blank." Reassurance came from still photos which were also sent in.

No. 55. March 5, 2:46–4:04 p.m.

Kathy Schroeder says that the kids were sent out "for their own safety . . . because there's no telling what these people are going to do to us." Dick is offended, being part of "these people," but Kathy insists, "we don't think they're just going to stand there and wait forever." Dick disagrees.

Sita Sonobe says her kids are to go to their grandparents. Dick says Sita can make her own mind up about being with her family; Dick can't make the decision. "No, when they came in, they made the decision when they start firing. . . . I'm just a simple person who just living her life, that's been, like, taken away . . . when I opened the curtains, they got out of their . . . vehicles and start shooting."

Steve says that Peter Gent is unaccounted for, and asks if he is in custody.

Koresh thought that Rodriguez "deeply convicted [conflicted?] over what I was showing him."

Koresh notes that he had been teaching since 1985 that police officers would attack them.

No. 56. March 5, 4:04–4:51 p.m.

Steve says they saw Waco *Tribune-Herald* newspaper exposé as the latest from Marc Breault, and thought "here we go again."

No. 57. March 5, 4:51–5:38 p.m.

Dick asks for kids as quid pro quo for tapes and photos, and suggests there will likely be a congressional investigation with Koresh as a probable witness. In declining sending out more kids, Koresh says his children are different from the other children who were sent out.

No. 58. March 5, 5:38–6:39 p.m.

Steve reports that they found Gent's body "in the compound . . . apparently hit in the back of the head."

Steve again asks about sending in milk. But he refuses to give kids for milk, and so withdraws the request for milk.

Dick insists that an adult accompany Gent's body or they won't take the body.

Steve complains about sandbagged entrenchments on their property and again about the Bradleys "crunching over buildings."

No. 59. March 5, 6:39–8:38 p.m.

Steve asks Dick why Rodriguez didn't come with a warrant, bemoaning "if you saw this building, how it's shot up where the women and children were. . . . Who's going to protect us from the government?"

Steve notes that they gave a kid but got no milk. Dick replies, yes, but you got the tapes. Steve replies that the tapes were the FBI's idea, not Koresh's. John Cox replaces Dick. Koresh again says that he wants to speak to Rodriguez.

Steve notes that Koresh jogs all the time and could have been taken. He goes to Wal-Mart. He insists that statements that he doesn't leave are a lie. Cox says no, it was a search warrant for the premises, not for Koresh. He denies there existed a warrant for his arrest. Steve's response: "Unbelievable." Cox relents, and acknowledges on further research that there was a warrant for Koresh's arrest.

Koresh says he told Rodriguez about the hellfire device. It came up before Rodriguez ever came and was cleared up with the sheriff.

No. 60. March 5, 8:38–9:25 p.m.

Recalling the initial BATF assault, Koresh says: "I says get back. I says there are women and children in the house, let's talk about this. I didn't want them running and rushing in all over the place." He again insists BATF admitted accidental shootings. "The ATF came in here and already the two agents already admitted they fired first. One said it was an accident." Koresh says, "it's plainly known by . . . all the people around here that I'm always available on the premises or off the premises. . . ."

Koresh notes that there were threats against his life by members of other religious groups.

Koresh says he tried to make it clear that he could be arrested without incident. He told Robert that you've got to do what you've got to do, and I've got to do what I've got to do.

No. 61. March 5, 9:25–10:12 p.m.

Both Steve and Koresh have indicated, says Cox, a desire to speak to Robert, since they think they were getting to him religiously. But Cox assures them, without convincing them, that's just how undercover cops act.

Recalling the morning of the raid, Koresh says he hoped Robert would recommend BATF just try speaking to him: "see if he'll come out to us, . . . 'cause . . . aggression is going to cause aggression . . . these people believe in God and they do not believe in being pushed over."

Koresh claims the prosecutor in 1987–88 convinced some jurors that just because guns were possessed, Koresh must be guilty.

On a possible trial, Cox tells, OK "the system that we have gives you a pretty good chance because you get to tell your side of the story . . . and a jury of your peers gets to listen to that. And you can bring in, literally, any statement, any evidence, anything you want before the court of law. [At the trial, the judge forbade the defendants to offer self-defense evidence.] And if you're not satisfied . . . we've got an appellate system, and it goes on and on. Plus, you have the opportunity to speak to the media. . . ." "You are presumed innocent until convicted in a court of law."

Koresh refers to National Gun Rights Association [he meant Gun Owners of America] and its film, whose title he remembers as, "The ATF: Breaking the Law in the Name of the Law."

No. 62. MARCH 5–6, 10:12 P.M.–12:15 A.M.

There is more autobiographical discussion by Koresh.

Koresh discusses child rearing and he warns Cox that the social workers'll put Cox's parents in jail for having spanked him.

Cox assures Steve there will be some media interviews when Koresh comes out, probably a pool, not 250 reporters, but a few. He further tries to reassure him by noting that not all adults were legally responsible even if they were inside the facility during the shootout, and the kids are not responsible.

Steve says Koresh was ready to come out on March 2, until God spoke to him. God hadn't spoken to Koresh for some time.

Cox confirms they have identified the body of Michael Schroeder. His son Bryan and three stepkids (children of Michael's wife Kathy by a previous marriage) are already out. Cox [incorrectly] says BATF injuries occurred in the shootout with Schroeder.

No. 63. MARCH 6, 12:15–1:02 A.M.

Cox is still insisting an adult must accompany Gent's body and remain outside, or they won't take the body. The adult and the body must go to the coroner, then the adult can help with next of kin, etc. Cox suggests Kathy Schroeder accompany Gent's body to "see that things are handled properly for two people, for not only Peter but for her own husband, and, then be with her children."

Steve says he was reading a book at the start of the raid.

Obviously, Koresh will be charged.

Steve says Koresh's warnings to Rodriguez were not in a bad way; there was nothing threatening or aggressive.

No. 64. MARCH 6, 1:02–1:50 A.M.

Some women express concern about seeing pictures of kids eating hot dogs. Cox assures them they were chicken or turkey or beef, not pork hot dogs.

Steve worries about tanks hurting the motorcycles.

Steve observes that "people here believe that that agency came here with actually the intention of murder." He says bullets just missed the kids. He goes on, "it wouldn't surprise me if they wouldn't want to get rid of the evidence. Because if this building's left standing, you will see the evidence of what took place." Cox says there will also be lots of evidence of guns, "peaceful . . . religious groups that would have LAW [light antitank weapons] rockets and machineguns . . . that's hard to fathom, isn't it?" Steve observes that the kids were upset that "they shot these dogs [the children's malamutes] right off."

No. 65. MARCH 6, 1:50–8:47 A.M.

Steve tells John Cox that Peter Gent was shot in the back of the head, with a response that this was while Gent was armed, he was not "waving a white flag up on top there."

Steve insists they called 911: "Who's at our door, because that was not made clear."

Steve expresses remorse regarding the four dead BATF agents, "totally regrettable . . . [the families] have our sympathy."

Cox assures Steve that not all Davidians will automatically be locked up; there'll be a magistrate at the airport [being used as headquarters, and the place the Davidians were to be taken on surrender].

Steve notes that an innocent man who didn't know what was going on [Mike Schroeder] was killed in the ravine.

Dick: "one of the questions apparently that David asked last night is why he was not arrested on the road while he was jogging or when he went to town." Dick's answer: That's simple, there was no arrest warrant. "You can't arrest him outside and then expect to execute the search warrant there. . . ."

Steve: "That doesn't make sense. Of course you could."

Steve says that videos of the raid would support Davidians' statements of events.

Regarding Marc Breault, Steve says he was "constantly harassing them [the sheriff's office] in regards to getting some kind of charges on us . . . the guy was relentless."

Steve notes three choppers shot up Koresh's room, and asserts [wrongly] that a child was killed by BATF.

No. 66. March 6, 8:47–10:15 a.m.

Dick expresses sympathy on the loss of Mike Schroeder and asks if there is anything he can do for Kathy Schroeder. She says he can get these Bradleys off. Dick sneeringly asks if she just wants to have the Bradleys, agents, and the press leave? "No, I'd like to have some open communication with the press. That would be nice." Dick says, okay, but not until they come out. She says she fears arrest.

"Kathy, if you shot somebody, then you have some concerns. If you did not shoot anybody, then you have very limited concerns."

Kathy asks what happened to the agent that killed a baby, and is told that the FBI will do an investigation of the shootout preliminary to prosecution of BATF and/or Davidians. But the Davidians can't speak to the press until they come out. "We have to do a crime scene investigation . . . to begin with." Kathy asks why the videotapes aren't made public.

Dick: It's for court.

Kathy: "I want it part of public knowledge." Dick says he saw the video of what happened on TV before he came over here.

Kathy complains that the Davidians wanted milk and got photos instead, "to pull on my heartstrings." Koresh sent out $1,000 with kids for milk and telephone.

Dick gives two options for getting the milk: "You can send the children out . . . or two, you can send me out the kids and I will send the milk in."

In response, Steve says get ready for a long winter, making it clear he means next winter, or "just come and kill us like you would like to do." And he asks, "Why do you have the press so far back?"

Steve indicates he's real upset over the games playing with the milk.

No. 67. March 6, 10:15 a.m.–3:59 p.m.

Steve complains that the press is being falsely told by Bob Ricks that people weren't free to leave the compound. Steve wants the press nearby, part of the negotiation process.

Dick cites the Rodney King case as evidence that police are sometimes prosecuted, and cites some cases where folks have been acquitted even though arrested by BATF.

No. 68. March 6, 3:59–4:58 p.m.

Differing from Steve, Koresh tells Dick that he's not concerned about the Bradleys, "that's why we haven't done nothing to them yet." Dick makes an offer: The FBI will remove the Bradleys after four kids and four women leave, if, once the Bradleys have left, everyone else comes out. Dick says the idea of the offer was given to Bob Ricks by God. Koresh wonders why God told two different things to two different people: "Maybe God's trying to get us to fight, or something."

Koresh requests to speak to Robert Rodriguez again: "When you put him on the phone and I talk to him, then Melissa's going to come out, okay?"

Melissa's the gal that wants to come out, Dick asks.

Steve says Melissa Morrison says she doesn't want to go but would go "if you allow us to talk to Robert Gonzalez[sic]." Melissa's mother doesn't want to come out. Dick says she could be with Melissa. She disagrees: not if the judicial system takes over. But she agrees to send Melissa as soon as the Davidians have spoken to Robert.

No. 69. March 6, 4:58–8:08 p.m.

Steve complains of agents giving the finger and mooning. He also complains that some women heard agents during the original raid refer to them as motherfuckers and use other foul language ("cocksuckers").

Dick wonders if Koresh has confidence in the sheriff.

Law enforcement forces at the scene are reported by Dick to include BATF, FBI, local sheriff, Texas Rangers, Austin Police Department, National Guard, and the DPS [Department of Protective Services].

Steve complains about Bradleys running over the cemetery, noting that's illegal in Texas.

No. 70. March 6, 8:08–8:55 p.m.

John Cox asks why they have LAW rockets and other such weaponry.

Bible babble.

No. 71. March 6, 8:55–9:42 p.m.

As part of Bible babble, Koresh quotes Revelation: "Babylon the great is fallen . . . and has become the habitation of devils." He says that God calls America Babylon.

No. 72. March 6, 9:42–10:28 p.m.

Bible babble, during which Koresh interprets chariots to be "tanks": "And I will burn her chariots in the smoke and the sword shall devour her young lions."

Koresh insists that "every weapon I have here I bought on the yellow sheet [BATF form 4473]," but he won't deny altering them since Cox wouldn't believe him anyway.

No. 73. March 6, 10:28–11:15 p.m.

John Cox offers to play a new tape to the media in exchange for releasing all of the women and kids.

He insists to Rita Riddle that the media are kept away by Koresh's weapons, and denies responsibility for the phone not being able to connect to the media. She says, "all we need is a telephone line."

"Well, you're not going to get it."

Cox denies to Neal Vaega that released kids are being seen by psychologists.

No. 74. March 6–7, 11:15 p.m.–12:32 a.m.

John Cox denies his group [the FBI] has weapons like the Davidians, which Lisa Farris doubts based on the tank in her yard. Lisa: "We don't have no LAW rockets."

Cox: "I know you do, so don't tell me that. You just don't know what a LAW rocket is, that's all." He notes in support of his statement that Steve and Koresh didn't deny it [nor did they affirm it, but Koresh said all weapons were registered on form 4473s, which cannot be used for rockets]. Cox insists Lisa just never saw a Barrett .50 rifle; that doesn't mean there are no such rifles at Mount Carmel.

No. 75. March 7, 12:31–1:18 a.m.

Bible babble.

No. 76. March 7, 1:18–2:05 a.m.

Bible babble.

Koresh: "I says, Robert, they're coming now." And what was his response? "He was confused. Same as Pilate. Pilate was confused. He wanted to let Christ go."

No. 77. March 7, 2:05–2:52 a.m.

Bible babble.

Cox promises no aggressive moves.

Koresh complains about young men mooning the Davidians.

No. 78. March 7, 2:52–9:25 a.m.

Koresh suggests to Cox that the kids are safe with him, aren't they? If there's no threat from the FBI, why the big deal about the kids staying with the Davidians?

Dick suggests that Steve send out four kids in exchange for milk. Steve says he would have to discuss it with Koresh. "You can't do this yourself? I mean this is just milk." Steve sees it as coercion. Koresh responds, via Steve, that milk was requested days ago. The request is getting sour. Why not send six gallons of ice cream in and give the Davidians two kids back?

No. 79. March 7, 9:25 a.m.–12:36 p.m.

Dick suggests milk is another Davidian rejection of FBI help. He suggests they will get the milk for two kids, after explaining that negotiations are tit for tat.

Sita Sonobe complains that the photos the FBI sent in show that the kids look unhappy and therefore they are probably eating pork hot dogs. Dick denies that, insisting they are all-beef hot dogs. She complains about mooning and the finger from agents.

Nicole Gent complains, with expletives, about tanks running around on their property, about the FBI not taking her brother's body away, and about the lack of milk. Dick tells her Koresh is not agreeable to the milk being sent in. Koresh disagrees. "I asked you for milk for the children. They're neutral."

To show that complaints about the BATF raid will be taken seriously, Dick quotes a Fort Worth newspaper columnist critical of the initial raid.

Sita complains about her released son's hair being cut; the FBI's defense is that it was at his request. She also complains about his not being sent to family. The defense is that the kids are being kept together, and they're not being sent to foster homes.

Dick complains this is not a game, and asks why there's a guy in camouflage face paint and balaclava cap. With regards to the tanks on their property, "when you fired on federal officers, you lost some of your property rights."

No. 80. March 7, 12:36 a.m.–3:16 p.m.

Koresh asks for milk. The response again is, send out the kids. Koresh attacks the FBI for saying on TV that Koresh rejected the milk offer. Dick says, well, you rejected our terms.

He complains about a Davidian looking aggressive with black paint on his face and camouflage. Steve says she's black, it's not paint, and sneers at the FBI being afraid while they are sitting in Bradleys.

Koresh: Agent "shot me . . . because I was going to say something to him, and he wasn't fired upon." Koresh admits he broke his word about coming out after the tape was played, but says FBI broke their word, too, with regard to such things as the treatment of kids who were supposed to go to families.

During some Bible babble, Koresh says, regarding the New American Standard Version, "what a sorry translation."

No. 81. March 7, 3:16–4:03 p.m.

Bible babble.

Koresh complains they're calling it "biblical babblings" to media.

Koresh: "I have no intention of . . . sitting here rotting and dying. I'd rather live in prison than to have to live here in this cold place."

With regard to the complaint that the Davidians have not given anything, Wayne Martin points out that the Davidians let the BATF wounded be taken away instead of killing the BATF agents.

No. 82. March 7, 4:03–5:50 p.m.

Davidians complain about an elderly woman being held and denial of media access. They offer to send out photos of kids. Julie Martinez expresses fear of being arrested if she comes out. Dick mentions possible self-defense defense.

Julie expresses concerns about the government mistreating the kids when they're released and thinking there is something wrong because they're well behaved. Dick insists that no one would mistreat a child. Julie: "Well, they did here. They came and shot at us when . . . they knew we had a lot of children here." She wants to talk to her brother, Joe Santoyo.

Dick has to explain the protective custody of the two elderly women as being temporary. And he promises Julie that she can talk to her brother after she comes out; she wants to before.

Kathy Schroeder complains that the kids aren't being taken where they're supposed to go. Dick refuses to give milk to Kathy except in exchange for the kids. She responds that they gave twenty-one kids already. If they give more, why would they need the milk?

No. 84. March 7, 6:27–7:15 p.m.

Steve says to John that Dick fails as negotiator; Jim Cavanaugh was the best.

John complains about an apparent rifle seen in a Davidian window. Steve: "with all the tanks, with all these muzzles and all these cannons pointed at us, and he's worried about . . ."

John: no, "rules of safety that we all agreed to."

Steven answers, "these things are on our property . . . [and they shouldn't be] which you agreed to [in the cease-fire], but which you haven't done."

Steve renews the complaint about mooning and about tanks running over the cemetery.

Steve observes that the first red flag they had was the FBI cutting phone lines—in response to sending out some children. The Davidian suspicion is that the FBI "don't want to let the media know what's going on."

John suggests sending out a videotape which the FBI will take in exchange for their sending out five kids. That is not what the Davidians want. Koresh says he sent out Mark and told the FBI to send in some milk, and that the FBI agreed. Then he sent out Kevin, too, because he was assured that milk was on the way. Then he sent out Heather. So they've sent out three kids and gotten no milk. John denies any discussion regarding milk for Heather.

Koresh says the Bradley's 25mm barrels are a threat. John denies they have barrels.

No. 85. March 7, 7:15–8:02 P.M.

Bible babble.

John insists they're just going to sit and wait; does Koresh understand that? Koresh: "When my father tells me to come out, we'll see what you do."

Rachel Sylvia, thirteen, daughter of Lorraine, says they are all free to leave but no one wants to. Her brother Joshua, seven, already left.

The FBI insists the video was not blank when they sent it in. [See tape no. 54.]

The FBI says it wouldn't be prudent or safe to come for Gent's body, but in exchange for an adult Davidian, "we'll be happy to take the body as a humanitarian gesture."

No. 86. March 7, 8:02–8:49 P.M.

Aisha tells John she knows she's free to leave but she doesn't want to. She is pregnant by David, seven to eight months; she also has a one-and-a-half-year-old. John perceives the $1,000 as being for caring for kids on the outside, and paying utility bills, not for milk to the inside. Aisha insists the money is also for the milk.

If the FBI didn't twist what was said, more Davidians might be willing to talk to John and other negotiators on the telephone.

Again, Steve says he will be sending out a video—and will probably bury Gent tomorrow.

The FBI assures them regarding the kids outside, "we're . . . getting them medical checkups, make sure they don't have any, any problems."

No. 87. March 7, 8:49–9:35 P.M.

Cox tells Rachel they were all-beef hot dogs in the photos. David Thibodeau says the Davidians are really nice people, but he's not very religious; he's there for the politics and the music, noting that there is lots of injustice around.

Thibodeau says the Davidians don't have LAW rockets, .50 cal rifles, and automatic weapons. Cox [inaccurately] says Koresh "admitted it. He told me that you did." Cox argues the Second Amendment, insisting it applies only to state governments, not private militias.

Thibodeau: "When the government exceeds . . . in weaponry what the private militia, what the people have, that's when it gets dangerous."

Cox says [inaccurately] LAW rockets, automatic weapons, and .50 cal. rifles are "against the law." [Rifles up to and including .50 caliber are subject to no special regulation; automatic weapons can be possessed if they are registered and the tax is paid.]

Thibodeau: "I see what you guys are feeding the media, man, we're toast."

Cox objects to the suggestion "we're feeding some false information to the media."

Koresh discusses his father.

No. 88. March 7, 9:35–11:00 P.M.

Rachel explains a fear of separation if they leave the compound, because she is worried that the self-defense claim won't be believed. Cox vaguely notes various legal protections.

Cyrus expresses fear of an assault on the compound. Cox explains that "the last thing that's going to happen is for the government to take any type of offensive action here. It's just not going to happen. You know, we don't hurt babies. You know, we don't hurt women. We don't do those types of things."

Asked by Rachel about the Weaver case, the negotiator denies much knowledge, just what he's read in the papers.

Rachel notes that kids who left the compound were supposed to be sent to their nearest kin. The agent says the nearest kin are in the compound.

No. 89. March 7, 11:00–11:47 p.m.

John explains that mooning and flipping the bird were "from frustration and anguish."

Sherri Jewell: "Why didn't he [Rodriguez] just arrest him right there? Why didn't he just serve him a warrant right there?"

John: "'Cause he wasn't supposed to."

Sherri: "He was supposed to wait for us to be slaughtered?"

John: "He was supposed to leave."

She complains about BATF firing first and using foul language, to which John offers her a day in court, but "David had a large role to play in that and he should have been concerned." He says that it's just her opinion that BATF did wrong.

Sherri: "Before Sunday, we were preparing for this event. We knew it was going to happen. . . . We were prepared . . . because we can't control."

John asks his usual question about why a church would have so many weapons.

Sherri: "If we didn't, we would have been slaughtered. . . . Christ said if my kingdom was of this world, my servants would fight."

She mentions rounds having been fired from helicopters, which John denies.

"We have a dead person [Gent], I think, because of that," she asserts.

John: "Well, you may have had more."

No. 90. March 7–8, 11:47 p.m.–2:57 a.m.

John says he'll see Sherri in court for her "day of justice."

Sherri nastily refers to Psalm 75 and its reference to horns [a symbolic penis, in her view], noting that those of the wicked will be cut off. He complains about her crudity, and she mentions that of the assaulting BATF agents who didn't say excuse me ahead of time, as she had.

She says the Branch Davidians are there of their own free will, and don't like the FBI suggesting otherwise in press conferences.

Oliver Gyarfas, brother of Aisha, complains about being called motherfuckers by BATF.

Regarding Gent, Koresh notes that BATF is all concerned about its own people, but doesn't care about Davidian dead.

John asks, for the press conference tomorrow, whether Koresh wants to be referred to as "the Lamb, as David, as Christ, or as the Lord."

Koresh: "My name is David Koresh . . . and that's what you need to call me by."

No. 91. March 8, 2:58 a.m.–1:12 p.m.

Steve and John-2 (John Dolan) discuss plans for the Branch Davidians to bury one of the dead.

No. 92. March 8, 1:12–3:36 p.m.

Rachel Koresh tells John Dolan that David Koresh can't talk right now, "He said no, he's in town buying milk." But when Dolan says that Sheriff Harwell wants to talk with him, Koresh comes to the phone.

Harwell and Koresh express their mutual respect. Harwell asks Koresh to tell him what can be done to resolve the negotiating stalemate immediately.

Koresh says that the FBI negotiators all sound the same: "Every one of them sounds like they came off the same cookie sheet. . . . There's not a genuine ounce of blood in these men."

Koresh complains about the milk, and Harwell replies that he will try to get that taken care of.

Later, when Harwell announces that the milk will be delivered, Koresh is delighted, and says that the Davidians will send out the videotape the FBI asked for.

No. 93. March 8, 3:36–10:47 p.m.

Steve tells John he is making a tape of the kids. John says, okay, you guys take in the milk and leave the tape in the same place. Steve says he hasn't made the tape yet; he's just starting. He lets them know when it is done and out.

Steve: "David just told me to tell you he just heard on the news that he threatened the FBI to have another war."

John: "Oh, he did? I'm not aware of that."

Steve: ". . . He wasn't aware of it either."

Steve complains of radio reports that the Davidians were making obscene gestures at authorities from the tower. Max blames the media; denies the FBI would say things like that.

Max says the Davidian videotape is impressive and will cause them to redouble their efforts to reach a "peaceful conclusion."

The FBI plays a tape message from Joe Santoyo to his sister, Julie Martinez, saying there might be some legal trouble at first, but it'll pass. On the tape, he says that BATF was there because of all the weapons, not to attack their religion, and she should come out.

No. 94. March 8, 10:47–11:34 p.m.

Julie Martinez is thinking about leaving, but her thirteen-year-old daughter doesn't want to. Max tries to get her to make the decision for the kid. Mom doesn't want to come out either.

Max: "How could the government, the ATF, the FBI, anybody now with all this spotlight shining on us do anything improper to you or anyone else?"

Julie: "They're going to do it." Max insists that everything is covered by the media. "Only what the FBI wants them to see."

Max plays the tape of Joe for Julie's mother, Ophelia, who still doesn't want to come out. Julie complains that tanks frighten the kids.

No. 95. March 8–9, 11:34 p.m.–12:20 a.m.

Julie raises concerns about the treatment of the two old ladies who first left the residence. Max: "Well, they're being treated just fine now." He suggests that even if she is arrested and the trial is a year off, as reported on radio, "even for the worst, people make bond."

Max: "nobody's going to run tanks through buildings that contain people."

Julie wonders why they took the media away, and complains that a bullet went six inches from her daughter's head.

No. 96. March 9, 12:20–1:30 a.m.

To Max, Steve says Marc Breault was responsible for Sherri Jewell and Steve going to Michigan in defense of Sherri's daughter Kiri. Steve won't say if Judy Schneider's baby is by Koresh, or whether Steve shares Judy with Koresh—or doesn't have her himself.

To Steve, the relationship to the FBI appears to be a one-way street; the Davidians give but don't get anything in return.

Max refuses to believe there were offensive choppers, intent to kill. Steve: ". . . you're with a different agency."

Max: "Yes, I am, but we work . . . under the same general umbrella. We have the same . . . guidelines."

Steve complains again that Koresh could have been arrested in town, or even in Dallas. "The sheriff could have come and got him. He knows these men." Steve denies he "had to give up my wife."

Max praises the Davidian video, a "beautiful group of children there."

Koresh says that while he's waiting for God's word, the FBI "could possibly speed things up by getting in touch with the religious personages of their . . . beliefs . . . , those who should know the Bible," and could disprove Koresh's interpretation to his satisfaction. He complains that the FBI is telling the media Koresh has threatened violence. [He had. See tapes 8 and 41.]

Koresh gives Sheriff Harwell credit for resolving the milk issue.

No. 97. March 9, 1:30–11:21 a.m.

Koresh recounts initial BATF assault: They were screaming, but "they were all screaming at one time . . . you've been to a football game and you hear a roar but you don't know what anybody's saying. . . ."

Max says courts can hear all sides and resolve the issue. Max asks if the Davidians have more videotapes they can use "in case you'd want to do it again."

Koresh agrees, "if you'd like."

Max mentions local police. Koresh: "tell them I appreciate talking to Mr. Harwell because . . . that's like talking to a relative. . . ." Sheriff Harwell and another guy from his office are "just real good down-to-earth people."

Steve asks that power be turned back on or there will be no more talk. John blames the tactical folks, and says it'll be back on so they can see the press conference.

Koresh wants to send out a tape, and says that parents in the residence would love to see the FBI tape showing the children on the outside. John wants to be able to show higher-ups, even in Washington, some progress. John notes support for Koresh from the public regarding the right to keep and bear arms, "anger at the ATF," support of the powerful NRA, and so on. And so, he suggests, send a child out. He also suggests sending out an elderly woman, leading to discussion of arrests of those sent out earlier, with Koresh noting that material witness status still means they pay bond.

No. 98. MARCH 9, 11:22 A.M.–3:52 P.M.

Koresh is told that, since the videotape has come out, the negotiators see him as a person, unlike some in D.C., who "don't have the same identification process. . . ."

Koresh: "Send them a tape."

The discussion reverts to some of the problems from the outset: They sent out twenty-one kids who were to go to kin and haven't, and instead are with strangers with sociological degrees.

John says that the government might not go along with BATF; look at Rodney King.

Regarding the milk issue, Koresh says, "I thank God for Mr. Jack Harwell . . . what you all were trying to do with this milk thing was a very cruel thing. . . . I'd already given up three kids since the milk was agreed upon." And then they just asked for four more. Koresh asks for tape. "I know the parents would really like to see this . . . I want everyone in this . . . complex . . . to feel their own conscience and to follow it."

John Dolan asks for one of the kids for the tape, which seems odd to Koresh who perceives the tape as a way to seduce parents out; maybe "They can see that there is some kind of normality . . . out there . . . you people are [a] very dark and scary and gloomy mist."

Steve notes that when the Davidians looked at the FBI tape of those sent outside, "He [Koresh] wasn't too happy because they seemed to be very misbehaved, jumping on furniture and all the rest."

John: Okay, other than "undisciplined and just being normal kids, was everything pretty good on the tape?"

Steve notes he didn't like CNN references to .50 caliber guns being used.

John says that was a mistake, they must have reused a tape, due to a shortage, and didn't intend to send in CNN footage. [John and Steve are referring to a videotape the FBI sent in.]

John says the claims about .50 caliber guns are BATF "trying to save face."

No. 99. MARCH 9, 3:52–5:30 P.M.

John Dolan: Scott, Jacob, and Kristin Mabb (Kathy Schroeder's kids by her first husband) have been released to the custody of their father.

Koresh: "Ah, great . . . Go get Kathy. . . . Good news. . . . At least he won't let them be jumping around all over the furniture."

The FBI is moving to expedite releases by "home studies of relatives to pursue placement."

Kathy worries about their half-brother Bryan.

Regarding jumping around, John describes it as "that's kids being kids. . . ."

Kathy: "Well, not our kids. Our kids are usually much better behaved than that. Usually."

He pretty much assures Kathy no legal hassle beyond material witness status if she comes out. [She ends up being charged with homicide.]

Steve's working on another Davidian video.

John wants to keep the momentum going—but the public address system is going up and he doesn't know what's to be played. He wants someone out with the video, suggesting Greg. "You mentioned about an adult coming out with the tape." As a negotiator, he says he needs a sign of progress.

Later, the "high-frequency sounds" from the FBI public address system make Koresh and everyone think the FBI is just planning to "move in here, and wipe us out." He suggests backing off and letting individuals make decisions about whether they want to come out. When John mentions needing something to show the commanders indicating progress, Koresh observes, "They want patience, and they want it now."

Koresh suggests sending in a doctor for Judy Schneider.

The Davidians heard the government just raided the Davidian's house in California, currently occupied by non-Davidian tenants.

John Dolan, referring to a Davidian baby [allegedly, but not actually] killed in the initial BATF raid, notes to Judy that they've got a good civil case. Judy reiterates Koresh's account of the raid, with him holding hands up and suggesting they talk.

Judy, commenting on the video the FBI sent in: The kids are "eating candy all day long, drinking soda pop . . . hyper as heck."

No. 100. March 9, 5:30–8:15 p.m.

John suggests Judy come out for treatment of her finger injury; Koresh says he will show pictures of her finger on video so that physicians can consult. Koresh complains about constricting communications so media are limited to one side of the story. He also complains about the treatment of released elderly women. He wonders whether they've arrested gun-dealer Henry McMahon in Florida, and reiterates that there are yellow sheets [BATF Form 4473] on all guns.

Koresh: "You know, I did extensive research on these things before I bought these things."

John: "Hey, I'm not saying you're wrong at all."

Rachel suggests sending a doctor in, noting that neither side would harm him, but John declines due to the liability issue, and insists the doctor can't sign a waiver; it's a "crisis site." He suggests Judy would probably be a material witness. He insists that everyone's entitled to bond, so reports that the trial would take a year doesn't mean a year of jail. [Ultimately, all the Davidians who were charged with crimes were held in jail until the trial ended in February 1994.] He notes that both the innocent and the guilty get off every day, and there are civil suits against law enforcement, and there could be serious liability if there really is a dead baby in there, as the Davidians say. He notes some self-defense acquittals for killing cops.

Steve complains about seventeen FBI people intruding on the grounds, and John says he'll check.

NO. 101. MARCH 9–10.

Davidians note they are sending out a videotape of Davidians inside, and negotiators comment on the nasty-looking finger of Judy's from that tape.

They discuss the fact that Perry Jones might be buried inside, too. Max asks about the infant who also was supposed to have died, and Steve says he honestly doesn't know if there is an infant death. Steve notes it also took a while to learn about Peter Gent. He says there are lots of kids and infants and he hasn't heard enough details to know.

Max notes that negotiators are losing "voting rights" to the tactical folks for want of people coming out despite improved communications and relations.

NO. 102. MARCH 10, 12:02–12:48 A.M.

The FBI suggests that Judy, an adult, come out as a show of good faith and credibility. They suggest Steve must still have influence with his wife. Max notes that all the kids came out when Koresh wanted them out, to which Steve insists that their mothers were consulted, it wasn't Koresh's decision alone.

Max admits there will be some people in legal difficulties when they all come out, but that the majority will just be "leaderless." He's trying to suggest Steve could lead the group while Koresh was in jail awaiting trial; Steve denies any intent to fill a void. Steve in effect defends giving Judy to Koresh on the grounds one is supposed to put God before family members. To Steve, Max criticizes Koresh's control, pointing out all that Koresh would lose in terms of money and power if he came out. Max insists that there's no way, with due process, that the system can abuse Koresh the way Koresh seems to fear.

NO. 103. MARCH 10, 12:48–10:11 A.M.

Steve: "Well, Max, . . . just think what, what it would have been like if say these agents would have come to the door, knocked at the door like, like Robert Gonzales and said now David, we want you to come with us . . . I know him . . . I swear he would have gone. . . . And pretty soon, you know, it opens up. Guys are running to the front door with their guns pointed and screaming and yelling, and nobody could make out what was being said."

To Steve's complaints about BATF's Dan Hartnett's statements to media, Max says it's because there's no Davidian outside to give their side.

Both agree Sheriff Harwell might be a good mediator.

Max tries to suggest a show of good faith to keep commanders and "tank drivers" happy, to which Steve suggests that the way to draw people out is to be nonthreatening, like by withdrawing the encroaching tanks from their property.

There is some discussion of the funerals for Perry Jones and others.

Steve complains about electricity being turned off, noting, as before, it doesn't spur folks to leave the compound, but makes negotiations more difficult.

Max denies the military are involved; they just trained FBI agents to drive the tanks. Steve thinks it's an erosion of the Constitution.

Steve is assured the electricity will be turned back on so they can see the morning press conference on television.

Steve complains that the stuff they're doing outside makes his job of convincing people to leave ten times harder. He again complains about the foul language BATF used in the initial assault, and insists BATF shot first and then the Davidians went for their weapons.

NO. 104. MARCH 10, 10:11–11:41 A.M.

In 1987, the Davidians were happy to see police after the shootout with Roden, but then they were treated badly.

Steve again complains about mooning and flipping the finger.

Again, Steve insists that a couple of BATF agents have admitted that an accidental firing started the shootout.

In response to insistence there is a presumption of innocence, Steve contends that in reality from traffic citations on upward, it's guilty till proved innocent.

The FBI insists again that cops can be punished and that self-defense for cop-killing may be valid; but the only example he can offer of a BATF agent being tried is for an agent who attempted to kill his own wife.

Steve complains about the Trilateral Commission, CFR, and the Rockefellers. On the other hand, he knows nothing about Rush Limbaugh, besides the name. He complains about the way the government reportedly took over the Davidian place in the Los Angeles area, and about statements by Hartnett. Steve denies there has ever been a hit list; that is just another lie of Breault.

The FBI tries to assure Steve that he's not chargeable since he wasn't involved in the shooting, and everyone seems to know that; Sage will testify for him. He'll be out on bond and can address the press. Steve's worried about other folks, and is told he can be spokesman, leader.

NO. 105. MARCH 10, 11:41 A.M.–2:39 P.M.

Steve gives another address they can search in California since Koresh has nothing to hide. There is discussion of Judy's finger and a bit of Bible babble by Steve and David Jones. Jones doesn't know who fired first.

Steve again asks about what's happened to the Weaver case.

NO. 106. MARCH 10, 2:39–7:04 P.M.

David Jones insists it was the other side which was guilty of homicide, but isn't sure that's the way it'll come out, and so there is fear about coming out. Steve mentions they are making another video. And he complains again of taunting, and of destroying motorcycles.

No. 107. March 10, 7:04–9:34 p.m.

To Steve's complaint about electricity, John counters that nothing positive has happened since Heather left four days ago. There is some talk of lawyers.

No. 108. March 10, 9:34–11:04 p.m.

Steve recounts that in addition to the "white house" in California, they should check out the "rock house." Koresh is trying to cooperate. It's the Bunds' house, but some of Koresh's stuff was left in the cellar. Steve recalls Koresh's getting into the gun business as an investment about a year and a half ago.

The negotiator complains about Davidians leaving the building without the FBI first being told. There is some discussion related to leaving: the sheriff, medical care, lawyers, etc. Negotiators report that Kendrick was arrested without incident, but with two handguns on him.

Steve complains about hyperactivity of kids on videos, but John insists it's just kids being kids.

John suggests Lynch and Sage would be testifying on Steve's and Wayne's behalf on their noninvolvement in the shootout.

No. 109. March 10–11, 11:04 p.m.–12:29 a.m.

John mentions Koresh's repeated assertions that if BATF had just come to the door, "it would have been a very peaceful thing." Steve agrees, referring to similar experiences with the sheriff. Well, John suggests, we're here and just waiting for an invitation, not breaking in, willing to supply medical attention. John assures him there'll be media attention and coverage when they come out.

Steve insists that at least six people saw three helicopters come over and start shooting at Koresh's room. In recounting the dead, John reminds him of the BATF dead, and pushes Steve to find the name of the dead baby.

No. 110. March 11, 12:49 a.m.–11:41 a.m.

Greg Summers. He raised many of the dogs, and complains about them being shot. The young puppies are currently at the ASPCA, and Summers wants them reunited with the children who have left.

Schneider says three males may come out tomorrow. During the night, Schneider calls to tell the FBI that an unidentified male is snooping around a Branch Davidian trailer. After checking with the HRT, the negotiator says that nobody is doing anything, and that the HRT would not want to interfere with the good rapport established during the day's negotiations. Schneider accepts his word. The next morning, Schneider reports that Oliver Gyarfas is interested in coming out, but wants to talk to David first. David has been asleep in his room for the past two days. According to Schneider, Koresh always tells people who are thinking about leaving that they should leave, if that is what they feel is best. But the implication is that the desire to leave springs from weak faith.

No. 111. March 11, 11:41 a.m.–4:17 p.m.

There is a problem speaking to Koresh, partly due to his physical condition.

Based on videos, doctors are worried about Judy's possible septicemia; they have some concern about Koresh, too, which is why the negotiators keep asking for vital signs.

Doctors' analysis of the videotape suggests possible deep-seated infection of Koresh, sero-sanguineous in left buttock, which, too, could develop septicemia. His grandmother, Mrs. Haldeman, has found a lawyer for Koresh, Dick DeGuerin.

Kathy Schroeder indicates she's planning to come out, but won't commit to a time, possibly today. FBI says they've got Bryan (her son) ready to meet her when she comes out, and she'll get to call back in. Also coming out will be Kevin Whitecliff, Brad Branch, and Oliver Gyarfas. The FBI wants to know if it will be this afternoon, but that remains uncertain.

No. 112. March 11, 1993 4:17 p.m.–7:31 p.m.

Schneider reports that Koresh has heard news reports about major astronomical activity, including a star moving rapidly toward the earth. Koresh thinks it is a sign, but is unsure of the meaning.

The negotiator tells Schneider about a story in the morning's *Houston Chronicle* describing the "Guitar Nebula"—a neutron star moving very rapidly through the Milky Way. The star, only ten miles in diameter, is the fastest-moving star ever found. Schneider is very interested, and asks the article be sent in. He also asks the FBI to send in the rest of the Waco *Tribune-Herald* series on Koresh, since the Branch Davidians only saw the first two articles.

Later, Schneider wakes Koresh up, and they listen to the negotiator read the entire article to them. As the star crashes through interstellar gas clouds of different densities, it gives off a glow which looks like a guitar. This phenomenon is called "bow shock," and the Guitar Nebula gives off the most spectacular bow shock ever observed. Koresh is not impressed, and he starts giving a science lesson, using the Bible to illustrate his thoughts about particle physics and astronomy. Koresh touts *Chariots of the Gods?* and then discusses Ezekiel's flaming chariot (in which the prophet sees a flaming ship with strange beings descend from the sky). Koresh begins a lesson about sea monsters described in the Bible.

No. 113. March 11, 7:31 p.m.–8:22 p.m.

Koresh recounts his conversation with Oliver Gyarfas. He told "Ollie" that if he left, he would have God's blessing. The negotiator encourages Koresh to give the three males (Gyarfas, Brad Branch, and Kevin Whitecliff) emotional support in deciding to come out. Koresh returns to the sea monsters discussed in the Book of Job. The "Leviathan" sea monsters will surface shortly after "the son of man" is destroyed by the current generation.

No. 114. MARCH 11, 8:22 P.M.–10:26 P.M.

Schneider reports Koresh's vital signs. Negotiators remain very concerned about his health.

Clive Doyle gets the negotiator to admit that every adult who exits will be arrested.

Kathy Schroeder is coming out tomorrow, and wants to make sure she can see her son Bryan.

No. 115. MARCH 11–12, 10:26 P.M.–11:04 A.M.

Kathy Schroeder and John discuss the need for more milk and the problem of electricity going on and off; John claims the electricity goes off and on for them too. Kathy's coming out, and it is agreed that the quid pro quo for her leaving will be more milk and copies of *Time* and *Newsweek,* which have articles on the standoff the Davidians want to see.

Then Oliver Gyarfas, Brad, and Kevin will be coming out. The FBI plans to tape videos of Kathy and her son Bryan to send back in. She clearly doesn't know whether she's to be held in custody as witness or criminal or not at all. She indicates that this time, they want whole milk—no two percent this time—and *Time* and *Newsweek* (temporarily sold out), and they're going to need toilet paper (no threat of stores running out of that, John Dolan assures her).

Steve adds Rita Riddle to the list of those soon to come out. They agree that it's good that momentum's continuing.

No. 116. MARCH 12, 11:04 A.M.–2:24 P.M.

At Schneider's request, the negotiators call a radio station which is interviewing a woman who claims to be connected to the Branch Davidians. Schneider said that they had never heard of her before, and the FBI promises to convey that to the radio station. Schneider complains about the daily FBI press briefing talking about when the Branch Davidians will be "releasing" people. Schneider insists that everyone can leave as they please. He also complains about a BATF claim that BATF was not allowed to carry away wounded and dead agents. He says a lot of people would be willing to come out, if led by an intermediary who went into the residence, such as talk-show host Ron Engelman.

No. 117. MARCH 12, 2:24–5:53 P.M.

Some telephone difficulties.

Judy says she is not coming out, so maybe they can discuss her finger problem with a medic over the telephone.

Kathy's call in is encouraging, assuring the Davidians that she has gotten decent treatment, as the first to come out recently. The FBI and Texas Rangers aren't asking anything about "the incident" but only about the situation now; she has neither waived rights nor seen a lawyer. Kathy thinks she's not going to be charged with anything when she sees a magistrate tomorrow (Saturday), but will just be held as a material witness.

No. 118. March 12, 5:53–7:47 p.m.

Some autobiographical recollections by Scott Sonobe, who'd like his father to get custody of his kids. Ollie's coming out now. And then the Davidians can pick up the milk. But the FBI is having trouble finding copies of the magazines and they're not available yet. Scott notes there are one or two subscribers to those magazines at the residence, but John tells him that mail in such situations is treated as for folks on vacation, and is being held until afterwards. An M.D. is willing to talk to Judy about her wound and Scott about his injury.

Discussion with Steve on phone problems. Steve is hoping for a video of Kiri Jewell on the "Donahue" show. Sherri Jewell is "very curious to know, you know, what the ex-husband pumped into her mind and what she had to say and is there any way to get" that video? He would also like the rest of the newspaper series on Koresh; the last one they got was the Sunday issue Robert brought just before the BATF raid.

No. 119. March 12, 7:47–8:44 p.m.

Continuing medical advice from Dr. John Hagmann. Judy's not sure whether to leave, says Steve. John Cox says that the Davidians can go outside to take care of the chickens, but not at night.

The command people are upset because they were expecting four people to come out. Steve denies making commitments about time. Steve: "I get kind of tired about hearing about these damn commanders or what, tell them to be human and to relax because it's working, just tell them to relax." As for their impatience, Steve notes that the FBI agents will soon be warm and eating steaks and watching TV, but it'll be different for those now on the inside. He objected to the FBI saying at the press conference that Koresh was "releasing" people; it was their decision, not Koresh's; they have free will, freedom of choice.

John Cox responds that if Steve wants to see videos and the notes of kids from outside, the FBI needs more cooperation in getting people out. Phone difficulties continue. Steve says Rita, Kevin, and/or Brad will be leaving in the morning.

No. 120. March 12, 8:50–10:46 p.m.

Steve got the package from the FBI but is wondering why Bradleys are still driving around. Ollie Gyaras is still with the probation people, so can't call in to talk to his sister Aisha. Steve liked that the video showed the negotiators, so he can see who he's talking to. Koresh doesn't plan to talk to the FBI today. Steve: "of course he likes sharing things with you. He, he likes you a lot you know."

John: "Well, I'm sure. He doesn't like me enough to come bouncing on out and shake my hand though, does he?"

Steve: "Well, he likes you enough to invite you in and sit you down right by his bed there. (Laughing.)"

Steve insists the folks inside are being talked to about leaving so much by Steve that they're getting the impression he's trying to kick them out. John credits Steve with working well to get folks out.

Koresh comes to the phone. "If I, if I wanted to, you know, if I had been under any violations as soon as the ATF boys moved in a month ahead of time next door. . . . We could have removed everything out of here. We could have hightailed it to any part of this country." Koresh insists it was the Davidians who called for the cease-fire, not BATF; that agents were even allowed in the building to take wounded agents, but none of this was revealed to the news media. He credits the FBI as folks stepping in to separate participants in a schoolyard fight.

No. 121. March 12–13, 10:46 p.m.–8:36 a.m.

The negotiators say they are looking forward to Rita, Brad, and Kevin in the morning.

Steve asks if the electricity is off because the bosses are antsy.

John responds, we've been making some progress, "So I guess they're going to let you go to sleep early, huh?" Really, John explains, it's that nothing had happened for five or six days, so the HRT responded. But now some people had come out and more were coming.

Steve: "Maybe what they want is what the ATF apparently came here to do in the first place?" Steve recounts complaining about the original raid, with choppers shooting in Koresh's room, and the shootout at the front door.

John insists that Kathy and Ollie are tangible progress but really would have liked Brad and Kevin. The Davidians note that Oliver Gyarfas was supposed to call back in. Dick blames tactical folks for Oliver not calling, saying it was opposed by negotiators. Steve recounts cattle trucks, and says they'll tell God and a court some day. Dick promises a congressional inquiry. Steve requests a talk with the Texas Rangers, whom Dick says will be handling the shooting incident review. Steve's says he is impressed with FBI Director Sessions.

No. 122. March 13, 8:36–9:21 a.m.

Steve: "She [Judy] says, why didn't Robert Gonzalez just bring a friend in? . . . When we watched, now listen to this, when we hear and watch this man, Dan [Hartnett] . . . from the ATF on the television, . . . it's so obvious, he . . . wants blood. He could give a crap about . . . justice. . . . He doesn't talk about his men ever being brought to justice or that there was any wrongdoing. It looks like the guy's got a vengeance to find some leak in the press and go for their throats and jugular also."

Brad Branch and Kevin Whitecliff are preparing to leave, Steve says. And maybe Rita. Dick notes, in response to complaints, the negotiators' frustration on learning what the tactical people did.

Steve was convinced by the method of approach that BATF was out to kill them. He thinks they want to destroy evidence, perhaps burn the building to destroy evidence, "because the evidence, from the door, will clearly show how many bullets and what happened, especially if there's, the press got video of this." But you've got the press miles back.

Kevin seems to have changed his mind about leaving due to the electricity being cut off. But, despite the temptation, Steve won't "pull the plug" on discussions.

Steve recalls Gary being okay as negotiator [even though earlier tapes suggested Steve hadn't thought much of him]. Steve complains about FBI complaints of Davidians at windows while the FBI has Bradleys running around and destroying property, and is lying to the press and keeping them away. Steve attacks BATF for assault on guns and freedom, even though Steve personally hates guns.

No. 123. MARCH 13, 9:21 A.M.–1:08 P.M.

Steve believes in the right to guns; Bush came in pretending to like the NRA, but he did three things against guns; and Clinton is attacking guns. Steve denounces the Trilateral Commission and CFR. But he's always had pride in the FBI.

Dick suggests that if Steve came out, he would probably just be held as a material witness, and likely released on bond within a day. Dick's not sure how long with church property being a crime scene, the Davidians would be kept away from there. Dick tries to convince Steve he has more influence than Steve thinks.

Steve says some of the Davidians were interested in gun shows as an investment with Henry [McMahon]. Others were more interested in the music, like Steve.

Steve's sister has asked Jack Zimmermann to represent him, he's told by Dick. A letter from Steve's sister curiously says if Steve doesn't let Zimmermann handle it, the message may come from Marc Breault. Steve's puzzled at first, since Marc's the avowed enemy; he said he would destroy the group. Eventually, Steve figures out that the letter means that Marc would be the winner if Steve doesn't get representation.

Steve notes that, but for the electricity being shut off, Brad would have been out of there; and says they can thank the commanders that Brad won't even talk about leaving now. Steve points out the senselessness of sending in six gallons of milk and then turning off the electricity which keeps it refrigerated.

There've been death threats against the Davidians, Steve recalls, but the Davidians never threatened to attack Waco, contrary to lies by the Bunds and Breault.

No. 124. MARCH 13, 1:08–3:52 P.M.

Steve recalls his complaints about Bradleys running around from the outset, running over shacks, etc., while the FBI complained about seeing someone wearing a balaclava, thus expanding Steve's vocabulary, since he didn't know what they were talking about.

Steve recalls that the first time milk was sent in was also followed immediately by the electricity being shut off.

In response to the suggestion that Steve send people out, Steve, clearly peeved, indicates there is freedom of choice. Steve: "So, if the commanders are the—actually the ones in control and no matter what you say it doesn't matter, they'll do their own thing, well, then, what's the sense of me having a phone line open to you in the first place?"

Steve suggests sending Judy out for treatment and then letting her go back to the residence? Okay, but it'll cost you, the FBI responds; you'll have to send out the kids. But they're mostly Koresh's. Then three adults? Two adults?

At first, it wasn't quid pro quo to Steve. More Davidians came out as they got more confidence in decent treatment from FBI. As Steve recalls, "there was no bargaining, nothing. They just came out because they had—gaining confidence in you people. I kept talking to them. They were gaining confidence. That's the reason." And Steve doesn't really care for the FBI's style, when they lie and say Judy isn't interested in medical care, because she's not interested in it on the FBI's terms. He says the government should be willing to treat her because she was a totally innocent person and the government came in and shot her.

He complains that the government seems to control all aspects of society, even the press.

The three adults refused to leave, so, since there is freedom of choice, there is no need to discuss the FBI's offer with Koresh.

Steve seems to perceive Dick's "commanders" as "commandos."

No. 125. March 13, 3:52–9:54 p.m.

Dick assures Steve that Kathy and Ollie have legal representation, but he's not sure whether they face any charges.

Koresh said one word to Steve, "electricity."

Clearly upset about denial of medical treatment for his wife, Steve complains about how inhumanitarian the government is. Also upset that when he says the electricity shut-off is making the kids cold, the FBI responds that therefore they should send the kids out.

Steve notes that only a few folks were able to see the video the FBI sent in since electricity was cut off before they could all see it.

The FBI tells Scott Sonobe that, if he comes out, he won't be thrown in jail without a trial, but that he may be held as material witness, like the others; first, he would get medical treatment, and then likely be sent to the Waco jail.

No. 126. March 13.

Surrender might give Scott an arrest record, but, if he is then released, the disposition record will note the absence of a conviction. Scott's worried about the treatment of his daughters, Angelique and Crystal, since a so-called expert complained of them being well behaved; he wants to know about their being sent to next of kin, even if out of state, by Texas authorities.

Oliver Gyarfas calls in to say the treatment he's gotten was okay, that he has an attorney.

Kathy, too, calls in. She is criticized by Steve for claiming to be a spokesperson and for referring to them as "Koreshians" or "Branch Davidians." She assures them they'll have no access to the press until they come out; Steve has been assured of that several times. But she has access to the press. The elderly women have been released on bond. She says she plans a wrongful death suit against BATF for Mike. Time isn't on their side, she notes; it's on the FBI's, and the FBI is very anxious for the standoff to come to a quick end. Steve observes that the FBI never wanted it to begin, and now they want it to end quickly. She notes the resources the FBI is using are tremendous— in costs for the FBI, Bradleys, holding her, etc. We can tell it to the media and to the courts, but not from the compound, she says. An FBI agent comes on the phone to assure Steve that Kathy didn't claim to be spokesman, it was the FBI's fault. She suggests the "Koreshian" came because "Branch Davidian Seventh-day Adventist" was too much for their computer. Steve suggests "Bible student" as the proper alternative.

Steve complains again about a tank near the lake, real close to the house and on Davidians' property, contrary to the agreements.

No. 127. March 14–15, 1:25 p.m.–11:02 a.m.

John insists the FBI didn't lie about Oliver Gyarfas; he checked and there was no promise he'd be allowed to call in; it was just a misunderstanding.

Local sheriff wants to talk to Steve. He suggests it's time for common sense to resolve this thing, without harping on the past. He notes they've generally had good relations in the past, and he assures them that lots of Davidians will be released quickly, and the property fairly quickly returned.

No. 128. March 15, 11:03 a.m.–2:45 p.m.

Sheriff Harwell talks to Koresh. Koresh discusses the sudden cut-off in electricity, the Klieg lights, not receiving the *Time* and *Newsweek* that were promised, the FBI knocking down their fence, and the new, abrupt demeanor of the negotiators. Harwell tells Koresh he's been talking with the neighbors, and none of them have anything bad to say about the Branch Davidians. A face-to-face meeting is planned between Harwell and Schneider. Schneider mentions his good rapport with negotiator John Dolan; Harwell informs him that Dolan has gone home.

No. 129. March 15, 2:45–7:55 p.m.

Discussions about preparations for a meeting of Steve and Wayne Martin with the sheriff and Byron Sage.

Steve asks, per Wayne's advice, about the sealed warrant, since they still don't know what Koresh's supposed to have done.

He requests batteries for videos. And Steve mentions Phillip Arnold as part of a potential solution to the seven seals issue.

No. 130. March 16, 7:55 p.m.–8:24 p.m.

Schneider recounts the meeting that he and Koresh had with Sheriff Harwell and FBI negotiator Byron Sage. He felt things went well. Schneider asks to hear more from Dr. Arnold.

No. 131. March 16–[March 17?], 9:30 p.m.–9:25 p.m. [Times based on transcript cover page.]

David Jones talks about being shot on February 28.

No. 132. March 18–19, 7:38 a.m.–8:21 a.m.

John assures Steve there is no threat; the vehicles are just moving trash. Steve gives his okay.

Steve is upset that FBI spokesman Bob Ricks is falsely saying the Davidians sometimes point guns from their windows. This just makes it harder for Steve: "does it bother you in any degree at all that the FBI and/or the government can control and have such power over the press . . . ? . . . I'm talking about how they've not been allowed to cover the story and they're all saying basically the same thing." When they come out, the press will basically say, "here's a bunch of loonies . . . and cultists. . . ."

Steve is told the FBI is removing the Davidian diesel tanks. Steve: "You guys are getting pretty serious now."

NO. 133. MARCH 19, 8:21–9:01 A.M.

John Dolan is back. John Dolan tells Steve that Jamar has been convinced to send in *Time, Newsweek,* a tape of Dr. Arnold, and the legal documents [the sealed warrant]. There is no trade; they're just to be sent in. Steve: Koresh says that he won't be in here forever; he's getting ready to come out.

Koresh complains of noise to Byron Sage. Try not to demolish more of the property, he says.

NO. 134. MARCH 19, 9:02 A.M.–2:35 P.M.

John Dolan. Bible talk. The three men don't want to come out during the sabbath, which begins that evening, and lasts until sunset the next evening.

NO. 135. MARCH 19, 2:35–7:41 P.M.

Koresh complains about his mother taking $5,000 from the media, and calls it "blood money." He recalls that when he was a child, she called him "weird" because he asked so many questions, and she sometimes said that he didn't really seem to be her child.

Schneider arranges details for the impending exit of one or two Davidians, after getting assurance that they can keep their Bibles with them. Schneider relays a demand from HRT (sent through negotiators) than an adult male who is outside get back into the house. Discussion of impending exit of Brad Branch and Kevin Whitecliff, which is delayed by their need to have a final Bible study with Koresh. Koresh says he has nineteen children.

NO. 136. MARCH 19, 7:41–8:41 P.M.

Discussion of details for Kevin and Brad's exit.

Koresh shares his understanding of the Bible, astrophysics, and carpentry.

NO. 137. MARCH 19, 8:41–9:28 P.M.

Koresh: "My mother . . . all my life she's been telling me she doesn't even know if I'm her kid or not."

John Dolan tells Koresh that Koresh should have just directly told undercover agent Robert Rodriguez to call the BATF raid off, rather than putting things in "roundabout" biblical terms. Koresh: "No, well, see, his soul's at stake here. You know, we're talking about Judas."

No. 138. March 19, 9:28–10:15 p.m.

Rita Riddle tells the negotiator that all the property destruction makes the negotiators' promises less credible. Negotiator promises that the federal government will pay for repairs of all damaged property.

Rachel Jones Koresh wonders if the government will stop being "nice" after negotiations are over and the Davidians are in custody.

David Koresh begins an extended Bible discussion, relating it to the American criminal justice system.

No. 139. March 19, 10:15–11:03 p.m.

Koresh notes the lack of a warrant, and says things have changed since February 28, so he's not necessarily ready to meet John outside with it; but he repeats that the warrant was never shown on the twenty-eighth. Bible babble.

Rita is expected out tomorrow. Steve suggests Brad and Kevin were sent out because they were abusing the system [drinking Koresh's scotch].

No. 140. March 19, 11:03–11:50 p.m.

Koresh suggests that perhaps it was just that a BATF agent's hand was resting on the trigger too tight, but they fired first, and that fact should be on the tape taken by the guys across the street. Melissa Morrison was going to come out, Koresh says, when we first had the problem with the milk. He denies flock suicide.

Bible babble. "I'll be talking to brick walls one day."

John says he'll still be talking to a lot of people.

Koresh is 99 percent sure Rita will be out, but she's scared.

John asks about a few folks. John: "And that—and Melissa, Sherri, my pal Sherri."
Koresh: "Um-hum."

John: "I'll never forget the 75th Psalm as long as I think of Sherri."
Koresh: "Talk about those horns chop chop, isn't it?"

John: "(Laughing.) She's a real silver tongue devil. Scott and Sita, David Thibodeau, Marguerita. They're all people that, that we have messages for out here."

No. 141. March 20.

Koresh discusses money, asserting there's still plenty left from the $1,000, and, if not, Jim was told Koresh would be happy to send out some more.

There is a panic call about someone outside with a bucket. Koresh teasingly says he's collecting water to throw on the Davidians and make them melt. Kevin and Brad are reportedly out, with John reporting the soft drinks they're getting.

Steve discusses details of jail for those out now and those who will come out in the future: rooms, clothes, material witness status, and bond. Also whether he could change lawyers if he is dissatisfied with the one his sister chose.

Steve on the Waco *Tribune-Herald* exposé: "ATF agent Robert Gonzalez. . . . He brought over Sunday's paper that morning even and we all looked at it, so he . . . saw the reaction . . . it was not a big deal."

Steve: "the ATF want blood. . . . I can see a number of individuals languishing away in prison."

No. 142. March 20, 1:34–6:41 P.M.

On the other hand, Steve sees potential money from book contracts.

Rita's coming out at 6:30; the delay to darkness is due to the sabbath. John hopes for an end soon; the guys are on thirty-day rotation, and he hopes they're out before the end of his rotation.

Steve expects to have more questions regarding the legal situation once they come out. Kevin and Brad are reportedly treated well by the sheriff, and all agree he's a swell guy.

The FBI discusses with Rachel the logistics of everyone leaving.

Steve asks to speak to Kevin and Brad.

Koresh gives Kevin and Brad a quick refresher Bible lesson, urging them to keep their faith.

No. 143. March 20, 6:41–7:27 P.M.

The Bible lesson continues, with Kevin also participating. Koresh ends by telling them "we're going to be sending some more people out."

No. 144. March 20–21, 7:28 P.M.–12:15 A.M.

John assures Koresh that, when he comes out, everyone gets legal representation and the right to practice his religion. He tries to get them to send out Victoria Hollingsworth, too; agreed to, in particular since she's lost a lot of weight since the siege began. The Davidians note that Rita Riddle had a nice Honda Prelude which a tank pushed around a lot a few days back. Having her car be vandalized was not what the Davidians meant when they asked if Rita could help Vicky come out.

In reference to all the studies with Koresh, John jokes that he won't have to go to church for six months.

Rita and Vicky will stay in until the morning; Rita's hesitant about leaving. Vicky will leave with Annetta Richards.

No. 145. March 21, 12:15–1:02 A.M.

Koresh recalls some rough treatment at the 1988 arrest, but nice treatment by a black deputy. Some discussion of the trial. Koresh distinguishes himself from Jim Jones and his group, and from rich preachers.

Bible babble.

No. 146. March 21, 1:02–1:50 A.M.

After listening patiently to a lengthy Bible study, John says that he and John Dolan may be sent home, because their bosses think that they're not getting anywhere with Koresh.

No. 147. March 21, 1:50–2:37 a.m.

John's Bible lesson continues.

No. 148. March 21, 2:37–3:20 a.m.

The Bible study concludes.

No. 149. March 21, 6:19–11:37 a.m.

Telephone problems are noted.

Rita Riddle and Gladys Ottman are about to depart. John wants to know when all the rest will come out, and Steve says he's being pushy. They discuss the possibility of getting Rita's red Prelude off the Mount Carmel property, so she can use it after she comes out.

Discussion of messages for various persons in the residence which have been received by the FBI.

Steve says that, despite what the FBI may have heard, in general, the Davidians are modest, and he objects to the fact that the women were frisked by male agents. John insists women are searched by women agents, but Steve replies that the Davidians saw the searches from a window. John's defense is that, with what the ladies were wearing, the FBI just couldn't tell if the women had weapons. Steve lodges an objection for the future.

No. 150. March 21, 11:37 a.m.–3:57 p.m.

Steve asks John-3 (John Hylar) to turn off the loudspeaker for a while; several people are ready to leave, and are having one final study with Koresh, but they can't hear what he's saying. Arrangements made for three more adults to leave. At Steve's request, John-3 arranges for the two exiting females to be frisked by a female FBI agent, out of respect for their modesty.

Later, Sheila Martin, now in custody at the sheriff's, calls to talk to her husband, Wayne Martin. Wayne also talks with their small children, who had been sent out earlier.

No. 151. March 21, 3:57–6:14 p.m.

There is a question as to how many Davidians are coming out next. Steve's unsure; he's talking to one of the largest groups yet, and still answering questions on Bible study, etc., in the absence of Koresh. He won't be pushed even for a ballpark figure by John. Steve says that Koresh is all but pushing the Davidians out, but it's a question of conscience, and he's not pushing them out. Steve suspects Gonzalez [Rodriguez] may still be a little tempted by Koresh's teachings.

Steve expresses concern when the building is searched, will it just be Texas Rangers (and FBI) or will biased BATF be involved as well? He fears BATF involvement, and John can't say they won't be involved.

Steve complains about the negotiating process where the FBI keep insisting he has to give them things; and the FBI has, among other advantages, sleep, since they work in shifts, and he doesn't, and the pressures on him are rather greater.

John doesn't want to push, he says, but the commanders want to see real progress. Steve replies there has been today. Steve can't just grab 'em by the neck and throw them out. Steve offers, if the FBI wants, to make a tape recording of what he tells people to assure them fair treatment. But if the FBI hadn't cut off electricity, over two-thirds would have been out already; "you know, if they start threatening or forcing, then I lose the ability to talk to them again."

John says that five or six Davidian departures a day is unacceptable.

"Then what—," asks Steve.

John pushes, saying call back with numbers.

Byron Sage telephones, saying it's important to speak to Koresh or Steve, Koresh more than to Steve, since he doesn't want to interrupt Steve, who's talking to Davidians.

Eventually John tells Steve about bulldozing go-karts and motorcycles: "it's not offensive. They're just moving them out." Now, John suggests to Steve, go back to trying to get folks out of there.

No. 152. March 21, 6:14–11:36 p.m.

John Cox tells Steve it's been a very successful day. Steve says not according to John-3 and Byron.

John mentions messages the FBI has for a variety of persons inside. Melissa Morrison's grandmother is anxious for her to come out safely. Melissa's looking forward to it, too, according to her mother; they shouldn't worry; it's all written in the Book. Rose Morrison is healthy and understands it's her decision as to when or whether to leave.

John Cox continues passing along messages to various residents.

Davidians complain about the radio blaring through the FBI public address speakers. Steve suggests the great commercial United States has repudiated its values of freedom and will be brought down as an example to the world.

John wants Steve to suggest something he can offer to get his superiors to shut off the music. Steve answers that he won't give anything to shut the speakers off; the noise is just going to prevent him talking others into leaving. Steve confirms that Koresh said that nobody is coming out.

No. 153. March 21–22, 11:36 p.m.–9:33 a.m.

Steve: "We're trying to give people an opportunity—he's letting them ask their questions, finalizing that with them, that they might be sure in their own mind and confident in why they even came here, that they go out. This [tactical pressure] of course is creating the opposite effect." We're reverting to the Dark Ages and the persecution of persons for their consciences.

John says if Steve will give a number coming out, they will shut off the music. Steve notes this is the reward for sending out seven between midnight and midnight. Steve bemoans that he's seen eroding of the Constitution for years. BATF attacks people for their religious beliefs. Is this what Jefferson et al. had in mind? Three weeks ago he was minding his own business, and now he'll probably go to prison, for what? He doesn't trust the system.

John just wants a number, and Steve just wants some sleep.

The next morning, John notes they got the music turned off; but Steve says he didn't notice; he was asleep. Negotiators need to know what Koresh's doing, Steve is told. He responds that Koresh is probably sleeping. John blames tactical guys for music.

Steve complains about destruction of go-karts and an Airstream trailer which belongs to a woman who's not even there now.

John suggests a civil suit, and uses Rodney King as example of possible prosecution of policemen who misbehave, noting it's the feds who are prosecuting the Los Angeles police.

Steve is not real convinced: "And the only thing that my innocency one day will only be shown in the light of the judgement of God. I'm serious. I believe that. I don't think this agency, this federal agency that came here for whatever purpose and intention, nothing is going to happen to them. I know they want blood. I've seen it in the eyes. I've seen it in the demeanor and in the statements of the spokesperson for them. And I'm afraid because you're a sister agency that somehow or other, you're going to be involved more—producing evidence. Maybe even suppressing it, I don't know. I hope not." Steve hopes all this stuff is on tapes and that the tapes are not destroyed. John insists they're evidence.

Steve indicates that he is not a big admirer of BATF and gun control: "I believe ATF has been brought about as an agency to take away those freedoms slowly but surely, insidiously. And I see that's what is happening, John. I believe that, unless somebody—I've got open ears. You can show me something else. But I feel over time it's going to be to the place where they're going to push for gun control. No one will have any guns. I think that the founding forefathers wanted individuals to be allowed to have guns against the tyranny and the possible tyranny of their own government."

Steve is told that Brad and Kevin are on a radio show.

NO. 154. MARCH 23, 9:33 A.M.–7:28 P.M.

Livingstone Fagan has decided to leave.

Steve complains about damage from vehicles and problems with communications. Steve says it is unclear what army they belong to, leading to a prompt "no army, no army" from a John. Steve complains about statements by BATF and misleading statements by the FBI at press conferences. So, John responds, come out and talk to the press yourselves.

Steve observes that a court defense will be costly even if they eventually go free.

NO. 155. MARCH 23, 7:28–11:52 P.M.

John tells Steve that the fact that no one came out after Heather Jones for six days set a bad precedent. Steve notes that it took quite a while for the milk to come in. Steve also notes that Koresh is upset with the approach of Byron Sage, which John defends as being imposed on Sage by the system.

John is offended by Koresh's making light of the siege by playing his guitar through the Davidian PA system, hurting John's credibility. But Steve says that Koresh sends out seven people and the reward is the destruction of property and phone lines, and weird music over the FBI PA.

No. 156. MARCH 23–24, 11:52 P.M.–6:40 A.M.

Steve says the fact that every adult who leaves is immediately taken into custody, and never released, is preventing other people from coming out. He is upset about what he sees as numerous violations of the Constitution. Steve wonders what happened to negotiator John Dolan, whom Steve greatly respected. Negotiator Tony has no idea. Schneider says that negotiator Byron is arrogant, and wants to do all the talking.

No. 157. MARCH 24, 6:40 A.M.–10:06 P.M.

A new negotiator, Jennifer, tells Steve Schneider that she has been talking daily to Steve's sister Judy, and has some things she wants to tell Steve. Steve is very interested, but can't talk during the sabbath.

John Cox is concerned that someone has been spotted banging on the Mount Carmel Center's front door. Steve has no idea who the guy is. [It is Louis Alaniz, a non-Davidian who has snuck past the FBI.] Alaniz comes on the phone briefly, and tells John Cox to "allow God to handle it," but Cox won't talk without knowing the name of who he's talking to, and Alaniz won't tell him. Steve rejects Cox's suggestion that the visitor be ejected immediately.

No. 158. MARCH 24–25, 10:06 P.M.–8:45 A.M.

Some phone problems discussed.

No. 159. MARCH 25, 8:45–10:20 A.M.

Dick questions Steve about Louis Alaniz, who is at the moment receiving a Bible study from Koresh. Steve wants to talk to Livingstone Fagan, currently at the sheriff's jail, but Dick says Livingstone does not want to talk.

Steve asks about Jennifer (see tape no. 157), and is told that she is gone and will not return. Steve is incredulous.

Steve says he doesn't believe Koresh's claim that Koresh hears audible voices, but follows Koresh anyway because of Koresh's exposition of the Bible.

No. 160. MARCH 25, 10:20 A.M.–12:00 NOON.

Steve expresses concern about constitutional violations. He is very concerned about reports that Davidians who have left have had their personal Bibles taken from them.

Wayne Martin and negotiator Dick discuss why Livingstone Fagan has not yet called in. Wayne doesn't believe FBI claims that it was technically impossible yesterday to make a phone connection from the county jail to the Mount Carmel phone, because a tank had accidentally cut a phone line.

Dick says that as soon as the Davidians come out, their request to meet with radio host Ron Engelman will be honored.

No. 161. MARCH 25, 12:00–12:35 P.M.

Wayne and Dick continue. As an attorney, Wayne knows that an FBI negotiator can't make legally binding promises, so he wants to talk to a United States Attorney. In particular, he is concerned that promises the Branch Davidians will be held in the Waco jail pending trial are not binding; legally, they could be sent to any federal detention facility.

Dick gets increasingly frustrated with Wayne, and hangs up on him.

No. 162. MARCH 25, 12:35 P.M.–6:35 P.M.

Dick relays to Steve the warning from Jamar that ten to twenty people must leave "by 4 P.M. today for safety reasons." If not, "certain actions will be taken. . . . This is not a threat, Steve, this is a promise."

When the Davidians fail to comply, the FBI destroys some property. Steve: "the motorcycle that they got happened to be mine." Steve says that Doris Fagan and Yvette Fagan would have left earlier if Livingstone Fagan had called in.

Asked to bring his wife and daughter and seven other people out, Steve says that Judy is adamant about not leaving, for fear that she will be separated from her two-year-old daughter, Mayanah, and never see her again.

He says that everyone would come out if one or two BATF raiders were arrested.

No. 163. MARCH 25, 6:25–8:30 P.M.

Steve gathers a group of people near the phone who are willing to go out with him tomorrow morning: Lisa Farris, Julie Martinez, Cliff Sellors, Clive Doyle, Pablo Cohen, David Thibodeau, Shari Doyle, David Jones, and Scott Sonobe. And Steve will try to talk Greg Summers into coming.

Steve again asks for Jennifer (see tapes no. 157, 159), and is told to forget about her.

Later, Steve says that all the other people who might come out are concerned that Livingstone Fagan has not phoned in.

John talks to Livingston Malcolm, relaying a message from his brother. John says that if ten people do not come out tomorrow morning, "something's going to happen."

No. 164. MARCH 25, 8:30–9:51 P.M.

Tony urges Steve to come out with his family.

No. 165. MARCH 25, 9:51–10:38 P.M.

More Tony and Steve.

Negotiator Linda Barry talks to Julie Martinez, mother-to-mother. Julie's mother had left earlier, but is being held as a material witness, increasing Julie's reluctance to leave. Julie is particularly reluctant to force her thirteen-year-old daughter to do something against her will.

No. 166. March 25–26, 10:38 p.m.–6:00 a.m.

Linda Barry talks with Lisa Farris. She is not interested in leaving, and says the FBI has broken its promises.

Tony talks with Judy Schneider. She is not going anywhere, but is waiting on David Koresh and his God. She says Steve's earlier interest in leaving was just because he was tired.

No. 167. March 26, 6:00 a.m.–11:15 a.m.

John-3 and Steve. The FBI thinks that Livingstone Fagan came out with the intention of not cooperating, so as to provide a pretext for other people to stay inside. The FBI loudspeakers have been playing Christian Broadcast Network tapes from Craig Smith's program, in which he criticizes Koresh. Steve says the Davidians think Smith is rude to his callers.

John-3: "Steve, the key word here is noon, and the key word is to come out and get this resolved. You come out."

Steve: "The key word though is God's word, His will, the seven seals."

Later, Steve says, "This is the first time that I'm aware of in the history of the United States that the government has used tanks against its own people. . . . That's a fulfillment, a direct fulfillment of the prophecy of Nahum."

No. 168. March 26, 11:15 a.m.–4:06 p.m.

John-3 calls to tell Steve that Livingstone Fagan was just on CNN. Steve has been talking to Floyd Houtman and Jeff Little about leaving. John-3 insists on a major exit by noon, in half an hour.

Nobody comes out. John-3 tells Steve that action will be taken.

That afternoon, negotiator Henry asks Rachel Koresh for a new tape of the children.

Henry wants to talk to Koresh to give him what he's always wanted: input from religious scholars. But Koresh is said to feel too sick to come to the phone.

No. 169. March 26–27, 4:06 p.m.–6:00 a.m.

The Davidians call to let the FBI know that in a little bit, an unarmed woman will be going outside to empty the toilet buckets. While the woman is outside, the tactical team announces that no one can leave the house for any reason: "Return to the house or suffer the consequences."

No. 170. March 27, 6:00 a.m.–1:42 p.m.

Steve is angry that BATF's Troy, at the morning press conference, falsely accused the Davidians of running a drug lab and of shooting the BATF agents before they even left the cattle trailers.

John-4 (John Denton), a new negotiator, talks with Steve about videotaping the children. Steve informs John-4 that a new person snuck into the compound last night, Jesse Amen.

The FBI is unsure if Koresh is still alive.

No. 171. March 27, 1:42–2:25 p.m.

During this conversation between John-4 and Steve, the tactical team begins ripping down the fence. Steve accuses them of destroying evidence.

Discussion about Jesse Amen: a longhaired, bearded man, from an Assembly of God church, who wanted to find out for himself about Koresh's message.

No. 172. March 27, 2:25–7:53 p.m.

Tony and Steve. The two men who sneaked in, Louis Alaniz and Jesse Amen, are currently receiving a Bible lesson. They are thinking about leaving tomorrow, as is Greg Summers.

During another of the discussions about Livingstone Fagan, someone in the background tells Steve that Fagan said on CNN that he was not allowed to call out.

Tony tries in vain to get Koresh on the phone, even if just for thirty seconds.

Tony talks briefly with Louis Alaniz and Jesse Amen, but they want to talk about the Bible message they're learning, and he is not interested.

No. 173. March 27, 7:35–9:57 p.m.

Steve complains about the tactical team destroying evidence, and breaking an $85,000 bulldozer that belongs to Waco Rental. He is also very concerned that Kathy Schroeder was not allowed to post bond and is being held on charges of attempted murder.

Negotiator Dek reads Steve a letter from Jack Zimmermann, offering to represent Steve, urging him to go through the legal process, and suggesting a meeting of Zimmermann, Schneider, Koresh, and Dick DeGuerin (the attorney that Koresh's mother has hired for Koresh).

No. 174. March 27, 9:57–10:47 p.m.

Steve asks if he can talk by phone with a Baylor University professor of religion.

No. 175. March 27, 10:47–11:34 p.m.

Linda Barry tries, without success, to get Steve to put Koresh on the phone. Steve hangs up for a minute to talk to someone in the room. When he calls back, the new negotiator is John-5 (John O'Neil's first appearance). When Steve asks what happened to Linda, John-5 temporizes, "Oh, she's a—something came up and you know how it is with the ladies."

"Nonsense," Steve replies.

John-5 offers to turn the electricity back on, if everyone will leave.

Steve: "Well, who's the electricity going to be for then, John-5?"

Steve denies that his wife, Judy, has had sex with David Koresh, or had a child by him. (This obvious lie probably played a role in the negotiators losing confidence in Schneider.)

Later, Steve suggests, "Throw a match to the building, people will have to come out."

NO. 176. MARCH 27–28, 11:34 P.M.–12:12 A.M.

John-5 offers the possibility of a meeting with Bible scholars, once Steve surrenders.

Schneider would prefer a discussion by telephone, without the surrender.

NO. 177. MARCH 28, 12:12–1:08 A.M.

Discussion on details of delivery of the videotape of the children.

John-5 wants Steve to wake up David Thibodeau, so Thibodeau can hear a tape from his mother.

NO. 178. MARCH 28, 1:08–6:00 A.M.

Steve's repeated requests to be allowed to go to sleep are ignored, but a new negotiator (from the Austin police) named Rick comes on the phone. Rick asks if Steve would like to talk to attorney Jack Zimmermann on the phone.

Rick continues the line of previous negotiators, telling Steve how influential and articulate Steve is, and reminding him of his responsibility for leading people out, based on his having recruited so many people to the group.

Shortly before Steve goes to bed, the loudspeaker noise changes to howling coyotes, a shift from the crying baby and the seagulls that had played earlier.

NO. 179. MARCH 28, 6:00 A.M.–12:06 P.M.

John-4 plays the tape for David Thibodeau from his mother. She is in Waco, where she will stay until he is safe. She is anguished and deeply concerned for his future.

Jim (new negotiator, also from the Austin police) tells Steve that the higher-ups are deeply concerned about the lack of contact with Koresh, and worried about the development of a Jim Jones-type situation. Jim offers to participate in a face-to-face meeting with Steve and Koresh, like the earlier meeting of Steve, Wayne Martin, Sheriff Harwell, and Byron Sage. Steve refuses, since Koresh is too sick.

Later, George (new negotiator from the FBI) phones to warn that unless ten people leave by 12:50 P.M., action will be taken.

NO. 180. MARCH 28, 12:06–2:19 P.M.

George reiterates the "safety" rules to Steve: no one should point a gun at the tactical personnel, etc.

The transcript states that the remainder of the tape is distorted, and could not be transcribed.

NO. 181. MARCH 28, 2:19–3:14 P.M.

Koresh finally comes on the phone. George asks if Koresh would like to talk with Dick DeGuerin.

NO. 182. MARCH 28, 3:14–3:55 P.M.

Koresh supplies a blow-by-blow account of the shootout with George Roden. He expresses great concern that his children will be taken away from him and from their mothers, and given to a "jerk" father who will feed them junk food.

NO. 183. MARCH 28, 3:55–7:17 P.M.

The battery for filming the video of the children ran out; negotiator George promises a new one.

Dick DeGuerin is patched in to talk to Koresh for fifteen minutes. Because conversation is a privileged attorney-client communication, the FBI does not listen, and the recording equipment is turned off.

NO. 184. MARCH 28, 7:17–10:24 P.M.

While Koresh and John talk, a Bradley tank drops off nineteen pints of milk, crackers, a fresh battery, and an article from the day's *New York Times* about Waco (reporting that BATF knew that surprise had been lost).

More talk about the video, then Koresh sighs, "Yeah, my babies. My life is over."

NO. 185. MARCH 28–29, 10:24 P.M.–6:00 A.M.

Steve is very impressed with the unbiased tone of the *New York Times* article.

John talks with Pablo Cohen, who has no interest in cutting short his Bible studies by leaving the compound.

NO. 186. MARCH 29, 6:00–11:59 A.M.

George tells Steve that the new video of the children and of David Thibodeau turned out fine. They make plans for a video of the adults who are wounded, so that a doctor can view the video and offer advice.

George pressures Koresh to have an immediate face-to-face meeting with DeGuerin. Koresh is willing to talk tomorrow, but won't be forced into an instant meeting and is too weak to walk into a field anyway. George offers to have DeGuerin come to a fence near the house, so that Koresh can sit by the front door and talk with him.

NO. 187. MARCH 29, 11:59 A.M.–6:20 P.M.

Steve worries that if Koresh is exposed, FBI snipers may kill him, hoping to destroy Branch Davidian cohesion.

NO. 188. MARCH 30 [MISLABELED MARCH 29], 6:00 A.M.–9:28 A.M.

DeGuerin and Koresh meet in-person for two hours. John is frustrated that Steve still won't commit to an exit. Steve accuses the FBI of bad faith for starting the loudspeaker barrage on the same day that seven people were leaving. John accuses Koresh of bad faith for only sending out people who were liabilities to him: other people's children, the elderly, or people with drinking problems. Fagan is the lone exception to this.

No. 189. MARCH 30–31, 9:28 A.M.–8:00 A.M.

Arrangements are discussed for Zimmermann and DeGuerin to meet with Steve and Koresh.

No. 190. APRIL 2.

DeGuerin calls from inside the compound and tells the FBI that the meeting is going very well.

Later, while John-1 (John Cox) and Judy Schneider talk, he is handed a postcard picturing the University of Wisconsin at Green Bay; the card reads: "Dear FBI: God said tell David 'Altoona' and he will surrender."

Judy, a Wisconsin native, has no idea what the card means. She is more interested in obtaining chicken feed for the twenty-five chickens; they used to eat table scraps.

No. 191. APRIL 2.

John-5 informs Judy Schneider that there will be no more attorney visits. He criticizes her for not removing her daughter from the unhealthy compound.

No. 192. APRIL 2.

Steve tells John-5 that Koresh asked God what to do, and God again told Koresh, "wait." This is one of the two commands that Koresh often hears, the other being "trust."

No. 193. APRIL 3.

John criticizes Koresh for the emotional and social damage being inflicted on the children during the siege.

Koresh: "Why don't you turn the music off on the outside out there? You know so much about social and psychological sciences and all that, buddy, what do you think you're doing?"

No. 194. [NO DATE], 9:01 A.M.–8:44 A.M.

The FBI wants Steve and Koresh to talk to the attorneys by phone, but they won't talk during the sabbath. The attorneys return to the compound, and report that they are having another productive meeting. Steve tells John that Jesse Amen will be coming out in half an hour; he came to bring peace, and with the arrangements with the attorneys working out, he sees that peace is coming. Louis Alaniz, however, has just learned the first three seals, and doesn't want to leave until he learns all seven.

No. 195. [NO DATE], 8:44 A.M.–8:37 A.M.

Steve refuses to provide an estimate for when they will leave.

No. 196. [No date], 8:37 a.m.–11:12 p.m.

John tells Steve that Jesse Amen is claiming that the moment Amen got inside the compound, Koresh came up with a bowl and a towel, and washed his feet. Steve recalls no such event.

John wants to talk to the two pregnant women, but Steve says only if the FBI will do something for them, like send them food.

Near the barn, about 350 yards north of the compound, two booms are heard, and a flare is seen; the Davidians say they heard somebody yell, "Yahoo." Neither Steve nor the negotiators have any idea what happened.

In response to John's question, Steve says that suicide is not a possibility; it is an unpardonable sin.

No. 197. April 8, 11:12 p.m.–11:59 p.m.

Steve complains about the FBI playing the music extra loud last night, during what they had been told was the Davidians' holiest night of the year.

Koresh refuses to be pinned down about what he will do when Passover is over.

No. 198. April 8–9, 11:59 p.m.–12:55 a.m.

Somebody shoots off another flare while Steve and Henry are talking.

No. 199. April 9 [mislabeled April 8], 12:55 a.m.–11:42 a.m.

Negotiator Jennifer tells Steve that DeGuerin says that Koresh and DeGuerin agreed on an exit by April 14.

Steve says that the Davidians were disappointed with the radio tape of Dr. Arnold which was sent in earlier, since the tape just repeated a radio program they had already heard; there was no opportunity for dialogue.

No. 200. April 8–9, 11:42 p.m.[?]–10:21 a.m.[?]

John suggests the world is going about its business, not really interested in the Davidians, while Steve suggests the world is going to hell in a handbasket, and he is somewhat dubious of John's earlier pleasant descriptions of jail. John defends the job of negotiator as bringing peaceful resolution, and suggests the Davidians don't want to be known as a Jonestown. He asks Steve to describe what he saw at the initial BATF assault.

Steve again complains about Bradleys and guys in them giving the finger to the women in the compound. He says nice things about a Bradley driver named Tom, who was involved in the meeting with Sage and the sheriff.

John asks about meals-ready-to-eat [survival food, of which the Davidians had large stocks], and suggests that pizza is better; and, if he comes out, he will take Steve to Pizza Hut. Steve fears that his reputation in Waco would fall if he went to Pizza Hut with shackles on. John insists media are interested, why else would they be there? But

Steve questions their willingness to come to jail for talks, and attacks Bob Ricks's statements to media.

Telephone troubles.

No. 201. April 9, 10:21 A.M.–12 NOON.

Steve complains to Byron Sage about the phone connection. Steve says Koresh objects to lies Ricks tells about Koresh's use of profanity.

Sage wants to make sure they can still hear press conferences. He agrees that it's a misrepresentation of recent calls to mention profanities, but that Ricks meant to describe all the calls over the forty-day period.

Steve indicates more irritation with BATF's Troy's comments. And he complains about Bradleys running over the grave of Peter Gent. Steve complains about the death of Jaydean Wendell, shot while in her bed, and of seeing Perry Jones shot. He says he liked Robert Gonzalez, and understood that Gonzalaz tried to call the raid off.

Steve says he'll be coming out, but he expects to be stuck in a cell with the press not coming to him, because they're going to want something sensational. Recounting the arrests of the women. He expects a worse time than the others, because he was the spokesperson. Sage disagrees, since Steve's done a good job. And, regarding Koresh, Sage notes that Christ went to meet the magistrate.

Sage notes that this siege can't go on indefinitely. It's been forty-one days, and Sage asks for a time frame, which he doesn't get.

Steve says Koresh's looking forward to jail, recalling that Koresh's first decent night's sleep in some time was on his arrest in 1987. Steve expresses fear of, at best, life imprisonment without possibility of parole, based on excessive powers of the federal government. And he notes that his attorneys' fees will be about $450,000.

Sage sort of defends Troy's statements to the press, noting Troy can't say some things because of pending issues.

No. 202. April 9, 12:00–3:31 P.M.

Friendly discussion between negotiator Byron Sage and Steve, in which Byron—like Steve a committed Christian—urges Steve to rely on the Bible, not the word of David.

No. 203. April 9, 3:31 P.M.–

Telephone line problems.

They discuss Koresh's talk of Lake Waco shaking, the dam bursting, etc. Negotiators wonder about timing since they're trying to facilitate everyone's leaving, with Steve responding that God's first, the timing is not. Steve still says they're coming out, but he is more concerned about waiting for God's call. Steve's sending out a letter from Koresh. He says analyze the letter. The FBI says maybe he had too much sugar on his Fruit Loops this morning, and Steve calls him a smart ass.

Byron complains about someone being on the roof; Steve goes to check. Byron says Koresh's letter is very threatening to FBI people there.

No. 204. April 10, 1:58–2:45 p.m.

Sage interprets Koresh's letter as threatening, but Steve argues that the letter is not one human being to another. In the letter, Steve says, Koresh merely warns of an earthquake breaking a dam, a natural disaster. Sage views the letter as a threat of a criminal act.

Steve still insists the plan remains to come out peacefully sometime. Sage says they're going to facilitate that by putting wire around to prevent anyone else from breaking into the compound. It'll also provide a clear exit path for when they leave. Sage notes there will be metal detectors to make sure no evidence is taken out by Davidians or taken in by others, a fear Wayne Martin had expressed. Steve complains that they had to bury Peter Gent, and then tanks have run over the grave, that BATF murdered Jaydean Wendell. Steve complains of the one-way street, where rules are given to Davidians about what not to do.

Steve notes that once the Davidians leave, they've lost all their bargaining chips.

Sage insists the government can't lie because the whole world is watching, while Steve insists the world is only hearing or seeing what the FBI wants it to. Sage insists that the only way Steve would lose his life if he left is through his own initiative. Steve objects to having a flashbang thrown at him when he was clearly harmless.

Bible babble.

Steve: "We hold life so highly. That's why I want it eternally."

No. 205. April 10, 2:45–7:23 p.m.

Byron Sage and Steve make plans for Steve to put Koresh's letter under a rock, for the tactical team to pick up. Yesterday, when Steve dropped off Koresh's letter of the day, he retrieved the only undemolished children's go-kart and brought it inside; the tactical team threw flashbangs at him for deviating from the conditions under which he was allowed to leave the building, and Steve is angry about the team's actions.

No. 206. April 10, 7:23–9:07 p.m.

Friendly conversation between Steve and Dek, which goes nowhere.

No. 207. April 10, 9:08–11:29 p.m.

Discussing Koresh's recent letters to the FBI, Steve says that Koresh has never written a word since Schneider met him, six-and-a-half years ago; these letters were produced by inspiration from God.

John O'Neil suggests to Steve that David Koresh is a fraud modeling himself after Cyrus R. Teed, a turn-of-the-century religious leader who changed his name to "Koresh" and whose followers were called "Koreshians."

No. 208. April 10–11, 11:29 p.m.–1:34 a.m.

Steve says that Zimmermann's fee more than doubled between Steve's first conversation with Schneider and his second.

No. 209. April 11, 1:34–11:25 a.m.

Negotiator Rick asks Steve about an incident with Koresh and a ten-year-old girl [Kiri Jewell] in a motel. Steve says he has no knowledge of the allegation, and that Koresh's youngest "wife" was fourteen.

Steve says that the Davidians don't worry that being isolated in the compound prevents them from disseminating God's message; if God wants the message to circulate, it will.

No. 210. April 11, 11:25 a.m.–7:38 p.m.

Easter morning, but not a Branch Davidian holiday, because they reject the holiday's pagan roots. [Passover is their biggest holiday.] He asks that the social workers caring for the children on the outside be asked not to take the children on Easter egg hunts, which are pagan.

Steve says three people are tentatively thinking about leaving.

More discussion about Cyrus Teed Koresh and the book by Elizabeth Bartosh, *Koreshianity: The New Age of Religion* (Koreshnan Foundation, 1971). Steve is eager to see the book, or even a photocopy, to check out FBI claims that David Koresh's whole routine is derivative. The FBI will only send in a copy in exchange for five people coming out. (David Koresh had read or learned about some of Cyrus Teed Koresh's six books, but the two Koreshes' philosophies had very little in common. As detailed in Robert Fogarty's chapter in *Armageddon at Waco,* edited by Stuart Wright, the first Koresh only dabbled in Revelation, and was mainly a Swedenborgian.)

Rick brings up another issue—one of the FBI's constants—why can't David continue to spread his message from prison, where he will have a larger audience than he does currently? Steve never answers this satisfactorily, because he only wants to give the answer through very lengthy Bible studies, which the FBI doesn't care to hear. (The answer is that Koresh and his followers, unlike, for example, Saint Paul or Mohammed, are not interested in evangelizing the whole world; they are interested in playing the role which they believe the Bible assigns them: to be a small, righteous community in a sinful world [like Noah's family] and [again like Noah's family] to be the only humans who survive [or, perhaps, who receive eternal life] after the imminent Armageddon. As detailed in chapter 2, social worker Joyce Sparks understands the Davidian Armageddon mentality, but federal law enforcement has been ignoring her insights.)

No. 211. April 11, 7:38–11:42 p.m.

Some discussion of Louis Alaniz. He came from a Pentecostal background, which, in Steve's view, relies excessively on emotion and excitement, guided by the Holy Spirit. The Davidians are much more sober in this regard, focusing on textual analysis of the Bible. Koresh is revered as leader solely because of his biblical expositions, certainly not because of his personality. Louis is not quite "a convert," but is very interested in what he's learning about the Bible.

John-5 jokingly threatens to send Jesse Amen back inside. Steve: "Basically, all he ever said was amen, brother, amen, brother." Jesse sometimes talks about his father, Lord Lightning Amen.

No. 212. APRIL 11–12, 11:42 P.M.–12:56 A.M.

John-4 takes over on the "graveyard shift" for John-5, and has another friendly, light-hearted conversation with Steve that goes nowhere.

No. 213. APRIL 12–14 [NO START TIME LISTED, ENDS AT 11:31 P.M.].

John-5: "Do you have any way of fighting fire in there?"
  Steve: "Only, only God."

No. 214. APRIL 13–14, 11:31 P.M.–12:25 A.M.

Steve wants to send out more videotapes of the Davidians, but the FBI will accept them only if everyone leaves and brings the tapes with them.
  At John-4's request, Greg Summers comes to the phone. He complains about BATF shooting the mother of the prize malamute puppies he was raising.

No. 215. APRIL 13, 12:25–1:10 A.M.

Dick DeGuerin will be coming back in.

No. 216. APRIL 13, 1:10–1:55 A.M.

John-4 tells Koresh that Koresh is like the Wizard of Oz.

No. 217. APRIL 13 [NO START TIME–2:41 A.M.].

As a child, Koresh was into sports and very fit. He tried alcohol and marijuana a few times, and hated the feeling of loss of control of his body.

No. 218. APRIL 13, 2:41–3:26 A.M.

Koresh discusses old cars with John. Koresh mentions people talking about the seven seals, and John mentions folks wondering when he's coming out. No one's going to hear his side of the story until he comes out.
  Bible babble.

No. 219. APRIL 13, 3:26–4:13 A.M.

John and Koresh find common ground; they both smoke Marlboro Lights.
  Bible babble.
  Koresh mentions the cult awareness people, and says he doesn't mind his group being called a "cult."

No. 221. APRIL 13, 4:59–5:44 A.M.

Koresh complains about the tanks driving over Peter Gent's grave, crushing the flowers on it.

No. 222. APRIL 14, 5:44 A.M.–1:38 P.M. [MISLABELED A.M.].

DeGuerin wants to meet with Koresh, but Steve says Koresh can't transact any business until after Passover ends, at sundown.

No. 223. APRIL 14, 1:38 P.M.[MISLABELED A.M.]–7:31 P.M.

DeGuerin's proposed legal representation agreement with Koresh has been delivered; Steve wants a typewriter sent in, to work on modifications. Steve eventually agrees to send out handwritten modifications by five o'clock.

No. 224. APRIL 14, 7:31–9:41 P.M.

Steve is working on modifications to his agreement with Jack Zimmermann; as before, Steve is extremely worried about the size of the fee. Judy Schneider will be represented by Jim Levine, Zimmermann's partner.

The Davidians are collecting rainwater in buckets, and Steve says that they also get water from holding tanks connected to a well.

Steve: If you think that the noise bombardment and the tank activities are "causing people to want to come out sooner, it has the opposite effect on these people. It's like they want to dig in all the more. It's like, you know, you're doing that on behalf of God's power to strengthen these people's faith."

No. 225. APRIL 14–15, 9:41 P.M.–1:20 A.M.

Steve tells Duane that he's exhausted and burnt out.

Clint van Zandt questions Scott Sonobe on the seven seals' meaning.

Clint asks about water and learns they can get some from the roof.

No. 227. APRIL 15, 3:23–4:10 P.M.

Discussion with Steve as to why Koresh doesn't do his manuscript on tape, and have it transcribed by a good typist, which would be quicker. Steve agrees that it's important to come out and get this thing taken care of.

At the beginning of the siege, Steve was scared because someone came to kill them; once they see the house they'll see evidence of BATF's murderous intent. By Tuesday [March 2], Steve had relaxed, because there was some hope of a future.

Rick asks Steve about the length of Koresh's hair, whether he has any tattoos, etc. There has been some talk of a burning-cross tattoo on Koresh's chest, but Steve says no. And Steve hasn't any tattoos, and is not sure anyone in the compound has any.

Rick suggests Steve can bring out the papers; Steve wonders if he means Koresh's analysis of the seals. No, Steve's papers. Steve answers, "But that's not even a consideration whether I come out or not. . . . Because I will anyway. . . . [Koresh] was almost like breathing a sigh of relief yesterday morning when I went to talk to him and he gave me this paper. And when I read the paper [the surrender letter], it kind of surprised me. . . . I was definitely upbeat and glad that, you know, there was something even for me to look at. . . . It seems like this is the thing that all of a sudden I think he's implying it would seem to me that some time from God's perspective has been allowed for people to start hearing something about seven seals, and now finally it's time for them to go out."

Steve complains about some of the intimidating statements which have been made to someone with such a deep love of freedom.

Steve denies having any way of knowing if the threatened natural disaster is supposed to occur, say, when Koresh reaches the sixth seal.

Rick wonders why Koresh's followers, knowing he's about to come out anyway, don't just come out now and wait for him to finish with them on the outside. Because we still get lessons from him in here, Steve answers. And when we come out, we won't all have direct access to him for questions and leadership.

No. 228. April 15, 4:10–6:24 p.m.

Steve notes that Koresh gets his information supernaturally and he's opening up the seals in his manuscript. "It's opening it up to the entire world. It will show you where that first seal is. He'll give you all the text that for you to read it on your own you will understand it."

Bible babble, the gist of which is things have different meanings for different generations of mankind.

Steve's been treated pretty well by the negotiators, and he's confident he'll come out; he likes all the negotiators. It's something else with BATF.

Among other things, Rick wants Steve to glance at Koresh's chest to check out the tattoo story.

Rick: Let's see if we're on the same wavelength in terms of deadlines.

In response to what Koresh has completed, no, Steve hasn't seen anything, but the news of yesterday [the surrender letter] was a surprise to him.

John: "Upon completion of the manuscript on the seven seals, you folks are planning on coming out forthwith?"

Steve: "Yes. Positively."

FBI wants to ask Koresh some questions but they don't want to take him away from his manuscript. But they would like to talk to Koresh about 7 p.m.

Koresh notes that he doesn't expect good treatment once he finishes his manuscript and leaves. And Steve says that Koresh says, "I'm coming out even though I'm going to be looked upon as an oddity, as a bizarre thing. And I don't believe even though the FBI they mean well about taking me through the system and, you know, harm and all that. He, he doesn't have a problem with that. But he just knows what it's going to be like. But irregardless, when he's told he'll do something he does it."

Steve expresses irritation again at a flashbang thrown at a Davidian.

No. 231. April 15, 8:17–9:04 p.m.

Koresh discusses the seals' meaning with Clint.

Bible babble. Clint asks if we're in the last days foretold in Revelation, to which Koresh says yes.

Koresh recounts briefly the opening assault, of jumping back from the door, etc.

No. 232. April 15, 9:04–9:51 p.m.

Clint talks with Koresh, self-described, repeatedly, as a mechanic and "I'm a carpenter."

Clint complains about references to different clocks; courts operate on man's.

Koresh: "I didn't bring these things on. You never found nothing illegal here."

After a long argument between Clint and Koresh about the seven seals, Koresh: "Do you want to know the seven seals or not?"

Clint: "No, David."

Koresh says he said he'd work on the seven seals: "Didn't I tell you I'd be out as soon as I finished my work?" Will he be out quickly? Is two thousand years quickly? the equivalent of two days in God's eyes?

Clint suggests Koresh might be stalling since he knows, once he's out, he won't be able to tell folks to turn to psalm this or that as he is now doing. Clint suggests that if Koresh came out now, he would have just as much time to complete the seals, and better conditions.

No. 233. April 15–16, 9:51 p.m.–2:00 a.m.

Unidentified agent says finish the seals and come out.

Then back to Dick and Steve. Dick says he came back to Waco because he heard they were coming out. But when? Steve again complains of Bradleys frightening the kids. Mankind wants to see something spectacular. Dick asks if that means more bloodshed.

Dick notes that his belief is that the seven seals manuscript is nothing more than a stalling tactic. Steve: "If you think we're stalling, what that tank just did, you can go get the big—you can get the Abrams. Go get 10 of those, if you'd like, and run right through the entire building. . . . You will see people—and I'd come out screaming and all the rest. If you think we're stalling, do what you feel or you know that you need to do, Dick, and I'm not—I'm telling you it's not a stalling tactic."

Dick: "Well, you still have to deal with the laws of man, do you not, Steve?"

Steve: "I do. I do. But God I fear first though, Dick."

Dick observes that when Koresh says they're coming, he doesn't say whether the exit will be today, tomorrow, next week, next month, or next year. Steve doesn't know the time frame, Dick says, and nobody does.

Steve denounces the overly powerful federal government where folks like Dick can't be voted out of office. He recounts the killing of Branch Davidians and sneers at the idea there will be punishment, suggesting it will be limited to having a few reprimands. Dick responds that the Branch Davidians were armed and prepared to shoot BATF. Steve: "I, I hope that the ATF themselves did take a video even before the first shot, because that'll exonerate us. It will. And I hope that the press were here."

Dick suggests Koresh is stalling out of fear, to which Steve notes he doesn't fear death, and Dick suggests it's not death he's facing, it's a court of law and telling his story.

No. 234. April 16, 2:00–2:45 a.m.

Steve denies that Koresh has taken the wives of Branch Davidians. Steve admits that "carnally" he often wishes he had never met David Koresh, but "spiritually" Steve fears "the unknown power" found in the Bible.

Koresh comes by, and Steve says that Koresh is working on the manuscript for the second seal.

No. 235. April 16, 2:45–3:30 a.m.

Koresh says his completed first seal manuscript, which still needs to be edited by Steve, is twenty-five to twenty-eight pages long. Koresh: "I'm one of the hottest guitar players LA ever saw." Koresh says that as soon as DeGuerin delivers the manuscript to the theologians, Koresh will come out with DeGuerin.

No. 236. April 16, 3:30 a.m.–11:06 p.m.

Steve complains that a Bradley bumped into a wall, causing minor injuries to Graeme Craddock and frightening Cyrus Koresh. Negotiator Henry is handed a note saying the incident was unintentional. Steve warns that he can't control everybody inside, and says that somebody may be provoked to do something.

Steve says the fourth seal is especially deep and complicated, leading Henry to wonder if it will take a long time to write. Steve thinks not, because Koresh writes by divine inspiration.

Judy Schneider says she has "maybe a couple pages" transcribed to disk.

No. 237. April 16–17, 11:06 p.m.–3:29 a.m.

Rick-1 and Phil Henry have a pleasant conversation, in which Phil does not accept Rick's suggestion than Phil is placing too much faith in one man.

Louis Alaniz calls and asks to be picked up by a Bradley. "I have seen something in which I've seen inside the Bible and which can cut all this out completely." He asks that the FBI have King James Bibles ready to study with him when he comes out.

The tape records Alaniz talking to an unidentified person inside the compound: "I know David is the Lamb." Alaniz wants to come out and share the message so that other people can be saved. But he reports that the other Davidians are "upset" that "I'm walking out of the body. . . . They said I'm going to be lost."

Louis acknowledges to Dwayne that Steve has been trying to talk Louis out of leaving. (This suggests that Steve's frequent claims to the FBI negotiators that he has been trying to talk people into leaving may now be lies. In fact, one reason that nobody wants to come out is because Steve is warning them that they will be damned forever if they do.)

Later, Koresh discusses Jesse Amen with Dwayne. Koresh says that Jesse Amen claimed that there are twenty thousand people waiting for a signal to come challenge the FBI and save the Davidians.

Koresh says he is finishing the second seal. In response to an FBI question, Koresh says he could send out the first two seals, rather than waiting for the entire manuscript to be finished.

No. 238. April 17, 3:29 a.m.–8:32 p.m.

Koresh is willing to send out the first seal once Judy gets done typing it.

No. 239. April 17, 8:32–9:26 p.m.

Steve discusses typewriter ribbons with John Cox. Judy Schneider suggests they don't need an office so much as electricity.

Louis Alaniz, debriefed, noted he was a little thirsty, and Steve explains they've had to ration water. Steve is praised for still having his sense of humor. Steve hints he hopes it won't go on much longer; he's certainly sick of the place. He says that Davidians are talking about gray walls [jail] as better than this place. Steve is asked if Koresh is "staying busy on this thing?" Yes, he responds, Koresh is upstairs working on it. He's working on the second seal; Steve has been waiting for him to give him the first. The FBI said in the press conference that Steve was already editing the first, which wasn't true. Koresh wants to redo a couple of things.

Steve notes that not all the FBI's bright lights are on anymore, semi-complaining that he had found a couple of places where he could use those lights to read.

Asked if he, too, is planning to write a book, Steve notes he may have to write a book just to pay for his attorneys, having seen some preliminary statements of the fees, based on their having to face the press. Steve expresses regret that the siege kept negotiators away from normal work and family for so long. The negotiator pressures Steve to get Koresh working on it, and Steve agrees.

Koresh hadn't thought of doing this before because he's not a writer but a speaker, and the Bible's already been written. The seven seals are like a movie preview.

Judy's finger is healed but splinted, so she can't bend it.

Bible babble.

Koresh came down to stretch his legs, he says. His hand's getting crampy; he's not used to writing so much. John suggests using a pair of secretaries and dictating to speed things along. Koresh notes that he was using tapes, but they weren't working too well.

They discuss jokingly the music the FBI should be playing.

No. 240. April 17–18, 9:26 p.m.–2:15 p.m.

This is the endgame and both sides know it, although it's not clear that the FBI knows the Branch Davidians know.

First, the FBI has good reason to believe that the seven seals manuscript is just a stall. Koresh sends out a drawing by one of his followers (the dream statue from the Book of Daniel), which has prophetic significance for the Branch Davidians (they interpret it to show that America is the fourth and final kingdom foretold in the dream), but the drawing does not get Koresh any closer to completion of his own manuscript.

Second, Steve notes that he's particularly curious to see what Koresh has to say about the seventh seal; he was just beginning to teach the topic at the time of the BATF raid. So while the part of the manuscript dealing with the first six seals would simply summarize existing teachings, the seventh seal portion would involve material new to Koresh, with potentially slower composition as a result.

Third, Koresh flatly refuses to provide an explanation why he must stay in the compound. Why isn't it true that he could work in jail? "Because it's just not," he says.

One of the motifs of the fifty-one days gets a final reprise: Steve hates hot, dry, barren Waco and the spartan conditions in the compound—what he calls "the anthill" —and hated them long before the BATF showed up. "This has always been a stumbling block for me being here." He never would have left his paradise-on-earth home in Hawaii, which he and Judy both loved, but for what Judy and he saw as the only path to eternal life.

Steve feels forgiving toward everyone, including the tactical team and the negotiators, but he wishes that just one of the negotiators had an interest in what will happen to them after death. [But in fact, two of them clearly do: Byron Sage is a strongly committed Christian, and Clinton van Zandt is a fundamentalist Sunday school teacher with a well-worn copy of the King James Bible. Both have tried to engage Koresh directly as Christians, but he has refused to answer questions directly, instead attempting to perform a mini-Bible study, in which the questioner will answer his own question after seeing the appropriate verses. Defenders of Koresh might point out that Jesus also tended to answer questions elliptically, using parables, or answering a question with a question. This is true, but does not change the fact that even the FBI's most religious negotiators could not open a genuine dialogue with Koresh. When a direct question did receive a direct answer, the answer was often false (as when Steve and Koresh denied that the fifth seal is in progress).]

The negotiators reprise their own key theme with Schneider: urging him to take responsibility for himself, his family, and his fellow Davidians by leading at least some of them out. [But there was no reason to believe he would ever do so. He came close once, in late March, when he was exhausted, but Judy Schneider apparently talked him out of it, and he has never weakened since then.]

Louis Alaniz left today. Henry asks, "Is anybody interested in exiting stage left?" No one is. [As discussed in earlier negotiations, none of the Davidians can just step out of the tragedy like Alaniz did. All the adults know that they will be arrested the moment they leave. At best, they face months in jail and will have to spend their life savings on defense attorneys.]

For the second time in a short period, David Jones has snuck out the back door and wandered around outside. Steve is apologetic and says he will talk to Koresh about whether they should kick Jones out.

The Jones incident provides the negotiators with a pretext for the final perimeter-tightening and ground-clearing before the upcoming tank assault. They tell Steve to keep people out of the tower, but he says their order will not be obeyed.

Any more milk has been out of the question for weeks now, but Henry suddenly inquires if the children have enough and indicates an openness to new requests.

The ground-clearing is about to destroy Koresh's prize 1968 Camaro. Steve passes on Koresh's warning that everything is now changed; cooperation is ended. Evoking prior FBI warnings to the Davidians, he hints at unspecified reactions. "We're going to be doing something different," says Steve.

Koresh comes on the phone, promising anger and wrath: "If this is the corner of the box you placed me into . . . ," and then he and Henry disagree on who put Koresh in the corner.

The FBI tells Koresh that fifty people must come out tomorrow, and if not, unspecified actions will be taken.

Koresh: "I'm not going to . . . you don't understand these people yet."

Henry: "And you don't understand about the people here either."

Steve says, "No one believes anyone will be coming back here again." Steve says he doesn't mind because "this world is not my place." Like Abraham in Hebrews 11, Steve is a sojourner on a way to a better home. Henry optimistically looks forward to a period "to rebuild, to resurrect." Steve agrees, but surprises Henry with his comment, "There will be a time to resurrect, but I'm talking from the dead."

No. 241. April 17, 2:15–2:17 p.m.

Unidentified male speaker: "We'll talk to them, okay?"

Koresh: "Well, you better do it right now."

No. 242. April 18, 2:17–5:42 [p.m.].

Steve complains to Dwayne about tanks being driven destructively, as if by kids.

Asked if he is frustrated by Koresh, Steve says he is, a bit. Dwayne says he knows Koresh is working on the manuscript but "out of nowhere" there is pressure to see where the manuscript stands.

Steve: "I'm not sure what he's going to do or not do. I think it may slow the whole process down."

Dwayne: "We didn't want anything to . . . slow that down."

Koresh was very upset by the new movements of the tanks, "extremely . . . he was . . . not a happy camper." Koresh was concerned about the evidence being destroyed by the tanks, the shell casings from "the ATF when they fired upon the building. . . ."

Dwayne insists that all the tank activity is for safety reasons, and doubts that the commanders will listen to him.

Dwayne tells Steve that no one's allowed on the water tower. Steve says that order won't be heeded. Dwayne insists that the vehicles they ran over with tanks looked to the FBI like hiding places. Steve is assured there won't be any shooting, but Steve assures Dwayne the orders to stay out of the tower won't be heeded even if it means shooting.

It's not just Koresh, Steve says, but all the Davidians have said they won't comply: "the Constitution has been so ripped apart and run over. . . . You tell the commanders that if they tell us to not stay in some portion of our building, you can tell them it's not going to be heeded. . . . They . . . can burn the place down."

Dwayne calls the new rules "rules of safety."

Steve infers that the commanders are itching for them to start something. The Davidians don't like being told what to do on their premises—"freedoms of being Americans." Steve still insists BATF came "intent for murder," based on shots through Koresh's ceiling and the front door.

Steve complains that even if he is acquitted, he will have to spend six months in jail. Dwayne asks if he got the idea of six months in jail from his attorney, Zimmermann? Steve says yes, that "my life has been affected by this government, not the people of America but by this government, by agencies that have become so powerful."

Steve recalls that the response to sending seven Davidians out was destruction and weird noises. Every time the Davidians did something to cooperate—like the manuscript—"all of a sudden, they do more destruction. It seems like it always coincides."

Today, Steve recalls, Henry brought up the milk idea. Yesterday typewriter ribbons were discussed, but they were discussed as part of a quid pro quo. Now, Steve says, the milk "really surprised the heck out of me."

Dwayne notes that the children are the "true innocents." Steve: "I think all of us are. I don't care if I'm a baby that's 43 years old. . . ."

Dwayne says that the commanders want evidence regarding the seals. "We don't have much hope that he's really doing this," so they want a show of good faith or progress. Dwayne wants evidence that Koresh is working on the manuscript. Steve says he's not right now; he just walked by. Dwayne: over the last few days?

Steve: "Oh, he has been but I don't know about now." Steve isn't sure if Koresh will continue after what's been done in front. "He's not working on it now, for the first time in the daytime."

Steve complains to Dek of folks in the helicopter flipping the finger.

Steve repeats that Koresh hasn't done any writing since the destruction in the front yard began. There's nothing for Steve to edit. Dwayne says that he's not trying to push but he would like it if Schneider could send the first seal out, something tangible to show the bosses, some of whom are skeptical of Koresh's and Steve's promises.

No. 243. April 18, 5:42–6:21 p.m.

Steve agrees with Dwayne's observation that Steve seems to "kind of live for the next life rather than this life." Steve recalls that he might have said some nasty things on the phone out of tiredness or frustration, but that he always apologizes. He recounts again that there were never plans to go and harm anyone. The guns were for investment, after meeting Henry [McMahon]; Mike Schroeder did a lot of the buying down at the Mag Bag.

Asked why the Davidians had so much ammunition, Steve says they had heard those prices were going to skyrocket, too.

Dwayne doesn't mean to push but is progress being made? Is Judy typing? Not really. Judy asked for a laptop computer, Dwayne recalls, but if the commanders won't send in batteries, they certainly won't send in a computer. "Things kinda went downhill from there. But I guess in coming back to that confirmation that, you know, they're asking me, now, look, you can't just send this in and have them say, well, no, we never agreed to send out the first manuscript when it's completed. That's your understanding and my understanding of the, the agreement."

Steve says Koresh has finished the first seal; he saw a stack of maybe twenty sheets.

Dwayne suggests having Judy start typing seal one while Koresh proceeds to seal two. He suggests again the use of the legal secretaries in the residence since Koresh is good at talking but not at writing. Dwayne wonders about whether tapes could be used, "I guess I have to ask you, if we send in the cassettes, the, the, you know, the cassettes for the Casio, can we count on the agreement that we set up yesterday?"

Steve: "I don't know now because of all that took place out front and all that. . . . I better talk to him."

Dwayne says he's not trying to push, just to reach an agreement on whether, if the FBI sends in ink cartridges, things will go more quickly. Dwayne notes that Koresh may ponder it for two or three days, or more than that. But then the commanders may perceive it as reneging on the agreement.

Steve says he's committed to doing what he's doing regardless of whether the FBI sends in milk and cassettes. Steve has asked Koresh for the first seal, but Koresh won't let him have it. Steve needs to make changes (especially because of all the errors from Koresh's bad grammar and spelling), and to tie the first seal manuscript into the second seal manuscript.

Dictating may help; Steve agrees, and says Koresh responded in a positive manner to the suggestion.

Dwayne asks if they don't want the cassette and some milk. Steve says they will take them, but not if the commanders think it means there has been some kind of promise.

Steve: "I think it would go a long way to showing that you definitely want to help us in getting it done."

Dwayne: "Well, I think maybe we're willing to make that gesture now."

Selected Bibliography

This selected bibliography lists sources which were particularly important to this book, or which would be especially useful to researchers wishing to investigate Waco further.

BOOKS AND MONOGRAPHS

Abrams, Norman, and Sara Sun Beale. *Federal Criminal Law*, 2d ed. St. Paul: West, 1993. A legal treatise surveying the vast scope of federal criminal powers.
Applegate, Rex. *Unpublished Report on FBI Planning and Operations Relating to the CS Gas Assault at Waco, Texas, February 28 to April 19, 1993*. Scottsburg, Oregon, 1995. An analysis of the FBI's plan and use of CS against the Branch Davidian residence by a leading authority on police and military riot control. The monograph is based on imprecise details of the layout of the residence, but fairly complete knowledge of CS. Appendices including manufacturers' warnings about the CS and its delivery systems.
Boyer, Paul. *When Time Shall Be No More: Prophecy Belief in Modern American Culture*. Cambridge, Mass.: Harvard University Press, 1992. The best survey of apocalypticism in the second half of the twentieth century in America.
Breault, Marc, and Martin King. *Inside the Cult*. New York: Signet, 1993. The story of Koresh's former chief advisor, turned apostate, as told to a television tabloid journalist. A very valuable original source, although seriously marred by King's sleazy approach and by Breault's unreliability on numerous factual issues.
Burnham, David. *Above the Law*. New York: Scribner, 1996. An excellent survey of the Department of Justice.
Chevigny, Paul. *Edge of the Knife: Police Violence in the Americas*. New York: The New Press, 1995. A multination look at police violence, and public attitudes toward it.

Chosen Vessel, The. *Seven Seals.* No publisher named, 1996. Two volumes of post-Koresh Branch Davidian theology. Apparently written by one or more Davidian prisoners.

Cole, Ron. *Sinister Twilight.* Longmont, Colo.: self-published, 1994. Story of Waco by a Branch Davidian convert.

DeVault, Jack. *The Waco Whitewash: The Mt. Carmel Episode Told by an Eyewitness to the Trial.* San Antonio: Rescue Press, 1994. A useful summary of the day-to-day trial proceedings and sentencing of the Branch Davidians, by someone openly sympathetic to the defendants. The book is prefaced with a summary of the assault and siege, and information about the participants in the judicial proceedings, and includes documents regarding the charges and various legal issues involved in those proceedings, as well as the transcript of the Davidians' 911 call to the local sheriff's office. Because DeVault was summarizing the evidence he heard, rather than relying on the transcripts, some of his interpretations of the testimony differ slightly from the transcribed testimony.

Failure Analysis Associates, Inc. *Investigation of the April 19, 1993 Assault on the Mt. Carmel Center, Waco, Texas.* Menlo Park, Calif., July 1995. An evaluation of the actual likely results of the various assaults on the Mount Carmel Center based on the amounts, manner, and timing of CS insertion into various parts of the building, and of the origins of the fire based upon FLIR and other photographic evidence.

Fawcett, Ken. *Blind Justice: A Chronology of the Historic Trial of Eleven Branch Davidians in January 1994,* 2d ed. Royse City, Tex.: Electropress, 1994. Similar to the DeVault book mentioned above. As with the DeVault book, there are some discrepancies between the author's recollection of the testimony and the trial transcript.

Hardy, David. *The B.A.T.F.'s War on Civil Liberties.* Bellevue, Wash.: Second Amendment Foundation, 1979. A thorough exposition of BATF abuses through the late 1970s. There are few violent incidents.

Hart, Paul 't. *Groupthink in Government: A Study of Small Groups and Policy Failure.* Amsterdam: Swets and Zeitlinger, 1990. A rigorous exploration of a sometimes amorphous concept.

Kessler, Ronald. *The FBI.* New York: Pocket Books, 1993. A good overview of the bureau, although limited by the author's "gee-whiz" attitude towards the G-men. The book helped cause the downfall of FBI Director William Sessions, when the author discovered certain improprieties involving Sessions and his wife.

Koresh, David. *The Decoded Message of the Seven Seals of the Book of Revelation.* Axtell, Tex.: General Association of Branch Davidian Seventh-day Adventists, 1994. The manuscript is reproduced as an appendix, with commentary by Phil Arnold and Jim Tabor, in Tabor and Gallagher, pp. 191–211. Also available from The Research Center at http://www.ime.net/~mswett, and Joint Hearings, part 2, pp. 227–45.

Lewis, James R., ed. *From the Ashes: Making Sense of Waco.* Lanham, Md.: Rowman and Littlefield, 1993. The first serious book about Waco, supplying a wealth of information and insights from numerous scholars. Supplanted, however, by Stuart Wright's collection of essays, published two years later.

Linedecker, Clifford L. *The Massacre at Waco, Texas.* New York: St. Martin's, 1993. Insta-trash. Mass-market paperbacks which go from concept to bookstore in a few weeks should not be criticized just because they are hastily written. But Line-decker's ready acceptance of federal propaganda and his antipathy toward the Branch Davidians, whom he spent little energy trying to understand, make this book an excellent exemplar of the mass media's complicity in the atmosphere of hate. Linedecker's other books include: *Thrill Killers* (Toronto: Paper Jacks, 1988), *Serial Thrill Killers* (New York: Knightsbridge, 1990), *Hell Ranch* (New York: Tob, 1990), and *The Man Who Killed Boys* (New York: St. Martin's, 1980).

McCarroll, James E., Carol S. Fullerton, Robert J. Ursano, and Joan M. Hermsen. *Psychological Stress of Forensic Dental Examinations: The Waco Disaster.* Washington, D.C.: Walter Reed Army Institute of Research, Division of Neuropsychiatry, Department of General Psychiatry, August 1, 1994. How the forensic dentists coped with the mental stress of identifying so many bodies.

McMahon, Henry Stanley, Jr., and Karen J. Kilpatrick. *In re: Interviews of Henry Stanley McMahon, Jr. and Karen J. Kilpatrick,* deposition taken May 25, 1993. An interview, under oath, of Koresh's gun dealers, involving their knowledge of Koresh, the guns and related items he owned and used, their experiences with the Davidians (Kilpatrick had more access to the women and children), and McMahon and Kilpatrick's treatment by the government following the initial assault on Mount Carmel. The interview occurred after the final assault and while it was unclear whether the government's intentions with regard to McMahon and Kilpatrick included prosecution or apology.

Moore, Carol. *The Davidian Massacre.* Frankin, Tenn.: Legacy Communications and Gunowners Foundation, 1995. 1–800–417–1486. Thoroughly documented, well-written, book-length argument in favor of the Branch Davidians, who are seen as entirely without fault. Earlier version of the book available on the Internet at http://www.shadeslanding.com/firearms/waco.massacre.html.

Reavis, Dick. *The Ashes of Waco: An Investigation.* New York: Simon and Schuster, 1995. The best journalistic account. Starts with the background of Koresh and the Branch Davidians and proceeds through the trial. The book is not interested in putting the incident in the wider context of trends in federal law enforcement, and avoids both the drawbacks and advantages of documentation and endnotes. Internet site for the book is http://rampages.onramp.net/~djreavis/.

Samples, Kenneth, Erwin de Castro, Richard Abanes, and Robert Lyle. *Prophets of the Apocalypse: David Koresh & Other American Messiahs.* Grand Rapids: Baker, 1994. Fundamentalist Christians examine the Branch Davidians, and detail their deviations from Christian orthodoxy. The best source for life at Mount Carmel in the early 1980s. Includes transcripts of interviews with apostate Branch Davidians, and Koresh's mother.

Scott, Alice. *The Incredible Power of Cults.* Colorado Springs: Blue River Publishing, 1994. Anticult book by mother of a man who joined the Branch Davidians for a while. A good summary of the basic anticult position, and a very interesting final chapter detailing her son's experiences.

Singer, Margaret Thaler. *Cults in Our Midst: The Hidden Menace in Our Everyday Lives.* San Francisco: Jossey-Bass, 1995. Shows the cutting edge of the anticult movement (cults should be considered a public health problem), along with a good deal of common sense (employees should not be forced to attend New Age motivational programs which infringe upon their religious beliefs).

Tabor, James D., and Eugene V. Gallagher. *Why Waco? Cults and the Battle for Religious Freedom in America.* Berkeley: University of California Press, 1995. The best analysis of Branch Davidian religious doctrine and its connection to mainstream religious thought. Also the best source for the story of the attempt by Professors Tabor and Arnold to convince Koresh that surrender would be religiously legitimate. Puts Waco in the context of religious intolerance. Promotional website is: http://www.neo.com/ucalpress/whywaco.

Wright, Stuart A., ed. *Armageddon in Waco: Critical Perspectives on the Branch Davidian Conflict.* Chicago: University of Chicago Press, 1995. Excellent, well-documented, thoughtful analyses of Waco by various scholars, with special emphasis on religious issues.

Journal, Newspaper, and Magazine Articles

The main newspapers consulted were the *New York Times*, *Washington Post*, *Washington Times*, and *Dallas Morning News*, from which we read nearly every Waco or Weaver article. The reporting in the first three of these newspapers was consistently better than the superficial, extremely slanted wire-service accounts which ran in many local newspapers. Jerry Seper of the *Washington Times* did a particularly thorough job of examining the issue of use of CS gas. The *Dallas Morning News* stories were uneven; daily reports tended to simply repeat the government version of the facts, while the longer, perspective stories were well-balanced and thought-provoking.

Adams, James. "FBI Brings out Secret Electronic Weapons as Waco Siege Drags On." London *Sunday Times*, March 21, 1993. The mainstream American press ignored this report of use of British military electronic warfare at Waco.

Bovard, James. "The New J. Edgar Hoover." *American Spectator* (August 1995): 28–35. A good review of how Louis Freeh has disappointed the high hopes held for him, and how he has used his political and media connections to enhance the power of the FBI and its director at the expense of the Bill of Rights.

Boyer, Peter J. "Children of Waco." *The New Yorker* (May 15, 1995). Examines the issue of child abuse at Waco in the context of Janet Reno's troubled childhood and her child abuse prosecutions in Miami.

Bradford, R. W. "There's No Kill Like Overkill." *Liberty* (August 1993). An impassioned libertarian critique of Waco, as part of a special Waco issue.

Dunlap, Charles J., Jr., "Welcome to the Junta: The Erosion of Civilian Control of the U.S. Military." 29 *Wake Forest Law Review* 341 (1994). An award-winning, frightening examination of current trends.

Hardy, David T. "Use of CS Gas at Waco." Available at http://www.indirect.com/www/dhardy/CS_Gas_at_Waco. Makes a powerful case that many people at Waco were incapacitated or killed by the CS.

Hennig, Karl. "Apocalyptic Rock: My Days with David Koresh." *Liberty* (July/August

1993). An ex-Davidian writes for a Seventh-day Adventist magazine. One of the first serious attempts to explain Koresh's theology. (This magazine is distinct from the libertarian magazine *Liberty* cited above.)

Hu, Howard, et al. "Tear Gas—Harassing Agent or Toxic Chemical Weapon?" *JAMA* (*Journal of the American Medical Association*) 262 (August 4, 1989): 660. The answer is the latter.

Larson, Erik. "ATF Under Siege." *Time* (July 24, 1995). BATF has its problems, but the new management is fixing them.

McLaughlin, Vance, and Steve Smith. "The Rodney King Syndrome," paper presented at the annual meeting of the Academy of Criminal Justice Sciences, 1993, forthcoming in *Journal on Firearms and Public Policy* 9 (1997). How law enforcement frustration can lead to violence.

Pate, James L. "ATF's Bloody Sunday." *Soldier of Fortune* (June 1993).

———. "Gun Gestapo's Day of Infamy." *Soldier of Fortune*, (June 1993).

———. "Waco Standoff Ends in Disaster." *Soldier of Fortune* (July 1993).

———. "No Longer Untouchable." *American Spectator* (August 1993). The fall of the BATF.

———. "Waco's Defective Warrants: No Probable Cause for Raid on Ranch Apocalypse." *Soldier of Fortune* (August 1993).

———. "What the Feds Don't Want You to Know about Waco." *Soldier of Fortune* (October 1993).

———. "Waco: Behind the Cover-Up." *Soldier of Fortune* (November 1993).

———. "One Hand Whitewashes the Other." *Soldier of Fortune* (February 1994).

———. "We Have Truth on Our Side: Jailhouse Interviews with Branch Davidians." *Soldier of Fortune* (July 1994).

———. "Wacogate." *Soldier of Fortune* (June 1995).

Pate's Waco series was given the Mencken Award by the Free Press Association "in recognition of his investigative articles about the Waco massacre for *Soldier of Fortune*." The award is established for "outstanding journalism in support of liberty as chosen by their professional peers."

Steinke, Darcey. "God Rocks." *Spin* (July 1993). Koresh's musical career in Waco clubs and California.

Tammeus, David. "Religion: The Overlooked Key to the Waco Tragedy." *Boulder Daily Camera* (April 24, 1994). Summary of how the FBI ignored the role of religion while besieging a group of religious zealots.

Vinzant, Carol. "ATF-Troop." *Spy* (March 1994). A good overview of how BATF's institutional culture created its current problems.

Wattenberg, Daniel. "Gunning for Koresh." *American Spectator* (August 1993). One of the first widely circulated articles to question the premises behind federal activities at Waco. A superb summary of the background and flaws in the BATF investigation of David Koresh.

GOVERNMENT REPORTS AND LEGISLATIVE TESTIMONY

Aguilera, Davy. "Application and Affidavit for Search and Arrest Warrants for Vernon Wayne Howell and the Residence of Vernon Wayne Howell, and Others." Waco, Texas, February 25, 1993. Available at http://www.shadeslanding.com/firearms/read6.html.

Bureau of Alcohol, Tobacco and Firearms. "Transcripts of BATF Tapes of the Negotiations between Federal Law Enforcement and the Branch Davidians, February 28–April 19, 1993" (cited as "Negot. Tapes").

Dennis, Edward S. G., Jr. *Evaluation of the Handling of the Branch Davidian Stand-Off in Waco, Texas, February 28 to April 19, 1993, Redacted Version* (Washington, D.C.: Department of Justice, October 8, 1993).

Dunagan, Earl. "Application and Affidavit for Search Warrant for the Residence of Vernon Wayne Howell, and Others, Waco, Texas, March 9, 1993" (cited as "Dunagan, Howell Affidavit").

———. "Criminal Complaint and Affidavit, United States v. Woodrow Hendricks" [*sic*, "Kendrick"], Waco, Texas, March 5, 1993 (cited as "Dunagan, Kendrick Affidavit").

Dunagan, Earl, and Davy Aguilera. "Application and Affidavit for Search of Residence of Vernon Wayne Howell, and Others," Waco, Texas, April 4, 1993.

Heymann, Phillip B. *Lessons of Waco: Proposed Changes in Federal Law Enforcement* (Washington, D.C.: Department of Justice, October 8, 1993).

KPOC TV. *Overview and General Information of Criminal Negligence by Agents of Federal Government*, report for U.S. Senate Judiciary Committee, August 1994.

Tarrant County Medical Examiner. Autopsy reports, including photos, are available at http://www.mnsinc.com/SkyWriter/WacoMuseum/death/map/d_list00.html.

Trial Transcript. *United States* v. *Brad Branch et al.*, Crim. Action No. W-93-CR-046 (W.D.Tex., 1994) (cited as "Trial Transcript").

U.S. Department of Justice. *Department of Justice Report Regarding Internal Investigation of Shootings at Ruby Ridge, Idaho, during Arrest of Randy Weaver* (cited as "DOJ Internal Investigation of Ruby Ridge"), available at http://www.courttv.com/library/government/ruby.html. The report has never been formally released. After withholding the report for years, the Department of Justice finally said that the report was so old it was not worth releasing.

———. *Recommendations of Experts for Improvements in Federal Law Enforcement After Waco* (Washington, D.C., 1993).

———. *Report on the Events at Waco, Texas, February 28 to April 19, 1993* (redacted version, Washington, D.C.: October 8, 1993) (cited as "Justice Report"). A useful, if biased, misleading, and sometimes dishonest summary of the FBI's efforts at Waco. Addresses some concerns, while generally white-washing any individual responsibility for the disaster.

U.S. Department of the Treasury. *Report on the Bureau of Alcohol, Tobacco, and Firearms, Investigation of Vernon Wayne Howell also known as David Koresh* (Washington, D.C.: Government Printing Office, September 1993) (cited as "Treasury Report"). A largely worthless and dishonest summary of the investigation of David

Koresh. More useful when it studies the planning of the February 28 raid and the damage control efforts which followed. Some of the material in the appendix is also useful.

U.S. House of Representatives. *Events Surrounding the Branch Davidian Cult Standoff in Waco, Texas*, Hearing before the Committee on the Judiciary, U.S. House of Representatives, 103rd Cong., 1st sess., April 28, 1993 (cited as "Hearing"). This early investigation provides some information, but is more interesting for how much the stories were changed for the 1995 congressional hearings.

————. Subcommittee on Crime of the Committee on the Judiciary and the Subcommittee on National Security, International Affairs, and Criminal Justice of the Committee on Government Reform and Oversight. *Joint Hearings on Activities of Federal Law Enforcement Agencies Toward the Branch Davidians*, 104th Cong., 1st sess., July 19–August 1, 1995 (Washington, D.C.: Government Printing Office, 1996) (cited as "Joint Hearings"). Even if the Joint Hearings failed to ask the right questions or follow up the wrong answers, they pried materials loose from the government which otherwise would have remained secret. And the published hearings provide a valuable collection of the views of all sides, along with some documents (often printed more than once). The published transcript version is often inaccurate and badly punctuated, inferior to the overnight transcripts. (Our favorite example is Rep. Peter Blute's and Prof. Alan Stone's discussion of infants, babies, and toddlers, which the published transcript translates as "totterers" [part 2, p. 403].)

————. Committee on Government Reform and Oversight in conjunction with the Committee on the Judiciary. *Investigation into the Activities of Federal Law Enforcement Agencies Toward the Branch Davidians*, Report 104–179, 104th Cong., 1st sess. (Washington, D.C.: Government Printing Office, August 2, 1996) (cited as "Committee Report"). While generally indifferent about the Fourth, Fifth, and Sixth Amendment issues affecting David Koresh and the other Branch Davidians, and overly political (preferring to blame high-level Democrats for failing to take control rather than blame career employees for deceits), the report provides an excellent summary of the planning, assaults, and siege at Waco, and—using documents elicited by the hearings—is especially strong in its analyses of the drug nexus/Defense Department and CS issues. The 110-page summary of the House Report can be obtained for free from House Documents, 3rd & D St. SW, Ford Building, Room B-18, Washington, DC 20515. (202) 225–3456. Also available from the congressional "Thomas" website: http://thomas.loc.gov.

VIDEOS

Branch Davidians home video. 117 min. P.O. Box 3390, St. Johns, AZ 85936. $30.00. Also available from the CAUSE Foundation, P.O. Box 1235, 1112½ Montreat Road Suite 1, Black Mountain, NC 28711. Tel (704) 669–5189. Fax (704) 669–5191. The home video was filmed by Steve Schneider, sent out in early March 1993, and kept from public view by the FBI until the siege was over. Schneider interviews almost all the Branch Davidian adults and children, including Koresh. This is an essential source for anyone making a serious effort to understand the Branch Davidians.

David Thibodeau: A Waco Survivor Speaks Out. Produced by Liberty Productions, P.O. Box 261, Elyria, OH 44036–0261. (216) 365–3040. $20.00. An interview and then a very long speech by David Thibodeau. The former drummer for Koresh's band comes across as an engaging and well-spoken young man. He was not part of the Koresh inner circle, so he was in some respects an observer of the Waco events rather than a shaper. The speech is particularly persuasive in explaining how the aggressive actions of the FBI tactical team undermined the Davidians' interest in coming out of their besieged home.

Day 51: The True Story of Waco. 60 min. Copyright listing is "UTV," but no further information is supplied on the box. Available from Mount Carmel Survivors Fund, address listed below under "Organizations." Professional quality, technically excellent video features Branch Davidian convert Ron Cole posing as an "investigator," and summarizing Branch Davidian perspective at Mount Carmel. Includes extensive interview with a Waco-area doctor who had several Branch Davidian patients. Like the Linda Thompson videos, this is a very important video among the Patriot/militia movements.

Gun Owners of America, *Breaking the Law . . . in the Name of the Law: The BATF Story.* Springfield, Va.: Gun Owners of America, 1989. This is the video that David Koresh showed to BATF undercover agent Robert Rodriguez, and which was cited in the search warrant application. The Fifth Circuit Court of Appeals uses the fact that the Branch Davidians watched the video as evidence of their participation in a conspiracy to murder BATF agents. The video details various abusive enforcement actions by BATF agents against American citizens, including police officers. The abuses tend to be improper prosecutions for technicalities rather than violent assaults or break-ins. That all of the BATF horror stories from the 1980s were nonviolent illustrates how far BATF has "evolved" in the 1990s.

KPOC television. David Hall, producer, *The Waco Incident*, television documentary, September 19, 1994 (Ponca City, Okla., channel 27). Available from: The FOREND Times, Inc., P.O. Box 2861, Covina, CA 91722. (800) 474–2861. Also available from: American Freedom Network. (800) 205–6245. Documentary exposé by small television station which initially supported government actions, but then became more skeptical. Cited as "KPOC."

———. *Atrocities at Ruby Ridge . . . The Randy Weaver Story* (Ponca City, Okla., channel 27, 1995). Available from: The FOREND Times, Inc., P.O. Box 2861, Covina, CA 91722. (800) 474–2861. Also available from: American Freedom Network. (800) 205–6245. Much of the film is video footage—with a camcorder feel—of Bo Gritz's speeches to the crowd of Weaver sympathizers who had gathered.

NBC. *In the Line of Duty: Ambush at Waco.* Made-for-television movie which began production while the siege was in progress. Even more distorted and deceptive than the Linda Thompson videos, but from a different political viewpoint. Although Koresh despised the NRA, NBC planned to place NRA decals in the television Davidians' home, but changed its decor under threat of a libel suit.

Thompson, Linda. *Waco: The Big Lie* and *The Big Lie Continues.* These videos are of no value in figuring out what actually happened, but their wide circulation has played an important role in arousing public anger over Waco. The video's assertions that the FBI used flamethrowing tanks on April 19 and that a special commando squad went inside the building and started the fire are implausible in the extreme.

WGBH, "Frontline." *Waco: The Inside Story.* 60 minutes. WGBH television, Boston. Available for purchase at (800) 255–9424. Public television documentary on Waco. Balanced and carefully researched. Focuses mainly on the negotiations and the conflict between the negotiators and the HRT. Even to a person who has spent thousands of hours studying Waco, the tape has an intense visual and emotional impact. It shows the tragedy of Waco, both in the innocent children who were killed and the anguish of the negotiators and Sheriff Harwell over their deaths. Website for the program is at http://www2.pbs.org/wgbh/pages/frontline/waco/flwacosite.html.

AUDIOTAPE

David Koresh, *Songs for Grandpa.* Mount Carmel Survivors Fund, Box 120, Axtell, TX 76624. $10.00. Koresh sings and plays acoustic guitar, and does some sermonizing. The music is folk rock, perhaps influenced by 1970s Jesus music, and with a little Pete Townshend-style strumming. Koresh plays about as well as would a person of average talent who put a great deal of time into guitar work.

COMPACT DISC

David Koresh, *Voice of Fire* (Otho, Iowa: Junior's, n.d.). Koresh's fifty-eight minute radio sermon from March 2, 1993, plus a pair of Koresh songs.

INTERNET SITES

Several Internet sites related to a particular book or document are cited above. In addition, the following Internet sites related to Waco may provide useful information.

Koresh's sermons. Gopher://wiretap.spies.com/00/Library/Religion/Fringe/koresh.txt.
Hidden Manna. http://www.sevenseals.com. Site contains a huge new book of Branch Davidian theology, as expounded from prison, and provides a theological explanation for the events at Waco.
Independence Institute Waco Page. http://i2i.org/SuptDocs/Waco/Waco.htm. The promotional site for this book. Contains a downloadable copy of a draft of the prologue, links to all the Internet resources listed in this bibliography, plus links to or copies of the Fifth Circuit Court of Appeals decision on the Waco appeals, trial judge Smith's sentencing memorandum, Judge Smith's memorandum reinstating the guilty verdicts, the jury instructions, the grand jury indictment, and other resources.

David Hardy Waco page. http://www.indirect.com/www/dhardy/CS_Gas_at_Waco. Maintained by attorney and historian David Hardy. Includes Hardy's excellent article "Use of CS Gas at Waco," as well as pictures and other resources.

Koresh Research Homepage. http://lark.cc.ukans.edu/~voss/. Maintained by Cary Voss. University of Kansas doctoral student writing a dissertation on the Waco Negotiations. Includes Voss's lengthy article on the history of the Branch Davidians, starting with the Millerite movement in the 1840s.

Mount Carmel today. http://www.softdisk.com/comp/dan/davidian.html. Photos of the property.

The "Mount Carmel Center" Information Center. http://www.flash.net/~wyla/. The transcript of the San Antonio trial.

The Research Center. http://www.ime.net/~mswett. Maintained by Mark Swett. The world's best electronic collection of Branch Davidian theology. Contains writings from David Koresh, Livingstone Fagan, Jaime Castillo, and Marc Breault. The site takes on-line orders for its large collection of Koresh Bible study tapes, as well as transcripts of the FBI negotiations with the Branch Davidians. Some negotiation transcripts on-line. Branch Davidian prisoners' speeches to the court before sentencing. The most information-packed of all the Waco web sites.

Shade's Landing Waco Archive. http://www.shadeslanding.com/firearms/read6. html. Includes the Search Warrant Application, the Jury Instructions, and various articles about Waco.

Waco Holocaust Electronic Museum. Maintained by Carol Valetine. http://www. mnsinc.com/SkyWriter/WacoMuseum/index.html. Many photos and other rare resources, as well as lots of conspiracy theorizing. Includes the full autopsy reports and many grisly photos of the corpses.

Waco Links Page. http://uts.cc.utexas.edu/~cwalker/waco/waco.html. Very large collection.

WGBH Television, Boston. "Frontline" special on Waco. http://www2.pbs.org/wgbh/pages/frontline/waco/flwacosite.html. Includes RealAudio tapes and transcripts for selected negotiations. Dr. Alan Stone's review of the Justice Department Report on Waco. Excerpts from WGBH interviews with Waco participants. Order form for the WGBH special, and a teacher's guide.

ORGANIZATIONS

Committee for Waco Justice. Carol Moore, Box 65518, Washington, DC 20035.

Mount Carmel Survivors Fund. Box 120, Axtell, TX 76624. Run by Branch Davidian elder Clive Doyle. Sells David Koresh music and sermon tapes, books, and other materials.

ADDRESSES OF BRANCH DAVIDIAN PRISONERS

Note: the addresses for the Waco Eight are subject to change without notice. Livingstone Fagan in particular has been moved from prison to prison, in response to his stance of passive noncooperation.

Renos Avraam, #60590–080
Federal Correctional Institution
Box 1500
El Reno, OK 73036

Brad Branch, #60536–080
Federal Correctional Institution
Box 4200
Three Rivers, TX 78071

Jaime Castillo, #60594–080
Federal Correctional Institution
Box 5000
Oakdale, LA 71463

Graeme Craddock, #60593–080
Federal Correctional Institution
Box 5000
Oakdale, LA 71463

Livingstone Fagan, #60550–080
Federal Correctional Institution
Box 1500, Unit 4–A
El Reno, OK 73036

Paul Fatta, #61154–079
Federal Correctional Institution
Box 3000
Anthony, NM 88021

Ruth Riddle, #60596–080
Federal Correctional Institution
33 1/2 Pembroke Rd.
Danbury, CT 06811

Kevin Whitecliff, #60537–080
Box 4200, KARNS–A
Three Rivers, TX 78071

Index

NATIONAL UNIVERSITY
LIBRARY

NATIONAL UNIVERSITY LIBRARY   SAN DIEGO